Contributions to Economics

The series *Contributions to Economics* provides an outlet for innovative research in all areas of economics. Books published in the series are primarily monographs and multiple author works that present new research results on a clearly defined topic, but contributed volumes and conference proceedings are also considered. All books are published in print and ebook and disseminated and promoted globally. The series and the volumes published in it are indexed by Scopus and ISI (selected volumes).

Mehmet Baha Karan · Wim Westerman ·
Jacob Wijngaard

A History of Banks

From the Knights Templar to the Present Era

Springer

Mehmet Baha Karan
Department of Business Administration
Hacettepe University
Cankaya, Ankara, Türkiye

Wim Westerman
Faculty of Economics and Business
University of Groningen
Groningen, The Netherlands

Jacob Wijngaard
Faculty of Economics and Business
University of Groningen
Groningen, The Netherlands

ISSN 1431-1933 ISSN 2197-7178 (electronic)
Contributions to Economics
ISBN 978-3-031-62296-0 ISBN 978-3-031-62297-7 (eBook)
https://doi.org/10.1007/978-3-031-62297-7

This Springer imprint is published by the registered company Springer Nature Switzerland AG
The registered company address is: Gewerbestrasse 11, 6330 Cham, Switzerland

Preface

Most of this book was originally written by Mehmet Baha Karan and published under the title "Para Banka ve Finansın Sırları: Tapınak Şövalyelerinden Modern Çağlara[1]" (Secrets of Money, Banking and Finance: From the Knights Templar to the Modern Ages) in 2022. He translated the Turkish text 1:1 into English, but felt that it should be taken out of its domestic context and that the cases described should also cover the last 100 years and developed. That is how Wim Westerman and Jacob Wijngaard became to be involved with the book. In the person of Johannes Glaeser, we found an enthusiastic supporter at Springer and this is how the project started. Soon, the authors found out that they could not write a text covering everything and that it would still be interesting to a broad public. Actually, this constraint, while being somewhat painful, helped us to keep on track in terms of both timing and content. We decided to merely focus on the most important banking episodes and to cover the recent period in a condensed way.

Writing is much about rewriting, and this counts even more for the present text. We wanted to agree on every word, despite our differing backgrounds. Mehmet Karan is proud to be from Turkey, and the other two authors are from the Netherlands. Jacob Wijngaard is specialized in supply chain issues and currently finds himself being involved with the design of future monetary systems. Mehmet Karan and Wim Westerman have a corporate finance and financial markets background, and Mehmet Karan also has a strong base of experience in energy finance and economics. Understandably, our political, cultural, and religious backgrounds differ, but perhaps surprisingly our values have much in common. Moreover, the three of us share an interest in case studies and feel that they can help to sketch a general picture. Finally, we agree that facts are first in science and that the reader should decide for herself, but science is by no means value-free, so we should not try to hide our own opinions.

Here it is, our book. If anything, we dedicate it to the people who showed us how decent banking works. We had them in mind, trying to honor them. Having said this, the book is actually written for you in person, whether you are a banker,

[1] Karan, Mehmet Baha. (2022). Para Banka ve Finansın Sırları: Tapınak Şövalyelerinden Modern Çağlara. Scala Publishing. ISBN-13: 9786057110107.

a financial economics or management professional, a policy maker, a student, a lecturer, a researcher, or just a curious individual. If you like to read about the history of banks rather than of banking systems, want to know how banks relate to authorities, are interested in what people actually do rather than in how markets function, and wonder about how the miracle of thousands of years of banking has come around, this book is especially meant for you.

Ankara, Türkiye — Mehmet Baha Karan
Winschoten, The Netherlands — Wim Westerman
Assen, The Netherlands — Jacob Wijngaard
April 2024

Contents

1 Introduction: The Origins and Fundamentals of Banking 1
1.1 The Magic of Manhattan 1
1.2 What Are the Tasks of Modern Banks 5
1.3 Banking from the Ancient to Medieval Times 7
1.3.1 Roman Banking 7
1.3.2 From Rome Until the Crusades 11
1.3.3 Trust, Reputation and the Maghribi Merchants 12
1.4 Banking in Medieval Times and the Knights Templar 14
1.5 Extending the Story of Banks into the Present 23
1.5.1 How the Power Dance of State and Banks is Developing 23
1.5.2 How the Banking Secrets Are Developing 26
References 28

2 The Medici Family: Bankers of the Renaissance (Fourteenth and Fifteenth Centuries) 31
2.1 Introduction 31
2.2 Politics at the End of the Middle Ages 32
2.3 Development of Commerce and Finance 34
2.4 The Bill of Exchange and Bookkeeping 35
2.5 Church and Bankers 39
2.6 Kings and Bankers 42
2.7 The Rise of the Medici Family 43
2.7.1 Giovanni Di Bicci de' Medici 43
2.7.2 Cosimo de' Medici 45
2.8 Structure and Organization of the Medici Bank 48
2.9 The Decline of the Medici Bank 52
2.9.1 Piero de Medici and Lorenzo the Magnificent 52
2.9.2 The Fall of the Medici House 58

2.10 The Banking Secrets of the Medici ... 60
2.10.1 Leadership ... 60
2.10.2 Holding Type of Company Structure ... 61
2.10.3 Public Relations ... 62
2.10.4 Risk Management and Diversification ... 63
2.10.5 Bookkeeping and Accounting ... 64
2.11 Conclusion ... 64
References ... 65

3 Corporations, Stock Exchanges, and the Amsterdam Bank of Exchange (Late Sixteenth and Seventeenth Centuries) ... 67
3.1 Introduction ... 67
3.2 Political Developments in Western Europe and the Birth of the Dutch Republic ... 70
3.3 Economic Developments in Western Europe and the Prosperity of the Dutch ... 74
3.4 The East and West India Companies ... 77
3.4.1 The Dutch East India Company ... 77
3.4.2 The Dutch West India Company ... 80
3.5 The Amsterdam Stock Exchange ... 82
3.6 The Amsterdam Bank of Exchange ... 83
3.7 The Dutch Banking Secrets ... 87
3.7.1 Liberal Economy and State Administration ... 87
3.7.2 Corporate Management Approach ... 89
3.7.3 Bank Money ... 90
3.7.4 Initial Public Offerings ... 90
3.7.5 Dutch Auction Method ... 91
3.7.6 Financial Center and Stock Exchange Transactions ... 92
3.7.7 Investment Banking and Mutual Funds ... 93
3.8 Conclusion ... 93
References ... 94

4 Goldsmith Bankers and the Birth of the Fractional Reserve System (Seventeenth and Early Eighteenth Centuries) ... 99
4.1 Introduction ... 99
4.2 Early Political and Economic Developments ... 101
4.2.1 From Tudor Reign to Stuart Reign ... 101
4.2.2 Royal Finance and Taxation ... 103
4.2.3 The Civil War ... 104
4.2.4 Economics and International Trade ... 105
4.3 The London Bankers ... 107
4.3.1 The Rise of the Goldsmiths ... 107
4.3.2 The Banking Products of the Goldsmiths ... 109
4.3.3 Edward Backwell and His Bank ... 111

4.4 Public Finance After the Restoration 113
4.5 The Glorious Revolution and Its Aftermath 114
4.6 Organizing the Government Debt 116
4.6.1 Loans/Lotteries and Exchequer Bills 116
4.6.2 Establishment of the Bank of England 117
4.6.3 The South Sea Company 119
4.7 London Banking Secrets 122
4.7.1 Endorsing and Discounting 122
4.7.2 Fractional Reserve Banking 123
4.7.3 Communication and Market Intelligence 124
4.7.4 Bank of England 125
4.7.5 Conversion of Government Debt into Company Shares 126
4.8 Conclusion 126
References 127

5 John Law: The Lord of Paper Money (Late Seventeenth and Early Eighteenth Centuries) 129
5.1 Introduction 129
5.2 John Law's Youth and Early Life 131
5.3 John Law, the Activistic Economist: Scotland, the Netherlands, Genoa, Turin 132
5.4 The Financial Problems of France at the Beginning of the Eighteenth Century 136
5.5 Further Development of Law's Ideas 140
5.6 Foundation of the Banque Générale 141
5.7 The Mississippi Company, the Conflict with the Parliament ... 144
5.8 The End of the Buying Fever and the Start of the Fall of Law 149
5.9 The Apotheosis 152
5.10 Foundation of the Bank of France 156
5.11 Conclusion 158
References 160

6 The Rothschilds: The Global Financial Empire (Eighteenth and Nineteenth Centuries) 163
6.1 Introduction 163
6.2 Mayer Rothschild and the Birth of the Rothschild Dynasty 167
6.3 Rothschild and Wellington 170
6.4 The Five Brothers Empire 173
6.4.1 Frankfurt House 175
6.4.2 London House 175
6.4.3 Paris House 177
6.4.4 Vienna House 179
6.4.5 Naples House 180

6.5 Other Notable Events in the Rothschild History ... 181
6.5.1 The Crisis of 1825 and the Bank of England ... 181
6.5.2 The Suez Canal Incident ... 184
6.5.3 The Rothschilds and the US Market ... 186
6.6 The Banking Secrets of the Rothschilds ... 187
6.6.1 Being Untouchable ... 188
6.6.2 Being a Family Business ... 188
6.6.3 International Multicenter Structure ... 189
6.6.4 Connection with Very Important People ... 190
6.6.5 Communication Skills ... 191
6.6.6 Developing the International Bond Market ... 192
6.7 Conclusion ... 194
References ... 195

7 J.P. Morgan: The Banker Who Saved America (Nineteenth and Twentieth Centuries) ... 199
7.1 Introduction ... 199
7.2 Banking in the United States ... 202
7.3 The Banking Empire of John Pierpont Morgan ... 205
7.3.1 J.P. Morgan's Youth and Early Years ... 205
7.3.2 The Railways Investments ... 208
7.3.3 The 1895 Crisis and J.P. Morgan's Gold ... 211
7.3.4 The Iron and Steel Investment ... 212
7.3.5 The 1907 Crisis ... 214
7.4 Establishment of the Federal Reserve Bank (Fed) ... 219
7.5 The Death of J.P. Morgan and the Future of His Bank ... 221
7.6 J.P. Morgan's Banking Secrets ... 222
7.6.1 Using Social Networks ... 222
7.6.2 Crisis Management ... 225
7.6.3 Morganization ... 226
7.6.4 Corsair Negotiation Method ... 227
7.7 Conclusion ... 228
References ... 229

8 The Ottoman Bank: State Bank of the Empire (Nineteenth and Twentieth Centuries) ... 233
8.1 Introduction ... 233
8.2 Politics and Economics in the Ottoman Empire ... 236
8.2.1 The Political Situation ... 236
8.2.2 The Economic Situation ... 241
8.2.3 The Monetary Mechanism ... 242
8.3 The Ottoman Bank ... 246
8.4 The Bank-i Osman-i Sahane (The Imperial Ottoman Bank) ... 248
8.5 The 1908 Revolution and Afterward ... 252

8.6 Imperialist Banking in the Nineteenth Century ... 255
8.6.1 Egypt: A Country in a Debt Trap ... 256
8.6.2 Greece: A Country Created by Debt ... 258
8.7 The Banking Secrets of the Ottoman Bank ... 260
8.7.1 Independence of Bank Management ... 260
8.7.2 Adaptability and Flexibility ... 263
8.8 Conclusion ... 264
References ... 265

9 The Rise (and Fall) of National Banking Champions (Nineteenth, Twentieth, and Early Twenty-First Centuries) ... 269
9.1 Introduction ... 269
9.2 Dutch Banking and ABN AMRO ... 274
9.3 German Banking and Deutsche Bank ... 280
9.4 Swiss Banking and Credit Suisse ... 286
9.5 Banking Secrets of the Champions ... 291
9.6 Conclusion ... 292
References ... 293

10 Citibank: A National Champion Going Beyond Limits (Twentieth and Early Twenty-First Centuries) ... 297
10.1 Introduction ... 297
10.2 The First Century ... 298
10.3 Citibank and the Crisis of 1929 ... 299
10.4 The Glass-Steagall Act and Its Impact ... 302
10.5 Wriston Wrestling with Regulations ... 305
10.5.1 The One-Bank-Holding Company Act and Amendments ... 305
10.5.2 Regulation Q and Reserve Requirements ... 307
10.6 Intermezzo: Bretton Woods ... 309
10.7 LDC Loans: Bankers as Warriors for America ... 312
10.8 John Reed and Consumer Banking ... 316
10.9 The Prelude to the Financial Crisis ... 319
10.9.1 Further Deregulation ... 319
10.9.2 Sanford Weill, the Deal Maker ... 322
10.9.3 The Faring of Citigroup ... 323
10.9.4 The Start of the Crisis ... 324
10.10 The Citibank Banking Secrets ... 325
10.11 Conclusion ... 326
References ... 327

11 Conclusion and General Discussion 329
11.1 Introduction 329
11.2 The Demise of the Gold Standard and the Failure of Lehman Brothers 331
11.3 The Global Financial Crisis and Its Aftermath 335
11.4 The Secrets of the Banks: From the Knights Templar to the Present 340
11.5 Banking and Politics: About Countervailing Power 347
11.6 The Power Game: Wall Street Versus Main Street 351
11.7 Central Bank Independence and Basel Accord 355
11.8 The Future of Fractional Reserve Banking 358
11.9 Conclusion 360
References 362

Chapter 1
Introduction: The Origins and Fundamentals of Banking

1.1 The Magic of Manhattan

At 8:45 a.m. on September 11, 2001, John Murphy, CEO of Oppenheimer Funds, was jogging in Manhattan's Battery Park, as usual, thinking about what he would address at his firm's reorganization meeting that afternoon. Suddenly, he heard an explosion. When he looked up, flames rose from the upper floors at the north tower of the World Trade Center (WTC), one of New York's most symbolic buildings. The first thing that came to his mind was a plane crash. He thought that, fortunately, the plane didn't crash into the South Tower; his office and 598 employees were there. However, just about fifteen minutes later, what he feared would come to pass, and a plane would crash into the South Tower (Argenti, 2002). Little later, other targets, including the Pentagon, would also come under attack. Al-Qaeda terrorists attempted to damage American capitalism by attacking landmark buildings in the Wall Street area and discrediting the financial system. The WTC's Twin Towers symbolized globalization and America's economic power and prosperity. Al-Qaeda hoped that attacking these American symbols would create widespread fear across the country, particularly in the financial markets, and severely weaken the US position in the world community. The United States was not the only country affected by the attacks. It created a snowball effect; stock exchanges, banks, and financial companies worldwide, including the London Stock Exchange, would be closed for a week due to fear of terrorism. The New York Stock Exchange was experiencing a long-term shutdown for the third time. The first occurred at the beginning of the First World War, and the second happened in March 1933, during the Great Depression.

In 2001, while gold prices rose 30%, stocks sharply declined globally in almost every stock market (Makinen, 2002). The attack on 9/11 was a complete disaster. Thousands of people, including many bankers and financial managers, died in this attack. Fortunately, for John Murphy, no Oppenheimer Funds employees were among them. Still, many financial firms, such as Cantor Fitzgerald Securities and Fuji Bank, were not so lucky (Casualties of the September 11, n.d.). John Murphy, who could not

M. B. Karan et al., *A History of Banks*, Contributions to Economics,
https://doi.org/10.1007/978-3-031-62297-7_1

recover from the event's influence for a long time, participated in the documentary film project "Rebirth" for the victims of September 11 ten years later and said that this terrorist attack exemplified the resilience of the human spirit (Stabile, 2011).

The WTC was located at the southwestern tip of New York City, Manhattan Island, near the shore of the Hudson River, a few blocks away from Wall Street. The city, particularly Manhattan, is known as the world's cultural, financial, media, and entertainment capital. It also hosts the United Nations headquarters. Also, many multinational media conglomerates are headquartered in Manhattan, and the borough has been the scene of numerous books, movies, and television shows. The Manhattan district has been cited as the economically most powerful city and the world's leading financial and fintech hub. Wall Street is in Manhattan's financial district, symbolizing globalization, high finance, and investment. The Street is home to the New York Stock and Nasdaq exchanges, the undisputed leader worldwide regarding average daily share trading volume and total market capitalization of its listed companies. Hundreds of financial centers' representatives worldwide and all major banks and players in financial markets are located on Wall Street. News agencies such as Bloomberg and Reuters constantly transmit developments on Wall Street to their audiences. Although the WTC is not located on Wall Street, the Twin Towers characterized the power of the finance sector, and an attack on the WTC is an attack on the financial sector.

The term "Wall Street" was originally used to refer to the elite large group of independent brokerages that dominate the US investment industry. But today, it also includes the largest investment and commercial banks, hedge funds, mutual funds, wealth management firms, insurance companies, brokers, currency and commodity traders, and financial institutions. Although many of these organizations are headquartered in other cities such as Chicago, Boston, and San Francisco, the media still refer to the US investment and financial industry as Wall Street. With the increase in the power of the USA after the Second World War, the world's most important financial institutions and stock markets began to take place on Wall Street. While the USA is the most powerful economy in the world, the Federal Reserve Bank has become the world's central bank, with the dollar being the reserve currency. Financial institutions on Wall Street provide various financial services to investors and can reach all countries directly or indirectly. Here, all short-term and long-term monetary transactions can be made, and all transactions that investors will be interested in, from stocks to bonds, from spot transactions to the most complex derivative transactions, can be made in the stock markets where trillions of dollars are traded. So, Wall Street is indeed the center of the Western world. Like the other financial centers, Wall Street has the best commercial and communications infrastructure where people conduct huge volumes of international and domestic trading transactions (Fig. 1.1).

Wall Street, where the slave trade took place in the seventeenth century, takes its name from the wall built by the Dutch in 1653 to protect its colony against English forces. This narrow, short street runs just seven blocks from Broadway to the East River in the southern part of Manhattan in New York. A bull statue placed two blocks south of Wall Street also attracts the attention of visitors. The bull symbolizes a strong stock market in which participants are optimistic and confident (Brooks, 1999). Along with the statue of the bull, the magnificent buildings and the New York

Fig. 1.1 : Wall Street, New York City https://commons.wikimedia.org/wiki/File:Wall_Street,_New_York_City.jpg

Stock Exchange stress the power of the financial sector. These buildings, which are also illuminated at night, bring to mind the phrase "Money never sleeps," as said by Gordon Gekko, the unforgettable character in the movie "Wall Street" (1987) starring Michael Douglas. The impressive skyscrapers in the financial centers are not exclusive to the USA; a similar image is valid for London, Frankfurt, Tokyo, and even Dubai. All these financial centers spread a sense of immunity to its surroundings. It looks as if the world is controlled here. Not only do their buildings stress the power of banks, but the rumors about banks are just as effective. Conspiracy theories claim that they shape world politics; they are behind the scenes in wars, revolutions, and turmoil worldwide. There is a widespread belief that the financial lobby rules the world (Farrell, 2013). Is it really so? How does it work?

The power of the financial world suggested by Wall Street, the City of London, and other financial centers contrasts sharply with the volatility of the financial processes and the fragility of the supporting organizations. Finance and accounting experts know that banks' balance sheets differ entirely from those in the industrial and commercial sectors. Since the financial ratios showing the financial performance of banks are different from the others, banking companies are analyzed separately from companies in other sectors. The specificity of bank financial structures comes from two essential features of banks. Firstly, banks' equity is very low relative to the total assets. While the ratio of a typical company's equity to its total assets is 30–70%, this ratio is as small as 5–10% for banks. Banks' primary source of funds is deposits and loans from other institutions. Banks record such funds as assets and give them to companies as loans. They have to keep some of their assets as cash reserves to meet the cash demands of their customer. When the average maturity of their resources and the average maturity of their assets do not match, a significant jump in interest or exchange rates endangers the bank's life.

Banks are institutions operating with a low capital base, which makes banks very sensitive to financial turmoil. Since a strong wind in the economy can destroy their equity immediately, they are greatly affected by crises in the market and their related non-performing loans. Moreover, since banks trade money, they can quickly lose their equity due to corruption and employee mistakes. Banks sometimes get greedy and self-destruct by entering high-risk business ventures, as Lehman Brothers did in 2008. The second feature of banks is that they have to repay their money when depositors demand it. In other words, the bank can hardly make long-term investments but keep cash reserves to repay the money at any time. In 2023, New York-based Signature Bank went bankrupt when depositors quickly withdrew their money. In banking jargon, this is called a "bank run". In this case, no bank can cover such great demand. All these features make banking more fragile than other sectors.

Banking crises injure not only the banking industry but also the whole economy. The bankruptcy of one bank can lead to a general decrease in the credibility of banks and the spread of this distrust to other banks. Depositors withdraw their money from the distrusted banks and, possibly, out of the country. The spread of such insecurity will cause a collapse in the country and the onset of a significant economic crisis by affecting the country's payment system. So, regulations are required to support the power of the banks and simultaneously prevent them from getting into a very risky position. These regulations support the fragile financial structures of banking, make it difficult for banks to go bankrupt, and ensure the stable functioning of the monetary system. It is a fact that the regulations for banks are stringent and heavy. Since this fragile structure of banks is known, they are subject to national and international regulations not seen in any other sector. Ironically, banks are not free to go bankrupt. The whole society depends on a stable financial system.

In an economy without banking, there are no intermediary activities, and the wheels of the whole economy will stop. Therefore, laws often prohibit the spreading of negative news or rumors about banks. Even mentioning such a possibility may harm a country's economy. In addition, banks conduct close business transactions with so-called near-banks, mutual fund partnerships, insurance companies, and even stock exchange organizations. A climate of insecurity can have pervasive consequences on them. For this reason, the asset-based interests of banks on their "reputation," "fame," and "wealth" have been deemed necessary to be specially protected

(Saritas, 2010). The financial system is delicate and needs protection because we depend on it.

There is some bitter irony in this: the destruction of the WTC was an attack on the heart of the financial system; it had a terrible impact, but the financial system itself recovered soon, while seven years later it appeared that the system almost destroyed itself. While regulations protect banks from bankruptcy, they can also reduce their profits by chaining their activities. So, banks tried to stretch these chains and circumvent or even eliminate them. That fueled the growth of banks and the economy, but made the system more fragile and vulnerable to shocks. Toward the end of 2007, many banks in the US came to the edge of bankruptcy. Timothy Geithner was president of the Federal Reserve Bank of New York then, and hence the supervisor of many of the big New York banks, e.g., Citibank (see Chap. 10). He saw how they had stretched the regulations and how that had caused the problems. In September 2008, Lehman Brothers collapsed because of too heavy involvement in the subprime mortgage crisis, causing a wave of new problems. It brought the system to the brink of a total meltdown, notwithstanding the involvement of the Fed and Treasury. In his memoirs, Geithner (2015) describes how he concluded that most of the banks were "too big to fail" and that the best way to proceed was to do whatever was possible to save them, also the banks that behaved irresponsibly. Even replacement of the bank management was not possible because it would create too much turmoil. That was what happened. Geithner was first involved as President of the New York Fed and from 2009 as Secretary of the Treasury.

If a bank has come to the edge of bankruptcy, central banks lend to save that institution; if this support is insufficient, the Treasury can directly intervene to the rescue. Banks may cover the losses with the people's taxes. The book "Too Big to Fail" by Andrew Ross Sorkin, describing the 2008 financial crisis and the collapse of Lehman Brothers, reveals the discourses between Wall Street CEOs and government officials. This book, later filmed, describes how the public had to bear the losses of poorly managed banks (Sorkin, 2009).

1.2 What Are the Tasks of Modern Banks

For a flourishing society, it is necessary to be able to settle and pay transactions. We need money for that, only bartering is very inconvenient. There are three types of money, coins, produced and issued by the Mint, banknotes issued by the Central Bank, and bank money, i.e., demand deposits, organized by the banks (Galbraith, 2017). Bank money is the most common form of money, certainly for the larger transactions. Banks create money while doing their regular business of taking deposits and making loans. For example, when you get a loan to buy a car, the bank opens an account for you, and money that did not exist before is deposited into your account. The amount deposited into this new account is the new money created by the bank. The cash amount will increase when you pay with this money by depositing it into the car dealer's bank account. When the car dealer uses this money to repay his debts, the amount will grow again. There is a well-known anecdote about this. John comes to a town hotel as a tourist and likes the room shown to him; he pays a 100-dollar deposit to the hotelier to keep the room for a few hours. Then, John leaves the hotel to consult his friends who are waiting nearby. When the hotel owner receives the money, he transfers it to the account of the greengrocer, whom he has owed money for a while. When the greengrocer sees the $100 in his statement, he pays the wholesaler in the primary vegetable market. The wholesaler happily takes the money and pays the prostitute he was with before, and the prostitute deposits her debt to the hotel's bank account. A few hours later, John returns to the hotel and demands his $100 deposit back, saying his friends prefer another hotel. The hotelier pays John the $100 credited to his account. Although the hotelier could not earn money at the end of this transaction, everyone in the town paid their debts due to the money created. When this process is done continuously by all banks, the amount of money made in the country will increase. When this situation comes to the point where the value of the money decreases, the Central Bank will step in. To stop the money supply that creates inflation, it takes the excess cash from the system by selling treasury bills to the market with an appropriate interest rate. If the liquidity in the market is insufficient, the Central Bank does the opposite of this process; that is, it gives cash to the market by purchasing back the treasury bills it sold before.

According to a famous professor at Harvard University, John Kenneth Galbraith, the money creation process of banks is so simple that even the mind does not accept it. Bankers love to use jargon such as letters of credit, forwards, and swaps that the ordinary person may not understand. They probably feel that people respect terms they do not understand and that it contributes to the image of a magic, powerful, unassailable, and trustworthy financial system. Professor Galbraith has been telling an anecdote about George W. Ball, a lawyer who started as a banking associate at Lehman Brothers in the 1960s. After seeing the profession's appeal, he said, "Why hasn't anyone told me about banking before?" (Galbraith, 2017).

Banks and other financial corporations provide a range of financial services: money transfer, foreign exchange, lending and borrowing, insurance, and trade in financial products. And there are many different financial products. Some follow right away from the execution of real transactions; others are intended to hedge the risk of real transactions. For all these transactions, it holds that intermediate parties temporarily possess the assets involved. That is why the whole system is threatened by uncertainty. If such a party goes bankrupt during the transaction, it leads to severe losses for the other parties. The transactions are halted because of the threat. Even a normal bank payment is not completely instantaneous and risky, therefore. Suppose actor **A**, with a deposit from bank A, wants to pay actor **B**, with a deposit from bank B. Then bank B may receive the money just before it goes bankrupt, blocking the further transfer. Geithner (2015) refers to the use of Repo's to organize daytime credit for security trading. A Repo is a repurchase agreement. The borrower sells some securities contracting that they can repurchase them at the end of the day, and they do that day after day. But what if there is a threat that the borrower is bankrupt during the day? The whole system stops if there is a broad risk of bankruptcy. It is very common for a third party to service this repeated sale and repurchase, but that makes the whole situation even more sensitive to bankruptcy risks. Regulations are necessary to limit that risk. The government has to establish and maintain those regulations.

We will describe several banking episodes in this book, starting with the Knights Templar in this chapter and finishing with Citibank and the Financial crisis of 2008 in the last two chapters. The tensions between the government, on the one hand, and banks or other financial intermediaries, on the other hand, are an essential element in the context of all these banking episodes. This field of tension changed dramatically between the Middle Ages, the age of the Knights Templars, and 2008, the start of the financial crisis, but the heavy interdependence remains. We give an impression of the development of banking through the ages and provide also attention to this field of tension between banks and governments.

1.3 Banking from the Ancient to Medieval Times

1.3.1 Roman Banking

The history of banking goes back further than the Middle Ages. To stress this, we give an impression of banking during the Roman period. The Mediterranean region was the most important trade center of the ancient times. From 700 BC to the first centuries AD, the Mediterranean experienced steady economic growth, particularly maritime trade. Economic activity in this period was dazzling; it could only be reached in the early modern era. While very different peoples belonging to other religions, cultures, races, or tribes lived in the regions on this trade route connecting the East and the West, the trade of goods and money developed. With the conquests of Alexander the Great, trade became even more open in the Mediterranean world. In the eastern sea basin, Greek became the language of international trade, as Latin would in the western one (Curtin, 1984). The power of the Roman Republic and later the Roman Empire brought the stability (the Pax Romana) necessary for the trade to develop. As Thomas Hobbes wrote in 1631, "*If a covenant be made, wherein neither of the parties performs presently, but trust one another; in the condition of mere nature... upon any reasonable suspicion, it is void: but if there be a common power set over them both, with right and force sufficient to compel performance, it is not void. For he that performeth first, has no assurance the other will perform after; the bonds of words are too weak to bridle men's ambition, avarice, anger, and other passions, without the fear of some coercive power.*" (Farrell, 1984).

A single state's unification of the Mediterranean Basin ameliorated economic conditions in practical ways: monetary and metrological systems were standardized, removing costly trade barriers. Legal rules were also standardized, which held the potential for an even more significant transaction-cost-reducing effect.

The first bankers, who took deposits from customers and used some money to make loans, were known as 'trapezites' in Athens in the second half of the fifth century. The word denoted that their work was "trapeza" (literally 'table'). Similar professionals first settled in the Forum in Rome between 318 and 310 BC (Andreau, 1999).

Millett (1991) categorizes financial loans and transactions in the fourth century BC Greece into three groups: (a) non-profit interest-free loans based on personal and social relationships; (b) loans and transactions made for some fee but only occasionally carried out by anyone without any financial expertise, i.e., non-professional interest-only loans; (c) 'professional money lending'. According to Millett, the last category falls into two groups. The first group includes transactions carried out by specialized financiers, who in some cases were profit-seeking and competent businessmen, but not practicing any urban profession, e.g., members of the elite who lent part of their wealth at interest to generate income or increase their inheritance; the second group includes professional men, moneylenders/bankers (trapezites and argentarii in Rome), merchants and wholesalers, who also engaged in financial business. Millett believes that the practice of free lending was widespread in Athens and was based on relationships of kinship, neighborhood, and civic solidarity (Andreau, 1999).

In Rome, bankers carried out the following activities: the assaying of coins; foreign exchange; the raising of credit and the collection of money at auctions; the taking of deposits, which formed the basis of bank accounts and the payments made by moneylenders/bankers; the advancement of loans; and all other transactions arising from the above. Verboven (2020) documents the existence of banker guilds in Rome and Ostia from the second and third centuries (AD) onwards. Rome had four banking-type professions: Argentarii, Nummularii, Coactores, and Coactores Argentarii. Argentarii were free citizens, independent of the state, and belonged to a guild that accepted a limited number of new members. There were also slaves who were argentarii, mainly belonging to the imperial family. But most of these argentarii slaves were goldsmiths or silversmiths, not bankers or coin assayers. The primary function of the Argentarii was deposit banking. They regularly attended auction sales to advance credit to buyers. Nummularii limited themselves to assaying coins and changing money. Subsequently, they became deposit bankers, like the Argentarii. By the middle of the second century (BC), a third group of professionals emerged. These were called Coactores. These were not bankers, but private buyers who received commissions on the sums they held for their clients. Finally, a fourth profession emerged in the first century (BC), the Coactores Argentarii, who were buyers, moneylenders/bankers. None of these bankers were women. Probably the profession of Argentarius was officially forbidden to women (Andreau, 1999).

There were two differences between Italy (Rome) and the non-Latin-speaking states, like Greece. In the Greek world, professional bankers were never regularly involved in auctions. Auctions were held in Greece, and buyers were free to borrow money to pay sellers for their purchases, however, trapezites did not take part in these sales. The second difference concerns the geographical distribution of these professions. While the Latin-speaking world adopted Italian tradition and seems to have been relatively homogeneous in this respect, regional peculiarities are striking in the Greek part of the Empire, especially in Egypt and Palestine.

No argentarii were documented in Italy after the early years of the third century (AD). With this disappearance, the word argentarius, used alone, came to be used for a different profession, the silversmith. Later, these silversmiths, known as argentarii, began to carry out money exchange and banking transactions (Andreau, 1999).

In Greco-Roman antiquity, especially in Italy, it was very common to sell goods at auction. All kinds of goods were auctioned in ports, fairs, wholesale and retail markets, at harvest times, as were estates, slaves, etc. Announcing an auction was a good way to advertise a sale. It was useful after a death, when heirs wanted to sell their jointly owned inheritance. Collateral for those who could not pay their debts was also sold at auctions. Cicero's correspondence gives several examples of auctions following a death in the family. It was the crier, the praeco, who presided over such auctions and gave the objects to the highest bidders. At auctions, there were money buyers (coactores), who did not lend money but received a commission for taking the money from the buyers and passing it on to the sellers. Where both seller and buyer were constantly on the move (as with itinerant merchants and absentee landowners), the services of a buyer became even more indispensable. A buyer was officially responsible for keeping detailed records (tabulae auctionariae or auctionales) of these auctions, noting dates, detailed descriptions of the objects sold, prices, and the names of sellers and buyers (Andreau, 1999).

The study of epigraphic records reveals the regular presence of private bankers in urban environments and marketplaces, some of whom were involved in auctions linked to the sale of specific goods. Examples from the city of Rome include a group of coactores and argentarii who dealt with fish auctions. However, professional bankers were rarely involved in the financial affairs of members of the socio-economic elite, such as the auctions of manors and patrimonial goods reported in Cicero's Correspondence. The receipts of the tabulae ceratae of L. Caecilius Iucundus (reign of Tiberius and Nero) found in Pompeii in 1875 represent the most revealing testimony to Roman professional bankers preserved. The coactor argentarius participated in organizing auctions, opened deposits, and provided loans to buyers (Morcillo, 2008).

Argentarii, coactores argentarii and (later) nummularii accepted deposits. One of the most essential activities of bankers was lending. Bankers were not averse to lending beyond a fraction of the funds entrusted to them. Sometimes, by special authorization, they also managed properties for their clients. Almost all we know about loans made during this period is when their repayments were due. They were due in a few months or, at most, a year. When a client was involved in a lawsuit, a banker's account book was required by law to be produced, even if it did not involve the banker personally (Andreau, 1999).

Credit for auction sales was very important for the argentarii, but banking in ancient Rome was more than that. The banker did not only lend his own money, but also some of the money he received from his customers. Once the customer deposited his money with the banker, he could leave it on deposit, withdraw it at any time, or ask the banker to pay him with it. For instance, according to Andreau (1999), the bankers applied interest on some of these deposits. There is no documentation on the interest rate charged. However, it is clear that bankers profit from their banking by charging a lower interest rate on customer deposits than they do on loans to those in need. A customer could withdraw his deposit all at once or little by little. He could also visit the bank with one of his creditors and ask the banker to pay him or—in some cases—send his creditor to the bank himself. In the latter case, the customer would give the banker a payment order and the creditor, if not recognized by the banker, would come to the bank with some kind of token by which he could be recognized. One type of deposit was a sealed deposit, also known as a regular deposit. These deposits, sometimes in the form of coins, sometimes in the form of goods or documents, had to be returned to their owners untouched by the person who accepted them as deposits. The depositor did not have the right to use the money or object or to earn a return by investing it. Such a deposit was kept in a sealed sack. When a text mentions the delivery of money in a sack to a person (in sacculo dare), it usually means the delivery of a sealed deposit. The point is that while there is no doubt that argentarii, coactores argentarii, and (later) nummularii accepted unsealed deposits, it is not certain that jurists recognized the existence of an irregular deposit contract to support this financial practice. Many legal historians believe that no such contract existed in the second and third centuries and that a deposit in a bank was legally recognized as a loan. Although some evidences indicate that the first traces of deposit banking date back to the Middle Ages, there is no consensus among historians on this issue. A few check-like practices have been found in the eastern Mediterranean. There are also examples of money transfers from one customer to another.

Apart from the bankers described above, four other groups in ancient Rome were engaged in finance. These were the entrepreneurs, usurers, high-interest moneylenders, and merchant-financiers. The entrepreneurs had strong social relationships. They were not only very socially mobile but also technically and professionally mobile. Their financial situation and cultural background allowed them to avoid any profession other than large-scale wholesaler or ship-owner. Their active lives were, therefore, much more flexible and versatile than those of professional bankers. Some had an inheritance that consisted partly of real estate and partly of movable assets. They managed the money of senators and nobles, looking for the best way to manage their inheritance. They adopted a profit strategy and took risks to succeed in their speculations. In private finance, they openly practiced lending practices, using both their funds and those of their friends and contacts. Moneylenders, on the other hand, included commercial financiers. They operated as both wholesalers and financiers, lending to merchants. There is limited information about high-interest lenders. Four wall inscriptions testify to their presence in Pompeii. The fourth category, merchant-financiers, mostly financed a one-way or round trip with a commercial loan, usually between a moneylender and a wholesaler or a ship-owner (Andreau, 1999).

In 1959, a building was discovered about 160 m south of the Stabiae Gate in Pompeii. The writing tablets in this building constitute the third major group of tablets found in towns in the Vesuvian region. They are known as either the Agro Murecine tablets, or the Murecine (the name of the place where they were found) tablets, or the Sulpicii archive, as the Sulpicii, a group of businessmen from Puteoli, guarded them. These tablets undoubtedly constitute examples of commercial loans granted in connection with activities in the port of Puteoli. The findings indicate they were involved as an intermediary in a maritime loan. The evidence is strong enough to dispel all doubts. Secondly, the Murecine tablets show that the Emperor's entourage and the retinue of some senators deposited money through the financiers of Puteoli. These investments are indicated in the Sulpicii archive. Several imperial slaves or freedmen lent money to Sulpicii or merchants in Puteoli. The Murejine tablets provide information about the role played by the warehouses where the collateral for these loans would be kept, as well as about the private grain trade. Thirdly, the tablets are concerned with the security of loans and the legal means of securing this security. If the money lent was not repaid, the creditor could put the property he had pledged as collateral or up for sale and cover his expenses from the price paid at the sale. If the sale proceeds exceeded the debt amount, he would transfer the excess to the debtor. The loan agreement would include the possibility of an auction, which would provide ample publicity for the sale (Andreau, 1999).

1.3.2 From Rome Until the Crusades

With the official acceptance of Christianity by the Roman Empire in 379 AD, religious pressures started on those who traded money in exchange for interest, and banking activities gradually disappeared. However, some still exchanged money with interest, primarily the Jews. Since Christians were banned from usury during this period, Jews became indispensable as moneylenders. While they could not lend money at interest to other Jews because of their religion, they could lend money to those of other faiths. They, therefore, filled a critical gap in the financial system. They provided much-needed capital for businesses and personal loans. They also performed banking practices such as deposit banking, currency exchange, and issuing of promissory notes. In addition, Jews traded various goods in local and interstate commerce. They were vital in establishing trade routes along the Silk Road, linking Europe to the eastern countries.

First, there were also Syrian and Greek merchants, but these turned their attention to the Eastern Roman Empire, and the Jewish merchants expanded their activities and dominated international trade with the Middle East (Jewish Virtual Library, n.d.). The concentration of Jews in trade and banking was a combination of push and pull. They were pushed from other areas, not being allowed to own land or become a member of guilds, but they were also pulled to such work because, in that way, they could use their lead in education. It was also more profitable (Botticini & Eckstein, 2003).

The Western Roman Empire collapsed in 476 AD. During the rule of the Merovingian kings (from 481), the Jews probably collected taxes and made advances on revenues to high officials, but they had to hide their activities due to Church pressure. The most powerful state in Western Europe after the collapse of the Western Roman Empire was the Holy Roman Empire under Charlemagne in the early ninth century and developing before. Charlemagne was rather tolerant with respect to Jewish contributions to economic development. It was a matter of pragmatism. They depended on the Jews for contacts with the Middle-Eastern trade centers. During the Carolingian dynasty, the Jews spread further over Western Europe, with the Rhineland as basis. A special community of Jews associated with the trade with the East is the community of the Radhanites. The travels of the Radhanites are described by a contemporary Muslim official from Iran (Ibn Khordadbeh, around 870). He wrote that there were four trade routes, from the Rhone valley all the way to China's east coast, and that they traded in slaves, furs, silk and swords (going east), cinnamon and other spices, and camphor (going west) (Radhanite, n.d.). There was only a fragmented legal framework for the role of the Radhanites. It relied mainly on their reputation.

1.3.3 Trust, Reputation and the Maghribi Merchants

There is another community of Jewish merchants that has been used extensively in the literature to investigate how it was possible to develop international trade in medieval times, when there was no integrated legal system. Trust in their dependability was provided by their reputation. Maintaining this reputation was also important for the community that provided the services, e.g., the Radhanites (early medieval Jewish merchants) and the Maghribi. Maghribi Jews were ethnic Jews who had traditionally lived in the Maghreb region of North Africa (al-Maghrib, Arabic for "the west") under Arab rule during the Middle Ages (yadvashem.org, n.d.). It was for these communities a very rational policy to develop and protect this reputation. At that time, there was great uncertainty about trade between countries, the duration of the ship's voyage, the conditions of the arrival of the goods, and the price; it was not clear which goods would be sold at what cost for example, the journey from Egypt to Sicily could take 13–50 days, and ships did not always reach their destination. The goods inside the vessels were not well protected and were often damaged in transit, and there was always the possibility that the ship's captain could extort the goods. If merchants did the shipment themselves, their business would suffer as they would be on boats or on the road for months. Therefore, merchants had to work with intermediaries. However, these intermediaries had to be reliable and reputable. They could confiscate the merchants' goods and not pay them. It was impossible to rely on the countries' laws in the trade carried out in such a large area. There was no legal mechanism to enforce the implementation of the contracts with intermediaries. The only thing one could do was to believe in their intermediaries and trust them. Over time, the intermediaries understood that their reputation was much more valuable than the money made in the short run. If this reputation were lost, no one would give them goods or cash for their trade (Buckley & Nixon, 2009).

Around AD 1055, Abun ben Zedaka, a Maghribi merchant living in Jerusalem, was an intermediary for African trade. Although successful, it turned out that he was probably overly ambitious or embezzling the other Maghribi merchant's money to meet a need. When the corruption was learned by other Maghribi merchants with whom he was doing business, he faced a considerable backlash. Those around him and the merchants with whom he did business in Sicily stopped trading with him. No one, not even his friends, could conduct a commercial transaction. Because this person was doing dishonest things as an intermediary, no one wanted to share the responsibility of their business by doing business with him. It would also not put any pressure on the intermediary. In particular, the sanction excluded a dishonest intermediary from that market. Where the law could not protect traders, the only thing to rely on was the community's or diaspora's rules. These rules were also tried to strengthen the merchants' reputations. Thus, nobody would work with Zedaka, as no one would want to sacrifice the lucrative mutual partnerships (Greif, 1993). Undoubtedly, economic sanctions were significant for this mechanism to work. Everyone would make money together, or all would be on their own. Avner Greif's work suggests that complex social networks and diasporas can create reputation-based enforcement mechanisms if formal rules do not work. These unique contractual enforcement mechanisms replaced a proper legal system. Greif's research showed that other institutions, like diasporas, besides courts and the rule of law, can support economic growth. Interestingly, Edwards and Ogilvie (2008) challenged Greif's views and argued that Maghribi traders had no more 'collectivist' cultural beliefs than their European counterparts. However, Greif (2008), on the other hand, challenged their argument by defending her views with some evidence.

Organization theory predicts that when cooperation leads to efficiency gains that the market and the legal system fail to capture, "private order" economic institutions will be established. Since agents were employed by Maghreb merchants and "trust" prevailed in agency relations, it is plausible that they would have established a "private order" institution. Reputation in repeated contractual relationships could provide the basis for such an economic institution. Theoretically, two types of reputation mechanisms can be distinguished in relation to agency relationships. The first allows an agent to signal that he is trustworthy because he fears God or because he has internalized the ideology of honesty. The second mechanism allows an agent to determine in advance that it is most profitable to be honest. The merchant, knowing this mechanism, will be able to trust the agent. Relations of diasporas rely upon the second mechanism and improve reputation among the merchants (Greif, 1989).

In the first decade of the eleventh century, Samhun ben Da'ud, a leading merchant in Tunis, sent a long letter to his business partner Joseph ben Awkal of Fustat. The letter is a historical document that reflects the merchants' awareness of the importance of the implied contract in governing their relationship. In this document, Joseph makes this clear when he makes his future dealings with Samhun dependent on her track record: "If you conduct my business properly, I will send you goods." The linking of future relationships to past behavior, i.e., the essence of reputation mechanisms, is well captured in this example. According to this letter, Joseph believed that Samhun was not sending his revenues on time and subsequently imposed economic sanctions by not providing him with agency services (Greif, 1989).

The diaspora connection enabled traders to reduce the transaction costs associated with agency relationships by reducing the wage premium that had to be paid to keep an intermediary honest and the cost of not working through intermediaries in relationships previously known to be short-lived. The traders' shared religious-ethnic origins created natural boundaries for the diaspora and gave credibility to its own traders and intermediaries. On the other hand, it motivated them to preserve their distinct identity within the Jewish world (Greif, 1989).

1.4 Banking in Medieval Times and the Knights Templar

From the third to the eleventh century, the church's prohibition of interest was quite effective and a significant institutional structure couldn't emerge in Europe except for individual money exchange or secret usury activities. However, the beginning of the Crusades created a significant change in Europe and the Middle East and increased the need for banking. This gap was to be filled by an organization that no one expected at the time. This organization was the Knights Templar.

The idea of the crusades began with the rise in self-confidence of the Christian world. The threat of more Moorish victories in Spain and France was gone and the invasion of Vikings and Huns had ended. But there were new threats form the East. The Seljuk Turks defeated the Byzantine army in Anatolia at the battle of Manzikert (1071) and continued their advance from the east. Pilgrimage to the Holy Land was complicated and dangerous. The Byzantine emperor Alexios I, who had established a good political relationship with the Pope, responded to Pope Urban II's appeal for his support. The Pope's aim was not only to capture Jerusalem by defeating the Muslims but also to control the "Heretical" Eastern Christians who did not adopt Catholic thought and to unite the Christian world under the Papacy. The Crusades were the largest and most comprehensive military campaigns of the Middle Ages and took place in a historical period of religious bigotry, greed, and poverty. In total, eight major Crusades were organized between 1096 and 1291. These bloody, violent, and often brutal conflicts were crucial to world history. They strengthened the position of European Christians for the first time, making them essential players in the territorial struggle in the Middle East. During these expeditions, tens of thousands of Europeans went to the Middle East, wars took place, and lands and cities changed hands. Beyond being a series of religious expeditions between Christians and Muslims to secure control of the holy places, this series of wars had significant cultural, sociological, and economic consequences. It began in 1099 when Christian armies conquered Jerusalem during the First Crusade and took it from Muslim control. Thus, groups of pilgrims from all over Western Europe began to visit the Holy Land. These pilgrims included soldiers, nobles, knights, and various groups of unarmed people who wanted to fulfill their religious duties. However, in the conditions of the time, it was not easy to reach the Middle East from Europe; the roads passed through lands inhabited by Muslim countries and peoples. Moreover, pilgrims traveled among deserters, and bandit groups, and many of them were robbed and killed during their journey. Thus, a number of problems related to the safety and health of Christian pilgrims arose during this period.

The Order of the Knights Templar was founded in 1118 by a French knight, Hugues de Payens, to protect the pilgrims who wanted to visit Jerusalem during the Crusades. They gained the support of the Pope as a religious order. The Templars got their name from their headquarters on the Temple Mount of Solomon in Jerusalem. Next to the Templars, there were the Knights Hospitaller and the Teutonic Knights, together the three great Masters or Houses. They played essential roles in logistics, health, and war issues in the Crusades. Each of these left their mark on history with different characteristics. However, the Knights Templar, the Crusaders' most important military and logistics power, established the first bank-like institutional organization in history.

Hugues de Payens, together with eight knights, with the support of Baldwin II, the ruler of Jerusalem, established a headquarters on the Temple Mount, where the Temple of Solomon was located. The knights quickly gained the official approval of the Catholic Church and the support of Bernard of Clairvaux, a prominent abbot, thanks to their demonstrated skills. When the Order started, the Templars were nothing more than a group of poor monks, but they became a powerful organization as their support grew. In his order rule, Bernard of Clairvaux described these warring men as monk warriors, calling them "*Knights of Christ*". The Templars and other Orders initially considered their mission to fight to protect pilgrims in the Holy Land. They said they would carry out this task by adhering to the three traditional vows of the Church known as poverty, chastity, and obedience like other orders. While maintaining them, the Templars would also take up arms and stand up to the threats posed by the infidels. In Bernard's words, "*They would have to be gentler than the lambs, but tougher than the lions.*" (Bellitto, 2017).

With the support of Bernard, the Templars gained land in many areas all over the world (Fig. 1.2). The most essential lands held by the Templars were in France, given by the King of France. They had also established a network of land and property in Ireland, England, Spain, Portugal, Italy, Hungary, Germany, and even as far as Cyprus. The Templars were skilled, resourceful people. The Order managed their holdings to maximize income and became excessively cash-rich and property-rich. By the thirteenth century, they had also developed the skills to move their wealth around in their territory. We know that during the Fifth Crusade from 1213 to 1221, the Pope used the Templars as tax collectors to reach different regions. Templars owned large tracts of land in Europe and the Middle East, were involved in manufacturing and import/export, and maintained a fleet of ships. The Templars operated a large logistics organization that grew in Europe to sustain the warriors in the Holy Land. It is estimated that at its peak, the order had 9,000 estates from Syria to Scotland; it also controlled ports and had a vast fort that served as its financial center just outside the walls of Paris (Wu, 2019).

The Knights Templar organization served as a military force in Europe and the Middle East for nearly two hundred years. At the Battle of Montgisard in 1177, they proved that a small force could defeat a much larger enemy under the right conditions. On the other hand, they became increasingly involved in logistics and finance operations (Fig. 1.3).

The success of the Templars depended heavily on their institutional structure as a multinational order of Christian monks maintaining high values. The members were highly reliable, reputable, creative, and flexible. Underlying the success of the Knights Templar was the rapidly growing trade in Europe and the Middle East due to

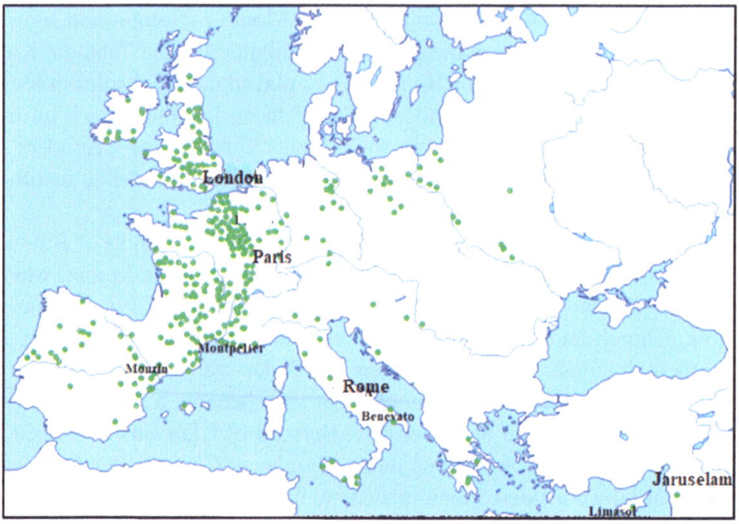

Fig. 1.2 Templar bases in Europe. *Source* It is redrawn by the author. https://en.wikipedia.org/wiki/List_of_Knights_Templar_sites#/media/File:Templerorden_in_Europa_1300.png

the crusades to the Holy Country of Palestine. The Templars were a critical institution that kept a social balance between kings and people. They inspired modern banking with corporate insights far beyond their contemporaries, leaving significant traces for 200 years.

This issue is especially evident in the relationship with the Church as an institution that carries out financial transactions. The Knights Templar were not affiliated with any country; their only link was to the Pope and the Church. They attached great importance to their relationship with them. Since the Templars were religious people, they tried to live up to their vows, paid attention to the relationship between worldly and spiritual affairs, and tried to act morally. Their relations with the Popes were excellent until their last days. In the latter's eyes, they were the guardians of Christianity. They especially cared about staying away from interest and usury, which the Church forbade. However, we know that not using interest in banking and money matters was not technically easy, and this issue was also very delicate for the Church. Therefore, the Templars needed more pragmatic interpretations. They had easy access to these comments and they discovered banking practices similar to Islamic finance methods used today to obtain the Pope's indulgence. While the Church was against the practice of interest, the Western and Eastern Churches' practices differed. In the East, moderately controlled lending was considered better than too strict control with no effect, especially for commercial ventures. In the Byzantine Empire at the beginning of the tenth century, Leo VI allowed lending with interest no higher than about 6% for most loans, and loans for high-risk commercial ventures were even allowed at 12% (Maniatis, 2016). Since the Templars in the West also developed other ways to cover the cost of the debt, they were not at odds with the

Fig. 1.3 Knight Templars (11–12th Centuries) https://commons.wikimedia.org/wiki/File:Knights-templar.jpg

Church. For example, some Templar loans in the South of France included a clause in the loan agreement that if the coin lost value between the time the loan was granted and the time of repayment, the borrower had to add a fixed amount to compensate the lender. Since the fixed sum would remain the same no matter how much the coin depreciated, an interest charge was likely embedded in this fixed sum. Again, if the land was pledged as collateral for the debt, the terms of the loan could stipulate that the produce from the land was not included in the repayment of the debt, but was an extra for the lender (Nicholson, 2014).

The Templars showed a similar flexible behavior while working with kings, especially the Kings of France. They met their special requests, lent them money, and rushed to the aid of the Kings, stretching their principles. In 1148, when King Louis VII of France arrived in Jerusalem, having lost most of his army and all of his treasury in a disastrous land crusade, the Knights Templar lent him so much cash to cover his expenses during his stay in the Holy Land that it brought the Order to the brink of financial ruin (Barber, 2012). During the Seventh Crusade, when King Louis IX of France ran out of money, the Templars voluntarily became involved in chartering organizations to supply the French armies and take the Crusaders to Egypt. Moreover, when the Muslims captured Louis IX, the Templars met the ransom demand (Worral, 2017). They saved the King by paying with money they had on their ships. It is written that the Templars hesitated for a while, considering that this money was not their own. Still, they stretched their rules regarding the King's situation (Nicholson, 2014).

The fall of Acre in 1291 and Ruad in 1302 also meant the destruction of the last Crusader temple in the Holy Land. Only Cyprus, the last stronghold of the Templars in the Eastern Mediterranean, remained. From here, the grand Master Jacques de Molay called on Pope Clement V to join forces with all the Kings, Hospitallers, and Teutonic orders to launch new crusades against the Muslims. He and most of the Templars would return to France to receive an answer to this call. France was where the Templars were strongest. They had several properties in France and had their headquarters here. Under the conditions of that day, the European Kings were trying to increase their power and take control of the church, and the support given to the Crusades was decreasing due to new wars. As a result, the power of the Pope was waning. In France, there was a powerful king: Philip IV. Seeking an undisputed monarchy, the king challenged his vassals with wars. He curtailed his feudal privileges, paving the way for France's transformation from a feudal country to a centralized early modern state. With the end of the crusades, kings no longer needed Knights Templar and could receive similar services from other important orders, like the Knights Hospitallers.

Inevitably, the Templars would encounter the intrigues of King Philip IV of France. The King, who owed the Templars 4000,000 florins, was jealous of their power and wealth. Philip had taken the loans as a way to finance his wars against Flanders and other rebel lords, as a way to create a personal army and increase his power. Another problem was that the exemption of the Knights Templar from priestly taxes gave them considerable autonomy to rule their lands, which annoyed the King. The opportunity King Philip sought, came to him in 1307. Pope Clement wrote a letter to King Philip IV regarding accusations made by a Templar, asking for his help. He would use this opportunity to launch an investigation incriminating the Templars. If the Templars disappeared, he would both clear his debt to them and seize the Templars' fortunes. King Philip IV began investigating and substantiating the alleged accusations and pressured French Pope Clement V to allow arrests. Pope Clement already had serious problems. He had inherited a papacy that had recently lost both prestige and power because of its involvement in factional conflicts and its inability to help the Latin Christians in the East. Clement complied with the King's request. He was also jealous of the Templars and worried about their growing religious influence during the Crusades. In November 1307, Pope Clement V issued a papal proclamation to arrest all Templars and confiscate their property. On Friday, October 13, 1307, every single Knight of the Templars in France, including Jacques de Molay, the grand Master of the Templars, was arrested in a raid, and handed over to the Inquisition for questioning, and all of the Order's property was confiscated. Many, including

Molay, were executed. The Pope gave an essential part of the possession of Templars to the Hospitallers, including Cyprus (Nicholson, 2014). Some surviving Templars are believed to have fled to Britain, Switzerland, and other countries, where they secretly carried out their activities.

A final claim about the Pope's stance is based on the Chinon Scroll, discovered in the Vatican archives in 2001. According to this claim, the Pope had sent his senior men and cardinals to Chinon, one of the most important bases of the Knights Templar, in western France in 1308 to take their statements and speak with the Knights. The events of the meeting between the knights and the cardinals were recorded on the Chinon Scroll. This scroll contained all the confessions of the knights and the decisions made by the Cardinals and the Pope. With the discovery of the scroll, we know more about the persecution of the Knights Templar in the thirteenth century and of an unsuccessful attempt by Pope Clement V to save the Knights Templar from King Philip IV. The Pope wrote that he pardoned all the knights who confessed heresy, allowing some to escape, to ensure less bloodshed. Later in 1310, Pope Clement intended to call for papal trials to prove the Templars' innocence, but King Philip IV blocked the attempt, threatening to take military action against the Church if the Templars were not disbanded (Nicholson, 2011).

The importance of the Knights Templar goes beyond their success on the battlefield, it is also based on their commercial and financial operations. The Templars owned many properties in various parts of Europe. They earned income by running farms, mills, or land. Most of the Templars' financial resources came primarily from donations from the Church and Kings, but the Order was also able to generate income for itself through independent economic and commercial activities both in the East and the West. In the Middle Ages, mills played a very important role in agriculture and were an excellent means of generating income. Because they were expensive to build and maintain, there were still relatively few mills in the twelfth century, and those who owned them could charge high fees for their use. Some of the Templars' mills worked on rivers, while others worked in coastal areas, thanks to the tide. The most famous of the Templar river-powered wheat mills was located at Da'uk on the Nahr Kurdaneh (Belus River), which flows from Recordane (Kurdaneh) to Acre. The Templars had tidal mills on the River Thames just west of the City of London and on the River Lea north-east of the City of London. The Templars also owned a windmill at Dunwich in Suffolk, given to them by King Richard I of England. It was not always economical for the Templars to run the mills themselves and they sometimes rented them out to a third party in exchange for money, grain, or other in-kind donations. They were also engaged in the extraction of coal and metal ores, smelting, and manufacturing of metals. In 1246, King Henry III of England gave the Templars two forges in Fleet Street, west of the City of London. The Templars had a saltworks at Pilgrim Castle on the Palestinian coast, where salt was produced by distilling seawater. There was a glass factory in the village of As-Sumairiya in the Kingdom of Jerusalem (Nicholson, 2014).

Using their wealth, Templars engaged in various activities that inspired modern-day bankers. These included a range of financial transactions such as property management, loan and deposit services, remittances, safe deposit boxes, and financial arbitration/accounting. The Templars had special agreements with landowners and pilgrims. Wealthy noble proprietors delegated their property management to the Templars as their trustees according to the "Common Law Trust" of medieval England. A common law trust is created by an agreement between the owners of a property or business and a trustee or group of trustees; the trustees have legal ownership of all the business's property and manage the joint venture's business. Thrust partners receive a proportional share of the income from the trust. When the trust is terminated, its revenue is shared pro rata. This practice was especially in demand during the Second Crusade, and documents related to the procedure were found in the Court of Chancery, which served as a High Court of Justice in the Medieval Age (Hudson, 2022). During the Crusades, finding an institutional structure to be trusted was significant for a pilgrim or knight who had to be away from home for a long time. The Templars managed this person's property until he returned to his country. Part of the trust agreement was often the bequeathing of part of the property income to the owner's relatives after his death. For example, when Peter of Alcalá made his will in 1214, he transferred all his deeds to the Temple to be held by the Order until the conditions of his will were fulfilled (Forey, 1973).

In Aragon, the Templars' lending activities date back to the 1130 s. All religious orders lent money, but since Christians were not allowed to charge interest, they had to find other ways to cover the cost of the debt. As we explained before in the loan agreement that if the coin lost value between the time the loan was made and repayment, the borrower had to add a fixed amount to compensate the lender. If land was given as the pledge for the debt it could be stipulated in the loan conditions that the produce from the land did not count toward the repayment of the loan (Nicholson, 2014). In time, most other religious organizations lost importance in this field; lending became and remained a very important Templar activity. Documents show that the Templars continued to lend frequently, until their arrest (Forey, 1973). For the Templars, lending was naturally an institutional activity undertaken on the advice of the Master and carried out over a long period. Given that very few of the Order's records have survived in the East, loans to private individuals cannot be expected to leave much of a trace in extant documents. But there are some. For example, documents mention that Bishop Aimery of Tripoli borrowed 3,000 bezants (a gold or silver coin originally minted at Byzantium) from the Templars in 1187, and Bohemund IV of Antioch received 6,000 bezants from them in 1199. In the twelfth century, bishops and monasteries were frequent sources of loans, and the Templars may have seen lending to the needy as an expected activity in their early days (Stuckey, 2017).

Such loans were normally for one year, and repayment was usually fixed for Easter, the Assumption of Mary, or All Saints' Day. Interest payments were hidden because of the prohibition of usury. As we explained previously, there were different approaches to interest in the West and East Christian world (Stuckey, 2017).

An excellent example is a Templar Loan agreement signed in 1250 by Robert, Count of Artois (1st cousin to King Philip III of France). In this contract, the Count wrote: "*I declare... I am indebted to Brother John, the Friar of Tours, Treasurer of the house of the Knights Templar in Paris, 1,578 Livres Parisis [Paris Pounds]. From my affairs ... For the settlement and full payment of the said loan.. I specifically state that ... my rents, incomes and rents and income from my Domfront-en-Passais towns ... until continuous payment is paid and liquidated ... the entire debt in question will be made to the treasurer*" (Barber & Bate, 2002). Another example is the loan King Edward of England demanded from the Templars to cover the expenses of the war in the Holy Land. The King was offering his commodities in France as collateral for the debt (Ferris, 1902). Sometimes debtors could not make their payments on time. If the borrower did not fulfill his or her commitment, a clause was added to the loan deed. In this case, the loan would be collected from the income from certain properties (Forey, 1973).

Another practice that the Knights Templar developed is a kind of Letter of Credit. It was true that there was a clear need for financial credit and cash transfers to help the pilgrims and crusaders. The Bibliotheque Nationale in Lavoix has a collection of manuscripts of contracts signed by the Crusaders in the Latin East with Italian bankers. Three hundred of these documents have survived, of which almost two hundred are payment orders or promissory notes, and the rest are drafts, letters of guarantee, and letters of credit. For example, in 1250, 200 livres parisis (Parisian livre) were sent to Jean de Haumont from the revenues of the lands of the abbot of Res, which were administered by the abbot in his absence. In another example, pilgrims borrowed cash from the Templars in Spain to take with them on their journey, in exchange for the assurance of the expected income from the land. Much more common is the letter of credit application. It is signed or rather sealed by a prince, a baron, or a bishop, in which he guarantees upon sufficient proof to reimburse anyone who has lent specified person sums of money up to a specified limit. In 1217, for example, the Dean of Arras in letters patent names four crusaders who are just setting out for Jerusalem and are to carry the letter with them: Baudouin de Henchin, up to 150 livres parisis a year; Gui de Hautecloque, up to 130 l.p.; Jean de Bouffles, up to 90 l.p.; and Pierre du Chatelet, also up to 90 Up. These are the estimated annual revenues of the properties which the said persons have entrusted to the Dean, and he will repay to the lender of money, or to his nominee, sums which the four men have harrowed, up to the stated limit against letters from them acknowledging what they owe. However, if a knight were killed in battle, such a debt would be difficult or impossible to collect. Therefore, the crusader had to sign a bill of law in which the lender was the beneficiary, and there had to be four witnesses (Forey, 1973).

The king and the army leaders had considerable dealings with Italian bankers through their local branches. According to historical documents, King Henry III of England borrowed from the Florence bankers. He paid the debt when it was due in Spain for a ship he bought over there and made the payment in London without the hassle of carrying money, relying only on a transmitted code, through the Templar's house in Florence. It was delivered to the banker by the Templars. This way, there was no need to transport money (Ferris, 1902). These examples clearly show how loans to individual Crusaders were achieved without physically transferring money from the West to the East (Stuckey, 2017).

In the Middle Ages, all religious orders were used by ordinary people as a vault for valuables, and they were asked to lend money when ordinary people needed cash. The Templars, in particular, were well-known for such financial services, being used by kings as treasurers and money carriers. In the West, the Order developed systems for collecting, safekeeping, and transporting large sums of cash and other valuables to the East. Merchants made extensive use of the New Temple in London and Paris to store their valuables. The Templar systems were highly secure and strictly secret (Nicholson, 2014). Various precious stones, gold, or jewelry were kept in these safes. These chests, found in the Templars' houses, were used by travelers or those who wanted to keep their valuable assets for a certain period. An example of a surviving receipt reads: "*We...we...we, who have been deposited in the house of the Monzon Temple, acknowledge that we have received and preserved all the jewels we have put for safekeeping. Therefore, we declare that the places of the temple and all our brethren have no affiliation with all the jewels in question*" (Barber & Bate, 2002). In Aragon, too, Templar houses served as depositories and were often used for this purpose by people of all classes. Gardeny Castle, Spain (west of Barcelona) even had a special "*deposit house.*" In the early thirteenth century, Gerald of Cabrera and his son had gold, silver, horses, and corn on deposit at Gardeny. But most of what was kept was jewelry, documents, or money (Forey, 1973). From the reign of King Philip Augustus (1180–1223) until their arrest by Philip IV in 1307, the Paris Temple served as the French royal treasury. From the second half of the twelfth century, the Papacy began using the Templars to deposit, exchange, and transfer money (Smith, 2016).

Since the Templars were widely engaged in banking and lending activities, it was giving their Master a natural place among the king's advisors. The Master in Spain often attended court and was regularly summoned to the Cortes Generales (the legislative chambers of Spain). The high-level Templars were occasionally entrusted with responsible finance tasks (Forey, 1973). In 1227, for example, disputed matters between James I and the nobles of Aragon were submitted for arbitration to the provincial Master Fulk of Montpesat, the archbishop of Tarragona, and the bishop of Lérida. The Templars seem to have been frequently employed as fiscal officials in collecting royal dues and taxes. In 1184, the Templar Master Pons in Azemar was among those who received accounts from the royal bailiffs of Tarragona and Cervera. Likewise, the commander of Palau, had temporarily appointed a Templar in both Aragon and Catalonia two years earlier. At the same time, at the end of 1222, the account of the profits arising from the changes made to the coins was taken from the coin holders, using the arbitration and accounting skills of the Templar masters (Forey, 1973). Ferdinand III of Castile (1199–11,252) issued a new coinage after his accession to the throne. This was probably intended to solve the problems caused by the new coinage issued by Ferdinand III of Castile (1199–11,252) (Todesca, 1988).

Smith (2016) gives two examples of practices in this context. The first example concerns a letter written by Pope Honorius in 1220. The Pope stated that the money collected for a fund was not sent to them, even though the Crusaders promised it. The Pope appointed the Templars as his deputies and demanded they collect the money and bring it to the Papacy. The second example also describes how the

Templars recorded land and similar immovable assets and used accounting to track movable assets such as wine and grain. Undoubtedly, a sound registration system was needed to carry out fiscal transactions. Historical documents indicate that the Templars consistently recorded their money and property and successfully controlled their branches and representations (Edwards, 2022).

According to one legend, after their activities ended, the Templars went underground, disguising themselves with various symbols. Those who fled to Switzerland also played an important role in the Swiss victory over the Habsburg army at the Battle of Morgarten (Nov. 15, 1315). They used their banking know-how in Switzerland to inspire the establishment of "*private banking*" centuries later, based on secret accounts. Although there is no serious evidence for this, many believe that the spirit of the Knights Templar lives in Switzerland (Butler et al., 2006). We will describe the origin of Swiss Banking later in this book.

1.5 Extending the Story of Banks into the Present

This book will continue to tell banking history by presenting nine banking episodes, stepping stones between the Templars and the Global Financial Crisis of the 2008/09 period. The differences between the Templars in the Medieval world and the Wall Street banks at the beginning of the twenty-first century are huge. By presenting nine episodes, we give an impression of the crucial developments. We are going to give attention to the banking products developed, and also to the political background. The political background determines the freedom that was needed to provide these products, and the contribution to the economy, banks had. There is always tension between the power of the banks and the power of the government. Only if there is some stability in this tension, albeit a dynamic one, a power dance, banks can prosper. We give extra attention to this power dance because it is the condition-sine-qua-non for a good functioning of the banks.

1.5.1 How the Power Dance of State and Banks is Developing

The Templars worked for the people, the nobility, the Church, and the Kings. They were protected by the Church and King to give them sufficient independence to be able to perform this work. Through this work, they acquired substantial power and wealth. As the crusades became less important, the interest in the Templar activity diminished and they became an attractive prey for a greedy King, insufficiently protected now by a hesitating and weakening Pope. The power of cities and merchants was yet insufficient to compensate. The power balance that was necessary for the banking function of the Templars crumbled and broke. It was not long before Orseme wrote his Treatment about the character of money and stressed that the king was not the owner of the money, but that it was for the service of the community and that the king had to take care of that (Martin, 2014).

At the beginning of the twenty-first century, in the US, there were other countervailing powers around banking and finance. In the first place, banking and finance itself, the total system of financial services corporations: "Wall Street". Wall Street has to work for the real economy. The real economy consists of "Main Street", representing the interests of everyday people and small business owners, together with the second party, and, next to that, the large national and international corporations, the third party. A fourth party is the government, in the U.S. including the Fed and other regulating bodies (= Fed +). The Church did not play a role anymore in this power game. The Fed + has as role to maintain the balance. Wall Street needs sufficient freedom to be able to service the real economy adequately. Some protection is necessary, therefore. But the freedom has to be restricted as well, to protect the interests of Main Street and the real economy in general. That leads to structural tensions, and the Fed + has to resolve this. But during the Financial Crisis of 2008/09, it appeared that Wall Street corporations were so large and mutually dependent that the Fed + could only decide to let it go and postpone interference. There was no balance anymore.

In describing this tension between government and banks, it is useful to refer to the book "The Narrow Corridor" by Acemoglu and Robinson (2019). It underlined the importance of establishing a balance of power between the state and society to develop economies. The authors use the concept of Leviathan, or the Content, Form, and Power of a Religion and World-State, as developed by Thomas Hobbes (1588–1679). They argued that societies need a state (Leviathan) to beware of an anarchic structure. However, if the institutional arrangements in the community do not balance the state's power within the society, oppressive and totalitarian administrations will emerge. If there are such institutional arrangements, the Leviathan can be chained to form a narrow corridor. Here, the state has enough power to maintain order but not enough to be oppressive. This preserves freedom and facilitates economic growth, and banking activities flourish. Given the opposing pulls exerted by state and society, maintaining this balance requires a never-ending struggle. Therefore, a sustainable institutional structure is needed.

We will travel with exciting stories from medieval monarchical structures to contemporary developed structures, following the intertwined footsteps of states and banks as they start from the Mediterranean coast and extend to northern Europe and the New World.

A most remarkable banking activity began in Italy after the Templars waned from history. The bankers, known as Lombardy bankers, lived in Northern Italy and were the region's main players. These merchant bankers were dealing with both trading and banking. From the fifteenth century onwards, one of them, the Medici Bank (Chap. 2), became a leading institution in Europe. Since then, no banker has been said to have had their glory (Galbraith, 2017). At a time when the political environment there was rather moderate, they were able to control money as well as administer the city-state in Florence.

From the sixteenth century onwards, the Netherlands and England were the driving forces of the banking sector, respectively. The Dutch experience (Chap. 3) was the first significant example of a more moderate political atmosphere, providing a power balance between society and state. On the other hand, England established the first modern central bank and the first fractional reserve system, in a parliamentary environment created after the Glorious Revolution (1689). Royal power was restricted in Britain, and then the narrow corridor mentioned by Acemoglu and Robinson in which banking could work comfortably began to form with a constitutional guarantee (Chap. 4). England became the most important country of the nineteenth century. With the invention of paper money, banks did what alchemists could not do and turned gold into paper money. As we will explain in this book, the transformation of money from metals such as gold and silver into paper money resulted from many historical events, wars, and economic developments. The actual champion of paper money was undoubtedly John Law, who created wealth for the French with the paper money issued by a French royal bank he founded, but then caused a great crisis (Chap. 5).

However, the newly formed United States of America was the real homeland of paper money. Although paper money has become widespread in this country, bankruptcies and frauds involving banks also created an atmosphere against banks. The early-nineteenth century US president Thomas Jefferson (1801–1809) said: "I believe that banking institutions are more dangerous to our liberties than standing armies (…) The issuing power should be taken from the banks and restored to the people, to whom it properly belongs" (Lenzner, 2011). Despite all the concerns, using paper money has become very common in the continent within the century. The fact that the bankers told the story of paper money to the public very well and convinced them might also have played a role in this success. Yuval Noah Harari, known for his book "Sapiens," holds that the difference between humans and other living beings is their ability to make mental fiction. Claiming that the line between fantasy and reality is unclear; if a compelling story is told to people and made to be believed, they will embrace that belief with passion. An example shows the value they attach to the piece of paper on which a king's picture is printed, namely paper money. According to Harari, religions, human rights, and even ideologies exist because people believe (Harari, 2015). Indeed, in a short time, the banking system, as an institution, has made society believe in paper money so much that people can give their lives for this cause (Greider, 1989).

In the nineteenth century, under the leadership of the Rothschild family in Europe, while Jews rose with banking, banks have become more and more influential in economy and politics (Chap. 6). While the conditions of the period led to the emergence of financial imperialism, some underdeveloped countries, such as the Ottomans and Egypt, fell into a debt trap (Chap. 8). Although somewhat contested by large banks from other countries ("National Champions") (Chap. 9), Wall Street became the engine of the US and the global economy from the beginning of the twentieth century onwards. American banks grew more vital in the corridor opened under a free economy and a liberal democracy. Banks like JP Morgan (Chap. 7) and Citibank (Chap. 10) heightened Wall Street's efficacy against Main Street in the twentieth century. However, when their greed and inadequate government control caused significant crises, such as in 1908 and 1929 in the early twentieth century, regulatory agencies established restrictive laws reducing Wall Street's power.

In response, interestingly, U.S. banks, have taken advantage of the widespread role of lobbying in the US political system and have begun to try to penetrate the views of legislators and regulators on significant issues. When entering the last quarter of the twentieth century, they removed several restrictions by persuading politicians and regulators to step back (Chap. 10). According to the International Monetary Fund (IMF), it is probable that banks can capture the regulators (Hardy, 2006). The concept of "regulatory capture" was introduced by Nobel laureate economist George Stigler. If regulators are captured, the dominance of the regulators could fall into the hands of the industries or interests they are supposed to regulate. Thus, an agency tasked with acting in the public interest instead would tend to work in a way that would benefit incumbent firms in the banks it needed to regulate (Stigler, 2021). As a result, while the 2008/09 crisis was related to covetousness of the banks, populist governments, and insufficient supervision of regulators, it became clear that deterioration of the balance of power in favor of banks could bring severe costs to the economies (Chap. 11).

As we will explain in this book via interesting banking stories, the struggle for the "narrow corridor" will continue forever. While the banks in developed countries seem to fight foremost against the regulations restricting their profits, the banks in oppressive regimes will continue to seek a way to open a narrow corridor in the twenty-first century.

1.5.2 How the Banking Secrets Are Developing

Through all of the cases, we focus on the tension between the power of the banks and other powers in society. While we think that the development and value creation of sound banking is related to democracy and freedom, it is certainly not just about that. The book covers the development of large corporate banking from the thirteenth century to the early twenty-first century, following the Knights Templar as the first bank-like institution. We bring it closer to the reader by giving attention to the actions and emotions of the protagonists. Each bank that is the subject of these stories not only affected its own country but also created turning points in the history of world banking. Together they established the banking innovations that contributed to this huge structure of modern finance and banking that is on one hand so powerful and unassailable and on the other hand so fragile and vulnerable. This contradiction looks almost mysterious and, to stress that, we speak of banking secrets. Beyond the struggles these banks put up in the transition from the era of despotic kings to the modern years, the traces they left behind in the history of political economy, as well as the methods they developed, will be discussed.

As we briefly explained above, the evolution of banking for hundreds of years is full of colorful events, and interestingly, it has a multinational character. From the

Crusades to the 80 Years War of the seventeenth century, from the Battle of Waterloo of 1813 to the twentieth century World Wars, events take us around various countries and cities, from Florence to Amsterdam, from London to New York, and confront the reader with exciting characters. Even though much of the origin of banking is in Italy, many countries have benefited from each other's experience, and each nation has contributed something of itself to banking practices. The historical adventure of banking is full of exciting stories that could be the subject of a novel or movie. Stories of the book contain wars, quests for freedom, political marriages, politics, greed, and dishonesty. The unavoidable rise in the power of the banks in this historical process and its political and political consequences are given strikingly between the lines of the stories.

It is thought that if the reader establishes a link between political and economic developments and the development process of banking, she (or he) will better understand the functions of banks. Therefore, the book tells the historical development process of banking through the stories of significant banker characters and banking organizations. These stories will enlighten us on the political and economic conditions in which banks can survive and show how the quest for freedom and democracy will play a vital role in the time travel of banking. While this book explains how banking developed historically, it also aims to reveal the dominant features that make it successful, and that contribute to this structure of modern finance and banking. Undoubtedly, every stage of banking evolution is full of various lessons. The reader will encounter many familiar stories and characters, having their counterparts in politics and business in virtually every country. We hope these stories will induce important insights for bankers, policymakers, and the public.

The development of banking is described in harmony with historical events, and definitions related to banking have been presented such that many can understand. Although this book has been prepared with an utterly scientific point of view, we tried to avoid the concepts and jargon used in the banking sector as much as possible. We try to initiate a broad group of readers into the "secrets of the banks". Historical events are often slightly dramatized at the beginning of each topic, encouraging the reader to be part of the story while avoiding the details. In addition, the topics themselves are embellished with lively stories.

Our study is limited to the modern era: from the thirteenth century, when banking was institutionalized, to the early 2000s. Because the banking story after the early twentieth century is much more comprehensive, contemporary banking is not covered at length but is presented condensed. After the introduction, the institutions that contributed to the development of international banking are narrated separately in Chap. 2 up until Chap. 7. Much emphasis has been given to post Middle Age developments in the Netherlands, Great Britain, France, and the USA. In Chap. 8, the story of the Ottoman Bank, a semi-colonial institution in the Ottoman State with its still feudal economic structure, is given. In Chaps. 9 and 10, we focus on a set of Western banks that have shown to be leaders in their home countries in the last century or longer, and we especially zoom in on the U.S. Citibank as a major developer and challenger of a complicated Bank-State relationship. In the final chapter (Chap. 11) we describe the financial crisis of 2008 and, from that perspective look back to the earlier chapters. We combine that with a modest look forward.

While telling the stories of the banks, especially the years when they were the most magnificent, are emphasized. For example, in Chap. 2, the golden period of the Medici Bank in the fourteenth and fifteenth centuries is noted, and the remaining years are shortly dealt with. Similarly, the activities of J.P. Morgan & Co., still part of a vital bank today, are examined in Chap. 8 only in the 19th and early twentieth centuries. Sometimes, a step back or ahead will be set, e.g., when referring to (semi-) colonial or other early activities by some banks in Chaps. 9 and 10. Although most of the banks' historical journeys being the subject of our book are success stories, John Law's early eighteenth century adventure in France, a success story at first, turned into a disaster and left many lessons to be learned in history. The stories in each chapter are written independently of each other. The chapters are designed to start reading from the book's first chapter, but it is also possible to quickly understand a subject by reading separate chapters.

One of the contributions lies in interpreting the factors underlying the banks' success in each chapter. It may not surprise the reader that almost all of these conditional factors are still valid today. A link between the stories of banks and some current developments will be established. At the end of each chapter, the organizational instruments and financial innovations they developed ("banking secrets") will be singled out. In doing so, the authors like to convey a positive note with their story.

References

Acemoglu, D., & Robinson, J. A. (2019). *The narrow corridor: States, societies, and the fate of liberty*. Penguin Books.

Andreau, J. (1999). *Banking and business in the roman world*. Translated by J. Lloyd. Cambridge University Press.

Argenti, P. A. (2002). Crisis communication: Lessons from 9/11. *Harvard Business Review*. https://hbr.org/2002/12/crisis-communication-lessons-from-911

Barber, M. (2012). *The new knighthood: A history of the order of the temple*. Cambridge University Press.

Barber, M., & Bate, K. (2002). *The templars: Selected sources*. Manchester University Press.

Bellitto, C.M. (2017). *Secrets of the Knights Templar | Franciscan Media*. Retrieved 11 July, 2022, from https://www.franciscanmedia.org/st-anthony-messenger/secrets-of-the-knights-templar/

Brooks, J. (1999). *Once in Golconda: A true drama of Wall Street 1920–1938*. Wiley.

Buckley, R., & Nixon, J. (2009). The role of reputation in banking. UNSW Law Research Paper No. 2009–18. *Journal of Banking and Finance Law and Practice, 20*, 37–50. https://papers.ssrn.com/sol3/papers.cfm?abstract_id=1420390

Botticini, M., & Eckstein, Z. (2003). *From farmers to merchants: A human capital interpretation of Jewish economic history*. Retrieved from https://www.bu.edu/econ/files/2012/11/dp124.pdf

Butler, A., & Dafoe, S. (2006). *The knights templar revealed*. Barnes & Noble.

Casualties of the September 11 attacks. (n.d.). Casualties of the September 11 attacks. *Wikipedia*. Retrieved 20, April 2021, from https://en.wikipedia.org/wiki/Casualties_of_the_September_11_attacks

Curtin, P. D. (1984). *Cross-cultural trade in world history*. Cambridge University Press.

Edwards, D. (2022). *Finance and the Crusades: England, c.1213–1337*. Routledge.
Edwards, J., & Ogilvie, S. (2008). Contract enforcement, institutions and social capital: The Maghribi traders reappraised. *CESifo Working Paper No. 2254*. https://doi.org/10.1111/j.1468-0289.2011.00635.x
Farrell, P. B. (2013). *Big banks conspiracy is destroying America*. MarketWatch. Retrieved from https://www.marketwatch.com/story/big-banks-conspiracy-is-destroying-america-2013-08-07
Farrell, D. M. (1984). Reason and Right in Hobbes' "Leviathan". *History of Philosophy Quarterly, 1*(3), 297–314. https://www.jstor.org/stable/27743688
Ferris, E. (1902). The financial relations of the knights Templars to the English crown. *The American Historical Review*, 1–17. https://www.jstor.org/stable/1832571
Forey, A. (1973). *The Templars in the Corona de Aragón*. Oxford University Press.
Galbraith, J. K. (2017). *Money: Whence it came, where it went*. Princeton University Press.
Geithner, T. F. (2015). *Stress test: Reflections on financial crises*. Crown.
Greider, W. (1989). *Secrets of the temple: How the Federal Reserve runs the country*. Simon and Schuster.
Greif, A. (1989). Reputation and coalitions in medieval trade: Evidence on the Maghribi traders. *The Journal of Economic History, 49*(4), 857–882. https://doi.org/10.1017/S0022050700009475
Greif, A. (1993). Contract enforceability and economic institutions in early trade: The Maghribi traders' coalition. *The American Economic Review, 83*(3), 525–548. https://www.jstor.org/stable/2117532
Greif, A. (2008). Contract enforcement and institutions among the Maghribi Traders: Refuting Edwards and Ogilvie. Retrieved from https://www.econstor.eu/bitstream/10419/26395/1/572272189.PDF
Harari, Y. N. (2015). *Sapiens: A brief history of mankind*. Vintage Books.
Hardy, D. (January 2006). Regulatory capture in banking. IMF Working Paper No. 06/34. Available at SSRN: https://ssrn.com/abstract=892925
Hudson, A. (2022). *Equity and trusts* (10th ed., p. 2013). Routledge.
Jewish Virtual Library, Ancient Jewish History: Banking & Bankers. Retrieved from https://www.jewishvirtuallibrary.org/banking-and-bankers
Lenzner, R. (2011). *Thomas Jefferson warned the nation to beware the power of the banks*. Forbes. Retrieved from https://www.forbes.com/sites/robertlenzner/2011/11/06/thomas-jefferson-warned-the-nation-about-the-power-of-the-banks/?sh=d4a829d2b18b.
Makinen, G. (2002). The economic effects of 9/11: A retrospective assessment. In *Report for congress. Congressional research service*. Retrieved from https://fas.org/irp/crs/RL31617.pdf
Maniatis, G. C. (2016). The economic institutions of the Byzantine State. *Byzantion, 86*, 205–259. https://www.jstor.org/stable/26768924
Martin, F. (2014). *Money: The unauthorised biography*. Random House.
Millett, P. (1991). *Lending and borrowing in ancient Athens*. Cambridge University Press.
Morcillo, M. G. (2008). *Auctions, bankers and public finances in the Roman world* (pp. 257–75)
Nicholson, H. (2011). *The proceedings against the Templars in the British Isles: Volume 2: The translation*. Routledge. https://doi.org/10.4324/9781315085487
Nicholson, H. (2014). *A brief history of the knights Templar*. Robinson.
Radhanite. (n.d.). Radhanite. *Wikipedia*. Retrieved 10, January 2024, from https://en.wikipedia.org/wiki/Radhanite
Saritas, E. (2010). Banka İtibarının Zedelenmesİ Suçu (The Crime of Damage to Bank Reputation). *Istanbul University Faculty of Law Journal, 68*(1–2), 121–150. https://dergipark.org.tr/en/download/article-file/97584
Smith, T. W. (2016). Pope Honorius III, the military orders and the financing of the fifth crusade: A culture of papal preference? In: J. Schenk, & M. Carr (Eds.), *The military orders volume VI (Part 1): Culture and conflict in the mediterranean world. The military orders* (pp. 54–61). Routledge. ISBN 9781315460888.
Sorkin, A. R. (2009). *Too big to fail: Inside the battle to save wall street*. Penguin Books.

Stabile, L. (2011). 9/11 10th anniversary: Survivors of attacks maintain life perspective. *Mass Live*. Retrieved from https://www.masslive.com/news/2011/09/911_10th_anniversary_survivors.html

Stigler, G. J. (2021). The theory of economic regulation. In *The political economy: Readings in the politics and economics of American public policy* (pp. 67–81). Routledge. https://doi.org/10.4324/9781315495811-8/theory-economic-regulation-george-stigler

Stuckey, J. (2017). *The Eastern Mediterranean frontier of Latin Christendom*. Routledge.

Todesca, J. J. (1988). The monetary history of Castile-Leon (ca. 1100–1300) in light of the Bourgey hoard. *Museum Notes (American Numismatic Society), 33*, 129–203. https://www.jstor.org/stable/43574156

Verboven, K. (2020). Bankers' guilds and the Roman monetary system. In: *Detur dignissimo: studies in honour of Johan Van Heesch. Cercle d'études numismatiques–European Centre for Numismatic Studies* (pp. 417–436). Retrieved from https://biblio.ugent.be/publication/8676522

Worral, S. (2017). The Templars got rich fighting for god—Then lost it all. *National Geographic*. Retrieved from https://www.nationalgeographic.com/history/article/knights-templar-crusades-dan-jones

Wu, N. (2019). Actions and receptions of the knights Templar from 1118–1192. Honors thesis, Duke University. Retrieved from https://dukespace.lib.duke.edu/items/2c2491fe-cc4e-4f2b-ab39-0c37e61be0db

yadvashem.org, (n.d.). The Jews of Algeria, Morocco and Tunisia. Retrieved from https://www.yadvashem.org/articles/general/the-jews-of-algeria-morocco-and-tunisia.htm

Chapter 2
The Medici Family: Bankers of the Renaissance (Fourteenth and Fifteenth Centuries)

2.1 Introduction

The Tuscany Valley, located on fertile lands in the central regions of Italy, has an awe-inspiring natural beauty with cypress trees stretching their heads among the vineyards, maquis, and olive groves in geography where hills are lined up. The most important and impressive city in the region is undoubtedly Florence. Florence, a big city with many squares, has a stylish appearance with the Arno River flowing in the middle and historical bridges. Florence is an open-air museum with works by artists such as Leonardo da Vinci, Michelangelo, Raphael, and Donatello, offering a feast of art to visitors worldwide. The Renaissance movement started right here, which enabled significant developments in art, science, philosophy, architecture, and even rediscovered man.

Florence was leading a new era in the early fifteenth century. While still living under the shadow of the Catholic Church, a vital institution known for its strict and conservative stance against change, a severe stir had begun in its society. The most important activities of the region were manufacturing, commerce, banking, art, and philosophical movement. Just as a wealth and tolerance environment created by the Islamic caliphs in the 900–1300 s led to enlightenment and brought forth scientists and thinkers such as Ibn Sina, Ibn Rushd, Farabi, and Ibn Khaldun, the first sprouts of the Renaissance movement grew in Florence. The Florence City Republic was highly developed due to the trade between Rome and France and gradually became the wealthiest and most powerful city in Europe. The most important activity of the economy was textile, which met the increasing demand for luxury clothing in Europe. Democracy began to revive in Italy, which was made up of city-states and created an environment suitable for change.

Bankers are the protagonists of our story with their creative practices. Although there were many merchants and bankers in Florence, one family would become far more critical and overshadow all the other players. The Medici is one of the most colorful families of their time, with conspiracy, assassination, politics, and marriages

M. B. Karan et al., *A History of Banks*, Contributions to Economics,
https://doi.org/10.1007/978-3-031-62297-7_2

having become the subject of many books and movies. When the Medici entered the scene at the end of the fourteenth century, a recession had begun in the Italian economy; the big Florentine bankers (the Bardi and Peruzzi) had gone bankrupt and only small ones were operating in the market. The Medici became prominent in business when ancestor Giovanni came to Florence and continued his banking activities there. However, the Medici owed their power and wealth to his son Cosimo di Giovanni de' Medici. A very creative and successful banker, known as "*il Vecchio (The Elder)*" or "*Father of the Fatherland*," Cosimo's success was not limited to banking alone. He was one of the main financiers of the Renaissance movement, as he made Florence stand out on the historical scene by protecting artists and investing in art with the money he earned. Cosimo di Giovanni de' Medici would have a significant role in the growth of the Italian Renaissance by taking the movement of art and humanism under his protection, and the Medici Bank would steer the European economy for about a century with its advanced financial methods.

2.2 Politics at the End of the Middle Ages

At the end of the Middle Ages, Italy's form of government was completely different from that of other European countries. While there were monarchical governments in European countries, some city-states of northern and central Italy did not recognize the Pope's authority and the Italian Kingdom's sovereignty. Northern Italy and upper Central Italy had city-states, the most powerful of which were Milan, Florence, Pisa, Siena, Genoa, Ferrara, Mantua, Verona, and Venice (Fig. 2.1). Northern Italy was further divided by a long-running war for supremacy between papal and Holy Roman Empire forces. Signoria ruled the cities. This form of government is a phase associated with the decline of the medieval commune system of government and the rise of the dynastic state. Contemporary observers and modern historians see the rise of the Signoria as a reaction to the failure of communion law to maintain order and suppress party strife and civil strife. In the anarchic conditions that often prevailed in medieval Italian city-states, people asked the strongmen to restore order and disarm the bloody elites (Encyclopedia Britannica, 1998). The growing merchant class and guilds believed that this institution provided a state structure where trade could be done more easily by reducing conflicts and anarchy. After all, Northern and Central Italy had become much more prosperous, and this region was the wealthiest in Europe. The new merchant ruling class, gaining their position with financial skills, adapted the feudal aristocratic model that dominated Europe in the Middle Ages for their purposes. The Signoria could be one lord or one family, like in Milan with the Visconti family, or a council, the ruling body of magistrates, like in Florence.

A kind of elitist democracy was practiced, in which guilds, the rich, and the nobility participated in political processes. In Italian city republics, elections were applied to get a political position, and the duration of office was limited (Ricciardelli, 2018). Still, only those with property and political power benefited from the right to elect and be elected.

Fig. 2.1 City-States of Italy (1494) https://commons.wikimedia.org/wiki/File:Italy_1494_AD.png

The free governance of cities facilitated commercial activities, motivated the business world, and provided opportunities. The most important institutional innovation was in the judiciary; a well-functioning legal system, security, and conflict resolution had become more accessible. A relatively fair tax system was established, and public order was maintained. Roads were securely guarded, and freedom of travel was ahead of its time. The East of Italy already had highly skilled sailors near the Byzantine Empire and the Muslim States. Demand for luxury goods such as silk and spices, which came from China and India via the Silk Road, increased. In England, sheep and goat farming was very well developed in the north, exporting high-quality wool all over Europe. International trade was developing, and the Italian city-states were central to this development (Robinson & Acemoglu, 2019).

The moderate environment in the region facilitated the organization of merchants under guilds that had power in political life. The Florence Signoria had nine members who were chosen from the ranks of the guilds of the city. The guilds had a secular administration based on strong family ties and were ruled by the city's prominent families. Guilds were, in fact, medieval institutions that organized every aspect of economic life. While protecting their members from competition from outsiders, their workshops were supervised, working hours were regulated, and they ensured a certain quality of work. Public services were also provided to their members, spouses, widows, and children. It is known that the first guild established in Florence in the 1150 s was the Arte di Calimala, the organization of cloth merchants (Staley, 1906). The Florentine government pursued a limited economic policy by the standards of the time, certainly compared to Venice. It took a laissez-faire attitude toward them, except in matters such as food supply and control of weights and measures, which De Roover describes as professional standards rather than economic regulation (De Roover, 1963). There were many large and small companies in the city. The structure of Florence's Renaissance economy, with its wide-ranging and dispersed activities and lack of central focus, prevented its various departments from being dependent on any one function, so it was almost impossible for any operator to hold the key. The business system structure in which the family companies of Florence, like the Medicis, operated and conditioned their business assumptions and approach to it, was more oriented toward remaining politically powerful than to direct competition (Goldthwaite, 1987).

2.3 Development of Commerce and Finance

Under the rule of the Byzantine Empire, the Italian city-states began to seize the Mediterranean trade networks. As the Italian trio of Venice, Pisa, and Genoa gained more and more wealth, they further expanded their trading arms, establishing trading posts in North Africa, gaining trade monopolies in parts of the Byzantine Empire, and expanding their transport networks, especially during the relocations of the crusader armies.

Bounded by a line from Florence to Ancona to the south and the Alps to the north, this area was arguably the heart of the Venice-centered world economy. Europe was bisected by a Venetian-Bruges-London axis running from south to north: both east and west of this line were large commercial zones that were much less mobile than the axis itself. The Venice city council, the Signoria, encouraged all such trade practices, offering equal opportunities to all participants. Venice's success resulted in its precocious capitalist organization: capitalism was born or invented in Venice and only later spread elsewhere. The characteristic problems regarding the relations between Capital, Labor, and the State were visible here (Braudel, 1992). Venice was not an isolated phenomenon; it grew up surrounded by a network of thriving towns, all inspired by similar reactions of the age in which they lived. Genuine innovations often did not come from Venice itself. In terms of banking or the formation of large companies, it was far behind the leading cities of Northern Italy. The first gold coins were minted in Genoa, not Venice, in the early thirteenth century, and Florence followed in 1250. Bills of Exchange and holding companies were invented in Florence, not Venice. Double-entry bookkeeping was also first practiced in Florence. The useful simplification of the marine insurance procedure by eliminating the need for a notary was enacted in Florence, not in the ports. The practices that maximized industrial activities had started again in Florence. Genoa made the first regular sea connection with Flanders via Gibraltar in 1277.

The main partners in a trade expedition were the investing partner, the commentator, and the traveling partner, the tractator. In a unilateral commenda, the investing partner paid all the investments and received 75% of the profit. Financial losses were completely for the investing partner. In a bilateral commenda, the traveling partner also invested, typically one-third of the investments and took also one-third of the losses. The profits were evenly split (Pryor, 1977). With trade growth, business relations became more complex by adding intermediaries and agents. Behind these large investors, consortia of smaller investors developed, who put their money into profit expectations but could not pay for an entire expedition. As noted by Florence Edler (De Roover, 1941), the American wife of the well-known Belgian Medici expert Raymond de Roover, the complex borrowing and lending mechanisms concerned many families.

2.4 The Bill of Exchange and Bookkeeping

The biggest problem in business was related to the difficulties in operating financing channels (Cartwright, 2019). According to historical documents, the transport of English wool to Florence required a somewhat complex process (Munro, 2012) (Fig. 2.2):

- Payment of tips and wine to officials, fees to customs guards and brokers, as well as duties to customs and export duties in London,

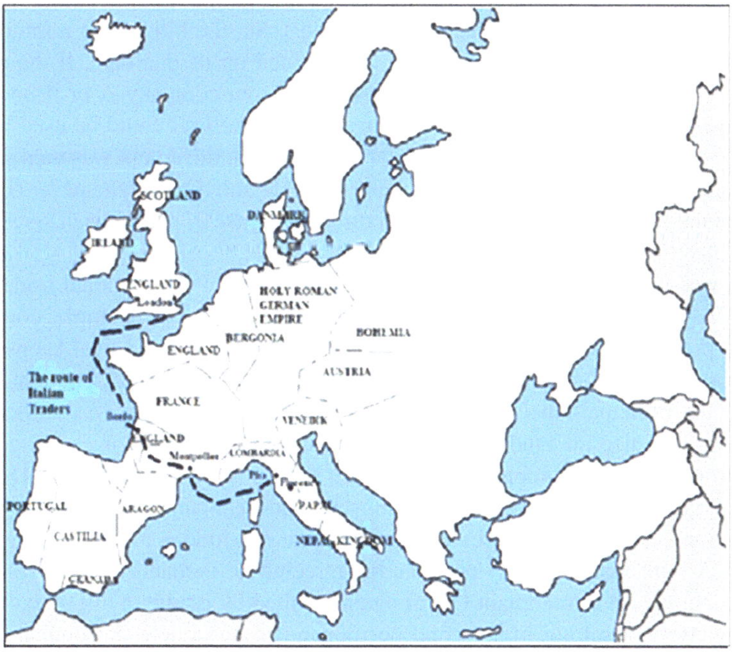

Fig. 2.2 British trade route of Italian traders

- Shipping wool from England to a port near Bordeaux (France) and paying innkeepers to store it temporarily there,
- Transport wool by land to Montpellier on the Mediterranean coast of France and then by sea to Pisa in Italy.
- Payment for port, warehouse, transport, and notary services in Pisa.
- Payment of tolls at three locations on the way to Florence.
- Payment of customs fees in Florence.

It was not easy to make these payments under the conditions of that time. In addition, financing was needed for each of these steps. Since different countries were involved, the necessity of considering the exchange rate and variations in it complicated the whole process.

To solve the difficulties of payments in such international trade, they used a new payment tool called "*bill of exchange*." A bill of exchange is a payment order, typically an order of some international trading company, A in country I, to a correspondent trading company, B in country II (or a subsidiary of trading company A in that country) to pay a specific party (merchant Q) at a specific time in the future a specific amount of money in the currency of that country (II). Suppose merchant P in country I wants to pay merchant Q in country II. He can buy such a bill of exchange from company A, paying in the local currency. He sends a copy of the bill of exchange to his counterparty Q, while company A sends a copy, plus instructions to pay this bill to his correspondent B. The due date of the bill was generally sufficiently far in the future ("*usance*") to be sure that merchant Q and trading company B had received their copies of the bill already then (Kohn, 1999). So, the bill would normally be presented before its due date and could be executed on its due date. If the payer, trading company B, had not received instructions from company A or if he had a lack of funds to honor the bill, he would refuse. This refusal could be used by the payee (merchant Q) to protest with a notary. The protest document was then sent to merchant P, who could sue trading company A for default. Only if the payer (B) had accepted the bill could the payee sue him directly in case of problems. There was a special merchant court for such cases.

This was the main pattern of payment in the world of international trade. The correspondent relationship was important in this pattern. In our example, company A is the principal, and company B is the correspondent. The principal keeps track of the correspondent's actions for him in a Nostro account. The correspondent keeps track of the principal's balance in a Vostro account. The pattern was sufficiently flexible to organize all kinds of financial transactions. The bill of exchange was a way to postpone a payment and combine it with a currency exchange. The ban on usury, the prohibition of interest established and maintained by the church (see next section), could be circumvented in this way; it was hidden in the exchange rate applied. A pure loan was also possible by agreeing beforehand that the resulting debt of company B to merchant Q was again fulfilled by issuing a bill of exchange on company A, resulting in a second postponement and a debt of company A to merchant B again. This was called dry exchange, and there was some discussion about whether it was allowed, given the ban on usury. But it was certainly applied in practice.

In the example above, we sketched the use of the bill of exchange for a bilateral payment. In many cases, the patterns were more complex. Kohn gives the example of a merchant from Lucca who pays a merchant in Genoa by selling a bill of exchange on a company in Champagne and taking care of sufficient funds in Champagne by buying in Lucca a bill of exchange on Champagne (Kohn, 1999). Patterns could become rather complex. A reason for Lucca merchants to pay Genoa merchants with a bill on Champagne could be that it was easier to borrow money there. Instead of taking care of sufficient funds in Champagne by buying Lucca a bill on Champagne, it could be attractive to settle the debt in Champagne by agreeing to let the Champagne bank issue a bill on Lucca. Of course, for a larger amount than the original one. This extensive use of bills of exchange was only possible due to the development of places where the demand and supply of bills of exchange could meet, a network of "*banking places.*" First, the cities of northern Italy and the Champagne (e.g., Troyes), later it extended over most of the commercial centers of western Europe, the Levant, and Spain. Interestingly, Florence was not a banking place. Important banking houses were from Florence, but the city itself was more directed to manufacturing. In the banking places, there were services available for money changers (the banchi del mercato in Italy), notaries, and brokers. The price of a bill of exchange was a matter of negotiation, but the involvement of brokers led to a certain uniformity in exchange rates. Apart from a concentration in place through the network of banking places, there was also a concentration in time, by adjusting the lead times of the bills, the usances, to the time between the fairs, realizing in this way that the bills were due during the fairs. During the fairs, the bills were netted with each other. The resulting debts could be paid in cash (1), in whatever currency (because of the presence of money changers), or it could be "*paid in bank*" (2) if the merchants had an account with a local bank, or new bills could be bought (3) or an inter-fair loan could be arranged (4), generally formalized through a letter obligatory. Interest was allowed on such credits because the fairs had a special position with respect to rules in general. There was a kind of "*freedom of the fairs.*" They were also exempted from the ban on usury. The other possibilities led to the situation that only a small fraction of the bills were eventually paid in cash. The tuning of the bills on the pattern of the fairs was important as long as the trade flows were not too massive.

Given how international trade was financed, it was natural that the international trading companies developed into banks, the banchi grossi. According to the fifteenth century historian Benedetto Dei, in 1469, there were thirty-three banchi grossi in Florence, and "*wherever there was commerce or money traffic, they dealt with goods and barter all over the world.*" These Florentine bankers were both merchants and bankers. They structured domestic and foreign trade not as a small-scale exchange of currency with coins but as the purchase and sale of bills in foreign currency consisting of larger payments. For most bankers, currency exchange was less critical than trading in goods though. Even the Medici, Florence's foremost merchant bankers, had emphasized that they were more merchants than bankers. Next to these banchi grossi, there were two other types of bank in Florence, banchi i pegno and banchi a minuto (De Roover, 1963). The first of them, the banchi di pegno, was despised among the people as scrupulous moneylenders. They were pawnshops operating under a public license that allowed them to issue loans at a cost (as commission) of up to 20% per year in exchange for pawned goods such as valuables and jewelry. The license was in fact a fine for breaking the ban on usury. The banchi a minuto formed with the banchi grossi, the money changers gild, the Arte del Cambio. Both exchanged different country and city currencies on stands and benches in public marketplaces. The origin of the word "*bank*" comes from them. It is known that these bankers, called money exchangers (cambiatori) or tavolieri, did business on a bench covered with a cloth, opening a ledger and a moneybag in front of them. By law, moneychangers were required to make transfers on their ledgers in the presence of their customers. Since checks were unknown, money orders were given orally and immediately written in the bank's books (De Roover, 1963). If these bankers went bankrupt, their benches were also removed. The English word "*bankruptcy*," meaning to go bankrupt, implies breaking or removing the bank (benches). The banchi a minuto were local and acted as retail banks in Florence.

The bill of exchange was the working horse of the international trading companies, well suited for long-distance trade with predictable and steady goods flows. In the case of local commerce or case long-distance commerce with a more erratic flow of goods, the commerce was performed by small merchants. Their main payment tool was the "*letter obligatory*." This was a promise to pay, instead of an order to pay, a promise to pay from a well-known bank. It also had a maturity date. We mentioned already that it was also used for inter-fair credits. This tool became especially important in France, the Netherlands, England, and later, Spain and the Hansa (Kohn, 1999). The demand and supply of bills of exchange and letters were well organized already in the fifteenth century, and the tools were therefore rather liquid. During the sixteenth century, this liquidity improved further by the possibility of reassigning bills and letters, transferring them to another actor, and by the possibility of discounting. In Chap. 4, we come back to this.

If a medieval merchant wanted to expand his business by forming a partnership, he needed an accounting system that satisfied both parties. As joint ventures increased and new alliances started to be established in Italy, this need began to be felt more than ever. For this reason, the double-sided bookkeeping system they developed had become increasingly necessary, as it constantly needed to verify itself. Of course, it was not easy to keep books and do basic mathematical calculations with the Roman numerals preferred by the Church (Durham, 1992). Later, with the numbering system known as Arabic numbering, more convenient methods related to bookkeeping began to develop. Arabic numerals were created according to the decimal system; zero was discovered. When you place a zero next to the numbers, ten, one hundred, and one thousand could be created. There would also be negative numbers if you go below zero. It was much easier to calculate this way. The Pisan mathematician Leonardo Fibonacci played an important role in introducing the Arabic numerals in Italy (Arabic Numerals, 2024). First, they were used alongside the Roman Numerals. The double-entry bookkeeping was developed in Venice and other Italian cities. In the first half of the fifteenth century, it was more or less common practice in Florence and within the Medici Bank (De Roover, 1963). Later, the system was formalized and published by Luca Pacioli (1447–1517), a Franciscan friar and mathematician. From then on it spread all over Europe.

2.5 Church and Bankers

In Italy, during the tenth and eleventh centuries, with the dynamics of the economy not fluently functioning, Jewish bankers had largely dominated monetary transactions and the credit market then. Because the Church forbade interest payments on loan transactions based on biblical interpretations of interest, Christians could not legally enter into the loan business. Despite the prohibition of interest in transactions between members of their religion, Judaism did not prohibit interest in monetary relations with people of other faiths. Jewish bankers were ahead in money matters, giving loans in return for interest. The Jews lived isolated and were despised in society. They were generally not allowed to own land, become a guild member, or have a government position. This situation inevitably led many of them to the bank business and made them specialize in the credit business. However, the increase in trade had made it inevitable for Christians to enter the market and forced Jewish players to exit the credit market. The crusades also led to more discrimination and isolation of the Jews.

With the expansion of commercial and monetary activities after the eleventh century, see also Chap. 1, the concept of interest began to be discussed more, and new interpretations were needed. For a while, a specific rate was accepted as the official rate in Byzantium. The third Lateran Council, in 1179, stressed the prohibition of usury and determined that people being engaged in usury had to be excommunicated. Usury was defined broadly as any return above the principal value of the loan (Munro, 2002). It was Canon number 25 of the Council. It was in the same spirit as Canon number 26 that forbade Jews and Muslims to have Christian servants. Two new religious orders, established in the early thirteenth century (Franciscans and Dominicans), were both working on further isolation of Jews and Jewish practices. The fourth Lateran Council (1215) issued a diatribe against the Jewish usury practices. Secular rulers were stimulated to enforce a ban on usury. From the thirteenth century on, openly admitted interest on a loan was unusual. A Dominican, Thomas Aquinas (1225–1274), was important in developing a philosophical basis for the ban on usury. He argued that charging for both the object and using that object would mean double charging. Aquinas said it would be morally wrong to sell a bottle of wine first and then charge the buyer to drink it. Money is a medium of exchange and will already be spent while using it. He stated that it is morally wrong to ask for a fee while using money after lending. He claimed that the usurer is, in a sense, selling time since he charges for the time the money is in the hands of the debtor. However, time is not a tradeable commodity. Also, whereas Aquinas condemned usury, this was based on Aristotle's newly discovered philosophical writings at the time. By interpreting Greek philosophy with Christian theology, Aquinas argued that natural law practices based on Aristotelian reason strengthened the perspective of Christianity. As Aristotle said, it is illogical to charge interest on money since money cannot reproduce itself as a pure element. For this reason, Aquinas argued that "*interest is inherently unjust; therefore, the person who receives interest is sinful.*" However, a completely different situation would arise when the money received was invested in a joint venture.

As an investor (venturer), the money provider would also have to share risk to deserve a profit. Just investing the money and waiting for it to be paid back, regardless of the venture's success, was to make money by usury. In contrast, according to Aquinas, an additional return could be expected for the risk taken in the joint venture. Therefore, a banker or lender would receive a fair remuneration, such as a commission, for the work or effort. In the 13th Century, Cardinal Hostiensis listed thirteen cases in which it was not immoral to pay interest. The most important of these allows the lender to charge a fee "*to compensate for profit from using the money elsewhere.*" This idea is very similar to the opportunity cost concept we use today. Although this idea was never officially accepted by the Roman Catholic Church, it would give Italian Bankers a vital opportunity to receive some commission instead of interest for the money to be used. They might receive a fair fee, such as a commission, for any work or effort they perform (De Roover, 1967). For this reason, while bankers preferred to receive commissions instead of interest in banking practices to avoid confronting the Church, they brought their merchant identities to the fore instead of their banker identities by intermingling their commercial and financing activities. As bankers, in the turbulent political environment of the time, they might easily be accused of usury and have lost their reputation. Indeed, the Medici were often blamed by their rivals for this reason. While bankers were opening savings deposit accounts to keep the merchants' money, they also started to give credit, money orders, and foreign exchange transactions.

In dealing with wealthy people, it was more complicated to hide interest. It was generally about time deposits, either implicitly or explicitly. The banker had the right to employ the funds in his business at his discretion. He was expected to return not only the principal, but also some extra, again at his discretion. Formally it was a gift and not a contractual obligation. But, of course, the deposit giver expected something reasonable. It was a gray area; some theologians saw this also as usury. But this was how the Medici bank (and other banks) practiced it, also for time deposits from cardinals and even the pope.

An extra reason to stay in line with the church's rules concerning usury was the importance of the church itself as a customer. Of all the profits of the Medici bank during the first twenty years of its existence (1397–1420), more than half came from the Rome branch. This was just the papal branch. They followed Eugene IV (1431–1447) when he stayed longer outside Rome (De Roover, 1963). The Pope was nine years away from Rome, and the "*Rome*" branch always followed him. That could be politically complex, certainly during a schism, a period with more than one pope. The start of the Medici bank fell in the so called Great Schism, or Great Western Schism, 1378–1417. From 1309 on the Popes resided in Avignon, partly due to continuous turmoil in Rome and partly because of the influence of the French king.

In 1477, Gregory XI moved the papacy back to Rome. But he died already in March 1378, before he could really settle in Rome. For the Italians, it was important to have an Italian Pope now. They managed to have Urban VI elected. He appeared to be rather autocratic and soon part of the cardinals protested and elected another pope, Clement VII, in September 1378. Urban stayed in Rome, Clement settled in Avignon. It was devastating for the functioning of the church and eventually, the cardinals of both popes organized the Council of Pisa, to unite the church (1409). They tried to depose both popes and elected a new one, Alexander V. However, it resulted in three popes instead of one. Alexander died already in 1410 and his successor was John XXIII, whose real name was Baldassarre Cossa. Under pressure from Sigismund, king of Germany, John had to convene a new council, the Council of Constance (1414–1417), to try to unite the church again. The council secured the resignation of Gregory XII, the Roman pope, the removal of John XXIII, and the excommunication of Benedict XIII, the Avignon pope, and elected Pope Martin V, finally ending the schism (Western Schism, 2024).

Baldassarre Cossa was a friend and customer of the Medici and one may presume that they used their influence to support his election, in 1410 (De Roover, 1963). Giovanni took a risk, took advantage of this chaotic situation, and became the papal banker. In this way, the Medici was able to manage the Church's money (Hallam & Trevor-Roper, 1988). Cossa accepted his dismissal only in 1419 and the Medici kept servicing him. It interrupted their role as papal bankers and Pope Marttin V took on the rival family Spini as a banker, but in 1420, the Spini suddenly went bankrupt, and the Medici family regained this role (Hibbert, 1975).

The papal treasury (Apostolic Chamber) was the counterpart of the banks. The Apostolic Treasurer was a high-ranking church official, but funds were deposited generally with a representative of one of the papal bankers, the Depositary General. During the fifteenth century, the manager of the Rome branch of the Medici bank was generally the Depositary General (De Roover, 1963). To comply with the regulations of the Apostolic Chamber, the depositary kept a special ledger recording all his receipts and payments separately and in chronological order. These account books were called "Introitus et Exitus"; for this audit, a balance was deducted at the end of each month and transferred to the following month. If the expenditures of a given month exceeded the revenues—either more or less than the previous month's balance—the Chamber had overdrawn its account and owed the difference to the depositary rather than having a credit in its favor. The revenues of the pope came from everywhere in Europe, and he depended on the large bankers to facilitate this movement of money. In places with a regular money market, bills of exchange could be used; in other places, they had to rely on more casual means, pilgrims, students, and traveling merchants. The banking places near the periphery were important in facilitating money transfers. Papal collectors did the collection itself. But the bank helped to smooth the collecting process and removed thresholds if necessary, not afraid of interfering in church business. De Roover gives a nice example (De Roover, 1963). In December 1448, the Bruges branch of the bank wrote to John Kemp, cardinal and archbishop of York, that they had succeeded in realizing the appointment of Thomas Kemp, a nephew of John, as bishop in London, in preference to a rival candidate supported by Henri VI. And they urged him (John Kemp) on the same occasion to pay his nephews dues within a month. Otherwise, to their regret, they would have to return the sealed bulls to Rome. Threats, bribes, and blackmailing were included in the tools to get the collection and depositing process going well.

2.6 Kings and Bankers

The greatest danger to medieval banking was giving loans to European monarchs to finance wars. The use of mercenaries increased the costs of organizing military operations. Some bankers could lend loans at commission (interest) rates, sometimes as high as 45–60%, when they financed a ruler's war. Most late Middle Ages and Renaissance bankruptcies resulted from large loans to princes and monarchs who refused to pay their debts. Bad debts would inevitably be a problem to the greedy Italian bankers. Indeed, Italian banks were damaged when Edward III had difficulty paying off loans to finance the Hundred Years' War (1337–1453). The two firms that suffered the most in this event were the Bardi and Peruzzi, known to medieval historians as the two largest commercial banking companies in Florence of the fourteenth century. Initially, only the Bardi were lending, and the credits were on a modest scale, gradually growing until the reign of Edward II. Between 1311 and 1326, it grew to almost £68,000. The pace of lending accelerated early in Edward III's reign and, by 1329, the Bardi became the Royal bankers. The Peruzzi started trading in England much later and avoided royal debt until 1336, on the eve of the Hundred Years' War, they could not resist the lure of the wool market (Hunt, 1990).

English wool was of the highest quality and essential for producing luxury fabrics. Italian companies contracted with growers for the material, which they sold to customer manufacturers in Flanders and Italy or turned into cloth in their mills in Florence. The Monasteries in England were important growers and always benefited from this credit. Another advantage of dealing with the monasteries was that the companies complemented the papal banking activities. When the papacy instructed the Bardi or Peruzzi to transfer funds accumulated in England to Avignon, the London branch would have the Florence headquarters provide the money from its resources. The papacy's cash would thus stay available in England to lend to the monasteries, which, in turn, would likely use some of the credits to pay their papal dues (Hunt, 1990).

Medieval rulers faced a constant cash flow problem because of the extra expenses and the resulting delays in the collection of tax revenues. The king promised to repay debts borrowed for the war and tempted the merchants with hidden interest, privileges in the trade, and "*gifts*" or "*losses.*" This attracted the Florentine families, but when Edward III defaulted on his debts, he owed 600,000 Florins to the Bardi and 474,000 Florins to the Peruzzi. This was an enormous sum for that day and contributed to the failure of the companies, although the Bardi and Peruzzi continued to be among the wealthiest families in Florence in the 1350 s (Hunt, 1990). It was the Medici Family's turn to take center stage.

2.7 The Rise of the Medici Family

2.7.1 *Giovanni Di Bicci de' Medici*

The Medicis were not a well-known and noble family like the Bardi and the Peruzzi. At first, no one could have guessed that they would become one of the most important historical figures in the Renaissance and the patrons of bankers, politicians, and artists. The story of the Medici begins with Giovanni de' Medici (1360–1429). Although Giovanni's father was wealthy, he had five sons, resulting in a relatively modest legacy for Giovanni. However, his uncle, Vieri de' Medici, was a prominent banker in Florence and had helped Giovanni start his career in the banking system by holding his hand. Giovanni succeeded in becoming a junior partner in the branch in Rome by working hard. After the retirement of Vieri de' Medici in 1393, the bank's management fell into the hands of Giovanni. However, he chose to go his own way and left his uncle's sons by establishing a new bank. He transferred his bank, called the Medici House, to Florence in 1397. According to the libro segreto (secret book) of the Medici Bank, the initial capital was 10,000 florins, of which more than 50 percent (5,500 florins) was provided by Giovanni di Bicci and the rest by his two partners (2,000 by Benedetto de' Bardi and 2,500 by Gentile Buoni). The partnership with Gentile Buoni did not last more than a few months, either because Gentile could not supply his share or because he and Giovanni could not agree. There is no record of why Giovanni de Bicci moved his headquarters from Rome, a source of funds, to Florence. Maybe the presence of other banking houses offered better investment opportunities. He also opened a branch in Venice. He aimed to find suitable investment opportunities for his deposits. By 1402, the bank had a capital of 20,000 florins. Of this, 8,000 florins were invested in Florence and Venice and 4,000 florins in Rome (De Roover, 1963).

In the fourteenth and fifteenth centuries, Florence was the center of an essential and prosperous wool industry in which many leading families were interested. On April 1, 1402, the Medici Bank decided to extend its activities into manufacturing by financing a bottega (workshop) to produce woolen cloth. The new firm was founded in the name of Giovanni's eldest son, Cosimo, who was only thirteen. In 1408, another partnership for the production of fabrics was created in the name of his second son. It was called "Lorenzo di Giovanni de' Medici e Co., lanaiuoli"; his second son was only thirteen years old then. Over time, the second bottega became more profitable than the first, thanks to exceptional management. The company didn't expand until 1426. By this date, in addition to the headquarters in Florence, the bank had two branches outside the city, one in Venice and one in Rome, and two industrial enterprises. Under the control of the Rome branch, there were also offices in Naples and Gaëta (opened in 1400). However, the Naples branch became an accomanda (limited partnership) in 1415, in which the Medici were silent or dormant partners; accordingly, they were only liable to the extent of their initial investment (De Roover, 1963).

One should not think that the House of Medici worked in imposing buildings like today's banks. In reality, medieval bankers transacted their business in small houses adorned with a bank or counter, a few desks, and in back rooms, the abacus on which the bookkeeper made his computations by casting his counters. According to the records in the Libro segreto, the payroll of the Medici Bank of March 24, 1402 included only seventeen names. Only five clerks worked at the headquarters in Florence, and the branches were even less staffed: Rome and Venice had four, and Naples and Gaëta had the same number of employees. In Florentine companies, the libro segreto was usually kept by one of the partners and kept in a locked cabinet. Such a ledger recorded data on capital investment, the allocation of profits among the partners, and the investments of significant clients such as cardinals and princes. (De Roover, 1963).

The Rome branch managed the papal (Curia) account most of the time during the leadership of Giovanni de Bicci. As custodian of the Camera Apostolica (Apostolic Chamber), Medici managed the funds of the papal treasury and became a center of attraction for the financial affairs of cardinals and prelates. The Curia was often a lender or depositor rather than a borrower. From 1397 to 1420, the Rome branch accounted for half of the total profits. In contrast, things were not going well at the Naples branch. This branch was closed in 1425 (De Roover, 1963).

Giovanni di Bicci withdrew from business when he was sixty years old (1420), and new business contracts were drawn up in the name of his sons Cosimo and Lorenzo. His older son Cosimo took over the business. Cosimo was fully informed about all the trade secrets and was ready to assume command. His younger son Lorenzo studied under the Italian Renaissance humanist Carlo Marsuppini. Lorenzo always supported the political activities of his brother Cosimo. Despite his dedication to banking activities, Lorenzo held various posts in the Florentine Republic and was ambassador to Pope Eugene IV and the Republic of Venice. In 1435, he moved to Rome to oversee the affairs of the Medici Bank at the papal court. He died very early in 1440. When Giovanni di Bicci de' Medici died on February 20, 1429, Cosimo Medici (1389–1464) was now the family leader.

Being a reasonably wealthy businessman, Giovanni mostly tried to live on a low profile. Taking care not to differentiate the Medici family from other citizens of Florence, he wanted to get himself and his sons to dress and behave like the average citizens of Florence. The behavior was partly due to Giovanni's desire not to draw undue attention to himself and his family and to maintain a favorable public image by avoiding conflicts with the rulers. His temperament is also evident in his words, as Reumont and Von Harrison (1876) quoted: "*Try to keep the people in peace and establish good relations with the powerful. Have no legal trouble because those who block the law perish by the law. Do not attract the attention of the public. Even if they give up on you, still be perfect.*" Giovanni di Bicci de Medici wanted a respectable societal position through marriages with Florence's rich and noble families. Therefore, he organized the marriage of his son Cosimo to Contessina de' Bardi from the Bardi family. The marriage with beautiful Contessina provided the Medici family with much-needed nobility, prestige, and military support (Tomas, 2005). When Giovanni de' Medici died in 1429 and left the bank's management to his sons Cosimo and Lorenzo, the Medici House was Europe's most profitable family business. (Hibbert, 1975). According to the Ricordi (book) of Lorenzo the

Magnificent, Giovanni left behind an estate worth approximately 180,000 florins when he died. At the time, one florin was equivalent to roughly ten days' wages for an unskilled laborer and 3.5 days' work for a skilled artisan (Calkins, 2014). According to De Roover, this figure is plausible, if not entirely accurate. Giovanni also refused to make a will. Possibly ordering extensive restitution in a testament, he could have denounced himself as a usurer and caused distress to his heirs.

2.7.2 *Cosimo de' Medici*

The Cosimo Medici era was a golden period for the family (Fig. 2.3). Their relations with the Curia improved, and profits from Rome increased to 63%. Until 1451, London and Pisa branches were constituted. They established another branch in Avignon (1444), the most crucial center in France. The Basel office existed in 1433 as a sub-branch of Geneva. As we will explain later in this section, the existence of the Basel Council, which was formed due to the schism that emerged in Christianity, led to the opening of this branch. In the fifteenth century, Ancona was essential for Florence as a port for shipping cloth to the Levant and importing grain from Apulia along the Adriatic coast. In addition, Cosimo acquired a silk shop in 1438. Political concerns were influential in the opening of some branches. Since the Florentine Republic had no vital interests in Flanders, political relations did not carry much weight when the decision was taken in 1439 to establish a branch in Bruges. His General Director, Giovanni Benci, was a very talented manager. He served successfully until he died in 1455. He would later be succeeded by Francesco Sassatti, who was not as skillful.

By 1451, the House of Medici consisted of the Tavola in Florence, with the investments made during the Givionni era, three branches in Italy (Pisa, Rome and Venice), four branches abroad (Avignon, Bruges, Geneva, and London) and three industrial enterprises (two wool shops and a silk shop), With the possible exception of Pisa, all these subsidiaries were under the control of, and partly or wholly owned by, the Medici Bank, just like a holding company today. The Tavola in Florence was run by a director entitled to one-eighth of its profits, even though he was a partner with no stake in the company. Tavola was a different entity from the head office in Florence. The head office was located in the scrittoio, or counting room, of the Medici palace and was staffed by the director general and a few assistants and secretaries. In contrast, the Tavola was located in the heart of the business district, two steps from the square that today still bears the name Mercato Nuovo. A branch was opened in Milan in 1452 or, at the latest, in 1453. The creation of the Milan branch was perhaps more a move on the chessboard of Italian politics than a decision driven by economic motives. The Geneva branch had an office in Lyons for a time before 1460. Francesco di Antonio Nori, one of the firm's factors, was already resident there in 1455. When the King of France, Louis XI restricted participation in the Geneva Fair to develop the Lyon Fair, the Medici branch moved its headquarters to Lyons. Still, the transfer

Fig. 2.3 Cosimo de Medici (1389–1464) https://commons.wikimedia.org/wiki/File:Italy_1494_AD.png

was not made at once and was not completed until 25 March 1466. However, the Medici had no branches in Spain, the Levant, or east of the Rhine (De Roover, 1963).

The main activity of the Medici family was the wool trade between England and Florence. They had textile workshops and companies in Italy. In 1464, Tommaso Portinari, one of the directors of the Medici branch, made it clear that "*trade was at the core of the firm's business, and most of the capital was directed to commercial affairs.*" (De Roover, 1963). They became importers and exporters of silk, spices, fruit, wool, and cloth; they supplied tapestries, relics, and horses to their clients and customers; they also dealt in alum, a mineral used in glass making and tanning, and, thanks to its close ties with the Papacy in this regard, the Medici Bank signed a treaty with the Pope in 1466 that gave the Medici the right to work in and profit from the alum mines near Civitavecchia in the Papal States and to sell their products locally and abroad. Eventually, the Medici Bank became a profitable institution throughout Europe and, in the words of the French historian Philippe de Commines, "*the greatest house of commerce that ever existed anywhere*" (Hibbert, 1975).

From 1435 to 1451, the profits of the Rome branch declined in absolute and relative terms compared to the first period of Cosimo (1420–1435). On the other hand, Geneva's position improved, both in absolute figures and as a percentage of total profits. The headquarters branch in Florence performed poorly from 1435 to 1441, perhaps because of the slow recovery after the exile of 1433–1434. The exile of Cosimo was one of the important events of the Medici House and will be explained later in this section. However, Florence was never a significant source of profit for the Medici Bank, probably because of the fierce rivalry between the town's families. Venice was important after Rome. As before, most of the profits (90%) came from trade and banking (De Roover1963).

While Cosimo was engaged in commercial activities, he was also an important political figure in Florentine politics. His whole life was spent in political struggle. He became interested in politics during the war with Lucca (1429). Although this war was successful, the damage it caused to the Florentine economy caused a rift between him and the Albizzi family, who ruled Florence at the time. The Albizzi family jealoused the power Cosimo and his family had gained in Florentine society and were, therefore, successful in driving the Medici away from Florence to Venice (1433–1434). Then, the war with Milan had failed. This failure encouraged his supporters, who went to great lengths to ensure the Albizzi's fall and the Medici's return. With the support of the Pope, Cosimo and the other exiled Medici could return to Florence. With the power he gained, he exiled Rinaldo degli Albizzi and his entire family from Florence. His supporters who fought for his return from exile pushed him into a decisive political role. He placed his family and friends in political office, thus guaranteeing his control over the government (Hibbert, 1975).

Cosimo's connection with the papacy consolidated his power in Florence, Italy, and Europe. He made a significant attempt to unite Christendom by persuading his friend Pope Eugene IV to transfer the General Council of the Greek Orthodox and Roman Catholic Church from Ferrara to Florence in 1439. He organized a major conference and the arrival of Greek intellectuals and scholars in Florence, which stimulated the development of classical knowledge, humanism, and the Renaissance, eventually paving the way for Florence to become the cradle of the Renaissance (Hibbert, 1975). The background of these events was very complicated. The Council of Basel was convened by Pope Martin V just before his death in Basel in 1431 to discuss unification with the Eastern Church and papal supremacy. The new Pope Eugene IV approved it. However, due to a dispute, Pope Eugene IV transferred the Council to Ferrara on January 8, 1438, where it was renamed the Council of Ferrara and succeeded in attracting some of the Byzantine envoys from Basel to Italy. With the support of Cosimo, the Council was moved to Florence. Some Council members remained in Basel, rejecting the papal decree: the Basel Council declared Eugene a heretic and then elected an antipope, Felix V, in November 1439. The Council of Florence ended in 1445 after negotiations for union with various eastern churches. The bridging of the Great Schism (the schism of 1054, of the Roman Catholic and Eastern Orthodox churches) was only temporary, a politically inspired movement to strengthen the position of Pope Eugene IV. In 1447, King Frederick III of Germany (later Holy Roman Emperor) supported the unification of the papacy by ordering the city of Basel to expel the Council of Basel. Upon the death of Eugene in 1447, his successor, Nicholas V, secured the abdication of Felix V and ended the council in April 1449. Cosimo supported Eugene financially, supplying the Pope with galleys and other necessities for his campaign against the Turks. After the Pope's death, the Medici lent money to help elect the new Pope; Nicholas V. Nicholas used the power and influence of the Medici to maintain his position as Pope (Hibbert, 1975).

During Cosimo's reign and also thereafter, the Medici Bank remained the Pope's bank, except for two short periods, as we will discuss in Sect. 2.9.1.

Growing his father's legacy several times with his political and business skills, Cosimo spent a substantial period of his 75-year life struggling with political conspiracies. These experiences not only improved his problem-solving skills but also gave him the ability to compromise and make strategic plans. Cosimo was more of a politician than a businessman and more of a community leader than a banker. However, although he was mighty and wealthy in the Florentine society, he never had an easy life (Martines, 2011). Cosimo's power over Florence stemmed from his wealth, which he used to control votes in Florence's city council, known as the Signoria. It is known that Cosimo, who pretended to have no political ambitions and often expressed his pride in Florence's democracy, repeatedly interfered in public affairs indirectly. The Bishop of Siena, Enea Silvio Piccolomini, who later became Pope Pius II, said about him (Hibbert, 1975): "*Political problems are resolved in Cosimo's house. The man he chooses is elected to public office ... He decides peace and war ... He is King in everything but his title.*"

Cosimo had a particular interest in art, always supporting artists and leading Italy to bring new works, even at the expense of conservative religious circles and the city's strong family structures. He gave work and reassurance to sculptors such as Lorenzo Ghiberti and Donatello and painters such as Andrea del Castagno, Fra Angelico, and Benozzo Gozzoli (Encyclopedia.com, 2018). He also opened the "*Plato Academy*" to revive Greek science. He invested in public construction projects around Florence. Especially when he was exiled to Venice, he needed to regain the support of the people that he had lost. Upon his death on August 1, 1464, the city was grateful to him and decided that 'Pater Patriae' (father of his country) should be inscribed on his tomb (Encyclopedia.com, 2018).

2.8 Structure and Organization of the Medici Bank

Giovanni had partnered with the Bardi family members at the beginning. He later formed partnerships with various people in the business model he developed. With family wealth limited then, the Florentine entrepreneurs had no choice but to partner with others to raise working capital; they invested separately in different partnerships. Giovanni was, therefore, able to avoid the problems created by the monolithic corporate structures of the turn of the century, that previously led to the downfall of the Bardi or Peruzzi companies. With the business model he started to build, he reached all the important European markets at that time by investing in essential centers in different countries. The fact that the conditions of the fifteenth century differed from those of the fourteenth century probably led him toward this business model (Goldthwaite, 1987).

In the Middle Ages, Florentine banking firms, including Bardi and Peruzzi banks, often had a centralized organizational structure. In contrast, the Medici Bank preferred a decentralized system, in other words, an organizational structure in which local companies participated in a significant portion of the decisions. Historian Raymond de Roover (1963) documented the most comprehensive information about the business organization of the Medici Bank. It was not a single company but a kind of corporate group of many partnership formations. All of the partner companies were organized as an independent company structure and were a separate legal entity or territorial unit and had their own style, capital, and ledgers. Each partnership was dealing with other subsidiaries as if they were non-group companies, and they also received commissions for their mutual work. Figure 2.4 shows the organizational structure of the company as of 1455. The President of the company was Cosimo Medici, while the General Manager and Partner was Giovanni Benci. He was also the head of the central branch in Florence. Accordingly, the company had three main divisions. These were Silk Manufacturing, managed by one partner, Cloth Manufacturing, managed by two partners, and Banking. The manufacturing division was divided into Purchases, Production, and Sales. The banking division was also divided into three. Apart from the Local Banking division, there were two separate divisions: branches beyond the Alps and branches in Italy. The branches in Italy were located in Milan, Rome, Pisa, and Venice, while the branches beyond the Alps were located as far away as Geneva, Bruges, London, and Avignon (Fig. 2.4).

Partner company managers were junior partners who received a share of the profits rather than a salary. These directors were appointed indefinitely, but according to the articles of association, the Medici had the right to terminate the partnership early

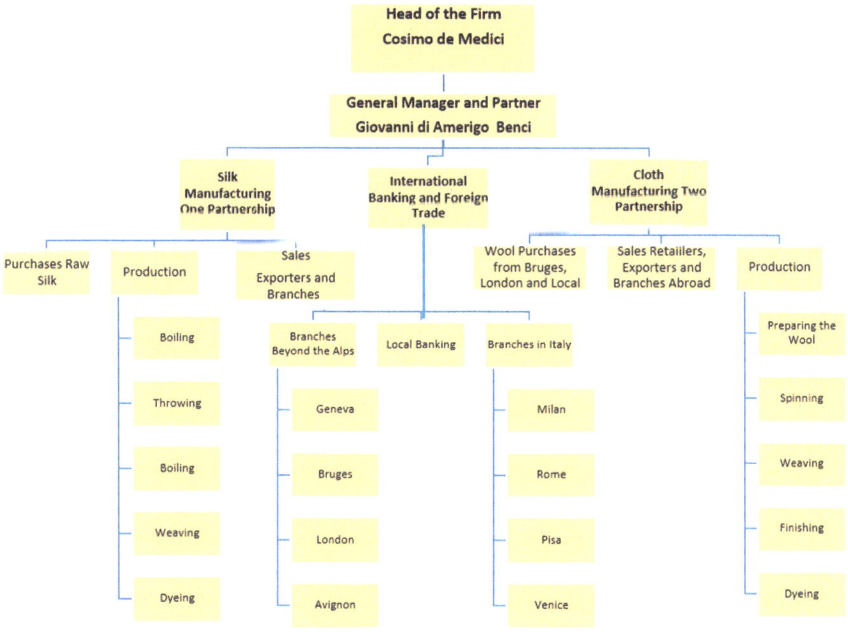

Fig. 2.4 Internal Organization of Medici Bank (1455) Source: De Roover, 1963

and dismiss them at any time. Company directors were called "*Governors*," while the Medici were called "*Seniors*." The use of these terms suggests that subsidiary company executives had the right to make managerial decisions, but that a Medici as the firm's head had the final say on all policy matters. The organization of the Medici banking house was largely similar to today's holding companies. The Medici owned at least 50 percent of the capital and controlled all the subsidiaries. The Medici had also taken care to require that ownership of their trademarks be retained after a partnership was dissolved (De Roover, 1963).

A case in the municipal court of Bruges in 1453 illustrates the structure of the Medici business organization. In this case, Damiano Ruffini of Milan sued Tommaso Portinari, acting manager of the Medici branch in Bruges, for the faulty packaging of nine bales of wool that the plaintiff had purchased from the Medici branch in London. The defendant argued that the bales never belonged to the Bruges branch and that the plaintiff should sue the London branch. The plaintiff responded to this claim: "*The Medici branch in Bruges and the branch in London were one company and had the same master*." Portinari testified under oath that the two branches were separate partnerships, that the bales of wool were sold to the plaintiff by the London partnership, that the Bruges partnership had nothing to do with the sale, and that it should be exempted from any liability and responsibility. In its judgment, the court rejected the claim presented by the plaintiff but upheld the right to sue Simone Nori, who was the manager of the London branch at the time.' If this case were today, the court would have ruled that the two companies would have different legal personality (De Roover, 1963).

The powers and responsibilities of the director head office in Florence were like those of a CEO or general manager in a modern company. The Director's duties included reviewing reports from subsidiary directors, preparing their instructions, auditing the balance sheets of different companies, discussing issues, and reporting all matters when the subsidy directors came to Florence every two or three years. The managers of the subsidiaries were operating as junior partners of the Medici Bank. Partnership agreements not only determined capital and profit levels, but they were also documents of fundamental importance, as they set out the obligations of the partners to each other. According to Medici partnership agreements, the senior partners had total power, while the junior partner managed the local enterprise. Their actions were subject to the approval of the senior partners, who could terminate the partnership at any time in case of dissatisfaction. The primary purpose of the Articles of Association was to define the managing partners' duties and restrict their powers (De Roover, 1963).

Cosimo did not ponder trivial administrative problems; managers or clerks were resolving them. For this reason, the initiative was given to local administrators, who were expected to be creative. In addition, their decentralized structure made it easier to keep up with the changing political and economic environment. The historical documents reveal that the heads of the Medici firm only made important decisions and set the general rules that the managers of the subsidiaries were expected to follow. Cosimo knew how to select and retain talented managers. He insisted that his instructions be followed; his dignity was so high that no one dared to ignore his orders

(De Roover, 1963). Angelo Tani, the director of Bruges, once incurred Cosimo's wrath. He had made an unfavorable deal with the Italian Bruges pawnbroking firm and had failed. Cosimo was so enraged when he learned of these transactions that he threatened to end the partnership and would have done so if his advisors had not intervened.

The Medici organized the transportation of goods such as wool, silk, and alum in various parts of Europe. In such an organization, communication and supervision had to be very good. With their strong branch networks, the Medici gathered news from every corner of Europe and tried to take advantage of the opportunities. The lack of a satisfactory audit and internal control system was a severe weakness of the Medici business organization. Even though they had frequent reports, these reports could sometimes be very delayed. They had no formal audit and control system. However, senior management relied heavily on frequent reports, written or oral, for audit purposes. This situation was perhaps the biggest reason why the managers were chosen meticulously. Although it is known that there were some mistakes in Cosimo's business life, he took an active role in the management and did not only rely on the judgments of his advisers but also intervened when necessary.

Branch managers were carefully selected. They were appointed by the headquarters in Florence, selected solely from factors with business training in one of the branches and knowledge of conditions abroad. The relations between the head office and the branches outside Florence can be understood from the partnership agreements signed between the Medici and the branch managers, the written instructions they gave when they left Florence, and the correspondence between the head office and the branches. Branch directors usually visited Florence every two or three years to report on working conditions and administrative problems. During these visits, branch managers were given verbal instructions and often met with senior partners and the managing director. No minutes of these meetings were found, but it is assumed that important decisions were often made by discussing managerial issues (De Roover, 1963).

Partnership agreements are of fundamental importance as they determine not only the division of capital and profits but also the obligations of the partners toward each other. According to the Medici partnership agreements, the senior partners retained all authority, but the junior partner bore the full burden of managing the joint venture. All his actions were subject to the approval of the senior partners, who had the right to terminate the partnership at any time if they were not satisfied. The main purpose of the articles of association was to define the duties and limit the powers of the managing partner.

It was customary to give the manager a share of the profits that was larger than corresponding to his capital contribution, as a reward for his services and an incentive to make a profit. No capital or profits could be taken from the company during the contract term, except for the junior partner, who could withdraw some money annually for living expenses. Losses would be shared equally with profits. The contract required the junior partner to reside in Bruges (or whatever branch) and confine his activities to "*lawful trade and licensed and honorable exchange transactions*" according to the instructions given by the Medici and the senior partners. The partnership agreements of 1455 also included some moral or behavioral constraints. For example, the junior partner was neither allowed to gamble nor to entertain a woman in his room.

2.9 The Decline of the Medici Bank

From 1455 onwards, the growth of the Medici Bank stagnated, and it soon entered a period of decline that began with Cosimo's death (1464). By the time he died, the peak of its prosperity had already passed, and the Medici Bank was going downhill. The political and business challenges of the end of his life had exhausted him. Cosimo was worried about his family's future, which looked rather bleak as he sighed when walking around his palace, "*Too big house for such a small family.*" (Encyclopedia Britannica, 2018). The decline of the Medici Bank covers thirty years from Cosimo's death in 1464 until the expulsion of the Medici from Florence in 1494. By 1494, the bank was effectively bankrupt. The London branch was struggling; other branches were experiencing increasing difficulties, and profits were falling. A few branches, such as Lyons, Rome, and Naples, were struggling to survive against severe difficulties. During these thirty years, leadership was assumed by three successive generations of Medici: Piero de' Medici (1464–1469), Lorenzo the Magnificent (1469–1492), and Piero the Unfortunate (1492–1494). Had Cosimo lived and retained his power, it might have been possible for the Medici Bank to recover its dwindling fortunes and halt its descent into the abyss. Unfortunately, his followers lacked his talents and were misled by those they trusted.

2.9.1 Piero de Medici and Lorenzo the Magnificent

Piero de Medici (1416–1469) succeeded his father, Cosimo, after dying in 1464. But Piero did not have the skills his father had, neither as a businessman nor a politician. Initially, Piero was not considered the successor, but his younger brother Giovanni (1421–1463), because Piero was often ill. Giovanni was much better educated, and for a time, he had worked as the general manager of the bank under the supervision of Francesco Sassetti, but Giovanni died before Cosimo, leaving Piero as the sole heir to the empire Cosimo had built. His death was a significant loss for the future of the Medici family. Piero was thoughtful, patient, and kind, but his health was not good, and he was always remembered for his long illnesses.

Piero had no practical training in business. Worse, he suffered from gout and was bedridden for most of the remaining five years of his life. Despite these handicaps, he performed much better than expected and tried to stem the tide by initiating a policy of austerity. It is known that shortly after his father's death, he ordered an investigation of his estate to see the company's financial situation and business interests. Business conditions in England, crucial to the Medici, had deteriorated due to a civil war known as the War of the Roses (1455–1487). In addition, the market had become increasingly unfavorable for the Italians, as British merchants competed with them, and the British Isle's wool was used domestically due to the rapid development of the British cloth industry (De Roover, 1947). When this audit probably revealed that the Medici company's affairs were not as prosperous as had been thought, Pietro embarked on a policy of economy. He took steps to terminate the Venice branch, tried to settle debts with Edward IV to relieve the London business, and limited the loan to Charles the Bold of Burgundy and the loans to the rulers of Milan. There was a wave of bankruptcies in Florence in 1464/1465, and some contemporaries blamed Piero for his policy of contraction, but the bankruptcies had more to do with the outbreak of a war between Venice and the Sultan. Piero tried to continue the policy of contraction, but had insufficient grip on the affairs to succeed. Branch managers protested because they feared loss of influence and stretched the directives. Piero realized that indeed the recall of loans would lead to the deterioration of existing relations. His energy and decisiveness were insufficient to execute the policy of contraction consistently.

Piero de' Medici died on December 2, 1469, and was succeeded by two young men: Lorenzo was twenty-one, and Giuliano was only sixteen. They had no experience and had to rely on their father's principles. Lorenzo de' Medici (1449–1492) took over the business and, within a few years, became one of the greatest statesmen of his time. On the other hand, Giuliano was impulsive, athletic, reckless, and liked dueling and jousting challenges. However, Giuliano had a level of affection for his elder brother Lorenzo and his family. Knowing his son Piero's weak points, Cosimo de' Medici gave great importance to his grandson's (Lorenzo) education and hired Greek, Latin, and philosophy teachers to ensure he received the best education of his time (Fig. 2.5). He eventually earned the title of "*Magnificent*." He was more like his grandfather, Cosimo, than his father. Like Cosimo, he followed his grandfather's example in many ways. He patronaged many artists, including Sandro Botticelli, Leonardo da Vinci, and Michelangelo. Unlike Cosimo, however, Lorenzo had been brought up with the expectation that he would rule Florence, and his education was pure and sound classical, literary, and philosophical. Compared to his grandfather Cosimo, he had learned very little about banking and commerce and consequently lacked Cosimo's financial courage (De Roover, 1963).

He did not devote much time to commercial matters and depended on the General Manager Francesco Sassetti. He did nothing without the advice and supervision of Sassetti, who was not as competent as the previous General Manager Giovanni d'Amerigo Benci. There were also general economic and political problems that neither he nor Sassetti could control. However, according to Machiavelli, "*Lorenzo the Magnificent had no luck in his commercial undertakings (fu, quanto alia mercanzia, infelicissimo); because of the mismanagement of his agents (il disordine de' suoi ministri) who conducted the business as if they were princes and not merely private persons, much of his wealth was lost in places abroad; as a result, the State had to support him with large sums of money.*" Some, citing Machiavelli, also

Fig. 2.5 Lorenzo the Magnificant https://upload.wikimedia.org/wikipedia/commons/2/2b/Lorenzo_de%27_Medici-ritratto.jpg

claim that Lorenzo the Magnificent had no luck and lacked aptitude for business (De Roover, 1963).

Due to Lorenzo's inadequate supervision and Francesco Sassetti's negligence, in the 1470 s, branch managers were given much more freedom, and the prohibition on lending to princes or governments was lifted. From time to time, instead of acting together as a team, the branch managers were often at odds, each defending his interests and ignoring the interests of the concern as a whole. For example, the Rome branch director (also Pietro's brother-in-law), Giovanni Tornabuoni, conflicted with Bruges and Lyons in 1464 over the alum trade. Initially, the alum needed for textiles came from Turkish territory. However, when the war with them started, the Italians were in trouble because they could not supply it, but they met their needs from the alum mine discovered in Tofla. The Medicis received a concession from the Pope and acquired a monopoly by operating the alum mine in 1470. The biggest markets for alum were Flanders and Britain. For this trade to be successful, the Rome and Bruges branches had to cooperate. However, there was fierce competition between the two managers of Bruges, Angelo Tani and Tommaso Portinari. Sassetti could not restore peace and coordinate the activities of the different branches.

The background to this rivalry was as follows. By 1450, the Bruges branch had become a full-fledged partnership under the direction of Angelo di Jacopo Tani (1415–1492). Tani's assistant was the ambitious Tommaso Portinari (1428–1501), son of Folco, former director of the Tavola of Florence, and brother of successive directors Pigello and Accerrito in Milan. In 1465, when it came time to renew the contract of the Bruges branch, Tommaso, now thirty-seven years old, had been working at the Medici Bank in Bruges for twenty years. After many years in Bruges, Portinari was fluent in French and had perhaps learned a little Flemish, the language of the people. He was at home at the Burgundian court where he served as advisor to the Count of Charolais, later Charles the Bold (1467–1477). He had been appointed to the Duke's council before Charles the Bold succeeded his father and took over. There were complaints that he spent too much time at court instead of attending to the affairs of the bank. Portinari became acting director on April 24, 1464, while Tani was in Florence on a mission. He had coveted Tani's job for some time and was doing his best to discredit his chief. But Tani did not want to retire and was quite willing to continue as director of the Bruges branch. Cosimo hesitated to appoint Tommaso Portinari as Tani's successor while he was still alive in the spring of 1464. After Cosimo's death, Piero, like his father, hesitated and Tommaso Portinari was appointed only in April 1465. He would remain in this position until 1480. Tani would still continue as a senior partner. However, disagreements would continue after 1465.

Moreover, the weaker branches were allowed to undermine the still financially sound branches. The relationship between Brugge and the London branch was a case in point. Initially, London's business was done from Bruges. After March 25, 1451, the London and Bruges branches separated. The London branch soon over-lent to the Crown, leaving it unable to collect its receivables. In 1467, the financial situation of the London branch of the Medici Bank was so bad that Piero di Cosimo, on Sassetti's advice, sent Angelo Tani to London to straighten out the mess and audit the accounts. Tani arrived in London in early January 1468 and learned that Edward IV owed an enormous debt of £10,500. Angelo Tani hinted that it was on the verge of bankruptcy without quick help from headquarters and other branches. He envisaged a gradual amortization of the debt by assigning some of the various sources of revenue and obtaining permission to export wool on the understanding that the customs duty of four marks per sack could be deducted from the debt until it was completely eliminated. Edward IV made a serious effort to liquidate his debt to da Medici, and some progress was made, with the redemption of the old debt exceeding the amount of the new loans. Having completed his mission, Angelo Tani returned to Italy in the spring of 1469, feeling that he had been able to save and put the London branch back on its feet. But the War of the Roses disrupted these plans and made things worse. Things were not going well in England. Following the advice of Francesco Sassetti, Tommaso Portinari agreed that the Bruges branch would take over the assets and liabilities of the London branch. The agreement between Sassetti and Portinari was certainly made without the knowledge of Angelo Tani, a partner in the Bruges branch but not in the London branch. When he found out, he wrote a strong protest in which he repeatedly emphasized that he was in no way responsible for the losses of the London branch. By assuming the liabilities of the London branch, the Bruges branch also assumed the interest burdens, which became a permanent burden and severely reduced its earning capacity. Indeed, this was one of the reasons that led to the collapse of the Bruges branch in 1478.

Sassetti's failure to supervise and discipline the branch managers led to another crisis in Bruges. Another person responsible for this crisis was the overly ambitious Tommaso Portinari. His excessive closeness with Charles the Bold had gone beyond rational business relations. He had raised the total debt of Charles the Bold, Duke of Burgundy and ruler of the Low Countries, to 6,000 pounds in 1470. This was twice the firm's total capital. In 1478, at the time of the Pazzi conspiracy, as explained below, the Low Countries government owed the Medici a large sum of money. Although Lorenzo the Magnificent and Sassetti were aware of the dangers of such loans, they approved it for political reasons. Charles the Bold launched a war against the Swiss and died at the siege of Nancy in 1477. This left the Low Countries government in desperate straits. Tommaso Portinari had to go to great expense to recover the money he had previously lent and to make additional loans to Charles the Bold's penniless son-in-law, Archduke Maximilian of Austria. Ultimately, only part of the debts were repaid over a long period (De Roover, 1963).

By the end of his career, General Manager Sassetti had probably become lax in discharging his duties, approving financial documents without adequate scrutiny. As a result of his carelessness, the mismanagement of Lionetto de' Rossi, the "governor" of the Lyons branch, was not discovered until it was too late for effective solutions to be implemented. The Lyons branch manager had caused a conflict with the Rome branch. Contrary to instructions, Lionetto reduced the bank's activities, causing funds to remain dormant. Besides, Lionetto did not promptly remit to Rome the proceeds from the expedition of papal bulls and the collation of benefices. Another difficulty was that the Lyons branch habitually borrowed money from Rome to cover its growing debt balance over the four fairs. Furthermore, Lionetto's balance sheet did not reflect reality. It had been falsified, the figures manipulated to hide massive losses. This dispute was prolonged rather than immediately terminated. Lionetto would eventually be arrested. This conflict, which began in 1476, lasted almost nine years. (De Roover, 1963).

From 1420 to 1443, which covered part of the papacy of Martin V and Eugene IV, there was a good relationship between the Popes and the Medici Bank. Mostly, they appointed the director of the Medici Rome branch as the Depositary General. In his last years, Pope Eugene IV, at odds with Cosimo's close friend Duke Sforza of Milan, stopped working with the Medici Bank and appointed another Florentine banker, Tommaso Spinelli, as depositary. Nicholas V (1447–1455) reappointed the Medici after he acceded to the papal throne, and the Medici Bank continued in this position until 1458, during the pontificate of Calixtus III (1455–1458). Pius II (1458–1464) entrusted the trusteeship to his fellow countryman, the banker Ambrogio Spannocch. After the election of Paul II (1464–1471), the Medici Bank took up the post again. However, the disagreement between the Rome and Bruges branches due to the alum trade affected their relations with Paul II (De Roover, 1963) and a year later the post of Depositary General was given to Giovanni Condolmer, a relative of the Pope. In 1471, Sixtus IV (1471–1484), gave the post to the Medici again. Despite the bankruptcy of Medici bank branches in some parts of Europe, the Rome branch flourished, and the

Medici remained the official bankers of the Church. However, Pope Sixtus IV was living beyond his means, creating a constant deficit between the introitus (income) and exitus (expenditure) of the trustee. In the first years of Sixtus IV's pontificate, the deficit rose already to 107,000 cameral florins. In March 1473 he was able to obtain an assignment over the salt mines in the Marches, which reduced the debt to 62,918 cameral florins according to an agreement approved by the Pope, but the general pattern was that he spent too much. The Medici's relations with Sixtus IV could not continue in this way. Lorenzo refused to accept Sixtus's request to provide him with financing to buy Imola, a town dominating the road from Rimini to Bologna because he had hopes of buying it for himself for political reasons (Hibbert, 1975). This led the Pope to turn to the Pazzi family, the Medici's newest business rival. Andrea Pazzi operated several companies in England, Bruges, Lyons, and Rome, almost as extensively as the Medici firm. They had developed friendly relations with Sixtus IV during a time of disagreement with the Medici in the political sphere. The Medici had come to power in Florence partly because of their influence over the papacy, and the Pazzi seemed a threat to them, possibly because they were following the same path (Goldthwaite, 1987).

With their help, the Pope managed to buy Imola and settled his nephew Girolamo there. The Pope also arranged a marriage for his other nephew, Giovanni Della Rovere with the daughter of the Duke of Urbino in 1474. Urbino was in the same region as Imola. The Pope aimed to have more territorial and political influence than the Florentines. These events strained relations between Lorenzo and the Church of Rome, bringing Florence and the Papacy to the brink of war and leading to the complete transfer of the Curia's accounts to the Pazzi. Then, that family hatched a murderous conspiracy with the support of the Pope against Lorenzo and his younger brother, Guiliano, which is called the Pazzi conspiracy. The conspirators include the Pazzi family, the archbishop of Pisa, a restive city under the control of Florence, and Giarolamo Riaro, nephew of Sixtus IV. Even the Pope gave his approval to do whatever it took. "*Lorenzo is a villain; once he is out of Florence, we could do whatever we like with the Republic, which would be very pleasing to us...*" (Hibbert, 1975). The Pazzi conspiracy aimed to overthrow the Medici regime and the Medici Bank. Lorenzo was wounded and barely escaped, and his brother Giuliano de' Medici was killed (April 26, 1478).

But Florence remained loyal to the Medici, and the people of Florence ensured that every conspirator paid for his betrayal. The failure of the Pazzi conspiracy aroused anger in Rome. The Pope excommunicated Lorenzo de' Medici and persuaded King Ferrante of Naples to go to war against Florence. Throughout 1479, the war was very painful, with territorial losses and the expenses of maintaining a mercenary army in the field. In December 1479, Lorenzo took a bold step that justified history's description of him as the Magnificent. As Florentine ambassador to Naples, he secretly traveled to Naples with a small group and threw himself recklessly into the king's power. He argued to the king that the war between the Italian powers increased the possibility of a French invasion. King Ferdinand of Naples was already fed up with a campaign more in the Pope's interest than his own. Lorenzo returned to Florence with a peace treaty (Hibbert, 1975). Despite the peace after the treaty, Sixtus made several attempts to remove Lorenzo from Florence, but these attempts were fruitless. Sixtus did not mend his relationship with the Medici and Florence until he died in 1484. Lorenzo had a new opportunity when Innocent VIII (1484 – 1492) came to power. He gained the Pope's friendship and trust (De Roover, 1963). Lorenzo's daughter, Maddalena, married one of the Pope's illegitimate sons, further increasing the Medici's influence over the Pope. The historian Christopher Hibbert called him "*the needle of the Italian compass.*"

2.9.2 The Fall of the Medici House

The Pazzi conspiracy broke out at a critical moment when financial difficulties peaked due to the losses suffered in Apulia, Flanders, England, and Milan. Sixtus had not only taken the alum mine from the Medicis but also confiscated all Medici properties, repudiated the Apostolic Chamber's debt to the Bank, and expelled the Rome branch manager Giovanni Tornabuoni from Rome. At the time of the Pazzi conspiracy in 1478, Lorenzo tended to rely heavily on his private resources or savings from the time of Cosimo. Another solution was to take up money by exchange, which was an expensive form of borrowing. Reliance on this was a significant factor in the heavy losses suffered by many Medici branches, notably in Bruges, London, and Lyons. Even the Roman branch collapsed as its funds were immobilized by loans to the Curia and the Orsini family (an Italian noble family that was one of the most influential princely families in Renaissance Rome). The generosity of Lorenzo the Magnificent was another problem. Between 1434 and 1471, the Medici family spent 663,755 florins on buildings, charities, and taxes, excluding household expenses. No attempt was made to rebuild the shaking structure from the foundations; plans for a complete renovation of the decrepit structure were presented to Lorenzo the Magnificent, but no action was taken. There are allegations that Lorenzo used Monte Dele Dote, a public fund, to pay off his debts. Monte delle Doti was a Florentine state fund that was created in 1425. The Florentine government guaranteed it and allowed fathers or guardians of single young women to provide a dowry for each of their daughters (Molho, 1994). Initially, the chroniclers, among them Pietro Parenti, were not believed because no documentary source corroborated their claims. However, according to De Roover (1963), it seems likely that the incriminating evidence was removed when the Medici returned to power after eighteen years of exile. It is possible that the bankruptcy after the Pazzi conspiracy was prevented in this way.

It is not correct to attribute the decline of the Medicis to mismanagement alone. The wars and political and economic events after 1470 harmed all branches. One of the main causes of the decline was the outbreak of the war between Venice and the Turks, which lasted from 1463 to 1479 and caused a wave of bankruptcies. During this period, silver lost value, creating monetary instability. Between 1422 and 1470, the number of international banks (banchi grossi) in the city fell from seventy-two to thirty-three. By 1494, there were less than half a dozen bankers left. Florence was a banking center in the sixteenth century, but it never regained its leading position as the financial capital of Western Europe. The War of the Roses, which lasted until 1487, had a negative impact on its activities in England.

The decline accelerated after the death of Lorenzo the Magnificent on April 8, 1492. His son Piero di Lorenzo (1472–1503), a healthy, arrogant, and sports-loving young man of twenty, possessed neither diplomatic skill nor administrative ability. His second son, Messer Giovanni (1475–1521), became a cardinal at just seventeen years of age and was more capable than Piero. Still, he had already shown a tendency to overspend, which hastened the collapse of the family bank and later ruined the finances of the papacy after he became Pope Leo X in 1513. After 1483, one of the main concerns of the Lyons branch was the future of Giovanni. Since the Medici had lost so much in their commercial ventures, they were determined to regain their wealth and prestige, if necessary at the expense of the Church. Everything was mobilized to secure privileges for Giovanni, and the spiritual interests of the Church were gladly sacrificed to the most naked and shocking greed. The growth of their position within the church was intended to recover what was lost in business (De Roover, 1963).

Piero Medici, known as Piero the Unfortunate, took over the bank's management. Like his predecessors, he was a dominant power in the administration of Florence. However, Piero had neither Cosimo's financial power nor Lorenzo's charm (Hibbert, 1975). Just as the bank's finances began to deteriorate from the time of his father, the turbulent political environment in Florence and the conflict between rival city-states worsened the situation. After a short period of relative calm, the fragile, peaceful balance between the Italian states, laboriously constructed by Lorenzo de' Medici, worsened. Piero faced a series of unfortunate events. Therefore, Florence called him the nickname of 'The Unfortunate'.

The events started in 1494 when the King of France, Charles VIII, claimed the kingdom of Naples, crossed the Alps with an army, and entered Italy. His contradictory decisions in this war and turmoil put Piero in a difficult position. Piero had to go into exile after a series of political events and conflicts. The Medici family was driven out of Florence. Piero proved his unfortunate nickname when he drowned in the Garigliano River while trying to flee after the Battle of Garigliano in 1503, where he fought side by side with his French allies.

In 1494, Florence had all its properties confiscated, including the Tavola. Geneva closed in 1466, the Venetian branch in 1470, and Avignon in 1483 had already been closed in 1483. Bruges, London, and the Naples branch closed in 1489, and Milan and Pisa in 1492. Finally, Lyons ceased its activity in 1497. This crisis was not limited to Florence; it affected European banking. Another wave of crises, in 1499, was repeated in Venice. Only in Spain did the medieval transfer and deposit banks weather the storm. This general crisis was probably one aspect of the disruption of European trade at the end of the fifteenth century (De Roover, 1963). Since the Medici Company never dominated the Florentine economy independently, their fall did not affect the economy as in the case of Bardi and Peruzzi (Goldthwaite, 1987).

The Medici House did not follow a sustainable policy after Cosimo. When new cracks appeared in their work life, they were covered with a patch, but this could not prevent the damage from covering the entire structure. The main factor for the Medici Bank's growth under Giovanni and Cosimo was the reinvestment of its earnings.

However, as the family rose politically and attained the status of prince, the family's expenditures and inner circle grew, and the profits reinvested each year dwindled after the death of Cosmo. As incomes decreased, the relative cost of capital increased, and the bank's working capital inevitably began to shrink.

The exile of the Medicis lasted until 1512. Then, with Cardinal Giovanni de Medici (the brother of Piero the unfortunate) becoming Pope Leo X (1513–1521), the family became politically powerful in Florence. The family's investment in him over many years had paid off. Now the future of the family was in his hands. Although the family lost its fortune, it maintained ties with the royal families through marriage and maintained its reputation and political power. Despite losing the family fortune, through his wise moves, the Medici maintained their ties to the royal families through marriage and retained their prestige and political power. Catherine de Medici (1519–1589), a grandchild of Piero the unfortunate, would become the queen of King Henry II (France). In 1523, Giulio de' Medici, a natural son of Giuliano, the brother of Lorenzo the Magnificent became Pope, taking the name Clement VII. The Medici family, which presented essential figures such as four Popes and many Dukes, maintained its reputation, albeit weakened, until the eighteenth century. However, the family and the Medici Bank would never reach the power and glory of Cosmo's time (Aboutflorence.com, n.d.).

2.10 The Banking Secrets of the Medici

The Medici benefited from Italy's growing economic activity and the momentum of the Renaissance. They developed a series of innovations that created the most important bank in Europe at the beginning of the new era.

2.10.1 Leadership

The political environment in Florence during the fourteenth and fifteenth centuries was quite slippery. However, it was a suitable atmosphere for developing business life and art. The leaders' ambitions, the strife between families, the rebellious poor, the pressure of the Church on society and politics, and France's desire to interfere in Italy's internal affairs created constant political turmoil. The economic success of family businesses also depended on gaining extraordinary political power in society. When families became weak in sustaining political relations, it was inevitable that they would encounter significant trade and banking business obstacles. Therefore, prominent families did not hesitate to resort to violence from time to time to gain a position in the political life of Florence.

With the administration and problem-solving capacity of Cosimo and Lorenzo, the Medici could preserve their wealth for a long time. Professor Uzzi (2015) says that Cosimo's success was based on "*multi-focused leadership*" and states that his leadership capacity was identified with the emotions and mentalities of different commercial and political groups in Florentine. Cosimo succeeded as a banker in an environment where many others failed despite lacking trading, merchandising, and other vital expertise. Apart from Cosimo's political rivals, he also had the powerful and wealthy Catholic Church to deal with constantly. Prof. Uzzi says that instead of directly facing competitors, Cosimo built new and joint-purpose bridges with them, with the collaborations resulting in a wider Florentine society that produced greater, more sustainable economic, social, and cultural value for all parties.

As a multi-focused leader, he dealt with what motivated the people around him, identified what would encourage others, and led the team to success by trusting them. Cosimo always had a plan; he could come up with creative solutions. Thus, he could maintain his power for a very long time. When multi-focused leaders work with different groups, they realize their weaknesses and determine their positions accordingly. Such leaders maintain order in business life by working with teams of people with different abilities, and they can manage for a long time to bring all team members into a unit focused on the same goal.

2.10.2 Holding Type of Company Structure

The Bardi and Peruzzi companies were centrally structured and power was vested in the company and family members in Florence. In the event of the deaths of family members and important disputes, the decision-making process sometimes did not work. In addition, due to the slow communication conditions of the time, it took a long time for the orders to reach the branches, which slowed down business processes. In addition, since these families mainly employed managers for a specific salary, it was not easy for managers to be motivated and to use their creativity sufficiently. The Medici Bank was established with a completely modern holding company model and, as the first of its kind, inspired many companies. Under the holding structure, each independent branch became a profit center. They had agents in the leading European fairs and trade centers, such as Lyons, Bruges, and Milan, and provided all kinds of information related to their business.

While de facto managing Florence, Cosimo emphasized teamwork and ensured that the people he trusted received authority. The most important benefit of this model for the Medici was that it could control a wide business network with limited capital and ensure the continuity of the management of partner companies. Instead of recruiting with a specific salary, as other banks did, in the Medici companies, staff payments were tied to firm performance for senior employees. Based on a sound accounting system, the company gave its members a share of the profits instead of salaries.

2.10.3 Public Relations

Public relations is not merely a marketing and advertising business. Going beyond this, it is meant to increase the prestige of an institution by making it accepted by society. In a broader definition, public relations help an organization or individual gain a positive reputation among the public through various traditional means of communication, personal interviews, and rumors. Public relations are a long-term effort. The most significant benefit of "*PR*" to the organizations engaged in this activity is to provide a kind of shield of protection against just or unfair campaigns against them.

Cosimo also understood that to be successful in Florence's very turbulent politics and business life, he had to establish a good relationship with the people of Florence. He undoubtedly had a good intuition. The people meant to him both potential business partners and political power in the imperfect democracy of Florence. He understood that he would lose his political power and worsen his bank's business if he could not find enough societal backing. Therefore, Cosimo and later Lorenzo began to use the funds provided by the Medici Bank to expand their influence over the city. After all, these activities had two main benefits; the first made them appear like a benevolent leader in society, and the second that it intimidated their opponents by making it clear to their enemies how powerful the Medici were in Florence.

One of the crucial discoveries of the 20th century is in understanding the connection between art and public relations. As art attracts people's attention, it is followed with interest by society with its aesthetic beauty, visualization, quality, and messages. When people in business have a close connection with artists, they can reach very different segments of society and increase their reputation (The PR Insider, 2016). Even if the public relations departments of today's companies use the arts as much as possible, they will never reach the level of the Medici's. It is not feasible for any family or company to be connected as much as the Medici's and artists were. Did the Medici do all these activities just deliberately? Undoubtedly, the answer to this question would be no. However, someone with the capacity for intelligent and multi-focused leadership like Cosimo must have understood the dignity and support art would give him and the Medici. About 400 years after the Medici, a famous US banker, JP Morgan, had a similar passion. In addition to paintings and sculptures, he collected rare books and manuscripts, bronzes, gold work, tapestries, snuff boxes, Chinese porcelain, medieval armor, and furniture. These people of great wealth perhaps thought that they could achieve immortality in this way.

Cosimo's descendants continued to patronize art and philosophy as a family tradition. In particular, his grandson, Lorenzo de' Medici, was impressed by his grandfather's interest in politics and arts. These two characters' outstanding public relations skills were important to the Medici family's success in maintaining their banking business when political activities went above the law and business traditions.

2.10.4 Risk Management and Diversification

Operating under medieval conditions, Italian bankers were businessmen who inevitably had to take huge risks. They operated in distant geographies, and shipping the goods they financed took weeks, even months. The jobs of the people they worked with were also not very reliable. However, they had learned about risk diversification, gaining experience by distributing their investments to different countries, people, and goods. In the Medici's shipment of goods, goods traveling by land were generally not insured. Conversely, Galleys were considered so safe that many merchants saw no need for insurance. They preferred to limit their risk by dividing their shipments into various sub-groups (De Roover, 1963). The Medici also paid attention to risk management by using their strong company network and relationships with correspondent bankers more intelligently in financial operations. The Medici had partners or correspondents in Europe's major financial centers. This extensive business network of subsidiaries and representatives made them aware of fluctuations in exchange rates and money markets. They had contacts with all the commercial regions of Europe. The way to earn high profits in exchange and borrowing activities was to exploit exchange rate differences and capital shortages. This led Medici Bank to diversify its portfolios by opening branches in different regions or working with correspondent bankers. The Medici, with the companies they founded throughout Europe, directed capital to the most demanded places. By this method, they enabled capital-rich entrepreneurs in Italy to invest in all the major financial centers of Europe by acting as intermediaries. While the Medici initially conducted their transactions with reliable people whose credit histories they knew, they had to work with lesser-known merchants in different geographies to expand their credit networks. When the Medici family saw a profitable opportunity for an investment in, e.g., Bruges, they could use their extensive network of relationships to verify the potential borrower's credibility through a local company and, if necessary, impose financial sanctions to recover their debt. Moreover, they kept reserves for uncollectible credits and prohibited credit granting to untrustworthy merchants. Their cooperation with the Church concerning the latter's excommunication practices on bad debtors helped them further mitigate their credit risks. The attention of the Medici family to the uncollectible credits shows us that this topic was relevant also at that time and not only nowadays (Fazzini et al., 2016). In a sense, their practices were forerunners of the risk management centers of the banks of today.

On the other hand, not only did they refrain from entering certain businesses because of the risk, but they also traded on commission, using consignment sales, which ensured that the ownership of the goods sent remained with the seller throughout the operation. The price of the product was paid according to the market conditions. This way, they protected themselves against the risk of exchange. For example, in 1441, the Medici company's subsidiary in Venice received ginger on consignment on behalf of the Bruges subsidiary. This transaction had no exchange risk since the payment and collection were made through the Venetian Duke (De Roover, 1963). Medici invested in many areas, entered into joint ventures with third parties, and diversified their risks with subsidiaries in different regions, with small investor partners involved in sharing risks.

2.10.5 Bookkeeping and Accounting

The Medici were not the inventors of modern accounting. Many Italian companies were using it already. They contributed significantly to professions accounting to improve the general ledger system by developing the double-entry system of tracking debits and credits or deposits and withdrawals. Research on the Medici indicates that their companies prepare balance sheets once a year. Senior partners received a copy of the balance sheet as of March 24. The directors of the subsidiaries were obliged to present a copy of their balance sheet anytime if requested by the senior partners. The tradition of medieval merchants, including the Medici, was to open a separate account for each new business venture. In such budgets, investment amounts and expenditures should be closed by the proceeds from sales. After the end of the business project, the remaining difference was transferred to the "Commodity Profit and Loss" account. This account showed the profit or loss of this venture. The Medici calculated the gains from trade and exchanges separately from each other. Opening separate accounts for each business is critical for risk accounting today (De Roover, 1963).

2.11 Conclusion

At some times in history, political struggle and social mobility created such a massive cloud of dust that many of those who lived in that period could not fully understand what was happening. All that happens are new searches of a society that has begun to change. Social occasions' direct or indirect contributions to culture, art, science, and even the economy cannot be felt immediately. Still, as time passes and the dust clears a little, it is realized that something extraordinary has happened. It was like that in 15th Century Florence. New ideas, art, and new business methods were flourishing.

Looking back today, the liberal environment that began to sprout in the city republics in northern and central Italy at the end of the Middle Ages, despite all the political turmoil, provided new opportunities for Florentines and opened the doors of the Renaissance. The main institution that undoubtedly left its mark on this period was the Medici Bank. The Medici Bank was founded by Giovanni de' Medici and lived its best period in the 15th Century with Cosimo and Lorenzo de' Medici. The bank pioneered commercial capitalism and ensured that Renaissance art peaked by promoting art and artists. The Medici's lives were not easy at all. In their lives full of political turmoil, exiles, assassinations, and conspiracies, they maintained their wealth for a long time with their leadership and problem-solving capacity while conducting their commercial activities. The Medici Bank was not only the most important bank of that time; it also laid the foundations of a company model that would mark the following centuries with its corporate structure. If we still remember the Medici today, it is because of their leadership and organizational skills in a complex political environment, reputation-building public relations, and exceptional risk management.

The two most influential leaders of the Medici, Cosimo and Lorenzo de' Medici, exhibited a type of leadership now defined as multi-focused. Thus, they established emotional and thought bonds with all segments of society, including their rivals, and enabled them to work together for a better Florence. In addition, by establishing a decentralized company structure, open to changes, they managed their subsidiaries, successfully motivated their managers, and increased corporate income. By selecting a good connection with society, they increased their prestige on the one hand. On the other hand, they intimidated their enemies with successful public relations activity, especially involving art and artists.

Apart from these, perhaps the most essential novelty they brought about is the holding type of company management, which was very different and far-fetched from what was established by the Knights Templar in earlier centuries. They had learned from the failure of the centrally managed Bardi and Peruzzi companies and created this structure. Hundreds of years later, the tycoons of America's Gilded Age rediscovered the holding company structure in the nineteenth century and established corporate empires.

A traveler visiting Florence today will most likely neither see the splendor of the Medici Bank nor the talents of Cosimo nor understand how magnificent Lorenzo was. Apart from the buildings that stood the test of time, travelers can only see awe-inspiring works of art made with the Medici Family's financial support, friendship, and interest. They will admire the works of Michelangelo, Leonardo da Vinci, and many other artists. Perhaps this was the legacy the Medici wanted to leave. They probably learned in their turbulent lives that money and power are temporary, while art is permanent.

References

Aboutflorence.com. (n.d.). About Florence, history of Florence. Retrieved from http://www.aboutflorence.com/history-of-Florence.html

Arabic Numerals. (2024). Wikipedia contributors. Retrieved from https://en.wikipedia.org/wiki/Arabic_numerals

Braudel, F. (1992). *The perspective of the world*. University of California Press.

Calkins, H. (2014). Can Florence in the Quatrocento help shape tax policy today. *Tax Law, 68*, 239.

Cartwright, M. (2019). Trade in Medieval Europe. World history encyclopaedia. Retrieved from https://www.worldhistory.org/article/1301/trade-in-medieval-europe//

Durham, J. W. (1992). The introduction of 'Arabic' numerals in European accounting. *Accounting Historians Journal, 19*(2), 25–55. https://doi.org/10.2308/0148-4184.19.2.25

Encyclopedia Britannica. (1998). Signoria | Italian Medieval Government. Retrieved from https://www.britannica.com/topic/signoria

Encyclopedia Britannica. (2018). Cosimo de'Medici | Ruler of Florence [1389–1464]. Retrieved from https://www.britannica.com/biography/Cosimo-de-Medici

Encyclopedia.com. (2018). Cosimo De' Medici. Retrieved from https://www.encyclopedia.com/people/history/italian-history-biographies/cosimo-de-medici
Fazzini, M., Fici, L., Montrone, A, & Terzani, S. (2016). A modern look at the Banco De' Medici: Governance and accountability systems. *International Business & Economics Research Journal*. https://doi.org/10.19030/iber.v15i6.9827
Goldthwaite, R. A. (1987). The Medici Bank and the world of Florentine capitalism. *Past & Present, 114*, 3–31.
Hallam, E. M., & Trevor-Roper, H. R. (1988). *The wars of the roses*. Weidenfeld & Nicolson.
Hibbert, C. (1975). *The Medici: The rise and fall*. Morrow Quill.
Hunt, E. S. (1990). A new look at the dealings of the Bardi and Peruzzi with Edward III. *The Journal of Economic History, 50*(1), 149–162. https://doi.org/10.1017/s0022050700035762
Kohn, M. (1999). Bills of exchange and the money market to 1600. Dartmouth college, department of economics working paper (99-04). Retrieved from https://bpb-us-e1.wpmucdn.com/sites.dartmouth.edu/dist/6/1163/files/2017/03/99-04.pdf
Martines, L. (2011). The social world of the Florentine humanists, 1390–1460. University of Toronto Press in association with The Renaissance Society of America.
Molho, A. (1994). *Marriage alliance in late medieval Florence* (Vol. 114). Harvard University Press.
Munro, J. H. (2002). The medieval origins of the 'Financial Revolution': usury, rentes and negotiability. MPRA Paper 10925. Retrieved from https://mpra.ub.uni-muenchen.de/10925/
Munro, J. H. (2012). The rise, expansion, and decline of the Italian wool-based textile industries, 1100–1730: A study in international competition, transaction costs, and comparative advantage. *Studies in Medieval and Renaissance History, 9*, 45–207. https://www.economics.utoronto.ca/index.php/index/research/workingPaperDetails/440
The PR Insider. (2016). The why art needs PR. Curzon PR. Retrieved from https://www.curzonpr.com/theprinsider/art-needs-pr-artists-public-relations-fine-art/
Pryor, J. H. (1977). The origins of the commenda contract. *Speculum, 52*(1), 5–37. https://doi.org/10.2307/2856894
De Roover, F. E. (1941). Partnership accounts in twelfth-century Genoa. *Business History Review, 15*(6), 87–92. https://doi.org/10.1017/S0007680500022753
De Roover, R. (1947). The decline of the Medici Bank. *The Journal of Economic History, 7*(1), 69–82. https://doi.org/10.1017/s0022050700053456
De Roover, R. (1963). *The rise and decline of the Medici Bank: 1397–1494*. Harvard University Press.
De Roover, R. (1967). The scholastics, usury, and foreign exchange. *Business History Review, 41*(3), 257–271. https://doi.org/10.2307/3112192
Reumont, A., & Von Harrison, R. (1876). *Lorenzo de'Medici, the magnificent*. Smith, Elder & Co.
Ricciardelli, F. (2018). Late Medieval City-States and the origins of modern democracy. Villa La Pietra. Retrieved from https://lapietra.nyu.edu/event/late-medieval-city-states-and-the-origins-of-modern-democracy/.
Robinson, J. A., & Acemoglu, D. (2019). *The narrow corridor*. Penguin Books Ltd.
Western Schism. (2024). Wikipedia contributors. Retrieved from https://en.wikipedia.org/wiki/Western_Schism
Staley, J. E. (1906). The guilds of Florence. In *Internet archive*. London, Methuen & co. Retrieved from https://archive.org/details/guildsofflorence00staluoft
Tomas, N. R. (2005). *The Medici women: Gender and power in Renaissance Florence*. Ashgate.
Uzzi, B. (2015). Great leaders can think like each member of their team. Harvard Business Review. Retrieved from https://hbr.org/2015/07/great-leaders-can-think-like-each-member-of-their-team.

Chapter 3
Corporations, Stock Exchanges, and the Amsterdam Bank of Exchange (Late Sixteenth and Seventeenth Centuries)

3.1 Introduction

Since 1585, Amsterdam was more crowded than ever before. The Catholic Spaniards were occupying the most important commercial center of the so-called Low Countries, Antwerp, and with the town being cut-off from the sea by a blockade, people flew to the city of Amsterdam. There was heavy traffic in the port. While some ships were carrying trade goods such as Far Eastern spices, American coffee, and Siberian fur, some ships were full of passengers, and many immigrants were unloading their belongings at the pier. Protestants, Calvinists, Jews, and people from various sub-identities and various countries and regions created a riot of colors in the streets with their different clothes. Some of the immigrants were quite wealthy, they had come with their cash and gold, and wanted to live and establish a business in Amsterdam. The city was free from religious oppression, under the moderate and tolerant administration of the later Dutch Republic, rebelling against Spain. Indeed, Amsterdam was increasingly becoming a center of tolerance and free trade.

Next to the Amstel River, the canal area of Amsterdam was a medieval city that had not yet assumed its present appearance; only a few canals were around and other canals were just being dug out. The "Amsterdammers" were gradually building red brick houses lined up around the channels (Fig. 3.1). Since the area was partially submerged, the land was not very suitable for the settlement of so many people. In a few decades, three more canals would be dug out and a city that would take the shape of a half-moon would emerge. Since the Heerengracht canal had the largest parcels of land, it attracted the wealthy's attention; they would soon buy two or three plots of land around it and built the most prominent houses (Rijksmuseum, 2020). Warehouses were also erected in the port area, and goods from all over the world were placed and replaced. Amsterdam was just at the beginning of the road.

Let us turn the wheels of time forward now and zoom in on July 12, 1614. Elias Trip was just appointed as Director of the Amsterdam Chamber of the VOC. Some pressure from Dordrecht had helped with that. The VOC was starting to get going and in Dordrecht there was some concern that it would be dominated too much by

M. B. Karan et al., *A History of Banks*, Contributions to Economics,
https://doi.org/10.1007/978-3-031-62297-7_3

Fig. 3.1 Amsterdam canal area. https://commons.wikimedia.org/wiki/File:Gerrit_Adriaensz._Berckheyde_-_De_bocht_van_de_Herengracht_te_Amsterdam.jpg

Amsterdam. Until now, Elias was trading from Dordrecht, just like a large part of his family. This involved salt trade and refinement, and the iron trade along the Meuse. Yet, he was already shifting his focus. The iron trade made him becoming involved in the bullet trade (from Liège) and thus in the much larger trade in cannons. In particular, he played a major role in the import of iron cannons from England, for the first time in 1612. In addition, he was involved in the trade in West Africa. There were all sorts of separate initiatives in that regard. It often went through so-called participation shipping companies, with two, three, or four partners. On the outward journey they carried textiles, copper, and ironware and on the way back, ideally, gold and ivory. When they came across a ship from an unfriendly nation, they hijacked it. The yields easily outweighed the extra crew required and the extra armament (cannons). The import of cannons served as a good match for this anyway. The States General easily granted rights to raid ships until 1606, but people did not take it narrowly even after. The accent did shift though. It was, of course, always an entrepreneurial venture with an adventure, just like any risky venture. Of an expedition in 1609, with three ships, only one returned safely.

Then, at the beginning of the Twelve Year's Truce, it was already clear that the Dutch Republic would be here to stay. Elias realized that, given the trade he was involved in, it was important to have a good connection with the rulers of the Republic. The core of the power was in Amsterdam. Here were the headquarters of the VOC, the main "trade army" of the republic and the big international traders were also around. So, when he was nominated as extraordinary director from Dordrecht, he welcomed it. He must have had a hand in it himself. That he had been given that position from Dordrecht was no longer noticeable later in his actions. He was also soon appointed as an ordinary director. He moved to Amsterdam in 1614. That worked out well for family life too. His first wife (Maria de Geer) had died in 1609 and he had remarried in 1611 to a much younger woman (Aelken Adriaensdr).

Elias was 44 when he started in Amsterdam. He was full of plans. In the first place, the arms trade: bullets, cannons, military equipment, rifles, gunpowder, saltpeter (raw material for gunpowder). The Republic and the VOC needed a lot of it and it could also be a good basis for further trade—iron trade in general, copper trade (also as a raw material for bronze cannons) and corn trade. In the arms trade, he would have to deal with all kinds of regulations with regard to imports and exports, with much dynamics in view of the fluctuating political relationships. England, for example, soon began to make a fuss about the export of cannons and then he had better be seated close to the fire. However, the role of the States General was also important in the more peaceful trade. They might or might not grant a monopoly. Because Amsterdam had an overwhelmingly large merchant fleet, a large part of the trade went through Amsterdam and a monopoly could therefore be very effective. As director of the VOC, he had a great place to exert influence and it was very beneficial in itself anyway. The directors received 1% of the equipment and of the proceeds of the net returns (another easily manipulated amount) and the directors were also given the opportunity to supply all kinds of things. For Elias as an arms dealer an opportunity not to be sneezed at. Indeed, the 12th of July of 1614 was a beautiful day to him.

Halfway the seventeenth-century Amsterdam was by far the world's most successful merchant city. There were now three new canals around the old city, mainly for luxurious merchant homes. Elias Trip bought one on the Heerengracht 54 in 1633, but unfortunately, he died in 1636, albeit as a rich man. On top of all of the Amsterdam buildings was the new city hall, however. The old one burned down in 1652, but the building of the new one was already underway then. It was designed by Jacob van Campen and it was finished in 1655. It was luxurious and huge, full of the message that Amsterdam had made it.

In this chapter, we are going to describe the Dutch "miracle," the enormous progress of the Dutch republic in terms of politics and economics, as a context for three institutions that are important for the development of finance and banking. We discuss the role of the United East India Company ("VOC") and its counterpart in the West Indies ("WIC"), the Amsterdam Exchange ("Beurs") and the Amsterdam Bank of Exchange ("Wisselbank"). The era from 1585 to 1672 was the heart of this period of progress and merchants like Elias Trip were the driving force and formed the ruling class. The just-mentioned appointment of Elias Trip was amidst the so-called Twelve Years' Truce. With the start of that Truce (1609), the Dutch Republic had reached independence from Spain. It was the result of 40 years of fighting. It is worthwhile to return to that period first, in order to put the developments in the financial sector in place. We start with the political developments in Western Europe and then cover its economic developments. In doing so, we will especially zoom in on the Netherlands.

3.2 Political Developments in Western Europe and the Birth of the Dutch Republic

The political balances of Europe in the sixteenth century were quite complicated. The political ambitions, family ties, and religious obsessions of kings were affecting all countries. One of the most common ways to strengthen the influence of European royal families was through dynasties' marriage. Because of these marriages, royal families claimed each other's thrones and ascended thrones by way of heritage. One of those who ascended the throne in this way was King Charles V, born of the marriage of Princess Juana, Princess of Aragon in Spain, and Felipe the Handsome, the German Habsburg Prince Felipe. King Charles V would later sit on the throne of both the German Habsburg and Spain. Besides Spain and Central Germany, the empire covered Southern Italy, some French regions, and the Netherlands, which also included Belgium and Luxembourg at the time, see Fig. 3.2.

In October 1555, Charles V began the gradual abdication of his several crowns. His son Philip II took over as sovereign of the Netherlands, which at the time was a personal union of 17 provinces with little in common beyond their sovereign and a constitutional framework. This framework, assembled during the preceding reigns of Burgundian and Habsburg rulers, divided power between city governments, local nobility, provincial States, royal governors, the States General of the Netherlands, and the central government (possibly represented by a Regent) assisted by three councils: the Council of State, the Privy Council, and the Council of Finances. The Governor-General of Habsburg Spain was responsible for the administration of the area. The Spaniards had established a central government that did not give much value to the Dutch merchants and notables of the cities. Moreover, since they were in conflict almost all over Europe, they were taxing this wealthy region in large sums (Israel, 1998). The people were overwhelmed by paying taxes, and unrest was growing in the region. Philip was going to stress the role of the central government and introduced a number of new councilors, to the chagrin of the Dutch nobles. When he left for Spain, in 1559, he appointed his half-sister, Margaret of Parma as regent and Governor-General.

Dutch Humanists such as Desiderius Erasmus (1466–1536) had called for reform long ago, criticizing the rigid practices of religion ("History of Religion"). Since then, Protestantism was rising in Central and Western Europe, especially in Germany. Many were done with the alleged ostentatious ceremonies and superficial piety and believed Protestantism, especially Calvinism, to be morally superior to the Roman Church. The Protestant movements established by Martin Luther, John Calvin, Menno Simons, and others had many adherents in The Netherlands. Philip was fiercely against these movements and prosecuted them, which caused widespread unrest. To support and strengthen his policy, Philip reorganized the Catholic Church in the Netherlands in 1559 and made Granvelle, as archbishop of Mechelen, the head of it. Granvelle became the focus of the opposition against the new governmental structure and the Dutch nobles, under the leadership of William of Orange, engineered his recall in 1564. In the summer of 1566, the protests exploded into an iconoclastic fury, the so-called "Beeldenstorm." Margaret restored order, but Philip had already dispatched the duke of Alba with an army to resolve the difficulties by military power. Alba took over the command and Margaret resigned. Alba started with the execution of about 1,000 of the nobles. William of Orange fled in exile, like many others.

As a result of this atmosphere of unrest, 17 states came together in 1568 and rebelled against Spanish domination, thus igniting 80 years of war. Their leader was Prince William of the Orange County in France, known for his quietness, honesty, and very determined personality. William I, also known as William the Silent, managed to unfurl the flag of rebellion. William was a clever commander; he sought military and financial help. This help came from the Ottoman Empire, which fought with the Spaniards at sea and the Habsburgs over land. Sultan Süleyman the Magnificent felt religiously close to the Protestants who also believed in one God and did not like the visible and touchable saints of the catholic church. It was also important for the Ottomans to divide the Christians politically. He backed William from the year 1566 onward (Karpat, 1974). The French and the British sympathized as well with the rebels, indirectly supporting the Dutch to balance the Habsburg power (Limm, 2014). William allied himself with Huguenots, French Protestants, while forming an army of primarily German mercenaries to fight the Duke of Alba. It invaded The Netherlands in 1568. However, the plan failed almost from the start. French royal troops defeated the Huguenots before participating in the mission and the army of German mercenaries was defeated (Tracy, 2008).

The first years of the Dutch Rebellion were rather chaotic. The cities and provinces adhered to their independence. Each of them had to cope with their own situation. The relations between the different religious groups varied and so did the economic opportunities and dependencies. The first wave of cities joining the revolt was due to the combined pressure of the "Watergeuzen" (Water Warriors), privateers acting in the name of William, and direct military actions by himself in the eastern provinces. For some cities the transition was voluntarily, inspired by the success of the Watergeuzen. Others had to be "convinced" militarily. Part of the cities were reconquered again by Spain. Others stayed loyal to king Philip anyway. Amsterdam, for instance, did so until 1578. It gave up after a blockade of its harbor. Between 1576 and 1578, there was an almost successful trial to combine all the Netherlands in a more moderate proposal to King Philip, the "Pacification of Ghent." It failed by Spanish greed and Calvinist intolerance. In 1579, the union of the 17 Dutch states was broken when the Southerners made a deal with Spain. The Netherlands in the North, including Zeeland, Utrecht, Holland, Utrecht, Gelre, Overijssel, and Groningen, joined each other in the rebellion against Spain by signing the treaty of Utrecht ("Union of

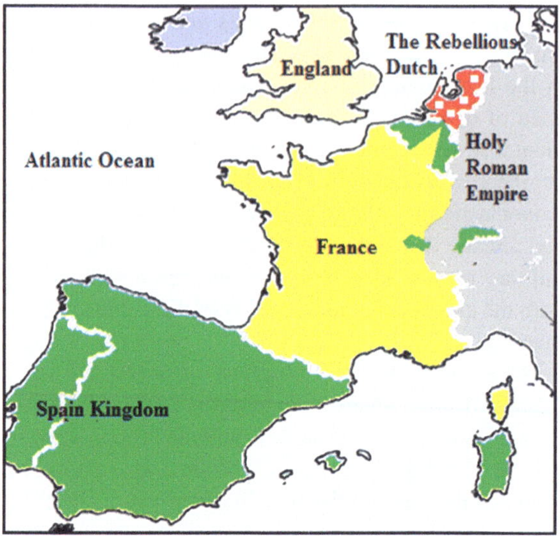

Fig. 3.2 Spanish empire (1580)

Utrecht"). Figure 3.2 shows the lands ruled by the Spanish Empire in the beginning years of the Dutch Rebellion.

During that time, there was a rather extreme Calvinist republic in Ghent, also containing Bruges and other cities in the neighborhood. This republic joined the North as well. Antwerp, also a republic at the time, joined it too. During the 1580 s, however, due to effective military actions of Spain, the revolt got concentrated in Holland and Zeeland. Groningen became royalist already in 1580, Ghent was defeated in 1584. Antwerp followed in 1585, leading to an effective separation between the North and the South. Meanwhile, William of Orange had been assassinated in 1584, in what is known as the first political assassination using a pistol against a president in Europe (Harvey, 1991). According to official records, his last words were: "*Lord, have mercy on my soul; God have mercy on these poor people*" (Edmundson, 1922). His murderer Balthasar Gérard was brutally tortured by soldiers and servants before being sentenced to death (Motley, 2004). The situation of the rebels was critical now.

The remaining provinces looked for support and protection in England. They agreed with Queen Elizabeth I to appoint the earl of Leicester to Governor-General of the Netherlands. It was not a success. They blamed him for the defeat of Zutphen and Deventer, in 1586. He was sent back and the rebelling provinces accepted that they had to decide to become really independent. In 1588, a new State was established: the Republic of the Seven United Netherlands (Holland, Zeeland, Utrecht, Gelre, Overijssel, Groningen, and Friesland). The two leaders were Johan van Oldenbarnevelt, the Advocate of the States of Holland and the Grand Pensionary, and Maurice of Orange, a son of William of Orange, who became the Stadholder (governor) of the core area Holland and Zeeland. Together with William's cousin William Louis, Stadholder of Friesland, they formed a terrific trio that worked very well together (Wintle, 2007).

The next 10 years were very successful, at least militarily. Maurice conquered many cities and with the defeat of Groningen in 1594, he completed the control of all of the seven provinces. Thereafter the failures and successes of the parties were more or less in balance. Both parties began to worry about the costs of the military operations. The Spanish Kingdom, which already had severe financial difficulties, could not pay its soldiers and went bankrupt several times. Spain's mobilization of most of its economic and human resources against the Ottoman Empire in the Mediterranean in the 1570 s was one of the primary reasons for its financial failure. The Dutch were also worried about the expenses. Van Oldenbarnevelt representing Holland (with Amsterdam) began to stress the importance of peace for the development of trade. In 1609, a ceasefire was signed for a period of 12 years. Maurice did not agree and would have preferred to continue fighting. The same was true for Zeeland, which was afraid of the competition by Antwerp, whose harbor was blocked by the Dutch until now. During the Twelve Years' Truce, the conflict between Maurice and Van Oldenbarnevelt sharpened. Maurice had the support of most of the provinces and used a religious conflict (between the Arminians and Gomarists) to accuse van Oldenbarnevelt of treason. Van Oldenbarnevelt was sentenced to death in 1619 ("Johan van Oldenbarnevelt").

The war that broke out again with Spain in 1621 would gradually have a global character, also including England, France, the Roman Empire, German Principalities, Sweden, Poland, Russia, and the Ottoman Empire. Although the war with Spain was partly in Europe, a sizeable part of the battles between the Spaniards and the Dutch would be overseas, in the colonies of both sides, and at sea. When Maurice died, his half-brother, Frederick Henry, succeeded him and had considerable success in the battle in Europe, e.g., by capturing the southern cities of Den Bosch (1629) and Maastricht (1632). When the war finally ended in 1648, with the Westphalian Peace that also included France and the Roman Empire, the Netherlands and Belgium had become completely separate entities. Little later, the Netherlands would start to fight with England and France on the hegemony of the world. British feelings of discomfort led to the Navigation Acts (1651), to restrict the Dutch role in shipping and trade, and thereafter to the first war between England and the Republic (1652–1654). After some mixed successes, e.g., including a victorious Dutch Raid on the Thames near London in 1667, the Dutch State had weakened militarily. The Republic became a toy of the French and the German Bishop of Münster in the "Distaster Year" 1672 that marked the end of the Dutch "Golden Age."

A major issue was that the Republic was a de-centralized state. The 7 provinces and 57 cities stuck to their independence (De Vries & Van der Woude, 1997). The Union of Utrecht (1579) was mainly a mutual defense pact. To organize the necessary central expenses, a Council of State ("Raad van State") was established. It had to draft a war budget and a budget for other central government expenditures. The seven provinces had to agree unanimously to make it effective. Once the budget was determined, all provinces had to pay a fixed quota but were free to decide how to organize the taxes to generate sufficient revenues. Holland started to introduce excise taxes as a main source and all provinces followed in some way. However, the provinces distinguished between provincial products and non-provincial products. It was left to the cities to implement the tax, which led to differences. There was one more universal tax, the tax on foreign trade. Its revenues would be spent completely on expenses for the Admiralty, to support the supremacy at sea. There were however five Admiralties: three in Holland, one in Zeeland, and one in Friesland. Moreover, the tax practices diverged in the course of time.

At the level of the Republic there was a structural conflict of interests between Holland, represented by the Advocate of the States of Holland, later called the Grand Pensionary, and the other provinces with the Stadholder. Holland was stressing the merchant interests, the importance of peace and the supremacy at sea and the other provinces and the Stadholder were stressing the importance of safety and military supremacy between the surrounding countries. It led to the already mentioned conviction and execution of Johan van Oldenbarnevelt in 1619, the start of an era without a Stadholder (1650–1672) and the murder of the then Grand Pensionary Johan de Witt, in 1672 (cf. Braudel, 1990). Moreover, the cities were most important. They competed internationally but also with each other in realizing an attractive trade and manufacturing environment, including a judicial system supporting a safe and dependable way of contracting (Gelderblom, 2000). All of these changes did not really interfere with the power of the merchants, especially those from Amsterdam and Holland. It remained all the time a government by and for merchants. The ruling institutions consisted of representatives of the merchants.

3.3 Economic Developments in Western Europe and the Prosperity of the Dutch

When our story begins in the sixteenth century, the Ottoman Empire governing the East of Europe was in its most glorious period under the reign of Suleiman the Magnificent. The most powerful and wealthiest region in Western Europe was the Iberian Peninsula, where the Mediterranean opened up to the oceans. The Umayyad State of Andalusia had collapsed here, and Prince Ferdinand of Aragon and Queen Isabella of Castile laid the foundations of the Spanish Kingdom. After Christopher Columbus discovered America in 1492, Spanish sailors had reached Africa, Asia, and especially Central and South America, enriching Spain and establishing a great empire. Another country in the Iberian Peninsula was Portugal, which was living its Golden Age somewhat before. The Portuguese sailed the seas like the Spaniards and made Lisbon port the distribution center of Far Eastern spices in Europe.

Already in the fifteenth century, the port of Antwerp had begun to become an important commercial center in the Netherlands—in between Italian merchants and the German Hanseatic League. While the Venetians brought precious jewels from the Far East, the Germans were trading fur and rye from Russia. England's trade was also conducted through the Netherlands. Merchants were welcomed in their inns and helped to barter and sell their goods. They also informed exchange rates to various banking centers in Europe, including Paris, Venice, and London, by collecting information from different countries. The van der Buerse family, for at least five generations from the 1200 s onward, ran the Ter Buerse inn in Bruges, which is on Belgian territory today. Groups of foreign merchants were gathering in tents on the square outside. Van der Buerse's important role in mediating economic trade during this period would lead to creating the word "beurs" or "bourse" that refers to exchange market in, respectively, Dutch and French. Although historians argue over whether the trading markets first emerged in Antwerp or Bruges, most agree that the first stock exchange building was the Handelsbeurs ("Trade exchange") in Antwerp. Initially built in 1531, it housed the city's Chamber of Commerce for nearly 500 years, but merchants would tend to trade debt securities rather than physical goods (Hunt, 2019).

To sustain the wealth, the Dutch had to rely on interregional and international markets for corn, cloth, timber, iron, etcetera. Already before 1585, Dutch skippers, mainly from Holland, controlled the Baltic trade (Braudel, 1990). Corn was an important product here. Interestingly, not only the Dutch had to import it. This is how Amsterdam came to staple corn and exported part of it to Spain, even during the revolt. The dependence on imported corn made the agriculture market oriented. The specialization was mainly on cattle and dairy. Cheese became a Dutch export product. In some cases, peat could also be exported (De Vries & Van der Woude, 1997). The prosperous local market offered an opportunity of creating new arable land by establishing a new polder as a rational investment for rich merchants. The Zaan shipbuilding district near Amsterdam was the world's first industrialized area, with around 900 industrial windmills. Industries using cheap fuel, such as papermaking, sugar refining, printing, the linen industry, and brewing and ceramics, also grew drastically. What the Dutch themselves could make available on the international markets was, e.g., fish, cheese, tulips, paintings, jewelry, and pottery. Developing regional trade relations helped to spread these goods across Europe (Blockmans, 2007).

The position of the Dutch on the North–South trade was strengthened by improved ship building. Given the central location of the Dutch harbors between Spain and the Baltic, these improvements made it possible to combine in one sailing season a trip to the Bay of Biscay, to load salt and wine and a trip to the Baltic, to load grain or timber (De Vries & Van der Woude, 1997). In the late sixteenth century, they developed a new type of ship (the "Fluit"), thus maximizing the loading space, minimizing the necessary crew, and also taking into account the way the Danish toll at Helsingor was determined. Taken together, it made the Dutch fleet much more efficient than the ones of competing countries such as France. The shipbuilding industry became also important in itself. Timber was imported from Norway and the Baltic; ships and (processed) wood were exported. The success in whaling and fishing, especially herring, helped also to strengthen the sea going power and hence the trading capacity. A bottleneck in sea fare was the crew. Immigrants filled part of the gaps and recruitment went sometimes by force.

The defeat of Antwerp, in 1585, accelerated the growth of Dutch trade. Textile workers from Flanders moved to the already existing textile industry in Haarlem and Leiden. A significant part of the merchants from Antwerp came, directly or indirectly, to Amsterdam, adding to the capital and entrepreneurship there. Amsterdam became the most important staple for Europe and attracted also merchants from other cities in the republic, including Elias Trip from Dordrecht as we saw earlier. Whereas the trade in Antwerp still followed the fair pattern, it was more permanent in Amsterdam. There was sufficient warehouse capacity and as soon as there was demand, it was possible to negotiate, close contracts and distribute. It was attractive for the merchants to use Amsterdam as entrepot, even when it was possible to transport directly. The United East India Company (Vereenigde Oostindische Compagnie, "VOC") and its counterpart in the West Indies ("WIC"), the Amsterdam Exchange ("Beurs"), and the Amsterdam Bank of Exchange ("Wisselbank") were important in facilitating the trade.

The Netherlands had long been entirely developed and wealthy by trading, but it always needed more income under war conditions. Therefore, from 1585 to 1620, the Dutch stumbled into innovations to establish a regular tax system, increase their savings quickly, and ensure that their resources were converted into investments successfully. They created various investment instruments through public and private financial institutions, including government (national, provincial, and municipal) debt securities, bills of exchange and acceptance loans (bills of exchange that are accepted without sufficient cover yet), maritime and other insurance investment instruments, and common stocks of publicly traded companies such as the East India Company. While institutional structures such as the Stock Exchange and the Amsterdam Bank of Exchange ensured the system's successful operation, merchant banks also contributed significantly to this system. The established system worked well and swiftly.

The problems emerging in the Dutch politics and a stagnating economy eventually caused the future investments to be mainly directed abroad. The Netherlands had meanwhile reached a position where it could lead international capital markets. However, following a series of economic crises in Europe, the economy deteriorated. The Netherlands owed its economic success in the 1585–1672 "Golden Age," unlike the previous Italian and other European states, by reaching out to overseas markets and directly controlling raw material sources and markets with naval fleets (Taylor, 2013). Until about the mid-1700s, the Dutch Republic's economic and financial system was the most advanced ever seen. At least between 1600 and 1720 and maybe longer, the Dutch had the highest per capita income globally (Kaletsky, 2011; Roser, 2013). Backing this success was an innovative corporate structure based on the East and West India Companies, the Amsterdam Stock Exchange, and the Amsterdam Bank of Exchange.

3.4 The East and West India Companies

3.4.1 The Dutch East India Company

In 1580, the Spanish conquered Portugal and included it in the Spanish Kingdom—a blow to the Dutch economy that traded with Portugal. Afterward, there was a risk of ship confiscations and of being cut off from the Lisbon spice markets. The Dutch tried to take control of the spice market now. They initially aimed to take the most practical method, which was attacking Portuguese and Spanish colonies in Africa, Asia, and South America, to build a global trade network. Meanwhile, they established the United East India Company (Vereenigde Oostindische Compagnie, VOC), to organize and finance international trade. This way, they sought to reap the economic benefits of military success. The VOC's outstanding achievements in the Indian Ocean would later prompt the establishment of a second company: the West India Company (WIC) that was established for colonial activities in South America. The Dutch attacks in the oceans began in 1602. The war in the oceans was an extension of the Eighty Years' War, but also a struggle to control trade and gain an overseas empire. As a result, the Dutch, though unsuccessful in the Portuguese colonies of Brazil and Angola, would establish settlements in the Cape of Good Hope and the East Indies, where they seized Malaysia, Ceylon, and the Malabar (India) Coast and they would rule Indonesia for a long time (see Fig. 3.3).

The first initiative leading to the erection of the VOC came from nine Amsterdam merchants, in 1594. Information about the opportunities came from Jan Huygen van Linschoten, who had been in Goa, the capital of Portuguese India. Also important was the involvement of Petrus Plancius, reverend and cartographer, who had a copy of

Fig. 3.3 Colonies and bases of the Dutch Republic (1650). *Source* https://en.wikipedia.org/wiki/File:Dutch-Empire-coloured.png

the maps of Bartholomeo de Lasso, the cartographer of the Spanish king (van Dillen, 1958; "Petrus Plancius"). The nine merchants, the directors of the company, provided the funds, together with some other participants. They prepared a fleet of three ships and a yacht. The fleet did not accomplish a plain success: only one ship returned. Nevertheless, it was clear that there were possibilities. The same company hurried to prepare a second trip. They teamed up with another initiative from Amsterdam. This trip was a big success. In between there were two competing initiatives from Zeeland (one from Middelburg and one from Veere) and two from Rotterdam. The fleets from Rotterdam explored the possibility to reach India through the Strait of Magellan. None of the ships of the first fleet returned. Of the four ships of the other fleet, only one returned; one ship reached Japan and the surviving crew could return a couple of years later. In this way, the contacts of the VOC with Japan started. As more initiatives were started, the competition became fierce, especially between the companies of Holland and Zeeland.

Already in 1598, the States General, with van Oldenbarnevelt in a leading role, started to stimulate coordination, cooperation, and centralization (cf. Ota, 2013). They feared that the fragmented Dutch initiatives would lose from the centralized Spanish, Portuguese, and English initiatives. After long deliberations and bargaining between Holland and Zeeland, this led to the establishment of the VOC in March 1602. It was a rather cumbersome organization, with six Chambers, one for each of the cities with already active companies: Amsterdam, Zeeland, Rotterdam, Delft, Enkhuizen, and Hoorn. Each Chamber was going to take care of a certain part of the investments: Amsterdam 1/2, Zeeland 1/4 and the other Chambers 1/16 each. The active direction was going to be a committee of 17 ("Heeren XVII"), selected from the wider group of (first 76, then reduced to 60) directors ("bewindhebbers") and consisting of eight representatives from Amsterdam, four from Zeeland, one from the other Chambers and one rotating between all of the Chambers less Amsterdam. This extra member was to limit the power of Amsterdam.

All of the directors participated financially. Next to them, there was a wide group of other participants. They were not linked to a single director, but to the VOC as a whole. Also, a participation was not for one voyage, but for the first 10 years of VOC activities. The VOC charter foresaw that liquidation would take place after 10 years; all participants would have their share to be returned and a new round would be organized. However, after 10 years, the States General concluded that liquidation was impossible. An important part of the investments was used to develop permanent trade relationships. The VOC appeared to be an ongoing corporation. The rule that directors were not liable for debts of the VOC fitted with the corporate character. The possibility to sell their shares made it possible for directors and participants to make their capital liquid. The VOC was the first effective joint-stock company (van Dillen, 1958).

The financial participation was broad, also from the cities not represented in the Chambers. The major of Dordrecht organized participation of city citizens (Klein, 1965). This led to the possibility to appoint the already mentioned Elias Trip as an extraordinary director in 1614. The information provision of the participants was weak. Before the VOC came up, company directors prepared the ships, organized the journey, and bought and sold the load. Next, they paid the original investment plus profit to the connected participants. There was a personal relationship—for one journey. This became different. The VOC directors received a provision of 1% of the costs of equipage. Moreover, they were paid for the costs made in organizing the journeys and had priority in buying the return load. Initially, there were no clear rules about the price allowed to ask for the services and the prices to be paid for the load. In 1616/17, for instance, Elias Trip belonged to a combination of merchants that bought all the pepper and indigo. Understandably, many participants wanted to see some dividend after the first couple of years, while the directors were not in a hurry at all. Eventually, the Heeren XVII were forced to pay the shareholders.

There was active trade in VOC shares on the Amsterdam Exchange, as well as a lot of speculation and short selling. Well known are the activities in this respect of the "Groote Compagnie" of Isaac le Maire, an important director and founder of one of the predecessor companies, the Brabantine Company. He had a conflict with the VOC regarding the way a journey to East India just before the start of the VOC was dealt with. He was forced to resign and to declare not to start competing trade again. It made him a bitter enemy of the VOC. In 1609, he tried to convince the French king Henri IV of the possibilities of a French East India company and helped to prepare for it. He combined all of this with short selling of VOC shares through the Groote Compagnie. Elias Trip was also participating (van Dillen et al., 2006; Klein, 1965). The initiative failed. It led to a new rule in that naked selling of shares was prohibited.

The VOC had to develop trade with the East, the area between Cape of Good Hope and Strait Magellan. First, it traded mainly in spices. Within the Republic, it had the monopoly for that trade. However, competition from England, Spain, and Portugal required military action. The Heeren XVII saw soon the necessity to realize stable physical presence in the East, with centralized political power, to be able to develop a network of settlements and coordinate the commerce within the East and at home. In 1610, they appointed the first governor-general, Pieter Both. In 1619, Jan Pietersz. Coen was the fourth. Elias Trip was one of the Heeren XVII who appointed him. Coen conquered Jakarta in the current Indonesia and made it the capital of the VOC. It was renamed Batavia. It was important of course to coordinate the activities of the VOC in Batavia with the interests of the republic. To that end, a sub-committee of the Heeren XVII ("Haagse Besogne") met in The Hague (Gaastra, 2002).

The VOC stumbled into an early modern corporate model of a global supply chain. It was a type of conglomerate tending to many commercial and industrial activities (Grenville, 2017). The main activities were shipbuilding, the production and trading of East Indian spices, the purchase and sale of commodities such as Indonesian coffee, sugar cane, and growing South African wine. It traded all kinds of goods, including even opium, when seeing the opportunity to make a profit (Derks, 2012). Besides of being the first multinational company in history, VOC was also the first publicly traded firm (Boettke & Coyne, 2015). With corporate innovations and business practices, the VOC set up the foundations for the rise of today's global companies and capital markets (Steensgaard, 1981). It inspired the British on how to operate their East India Company (Ferguson, 2004). The VOC evolved from a corporate structure to a state governing a country such as Indonesia. The company would protect its economic interests by purchasing new ports as trading bases and capturing surrounding areas. It had semi-government powers to imprison and execute prisoners in its foreign colonies, negotiate treaties, issue its currency, and establish colonies (Ames, 2008). The VOC, along with the WIC, was seen as the international arm of the Republic, symbolizing the power of the Dutch Empire ("Dutch East India Company").

While most of its shareholders were Dutch, about a quarter of the shareholders were investors living in the area that includes today's Germany, Belgium, and Luxembourg (De Vries & Van der Woude, 1997). The VOC had two types of shareholders, as was custom in Dutch companies at the time. A significant part of them did not have voting rights; around 60–70 investors could vote on the general management. VOC investors had limited liability for the company's operations in terms of the shares they owned. Investors wishing to sell their shares could only do so by transferring their shares to others on the Amsterdam Stock Exchange. During the seventeenth century, the share price increased to 600 percent, and in 1720 there was a peak price of 1200, corresponding to the Mississippi bubble and the South Sea bubble (see Chaps. 4 and 5). And the dividend was in average about 20% of the original price of the shares. After 1730, a period of difficulties and decline started, partly because of more competition, but also due to corruption and mismanagement (De Vries & Van der Woude, 1997). The company ceased its activities at the end of the eighteenth century.

3.4.2 The Dutch West India Company

The Dutch did not initially enter the Atlantic trade strongly. They became interested in the west coast of the Atlantic in the late 1620 s to take advantage of commercial opportunities. Previously, traders in the Holland and Zeeland Provinces established small companies to trade gold and ivory with West Africa and fur trade with North America. Some private companies even sent their ships to South America and the Caribbean Islands to find sources of wood and salt. Zeeland merchants developed settlements on the coast of what is now Guyana, to develop agriculture. However, as trade in the region expanded, small companies and private ship owners were staying unprotected from Spanish and Portuguese harassment. During the Twelve Years' Truce, new plans were developed, and after a lengthy discussion, it was decided to establish the Dutch West India Company (WIC, in Dutch: Geoctroyeerde West-Indische Compagnie) on June 3, 1621. According to the company charter, the WIC would have a monopoly in shipping and trade in a region covering South Africa, the Americas and the Cape of Good Hope, and the Pacific Islands. The WIC was empowered to establish colonies on these lands, sign treaties with local rulers, build forts, and wage war on the enemies (Encyclopedia, 2019).

The WIC was set up alike the VOC and listed at the Amsterdam Exchange. The company had a federal structure of five district councils: Amsterdam, Zeeland,

Rotterdam, West-Friesland, and Groningen. Each Chamber was headed by its directors, while the corporate policy was determined by a central board known as Heeren XIX. Since the weights of participation in the trade were different from those in the trade to East India, there were 19 "Heeren" instead of 17. Central board meetings were held two or three times a year to plan the equipment of war fleets and merchants, fix the value of the cargo, and oversee the company's finances. The primary purpose of the WIC was to establish a commercial network in the Atlantic and to defend the colonies. In 1623, the Central Governing Body developed a "grand design" strategy. As it was too risky to occupy the Spanish colonies, it was planned to attack enemy ships in the Caribbean, and vessels suitable for naval warfare were built. By employing the plan, the WIC captured or destroyed 547 enemy ships between 1623 and 1636 (Encyclopedia, 2019). The capture of the silver fleet, by Piet Hein in 1628, was the West India Company's most significant victory in the Caribbean, with the money covering the Dutch army's expenses for 8 months and paying its investors a 75% dividend that year ("Battle in the Bay of Matanzas."). It was the only dividend ever paid.

Getting intelligence that Portugal could not adequately protect its bases in South America and West Africa, WIC executives and the Dutch State agreed on a plan covering the conquest of Salvador, a vital sugar production center for the Portuguese. Although the project was initially unsuccessful, the company would occupy the northern states of Brazil between 1630 and 1654 and called it New Holland. Then, realizing that there was a growing demand for slaves in Brazil during these conflicts, the WIC turned to the slave trade and captured the Angola region in Southwest Africa. The WIC also captured Portuguese forts and mills on the African Gold Coast and shipped over 320,000 oz of gold, ivory, wax, and other tropical products to the Republic between 1623 and 1674 (Encyclopedia, 2019). The Dutch occupied the Caribbean Island of Curaçao, which is still part of their State, in 1634. It served as an essential warehouse for commodities and slave trade from the 1650 s onward, facing a bitter history of slave revolts and torture ("History of Curaçao"). The WIC traded close to half a million African slaves (Slaveryandremembrance.org, n.d.). The Dutch were also already active in North America, along the Hudson River and later also in what had been a Swedish colony. Colonial wars in the Atlantic eventually depleted the WIC's resources and by the 1650 s, the financial situation had deteriorated. In what is dubbed to be the worst real estate deal ever, "New Netherlands" was swapped for Surinam with the British in 1674 and it was renamed as New York. When the British realized their supremacy in the Caribbeans, the opportunities for the Dutch reduced and the WIC went bankrupt, in 1674. A new WIC was started a couple of years later, even more focused on slave trade. Yet, there were many competitors, partly financed by Dutch merchants, and its role was marginal. Altogether, the WIC was a commercial failure. Maybe the Dutch had been too late or perhaps there was insufficient focus.

3.5 The Amsterdam Stock Exchange

Whereas the Amsterdam Stock Exchange is often considered as the world's oldest and most modern securities market, earlier stock exchanges were previously established in, e.g., Lyon and Bruges. Antwerp built a new exchange ("Beurs") in 1531. Elizabeth I opened the Royal Exchange in London in 1571; it was founded by Thomas Gresham (see Chap. 4). Likewise, it was also important for a city like Amsterdam to create a merchant friendly environment, to have sufficient storage and handling facilities, to facilitate information gathering and finding right contacts, and to have a proper meeting place and transparency about the requirements for lawful contracts. The meeting place was first rather informal in Amsterdam. Merchants met in the Warmoesstraat and later on a bridge or in a church. The stock market is considered as founded by the Dutch East India Company (VOC) in 1602, when it began issuing transferable stocks and bonds (Euronext, 2020). The transfer of shares was recorded in the company registry with a record witnessed by the company executives. The secondary market for VOC shares soon proved to be quite successful, and the share price had soared to 1200 percent by the 1720s. The company policy initially distributed a low dividend rate, and a significant portion of its earnings was reinvested (De Vries & Van der Woude, 1997). The company's high earnings also made the stock market increasingly attractive.

Amsterdam started to build its Beurs in 1608. Hendrik de Keyser was the architect. He was also the architect of the offices of the Amsterdam Chamber of the VOC (Oost-Indisch Huis). The Beurs was finished in 1611. Together with the nearby corn exchange (Korenbeurs, built in 1617, also by Hendrick de Keyser) and the Amsterdam Bank of Exchange (Wisselbank, in the (old) town hall at the Dam) the city had now an attractive business quarter, fitting with the role of Amsterdam. The city used its opening to organize trade more orderly. To concentrate the trade, the opening hours were limited. Brokers were important in organizing the trade. Earlier, brokerage was often combined with having a hostel. This became forbidden. Brokers also had to be registered and could not stay in the vicinity of the Beurs outside opening hours. Tariffs for brokering ware adjusted. The tariff list of 1613 contained 173 items (Gelderblom, 2013). In 1618, the total number of registered brokers equaled 430. Many of them came from abroad, from current Belgian and German areas, and even way beyond, which was important to serve merchants of many different origins. To make their knowledge available, the brokers were also charged in 1613 with the publication of a twice-weekly price list: the "Officieele Prijscourant."

The Amsterdam stock market developed rapidly in a short time, reaching a much larger trading volume than the Antwerp stock market. As of 1661, 300 brokers and 600 people working for them operated in the stock market. Until 1671, only the shares of East and West India Companies were traded in the stock market, while in 1672, the Dutch Government offered government bonds for the first time on the Amsterdam Exchange, to finance the war with the Catholic France. By 1750, the stock market had assumed the identity of a genuine international market. It had six joint-stock companies listed, three of which were based in the Netherlands and three in England. In addition, 25 bonds of the Dutch Government and debt securities of 13 foreign governments, including the Government of France and England, were traded on the exchange (Allen, 2001).

Because the commercial voyages of the Indian trade companies were risky, reckless investors sought high returns. For this reason, stock market speculation increased rapidly soon. Investors who hoped that prices would rise were called "lovers" and those who expected that prices would fall "miners." Today, with the grown effect of U.S. markets, bull and bear market expressions are used instead of these concepts. When Isaac Le Maire, an unhappy investor, started shorting VOC shares in 1609, initial steps on the development of a futures markets were taken, followed by a market on options trading (De Vries & Van der Woude, 1997). Since these transaction contracts are not securities in itself, but are linked to another financial instrument, these so-called derivative investments were called "windhandel" in the Netherlands, to suggest a footloose character. Yet, although being hazardous for the investor, they can protect against risks when used wisely. The Dutch Government took some measures to curb excessive speculation and did not allow the West India Company shares to be subject to futures contracts (Allen, 2001).

The event that made the Amsterdam Stock Exchange known worldwide was the Tulip Mania in the 1630 s and the stock market crisis that followed. When the tulip bulbs, brought from Istanbul, started to be planted in the Netherlands, they soon became popular among the people and began to be traded in the stock market. Later, these investments turned into frenzy speculation, and tulip bulbs were planted in a significant part of the cultivated areas in the Netherlands. Forward contracts were also started to be made months in advance for deliveries to be made in the spring. The tulip craze took on a new dimension when it was discovered by coincidence that a virus infecting tulip bulbs had caused the production of tulips of many different colors. Tulip prices increased so much that a single rare tulip bulb is known to be swapped for a leading brewery in France during this period. The Tulip Mania and "windhandel," which were increasingly dominating the stock market, caused the world's first stock market crisis in 1637. Parts of the Dutch economy entered also in a prolonged depression, while the courts were incapable of dealing with lawsuits over tulip contracts (Allen, 2001). However, most of the economy was quite unaffected.

3.6 The Amsterdam Bank of Exchange

In medieval Europe, metal coins were made with gold and silver, and the value of coins varied depending on the gold and silver in them. Therefore, coins made from precious metals with high precious metal content were often the most stable and liquid assets available. Regional states such as Venice, Hamburg, and (in fact also) Amsterdam in Europe did not have their own currency and had to use the currencies of neighboring areas. However, due to the distrust on these coins, it was necessary to control their contents. Metal money was not easy to use, as it had transaction costs such as costs of analysis and preservation. In addition, due to the diversity of coins, conflicts could arise between the parties while bartering in commercial centers. For example, in the coin regulation of the Dutch Republic of 1606, 25 gold and 14 silver coins were officially recognized as money, although there were hundreds of different coins on the market (Quinn & Roberts, 2014a). Over time, these coins would worn out or, also, shrewd people were trying to profit by rasping the gold coin. As the famous English economist Thomas Gresham said: "bad money drives out good money." People kept the scatheless coins to themselves and spent the worn-out ones. When bad coins, clipped and worn out, circulated excessively in the market, it lowered the value of the currency and created Inflation. A country's minted coins were more valuable when being very new to the market. They were making a premium in exchange. Shortly after being minted, the coin's actual value could exceed the written value ("Bank of Amsterdam").

After the fifteenth century, the merchants of Amsterdam, already one of the most important trade centers of northern Europe, were quite disturbed by the constant decrease in the value of coins due to the issues mentioned above. A resolution of the Amsterdam City Council of May 1606 shows that it saw opportunities in the establishment of a public deposit bank like the Venetian Banco di Rialto, to facilitate safe storage of money and safe payments (van Dillen, 1934). In Venice, this measure was taken because of the frequent bankruptcy of the private banks of transfer. The problems were different in Amsterdam, however, the convenience and security of such a system was appealing. It led to the establishment of the Amsterdam Bank of Exchange ("Wisselbank") in 1609. Other Dutch cities followed: Middelburg in 1616, Delft in 1621, and Rotterdam in 1635. We restrict ourselves to the Amsterdam Bank. The Amsterdam Bank of Exchange founders' chief motive was not to resolve the unreliability of the private bankers as in Venice, but the improvement of monetary conditions (van Dillen, 1934). The Bank was given a four-stage task (Dehing, 2012):

1. ensuring that the value of money entrusted to the bank by traders remains constant;
2. to solve domestic payment problems, due to a chaotic situation with many different coins being used;
3. to facilitate international payments through an adequate accounting and transfer system and by creating a sufficient supply of valuable gold and silver money (merchants were required to make all bills of exchange of more than 600 guilders payable via the Bank);
4. to protect the Bank's foreign exchange reserves from the entry of lower value currencies.

The Bank was not supposed to trade in bullion, but exactly this trade developed into a very profitable activity. The Bank was determining the actual metal values of the foreign and local currencies it collected and examined. After deducting a small management fee from that value, it was being recorded in the customer's account in guilders, with nominal value of "20 stuivers" per guilder. This money was called "bank money" and since it was always traded at face value, it was more valuable than real metal coins whose value decreased as they wore off. There was a long list of coins that were acceptable and each coin had a tariff. If the bank money was refunded and currency was requested, the bank applied the same tariff, but it was allowed to charge a withdrawal fee of up to 2.5%. Popular coins were, as from 1619, the "patacon" and the "ducaton," issued by the Habsburg (Spanish) government in Brussels. The silver content of these coins was 4% lower than in case of the two corresponding coins in the Republic. The patacon and the ducaton circulated in the Republic with stuiver values equal to the heavier Dutch coins and hence drove these heavier coins out of circulation (cf. Gresham's Law). The patacon was 50 stuivers, just as the corresponding but heavier Dutch rijksdaalder. However, the Bank tried to keep the real value and gave only 48 stuivers for a patacon. Only legal coins were to be deposited into accounts with the Bank. Bullion and illegal coins would directly be transferred to the local mint, who would convert them into Bank currency, and the depositor would receive bank money as much as the actual value of the gold or foreign currency on that day (Quinn & Roberts, 2005).

Unusually for its time, the guilder was not a coin, and its value was not synonymous with the value of any currency. Instead, it was bank money, which was only available on record in the accounts of the Bank, being an early application of the modern paper money (Gillard, 2004). The main advantage of bank money is that it has a stable value, as it can protect merchants from theft, fire, and money fraud, since a bank backs it. This money was also relatively easy to count, to transfer, and to pay off. Bills could be paid in bank currency rather than other countries' coins. While coin deposits made up a small portion of its capital, most of this came from high-value gold and silver bullion deposits. The Amsterdam Bank of Exchange was not the only bank in the Netherlands. Many merchant banks supported its activities. Merchants and bankers also increasingly had trusted and got used to this system, using the bank money without withdrawing the foreign currency or gold they deposited, not to pay extra cash. However, the value of the currency decreased a little over time. For example, the rate of the guilder to the British pound was fixed in the early years, but its value began to decline gradually as some more valuable coins were withdrawn from the bank reserves and replaced with less precious ones (Quinn & Roberts, 2005).

A current account could be used to execute payments to other account holders. At first there was a small fee for these payments, but because of objections of the merchants this was skipped soon, and until 1683, transfers were free. It was forbidden to overdraw the account. The fine was 3% of the amount assigned. In principle, the Bank was a full reserve bank, just like the Banco Rialto in Venice, and not directed to granting credit. Yet, it gave regularly credits to three sister organizations: the VOC, the Amsterdam municipality, and the Lombard ("Bank van Leening"). The VOC was always short of cash and had to bridge the gap between the preparation of the new fleet and the arrival of the returning one. Here the Bank helped in giving short-term loans—generally for a couple of months. For the municipality the loans were longer term, but the City owned the Bank and the Bank did not pay out its profit. Instead of this, profits were added to a reserve fund, which was not actually necessary for a bank like this. The differences between reserve fund and municipality loan remained small. The Amsterdam Lombard, established in 1614, was financed partly by short-term debentures. The Bank participated in this financing. It is not clear how heavy, because the timing may have been such that it did not appear in its balance sheets, and other information is fragmented. Anyway, from the balance sheets it is clear that the liquidity of the Bank remained close to 100% until 1781, at the start of the fourth war with England (1780–1784). That was the beginning of a very problematic period for VOC, the City and the Republic.

Interestingly, of the 764 merchants opening an account at the Amsterdam Bank of Exchange at its start in 1609, more than 30% was from the Southern Netherlands (Gelderblom, 2000). The number of accounts later fluctuated between 2,000 and 3,000. To compel merchants to open an account, it was determined that bills of exchange of more than 600 guilders were to be made payable at the Bank. Simultaneously with the establishment of the Bank, the trade of private moneychangers and cashiers was prohibited. This measure had to be revoked soon though. The cashiers' receipts, expressed in current money, were too important for domestic transactions (De Vries & Van der Woude, 1997). The Bank itself was more focused on international trade. Because of the difference between current value and bank tariff, it became interesting for buyers and sellers of bank money to meet each other outside of the City Hall and see whether it was possible to close a deal that were more attractive than going to the Bank. Cashiers with an Amsterdam Bank of Exchange account played an important role here. It led to a more or less official exchange rate of current money and bank money, mentioned at the price list of the Amsterdam Exchange. The difference ("agio") generally fluctuated between 3% and 4.5%.

The position of Amsterdam in the bullion trade was important already in the first half of the sixteenth century, but even more so after the peace with Spain. "Every year, in the autumn, a silver fleet composed of from thirty to fifty ships, escorted by war vessels, coming from Cadiz, arrived at the port of Amsterdam" (van Dillen, 1934, p. 104). Amsterdam was able to preserve this position for a long time due to a new bank product (1683): advances on "specie" (coins of all kinds) and bullion. Merchants could deposit a quantity of specie and bullion for half a year at a very modest price of 0.5% for gold and 0.25% for silver. In between they could immediately dispose of a sum only slightly less than the actual value; it was added to their account. After half a year, they could buy back the deposit at the same price if their account was sufficient or they could extend the arrangement. The receipt could be transferred. It functioned as an option to buy the specie/bullion against a fixed price. Its value equaled the difference between the current price of the deposit and the amount advanced on it. The receipts ("recepisses") were eagerly traded at the Amsterdam Exchange. The commissioners of the Bank participated also in this trade, to smooth the fluctuations in the agio. Buying a receipt is buying specie/bullion, selling a receipt is buying bank money. Dehing (2012) and Quinn and Roberts (2014b) compare this with the open market operations of a modern central bank. An interesting related development at the end of the seventeenth century was that the Bank ceased to pay balances in specie. The introduction of advances on specie made it apparently less necessary to have specie paid to holders of current accounts. Of course, this measure made the Bank even more look like modern central banks. Transfers remained possible although the number of transfers declined, also because the Bank demanded a small remuneration for it.

The Amsterdam Bank of Exchange fulfilled three functions performed by all central banks today as part of their activities. It was operating a payment system, creating a non-bank reserve currency, and managing its value through an open market operation (Quinn & Roberts, 2014b). The Bank rarely gave loans, except to sister organizations later on. With this feature, it was completely different from today's (commercial) banking system; it performed most of today's central banking functions. A state bank model is exemplified in many European countries, including the Swedish Riksbank (1668) and the Bank of England (1694) (Johnson, 2000). The Amsterdam Bank of Exchange presented the concept of bank money, as considered by the father of economics, Adam Smith, who explains at length how the Dutch guilder works in his famous book "The Wealth of Nations" (1776). The Amsterdam Bank of Exchange guilder was the most common international currency of the late seventeenth and early eighteenth centuries. Its stability and security (backed by a full reserve bank) made it also attractive to make bills of exchange payable in it. The strong position of the Bank lasted longer than Amsterdam's supremacy in international trade. That position was already overtaken by London during the second half of the seventeenth century, while the Bank kept its strong position for one more century. However, the British pound replaced the guilder in the nineteenth century and as late as after the Second World War, the US dollar would take the lead.

3.7 The Dutch Banking Secrets

The Dutch merchants, stock exchange and bankers' most incredible fortune was the country's remarkable economic development in the first half of the seventeenth century. The Dutch expanded their economies through colonization and made significant investments all over the country. While the banking and finance sector enabled the country's resources to be used more effectively, liberal state management and corporate governance practices opened the life channels of the banking sector. New financial practices and products followed suit, extending into far of the eighteenth century.

3.7.1 Liberal Economy and State Administration

One of the periods in which the first freedom of thought and scientific development in world history was formed was the ancient Greek civilization, which existed in 500–300 BC. Historians attribute the formation of such an impressive civilization in the Mediterranean geography to the countries' administrative and economic structures (McNeill, 1989). In ancient Greece, which consisted of city-states, there were no powerful kingdoms and no religious pressure. A middle class had emerged in the region, enriched by Mediterranean trade. These conditions provided freedom of thought and an intellectual environment in the country, leading to the emergence of such an influential civilization. A somewhat similar liberal atmosphere also existed in the Netherlands. As in ancient Greece, there were many democratic mini-states. The republic became a loosely coupled system of provinces and cities, with Holland and Amsterdam as natural leaders. There was no dictator or absolute monarchy. While establishing an administrative structure in Holland where the merchant class was intense, away from the religious pressures of the Catholic Church, the mild environment created, provided one of the most important backgrounds for the development of the country in the fields of art and science. The Dutch had talented painters like Rembrandt van Rijn (1606–1669) and Johannes Vermeer (1632–1675). At that time, Christiaan Huygens (1629–1695) was exploring the rings of the planet Saturn, Anton van Leeuwenhoek (1632–1723) was contributing to the construction of Galileo's telescope, and Philips Vingboons (1607–1678) was building the Amsterdam canal system. There was also Simon Stevin, a great Bruges born mathematician, philosopher, and developer of windmills ("Simon Stevin"). The Dutch achievements were not limited to the just-mentioned; they made remarkable progress from war technology to philosophy and achieved extraordinary successful results in agriculture.

The Dutch economy had turned into a well-functioning market economy from the late sixteenth century onward, making the Netherlands the first capitalist country in history (Lachmann, 2000). Before Amsterdam was yet a financial center, the Netherlands had already two liberal stock market experiences, in Bruges and in Antwerp. On the Antwerp Bourse wall, the inscription "open to all traders, regardless of nationality or language" was written. People were trading goods and securities on the Antwerp exchange, and governments were borrowing through it. All news that came to the stock market was reflected in the prices immediately and was causing significant fluctuations in prices. A market expert named Christoper Kurz even created an astrological system that predicted prices of commodities such as black pepper, ginger, and debt securities (Allen, 2001). When the Nobel Prize-winning economist Eugene Fama, 400 years later, described markets where all kinds of news are reflected in the prices, in "The Theory of Effective Markets" (Fama, 1970), he perhaps took inspiration from the Antwerp Bourse.

In the seventeenth century, the Amsterdam stock market was on the rise, covering the prices of many goods and stocks and Indian companies' stocks. While there was a tulip frenzy, on the one hand, common stocks of the companies were also circulating, on the other hand. The market was quite liberal. Also, the trade had much of an international flavor. Such an environment was exceptionally favorable for banks, but some arrangements would be required for the market to function well. The most important of these was the creation of a currency whose value could be trusted. The Amsterdam Bank of Exchange made a significant contribution to the growth of the Dutch economy with the payments system it developed. It also ensured a more reliable trade by creating stable bank money and the clearing activity it offers. The price stability created by the Bank was not a natural result of the establishment of an early central bank; the main reason for the formation of a stable currency was the solid political support the Bank received from the Dutch Republic and especially the city of Amsterdam. Elsewhere, not always enjoying the same degree of political support, banks have been less successful and failed to stabilize currencies (Quinn & Roberts, 2005).

3.7.2 Corporate Management Approach

While Dutch capital markets were being shaped in the seventeenth century, businessmen contributed to the foundations of modern corporate governance. Shareholders (participants) did not have influence on the policy of the VOC, except, maybe, some influence on the payment of dividend. Remarkable is that the Church played a role in keeping a certain balance in the interests of participants and directors (van Dillen, 1934). Isaac Le Maire, a major shareholder of the East India Dutch Company, was the first investor to draw attention to corporate governance problems. He filed a petition against the VOC in 1609, complaining that the corporate governance of the VOC was rather inadequate. In this first recorded corporate governance dispute, an investor had complained about executives who unnecessarily long held someone else's money or used their money in ways other than the investor's demands (Mueller, 2012). A shareholder revolt occurred in 1622. On this date, VOC investors, claiming that the company's ledgers were fed to dogs and covered with bacon to eliminate them, requested that the accounts be mutually controlled (Soll, 2014). At the general meeting of the VOC in 1622, the first corporate governance demands in the capital markets began to appear, as some shareholders complained about the secrecy of operations and distributed brochures and asked management to provide more information (Jongh, 2011).

Being by far the largest employer of the Republic, the number of employees of the VOC was already about 8,000 in 1625 and it increased to more than 35,000 later on (De Vries & Van der Woude, 1997). The employees were from different countries and even continents. The contracts signed by the East India Company with its employees were prepared in accordance with the corporate governance approach as in modern multinational companies. Managers allowed employees to use company resources for private business dealings on their behalf in the Asian market. In this way, the VOC had encouraged its employees to stay committed to the company and develop the necessary skills, while doing the company's work. Those who could not put enough effort into their company work were dismissed (Hejeebu, 2005). As early as the seventeenth century in the Netherlands, the demands for a better corporate governance approach by investors reacting to the practices of banks and companies probably contributed significantly to the success of the companies and the banks alike. Since the Dutch society successfully formed a balance of institutions, traders, and investors, both the Indian Companies' and the Amsterdam Bank of Exchange managers developed corporate culture. In doing so, they managed companies and banks for a long time without engaging them in too much commercial adventure.

3.7.3 Bank Money

Until the seventeenth century, when talking about money in Europe, mainly coins made of precious metals such as gold or silver came to mind. People attributed a value to these coins, depending on the amount of gold or silver in them. The source of trust in money was the amount of precious metals in it. This situation would change with the practices of the Amsterdam Bank of Exchange. After that, the basis of money would not be a precious metal but a bank or state reputation over time. The bank money practice of the Amsterdam Bank of Exchange was one of the first examples of the paper money practices of today's central banks, as the bullion receipts of the Bank could be endorsed as of 1683. The introduction of recepisses helped to keep a strong position in financial affairs, also affecting the activities on the Amsterdam Exchange, until long after Amsterdam's supremacy in trade itself had vanished. The Bank reserves gave merchants considerable confidence. The strong reputation of the Bank was largely due to the promise that deposits could be fully withdrawn at any time. The Bank contributed to the stability of the monetary system by, in general, not using its money reserves for lending (Westerhuis & Zanden, 2018). The success of the Bank inspired also the process of creating the Bank of England. Later, the practice would be developed by John Law although leading to a crisis in France in the end, and it was finally used extensively in American banking from the eighteenth century onward.

Currently, central banks are known as institutions that issue treasury bills, direct interest rates, and conduct open market operations in money markets to stabilize the country's currency. The most crucial point to remember is that the institution's activity, which was established as the teller of foreign currency accounts, evolved and turned into a modern structure. The Amsterdam Bank of Exchange made a historical contribution to the level of use of paper money today. While reaching this goal, it did not issue public papers and opened discount windows like modern central banks. Instead, the Bank's power stemmed from its legal monopoly over the operation of the Dutch currency clearing system. The driving force of this innovation was its successful cooperation with the Amsterdam Exchange and the Dutch Republic, as it was basically led by the world's last leading "city state": Amsterdam.

3.7.4 Initial Public Offerings

Today, for a company to go public, it must first present and promote itself to the market participants through a brokerage firm and then sell its stocks to the investors. The money received in return for the shares sold is added to the company's equity. Strengthening the equity capital reduces the financial risk of the company. It is a permanent resource for the company, unlike the funds obtained from bonds or other foreign capital instruments, since there is no specific repayment term; that is, it will always remain on the company's balance sheet. On the other hand, shareholders will be able to transfer this stock at any time by selling it to other investors in the secondary market, which is the stock market. In 1602, the VOC became the first company up to today's standards to issue shares in this way, successfully holding the first modern initial public offering (IPO). Shortly after the establishment of the VOC, it raised a capital of 6,424,588 guilders (Chorafas, 2005).

In the first decade of the seventeenth century, the VOC was the first registered company to pay regular dividends to encourage investors to buy shares. According to Euronext Amsterdam Company Historian Cherelt Kroeze, by the end of the seventeenth century, the Dutch East India Company stock had increased in value by 400 to 500 percent. In the years of prosperity around 1720, dizzying returns of 1,500 percent were achieved. For a long time, the dividends were quite high, around 1720 more than 30% of the original share price. A simple calculation is that if a VOC shareholder had held stock from its inception in 1602 until the end of 1795, (s)he would have earned a 3,600 percent return with dividends (Kroeze, n.d.). However, the shareholders of the Dutch West India Company were less fortunate: it went bankrupt after having paid dividend only once, namely, after a raid on a Spanish fleet.

3.7.5 *Dutch Auction Method*

Unlike a traditional auction, a Dutch auction is a price-building process in which the auctioneer starts with the highest price and lowers it until the bids received are reduced to a price level at which the entire bid amount will be covered. The method dates back to the sixteenth century and is in the Netherlands much related to the sale of flowers (Adam et al., 2017). It is more suitable for situations where products such as stocks or bonds are offered for sale in large quantities instead of a single product such as paintings and sculptures, albeit that in the Netherlands the method is often used for these purposes as well. During the public offering tender process, the brokerage house does not set a fixed price for the shares to be sold. After the company decides on the number of shares it wants to sell, the final auction price is determined by the bids of the investors participating in the tender. Buyers bid by specifying the number of shares they want to buy at a specific purchase price, and a list is created with the highest bid at the top. After listing the list of bidders until the total number of shares requested is sold, the bid price will be the final price covering the entire bid. All bidders will pay the same price per share. The Dutch auction encourages high bidding because those who want to buy the stock have to act quickly.

The most important advantage of the Dutch auction method is that it makes it easier for small investors to access stock initial public offerings (IPOs). In traditional auctions, brokerage houses usually set the stock prices at a low level and try to offer them to their best customers at this price to sell the stock more quickly. For this reason, the price rises in the second-hand market right after the tender in the first public offering. The high earnings made within a few days indicate that the prices were sold lower than they should have been ("underpricing") (Aktas et al., 2003). However, small investors often have to wait for large investors to buy the stocks they have reserved through the brokerage house. Another benefit of the Dutch auction method is that the prices do not rise by making a premium immediately after the stocks are sold. In such a case, the brokerage house that issued the tender will not be faced with an accusation that the prices are determined cheaply. However, analysts suggest that impatient buyers pay more for the stocks sold, as prices start at the top and go down at a Dutch auction. Also, it is open to some tricks and forces buyers to participate in the tender in a more strategic and prepared way (Rothkopf et al., 1990). Today, this method is used for the IPOs of U.S. Treasury securities and share repurchases of many U.S. companies (Tracy, 2020). Yet, although, e.g., applied by Google with its IPO in 2004, the method is not widespread in the markets.

3.7.6 Financial Center and Stock Exchange Transactions

With its supremacy later taken over by a nation state: England, Braudel (1990) holds that Amsterdam was the last of the ruling cities (Venice > Genoa > Antwerp > Amsterdam). It was therefore no coincidence that Amsterdam became the world's first international financial center. The Netherlands was the first global trading country of the time; it had stock market experiences like Bruges and Antwerp, which were established earlier in the South of the then still united country. Perhaps most importantly, the (North) Netherlands was the world's first capitalist country under a moderate political regime. Amsterdam made the necessary reforms in the spirit of the time and developed a financial system with a central bank and full-fledged capital markets, certain types of financial instruments, as well as public multinational companies. Not only did Amsterdam become the world's most important financial center for over a century, but it also introduced a modern model of a global financial center.

The most Important institution of the Amsterdam financial center was undoubtedly its stock exchange. Securities trading operations, which started with Bruges and Antwerp markets, have turned into an institution in the modern sense with the Amsterdam stock exchange. The Amsterdam Exchange was the world's first official market for trading the VOC's securities by investors. The financial techniques used in the Amsterdam financial markets in 1680 were as complex as those applied today. Commercial banking, bond issuances, and other speculative instruments could be traded and various transactions like stock futures, stock options, short selling, and debt-equity swaps developed. The first known technical analysis application in history was also employed in the Amsterdam Exchange. An investor named Joseph de la Vega is known to draw the charts used in technical analysis today.

The practice of short selling, known as taking advantage of price decreases by selling stocks that one does not own, was also discovered on the Amsterdam Exchange. The first recorded ban on short selling was also implemented in the Dutch Republic in the same year. In the first decades of the seventeenth century, the VOC was the first registered company to pay regular dividends to encourage investors to buy shares. Over time, it paid out annual dividends worth about 18% of the value of the shares. In addition, the Dutch experienced the first recorded stock market crash in history, with the Tulip Crisis of 1636–1637 (Micklethwait & Woolridge, 2003). After all, we may be grateful to the Dutch for creating the capital markets and developing investment methods known in the stock market today.

3.7.7 Investment Banking and Mutual Funds

Investment banking is a very different field from commercial banking. Commercial banking institutions lend money in the form of short-term deposits and loans to companies, mostly with maturities not exceeding 1 year. Investment banks tend to prefer long-term businesses and diversify their investments and try to increase their returns by turning to more risky projects in different fields. They also engage in acquisitions and mergers. Because of the differing riskiness, investment and commercial banking activities are legally separated in many countries—organizations cannot operate in each other's fields. Dutch bankers, who liked to take risks, were the first investment bankers to direct their funds to different investments (Cross & Prentice, 2007). In addition, the Dutch established its first investment partnership in 1774. In the 1770s, a Dutch banker named Adriaan van Ketwich became a pioneer in this field by establishing an investment partnership called Eendragt Maakt Magt, offering small investors the opportunity to diversify (Goetzmann et al., 2005). The name of this fund can be translated as "*unity is strength.*" In addition, the first (indirect) mutual funds were established in Amsterdam in 1774. Abraham van Ketwich founded the first mutual fund in history. The first mutual fund outside the Netherlands would be set up in London a hundred years later (Rouwenhorst, 2004).

3.8 Conclusion

At the beginning of the seventeenth century, the bank money issued by the Amsterdam Bank of Exchange was a hundred percent gold reserve equivalent. Behind it was a powerful institution. Since it is not easy at all to assign a value to a piece of paper instead of metal coins, it was only natural that Amsterdam merchants kept aloof from money recorded in the Bank's books at the beginning, similar to the skepticism about virtual currencies today. The Bank solved this problem quickly with the trust it gave to society and so it became the first institution in history to issue fiat money. The State supported the banking system, and unlike many other countries, it did not demand unrequited funds despite the war conditions and did not confiscate any money. The Dutch Republic successfully maintained its reputation in the seventeenth and eighteenth centuries, respecting the Bank's independence. In addition, traders and investors also claimed their rights as market players. By demanding a greater understanding of corporate governance, they struck a balance between corporate goals and public expectations. An important reason for this success is undoubtedly the remarkable adaptation of the state administration to economic development. The State did not burden economic growth, being the first example of this in Europe. On top of this, the Dutch developed a consensus-based model of decision-making ("polder model"), which has remained influential in determining Dutch practice and culture up until present times.

Interestingly, Turkey has been aiming to turn Istanbul into a financial center since 2009, as Amsterdam did hundreds of years ago. For this purpose, the State has assigned a region in Istanbul, Ataşehir, and has spent millions of dollars by having huge buildings built here. Undoubtedly, such a center will both increase the country's reputation and attract international investments to Turkey. Within this project's scope, regulatory bodies, including all of the country's public banks, were moved to Istanbul. In addition, international banks, funds, and investment institutions are expected to open branches in Istanbul. At first glance, Istanbul seems to be quite suitable for such a center. Istanbul is ideal for being a financial center with its location between oil-rich Middle Eastern countries, developed European economies, and Asian countries with growing economies. While geographical location, infrastructure, and completion of buildings are undoubtedly crucial for such a project, many experts point out that it is difficult to achieve this goal in Turkey without reforms on law, freedom of the media, freedom of the press, and central bank independence, or, generally speaking, a state not interfering too much in finance and business (Egilmez, n.d.).

The Dutch created money and capital markets centuries ago, leading the way for other countries. Apart from bank money, they have constituted the auction system, short selling, initial public offering, technical analysis, investment banking, and investment partnerships and funds since the seventeenth century. Faced with financial crises and a stock market bubble, they inspired the science of economics in a practical way by producing hands-on solutions. Undoubtedly, the financial markets owe a lot to the Dutch. While the money and capital markets have developed with an ever-increasing volume of transactions for 400 years, market players, like Dutch investors, have gravitated toward a safer currency and better functioning markets. When they moved from the barter economy to coins, from coins to cash and paper money, and partially to cryptocurrencies now, they acted with similar expectations and impulses. In the 1929, 1987, and 2008 crises, the passion of investors who were caught in a wave of extreme optimism was probably a reflection of the emotions and expectations of investors in the Amsterdam Stock Exchange during the historical Tulip Mania, created by a beautiful type of bulb imported from Turkey.

References

Adam, M. T. P., Eidels, A., & Teuber, T. (2017). Bidding behavior in Dutch auctions: Insights from a structured literature review. *International Journal of Electronic Commerce*. https://doi.org/10.1080/10864415.2016.1319222

Aktas, R., Karan, M., & Aydogan, K. (2003). Forecasting short run performance of initial public offerings in the Istanbul Stock exchange. *Journal of Entrepreneurial Finance and Business Ventures, 8*(1), 69–85. https://doi.org/10.57229/2373-1761.1211

Allen, L. (2001). *The global financial system, 1750–2000*. Reaktion Books.

Ames, G. J. (2008). *The globe encompassed: The age of European discovery, 1500–1700*. Pearson Prentice Hall.

Bank of Amsterdam. (n.d.). Bank of Amsterdam. *Wikipedia*. Retrieved from https://en.wikipedia.org/wiki/Amsterdam_Wisselbank

Battle in the Bay of Matanzas. (n.d.). Battle in the Bay of Matanzas. *Wikipedia*. Retrieved from https://en.wikipedia.org/wiki/Battle_in_the_Bay_of_Matanzas

Blockmans, W. (2007). *History of the low countries—Economic structure*. Encyclopaedia Britannica. https://www.britannica.com/topic/history-of-the-Low-Countries/Economic-structure

Boettke, P. J., & Coyne, C. J. (2015). *The Oxford handbook of Austrian economics* (pp. 324–340). Oxford University Press.

Braudel, F. (1990). *Beschaving, Economie en Kapitalisme (15e–18e Eeuw), Deel IIII, De Tijd van de Wereld (Civilization, economy and capitalism (15th–18th Centuries) Part III, The Time of the World)*. Contact.

Chorafas, D. N. (2005). *The management of equity investments*. Elsevier.

Cross, F. B., & Prentice, R. A. (2007). *Law and corporate finance*. Edward Elgar.

Dehing, P. (2012). Geld in Amsterdam. Wisselbank en Wisselkoersen, 1650–1725 (Money in Amsterdam. Currency exchange and exchange rates, 1650–1725). University of Amsterdam. Retrieved from https://hdl.handle.net/11245/1.378147

Derks, H. (2012). History of the opium problem: The Assault on the East, ca. 1600–1950. Brill Publishing.

van Dillen, J. G. (1934). The bank of Amsterdam. *History of the principal public banks* (pp. 79–124). Nijhoff.

van Dillen, J. G. (1958). *Het Oudste Aandeelhoudersregister van de Kamer van Amsterdam der Oostindische Compagnie (The Oldest Shareholders Register of the Chamber of Amsterdam of the East India Company)*. Nijhoff.

van Dillen, J.G., Poitras, G., & Majithia, A. (2006). Isaac Le Maire and the early trading in Dutch East India company shares. In *Pioneers of financial economics* (Vol. 1). Edward Elgar Publishing.

Dutch East India Company. (n.d.). Dutch East India Company. *Wikipedia*. Retrieved from https://en.wikipedia.org/wiki/Dutch_East_India_Company

Edmundson, G. (1922). William the silent. In: H. Chisholm (Ed.), *History of Holland*. Cambridge University Press.

Egilmez, M. (n.d.). *Could Istanbul become a financial center?* Mahfiegilmez.com https://www.mahfiegilmez.com/2020/02/istanbul-finans-merkezi-olkazan-mi.html

Encyclopedia. (2019). *Dutch West India Company*. Retrieved from https://www.encyclopedia.com/history/modern-europe/benelux history/dutch west india company

Euronext. (2020). *Amsterdam*. Retrieved from https://www.euronext.com/nl/markets/amsterdam

Fama, E. F. (1970). Efficient capital markets: A Review of theory and empirical work. *The Journal of Finance, 25*(2), 383–417. https://doi.org/10.2307/2325486

Ferguson, N. (2004). *Empire: The rise and demise of the british world order and the lessons for global power*. Basic Books.

Gaastra, F. S. (2002). *De Geschiedenis van de VOC (The History of the East India Company)*. Walburg Press.

Gelderblom, O. (2000). *Zuid-Nederlandse Kooplieden en de Opkomst van de Amsterdamse Stapelmarkt (Southern Dutch Merchants and the Emergence of the Amsterdam Staple Market)*. Verloren.

Gelderblom, O. (2013). *Cities of commerce; the institutional foundations of international trade in the low countries, 1250–1650*. Princeton University Press.

Gillard, L. (2004). *La Banque d'Amsterdam et le Florin Européen: Au Temps de la République Néerlandaise (1610–1820) (The Bank of Amsterdam and the European Guilder: In the Time of the Dutch Republic (1610–1820))*. Ecole Des Hautes-Études En Sciences Sociales.

Goetzmann, W. N., Li, L., & Rouwenhorst, K. G. (2005). Long-term global market correlations. *The Journal of Business, 78*(1), 1–38. https://doi.org/10.2139/ssrn.288421

Grenville, S. (2017). *The first global supply chain*. Lowy Institute.Retrieved from https://www.lowyinstitute.org/the-interpreter/starting-point-first-global-supply-chain
Harvey, A. D. (1991). The pistol as assassination weapon: A case of technological lag. *Terrorism and Political Violence, 3*(2), 92–98. https://doi.org/10.1080/09546559108427107
Hejeebu, S. (2005). Contract enforcement in the English East India Company. *The Journal of Economic History, 65*(02). https://doi.org/10.1017/s0022050705000173
History of Curaçao. (n.d.). History of Curaçao. *Wikipedia*. Retrieved from https://en.wikipedia.org/wiki/History_of_Cura%C3%A7ao
History of Religion. (n.d.). History of religion in the Netherlands. *Wikipedia*. Retrieved from https://en.wikipedia.org/wiki/History_of_religion_in_the_Netherlands
Hunt, M. (2019, June 28). *How Belgium created and almost lost the world's first stock exchange*. The Brussels Times. Retrieved from https://www.brusselstimes.com/belgium/59675/how-belgium-created-and-almost-lost-the-worlds-first-stock-exchange/
Israel, J. I. (1998). *The Dutch Republic: Its rise, greatness and fall, 1477–1806*. Oxford University Press.
Johan van Oldenbarnevelt. (n.d.). Johan van Oldenbarnevelt. *Wikipedia*. Retrieved from https://en.wikipedia.org/wiki/Johan_van_Oldenbarnevelt
Johnson, H. J. (2000). *Banking alliances*. World Scientific.
De Jongh, M. (2011). Shareholder activism at the Dutch East India company 1622–1625. In *Origins of shareholder advocacy*. Palgrave Macmillan.
Kaletsky, A. (2011). *Capitalism 4.0: The birth of a new economy in the aftermath of crisis*. Public Affairs.
Karpat, K. H. (1974). *The Ottoman State and its place in world history*. Brill.
Klein, P. W. (1965). *De Trippen in de 17^{e} Eeuw (The Trippen in the 17th Century)*. Van Gorcum.
Kroeze, C. (n.d.). *Unpublished work*.
Lachmann, R. (2000). *Capitalists in spite of themselves: Elite conflict and economic transitions in early modern Europe*. Oxford University Press.
Limm, P. (2014). *The Dutch Revolt, 1559–1648* (1st ed.). Routledge.
McNeill, W. H. (1989). *A world history* (10th ed.). Image Bookstore.
Micklethwait, J., & Wooldridge, A. (2003). *The company: A short history of a revolutionary idea*. Random House.
Military history of the Netherlands. (n.d.). Military history of the Netherlands. *Wikipedia*. Retrieved from https://en.wikipedia.org/wiki/Military_history_of_the_Netherlands
Motley, J. L. (2004). *Rise of the Dutch Republic I. (of 3) 1555–66, by John Lothrop Motley*. Project Gutenberg. Retrieved from https://www.gutenberg.org/files/4811/4811-h/4811-h.htm
Mueller, D. C. (2012). *The Oxford handbook of capitalism*. Oxford University Press.
Ota, A. (2013). *The Dutch East India company and the rise of Intra-Asian commerce*. Nippon. Retrieved from https://www.nippon.com/en/features/c00105/
Petrus Plancius. (n.d.). Petrus Plancius. *Wikipedia*. Retrieved from https://nl.wikipedia.org/wiki/Petrus_Plancius
Roser, M. (2013). Economic growth. *Our World in Data*. Retrieved from https://ourworldindata.org/economic-growth
Quinn, S., & Roberts, W. (2005). The big problem of large bills: The bank of Amsterdam and the origins of central banking. *SSRN Electronic Journal* (Working Paper). Retrieved from https://doi.org/10.2139/ssrn.814004
Quinn, S., & Roberts, W. (2014a). How Amsterdam got fiat money. *Journal of Monetary Economics., 66*, 1–12. https://doi.org/10.1016/j.jmoneco.2014.03.004
Quinn, S., & Roberts, W. (2014b). The Bank of Amsterdam through the lens of monetary competition. In *Explaining monetary and financial innovation*. Springer. Retrieved from https://doi.org/10.1007/978-3-319-06109-2_11
Rijksmuseum. (2020). *1600–1665 Amsterdam's prosperity—Timeline Dutch history—Rijksstudio*. Retrieved from https://www.rijksmuseum.nl/en/rijksstudio/timeline-dutch-history/1600-1665-amsterdams-prosperity

Rothkopf, M. H., Teisberg, T. J., & Kahn, E. P. (1990). Why are Vickrey auctions rare? *Journal of Political Economy, 98*(1), 94–109. https://doi.org/10.1086/261670

Rouwenhorst, K. G. (2004). The origins of mutual funds. *SSRN*. Yale ICF Working Paper No. 04-48. Retrieved from https://papers.ssrn.com/sol3/papers.cfm?abstract_id=636146

Simon Stevin. (n.d.). Simon Stevin. *Wikipedia*. Retrieved from https://en.wikipedia.org/wiki/Simon_Stevin

Slaveryandremembrance.org. (n.d.). *Dutch slave trade*. Retrieved from http://slaveryandremembrance.org/articles/article/?id=A0145

Smith, A. (1776). *The wealth of nations*. Published in 2002. Bibliomania.com Ltd. Retrieved from http://www.bibliomania.com/2/1/65/112/

Soll, J. (2014). No accounting skills? No Moral Reckoning. *Opinionator—New York Times*. Retrieved from https://opinionator.blogs.nytimes.com/2014/04/27/no-accounting-skills-no-moral-reckoning/

Steensgaard, N. (1981). The Dutch East India company as an institutional innovation. In M. Aymard (Ed.), *Dutch capitalism and world capitalism*. Cambridge University Press.

Taylor, B. (2013). How 3 countries lost their position as the world's dominant financial power over the last 800 years. *Business Insider*. Retrieved from https://www.businessinsider.com/700-years-of-government-bond-yields-2013-12?international=true&r=US&IR=T

Tracy, J. D. (2008). *The founding of the Dutch Republic: War, finance, and politics in Holland 1572–1588*. Oxford University Press.

Tracy, P. (2020). Dutch auction. *Investing Answers*. Retrieved from https://investinganswers.com/dictionary/d/dutch-auction

Union of Utrecht. (n.d.). Union of Utrecht. *Wikipedia*. Retrieved from https://en.wikipedia.org/wiki/Union_of_Utrecht

de Vries, J., & van der Woude, A. (1997). *The first modern economy: Success, failure, and perseverance of the Dutch economy, 1500–1815*. Cambridge University Press.

Westerhuis, G., & van Zanden, J. (2018). Four hundred years of central banking in the Netherlands, 1609–2016. In *Sveriges Riksbank and the history of central banking* (pp. 242–264). Cambridge University Press. Retrieved from https://doi.org/10.1017/9781108140430.007

Wintle, M. J. (2007). Maurice I Stadholder of The Netherlands. *Encyclopedia Britannica*. Retrieved from https://www.britannica.com/biography/Maurice-stadholder-of-The-Netherlands.

Chapter 4
Goldsmith Bankers and the Birth of the Fractional Reserve System (Seventeenth and Early Eighteenth Centuries)

4.1 Introduction

One of the places the British are most proud of is the Financial Center in London. In this center, where trillions of pounds are traded, hundreds of financial companies, from the Bank of England to the London Stock Exchange, from the world's largest commercial banks to vast insurance companies, are located. The famous Lombard Street, where the most critical developments in the history of British rulings have been experienced, lies in the middle of this area. Here one realizes how vital the role of financial markets is in the UK's economic development that started in the seventeenth century, and that economic freedom can be related to democracy. Above all, the bankers of Lombard Street inspired modern banking by creating a new banking system. This is the system on which today's banking is based, i.e., "Fractional Reserve Banking." While the first seeds of this formation were planted, dozens of buildings such as Lloyd's coffee shop and the Historical Post Office have witnessed this development.

In the fourteenth and fifteenth centuries, Lombard Street was where Italian merchant banks provided in the financing needs of both the wool trade and the English kings (Bagehot, 1873). Lending to the kings gave them access to the wool trade. Over time, the British, who basically learned banking from the Italians and the Dutch, began to show their maturity. Goldsmiths, whose main business was in jewelry, gained more and more importance as bankers. They exchanged foreign currency, gave loans to those who needed cash, and preserved people's money. Over time, they also leased the Royal Mint, in the Tower of London, close by. Yet, most important was the trust that could be put in them and their reputation rose above that of the King. Without the approval of the bankers, the rulers would not be able to make vital decisions. Even more, a chain of events that began in Lombard Street contributed to the story of British democracy.

While the markets were developing, an event triggered a shock in England, the king seized the Goldsmith's money in the Mint (Gordin, 2017). One of the biggest

M. B. Karan et al., *A History of Banks*, Contributions to Economics,
https://doi.org/10.1007/978-3-031-62297-7_4

problems of the English kings, lacking a proper financial system, was to collect taxes. After the thirteenth century, to prevent the King from levying taxes whenever wanted, decisions on taxes were subject to Parliament approval. Charles I, being king from 1625 onward, had problems in getting the consent of the Parliament for his tax proposals. Therefore he stopped to convene it. He managed financially, more or less, by reducing his expenses, by borrowing, by stopping the war with Spain and France and by exploiting all kind of old feudal rights. Yet, at the end of the 30s he got in a war with Scotland, one of his two kingdoms, and he really needed extra money to fight this war. He convened the Parliament again in 1640. However the Parliament appeared not to agree with the war and Charles dissolved it again. Desperate then, he seized the money kept by the British Mint, most of which belonged to the bankers. With the King's seizure of private property in this way, the trust in the King bottomed.

In this chapter, we are going to sketch the development of banking in England during a large part of the seventeenth century and the first decades of the eighteenth century. An important element in this development is the structural government deficit, worsened by the many wars England was involved in during this period ("List of Wars"). This problem was extra complicated because of the tensions between King and Parliament—the King responsible for international policy and war fare, but the consent of Parliament required for new taxation. The "Seizure of the Mint" mentioned above is an iconic illustration of this tension. The role of the Parliament was broadened during this period. Important steps were the Civil War (1640–1649) and the Republican period thereafter (1649–1660), the Restoration (1660) and the Glorious Revolution of 1688 when the Parliament brought Queen Mary and her Dutch husband, William III to the throne. An important element is the relative weak position of England in international trade until the end of the seventeenth century and the shortage of money as a consequence of that. The Navigation Acts and the resulting Anglo-Dutch wars (1652–1654, 1655–1657 and 1672–1674) were intended to improve this.

The Goldsmiths acquired a powerful position in accepting deposits from wealthy citizens and using this to finance the King. They were trusted and the King was not. The receipts for the deposits were going to be used as an alternative form of money. But in the long run, in 1672, at the start of the third Anglo-Dutch war, when huge expenses were necessary, this dependence of the King's finance on the Goldsmiths became overstressed, leading to the Stop of the Exchequer, another iconic moment in the development of the King's finance. The King stopped all payments. Now it was Charles II, the son of Charles I. The event led to the bankruptcy of an important Goldsmith, Edward Backwell. It was clear that there were other measures necessary to manage the government finances. The government started to issue loans and lotteries and Exchequer bills, interest-bearing notes that could be used to pay taxes. Also, it established the Bank of England, a joint-stock company intended to issue bank notes for specie (minted money) and lending the specie to the government. It acted more or less similar to the Goldsmiths, but with more control by the government. Finally the main part of the government debt was transferred to South Sea Company equity. This huge debt-equity swap was executed during the South Sea Bubble (1720) and was in fact only possible because of this bubble. It made the government debt tradeable and more attractive for citizens to invest in.

4.2 Early Political and Economic Developments

The period around 1640 was a difficult and complicated one for England, both economically and politically. To understand the development of Goldsmiths banking and the role of the Bank of England, it is necessary to explain these difficulties. They are related to the conflicts of the first two Stuart kings, James I and Charles I, with the English Parliament, mainly due to problems with the royal finances and poor taxation methods, and contributing to the start of the Civil War. Below, we give attention to the transfer of Tudor reign to Stuart reign in 1603, to the problems with royal finance and taxation, as well as to the Civil War and the period without a king (1649–1660). All of this has to be understood against the background of the development of economics and international trade.

4.2.1 From Tudor Reign to Stuart Reign

Undoubtedly, King Henry VIII was one of the most colorful Kings in British history, who married six times. His daughter, Queen Elizabeth I (the last Tudor) died unmarried and childless in 1603. The Stuarts were related to the Tudors and had ruled in Scotland for long ("Mary, Queen of Scots"). Mary Stuart (1542–1587), the only surviving legitimate child of James V of Scotland, was raised in France, married the son of the French king and was queen consort for a short time, until her husband died. Then she returned to Scotland and resumed the queenship, aged 18. Her catholic background was a serious handicap, since Scotland had turned protestant in between, but she managed. Her marriage in 1565, with Henry Stuart, a cousin, led to more serious difficulties. He was murdered by the Scottish nobility in February 1567, their son James being 1 year old. Mary quickly remarried with James Hepburn. He was also unacceptable for the Scottish nobility that imprisoned and deposed her, in favor of her son, James. Her half-brother James Moray became regent.

The young James (VI of Scotland) was educated in a protestant environment ("James VI and I"). He came under the influence of the converted noble Lennox, was kidnapped by protestant earls, but escaped a year later. From then on he became more independent and started to pursue his own policies as king. He was able to balance the interests of the different factions of the Scottish nobility. One of his chief purposes was to consolidate his claim on the throne of England, as successor of the childless Elizabeth. In 1585/86 he concluded an alliance with England. He was a convinced Presbyterian and whereas this church is unhierarchic he tweaked it and made himself the Head of the Presbyterian Church of Scotland, thus creating more similarity with the situation in the Anglican Church of England. In 1603, with the help of Robert Cecil, the Chief Minister of Elizabeth, he succeeded her as ruler of England, Wales and Ireland. The Union with Scotland was a personal one; he was James VI of Scotland and James I of England.

Other than when dealing with the Scottish nobility, the English Parliament had to be consulted about all measures regarding religious, social, and economic life. An important right of the Parliament was to decide about new taxes and to allow the King to use the yield to support royal expenditure. Generally this was only allowed in case of emergency, war, or threat of war. For the normal expenses the King had to rely on rents and revenues of the own property, on feudal fines for other landowners and on customs. The Parliament was not permanently available. When needing Parliament consent, the King had to convene one. The most important topic of the first Parliament of James (1604–1611) was a proposal to re-organize royal finance, skip some feudal fines, and establish some new taxations by way of the "Great Contract," designed by Robert Cecil, now the Lord Treasurer. It was not accepted. James convened the next Parliament in 1614, because of the deteriorating financial position. It lasted only 2 months and failed completely. The third Parliament (1621–1622) granted some subsidies, but ended in a conflict about the plans of James to organize a marriage between his son and heir, Charles, and a Spanish princess. The Parliament suggested taking a protestant wife and the hazzling went on. The fourth and last Parliament (1624–1625) was short again, because of the illness and death of James, in 1625.

James was succeeded by his son, Charles I, born in 1600 ("Charles I"). He was different: more modest and more interested in art, but shared his father's opinion about kingship: it should be absolute. This led to many problems with the Parliament ("Parliament of England"). It started already with the first Parliament convened in 1625. Charles demanded that it would grant him certain import and export taxes for his lifetime, but the Parliament wanted more control and gave the rights only for 1 year. It mistrusted Charles' tendency to engage more in the Thirty Years' War and his pattern of expenses in general. The second Parliament (1626) was again convened because of the financial difficulties. To prevent impeachment of his main advisor, Buckingham, Charles readily dissolved it. The third Parliament (1628–1629) was again needed because of finances. With a Petition of Right, confirming the rights of an individual as against the divine right of the King, being put forward, the King gave in and the Parliament granted some subsidies to the King, also the import and export taxes discussed before. Yet, re-convening the next year, the Parliament recalled this decision. Charles then dissolved the Parliament and arrested nine of his opponents. The Parliament was not convened then until 1640. Lack of finance forced Charles to finish the wars with Spain and France. He held out by reducing his expenses, granting all kinds of rights and levying some incidental taxes.

Toward the end of the 1630s, Charles ran into a war with Scotland ("Charles I"). The direct reason for the "Bishops War" was a religious one. Charles ruled that the Scottish (Presbyterian) churches had to adopt the standard English book of common prayers. This was agreed upon by the Scottish bishops, but the local churches were more collegial and refused. The bishops were expelled and this movement (covenant) organized an army; when Charles went to Scotland with an army to enforce the measure, he was defeated (1639). Then Charles decided to convene a Parliament

(1640) to get money to fight against Scotland. But when the Parliament appeared to disagree with the war, Charles dissolved it again. The war went on, but when the Scots defeated the English army and crossed the border, Charles had to convene a Parliament again (1640). It was the prelude to the Civil War, to be discussed shortly. It was also at this time that Charles "seized" the Mint. We put this major financial history event in the context of royal finance and taxation.

4.2.2 *Royal Finance and Taxation*

Around 1600, the normal royal income was mainly feudal: rents and revenues from the royal properties and the yield of the "Court of Wards" (The National Archives, n.d.). The right of wardship meant that the Crown took on responsibility for orphaned heirs where their father had been a tenant in chief of the crown. This included rights over the deceased's estate. Being a medieval right, it was renewed by the Stuarts and applied rather arbitrarily. Comparable to this were church taxes and fines on Roman Catholics. The only regular tax income were the customs. In case of emergency or other special occasions, the King could ask the Parliament for a tax on land or on goods organized at county level. Elizabeth I was not a big spender, but even for her the normal royal income did not cover the normal expenditures. She had to sell property or to borrow. King James I needed more money. Therefore, Robert Cecil, his Lord Treasurer, devised the "Great Contract," a proposal to replace the yield of the wardship and some related feudal rights by a permanent subsidy, paid for by extra customs or some excise tax. It did not pass Parliament, because of merchant opposition. They knew about such a taxation from Dutch practices in the Netherlands. The underlying issue was mistrust.

James, and later his son Charles, had to rely on their "prerogative power" to find ways to supplement their income and/or they had to accept an increasing debt (Banknotes of the Pound Sterling, n.d.). English kings had the right in wartime to require maritime towns and counties to furnish ships and this duty could be commuted for a money payment: Ship Money. Charles applied it during peacetime, also to inland counties. It led to severe protests and the Parliament wanted to discuss this first when convened again. Another field was that of patents and monopolies. For example, in 1616, a group of pin makers was allowed to form a monopoly. The King received a commission for all pins sold in the next 40 years. There were many of such patents and monopolies and the suspicion grew that it was just concealed taxation (Wilson, 1984). Yet another possibility was to become involved in agricultural land improvement. An interesting example is Hatfield Chase, where drainage could improve the agricultural capacity of the land. Charles appointed a Dutch engineer (Vermuyden) to organize the work. It led to problems with the commoners. The measure to extinguish common rights was to lay a skyhigh tax on land being "hurtfully surrounded by water." If the tax remained unpaid, the commons could be sold to someone who could pay the draining. Charles himself took a large part of the land.

All measures were anyway insufficient to keep income and expenditures balanced. The royal debt raised and raised. It was necessary to borrow. A straightforward possibility was to get advances from the customs farmers (Wilson, 1984). Gradually, the farmers became as actual lenders, bankers to the Crown. They lent the King their future revenue. Other private, wealthy individuals contributed to it through the farmers. There were also direct loans from domestic or foreign parties. An important domestic party was the Corporation of London. Yet, to get long-term loans appeared to be more and more difficult for Charles. Little possibilities were left, when the Parliament of April 1640 made the conflicts to sharpen. Finally, Charles took some extreme measures, foremost the "Seizure of the Mint" (Milevsky, 2017). He took £200,000, most of which was deposited by Goldsmiths, trusting it would be save there. Charles saw it as a forced loan and promised to pay it back at 8% interest. Following wide protests, he released part of it right away and kept the rest as a forced loan for a while. More or less in the same spirit, he forced the East India Company to sell him the pepper stocks for an attractive price and required a credit to pay it later. In the turmoil of the Civil War, these payments got delayed further and further.

4.2.3 The Civil War

After the stable Elizabethan order had been collapsed, scandals and discontent caused by a decaying political system provoked a series of civil wars. Already in 1640, the country was divided into supporters of Charles I and supporters of the Parliament. The conflicts became irreversible when the Parliament decided that it had the control over the appointment of army and navy commanders. It did not support the war with Scotland, but Charles continued it. In 1642 Charles fled to Oxford and formed a Parliament there. There were nobles, merchants, and ordinary people from all walks of life on both sides. The differences between Scotland, Ireland, and England played also a role. Maybe most important were religious conflicts between Puritans, mostly Presbyterians, and members of the Church of England, and the fear of Roman Catholic influence. It was going to be a devastating war. About 100,000 British were killed. Thousands of people in Ireland died of massacre or starvation. Many others were injured or taken prisoner. Major cities were besieged and plundered. Cathedrals and churches were desecrated and pillaged. Homes were looted, farms burned, Cottswool sheep slaughtered (Wilson, 1984).

The Civil War was in fact a series of three wars ("English Civil War"). The First Civil War (1642–1646) went along with the continuation of the Bishops' Wars. It ended when the Scots imprisoned Charles and handed him over to the Parliament. Then, conflicts arose both in the Parliament and between the Parliament and its "New Model Army." Charles used it and made an agreement with the Scots, starting the Second Civil War (1648–1649) against the New Model Army. It ended with Charles' defeat. Because of conflicts within the Parliament, the army took control and forced its loyal part to set up a high court to sentence the King for treason. This happened in January 1649, Charles was beheaded publicly. Oliver Cromwell, a member of the

Parliament and then leader of the army, took the power. After the King's execution, a republic was declared, the Commonwealth of England. The eldest living son of Charles I was proclaimed to be King Charles II by the Royalists. With the help of Irish and Scottish allies he succeeded to conquer parts of England during the Third Civil War (1649–1651). He was defeated finally in 1651 and escaped to France.

Oliver Cromwell (1599–1658), a member of the English Parliament, was a well-spoken, gifted administrator and a devout Protestant. He organized a couple of parliaments that he could control well. He became named Lord Protector of the Commonwealth, a position he retained until his death in 1658. Cromwell's public finances were by no means exempt from difficulties. Just as during the James I and Charles I reigns, there was a structural government deficit. Taxation had to be reorganized. The Land tax was most important. It was derived administratively from the Ship Money; county committees were responsible for collecting it. The tax farmers of Customs were temporarily replaced by a public system. The tariffs remained the same, but the volume increased and the administration was made more efficient. Altogether, there was more control, with still the same potential financiers: tax farmers and London merchants. Cromwell's son Richard succeeded him. But he was a weak leader and had no power base in the Parliament. During these chaotic years, support for Charles II grew. In 1660, he was recalled to England. Cromwell's body was removed from his grave and he was posthumously executed.

4.2.4 Economics and International Trade

International trade gained importance over time, with the further exploration and exploitation of the East and the West. Spain was losing its hegemony. England was in a good position to benefit, but it did not meet the expectations yet. The center of gravity of international trade was shifting from the Mediterranean to the North Sea, but more to The Netherlands, first the South and then to the North, than to England. Only about 10% of the 5.5 million people in England and Wales worked in trade and manufacturing in 1600. Also, agriculture became more commercial and market oriented. It was vulnerable for fluctuations in international trade though. Wool was the main export product. The export consisted for 90% of the export of undressed woolen cloth to northern Europe (Wilson, 1984). This export dropped dramatically to less than half between 1614 and 1640. War in Europe played an important role, and the accompanying currency debasements in Germany and Poland made the import from England too expensive.

However, there was also the Cockayne project, illustrative for the way England tried to deal with its trade. The Merchant Adventurers ("Company of Merchant Adventurers") was a group of merchants chartered to perform and control the trade in woolen cloth with northern Europe. They exported only undyed and undressed cloth, leaving more than half of the added value to northern Europe, mainly Holland. Then William Cockayne suggested to King James, to protect the English economy against Dutch competition, to forbid the export of undyed cloth, develop dying capacity, and establish a new company for the export of dyed cloth to northern Europe. Of course, the King was tempted because he was going to earn some percentage of the turnover of this new company and for Cockayne it was attractive because he was going to be the leader of the company. This experiment appeared to be a complete failure. It lasted for 3 years with a dramatic drop of the export as consequence of mismanagement and Dutch measures. The privileges of the Merchant Adventurers were restored, but that did not solve the problems.

Meanwhile, England built up a big colony base (see Fig. 4.1). In exchange for financial help, Cromwell gave the East India Company a charter in 1657. However, the contribution of this peer of the Dutch colonial trade firm (see Chap. 3) was very restricted, it being dependent on Dutch shipping for the re-export to Europe of what was acquired far away. Cross-border trade was mainly sea trade and England was ideally located to be the most important player. However, the "English economy was, in many respects, still a junior partner in a system of European and extra-European trade" (Wilson, 1984, p. 41). Indeed, "a sizeable proportion of the trade with England came and went in Dutch ships, especially in the newly designed 'flyboats', built for cheap freightage. In all the arts of commerce, and many of industry, the Dutch were indisputably ahead. They dominated world markets, standing at all points between the English and their suppliers and customers. Their demand for wool drove up prices to the English clothier. They removed a half-finished cloth and extracted the largest profit margin from dyeing it. They stood in the way of the direct shipment of naval stores and colonial wares from their place of origin to England. England, it seemed, stood only on the periphery of an international system of trade, manipulated by Dutch cunning."

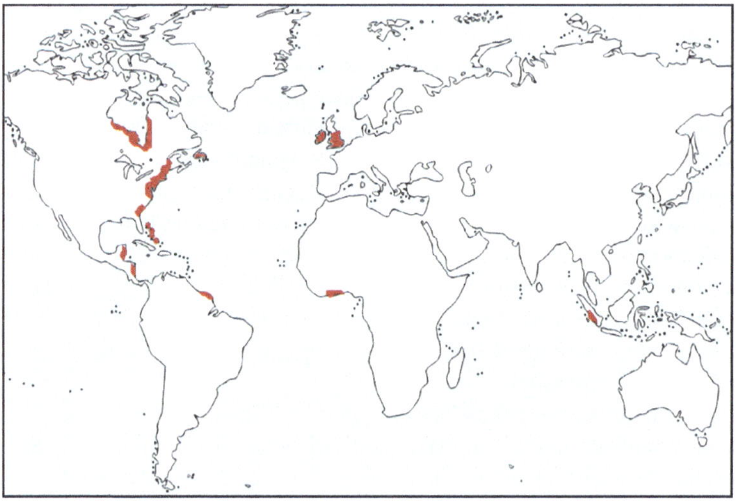

Fig. 4.1 England and its colonies at the end of the 17th century. https://en.wikipedia.org/wiki/English_overseas_possessions

This view on the lack of economic progress led to the "Navigation Acts" and to wars with the Dutch Republic. The first Anglo-Dutch war (1652–1654) was during the protectorate of Cromwell. England was successful in the war, but the Dutch bypassed this first Navigation Act. One of the loopholes was New Amsterdam, with Virginian tobacco being shipped via this Dutch colony. The loophole was closed with its capture in 1664. Together with the new Navigation Act, this led to the second Anglo-Dutch War (1665–1667), under the reign of Charles II. As a result, the English merchants received more freedom. Moreover, there was more variety in trade: manufactured products to the new colonies, tobacco from Virginia, sugar from the West Indies (Barbados, Jamaica), cod from Newfoundland, and cotton-based textile from India. This was combined with the development of shipbuilding (Wilson, 1984). The English balance of trade was structurally negative however. The deficit during most of the seventeenth century led to a situation with a shortage of money and high interest rates. The latter was considered to be one of the important factors hindering the economic development. It contributed certainly to the difficulties of royal finance during the reign of Charles II.

4.3 The London Bankers

4.3.1 The Rise of the Goldsmiths

Following William the Conqueror of Normandy, who invaded the British Isles in 1066, the Jews came in England. Although the Jewish Holy Books forbade lending money with interest among themselves, they could ask for an interest income in money trade with Christians, who were not allowed to lend money with interest at all (compare Chap. 2). As in all of Europe, the Jews were barred from many types of work, but the Crown encouraged or even forced the Jews to lend money with interest (BBC Bitesize, n.d.). In doing so, they met the financial needs of society. However, the Jews became increasingly racially hatred because of their way of life and beliefs. That some of them were very rich due to usury further fueled this hatred. They survived only thanks to protection by the King's troops. When Italian bankers came in for trade after 1200, they became an alternative for the Jews, who were then exiled from England (Gordin, 2017). They settled on the London street that would be called Lombard.

Instead of selling their wool to Italian merchant banks, the British eventually established textile workshops and they no longer needed Italian bankers. They also started credit connections with the leading financial centers Antwerp and Amsterdam. Tired of the endless royal demands for loans and the growing hostility of local merchants and bankers, the Italians began to leave the Island. As mentioned in Chap. 2, these developments had a very negative impact on the Medici Bank. The traders and experts in the centers were skilled in commercial affairs, understood complex financial transactions, and even produced creative solutions. The figurehead of English maturity in financial affairs in the sixteenth century is Thomas Gresham (1519–1579). He was a merchant, from an important merchant family, who served the English kings and queens from 1551 onward as banker in Antwerp. First Edward VI (1537–1553), then 14 years old, with the duke of Northumberland as the chairman of the regency council. Thereafter, Queen Mary (1516–1558) and Queen Elizabeth I (1533–1603). All three were children of Henry VIII. Before Gresham, William Damsell was the banker for Henry VIII and Edward VI. He had great difficulties in getting sufficient funds in Antwerp and Gresham used these difficulties to have Damsell replaced and become his successor. He made more than 120 trips to Antwerp (Guy, 2019) and was able to survive the transition from the protestant reign of Edward VI to the fiercely catholic reign of Mary and thereafter to the protestant reign of Elizabeth I again. He knew how the exchange markets and loan markets worked and was able to manipulate these markets with small actions. He saw the possibilities of the differences between nominal value and face value of the different coins in the different countries and knew the world of smuggling. Gresham's law, saying that "bad money drives out good money," is also attributed to him, although that is based on a misinterpretation of a fragment of an introductory letter from him to Elizabeth I; the phenomenon was already known by the Greek and was also formulated by Nicholas Oresme and Copernicus (Guy, 2019).

Already during the Middle Ages, the London Goldsmiths formed an important guild that was later transformed into corporations with also substantial political power. Given their profession as gold and silver workers, the step into financial services was rather natural. They met wealthy people, were active in gold and silver trade, and had facilities to store valuables securely. It was straightforward to offer safe deposit services and to act as pawn brokers. Merchants with cash surpluses used this safe deposit service as well. One of the secure places to store the money was the Mint. When Charles I "seized the Mint," however, this appeared to be not so secure. It was an important incentive to try to look for other possibilities, with keeping using it being an interesting one. Given the structural lack of money, this was by far the most attractive alternative. This is how goldsmiths turned into bankers. That happened mainly during the Commonwealth period and the reign of Charles II (Richards, 1958). Before the 1640s, there was a strict royal monopoly on the trade in bullion and money, because of the scarcity of money, and there were no real deposit banks, like the Banco de Rialto (Munro, 2002).

The Goldsmiths were not the only group of people performing financial services. There were also the "Merchants," the "Brokers," and the "Scriveners" (Richards, 1958). Some of the merchants developed into "exchanging" merchants, like, much earlier, the Medici in Florence. These merchants carried out Bill of Exchange operations and were active in international money and bullion trade. They were important financiers of the rulers. There were pawn brokers and "exchange" brokers. The last group of brokers were sworn in and traded under official authority. They were active in the exchange business and fitted in the monopoly of the King. The first group was not well respected. They applied usury and received stolen goods. The original role of the "Scrivener" was the writing of bonds and contracts. In this position the scrivener had ample possibilities of acquitting knowledge about finance and trade and to develop into a money lender, accepting deposits from customers and lending these to other customers. From 1545 on it was lawful to ask interest, capped at 10%. This law was repealed in 1552, but revived again in 1571 by Elizabeth I, and the official interest was fixed at 6%. Next to these groups of broad intermediaries, there were more specialized financial agents, active in the wool or corn trade. They advanced money on the future supply of wool or corn. All in all the Goldsmiths were not the only financial intermediaries, but certainly the most important during the second half of the seventeenth century. They serviced the King as tax farmers, lenders, transporters of money, and bullion, as well as the execution of payments.

4.3.2 The Banking Products of the Goldsmiths

The banking products of the Goldsmiths were manifold (Richards, 1958). As indicated above, they all started with deposit taking. A distinction was made between deposits that could be withdrawn immediately and deposits where the withdrawal had to be announced beforehand, the equivalent of demand deposits and time deposits. The whole system was directed then already to the use of the deposits for loans to customers, making it possible to give interest to the depositor. The depositors came from everywhere in England. The promissory note originated as a receipt given by a goldsmith for money that was given in custody to him. Such a note was really just a receipt that could not be assigned to another person. When it became a receipt for a money deposit that the goldsmith was allowed to use to give loans to other customers, it developed into an assignable banking product. Ultimately such notes were also issued by the Goldsmiths in the form of loans, so not necessarily backed by coins or bullion. In this way the goldsmith became a purveyor of extra currency. The promissory note developed into a bearer instrument, a banknote.

Originally the bill of exchange was for international trade, and the parties involved were merchants, but later it was also used for inland trade and the parties involved were not necessarily only merchants. The Goldsmiths participated in all necessary bill of exchange operations. It was possible to assign a bill to a goldsmith and use that to get paid or get a loan or a customer of a Goldsmith could issue a bill of exchange on the Goldsmith. A bill of exchange could be used as a means of payment by assigning it to a new payee. In case of payment problems, e.g., the party that was supposed to pay the bill refuses to pay or is not able to pay, it was not right away clear who had to sue the supposed payer. That is how the practice of endorsing started. Each new assignee endorsed the bill with a signature on the back of the bill. In case of payment problems all assignees were involved. It helped to settle more transactions without cash. A bill could have 10–20 or even more endorsing signatures (Kohn, 1999). The same practice was also developed with respect to letters obligatory. That was even a little easier, because then the issuing company was the same as the company who was supposed to pay. The difference between a promissory note as we use the concept in the previous paragraph and a letter obligatory as defined by Kohn (1999) is small. A promissory note is issued by a bank to confirm a deposit. A letter obligatory is an informal merchant document, to confirm how a debt is going to be settled. The liquidity of an assignable letter obligatory or bill of exchange depended of course on the reputation of the issuer.

In the sixteenth century the ban on usury was loosened in the Habsburg Netherlands and in England. Henry VIII and his parliament enacted legislation that determined that interest of up to 10% was allowed. This made it possible to discount bills of exchange and letters obligatory that were not yet mature. The law was repealed during the reign of Edward VI in 1552, but restored by Elizabeth I in 1571. Munro (2002) relates the relatively early practice of discounting in England to the non-existence of deposit banks and the need of other possibilities to pay without cash. Kohn (1999) is skeptical about this. But the general scarcity of money in England may have been a factor indeed.

The Goldsmith deposits became the best option for the wealthy people over time. Under the moderate Republican regime created by Cromwell, depositors transferred their lending rights to the banks, allowing the Goldsmiths to own their loans and receivables. While the Goldsmiths kept some of the gold as reserves, they lended part of it (Richards, 1958). Thus, the amount of gold or money that the Crown could confiscate was also minimized. A significant part of the money was circulating in the market. The Goldsmiths did not initially charge any fees for their services; the money entrusted to them was a kind of interest-free deposit and was seen as a costless debt for them. After the Mint Seize event, landlords and rich people tended to secure their money by entrusting them to trusted servants. Goldsmiths, who wanted to expand their business in this direction, gave these individuals a daily commission, encouraging them to invest their master's money in them. Over time, these accounts would form the central part of their business. Those who initially deposited with the Goldsmiths began to watch their money closely on if it was safe. Although they were a little worried that the bankers gave it to third parties as a loan, their confidence in the Goldsmiths increased. They learned that people received some interest for the money they gave and could get their cash back when demanded. They were now shopping with notes (banknotes) that the bankers gave them in return for deposits. These bills were increasingly used as money. The Goldsmiths were giving the money in their custody as loans. In doing so, the bank business started to work at an increasing pace.

Bankers initially started lending in short term to avoid a cash bottleneck. However, when they saw that the depositors were not in a hurry to ask for their money, the maturities began to get longer. For this reason, the Goldsmiths switched from weekly loans to monthly loans and from monthly to annual loans after holding a certain percentage of the money, anticipating on the possibility that their owners might demand cash (Cantillon, 1755). They might even keep only 10%–20% of the gold given to them as reserves. The cash ratio varied, according to the Irish-French economist Richard Cantillon (1680–1774), from 10% to around 66%, depending on the practice and conduct of the clients. This fractional reserve broke the direct representation between the notes being circulated from hand to hand and the cash kept in vaults and it then transformed the notes into paper credit. If the gold holders thought their wealth was in safe hands, there was no danger that it would be suddenly repealed. The promissory notes they gave as deposits were circulating among the people like cash. The clients for loans included large landlords, heirs, and merchants, many of whom were loaned with personal guarantees. They also provided loans to the Cromwell government at reasonable interest rates.

4.3.3 Edward Backwell and His Bank

Many of the Goldsmith bankers' applications were developed by the "shop" of Edward Backwell (1618–1683, see Fig. 4.2), the largest bank in the Lombard Street area. Backwell was a well-known politician and accepted as the creator of the English banking system by some scholars (Henderson, 1885). Born in a town near London, he moved to London where he married a merchant daughter. He was apprenticed to Thomas Vyner, one of London's leading Goldsmith bankers, in 1635. After working in the state finance for a period, he founded his Goldsmith company in 1651. He made a pretty good profit by buying the park at Hampton Court, a former Royal property, and reselling it to the government. Backwell was also one of the first to enter the business of collecting deposits and lending. During the Civil War, he collected low interest money, turned it into high interest loans, and earned huge incomes. He ran his business by issuing banknotes to depositors. He was a widely recognized keeper of deposits, patronized by many provincial and metropolitan customers. Backwell was not only a powerful bullion merchant, a big dealer in both "inland" and "outland" bills of exchange and Treasury Exchequer payment orders, but also an essential accountant, cashier, and tax farmer (Richards, 1958). He also collected money as deposits in exchange for daily interest by bribing servants who kept their masters' cash (Aylmer, 2008). Backwell relied on a network of foreign merchants and gave them loans to improve relations with overseas counterparts. To take better advantage of the merchants, the Goldsmiths had turned them into stakeholders who would gain various benefits from their banking activities. The information acquired in this way was very important and occasionally Backwell was entering into joint ventures with them (Richards, 1958). Backwell's preserved documents indicate that the opportunity to profit by buying foreign currencies in different countries and converting them to currency in another country began in the London market in the mid-seventeenth century.

Having a pragmatic personality, Edward, in addition to working with all segments of the society, established a close relationship with Oliver Cromwell, helping him with his financial problems and earning a high level of income from these works. In 1656, when Cromwell's navy plundered the Spanish fleet carrying silver from America to Spain, the precious silver from the ships was sold to Edward Backwell at a very affordable price. Edward turned the silver into money in the Mint and made a considerable profit from this business (Richards, 1928). After Cromwell's death, Backwell skillfully approached the new ruler, King Charles II, impressed him, and established excellent relations. He ran a lucrative banking business under the King's auspices and was sent to various places to negotiate international monetary transactions as the King's envoy. Interestingly, the King was comfortable with his

Fig. 4.2 Edward Backwell (1618–1683). https://en.wikipedia.org/wiki/File:Edward_Backwell.jpg

former relation with the old enemy, Cromwell. Backwell, as soon as the Parliament authorized the King to collect taxes, gave a loan to the Crown in bulk and then collected the taxes in weekly installments over 3–4 years from tax farming. Although a charge of corruption was brought against Backwell, no evidence was found. The incident might have been caused by jealousy. Apart from the King and Queen, most of the nobles and politicians and the East India Company and various companies, and all the leading Goldsmiths had accounts at Backwell. He owned several farms and bought property in Huntingdonshire in 1668. In addition, he was recorded in many town and city correspondences as a temporary proprietor; these real estates were probably acquired from those who could not pay their debts (Henderson, 1885).

While Backwell served King Charles II by taking important diplomatic missions from the state, he received generous payments from the King in return for these duties. Backwell was sent to Paris to collect the price of Dunkirk that was sold to France. In October 1662, he entered into secret negotiations with the French on behalf of the King. He often acted as an intermediary in money transactions between Charles and King Louis of France. The State Papers of January 21, 1666 had an "Order for Edward Backwell to be baronet," but he probably rejected this offer (Henderson, 1885). Despite such good relations with the King, Backwell was dealt the most brutal blow when the Exchequer stopped paying its debts in 1672. Twenty-two percent of the entire Treasury debt was his money. Perhaps the King recalled that he had once helped his nemesis, Oliver Cromwell. We cannot know this, but as the famous first-century Indian philosopher Beydeba said: "Friendship with kings is like carrying a snake in your chest; you don't know when the snake will bite." The action was a massive blow to his bank and he could not afford the loss. While it does not appear in court documents whether his creditors gave him a stay order, he is thought to have sought refuge in the Netherlands at the time, as many others did. However, he continued his relations with the King and was commissioned to help some people from abroad collect debts (Aylmer, 2008).

Although Backwell lost all his money and went bankrupt, his heirs somehow achieved a refund, or at least partially. See next section. Edward Backwell, who went bankrupt in 1682, died in Holland. He was a banker who was not afraid to take risks. His most important achievement was taking high risks while adapting hitherto unused methods to banking. Edward knew where his interests lay and could easily change his political position (Henderson, 1885).

4.4 Public Finance After the Restoration

When Charles II came to the throne, a hereditary revenue was agreed with the Parliament and in return Charles gave up ancient feudal dues, like wardship and knight service (Wilson, 1984). The three main sources of this revenue were the Customs, the Excise, and the Hearth tax. The Excise was very unpopular, but accepted. The Hearth tax was most debated because of the arbitrariness of its application: "what is a chimney?" It was dropped finally in 1689. In case of rare expenditures, like on wars, it was possible for the King to ask the Parliament for extra money. The burden of these subsidies was spread over counties and cities and finally reallocated to parishes and individuals. The hereditary income was insufficient to cover the normal expenses. The King depended on tax farmers and bankers, mainly Goldsmiths, to cover the income shortages and irregularities. It gave the bankers a privileged position. In 1664/65, for instance, Edward Backwell gave a loan of £280,000 with an interest of 6%, but received above that, privately, a free additional interest of £8,000. There was a lot of critique on how the bankers managed to screw so much interest out of the Exchequer. When the Parliament voted for additional funding of the second Anglo-Dutch War, the teller of the Exchequer, George Downing (indeed, the one after whom a famous London street was named) got Parliamentary support for a rule that such subsidies should be combined with the possibility for the country at large to lend directly to the Exchequer, that such loans should be repaid first-in-first-out and that these repayment orders could be assigned, enabling the creditor to go to a banker to cash it. To further restrain the bankers, Downing persuaded the Parliament, in 1671, to impose a tax on the bankers for loans with a higher interest than 6%. Such a well-organized public debt system as Downing had in mind was not going to be realized until in the early eighteenth century, with the Bank of England as an important instrument.

In 1672 the debt had increased to £2,250,000, two times the nominal hereditary royal income. Part of it was public, but uncontrolled. The government issued too easily payment orders. Next to that, it started to issue fiduciary orders that were not linked to a loan. These orders were also "secured" on certain segments of the hereditary income, but there was no serious check on whether these income segments were sufficient. The fiduciary orders were distributed to government agencies to cover their expenses. They had the order discounted or used it to get a loan. Both types of orders (payment orders and fiduciary orders) were interest bearing and assignable. The interest was generally 6%, and a gratuity of 4% for loans was normal (Richards, 1958). Most of the orders eventually arrived at the Goldsmiths for discounting. Part of it was sold again by them to their customers, for raising money that was urgently needed by the King to pay for 82 new ships for the war against the Dutch Republic. Finally, the vicious circle broke. The Goldsmiths ran out of money and could no longer satisfy the needs of the King, who was doing bad in the war anyway (Roseveare, 2019). Then, on January 2, 1672, the King stopped all repayments and payments of interest: the "Stop of the Exchequer," with the incoming money being purely used for war expenses. It was first meant for a year, but then it was extended till January 1674.

The event led to a debt chaos. In July 1674, Charles allocated £140,000 of his hereditary income to pay the interest, but it lasted until 1677 before the debt was well administrated. The total debt to the Goldsmiths was more than £1.3 million, more than £400,000 to Vyner and almost £300,000 to Backwell. The King decided to pay annually the 6% interest due on it. That happened indeed when Thomas Hornby was Lord Treasurer (1673–1679), but from 1680 on, payments became more erratic. A proportional part of the payment had to be distributed to the Goldsmiths' customers who had bought these payment orders (assignees). The first of the Vyner assignees who accepted this was "William Newbold of the parish of St. Stephen, Coleman Street, London" (Richards, 1958). He received an Exchequer order or a "bankers annuity order" as proof, presentable for payment at the Excise Office. The bankers annuity orders could be assigned to others. When the payments got erratic, this resulted in severe value reduction. Eventually Backwell went bankrupt in 1682, Vyner in 1684. The aftermath of the Stop lasted very long, but the Parliament legislated a definitive settlement in 1701. The creditors received a yearly income of 3% from 1705 onward. It was only half the interest agreed upon earlier. No compensation for missed interest was given. Burnet (1979) wrote that "*the bankers were broken, and this dishonorable and perfidious action ruined multitudes who had put their money in their hands.*" The withdrawal of such a large amount of money from the market also hindered the early buildout of commercial banking in London. The King had won the case, but is known to have admitted later that it was very wrong (McMullen Rigg, 1898).

4.5 The Glorious Revolution and Its Aftermath

After King Charles II spent his last years in constant conflict with the Parliament, he died without leaving a son and was succeeded by his brother James II (1633–1701), a staunch Catholic ("James II of England"). In the new period, financial issues and religious quarrels intensified. After a long time, a Catholic King had ascended the throne. The Anglican-dominated Parliament worried about the King's acts and behavior. When James II became King and took power in 1685, he quickly took first steps to convert England to the Catholic denomination and began to try to repeal the anti-Catholic laws. Since he had only two, protestantly educated daughters from his first marriage, Mary (1662–1694) and Anne (1665–1714), and his second marriage was already childless for 11 years, more pragmatic and moderate people did not care much. Yet, in 1688 a boy was born (James Francis Edward) and James was going to raise his son, whom he had designated as the heir, into full Catholic faith. Again, England was on the brink of a religious conversion. When the Parliament blocked the King's laws, the King suspended the Parliament.

Upon this decision of the King, a much-debated decision was taken in the history of England, with seven Members of the Parliament writing a letter to the Dutch General Commander and Prince of Orange, William III, offering him to invade England and sit on the throne. William III, Prince of Orange (1650–1702), was the grandson of the national Dutch hero William I (William the Silent) and he was a very successful military commander ("William III of England"). His mother was a daughter of Charles I and, most importantly, his wife Mary was the eldest daughter of King James II. That Mary was brought up with a Protestant education was also very welcome to the Parliament. The Lombard Street bankers, who closely followed Dutch markets, hoped for economic reforms (Wennerlind, 2011). William forced James II to flee and would rule England as King William III together with his wife, Queen Mary II. For the first time in history, two people shared the throne. It was combined with a contract between Parliament and King, the Bill of Rights, enacted in 1688. This enabled the Parliament to consolidate its supremacy over the Crown with peaceful means, the King could not suspend anymore laws passed by the Parliament (Davies, 1999). It also determined that King and/or Queen had to be Protestant. This major sequence of events is generally known as the "Glorious Revolution" or also "Bloodless Revolution." As the monarchy's influence waned in the years following, when eventually Mary's sister, Queen Anne, took over and later a distant, but protestant relative was called in from Hanover in Germany to be King George I in 1714, Parliament's power in Britain would continue to grow and England would become one of the world's best models of democracy. Britain's decision to democratize had essential repercussions on its young colonies in North America. When the news of the revolution came in, first movements of revolt began in territories such as Boston, New York, and Maryland.

The financial situation was no easier for William and Mary, as well as later rulers, than it was for Charles II, also because a long series of wars was coming up, the "Nine Years War" (1688–1697) against France, thereafter followed by the "Spanish Succession War" (1701–1714), also being mainly against France. The average deficit during the reign of William (1689–1702) was going to be £1 mio. per year, 20% of the total expenditures (Wilson, 1984). However, there were important changes as compared to the Stuart reign. Basically, there was a better flourishing economy, although it was severely hurt by warfare. There was also more clarity and mutual agreement about the role of Parliament and the role of the King. And a new taxation system was developed: the Hearth tax was dropped and instead of that a renewed Land tax was introduced and the tax farmers were replaced by commissioners as collectioners. Finally, the rulers started to organize the national debt instead of letting it go. It was not a complete design, of course, but rather a process of trial and error. Important elements were

- issuance of State loans and lotteries as well as the introduction of Exchequer bills;
- establishment of the Bank of England as a central bank;
- conversion of long-term government debt into South Sea Company participations.

4.6 Organizing the Government Debt

4.6.1 Loans/Lotteries and Exchequer Bills

For the Million Loan of 1693, people were invited to contribute £1 mio. for warfare against France. It was a so-called tontine. It worked roughly as follows. Subscribers received 7% per year, for 99 years or as long as they, or their nominees, lived. The total sum paid did not change however. So, if half of the people had died after, say 20 years, the rest of the contributors received twice as much. The contributor capital was not rebuted. The minimum subscription was £100. The loan payment was embedded in a Parliament arrangement on specified tax income drawings, an excise tax on beer and liquors (Milevsky, 2015). The chance element made the tontine attractive, implying that the interest, the annuity, could be kept a little lower. In the Million Lottery Loan or Million Adventure of 1694 there was a more explicit chance element. Tickets of £10 were sold, totaling to £1,000,000. The interest was 10% per year, for 16 years. So, an interest of £100,000 was due each year, but an extra fund of £40,000 per year was available for 2,500 "fortunate tickets" with an additional interest of £10–£1,000. Prices were drawn in November 1694. To manage the subscriber assets, the "Million Adventure Bank" was established in 1695. The contributor capital was not rebuted, just as in the case of the Million Loan, but it was yet very expensive for the government. It appeared to be impossible indeed to pay the interest complete and in time, with as consequence the rise of a secondary market for tickets without a price (Murphy, 2005). The pattern of lotteries and annuities continued. Between 1693 and 1712, the government raised over £10 million from the sale of annuities and around £11 million from the enormously popular lottery loans.

Short-term financial problems of the government due to the time lags of tax receipts or loan receipts could be solved by the issuance of tallies, short-term loans linked to a specified future tax income, promises to pay as soon as the tax would be available. They were interest bearing and tradeable and generally in denominations of 500 or 1,000. The establishment of the Bank of England, to be discussed shortly, helped to relieve liquidity deficits.

During its first years, an important experiment was started: the issuance of Exchequer Bills. Charles Montagu, then Chancellor of the Exchequer, was the main initiator of the Bank of England as well as of these bills. In 1696, there was a severe shortage of money, making it very hard to pay the army in Flanders. Montagu suggested to issue a new type of paper money, the Exchequer Bill, "to overcome the shortage of money and provide a breathing space until the war ended and enough tax was gathered to redeem the bills" (Graham, 2019). They would be accepted as payment of taxes and would carry a moderate interest rate. This possibility to pay tax with it was the main difference with the notes issued by the Bank of England. The first tranche was at 4% interest. But this turned out to be insufficient. The few bills that started to circulate were converted into money again very soon, at high discount rates. In 1697, the design was improved with the establishment of a fund that could be used to convert bills for money. Montagu tempted and pushed important London money market players to participate. This was made attractive by granting about 10% interest on the whole sum subscribed, also when the whole sum was not called right away. To create broad confidence the subscriptions were made public. The East India Company subscribed for £40,000, the Bank of England did not, but several of its directors did, for more than £30,000 in total. The Mayor of London subscribed for £5,000. Contractors involved in the transport of money to the army in Flanders participated also for about £50,000. When the total was £360,000, it was expected to be sufficient to issue the whole tranche of £1.5 mio. In between, the issuing had already started. Since people offered large quantities of bills for mutual payments, difficulties arose to get these accepted and a discount of up to 10% emerged. The initiative was more or less saved due to rumors about a peace treaty. The Exchequer Bills functioned well in covering a financially difficult period. Thereafter they disappeared gradually. However, at the end of the Spanish Succession War, the instrument was revived. The Bank of England took the responsibility then (1707).

4.6.2 Establishment of the Bank of England

It is tempting to compare the Bank of England with the Amsterdam Bank of Exchange, established almost a century earlier (see Chap. 3). The latter was already successful, people in England knew it of course and King William and his environs were familiar with it. Yet, it was in the first place a deposit bank, facilitating payments between merchants in a stable currency and thus circumventing the chaos of so many different types of money, while the Bank of England was in the first place an issuance bank, directed to creating "paper money," satisfying a need for more money and enabling the government to use the little silver and gold money that was available for necessary war expenses. "It did not monopolize the London exchange business, for the goldsmith bankers or any other financiers, alien or native, were allowed to engage in such transactions. Here was no guarantee for its security from the State or even from the City of London. City magistrates, as in case of the Bank of Amsterdam, had no controlling interest in its affairs" (Richards, 1958).

The need for a modern economy that could provide steady resources was growing and the expansion of the British Empire had to be funded. Even if the Goldsmiths partially met this need, the circulation speed of the banker's bills offered by them was no longer sufficient. Given the economic realities of the time, most of the Goldsmith bankers' customers were borrowers rather than depositors (Clapham, 1944). While the Goldsmiths financed the Treasury, they also ran a wide variety of banking businesses. They lent the money they collected at an average interest rate of around 6% as loans in exchange for banknotes issued in their name. They bought gold for their customers, exchanged currency, and discounted bills. Even though the Goldsmiths increased the speed of banknote circulation, there was a limit to the banknotes they could issue. The shortage of money was also partly due to the poor state of the coinage. Due to price increases, the metal value of the coins was higher than the nominal value and people started to clip the coins. A recoinage project, also led by Charles Montagu, started in 1696 and took 3 years. This shortage of money helped in accepting other forms of money like the Exchequer Bills or the various notes issued by the Bank of England.

The Bank of England grew out of the State's need to organize its huge debts. The Bank was established under the Tunnage Act of 1694, for "the better raising and paying into the Receipt of the Exchequer the sum of twelve hundred thousand pounds." This £1,200,000 was a loan to the Exchequer. The agreed interest was 8%, so £96,000 per year. The government agreed to pay £100,000 per year, this interest plus an allowance of £4,000 per year to be able to organize the bank properly. Individual people and corporates could subscribe. The maximum subscription was £20,000. The Bank was a joint-stock corporation. Some Goldsmiths were worried about the competition of the bank and protested, but there were also Goldsmiths among the first subscribers. A couple of years later the capital was extended until about £5 mio. Important was a contribution of 2 mio. of the New East India Company and the more than £1 mio. of the Malt lottery (Galais-Hamonno & Rietsch, 2013). In 1697 and 1707, the bank was granted the monopoly for joint-stock banking by the Parliament. Other partnerships of more than six persons were also excluded.

The £1.2 mio. was neither received nor paid right away. In between, the Bank started with her banking activities. It accepted and discounted tallies, issued by the Exchequer. It accepted Goldsmith promissory notes, but cashed these notes right away at the respective Goldsmiths at first. It accepted deposits and issued assignable promissory notes. It traded in bullion, for the first time on April 1, 1695, in Amsterdam. It discounted bills of exchange right from the start. It must have been very difficult to remain liquid during these first years. That was undoubtedly also the reason for being cautious with subscribing to the initial Exchequer Bill subscriptions, as noted above. Only in 1707, this was extended to £1,500,000, when the Bank became the main actor in circulating these bills. This was after a consortium of merchants and Goldsmiths offered to lend £1.5 mio. to the government by means of Exchequer Bills (Kleer, 2015). The loan was needed for the expenses due to the Spanish Succession War. Right from the beginning there were three types of notes (Bank of England, 1969): (1) interest-bearing "sealed bills" (promissory notes for sealed deposits); (2) "running-cash notes," payable to bearer; and (3) "accomptable" notes, a forerunner of the cheque. The running-cash notes were easy to use and most important then. They were at first hand written and made out for odd amounts, with the actual sum deposited, but soon they were being made out for round amounts and partly printed.

The Bank of England was initiated by the "Whigs." There was a competing initiative that was anti-Whig and anti-City, the Land Bank. The plan was to issue notes on the security of land, realizing in this way also the possibility to provide loans to the Exchequer. An amount of £2.6 million was suggested. In April 1696, the Parliament passed an act allowing a National Land Bank to start. It was the same act that allowed the issuance of Exchequer bills, in case the Land bank failed, which it actually did. The Bank of England helped to make this failure happen by guaranteeing the same amount of loans to the Exchequer. The course of the war made these loans necessary and it led to a period with very poor liquidity, but the bank survived and the Land Bank disappeared (Kynaston, 2017).

4.6.3 The South Sea Company

Public finance improved with the Bank of England, but remained precarious and a broader and more robust base was looked for. Citizens would be easier tempted by investing in companies than by investing in government debt. At the end of the seventeenth century, the discounts on government tallies were between 20 and 40% (Dale, 2004). Tallies were tradeable, but the transfer was cumbersome and risky. That made it attractive, also for creditors, to look for possibilities to convert the government debt into equity. At the end of the Spanish Succession War, the situation got urgent. The establishment of the South Sea Company, in 1711, was a welcome opportunity for the "Tory"-oriented government, led by Robert Harley, to explore the possibility to convert part of the government debt. The other two big government-related companies were the Bank of England and the East India Company, both controlled by "Whigs." It was attractive for the Tories to have their own vehicle to control the government debt. The South Sea Company (see Fig. 4.3) was meant to increase the English presence in the Spanish West Indies. Its establishment was combined with an offer to owners of short-term government debt to convert their tallies to company shares. This type of debt then equalled to £9.5 mio. and the discount on tallies was about 30%, making the conversion attractive as long as the share price would remain above 70%. The commercial potential of the South Sea Company was not very clear, but sounded promising. The alternative of the offer was kept vague, giving the creditors in fact no other option than to accept. The interest due by the government on the £9.5 mio. was 6%. It was planned to be used from now on to pay the yearly dividend. The price of the shares indeed remained above 70% during the first years. The government, however, appeared not to be able to pay interest in time. Part of it was added to the debt, increasing the company's capital to more than £10 mio. in 1716. The dividend of 1715 and 1716 was paid in stock. In 1713, when the "Peace of Utrecht" ended the war, the company acquired the "Asiento," the right to supply Spain's American colonies with slaves from West Africa. The commercial results of the company on both the slave trade and the rest of its trade were rather

Fig. 4.3 The South Sea House on Bishopsgate street in London, by Thomas Bowels III, Harvard University. https://commons.wikimedia.org/wiki/File:SouthSeaHouse_Stowe%27sSurveyOfLondon_1754.PNG

mediocre. Dale gives an estimate of £20,000 per year during the period 1714–1718, being very small compared to the interest income (Dale, 2004). It did not affect the share price significantly though. It rose steadily, also due to a reduction of the market interest. In 1719 the price was about 115%. The interest due by the government to the company was also reduced, from 6 to 5% in 1718.

In 1719 the company took the initiative to convert also part of the long-term government debt, the debt due to the £1.5 mio. lottery loan of 1710. The original maturity was 32 years; there were still 23.5 years to go. The annuity on this lottery was 9%, £135,000 per year. The company offered to convert these annuities by valuing the total sum of annuities at 11.5 times the yearly sum, more than £1.5 mio., and have the owners to exchange their annuities for shares at par. Since the payment of the annuities was at arrear, this was added to the loan and to make it more attractive for the government, an extra loan of almost £800,000 was added, financed by an issue of new shares. The total loan to add in this way would be £2.5 mio. The interest on this new debt was 5%. However, only 70% of the annuities was offered for conversion, making the total loan £1.75 mio. The attractiveness of the debt-equity swap for the owners of annuities depended strongly on the price of the shares. During 1719, this price increased from (about) 115% to (about) 128%. With this price, it was certainly attractive.

In 1720, this conversion scheme was going to be applied much broader, inspired by John Law's success with the "Mississippi Company" in France (see Chap. 5). The total government debt was now about £50 mio. Some £18.3 mio. was credited to the three big companies, the Bank of England, the East India Company, and the South Sea Company. Another compartment consisted of the annuities, most of which (£13.3 mio.) had an expiry date of around 1800 and some (£1.7 mio.) with a much closer expiry date (1742). The rest (£16.5 mio.) was redeemable government stock (tallies etc.), redeemable at a year's notice. The South Sea Company offered to exchange the £31.5 mio. of debt into shares. The House of Commons insisted that rival tenders would be considered and so the Bank of England submitted its own proposal. Reacting, the South Sea Company improved her bid. Finally this complex offer of the South Sea Company, in terms of interest rates due and timing of payments, was accepted (Dale, 2004):

1. The South Sea Company was going to be prepared to convert all outstanding annuities and redeemable debts, totaling £31.5 mio.
2. The company agreed to pay 4 mio. unconditionally and a further conditional sum equal to, maximally 3.6 mio.
3. The government would credit the Company with an increase of £31.5 million both in its nominal capital and in the amount owed to it by the state if all the debts were exchanged. The basis on which debts were capitalized for this purpose was: 20 years' purchase for the long annuities, 14 years for the short and par value for the redeemables.
4. The government agreed to pay interest on the increased debt partly at 5% and partly at 4% until midsummer 1727 when interest on all the debt owed to the Company would be reduced to 4%.
5. The government could start to pay off debts subscribed into the South Sea Company from midsummer 1727, that is, the entire debt had become redeemable.
6. The government agreed to lend the Company £1 million in Exchequer Bills as an immediate source of liquidity.

The South Sea Trade itself had only very limited profit potential, so the cash to pay to the government had to come mainly from the issuance of new stock. New stock leads to a wider spreading of the dividend ("dilution"), also over the new stockholders, making the conversion less attractive to holders of government debt. This had to be made up by expectations of further stock price increases. This was easy at the time: the stock market was positively feverish. The fever was enhanced by fake news about the trade potential of the South Sea Company, by giving a too positive image of the value of the stocks, by tempting important people to buy new stock by giving them (e.g., the King and his mistresses) cheap options to do so and by restricting the fraction of down payment that had to be paid right away for stock. The actions were effective. The stock price rose from 300% at the beginning of 1620 to 1,000% halfway the year. In June £5 mio. (nominal) stocks were offered for sale at a price of £1,000 and a down payment of 10% and it was no problem at all to sell it all. In total more than 80% of the government debt of £31.5 mio. was converted.

Of course, the bubble had to burst. That lasted a bit longer because of the bursting of the Mississippi bubble earlier that year and the flight of the capital from there to the South Sea Company. But it burst before the end of the year. In October, the stock price was only £170. It infected the whole stock market. The stock prices of the South Sea Company fell 80%, but the stock prices of the Bank of England and the East India Company fell also about 50% between July and October. It was a disaster for many investors and also for the South Sea Company itself. The down payments were insufficient to pay the government the agreed amount, so it had to borrow, which was very complicated now. The subscribers to stock issues refused to pay further terms. The Company reacted by reducing ex-post the conversion prices of the stocks and the stock price of the last and most expensive issuance. But it was insufficient. Finally, the government enforced a settlement, distributing the misery over the different players. For the government itself the misery was restricted. The major part of the government debt had been converted into a debt to the South Sea Company, with conditions regarding interest and redemption being far more attractive than beforehand.

4.7 London Banking Secrets

4.7.1 Endorsing and Discounting

In medieval Italy and Spain the deposit bank was very common. They served in the first place to facilitate payment. Payment with specie could be cumbersome and dangerous. Using a bank deposit was more convenient. If the payee had an account with the same bank as the payer, it was just a matter of transferring ownership of the agreed amount. If not, the payee could get a temporary account or he could ask transfer to his own bank. If the banks had accounts with each other it was not right away necessary to transport the specie. The banker was also used as the cashier for the merchant. They could provide good coin for disbursements and check the quality of coin received. And they provided a record of the transactions that could serve as a legal proof (Kohn, 1999). The banker was generally also a moneychanger. In England this was not yet well developed in the Middle Ages. Because of the scarcity of specie, there was a royal monopoly of the trade in specie and bullion. Of course, payer and payee could settle a transaction if they both had a positive deposit with the same banker, but the bankers could not develop into a complete combination of banker and cashier. Because of this it was important to develop other ways to pay cashless. And already circulating bills of exchange and letters obligatory formed a good possibility. A merchant who received a bill or letter could use that for his payments by endorsing it and assigning it to a new payee (see Sect. 4.3.2). First only mature bills and letters, later, when the ban on usury was eased, it could be also done with immature bills and letters. The lack of specie helped to develop this practice. And it was also possible of course to issue letters and bills. This was especially attractive for banks. The weakness appeared to be an opportunity.

4.7.2 Fractional Reserve Banking

After 1640 the royal monopoly was not enforced any longer, due to the civil war and the regime shift. The Goldsmiths could now develop into more complete deposit banks. With the seizure of the mint fresh in their mind, they realized that a way to keep the deposited money safe was to let it circulate, by lending it to people who needed it. This practice was, maybe, inspired by the mid-seventeenth-century bankers in Seville, who lent most of their deposits to private entrepreneurs and commerce to avoid an attempt to seize the gold kept in the vaults of King Charles V of Spain (De Soto, 2006). The Goldsmith bankers in England were more innovative and combined it with setting up a system of transferable banknotes. By creating simultaneous property rights for borrowers and depositors, they wanted the Crown to know that there would be significant opposition in the society if it dared to do something devastating such as confiscation. This approach was a typical confidence-building plan that had two main features: "permanent indebtedness" and "transferability of depositor's right" (Kim, 2011). The scarcity of money in England helped this approach to succeed. By developing this system, Goldsmiths bankers have earned the title of inventor of fractional banking more than anyone else (Selgin, 2012).

Initially, the Goldsmiths received a commission in return for the valuables, money, and gold they kept. While giving various promissory notes and receipts in return for the gold entrusted to them, they also provided loans to those in need. Meanwhile, the Goldsmiths made a significant discovery. If depositors did not lose their trust in them, they were in no hurry to ask their money back, and they preferred to shop using banker's notes they bought from Goldsmiths. This situation inspired them to give a significant portion of the money they collected as a loan. This practice accelerated deposit and loan services. Since the Goldsmiths, British banking has been based on permanent debt arising from its deposits. The depositor does his shopping with the banknotes he receives in return for his deposits, without touching his money in the bank. He will not demand his principal as long as the circulation continues. Thus, the bank will remain in debt to the people permanently. The new deposits that are constantly entering the system will relieve the banker's hand against those who occasionally withdraw their money. Based on the trust factor, the bank will convert this money into capital after making the debt permanent. From the bank's perspective, the depositors' money will be recorded in the balance sheet as foreign capital. Like its own money, the bank will lend it to third parties in need, and thus the rights of the depositors will be transferred to the bank. The promissory notes received in return for these loans will also be assets of the bank. Thus, the bank transformed the deposits it collected from the public into assets through a banking operation. For the money that is deposited with no future maturity date, it is always possible for the depositor to request his money from the bank. It is known that Goldsmiths kept 10–66% of their deposits as a reserve for this reason (Kim, 2011). While the Goldsmith approach was initially poorly regulated, it gradually developed into a business culture that permeated the upper and middle classes in England, and the element of trust was at the heart of it (Kim, 2011). Beyond the creation of a local payment system based on transferable deposits and notes backed only by fractional coin reserves, London's Goldsmiths provided the "critical background" for Britain's financial revolution through the financial innovations they developed (Quinn, 2001).

4.7.3 Communication and Market Intelligence

Undoubtedly, the Goldsmiths understood the importance of communication and market intelligence. London-based bankers used a network of merchants and bankers evolving around Lombard Street which could draw on the business expertise of various nations and religions. Thanks to this network, they had the ability to arbitrage. This business network was far more extensive than the kinship groups, religious affiliations, or guilds on which medieval banking depended. Relations were more institutional than in the Medici period now, making the ties much more secure. The effectiveness of the network varied with the nature of the legal systems of the various nations. While the autocratic tendencies of France diminished the credibility of its representatives, the Dutch and British merchants' adherence to international commercial practices allowed them to conduct overseas banking operations (Neal & Quinn, 2001). A complex problem of Goldsmiths was on agency relations in foreign ports with the provision of international services. A bank like the Amsterdam Bank of Exchange that did currency exchange provided significant advantages to payments in the Netherlands. This reduced costs, as well as the risk of non-payment (Neal & Quinn, 2001).

London-based bankers successfully specialized in generating international finance, with information sources reaching virtually every point in Northwest Europe. The most significant players of this network were traders. The information that could be obtained from them was diverse and highly strategic. Merchants also took advantage of the services of bankers in exchange for the information they had, to benefit effectively from the banks' facilities. There was not a single institution in London to coordinate the information required for the developing financial system. Still, bankers and traders who knew each other used this information effectively by sharing it. In this way, an important communication network was established as early as 1670. When the Bank of England was founded in 1694, the London market had more knowledge and skills to run the international financing and payments system than its Dutch counterpart (Neal & Quinn, 2001). Although no bank in London was a dominant force in the securities market, they exchanged physical securities and shared market information at various frequented social venues. The London Stock Exchange and Lloyds Insurance Exchange had meanwhile started their business activities in London coffee houses as a social space.

4.7.4 Bank of England

An important driver of the innovations regarding the English financial system during the last decade of the seventeenth and the first of the eighteenth century was the almost uncontrollable government debt, mainly due to the two subsequent wars with France, the "Nine Years War" (1688–1697) and the "War of the Spanish Succession" (1701–1714). The issuance of loans and lotteries was expensive for the government, and insufficient. Shortages were covered by the issuance of tallies and short-term loans. The corresponding certificates were not very popular and were offered at a discount to the Goldsmiths; people preferred Goldsmith banknotes above the government tallies and certificates, implying that the profit of creating extra money was for the Goldsmiths. An important step in improving this situation was the establishment of the Bank of England. The establishment of the Bank of England as a private organization closely related to the government helped directly and indirectly in softening the pressure of the government debt. The money of the private investors in the Bank could be lent to the government and the Bank relieved the shortage of money by issuing bank notes. Of course, it also applied fractional reserve banking. The reserve fraction was even so small that contemporaries were surprised that the bank did not fail right away. Richards (1958) writes: "Its establishment under such extraordinary financial conditions was, as that able economist of the day, Daniel Defoe, has truly stated, a 'particular glory' to the English nation."

The Bank survived. There was broad interest to participate in the capital required, already from the start and later, the New East India Company and the Malt lottery participated also for £2 and £1 million. They performed all kind of banking functions and were soon central in managing the government debt. The issuance of banknotes (mainly running-cash notes) started right away and got concentrated more and more in the Bank. In the second half of the eighteenth century, the bank began to issue fixed-denominated notes (Bank of England, 1969). As of the nineteenth century, the Bank of England had largely become a modern central bank. The bank was functioning as a "commitment instrument" on Crown obligations and guaranteed the government to pay off its debts reliably. In addition, while creating transparent regulations for all financial transactions, banknotes were readily accepted across the country with the confidence it made in the market. The gold system was adopted in Britain in 1844. By creating a ratio between the bank's gold reserves and the banknotes it could issue, it took the monopoly of issuing banknotes on behalf of England. As a result, the Bank of England provided the capital and reputation as a vanguard institution of the increasingly institutionalized British democracy. It enabled England to become the greatest world power for long. As a side note, until 1930, other banks with concessions would continue to issue banknotes, as they do in some parts of the United Kingdom (Scotland and Northern Ireland) even up until the present day. But they play a very limited role, because they are required to have the same amount of reserves in Bank of England notes or gold ("Banknotes of the pound sterling").

4.7.5 Conversion of Government Debt into Company Shares

The stock exchange was well developed. The trade in stocks was relatively easy and had a broad participation under the public. That made it attractive for the government to transfer its debt to government dependent joint-stock companies, the Bank of England, the (Old and New) East India Company, and later the South Sea Company. The decreasing market interest of the beginning of the eighteenth century made it necessary to restructure the government debt anyway. The final move in organizing the government debt was the conversion to South Sea company stock. The bursting of the bubble did not interfere with the success of this conversion. It was not like in France where the government was almost completely included in the Mississippi company. In England, the government was able to correct the market and to assign a more or less balanced distribution of the losses over the various players.

4.8 Conclusion

In the 1970s, new history was made in Lombard Street. After the oil crises, Arab and Soviet oil producers began depositing their revenues from dollar-denominated oil sales with London banks. This was the unofficial confirmation of London being the most important financial center in the world. It was announced that the floating interest rate, known as the London Interbank Rate (Libor) formed by hundreds of banks in the London money market, would be used as the reference rate of the so-called Eurodollar market (see also Chap. 10). International market players would focus on this rate, which could change at any time of the day. The story of England's becoming such an important financial center in the seventeenth century is exciting and full of lessons on democracy. Undoubtedly, the British Parliament and the struggle of the bourgeoisie against absolute monarchy played a vital role in this development.

The events that the Kings of England seized the bankers' money or stopped them from paying their debts in 1640 and 1672, extending into the shrewd government debt-equity swap in 1720, combined with the economic activity of the English society that started with geographical discoveries, had significant consequences. While the Parliament and later the Bank of England sought for a solution to the simultaneous expectations of the merchants, bankers and rapidly urbanizing people who wanted a new political structure for the country, England from an absolute monarchy to an island of increasing democracy. One of the important actors of these developments were the Goldsmith bankers, predecessors of big banks such as Lloyds and Barclays, who contributed to economic growth by creating a financial pillar of this transformation with the banking methods they developed. The Goldsmiths benefited from the economic opportunities with the communication networks they established in Europe of that day and protected themselves against the risks of the market. Beyond this, establishing a system based on trust created a new culture and understanding in society and strengthened their resources.

Goldsmiths were highly flexible and pragmatic people. Many instruments developed by them under the conditions of their era are still used in today's banking. The discounting of debt securities and the issuance of banknotes were primarily inventions of Goldsmith bankers. The Bank of England was established based on economic conditions and experiences created by the bankers. It became a reputable institution imitated by central banks worldwide. Above all, the most important legacy left by the Goldsmith bankers to human history is the "Fractional Reserve System." This system forms the basis of modern banking. Currently, the money creation mechanism of countries has been connected to the loans given by the banking system. As a result, the shadows of the bankers of Lombard Street do not just roam today only in London or in Great Britain, but also in the corridors of the European Central Bank, the U.S. Federal Reserve System, the IMF, the World Bank, and virtually all banks around the globe.

References

Aylmer, G. E. (2008). Backwell, Edward. In L Stephen, & S. Lee (Eds.), *The Oxford dictionary of national biography*, Oxford University Press.

Bagehot, W. (1873). *Lombard street: A description of the money market* (1st ed.). Scribner, Armstrong & Co.

Bank of England. (1969). *The Bank of England note: A short history*. https://www.bankofengland.co.uk/-/media/boe/files/quarterly-bulletin/1969/the-boe-note-a-short-history.pdf?la=en&hash=1B8B077EB3D127B2CF2D3D5F020F6199AD97C5B8

BBC. (n.d.). *Reasons for coming to England—Jewish communities and their expulsion from England in 1290—OCR B—GCSE history revision*. BBC Bitesize. https://www.bbc.co.uk/bitesize/guides/zpbs7hv/revision/1

Burnet, G. (1979). *History of his own time*. Everyman's Library.

Charles I. (n.d.). Charles I. *Wikipedia*. https://en.wikipedia.org/wiki/Charles_I_of_England

Clapham, J. (1944). *Bank of England: A history. Vol. 1: 1694–1797*. Cambridge University Press.

Company of Merchant Adventurers. (n.d.). Company of Merchant Adventurers of London. *Wikipedia*. https://en.wikipedia.org/wiki/Company_of_Merchant_Adventurers_of_London

Dale, R. (2004). *The first crash: Lessons from the South Sea Bubble*. Princeton University Press.

Davies, N. (1999). *The isles: A history*. Oxford University Press.

De Cantillon, P. (1755). *Essai Sur la Nature du Commerce en Général (Essay on the Nature of Trade in General)*. Fletcher Gyles.

De Soto, J. H. (2006). *Money, bank credit, and economic cycles*. Ludwig Von Mises Institute.

English Civil War. (n.d.). English Civil War. *Wikipedia*. https://en.wikipedia.org/wiki/English_Civil_War

Galais-Hamonno, G., & Rietsch, C. (2013). Learning by doing: The failure of the 1697 Malt Lottery loan. *Financial History Review, 20*, 259–277. https://doi.org/10.1017/S0968565013000127

Gordin, A. (2017). *From goldsmiths to bankers*. Fluent In Foreign Business. https://fluentinforeign.wordpress.com/2017/06/24/early-history-of-english-merchant-banking/amp/

Graham, A. (2019). Credit confidence and the circulation of exchequer bills in the early financial revolution. *Financial History Review, 26*, 63–80. https://doi.org/10.1017/S0968565018000161

Guy, J. (2019). *Gresham's law*. Profile Books.

Henderson, T. F. (1885). Backwell, Edward. In L. Stephen, & S. Lee (Eds.), *Dictionary of national biography*. Smith, Elder & Co.

James II of England. (n.d.). James II of England. *Wikipedia.* https://en.wikipedia.org/wiki/James_II_of_England
James VI and I. (n.d.). James VI and I. *Wikipedia.* https://en.wikipedia.org/wiki/James_VI_and_I
Kim, J. (2011). How modern banking originated: The London goldsmith-bankers' institutionalisation of trust. *Business History, 53*(6), 939–959. https://doi.org/10.1080/00076791.2011.578132
Kleer, R. A. (2015). A new species of money: British exchequer bills, 1701–1711. *Financial History Review* (Cambridge University Press), *22*(2), 179–203. https://doi.org/10.1017/S0968565015000153
Kohn, M. (1999). *Bills of exchange and the money market to 1600.* Dartmouth College, Department of Economics Working Paper (99-04). https://bpb-us-e1.wpmucdn.com/sites.dartmouth.edu/dist/6/1163/files/2017/03/99-04.pdf
Kynaston, D. (2017). *Till time's last sand; A history of the Bank of England, 1694–2013.* Bloomsbury Publishing.
List of Wars. (n.d.). List of wars involving England. *Wikipedia.* https://en.wikipedia.org/wiki/List_of_wars_involving_England#17th_century
Mary, Queen of Scots. (n.d.). Mary, Queen of Scots. *Wikipedia.* https://en.wikipedia.org/wiki/Mary,_Queen_of_Scots
McMullen Rigg, J. (1898). Somers, John. In L. Stephen, & S. Lee (Eds.), *Dictionary of national biography* (Vol. 53). https://en.wikisource.org/wiki/Dictionary_of_National_Biography
Milevsky, M. A. (2017). *The day the King Defaulted.* Springer International Publishing.
Milevsky, M. A. (2015). *King William's tontine.* Cambridge University Press.
Munro, J. H. (2002). *The medieval origins of the 'Financial Revolution': Usury, rentes and negotiability.* MPRA Paper 10925. https://mpra.ub.uni-muenchen.de/10925/
Murphy, A. E. (2005). Lotteries in the 1690s: Investment or gamble. *Financial History Review, 12*(2), 227–246.
Neal, L., & Quinn, S. (2001). Networks of information, markets, and institutions in the rise of London as a financial centre, 1660–1720. *Financial History Review, 8*(1), 7–26.
Parliament of England. (n.d.). Parliament of England. *Wikipedia.* https://en.wikipedia.org/wiki/Parliament_of_England
Personal Rule. (n.d.). Personal Rule. *Wikipedia.* https://en.wikipedia.org/wiki/Personal_Rule
Quinn, S. (2001). The glorious revolution's effect on English private finances: A microhistory, 1680–1705. *The Journal of Economic History, 61*(3), 593–615. https://doi.org/10.1017/S0022050701030017
Richards, R. D. (1958). *The early history of banking in England.* Routledge (The first edition is from 1929. We use a reprint by Routledge of the 1958 edition).
Richards, R. D. (1928). A pre-bank of England English banker—Edward Backwell. *The Economic Journal, 38*(Supplement 1), 335–355. https://doi.org/10.1093/ej/38.Supplement_1.356
Roseveare, H. G. (2019). *Charles II | Biography, accomplishments, & facts.* Encyclopaedia Britannica. https://www.britannica.com/biography/Charles-II-king-of-Great-Britain-and-Ireland
Selgin, G. (2012). Those dishonest goldsmiths. *financial. History Review, 19*(3), 269–288. https://doi.org/10.1017/s0968565012000169
Sterling. (n.d.). Sterling. *Wikipedia.* https://en.wikipedia.org/wiki/Banknotes_of_the_pound_sterling
The National Archives. (n.d.). *Land inheritance in the court of wards and liveries.* https://www.nationalarchives.gov.uk/help-with-your-research/research-guides/land-inheritance-court-of-wards-liveries-1540-1645/
Wennerlind, C. (2011). *Casualties of credit: The English financial revolution, 1620–1720.* Harvard University Press.
William III of England. (n.d.). William III of England. *Wikipedia.* https://en.wikipedia.org/wiki/William_III_of_England
Wilson, C. (1984). *England's apprenticeship* 1603–1763 (2nd ed.). Longman.

Chapter 5
John Law: The Lord of Paper Money (Late Seventeenth and Early Eighteenth Centuries)

5.1 Introduction

It was misty in the early morning of April 9, 1694, as often in London. Dawn had just broken; the sunlight had not fully illuminated the city. Nature had just begun to awaken on Southampton Square (now Bloomsbury Square), surrounded on three sides by the big houses of the wealthy and adorned with lush green meadows filled with flowers and fruit trees. Some of the trees had blossomed, and some had begun to bud. As it was secluded and far from the city's crowds, this square, where lovers usually encountered, was tranquil that morning. Only the chirping of starlings flying among the branches could be heard. The birds suddenly took off with a hum, frightened by the clanking of swords ringing in the square. Two English gentlemen were dueling with their long, slender swords in a secluded corner of the park while four men in bowler hats and long jackets watched them. The duel would not last long; the more athletic one, John Law, would kill his opponent, Edward Wilson, by wounding him with a sword blow. The *Greenwich Hospital News Lettere* writes the next morning: *Yesterday morning, one Mr. Wilson, the "mirror" of the town, having lived for five years past at the rate of £4,000 or £5,000 per annum, without either estate or visible way of getting a penny or running in any man's debt, was killed by one Mr. Laws, a Scotchman, upon a slight quarrel* (Murphy, 1997). Both men were "beau's," nicknamed Beau Law and Beau Wilson. Mary Astell, a protofeminist of that time, characterized a beau as "*one that has more learning in his heels than his head, which is better covered than filled. His tailor and his barber are his caninet council, to whom he is more beholding for what he is, than to his maker.*" Some biographers of John Law state that he had fought for Elizabeth Villiers, one of the most charming women of the time, who had been humiliated by Wilson. Elizabeth Villiers was the official mistress of William III, who led the "Magnificent Revolution" in England in 1689 and turned the country's direction toward democracy. She had a little fling with Edward Wilson and came to John Law to protect her shattered reputation. This fling could explain the rich pattern of living of Wilson, a man with hardly any income.

M. B. Karan et al., *A History of Banks*, Contributions to Economics,
https://doi.org/10.1007/978-3-031-62297-7_5

But Murphy gives a rather convincing alternative explanation: Maybe Wilson had a fling with William III instead, and was the duel related to that somehow? That could also clarify some of the further developments around the imprisonment of John Law and his escape. We have to be careful here; however, there was also a lot of gossip about William III's sexual tendencies, especially in England (Noordam, 1995).

All of Law's life would change now. John Law (1671–1729) is one of the most exciting figures in the history of European finance. Born in Scotland, the son of a Goldsmith banker, Law had extreme ups and downs and left an essential mark behind him with the storms he created in the history of the world economy (Fig. 5.1).

Unlike many of the events described in other parts of our book, John Law's life is not a success story but a collapse from which many lessons can be learned. While this chapter focuses on a single character, it is generally about France in the first decades of the eighteenth century. The events in France were so crucial that they significantly affected Europe's newly developing banking and financial system and paved the way for the French Revolution of 1789. This collapse was neither the first nor the last, but perhaps the most striking of all the past and future financial crises.

Fig. 5.1 John Law (1671–1729). https://commons.wikimedia.org/wiki/File:John_LAW.jpg

5.2 John Law's Youth and Early Life

John Law was born into a Scottish family of goldsmiths. This profession was highly lucrative at the time and incurred a high position in society. Just like in London, the goldsmiths in Edinburgh were also bankers. William Law, the father of John, was one of the important goldsmiths in Edinburgh. He made a fortune and bought Lauriston Castle, near Edinburgh. After that, they were entitled to call themselves Law of Lauriston. Father William had lost his first wife (Violet Cleghorne, a goldsmith daughter) early, and John Law was born to his second wife, Jean Campbell, in 1671. The family had 12 children, but only 4 survived under the day's circumstances. John was the eldest remaining son. His father cared about his sons' education and sent John to Edinburgh High School. John was a smart cookie, quite intelligent, and especially good with numbers; he studied religion, mathematics, Latin, and possibly modern languages. Father William would not see the further development of his son; he died in Paris after an operation to have a stone removed from his bladder. John was only 12 years old then, and it was a terrible blow to the family (Buchan, 2018).

His mother was a smart woman; she took over the family business. Being the eldest son, John Law also inherited the castle of Lauriston, according to the laws of the day. After his father's death, John Law continued his education and was raised like a gentleman, taking also fencing and tennis lessons. However, he was somewhat adventurous and interested in women and gambling. He did not want to attend university, so he tried to seek his fortune in London. With a population of 750,000 at the time, London was a fascinating place for a young man. John quickly adjusted to London life. He frequented stylish pubs and spent his money on gambling and women with the excitement of youth. When the year 1692 came, he was penniless and in significant debt. His mother came to his aid; she bought the castle of Lauriston from him. Interestingly, this event did not make him quit gambling but instead caused him to interpret gambling more scientifically, focusing on reducing the probability of loss. He began researching mathematics and probability theory. From now on, John Law would approach gambling more professionally; at least, he made a living from gambling. Maybe during this time, he learned that it was better to have the role of the bank in gambling, offering others bets devised by himself (Wiston-Glynn, 2022).

During these years, while gambling and wandering in luxury clubs, John Law met Edward "Beau" Wilson and Elizabeth Villiers, the mistress of King William III. Somehow, it is not quite clear how, it led to a conflict of Law with Wilson and eventually to this confrontation on Southampton Square and the death of Wilson. Dueling was forbidden, and Law was arrested, sentenced to death, and thrown into the then-notorious Newgate prison. Relatives of Law requested a pardon from the king, who was inclined to give that. But the deceased Edward Wilson had strong supporters, and his brother, Robert Wilson, countered this pardon in the Court of the King's Bench by appealing for murder. Law was removed from Newgate and moved to the King's Bench prison in Southwark (June 23), awaiting this appeal. Law, first, awaited the appeal with some confidence. Still, when this lasted too long, he escaped in January 1695, probably with government officials' help, maybe with King William's support (Murphy, 1997).

It is known that John Law fled from England to the Netherlands and then to France, the Netherlands again, Scotland, and Italy. But his precise traveling is unknown. His contemporary biographers agree that he earned sufficient money by gambling to realize a luxurious pattern of living. See the book by Gray, "The Memoirs Life and Character of the Great Mr. Law and His Brother at Paris" (1721), and Mammont Du Hautchamp's "Histoire du systeme des finances en 1719 et 1720" (1739). Gray describes how Law started to build a gambling fortune by finding "cullies enough to pick up a great deal of money from," and Du Hautchamp reported that Law was expelled from Paris ... because he knew too much about the game he introduced into the capital. Law was always the "banker" in gambling, devising the game's rules. A very simple one was described in the following quote: "He is always happy when gambling and each day proposes different games. He offered 10,000 sequins to any who could throw six times a six in a row, but each time they fail to do so, they give him a sequin" (Murphy, 1997). No wonder he got rich with such games.

On June 19, 1702, Law was granted a passport to leave France with two Scottish servants and a lady, Catherine Sennior, and her valet. This is Catherine Knollys, married to a Mr. Seigneur, of whom we don't know much further. Catherine Knollys and John Law formed a couple. James Buchan suggests that John Law and Mr. Seigneur are the same (Buchan, 2018). That would explain why no traces can be found of Law during the last years of the seventeenth century. The couple had two children, William, born in The Hague in 1705 or 1706, and Mary Catherine, born in Genoa in 1710. Catherine was a daughter of Nicolas, the third Earl of Banbury, distant family of Anna Boleyn, one of the wives of Henry VIII and the mother of Queen Elizabeth I.

5.3 John Law, the Activistic Economist: Scotland, the Netherlands, Genoa, Turin

During his travels, Law got interested in money and banking. In 1702, Law and Catherine settled in The Hague, in The Netherlands. The Netherlands was the wealthiest country then and quite strong in trade and finance. Dutch trade, scientific developments, art, and overseas colonization were among the most important in Europe. The Amsterdam Bank of Exchange was established in 1609 as a clearing bank and began to issue bank money in exchange for gold coins, and the activities of the Amsterdam Stock Exchange and the East India Company were dazzling at that time. It may be assumed that Law also got acquainted with the many possibilities to speculate there, the options trade and "short selling" (of what you do not own yet). Both could be used to hedge real transactions but were mainly used to speculate. In contrast, Scotland was a poor, rural, agricultural society with a population of 1.3 million. There was also famine, economic distress, and inflation during this period. People were migrating to the New World.

While John Law made good money with gambling and speculation, he also started working on financial theories. He was now confident about his possibilities to play an essential role in the European financial world. In 1704, he was back in Scotland, still independent then but with the same king as England had. There, he petitioned Queen Anne for pardon for the death of Wilson and for breaking from prison (Buchan, 2018). The request was rejected, however. Queen Anne detested dueling, and the relationship between England and Scotland was deteriorating during that time. But Law stayed in Scotland to be able to submit his proposals for financial reform to the Scottish Parliament. He published an essay on the Scottish situation titled "Money and Trade Considered; with a Proposal for Supplying the Nation with Money." It was a proposal to establish a Land Bank. It was printed and published by his aunt, Agnes Campbell. He wrote an essay in the same spirit a year earlier but directed more to the English situation: "Essay on a Land Bank." There is some uncertainty about the author of this pamphlet because it was unsigned, but Murphy had good reasons to ascribe it to John Law (Murphy, 1997). There were more land bank proposals around that time, and in England, it was tried to establish one in 1696/97, with the commitment of the Parliament, but it failed. In the "Essay ..." Law stresses that land is more suitable a basis for money than silver, especially because of the fluctuations in the availability of silver. He argues that land is relatively stable in value and that it also possesses "the other qualities needful in money: that it is (1) durable, (2) divisible, (3) capable of delivery and (4) of a stamp to denote the value." And he proposes, therefore, to establish a Land Mint, issuing 1,000 shares, each for £1,000. This Land Mint could then coin notes and sell these for land. The value of the coins keeps up with the value of the land (Murphy, 1997).

Law's "Money and Trade" focuses on the Scottish situation and is broader than the essay. He enlarged it with showing that the economy needed more money to create trade and employment. In doing this, he touched on a broad set of interrelated economic concepts like supply and demand analysis, value theory, balance of trade, inflation, etcetera, and many of his contributions were fresh and useful (Murphy, 1997). In the last chapters, he argues that a controlled money increase was possible with such a land bank. He writes: *"Since it is very practicable to make land money, it would be contrary to reason to limit the industry of people by making it depend on a species that is not in our power, but in the power of our enemies; when we have a species of our own every way more qualified."* In his opinion, Scottish poverty resulted from a poor administration, unable to create sufficient money due to the focus on species.

His proposal came at a difficult time for the Scots. Scotland was poor around that time, and unemployment was high. Many pamphletists blamed the lack of money. So, in that respect, John Law was not the only prophet. The failure of the Darien company had aggravated the situation. The official name of the Darien company was "The Company of Scotland trading to Africa and the Indies." It was established in 1695 and had, within Scotland, the exclusive trading rights to Africa and the Indies, more or less comparable to its much larger counterpart, the English East India Company. The directors of this company were afraid of competition and made it impossible for English people to invest in their Scottish counterparts. That complicated the start of the Darien company and made a more significant part of the investment come from Scotland, further reducing the amount of money available there. In 1698, the Darien company started with an expedition to Darien in Panama. One of the leaders was William Paterson, one of the founders of the Bank of England. They established a colony in Darien and called it Caledonia (the Latin name for Scotland used in the Roman Empire). Yet, after 8 months, they had to abandon it. Of the 1200 colonists, there were only 250 survivors, including Paterson. In between, a second expedition left Scotland, but this one was even less successful. The Darien failure led to a sharper money shortage in Scotland and liquidity problems for the Bank of Scotland (Prebble, 1969). The Bank of Scotland was established in 1695, right after the establishment of the Bank of England. The liquidity problems led to a run on the bank in the last months of 1704 and then to the suspension of the payments in December (Buchan, 2018).

No wonder the Parliament of Scotland welcomed serious proposals for another monetary system and more money. John Law had the handicap of being known as a duellist and gambler. Still, soon, he got acquainted with the Duke of Argyll, the High Commissioner of Queen Anne to the Scottish Parliament, to help prepare the union of Scotland with England. Law could be very convincing, and it became clear that he was to be taken seriously in this kind of money affairs. A competing proposal, also taken seriously by the Parliament, was that of Dr. Chamberlen. Chamberlen was a physician but also actively writing about and initiating banks, like his father and brother. In 1665, he wrote a proposal for a Lombard bank, a kind of pawn shop, and from 1689 on, he was active in trying to create support for land banks in England, Ireland, and Scotland. John Law was eager and devoted an entire chapter on "Money and Trade" to Chamberlen's proposals, explaining why his proposals were better. He supported his position by publishing a flyer with his proposal's most important points, distributing it to influential officials, and making it available in coffee houses. It summarized the proposal in the following way (Murphy, 1997):

"Proposal for supplying the nation with money.

(1) *That commissioners be appointed with power to coin notes, and to give them out upon land securities.*
(2) *That these notes be received in payments.*
(3) *That a committee be appointed to inspect the management.*
(4) *That any person who has such notes may have these securities assigned to them upon paying in the value to the commission.*
(5) *That the revenue of the Commission, over what pays the charges, and what part the Parliament think needful to make good any losses may happen to the Commission, be applied by way of drawback, for incouraging the export and manufacture of the Nation.*
(6) *That the gold and silver be reformed to the English standard."*

In "Money and Trade...", with respect to point (1), Law distinguishes three ways to issue (land) notes: (a) lend notes on land security; (b) mortgage the land for a certain period, and give a proportional amount of notes; and (c) sell the land. Concerning point (2) he stresses that the notes should be used in payments. Point (3) shows that the governance of the organization is taken seriously. Point (4) states that the notes can be turned in again, and the security canceled or the sale reversed. In point (5), he suggests that Commission revenues should be used to subsidize exports. Point (6) refers to the chaotic exchange value of Scotland's silver species at the time.

The Parliament treated the proposals in July 1705. It led to fierce debates, but the final decision was that organizing credit in this way was not the role of the government. It finished the role of Law in Scotland. The unification of Scotland and England was nearing, and then Law would no longer be safe in Scotland. So, he left for Europe in late 1705 or early 1706 (Buchan, 2018), looking for other possibilities to implement his ideas.

Together with Catherine, he went to the Netherlands, where their son William was born (1705/6), and then, via a stay in Paris, to Genoa. It was clear from the proposals to Scotland already that John Law tended to treat a country as a company. Genoa was, therefore, an interesting city because of the Casa di San Giorgio (Bank of St. George). Most of the state revenues went through this company. It acted as a buffer for the state balance of payments, like the tax farmers of Charles I and II in England. Of course, it was against an attractive interest to the owners. Law was very enthusiastic about the bank and called it "the best governed in Italy" (Buchan, 2018). The Casa di San Giorgio also operated a real bank, and Law had an account there. Through this account, it is possible to follow Law's economic activities, at least to get an idea. Because of the Spanish Succession War, the army of England was in Spain and was sourced from Genoa then. Law was probably involved in organizing and financing the supplies. He deposited and withdrew large sums of money around that time. At the end of 1710, he had a balance of more than 65,000 lire. To grasp the sum, it helps to know that a laborer earned one or two lire a day. His depositors were mainly army contractors. It is quite possible, of course, that he also continued gambling. Genoa was known for it.

Around that time, England got tired of the war, and the Law family decided to go back to The Netherlands; there, the turbulence of the war and the accompanying financial problems continued, hence the opportunities for experts in finance. The family left in May 1712. It may have been attractive for them to go via Turin. Turin was then the capital of Savoy, an independent Duchess and ally of England in the war against Spain. So, it also suffered financial problems. Law had already corresponded extensively with Duke Viktor Amadeus II about possibilities to deal with these problems. He was rather impressed by the Bank of England's performances and advised establishing a Bank of Turin along the same lines. Similar, of course, to the principles of the Bank of St. George in Genoa. From now on, he dropped the Land Bank principle and switched to other assets backing the bank notes, government liabilities, for instance, instead of land. He was not afraid of changing his convictions and was just as convincing in explaining and defending the new one as he was in explaining and defending the previous one. However, Victor Amadeus expected the war to finish soon and judged it was better to await that instead of hurrying into new financial adventures. Later, when Victor Amadeus became also king of Sicily due to the peace agreement of Utrecht in 1713, they had contact again about the possibility of straightening the financial complexities in Sicily (Buchan, 2018).

In The Netherlands, the family bought a rather expensive house in The Hague. It fitted to show success. The Netherlands was severely in debt then, and Law's gambling expertise would turn out to be profitable. Holland's debt service exceeded the ordinary tax income, the normal credit instruments appeared to be insufficient, and it tried lottery bonds instead, hoping that this would make them more attractive (De Vries & Woude, 1997). In July 1712, the Council of State issued a lottery loan of 17,500 tickets at 200 guilders each. Later, it was increased to 30,000 tickets. The ratio of prizes to blanks was fixed at about one to seven (Buchan, 2018). The lottery bond was attractive, and Law bought for himself and his friends. Since there was more demand than could be facilitated, maybe also due to the growing expectations of a soon peace, there was a lively secondary market with many possibilities to speculate, and Law did. But he liked to play it grand and published an ad in the Gazette d'Amsterdam with the offer to insure the ticketholders for not having a prize. Ticketholders could choose between different options. One option was to insure a set of 10 tickets for not containing a prize. The insurance cost was 100 guilders; if there were no prize, the reward would be 300 guilders. Another option was to buy the prize chance of a ticket for 40 guilders per ticket. In his book on probability, the Dutch mathematician Nicolaas Struyck refers to the first option and calculates that the expected profit was more than 20% (Struyck, 1716). It depended only on the probability of winning, not on the price size. The probability of no price was equal to p^{10}, with p the probability of no price for a single ticket; in this case, about 7/8. The second option's profitability depended on the size of the prices. The total prize sum was equal to 1.83 million guilders, a fraction of 1.83/6 of the total sum of the tickets. That was more than 30%, while 40 guilders for a ticket of 200 guilders was only 20%. So, this was another very profitable action for Law.

The peace treaties of Utrecht were signed in April 1713. This made it possible for Law to settle in France without interfering with the possibility to get a pardon in England for his duel and escape. He knew the difficult financial situation of France. A couple of years earlier, he sent already two proposals to Chamillard, the controller general of France, to improve the situation by establishing a Land Bank, more or less along the same lines as the earlier proposal to Scotland. The proposals got ample attention but did not lead to further actions. But now, the peace made the situation different. Law left The Hague in June to go to Paris (Buchan, 2018).

5.4 The Financial Problems of France at the Beginning of the Eighteenth Century

From 1688 until 1714, France was almost continuously involved in a war with the "Grand Alliance," headed by England and The Dutch Republic. The war was fought in Italy, Germany, Spain, The Netherlands, at sea and in the colonies and was very costly. It wrecked the finances of Louis XIV during the last decades of his reign and had a huge impact on the performance of his troops. For the costs of the war, Rowlands

(2012) refers to estimates of Francois Veron de Forbonnais, a French historian of the mid-eighteenth century. According to these estimates, the yearly costs for the war on land only, so excluding those on the navy, varied between 80 and 150 million livres, while the average royal income was only about 100 million livres. The deficits had to be borrowed. The organizations involved with taxation were also most important in organizing the short-time borrowing, the fisco-financiers. The combination of heavy borrowing with an inefficient and untransparent way of taxation led to increasing difficulties.

The main direct tax was the "taille," levied on individuals. There were some related taxes, organized in the same way, but for sake of easiness we speak of the taille only. The taille was organized per fiscal province (Géneralité). The total amount demanded each year was determined by the central government, then divided over the different provinces and per province over the different parishes. The actual collection was done within the parishes, then transferred to district receivers and then to the receiver general of the fiscal province. The posts of receivers general were venal offices, worth from 200 thousand to 1.5 million livres. The holders of such a post received gages of about 5% of the investment in the post, and to cover the costs of the administration, they were allowed to withdraw about 3% of the taxes received (Rowlands, 2012). The district receivers general were contracted by the receivers general to pay each month a certain amount. It was important to smooth the fluctuations in the tax reception. If necessary, the district receivers could borrow or they could issue promissory notes. If the total of payments by the district receivers were insufficient, the receiver general had to make advances. Of course, in case the total of payments by the district receivers was more than immediately necessary, the receivers general could use this for their own profit. The whole organization was looked upon by the royal intendant but its management was done by the receivers general. The royal intendent did not have much direct influence and it was easy to abuse the system. For instance, the district receivers could claim that local tax payments were insufficient, that they had to borrow therefore, to satisfy the contractual monthly payments, and ask the controller general for remittance of the costs of borrowing. The accounting procedures were not very transparent and there were many different institutions, all with some independence to solve their own financial problems. There was a secondary market for the promissory notes issued by all these institutions. Because of the poor state of government finance in general, the promissory notes were traded at substantial discounts and government institutes were also active on this market. The district receivers could buy promissory notes of the receivers general at a discount and use these to settle the payments to the receivers general.

The yield of the taille was about 40 million livres during the last seventeenth-century decade. It decreased during the next decade. To compensate, a new tax, the "capitation," was introduced, a poll tax. People were divided over 22 classes, with many more subclasses and had to pay a tax that just depended on their wealth—not a simple system either. Toward the end of the Spanish Succession War, yet another tax was added, the "dixieme": a 10% tax on all revenues. But the total of direct taxes did not increase much.

The indirect taxes consisted of excises on commodities (the "gabelle"), taxes on tobacco, wines and spirits, internal and external customs and tax on notarial acts and other formal registrations. This taxation was contracted to a group of tax farmers, from 1691 on acting as an association, the "ferme générale." There were 40 associates, each paying 450,000 livres for a 7 year contract. They had to organize the taxation and were due to deliver the contracted amount per year. They were allowed to keep 2.5% of the tax income. For the 1691 contract, the contracted sum was 61 million livres (Rowlands, 2012). Unfortunately, this was too high and the controller general had to accept that the difference was to be covered by the King. After 5 years, the cumulative shortage was 17 million livres. This corroded the whole system of a fixed tax income for the King. In subsequent years, the system further deteriorated, lacking a simple and transparent risk coverage rule.

The poor organization of the taxation also spoiled the short-time borrowing. Generally, the receivers and the tax farmers had to pay the tax they were going to receive in advance to the King. If the tax reception was delayed and/or was less than planned, they had to borrow by issuing promissory notes. The interest paid by the King on the advances could also be used to pay interest on the promissory notes or, rather, to offer the notes at a discount.

The tax farmers organized a system through "caisse emprunts." People could use their superfluous cash to give medium-term credit to the Caisse by buying "billets de ferme." The interest was attractive, 8%. Because of the fundamental problems with tax reception, the acquittal of the credits was far from perfect and the interest was not always paid in time. Therefore, the billets could only be traded at large discounts. Because of the underlying tax collection problems, the Caisse developed into a long-term savings bank in the first decade of the eighteenth century. Return of the deposited sum was very uncertain, and at the end of the decade, even the interest payments were hampering. The discounts at which the promissory notes of the Caisse were traded were huge at the end of the war, up to 80%.

In the second part of the Spanish Succession War, the controller general, Desmaretz, organized, together with some of the receivers, a joint caisse to have easier access to credit, the "Caisse Legedre." By assigning the most dependable revenue flows to this caisse, its operation was first rather dependable; billets were traded at modest discounts of about 10%. But at the very end of the war, this deteriorated as well because of the increasing difficulties with tax collection and general lack of confidence in the financial system.

Next to the borrowing, there were the "rentes." A "rente" was a way for an individual citizen or a family to buy a permanent allowance from the King and, for the King, a way to get money now at the cost of regular future payments. The allowance was a certain percentage of the principal as interest. The King could pay the principal back, but this was not practiced, since he was always in need of money. Citizens could not claim the principal. There were lifetime rentes and rentes that were heritable. The life time rentes could also be in the form of "tontines," meaning that the allowance of the citizen that died was added to the allowance of the citizens still alive. The rentes were organized through the Paris Hôtel de Ville. The allowances were paid with priority from previously indicated revenue flows. The heritable rentes were most important. The post-war total liability concerning them was estimated to equal 1.4 billion livres. The interest on these rentes was about 7%, but the Hôtel de Ville was bureaucratic and not very dependable with the payment of the annuities. It was also difficult to trade the rentes because they were dealt with as immovables, with the accompanying bureaucratic procedures and fees. Moreover, the controller general unilaterally reduced the interest rates now and then. In 1709 and 1710, half of the annuities were even canceled. On top of this, there was continuous manipulation of the domestic exchange rate-diminutions making the value of the coins, expressed in livres, smaller, and augmentations that made the coin value larger. The average trend was augmentation, reducing the coin yield, since the debts were expressed in livres. The rentes were unpopular because of the complexities and uncertainties and were issued at substantial discounts.

Augmentations were generally combined with a light recoinage, only over-stamping the face of the coins. In some cases, full recoinage was necessary to make completely new coins. The King earned seigniorage through the recoinage. The old coins that were offered to the mints for recoinage were accepted against the "mint specie price," a price close to the old value in livres; after recoinage, the people got back a number of coins for the same value in livres, but now the coins had their new, higher value. The difference between the new value and the mint species price was the revenue for the King. During the war, seigniorage resulted in an average income for the King of about 5 million per year (Rowlands, 2012). If the mint specie price was set too low, people looked for other ways to spend their old coins, on foreign markets or alternative markets within France, using the bullion value of the coins, complete with false coining.

An important step was that the receipts for the old coins turned in were made suitable for use as a substitute for cash, the mint bills. This made it tempting to issue more mint bills than only for the receipt of coins turned in. To make it attractive, it was combined with an interest of 4% and later even 8% (Rowlands, 2012). First, the number of mint bills in circulation was modest, about 7 million livres by the end of 1703, and the bills were accepted at a relatively low discount (18%). Yet, by the end of 1706, the amount of mint bills was already more than 170 million livres (Murphy, 1997). The public confidence had vanished in between though. The discount was up to 75%. It was attempted to make the bills more attractive by determining that rentes or promises of the caisse emprunts could be paid for with 50% mint bills, but it did not help much. And finally, from February 1711 on, mint bills could no longer be used in payments. The remaining bills could be converted into rentes.

During the war, the controller general had to rely, every now on and then, on rather unconventional and rough measures to squeeze more from the country to keep the war going. These were the "affairs extraordinaires," with people that had a sharp eye for places where money could be found. The tool was mainly the introduction of new venal offices and/or increasing fees for existing venal offices. In 1704, there was a peak in the contracted sum of more than 90 million livres. Later, it diminished to less than 20 million per year. The King received only about two-thirds of it and the measures cannibalized the effectiveness of other tax measures.

At the war-end, the King was basically bankrupt. His debt was about 2 billion livres. Per head of the population, this was not more than in England, but the financial system of France was too fragmented and chaotic to be able to service it. The King could not pay his creditors, and they could not pay merchants who supplied them with goods. There was a deflationary domino effect in the financial system (Buchan, 2018). It made France the ideal arena for Law.

5.5 Further Development of Law's Ideas

Law's ideas were developing during this period. He went beyond the concept of money backed by land. According to Law's theory, a system of paper credit should be established to replace the actual form of money based on silver and gold. He tried to show that it was possible to supplement the insufficient supply of money in the case of England and Scotland with paper money collateralized by land. In the French economy, the situation was somewhat different. There was not only a monetary crisis, but also a fiscal crisis. The French national debt was unmanageable. There, the monetary policy had to be accompanied by a debt management policy, a necessary condition for revitalizing the French economy. In his early works, he already hinted that it was possible to envision a broader concept of money supply, including shares of large trading companies. In a later note, directed to the French situation, Law stressed that an important advantage of shares as money was that they were inflation-proof (Murphy, 1997). He reasoned that the capital of the trading companies was not in money but in productive facilities and merchandise. In England, the Bank of England and large trading companies, such as the East India Company and the South Sea Company, were designed to deal with the Crown's debt management problems. The liabilities of these companies, i.e., their shares, were partly covered by state debt. It led Law to conceptualize a system encompassing these interconnections between the money supply and government debt (Berdell, 2017). These companies could act as a conduit for transferring funds from the private to the public sector. In exchange for obtaining a monopoly trading privilege, the companies undertook lendings to the government at favorable interest rates or take over existing government debt. Government debt occupied an important place on the asset side of the corporate balance sheet. On the liability side, capital had to be raised from the private sector to lend this money to the state. This capital could be provided by the moneyed people attracted by the combination of interest on public debt and the productive capacity of the corporations. The interest on government debt had to be paid from taxation, but it was only a small step to include the processes of levying the taxation in the company. In other words, he tended to consider France as a company, with the Bank of St. George as an important point of reference: all state revenues would flow through it.

5.6 Foundation of the Banque Générale

At the end of 1714, John Law settled in the Place de Vendôme, on the western edge of Paris, in the midst of monasteries, market gardens, and vacant lots. He wanted to present his ideas to Nicolas Desmaretz, the King's controller general of finance. Law then sent a letter to Desmaretz requesting free passage to Paris for his furniture and luggage that had arrived by ship from the Netherlands to Rouen, a letter that could provide an opportunity to meet with him. Meanwhile, on the death of Queen Anne, Law wrote a series of letters to the Scottish nobility to lobby the new King George to pardon him. Law also called on the new British Ambassador in Paris, the Earl of Stair, on January 23, 1715. They knew each other already from Holland, also from gambling. Stair believed their primary mission in Paris was to keep France weak and thwart the exiled catholic nationalist Jacobites' attempts to capitalize on King George I's impopularity. In the winter of 1715, Stair wrote a letter of praise about John Law to both Foreign Secretary Stanhope and Lord of the Treasury, Charles Montagu (Buchan, 2018). The answers were discouraging; there was insufficient support for a return of Law to England. Law would meanwhile befriend the King's nephew, Philippe II, the Duc d'Orléans (1674–1723). Interestingly, the two had much in common (Fig. 5.2), being intellectuals of similar age, handsome and interested in games and gambling (Wiston-Glynn, 2022).

In May 1715, Law met with Desmaretz. He presented a program to establish a bank, reduce France's unsecured or floating debts over time, and make Paris the world's financial capital. He also offered to put a substantial sum of 500,000 pounds into the bank. If it failed, this money would be distributed to the poor in France. This move scared Stair, and he wrote privately to the Duke of Montrose, a Scottish nobleman who contributed to the unification of Scotland and England: "When I first came here, I insisted that Laws be pardoned because I thought he might be useful to us in Britain. I was very determined to get him out of this country because I saw that he would greatly benefit the French. It was neglected when it should have been done, and now it is too late. I am afraid he is on board or about to be on board with them, but that is only for you; I don't think the government should now find a way to have him or go any further in granting him amnesty, which is only to raise his price here. I will be very pleased that his negotiation with this court has failed; it always happens, but his demands are too high. I will put a spoke in his wheel if I can" (Buchan, 2018). Law asked for a 20 year concession for a bank, initially limited to Paris and jointly owned by the King. Although Law would bear the costs of setting up the bank and managing the business, three-quarters of the profits would belong to the King and one-quarter to Law. The King's share of the profits would allow him to pay interest on his debts and eventually to pay off part of his debt. Using the Bank of England as a model, the new bank would issue banknotes as receipts for deposits of coins. Banknotes would be valid for tax and other public payments but would not be compulsory for trade. Law believed that these banknotes would be preferred, being

Fig. 5.2 Philippe II, Duke of Orleans (1674–1723). https://commons.wikimedia.org/wiki/File:Portrait_of_Philippe_d%27Orl%C3%A9ans,_Duke_of_Orl%C3%A9ans_in_armour_by_Jean-Baptiste_Santerre.png

more convenient than coins (Buchan, 2018). The plans developed fast, and on July 31, Law wrote Desmaretz that he was prepared to start in the course of August.

However, then Louis XIV got ill and died 3 weeks later (September 1, 1715). His son, the Grand Dauphin, died already in 1711, and a year later the son of the Grand Dauphin, the Petit Dauphin, died of measles, just like his wife and their eldest son. The future Louis XV, the second son had also measles but recovered, maybe because his governess forbade the doctors to apply the traditional treatment: bloodletting. The Duc d'Orléans was expected to become the regent, but Louis XIV left rather ambiguous instructions with respect to the regency. The Duc d'Orléans was appointed Head of a Regency Council, but the Duc de Maine, an illegitimate son of Louis XIV, was made responsible for the education of the young King and was also chief of the household guard. To correct this situation, the Duc d'Orléans convened the Parliament de Paris right away and requested to overturn these provisions, and declare him to be regent with full powers rather than only head of the Regency Council, while promising to give the Parliament a more important role in the government. There were 13 parliaments in France. A parliament was basically just a court of appeal. Laws and edicts issued by the crown were not official until the parliament gave assent by publishing them. The members of the parliaments ("nobles de robe") bought or inherited their offices and were independent of the king. The Parliament of Paris was especially always trying to broaden its role and get a say in establishing laws and regulations. Louis XIV had cut that off by stating "l'etat c'est moi." Yet, now they had an opportunity. To organize a broader involvement, the Duke introduced, next to the Regency Council, six other councils, one of them for finance. The Council of Finances was the most important. The Duc de Noailles, successor of Desmaretz, headed it. The anger of the Duc de Maine family was softened by appointing his nephew, the 23 year-old Duc de Bourbon, Head of the Regency Council ("Louis XV", Murphy, 1997).

Law's plan to establish a bank "in the King's name and for the King's account" was presented to the Conseil de Finances on October 24, 1715. Undoubtedly, it was helpful that Law and the regent knew each other already, whereas the financial situation was dramatic and necessitated unusual measures. However, after hearing a presentation of Law's project, emphasizing that the Bank would only issue banknotes for an equivalent deposit of coins, the Council, taking into account the opinions of 13 bankers and businessmen, including Samuel Bernard (1686–1753), the financier of Louis XIV, rejected the proposal (Buchan, 2018). An important objection was that, given the poor state of royal finance, the King would be tempted to "borrow" from the Bank, resulting in less backing of its notes.

After Law's proposal was rejected, the Duc de Noailles had to make the debt more manageable. In December 1715, he reduced the interest on the rentes to 4% and initiated a domestic devaluation (an augmentation). The revenue generated from the devaluation was far less than anticipated—the State gained only 110 million livres. Although persons caught altering the coinage faced severe penalties, human ingenuity created a secondary market for unreformed coins. They were smuggled to the Netherlands and neighboring countries, where private workshops stamped or melted them. The proceeds were transferred to France via bills of exchange (Murphy, 1997).

The interest reduction and the devaluation were insufficient; special measures were necessary. So, also in December 1715, the Crown issued a declaration, inviting wartime financiers and contractors to present their claims and announcing that claims would be subject to a general audit, "the Visa of 1716." Accordingly, more than half of the claims were canceled. At the same time, the remaining 200 million were converted into standard banknotes, or "billets d'état," payable to the bearer rather than to a named individual and bearing a uniform interest rate of 4%. Noailles seized the opportunity to issue also new billets d'etat for 50 million livres (Murphy, 1997). Since Noailles did not set a date for repayment of the notes and did not allocate any revenue to pay the 4% coupon, the notes changed hands for less than half their face value. In March 1716, the Regency launched an even more drastic approach to reduce the debts, a judicial investigation of "contractors and businessmen, their clerks and employees, who in the late two wars by their exactions forced the public to pay much more than was required by the exigencies of the time" (Buchan, 2018). All those involved in the King's affairs since January 1, 1689 were commended to appear before the "Chambre de justice." The decree read: "The vast and sudden fortunes of those who prospered from these criminal acts, the excess of their luxury and display ... are already a glaring proof of their malversations." Some were sent to the galleys, and there were even death sentences, but most of them were pardoned on payment of a penalty. Yet, the penalties were generally paid with the same "billets d'etat," and at the end of the day, the yield in cash was only (about) 50 million livres. Law opposed the "Chambre" because the effect on the development of credit and commerce was devastating, but it helped to set the stage for his plans (Buchan, 2018).

The Regent urged Law to pursue a more modest plan on a private bank. On May 2, Noailles submitted a motion to the Regency Council to authorize Law to establish a bank. A letter patent, issued in the name of the King, granted a 20 year license to "Mr. Law and Company" for a "Banque Générale" with authority to issue banknotes named "bank crowns" (écus de Banque) (Buchan, 2018). On May 20, the King authorized the bank to issue 1,200 shares of 1,000 "bank crowns," each at 5 livres per crown, or 6 million livres. There were to be general meetings in June and December to elect directors and approve the division of the profits. On May 26, the Paris Parliament registered letters of naturalization for John Law. Subscriptions for shares opened on June 1, and by June 12, as the Gazette d'Amsterdam reported in a letter sent from Paris that day, "all the subscriptions for the new bank have been filled for several days." Shareholders could subscribe not only in cash but also with billets d'état, which were discounted in the market by 60% but could be used here at face value. Law put in 1.5 million livres, or a quarter of the capital, probably his entire fortune. The Regent helped with its success. One of the Paris brothers, leaders of the Fermes Générale, wrote: "The Duke of Orléans, who wanted to give some credit to that establishment, was of the wish that we should take part and allocated us a certain number of shares. We obeyed, and that caused us to attend two general meetings of the bank, with that prince in the chair, and to enter into some relation with Mr. Law" (Buchan, 2018).

The Bank was a success. On December 22, at the first shareholders' meeting, Law announced a dividend of 8% of the issue price of the shares. In a private letter, Stair's secretary, Thomas Crawford, wrote the following: "Law's bank has ruined all the bankers here because he gives discounts on bills and in every foreign place he buys and gives bills one percent cheaper than all of them." An important success factor was that the banknotes issued were claims on fixed weight and quality silver coins, safe for devaluations. Law became an increasingly important figure—within 12 months, he had become the largest European banker (Buchan, 2018).

5.7 The Mississippi Company, the Conflict with the Parliament

The next step in the plan of Law was to establish a company, something like the South Sea Company in England, but strong enough to carry France's complete finance. The opportunity came in the form of the French colony of Louisiana in America (Fig. 5.3). This colony encompassed a vast territory stretching from the mouth of the Mississippi River into the north and including areas in the present states of Louisiana, Mississippi, Arkansas, Missouri, Illinois, Iowa, Wisconsin, Minnesota, and up to Canada. It had not yet been well discovered—only a few settlers lived there in Indian territory. Earlier, the Marquis de Chastel Antoine Crozat had formed a Louisiana Company with two partners to develop the colony; on September 14, 1712, the King granted Crozat's company a 15 year commercial monopoly over the entire territory from New Mexico to "the English in Carolina" and from the Gulf to the Illinois River. Crozat had made a fortune collecting taxes in France and from slavery and trading ventures abroad. Yet, the "Chambre de justice" had fined him for paying 6.6 million livres during the 1716 Visa, and his enthusiasm to develop Louisiana diminished because of that. He withdrew and offered his ships, sunk costs, and the unexpired portion of his concession as a (partial) payment of the Visa tax. To justify a large compensation, "he talked up the colony and peppered ministers with proposals to develop it" (Buchan, 2018). He suggested a joint enterprise with the King with a capital of 1.5 million livres. Fearing that even this modest sum would be difficult to acquire, he envisaged the capital to be subscribed in the depreciated billets d'etat. At this stage, Law got involved. The financial power of his bank enabled to enlarge the project substantially.

The enterprise was christened "Company of the West" but was known as the Mississippi Company. In August 1717, it was chartered by the King. The company acquired the sole right to trade and mine in the province of Louisiana and import beaver skins from Canada, both for 25 years. The King granted the company all fortifications and vessels available over there and the right to raise troops, build warships, dig mines, appoint judges and civil officers, enter into treaties with American nations, and call on the help of the King in case of interferences. In return for these privileges, the company was required to transport to the territory "six thousand whites and at least three thousand blacks," build churches of the Roman Catholic faith in all settlements, and furnish them with clergy subject to the Bishop of Quebec (Buchan, 2018). The regent appointed John Law as senior director. There were eight other directors; Crozat was one of them but seemed not to have been active as such (Murphy, 1997).

Fig. 5.3 Boundaries of the French colony of Louisiana

The shares were in denominations of 500 livres, payable only in billets d'etat. The final capital was left vague, but turned out to be 100 million. The 4% interest on the billets d'etat was transformed into a dividend of 4% on the company shares, to be paid from the revenues of a stamp duty on notarial acts. The billets d'etat were burned. The holders of billets d'etat who bought shares replaced the King as debtor for John Law as debtor. Both came with huge uncertainties; Canada and Louisiana had not been very successful until then. The subscription opened on September 14. Law bought right away 12,000 shares (6 million livres), but other subscriptions came only slowly. Only 24 million of the capital was invested by February next year. The company tried to bring positive news about Louisiana and the company, but that was not so easy yet, and the public opinion was not positive. Buchan quotes part of a song going around: "And since solidity is the word, they have put in charge a gallows bird who dodged the road abroad," referring to Law's death sentence in England. The first convoy to Louisiana, in October 1717, with the "Dauphine" as the main ship, was probably financed by Law himself. During the trip of the Dauphine, New Orléans was established, the name indicating the support of the Regent. But that was not very substantial yet and Law blamed De Noailles for lack of support.

In between, negotiations were going on for a longer peace between England and France, initiated by the Regent. The position of Law was of growing importance for France, and during the negotiations, Stanhope, the Chancellor of the Exchequer and effective prime minister, pleaded for a pardon for Law for his killing of Wilson. On December 13, the pardon was signed on behalf of King George. The document was delivered to Law, but Law handed it into the Regent, expressing that he was not going to use it to go back to England.

Yet, there was still a growing opposition, not only against Law but also against the Regent. It consisted of the Parliament of Paris, which had a strong link with the rich aristocracy, and the people who did not like the closer relationship with England and preferred a warm bond with Spain. From January 14 to 19, the Paris Parliament devoted four sessions to the country's finances. Although the speakers did not mention Law by name, they indirectly denounced him. The Parliament accused the Regency of bringing the King into disrepute and impoverishing his subjects. In turn, the Regent dismissed Chancellor Aguesseau and Noailles, the president of the Council of Finance. In place of both men, he appointed the Marquis d'Argenson. The Regent started to discuss the financial affairs of the kingdom with Law and Argenson and the Council of Finance did not meet regularly anymore. Adding to the tension was Argenson's decision (end of May) to devalue the livre drastically, by way of an augmentation, reducing the value of the livre in terms of gold or silver by about a third, thus reducing the debt of the King. It was combined with a recoinage. These measures were taken without consultation of the Parliament of Paris. Argenson sent the decree to a subsidiary court, the "cour de monnaie." The Parliament was furious and forbade all individuals from using the new coins and notaries to write contracts based on the new value of the livre. Argenson called the protests of the Parliament an insult to the King and accused the Parlement of just protecting the privileges of the magistrates. In August, the Parliament attacked Law's role explicitly and banned all foreigners from direct or indirect involvement in the King's finances. The countermeasure of the Regent and his allies was to organize a "lit de justice," the first for nearly 50 years. The Parliament derived its power from the King. A lit de justice was a meeting of the Parliament, preceded by the King, limiting the authority of the Parliament. It could ensure the registration of laws the Parliament was opposing. A decision of a lit de justice could only be stamped by the Parliament (Murphy, 1997). That is what happened: a lit de justice with the young King present, overruling the decisions of the Parliament. To prevent political actions while preparing it, it was kept secret until the last moment. After the meeting, three of the most outspoken members of the Parliament were arrested. All this happened while the internal conflicts with respect to the treaty with England and war with Spain were deepening. However, for the next one-and-a-half year, the Parliament was bridled in her actions against Law.

On December 4, the conversion of the General Bank into the Royal Bank was announced. The King was going to be the sole owner. The other shareholders were bought out at the face value of the shares (5,000 livres per share). The original 6 million in billets d'etat were gone in the subscription for the Company of the West, and the King left it so. At that moment, there were about 40 million livres of banknotes in circulation, and the reserves in species were about 10 million. Assuming that the difference was the result of loans with, on average, at least 4% interest, leads to an estimate of the earning power of about 1.2 million livres per year. The payback period for the six million livres investment was going to be limited. It was a good deal for the King (Buchan, 2018). The bank had branches in Lyons, La Rochelle, Tours, Orléans and Amiens. It was determined that in these towns, all transactions over 600 livres had to be paid in banknotes. In January 1719, the 100 million shares were finally fully subscribed. The first annual general meeting of the Company, held on Monday, March 27, 1719, was a success.

It was important now to enlarge the Company of the West, to be able to make it the pillar of the finance of France. The first step was taken already in December 1718 with the takeover of the Compagnie royale du Senegal. The Compagnie Royale du Senegal was founded in 1696 and under the control of financiers from Rouens. Its trade was in Arabic gum (for the textile industry) and slaves for American plantations. The Rouennais were kept in place to manage the business. In the same spirit was the plan to take over the Compagnie des Indes Orientales and the Compagnie de Chine. Both companies needed recapitalization. The price of the old shares was still under par (about 490), but Law proposed to sell 50,000 new shares for 550 livres each, with a down payment of 50 livres and the rest at 25 livres per month. His confidence was also fed by his insight into the effect of the issuing of another 110 million in banknotes by the Banque Royale that spring. To enforce a decision, Law offered to buy all new shares with a down payment of 2.5 million livres. This offer was public and led to an increase in the market price of the old shares to 600 livres. Law did not exploit this success for his own gain; however, he proposed instead to give old shareholders the right to buy the new shares. Each four old shares ("mothers") gave the right to buy one new share ("daughter") for 550 livres. That is what happened then. The Company of the West was called the Compagnie des Indes from then on. It contained the main parts of French foreign trade. It even had its own harbor (Lorient,

Brittany), which was developed for the navy but was transferred to the Compagnie des Indes now. The price of the old shares was increasing further (more than 1000 on July 21).

On July 20, the Company acquired the monopoly of minting coins (Murphy, 1997), a very different branch on the Company tree but completely consistent with Law's longer term plans. It had to pay 50 million livres over 15 months. To raise the amount, it initiated a third issue, now of 50,000 shares priced at 1,000 livres each. The dividend was increased from 20 livres per share to 60 livres per share (old and new shares). To buy a new share, a granddaughter, one had to have four mothers and one daughter. Everything was directed at building and keeping the investor's loyalty. The Banque Royale smoothed the demand for liquidity by issuing more banknotes, 240 million livres on July 25. The share price rocketed to 1,750 livres on July 28 and 2,500 livres on August 4 (Buchan, 2018).

The Company was strong enough now to take over all the debts of the King. At the end of August, it was announced that the Company would lend the King 1,200 million livres to buy out all his creditors. Law had prepared the move by offering, on August 17, to pay the pension arrears owed by the King. The interest to be paid by the King was 3%. The Company was allowed to issue annuities with an interest of 3%. It was a shock for all people used to having annuities of the King, yielding 4%. They could now choose between Company annuities or trying to acquire shares. The measure was combined with acquiring the rights to collect the excises. This right had so far been exploited by the Fermes Générales, a syndicate led by the Paris brothers. The Company had to pay 52 million livres per year for this right. Of course, it could subtract the 36 million livres interest for the 1,200 million livres loan. The Paris brothers became fierce opponents of Law from then on. The price of the shares soared to 3,500 livres on August 28 and 5,000 livres on September 12 (Murphy, 1997).

In July, Law had already widened the Company's scope by buying the complete trade in tobacco. Competing with other financiers, he had to promise the King more than 4 million livres per year to acquire the monopoly. It was a significant step and one of the actions of Law the Parliament tried to reverse. Law was close to his ultimate goal. The Company covered most of the foreign trade of France and was developing this further; Louisiana was developing, the city of Rouen was developing into an international staple, and the mint and the collection of excises were included and upgraded. There were also new industrial activities, new shipyards, for instance, and the manufacturing of new types of watches that could be used to determine the position at sea, but also of the manufacturing of more general steel products. Moreover, Law himself had bought and developed real estate, also to exhibit his success. The Company was the sole creditor of the King. The people were used to paying with banknotes. The shares in the company were popular not only in France but also in the UK and The Netherlands. Also, there were good possibilities to manipulate the price by adding liquidity through more banknotes and by adequate communication. With the support of the Regent, the situation improved. More revenues of the King were allocated to the company, including revenues from the monopoly of tobacco and the postal service.

However, the project had not yet been finalized. Law aimed at a situation with shares as the main form of money. He knew that more stability was required to accomplish that. Earlier he argued already that land was suitable as a basis for money because its value was stable. He realized that he had to fix the price of shares somehow. But at what level and how many shares should be issued? Law realized that the backing of the Regent was essential. Yet, he already experienced that political freedom was not unlimited even with that backing. He trusted, however, that there would be opportunities and was confident that he would be sufficiently alert to grasp these in time. The money received was to be used to repay the long-term state debts on the Hôtel de Ville (les rentes), the remaining billets d'état, the cost of offices that had been or would be suppressed and the shares of the tax farms.

5.8 The End of the Buying Fever and the Start of the Fall of Law

From the summer of 1719, the buying of shares got feverish. Daniel Defoe described his outlook during the most active days of the market: "The inconvenience of the darkest and nastiest street in Paris does not prevent the crowds of people ... coming to buy and sell their stocks ... up to their ankles in the dirt" (Defoe, 2013). Parisian society was stunned by the number of poor people making money from shares in Law's companies. The merchants on Quincampoix Street were selling like crazy. Prices at one end of the road could quite differ from those at the other, with fortunes made in one hour and lost in the next. John Law was now an international personality. Princes and priests raced to meet him; he was well-liked by the people, and as he passed through the streets, "God bless the King and Monsieur Law!", they were calling. The writer Voltaire asked a friend, "How nice to come to the country ... Have you all gone mad in Paris? I only hear talk of millions." Indeed, almost half the nation acted as if they had found magic in paper money. Was John Law a god or a criminal giving people a drug? (Wiston-Glynn, 2022). Elisabeth Charlotte, the Regent's mother, was astonished by the account of a duchess kissing Law's hand. She later added: "The French ladies would be happy to kiss his ass—excuse me—if Mr. Law asked them to."

Law knew he needed stability for the longer term, but first, he used the buying fever to get the money required for the loan to the King cheaply. On September 13, the Company announced an issue of 100,000 shares with a nominal value of 500 Livres, which now cost 5,000 livres in cash—a much cheaper option than issuing annuities with an interest of 3%: a dividend of 60 on a share sold for 5,000 is only 1.2%. The new shares were already five times oversubscribed on the first day of issue. So, another issue of 100,000 shares was announced for September 28. This time, the shares would be payable not in cash but in government debt, annuities, rents, etcetera. Again, it was subscribed fully on a whim. So, a third issue was announced for October 2. The Regent announced it to be the last one. The Company loan to the King stood at 1,600 million livres, yielding an interest of 48 million annually (Buchan, 2018).

The various Company activities were very different from each other. On the one hand, there was the development of Louisiana and of the other trading companies; on the other hand, there was the collection of the excises and the mint. The two sides of the Company were put in two separately managed entities. On October 12, the Regent also added the collection of direct taxes (tailles, etcetera) to the Company. He expected more transparency and efficiency from Law and also more justice in the allocation of the taxes than he was used to with the existing organization.

Concerning income flow, the trading side of the Company was only small. But in the public opinion, this side was very important. For the public, the Company was the Mississippi Company. Louisiana's development was difficult, also because of the war with Spain. Although, in Law's pictures, it looked like the French Riviera of New Orléans, the colony's inhabitants actually struggled to survive. About half of the thousands of refugees had died on the way or were distraught and disappointed. There was no trace of gold, silver, or precious stones. Another problem was that very few people wanted to go to Louisiana. While Law offered rewards to encourage people to go to the colony, every criminal, beggar, and unemployed servant was enlisted and sent to the settlement. Promises to find a wife for singles had not worked either. The Mississippi Company formed an army-sized troop of mercenaries to capture people and take them to ships. Some people took advantage of this situation and paid the soldiers to get rid of their enemies. While thousands of people were forcibly sent to America in this fury, the soldiers were even kidnapping children. The people gathered were brutally treated, starved, and imprisoned. As a gambler, John Law was bluffing by showing his hand bigger than it was. He hoped the colony would thrive as expected with enough time and money. Confidence in all stocks and paper money depended on the widespread belief that the settlement was wealthy and would become increasingly attractive. John Law had no other choice (Wiston-Glynn, 2022).

The share price increased further during the Fall of 1719, but it was vulnerable for rumors about the Mississippi Company. Law got very nervous about an article in a gazette that called the Company a chimera, an illusion. The next day there was a run on the bank, probably orchestrated by Stair, because he did not trust Law's increasing contacts with the Jacobites (Buchan, 2018). Law reacted by issuing a decree that all public payments must be made in banknotes. Yet, the shares lost a quarter of their price due to that, resulting in a price of 7,430 livres on December 14. The weeks thereafter the price increased again to more than 9,000 livres. The share price peaked to 10,100 at January 6. Maybe the edict of December 21 to ban the use of silver for all payments above 10 livres and the use of gold for all payments above 300 livres helped here. It did not lead to problems during the second general assembly of the Company. The main measure announced then was the increase of the dividend per share from 60 to 200 livres. Law was aiming at a stable price of about 10,000 livres per share and a market interest of 2%. But he was too much a gambler to just let it happen without the possibility of profiting from the greedy market. The expectations were that the price would increase further and on the market, there was a heavy trade in futures. On this futures market, the price of a share to deliver in March was estimated to be between 12,000 and 14,000 livres (Murphy, 1997). Law issued so-called primes for 1,000 livres. A prime gave the right to buy a share for 10,000 livres somewhere during the next 6 months. The primes were very popular. The trade in primes even cannibalized the trade in shares; people sold their shares to buy more primes. It caused a temporary slide down of the actual share prices (Murphy, 1997). In total, 300,000 primes were sold for 300 million livres. The run on primes lasted less than 2 weeks, from January 9 until about January 19. Such sales allowed the owners of the primes to buy 3 billion livres of shares. If the primes had been applied, it would have increased the company's market capitalization by nearly 50% (Murphy, 1997). The run on the primes was the final stage of the Mississippi shares bull run.

On January 4, Law was appointed Controller General of France. Given his influence, it was a very logical decision, but his religion used to be a serious threshold. This threshold was removed in September of the previous year when Law adopted Roman Catholicism. He knew that it was important for the Regent, and maybe he had considered it before, but Lady Katherine was the problem. They were not married, and a marriage now would lead to scandals. But his strong position and the access to some shares for the family of Pierre de Tencin, the vicar general of the diocese of Sens, resolved the problems. Argenson remained Chancellor and acquired important positions for his sons. Law had all the power he could wish. Now, he had to stabilize the monetary and financial situation. The challenges were huge and clear. To support the price of the shares, Law established on December 30 a "Bureau d'achat et de vente." Between December 30 and February 22, the bureau had already bought shares for about 800 million livres. They were paid, of course, with newly printed paper money. It destroyed the confidence in paper money, which was already only very superficial. On January 27, the graziers at the livestock market at Poissy had already refused to accept banknotes and would not drive the cattle to the market unless the city butchers paid in coin. People started to hoard species or spend it abroad. The flood of paper money led to price increases and a fall in the exchange rates with England and The Netherlands. Between January 7 and February 11, the exchange rate with England fell by about 20% (Buchan, 2018).

Law tried to tempt people to convert their species into banknotes by manipulating the domestic exchange rate of gold. The value of the Louis d'or decreased gradually during the year 1719, from 36 to 31 livres, to suggest a further decrease, hoping that people would convert. It led to an unrealistically low value, and on January 26, it was reset to 36 livres, but with the threat that it would be reduced to 34 livres. That happened indeed, but it was ineffective, and on February 25, it was reset to 36. More measures to drive gold and silver out of circulation came up. On January 28, exporting species and bullion was prohibited, followed by, on February 18, a ban on the production, sale or export of gold and silver objects. On February 27, specie holdings of more than 500 livres per person were forbidden. All payments above 100 livres had to be in banknotes.

On February 22, Law revised his policy drastically. It was the date that the Bank and the Company were finally merged. That was just as expected, but his policy change was not. He stopped supporting the price of the shares by buying shares, and the Bureau d'achat et de Vente was closed. Maybe Law realized that the share price was too high to be sustainable. It was also decided then that new banknotes could not be issued without deliberations in the Company's general meeting. This led to a fall in the share price from 9,500 livres to less than 8,000 livres in a week. There were many protests, making clear that most share owners were more interested in share price increases than in dividends. The pressure led to another u-turn. From March 20 on, the share price would be kept equal to 9,000 livres. Buying and selling was going to be performed by a *bureau de conversions*. The decision made shares and banknotes completely equivalent. Clearly, Law was off track in his quest for the ideal system. Cantillon, a colleague banker and economist who earned a lot of money from the bull run on the shares, came back to Paris during the 1720 spring, saw the chaotic situation, and started to speculate against the system, anticipating a loss for the shares, and further drops in the exchange rates with England and of banknotes with specie.

5.9 The Apotheosis

Not all was lost at once. With the bull run on shares in 1719, interest in Louisiana also increased, and new companies and partnerships were established to start plantations in Louisiana. And John Law made impressive investments in new ships. The fleet of the Company consisted, at the end of 1719, of 38 vessels. This was going to double in 1720. The two largest ships were built on the Thames. The treaty with England was so stable that that was possible. To let the Company grow, Law planned to take over the colony of Saint-Domingo in the Caribbean. He revived the contacts with Iran, with trade in coffee from Jemen, pepper from the Malabar coast, and trade on the Philippines and Bengal as side products. He sent agents to Switzerland and the Palatinate to recruit settlers for Louisiana and the extensions toward Arkansas. Another source of settlers were beggars and vagabonds. On March 10, it was determined that such people could be arrested and, after 8 days, sent to Louisiana. Of course, this measure led to much arbitrariness.

The March policy change was combined with measures to remove species from circulation. On March 5, the domestic exchange rate was 48 livres for a Louis d'or. But there was an immediate warning that this was exceptionally high and would last only a few days. On March 11, the rate was put on 42 livres and it was announced that gold and silver would be removed from circulation during the summer. Clearly, people were reluctant to abandon their species. The measures became ever stronger and were combined with possibilities for the authorities to search buildings and coaches for species and jewels. The liberal side of Law was replaced by Law the improviser and regulator (Murphy, 1997). Anyone disobeying would be punished, and whistleblowers would be encouraged by great rewards. Servants began to slander their employers and children their parents. Law frightened people so much that they felt more secure when handing over their silver and gold to the bank and returning home with a handful of papers. It worked. For a time, gold and silver poured in. Yet, many citizens found ways to keep their gold and silver. Later on, the South Sea Company attracted a large part of the superfluous species.

During the spring, the Parliament started to protest again, after a silence of almost one-and-a-half year. The debt of the King was still partly financed by issuing 3% annuities. Law was continuously trying to have these replaced by shares. Now he announced to reduce the interest rate to 2%. That would make shares, with their dividend of 200 livres, more attractive than annuities. But whole financial France and all Parliaments protested. The protests against the reduction of the interest were combined with complaints about the arbitrariness in arresting beggars and vagabonds and in the search for forbidden quantities of silver and gold. The police were too much a tool of the Company. These complaints were taken seriously, but the protests against the reduction of the interest on annuities had no effect.

The printing of paper money continued at full speed. By May 1720, there were 2.6 billion livres placed on the market, twice the amount in January. The country was drowned in paper. That was also clear to Law. Also, he sensed that the share price was far too high to be sustainable. He knew that already from the market reaction when he stopped the share price support. Leaving things to the market had turned out to be unacceptable, so now he had to make the corrections that were necessary by himself. He estimated that a good first move would be reducing the share price from 9,000 livres to 5,000 livres. He announced the measures when the markets were closed, the Tuesday after Pentecost 1720. On May 21, Law announced that the value of shares of the Indies Company, which had a price of 9,000 livres, would be gradually reduced to only 5,000 by December (Garber, 1990). The value of the banknotes would be reduced accordingly. For payment of taxes and annuities, the devaluation was postponed until January 1721. Law stressed that the measure was needed because the prices of banknotes and shares, on the one hand, and specie, on the other hand, were out of balance. The reductions in the price of specie of March had to be accompanied by a reduction in the price of shares and banknotes. The dividend remained 200 livres, but it became a higher percentage of the share price, 4%. It would also help to stop the downward pressure on the exchange rate with England.

Maybe people would have accepted it when it had been done right away, together with the depreciation of the species in March, but now people were just confused and angry. An English official, Pulteney, wrote: "It is in everyone's mouth that they are robbed of the half they are worth; that is the most notorious cheat that ever was committed." The Parliament protested, the Regent was stressed, and his advisor (Antin) convinced him that Law was wrong. The Regent started to lose his confidence in Law and decided to annul the decree. It was revoked already on May 27. In a meeting of the Regency Council that day, Law offered his resignation. Two days later, he was removed from his office as Controller General and put under house arrest. That was the end of the system Law had envisaged, but not yet the end of Law himself. Many people realized that they needed Law to operate the Company (the bank included) and he was called back on June 2 as Intendant-General du Commerce and director general of the bank. His freedom was much smaller now, however.

Annuities were reintroduced. First, it was for 500 million livres, which was later extended to 1 billion livres. The Regent determined the interest at 2.5%, which was already higher than the interest Law aimed for, but much lower than the interest the Parliament asked for (5%); Law still influenced the Regent. The introduction of annuities helped to reduce the number of banknotes in circulation; the banknotes used to buy the annuities could be destroyed. Because of the guaranteed price for shares until May 21, the number of shares with the public had reduced to about 200,000. The shares turned in were superfluous and could be destroyed as well. To meet the general public's discontent with Law's system, the superfluous shares and banknotes were publicly burned. Of course, each fire further reduced confidence in the paper system and created panic in the street of Quincampoix, while increasing the demand for coins (Fig. 5.4).

There was another measure that made the banknotes superfluous: the introduction of bank accounts that could be used to pay bills of exchange, like those introduced by the Amsterdam Bank of Exchange. The banknotes used to fill the accounts were superfluous thereafter. This measure fitted better with Law's ideas, but was not a big success. At the introduction, in July, a limit of 600 million livres was established. It was not realized, not more than about 200 million livres. Maybe, it should have come earlier. Law supported also a proposal to ask shareholders to pay a supplement of 3,000 livres. The normal dividend was 200 livres per share; with this supplement, it would be 360 livres per share. It helped make shares more interesting, and the price

Fig. 5.4 Panic on Quincampoix street 1720. https://upload.wikimedia.org/wikipedia/commons/f/f6/Estampe_satirique_sur_le_fonctionement_du_systeme_de_Law_et_sa_banqueroute_1720.jpg

increased slightly, from 5,780 to 6,350 (June 6). Later, there were also new share issues, to absorb large denomination banknotes.

So, Law was still influential, because he was the sole expert of how the system worked and he could use this expertise now and then to sneak in measures that supported his system, but the political situation had changed drastically and the general trend was to demolish what he had built. Murphy (1997) gives a revealing list of important measures: June 1, revocation of the prohibition to hold more than 500 livres in gold and silver; June 3, creation of annuities; August 15, high-denomination banknotes to be demonetized from October 1; September 15, high-denomination banknotes could only be used if half of the amount was paid in specie; October 10, banknotes no longer legal tender and taxes could not be paid in banknotes anymore. The public was also against John Law. The Bank could only very limitedly convert banknotes into specie. This led to chaos on market days, and riots. On July 17, there was a stampede, and several people were crushed. Mounted police and Swiss guards had to restore order. The Bank remained closed to the public, and then the Royal Bank of France went bankrupt.

Foreign investors had lost confidence as well, also because from May 1720, the French currency lost value significantly. In May, the British Pound was worth 39 livres; by September, it had risen to 92 livres. One of the investors who earned considerable money because of this fall of the French currency was Richard Cantillon. Since he expected the French currency to depreciate, he had made a great fortune through various agreements in different countries. Law and Cantillon cooperated in developing Louisiana, but when Cantillon started to speculate against the French currency, Law forced Cantillon to leave France by threat. In August, he invited Cantillon back because he appreciated his insights, but Cantillon refused.

Maybe the announcements of September 15 dealt the final blow to Law's career. It was a further step in the demonetization of the banknotes. High-denomination banknotes were going to be demonetized on October 1 and could be used in between only in combination with 50% in species. This was more or less as expected. Yet, there was also a drastic change in the way the just-introduced bank accounts were treated. The value of the accounts would be reduced to just one-quarter of their current value. It was also determined that from now on, all bills of exchange, all commercial transactions, and all large transactions of goods had to be paid using these accounts. To soften the measure, it was determined that the accounts could also be converted to high-denomination banknotes, the notes that could not be used anymore after October 1. Another possibility was to buy shares for 2,000 livres (bank account money) per share. Apparently, Law switched from developing a system with banknotes to developing a system with bank accounts. Maybe it was a good idea, but he had lost contact with political reality. It was impossible to understand, for instance, for merchants using the accounts already. The six merchant guilds of Paris protested with the Regent, but for the moment, the Regent was still covering the decisions of Law.

There were negative opinions and expressions toward John Law all over Europe. While cartoons on him were being printed in the newspapers, Law struggled desperately to defend himself. For the Regent, John Law had become a burden. The public was hopeless and thought that economic recovery would never happen. The Regent secretly sought help, appealing to various bankers and wealthy people to find gold or coins, but received only advice in return. The people he referred to suggested that returning to the old monetary system would alleviate some of the problems. That was in between also the advice of the English allies. They were envious first of the earlier successes of Law, but their belief in the system had vanished. The bursting of the South Sea bubble contributed to this change. People started to leave France with as much of their money as possible. The craftsmen hired in England to develop industrial activity also returned; payment in French banknotes was no longer attractive for them.

Law knew that the support of the Regent that was left, depended upon his possibility to provide him with sufficient species. At the end of October, he developed a last offer, depending partly on the contribution of all shareholders and combined with measures to prevent speculation. The company's directors, including Law himself, were also asked to use their position to raise money for the company. It turned out to be too little. On Monday, December 9, Law gave up (Buchan, 2018); he asked the Regent to be released from his service and permission to leave for Rome with just the one-and-a-halve million livres in cash that he brought with him when he came to France, in 1713. He left his land and estate in France to cover his debts and obligations. The Regent suggested staying close to help sort out his financial affairs. But Law preferred to go further away, given the political turmoil around him. The Regent issued passports for him, his son William, and two servants. They left Paris on December 18.

Law settled in Venice, where he took up his gambling career again. He hoped his wife and daughter would join him, but they stayed in Paris. Law was also for a time in England and tried from there to contact the Regent again about a possible come-back. That did not work right away, and when the Regent died in 1723, the possibility was gone. Law died on March 21 of 1729 and was buried in Venice.

5.10 Foundation of the Bank of France

Cleaning up the wreckage left by John Law was not easy, and there was long fear of the word "bank" in France. For this reason, the French did not dare to establish a public bank again for a long time. However, a central bank project modeled on the Bank of England by Isaac Panchaud, a London-born banker who moved to Paris in 1763, had the support of the French Minister of Finance Anne-Robert-Jacques Turgot. The new bank was called Caisse d'Escompte. Marion (1934) explained this situation as follows: "The disaster of the system of John Law was making the term 'Bank' so unpopular that one had to wait for long before trying again something with the slightest resemblance to a bank. It was only in 1776, 56 years after the system's fall, that Turgot believed to be able to equip France with an establishment discounting bills of exchange...".

The Caisse d'Escompte began by discounting promissory notes and issuing banknotes. This was very profitable when it came to lending to the public, and the circulation of banknotes reached 70 million livres by 1783, although its field of activity was limited to Paris (Kindleberger, 2015). A contemporary writer called this development a feat no other city had ever attained (Marion, 1934). The bank, however, would lose the public's confidence in 1787 when it was pressed to lend to the King in exchange for a 30 year extension of its charter. The bank's reserves would soon fall, and the conversion of its banknotes into gold would be suspended. The Caisse d'Escompte was to be liquidated in 1788, a year before the French Revolution (Kindleberger, 2015). Yet, it would be remembered as an essential institution that inspired the creation of the later Bank of France. Of course, financial activities continued outside of this bank.

Individuals other than government officials borrowed by way of notes ("billets"), passing from hand to hand in France as paper money. Royal Officers, who had official duties such as collecting, receiving, and paying royal revenues, could be bankers. For example, by borrowing from the public at 5%, they could lend to the Crown at a higher rate. Also, some wealthy people acted as bankers, lending to those in need (Bosher, 1972). Moreover, notaries played a significant role (Hoffman et al., 1995).

After the 1789 revolution, the income of the French state began to decline rapidly. Excises and Church tax were abandoned in response to public demand. Instead, Charles Maurice de Talleyrand (1754–1838), Bishop of Autun and later diplomat and politician, proposed expropriating church property. This land, whose total value was estimated at 2–3 billion livres, had the potential to pay the nation's debt. So, in December 1789, the National Assembly issued "assignats," 5% interest-bearing bonds, with expropriated church lands as collateral, to pay off urgent debts. The idea was similar to the notes John Law proposed to issue for land in 1705. In September 1790, the Assembly converted assignats into paper currency, and the amount in circulation was increased from 400,000,000 livres to 1,200,000,000 livres. The initial impact of paper currency was beneficial, stimulating economic growth and eliminating money shortages. Yet, the public's deep distrust of paper money and the fear that the currency would be worthless when the Revolutionary regime collapsed soon, caused assignats to depreciate (Encyclopaedia Britannica, 2011). It deepened the paranoia about paper money and banks in the French subconscious and helped establish Napoleon successively as consul and emperor (Kindleberger, 2015).

When Napoleon came to power, the country's financial situation was very bad, and a solution had to be found. As an economic thinker, Napoleon was idiosyncratic. He strongly objected to paper money, government debt, speculation, and free markets (Kindleberger, 2015). He always preferred metal coins to paper money and received loyalty from his army by paying coins. Napoleon did not trust bankers, choosing to control the finances himself. He said (Anderson, 1992): "When a government is dependent upon bankers for money, they, and not the government leaders, control the situation, since the hand that gives is above the hand that takes. Money has no motherland; financiers lack patriotism and decency; their sole object is to gain." Napoleon tried to control money wherever he could, in his Empire and satellite countries such as Italy, Westphalia, Naples, and Holland. Since he needed a circulation bank more than a deposit one to support economic recovery, he founded the Banque de France (Kindleberger, 2015). This new institution was tasked with issuing promissory notes to be paid to the bearer in exchange for discounting commercial bonds. Initially, it began as a private institution for managing state debts and issuing notes. It was responsible for the French government's accounts, managing them, and facilitating payments for the Treasury and some public companies. In the beginning, the management of the Bank was very cautious, and its operations were initially limited to Paris. To ensure the stability and reliability of this new institution, it was guaranteed to find the equivalent of gold of the same value for anyone who wished. Fearing to be deceived by the banks three times in a century, the French were initially highly suspicious. Then, gradually, they began to rely on the new money. The Emperor's personal, fierce, and irresistible participation was important in this success. He entrusted some of his own money and that of his relatives to the Bank. Together with the capital provided by wealthy shareholders, it provided the institution with the substantial capital needed. Soon, the Banque de France became the only bank authorized to issue monetary values (Brie, 2019).

5.11 Conclusion

Millions of tourists come to Venice every year to visit many impressive historical monuments, churches, and art galleries. One of them is the church of San Moise, located very close to the famous St. Mark's Square. The church was built in the seventh century and dedicated to Moses, but the name also honored Moise Venier, the aristocrat who rebuilt the church in the ninth century. Only very watchful eyes will notice the writing on the church floor, disappearing under the feet of the tourist crowds. It reads: "John Law, Son of William, born to the highest estate in Edinburgh, in Scotland, superintendent of the Royal Treasury in France, died in Venice, in the year of grace 1729 at the true age of fifty-eight" (Buchan, 2018).

John Law was from a family of Scottish bankers/goldsmiths in Edinburgh. As a youngster, he liked gambling already, and he was good at it. Edinburgh was too small for him, so he went for the adventures of London. His gambling did not bring him fortune right away, but later, he developed a preference for acting as the bank in gambling; he determined the conditions such that they looked attractive for his opponents while he knew that in the long run, he would profit. In that way, he made a good living. Yet, of course, it also brought him in conflicting situations, with money, women, and honor. And so, he got involved in a duel and, unfortunately, killed his opponent. He was sentenced to death, but through all kind of scheming had the opportunity to escape.

That started his travels through Europe, the Dutch Republic, Genoa, and France. There, he got acquainted with the big money, banks, shares, and speculation. And he enjoyed it. He saw how it worked and developed ideas about the relationship between money on the one hand and trade and industry on the other hand. There was plenty of money in the Dutch Republic and a lack of money in France, England,

and Scotland. He realized that silver and gold were poor bases for money because of their availability. There were already initiatives to have land as basis. He worked it out in his "Essay on a Land Bank," arguing that land is relatively stable in value and that it also possesses "the other qualities needful in money: that it is (1) durable, (2) divisible, (3) capable of delivery and (4) of a stamp to denote the value." Later, he made it more specific by projecting it on the Scottish situation in his "Money and Trade Considered; with a Proposal for Supplying the Nation with Money." He was then in Scotland to defend his proposal (1705). It was safe for him to be there as long as Scotland and England were not united. They had the same king already but were not united yet. The proposal received serious attention, but was not accepted in the end. Law had to leave Scotland then because of the near unification.

Later, Law realized that shares in a national company had even better properties as basis for money, because they were inflation-proof. The capital of the company was not in money, but in productive facilities and merchandise and, with good management, it would be growing. Also, he saw already in England that such a company could help also in solving the Crown's debt problems. The Bank of St. George in Genoa was his clearest example. It was not just a bank; most of the state's revenues went through this company. His goal was to apply this principle in France. France was in deep trouble regarding the King's debt and the lack of money to develop trade and industry. France was an absolute monarchy—given the support of the King, it would be quite easy to take the necessary steps. He realized that many steps were needed to arrive at his goal. It would be a game with many moves, and his opponents, the financiers, and the general public would come with unexpected ones. Yet, he was confident that, given the superior properties of shares as a basis for money and the King's support, he would succeed.

So, John Law confidently arrived in France in 1713 and hoped to get a chance to create an economic miracle. He got that chance because Louis XIV died. Louis XV was only a child then, and the Regent, the Duke of Orléans, was very accessible to Law. He established the Banque Générale (1716) and later the Mississippi Company (1717), having a business monopoly in French colonies. Then, the bank evolved into the Royal Bank with the King as sole owner (1718). The company was empowered with tax collection and the conversion of the King's debts with the financiers and the general public to debts with the Company only (1719). The role the combination of Royal Bank and Company had was already close to the role of the Bank of St. George in Genoa. The conversion of the King's debts was mainly financed by issuing new shares, and printing more banknotes facilitated this. It led to a bull run on the shares, leading to a price of more than 10,000 livres for a share of nominally 500 livres. Law was appointed to Controller General of France in between. The next step was to stabilize the stock price. In March 1720, Law chose to stabilize the price at 9,000 livres. That was far too high, and he knew that, but the political reality required it then; it could only be realized by heavily buying newly issued banknotes. He had to stop this in May and reduce the price by 50%. Here, he lost most of his support. People did not accept to lose their speculative gains. Under pressure from the Parliament of Paris and the financiers, the Regent had to fire him as Controller

General. A couple of days later, he hired Law again because of his expertise with the system he developed, but his role was more restricted then, and his goal was out of scope.

Law's mission failed. He failed, not because of shortcomings or mistakes in his ideas or abilities but because of his impatience (Murphy, 1997). His biggest mistake was that the Mississippi Company moved too fast in stock sales. While he did his best to increase the stock price, he created massive inflation with low interest rates and excessive money printing. He created a bubble in the stock price. John Law later admitted his mistake. He said, "I do not pretend I did not make a mistake, I admit that I did it all, I wish I could start over ... I would go slower but more carefully" (Masson, 1950). Moreover, probably, he underestimated the political power of the financial world and overestimated the possibilities in an absolute monarchy to control this power.

Paper money would not be used in France for a long time. The French hated the word "bank" for a long time, and when new banks were established, they were not called banks but typically would be called "caisse," "credit," "societé," or "comptoir" (Kindleberger, 2015). During the French Revolution, issuing new paper money, with a real estate bank to be established, in return for the church's land and property, was unsuccessful, also because the public saw many similarities with John Law's proposals. The Mississippi bubble hampered France's financial development, keeping the French away from paper money and stock markets for generations.

References

Anderson, B. (1992). The new world disorder. *New Left Review, I/193*, 3–13.

Berdell, J. (2017). The structure and stability of John Law's early land bank proposals. *Oeconomia, 7*(4), 459–479. https://doi.org/10.4000/oeconomia.2622

Bosher, J. F. (1972). The French crisis of 1770. *History, 57*(189), 17–30.

Brie, M. (2019, October 19). *Creation of the Bank of France by Napoleon Bonaparte*. Napoleon Cologne Le Blog. https://blog.napoleon-cologne.fr/en/creation-of-the-bank-of-france-by-napoleon-bonaparte-2-2/

Buchan, J. (2018). *John Law: A Scottish adventurer of the eighteenth century*. Maclehose Press.

De Vries, J., & Van der Woude, A. (1997). *The first modern economy: Success, failure, and perseverance of the Dutch economy, 1500–1815*. Cambridge University Press.

Defoe, D. (2013). *John Law and the Mississippi scheme: An anthology*. Newton Page.

Encyclopaedia Britannica. (2011, September 26). *Assignat*. Editors of Encyclopedia Britannica. https://www.britannica.com/topic/assignat

Garber, P. M. (1990). Famous first bubbles. *Journal of Economic Perspectives, 4*(2), 35–54. https://doi.org/10.1257/jep.4.2.35

Gray, W. (1721). *The memoirs life and character of the great Mr. Law and his brother at Paris* (Reprint 2014). Newton Page.

Hoffman, P. T., Postel-Vinay, G., & Rosenthal, J.-L. (1995). Redistribution and long-term private debt in Paris, 1660–1726. *The Journal of Economic History, 55*(2), 256–284. https://doi.org/10.1017/S002205070004105X

Kindleberger, C. P. (2015). *A financial history of Western Europe*. Routledge.

Louis XV. (n.d.). Louis XV. *Wikipedia*. https://en.wikipedia.org/wiki/Louis_XV

Mammont Du Hautchamp's "Histoire du systeme des finances en 1719 et 1720" (1739).
Marion, M. (1934). La Fondation de la Banque de France et ses Premieres Années (1800–1814). In J. G. van Dillen (Ed.), *History of the principal public banks, Den Haag* (pp. 301–318, Reprinted 1964). Fran Cass & Co.
Masson, A. (1950). *Oeuvres Complètes de Montesquieu*. Nagel.
Murphy, A. E. (1997). *John Law: Economic theorist and policy-maker*. Oxford University Press.
Noordam, D. J. (1995). *Riskante relaties; vijf eeuwen homoseksualiteit in Nederland, 1233–1733*. Verloren, Hilversum.
Prebble, J. (1969). *The Darien disaster: A Scots colony in the new world, 1698–1700*. Holt, Rinehart, and Winston.
Rowlands, G. (2012). *The financial decline of a great power: War, influence and money in Louis XIV's France*. Oxford University Press.
Struyck, N. (1716). *Uytreekening der Kanssen in het Speelen door de Arithmetica en Algebra*. Salomon Schouten. https://books.google.nl/books/about/Uytreekening_der_kanssen_in_het_speelen.html?id=FDvHaqnvwzoC&redir_esc=y
Wiston-Glynn, A. W. (2022). *John Law of Lauriston: Financier and Statesman, Founder of the Bank of France, Originator of the Mississippi scheme, etc*. Project Gutenberg. https://www.gutenberg.org/files/63453/63453-h/63453-h.htm

Chapter 6
The Rothschilds: The Global Financial Empire (Eighteenth and Nineteenth Centuries)

6.1 Introduction

If you have ever been to Belgium, one of the places you should see is the battlefield of Waterloo, some 25 km south of Brussels. Visitors to the Waterloo site have lush green fields stretching as far as possible, and small groups of trees and groves are interspersed with them. The view in spring resembles an impressionist painter's painting. As Monet did with small brushstrokes, the rays of sunlight filtering through the clouds break the colors of nature and offer a great feast to the eyes. The most striking thing in the field is a lion statue on a high hill that can be seen from all sides. The lion's right foot rests on a globe that symbolizes the world. It depicts the courage of those who fought in this war with all its glory. Dutch King William I built this statue for his son, who was injured in the war. This great war, which affected the history of Europe, was memorized (Coleman, n.d.). The Battle of Waterloo, where both sides fought bravely, brought two famous commanders of history against each other. At the head of the British army was Arthur Wellesley (Fig. 6.1), the cold-blooded and arrogant Duke of Wellington, who had been fighting against Napoleon's troops on various fronts in Europe for years. The Dutch and Prussians were his allies. The French army was commanded by Napoleon Bonaparte (Fig. 6.2). Napoleon became the emperor of France in 1804 following the turmoil of the French Revolution. After conquering much of Europe, he returned from his Moscow expedition with a defeat. Then, he was exiled to the island of Elbe in July 1814, losing his throne. Napoleon escaped from this island 9 months later, dominated the country's administration, and became the head of his army. The outcome of this war would show who would determine the future of Europe. The French, whose economy is based on military power and taxes from occupied territories? Or the British, whose system is tied to borrowing and banking? Undoubtedly, securities investors and bankers were among the most curious about the outcome of this war.

On the afternoon of June 18, 1815, Napoleon Bonaparte, riding his gray horse, Marengo, back and forth on a hill in the south of the Waterloo plain, carefully watched

M. B. Karan et al., *A History of Banks*, Contributions to Economics,
https://doi.org/10.1007/978-3-031-62297-7_6

Fig. 6.1 Duke of Wellington Arthur Wellesley (1763–1852). https://en.wikipedia.org/wiki/Arthur_Wellesley,_1st_Duke_of_Wellington#/media/File:Sir_Arthur_Wellesley,_1st_Duke_of_Wellington.png

the movements of the British army. Marengo, who had been wounded eight times in the battles he participated in, was accustomed to such fighting and was never frightened by the sounds of cannons that made the earth groan (Morengo (horse), n.d.). Napoleon was very impatient. He wanted to give orders and start the battle as soon as possible. The Prussian army that had entered the war on the English side troubled him. He did not know exactly where they were, so he had to end the combat before they reached the battlefield. Since the weather was stormy and the places were slippery, he could only start the war at noon. The fight initiated with an attack of the French infantry battalions; at two o'clock, the British lines had begun to split, and the enemy soldiers were retreating rapidly. Confident that he would win, Napoleon said to the colonel next to him, "*Send a message to Paris; we have won this war.*" Before this news reached Paris, it was already halfway to London.

Napoleon was too hasty to send this news. By three o'clock, the Prussian army would appear behind the hill. What Napoleon feared was happening to him, now he would be stuck between two armies. In contrast, he had won the battle with the Prussians 2 days ago at Ligny and driven them north. Thus, the troops of the enemy had split into two parts as the British and the Prussian army. It would be much easier if he fought them separately. He had sent one of his most trusted generals,

Fig. 6.2 Napoleon Bonaparte (1769–1852). https://upload.wikimedia.org/wikipedia/commons/4/4d/Napoleon_at_the_Great_St._Bernard_-_Jacques-Louis_David_-_Google_Cultural_Institute.jpg

Emmanuel de Grouchy, and 33,000 soldiers to pursue the Prussians and keep them out of the battlefield. This division made up almost a third of his army. However, an experienced soldier, the Prussian commander Blücher, with a skillful maneuver, hid from De Grouchy who was following him and reached the battlefield. De Grouchy was still looking for him beyond the hills (Barbero, 2005).

The escape of Napoleon from Elba, the hundred days thereafter, and, finally, the battle of Waterloo formed the apotheosis of the Napoleonic wars. England was the main opponent of Napoleon and Wellington was its most important general. Maybe his most significant contribution to the final defeat of Napoleon was not the victory of Waterloo, but the Peninsular campaign. In 1806, Napoleon decided to embargo all traffic between Europe and Great Britain, the Continental System, to hurt Britain economically. He tried to seal off the entire coastline of Europe, including Portugal. In 1808, the land war with France was not going well from a British perspective, but the Iberian peninsula was the one theatre where they, with the Portuguese, had provided strong resistance (Arthur Wellesley, n.d.). Wellesley made a proposal of how to defend Portugal and was appointed head of all British forces in Portugal. When Wellingto arrived in Portugal, in 1809, he had an army of 20,000 British and 20,000 Portuguese. The French army there was much more prominent. Wellington's strategy was based on the insight that a large French army could not stay very long in one place. That was because they had to live off what was locally available. And that was not much in most of the peninsula. Wellington's army was supplied over the sea, with Lisbon as the main harbor. He combined that with an extensive network of depots. The logistics were challenging. But next to the logistics challenges, there was a financial challenge. Part of what was needed could be bought locally, but only with the right type of specie. Oxes and mules necessary for transportation disappeared when no acceptable species existed (Oman). The soldiers had to be paid in specie, at least partly. The Portuguese army was also paid partly by Britain. The Portuguese were not able to take care of their troops. Wellington made numerous suggestions to improve this but without much result. In 1811, he wrote to the Commissary in London: *The (Portuguese) Commissaries have no money to purchase anything in the country. I will not allow the soldiers to pillage. The government has no money to pay for the transport of provisions from the magazines on the coast to the army, are bankrupt in credit, and are unwilling to execute their own law to force means of transport; and the result is that the troops get nothing, and every department and branch of the service is paralyzed* (Kirby, 2011). To support the Portuguese, sending money to the right species was also necessary. The Peninsular Campaign lasted until 1814, and the need for money for the right species became structural during all these years. In 1812, the strategy changed to a more offensive one. Once in France, the difficulties got even worse because the French peasantry refused to accept Spanish or Portuguese currency. *In the winter of 1813/14, Wellington determined even to set up a mint of his own, to melt down Spanish and Portuguese silver and remint it in the form of five-franc pieces* (Oman, 2015). It is not surprising that the London Government called for the help of the Rothschilds in this respect. The role of the Rothschilds, especially Nathan Rothschild, in supporting the British with sufficient money for the suitable species in their war against Napoleon was very profitable for the Rothschilds and an important step for them in gaining international recognition. And Nathan was delighted with these actions. *In* 1834, 2 years before he died, he declared that *"the best business I ever did" was buying and shipping coins for the payment of Wellington's army in the Peninsula* (Cathcart, 2015).

This chapter will focus on the Rothschild family. That is complicated because they are focal in many of the world's most curious and various conspiracy theories. According to it, this family can determine the world gold prices, manage the world financial markets, and benefit from all kinds of wars and economic crises. Some of these conspiracy theories are very persistent. That is not only because the Rothschilds are rich and bankers but also due to the structural anti-semitism in Europe. See Chaps. 1 and 2 for a more extensive description of the role of the Jews in the Middle Ages. On the one hand, medieval society depended heavily on Jews for lending. Christians were not allowed to ask for interest, and Jews were, at least, for loans to Christians. On the other hand, the Church tried to push away Jews and Jewish practices as far as possible.

Although the troubles of the Jews continued in the New Age, they began to take a more important place in usury and banking activities. Although the general religious atmosphere softened somewhat during the Protestant Reformation, anti-Semitism continued. Martin Luther, a founder of the Protestant religion, is known to have been angry with the Jews for their rejection of Jesus.

In the middle of the eighteenth century, Jews living in German lands were living under the authority of the Jewish community, separated from the rest of the society by religious traditions and family structure, although gradually beginning to feel the effects of the political, social, and intellectual changes of the modern world. The reforms implemented by Emperor Joseph II in the "Decree of Tolerance" of 1781 had a more immediate impact on the plight of the Jews. However, the legal status of the Jews was still weak until the German reunification in 1871. Meanwhile, the Jewish community had educated and intellectual families and bankers like the Oppenheims (Abraham Oppenheim, n.d.). They started to establish more stable relations with German society by getting rid of the influence of the clergy (Gillerman, 2005). One of them was Mayer Rothschild.

Further in the chapter, we return to some of the conspiracy theories concerning the Rothschilds, i.e., the rumor that Nathan knew very early the outcome of the Waterloo battle and, instead of communicating it to the government and the London people, used that information on the London Exchange to trade government bonds, with huge profit.

6.2 Mayer Rothschild and the Birth of the Rothschild Dynasty

The person who led the Rothschild family to this stage of history is the main character of this story, Mayer Rothschild. This family would certainly not have had such great wealth without his talent and skill.

Mayer Amschel Rothschild (1744–1812) was born in Frankfurt's Judengasse, one of Frankfurt's oldest Jewish ghettos, where Jews had lived for 500 years (Fig. 6.3). The House where Mayer was born was inferior; the author and statesman Johann Wolfgang Von Goethe, while describing this area, mentioned that it was a shabby, dirty, and smelly place and that the Jews living in these neighborhoods were misfits (Reeves, 2012). His father, Amschel Moses, owned a small shop and was engaged in the silk trade while exchanging money. His wife's name was Lechnich and they had eight children. All five of his children who survived to adulthood were boys. Mayer Amschel (1744–1812) was the fourth child and lost his parents when he was just 12 years old. His relatives immediately took care of him, and he was sent to a Jewish school that provided religious education. Although he attended this school for a while, he left the school, thinking that theology was unsuitable. Little Mayer, already accustomed to trading with his father, wanted to start a business at that age; maybe he had a natural talent. Perhaps being an orphan fueled his ambition. He quickly adapted to business life, bargaining well and using his intelligence wisely in trade. He had started collecting old coins and coats of arms while studying. When he began doing business independently, he began developing his old coin collection.

Meanwhile, his diligence was beginning to be heard around. He was looking for an opportunity to develop his talents; he did not want to spend his life in a poor

Fig. 6.3 Mayer Amschel Rothschild (1744–1812). https://commons.wikimedia.org/wiki/File:Mayer_Amschel_Rothschild_-_The_Jewish_Encyclopedia_1907.png

community. He accepted the offer of a banking firm called Oppenheim in Hannover and started working there. The owners of this bank, which continues its banking activities today, were Jewish and a well-established Frankfurt firm. The Oppenheims would become related years later by marrying the Rothschilds (Abraham Oppenheim, n.d.). Mayer thought the firm would open up new possibilities for him, and he took the job because he hoped it would improve his environment. After working for a few years, his work was appreciated, and he was promoted to assistant manager. He had also saved some money while learning his trade. However, his whole purpose was to open a shop and earn money from the trade in antiques and gold. He had no hesitation in quitting his job once he started to feel a little confident. Although he had challenging times initially, he improved his situation within a few years and married Gudula Schnappe in 1770. He started living in his father's house and running his business there.

There was a coat of arms in the form of a red shield on the door of the family house. Although it is not known what this red shield means, this coat of arms was not given a particular meaning since it was customary to put such coats of arms on houses at that time. The fact that the purpose of the red shield in German is Rothschild was probably the main reason he chose this name (Ferguson, 1998). Mayer was known as a risk-seeking trader. He was very calm when he speculated and was known around him for his solid character and trustworthiness. His first investment was to buy his father's house. Everyone around him called him an "*honest Jew.*" People he worked with recommended him to others, and the business grew. His former employer, Oppenheim, encouraged him while helping him find new clients (Ferguson, 1998).

During Mayer Amschel's apprenticeship at Oppenheim, he met General Baron von Estorff and won his support by doing business dealings on his behalf. Baron von Estorff was also a close friend of Prince William IX of Hesse-Kassel, an independent region in the then Holy Roman German Empire. In 1794, William offered Mayer the position of principality treasury manager, probably on the advice of the Oppenheims. Prince William was one of the wealthiest people in Europe at the time. The Prince, who had business acumen, earned this fortune from financing various wars.

In 1804, Mayer Rothschild's contract with the Danish Government on a four-million Guilder loan showed that his power increased and his circle expanded. Maybe the wisest move of Mayer Rothschild, who started to develop his business by taking advantage of his increasing influence, was establishing a European banking network by sending his sons to different countries. Mayer and his eldest son Amschel ran the growing business from Frankfurt, while Nathan founded a branch in London in 1804, and James (Jacob) settled in Paris in 1812. After his death, in the 1820s, Salomon and Carl would open offices in Vienna and Naples, respectively. Through these branches, the family had a better view of what was going on globally, and considering wars as an opportunity, they lent money to kings and princes.

Meanwhile, significant developments were taking place in European politics. Napoleon Bonaparte, the King of France, increased his power and conducted military operations against Western Europe. Like the British and other Western European Kingdoms, Prince William was uncomfortable with Napoleon's rise to power in this way. He was in a close link with the British and could increase his already enormous wealth by placing his troops at the disposal of the Prussian and British governments and receiving some financial support in return. Observing his behavior, Napoleon was enraged. He decided to punish Prince William severely by plundering Kassel, and in 1806, he sent a part of his army to Germany. The most critical issue for the Prince, who heard that the French were approaching his land, was how to hide his vast wealth. At this point, Mayer Rothschild enters the story. However, Mayer's role in hiding this wealth is not well known, and there are conflicting interpretations. This event will remain one of the most important secrets in the history of the Rothschilds, and the truth may never be revealed. According to John Coleman (2006), known for his conspiracy theories, William first sent his fortune to Mayer Rothschild in Frankfurt for safekeeping. However, he says that Mayer Rothschild never returned the money and suggests that the fortune smuggled from the Prince was the primary source of the Rothschild's fortune. On the other hand, historian Niall Ferguson suggests that Prince William, in the face of Napoleon's impending threat, had his money in various pieces and different places. William's continued management of his assets gives the impression that the latter story is more credible.

Mayer Amschel Rothschild died on September 12, 1812, as Napoleon's army approached Moscow. After Napoleon's loss of power and his fall in 1814, the political and financial crisis shook the Rothschilds' newly established (1812) Paris and old Frankfurt banks, almost jeopardizing their international structure. When Mayer Rothschild died, he left a great fortune to his sons. In keeping with Jewish traditions, their children never forgot his advice when they buried their father: "Stay faithful to the law of Moses, be united to the end, and do nothing without first consulting your mother. If you follow these orders, you will soon be rich among the richest, and the world will belong to you." His wife, Gudula, died in 1849. She was 96 years old and lived long enough to see her sons follow their father's advice and join among the wealthiest people in the world. She had experienced how they had gone from rags to riches in years. Later, his children would run the bank like Mayer showed them, and even if they ran separate companies in different countries, they would always act together on important events. This unity of purpose and action would enable them to enjoy fame and incredible wealth simultaneously (Reeves, 2012).

Fraternity was the first principle on which the Rothschild Bank Association was founded. In the will of Mayer Amschel Rothschild, written on his deathbed in September 1812, he called on his sons to maintain this fraternal friendship. When faced with adversity or crisis, the sons always remembered their father's words. There was another rule of the family; this rule was about male supremacy. Following religious references and the spirit of that time in Europe, men's rights in management and property always took precedence over women. According to this rule, until 1960, only Rothschild men were eligible to become company partners. This condition was accepted in the first partnership agreement in 1810, not allowing his wife and children to see the bank's accounting records in case of a partner's death (Ferguson, 1998).

Mayer Amschel Rothschild's acquisition of such a fortune was mainly due to the exceptional situation of the world, financial life, and turmoil in the political world. Napoleon changed the political structure of Europe and invaded Spain, Italy, Central Europe, and Russia. Mayer Rothschild probably would not have achieved this feat had he lived in more peaceful times. The years of the Napoleonic wars were a perfect time for a clever and daring speculator. Especially when prices fluctuate excessively, and all kinds of rumors affect prices, if somebody has good sources of information, he might make a great fortune by using it wisely.

6.3 Rothschild and Wellington

The Rothschilds had their first significant gains during the British campaign against Napoleon's armies in Spain between 1808 and 1814. When Duke Wellington did not receive sufficient support from the British Government, he sought help from the bankers. When no banker wanted to send that much gold to Spain, the Rothschilds stepped in and sent gold and coins to Spain in return for a hefty commission by violating the trade blockade of Napoleon between England and Europe. Behind this success is Nathan Rothschild's significant experience as a gold trader and perhaps smuggler in Continental Europe. Most probably, the French condoned the gold trade because an outflow of gold from England would harm the British economy, according to the Mercantilist economic understanding prevailing at the time. In January 1814, the British Secretary of the Exchequer, John Charles Herries, had authorized Nathan to secretly collect large quantities of French gold and silver coins in Germany, France, and the Netherlands. Within two months, the gold to be procured was delivered to British ships in the Dutch port of Hellevoetsluis and sent to Duke Wellington, crossing the Pyrenees to France. This massive operation showcased the Rothschild brothers' ability to access cross-country credit networks and manage large-scale bullion transfers. This project was so successful that Wellington soon declared his gratitude for this service: "*Rothschild has performed admirably well the various services entrusted to him, although he is a Jew, we rely heavily on him* (Ferguson, 1998)."

By May 1814, Nathan had loaned the government about £12 million, twice the amount envisaged in the original plan. It was risky to transfer such large amounts of gold even at the war's end, so the Rothschilds undoubtedly deserved the hefty commission required for this risk. What made them so fit for the task was that the brothers had a ready-made banking network within the family. Nathan worked in London, Amschel in Frankfurt, James in Paris, Carl in Naples, and Salomon went wherever Nathan saw fit. By building a European network, they used the method known as arbitrage: their ability to make money by taking advantage of price and exchange rate differences between markets. For example, when the price of gold in Paris was higher than in London, James in Paris would sell gold for bills of exchange and send it to London, where Nathan would use it to buy more gold. The fact that the price differences between countries were quite substantial contributed to the profits of the Rothschilds. In addition, the Rothschilds benefited from subsidies from the British Government to the Allies. Prime Minister Robert Jenkinson is known to have said, "*Mr. Rothschild is a beneficial friend; I don't know what we would have done without him.*" Since this payment continued throughout the war, it is estimated that they made quite a lot of money from this work (Ferguson, 2008).

In the last decades of the eighteenth century, many European countries struggled to cope with their debts. After the 1720 Mississippi economic crisis, the French economy faced the harsh economic conditions caused by the 1789 French Revolution. Napoleon developed the economy by establishing military action and occupation. The Netherlands and Russia, exhausted by wars, also had financial difficulties. Russia almost went bankrupt during this period. In 1797 and 1815, they improved their situation to some extent with two foreign debt negotiations.

On the other hand, Britain was a colonial empire that relied heavily on debt. Also, since they had been fighting for so long, their financial troubles were mounting, and they had borrowed to finance this war by issuing record amounts of bonds. Between 1793 and 1815, Britain's national debt had tripled to 745 million euros in today's money, more than double the annual output of the UK economy. The British issued "Consols," bonds with infinite maturity and fixed interest forever. Interest on this debt instrument is still paid by the British treasury today. The coupon rate (the nominal interest) was around 3% (Consol (Bond), n.d.). Let us write a note here to inform our readers. If interest rates rise due to risk or inflation, the bond price will fall because else no one will buy the 3% bond. Conversely, if the interest rates fall below 3%, the bond price will rise, as the interest rate will be attractive. Since February 1792, a typical £100 consol price had fallen from £96 to less than £60 on the eve of the Battle of Waterloo. In addition, England was heavily indebted, and the public held substantial bonds. British society was constantly lending to the state. If Napoleon won, interest rates would rise, and the people could sell their bonds only at a lower price (Ferguson, 1998). The Battle of Waterloo in 1815 raised the importance of the sovereign bond market in England. The development in England had a positive impact on other countries.

According to a popular legend, the Rothschild family owed their first millions of fortunes to speculation after the Battle of Waterloo. Nathan had learned the war's outcome before anyone else and had made a formidable fortune by using his cunning strategy to buy British bonds cheaply and then sell them at a high price when the actual result came to light. Georges Dairnvaell (1846), a French journalist and pamphleteer using the pen name Satan, claimed that Nathan Rothschild was a privileged audience at the Waterloo battle on Sunday. As soon as Rothschild saw with his own eyes how Napoleon had lost the war, he hurried to the port of Ostend, giving gold to the sailors in stormy weather and convincing them to move their boats, crossing the English Channel and returning to England. This way, Nathan Rothschild was 24 h ahead of Wellington's official messenger. A writer of the same period, John Reeves (1887), also elaborated on this story and wrote that everyone would see Nathan as in poor health and mood on Tuesday. He deliberately panicked investors by declaring the news of the defeat of Britain's Prussian allies at Ligny and appearing too worried about the outcome of the subsequent battle of Waterloo. The bad news spread like wildfire all over the city. Funds plummeted. But the next afternoon, a sudden, wild reaction began. Now, everyone knew Wellington had won. Many gentlemen took pity on Rothschild for the enormous losses he suffered; no one suspected him. Nathan and his brothers were told to have manipulated the Stock Exchange in one big hit, gaining almost a million pounds.

It was a very widely spread and very persistent story. European people liked to believe it, and ultimately, the Nazis used it greedily for a film: "The Rothschilds, Shares in Waterloo." In part of the story, Nathan Rothschild is mixed up with the famous economist Ricardo, a Jew. In that form, it has even been spread by Paul Samuelson (Parys, 2024). Cathcart (2015) investigated all possibilities extensively and explained that it was utterly impossible; Nathan Rothschild was not in Waterloo, the weather was not stormy, the price of the consols developed differently, Nathan Rothschild (as well as Ricardo) did not trade on the London Exchange then, etc.

Historian Niall Ferguson's assessment was based on further evidence; the Rothschilds faced a severe loss from Wellington's victory, let alone that they were making money. According to the author, they made their fortune not because of Waterloo but despite it. Based on the experience gained from the Spanish war, Nathan Rothschild decided to continue his gold purchases. He predicted the new war would last years (Ferguson, 1998).

Wasting no time, they bought all the bullion and coins he and his brothers could find and submitted them to the British Treasury to be sent to Wellington. The Rothschilds are estimated to have supplied more than approximately £2 million in gold coins, enough to fill 884 cans and 55 barrels. At the same time, the sum of his transactions with the British Treasury in 1815 approached £9.8 million as Britain decided to create a new financial support package with its allies such as the Netherlands and Germany. Since commissions for all these businesses were between 2 and 6%, he expected to make a tremendous fortune from these transactions. However, Nathan had got into a risky position, assuming the war would be extended. If the war lasted short, there would be no need for that much gold, and gold's price would drop. What they feared came to pass, and on the evening of June 18, the battle resulted in a decisive victory for the Duke of Wellington. Nathan Rothschild and his brothers, who shared the news received early with the British Government, were left alone with a pile of gold they were preparing for war. There was only one way out for them: to plan another speculation. Britain's economy, which was unrivaled in Europe, could develop in the coming years, and the prices of the bonds, which were not attractive enough, could rise very high at the end of the war. The Rothschilds would use their gold to invest in the bonds of England, which was beginning to heal their wounds.

With the peaceful period that started after Waterloo, the British Government's reduction in debt reduced the risks. Bond prices began to rise as interest rates fell. Nathan bought more and more bonds, not selling his holdings even though prices were rising, waiting for prices to increase even more. When he sold it in 1817, prices had risen 40%, and he had made £600 million in today's money. In the words of one of the partners of Barings Bank, one of the Rothschilds' biggest rivals at the time, "I must sincerely admit that I lack the courage for his operations. They were generally well-planned, with great wit and skill in execution. He has as much money and fund management skills as Napoleon's skills in war" (Ferguson, 1998).

6.4 The Five Brothers Empire

Toward the end of the Napoleonic wars, Hamburg quickly gained importance as an additional focus of the network. The network of agents expanded tremendously during the rapid rise of the Rothschilds from the 1820s. The importance of North Sea ports increased, and numerous agencies were established in France, the Mediterranean, and Eastern Europe. These conditions allowed the Rothschild brothers to establish an extensive European network by opening branches. After the death of their father, one in five brothers (Amschel) remained in Frankfurt, Nathan (Fig. 6.4) set up a branch already in London, while the other three set up their businesses in Paris (1812), Vienna (1820) and Naples (1821). After the father, naturally, the eldest brother, Amschel, would be the head of the family. Nevertheless, the family accepted Nathan's leadership, with this exception to the rule. Nathan Rothschild was the more talented businessman among them.

Fig. 6.4 Nathan Mayer Rothschild (1777–1836). https://commons.wikimedia.org/wiki/File:Nathan_Mayer_Rothschild.jpg

During this period, the Rothschilds had become not only a European but, to some extent, a global financial power. Representatives were often located in locations that were the headquarters of certain businesses, such as ports, but also in numerous political decision-making centers, reflecting the political fragmentation of the European continent at the time. This was especially true of pre-unification Italy, France, and Spain. After 1820, government loans grew and required exceptionally reliable political information. Salvador (Bahia), Valparaiso, and Havana have joined Rio as focal points for Rothschild agencies in Latin America. There was more trade in commodities such as cotton, sugar, tobacco, silver, and gold than in financial services.

The Rothschild brothers had treated their network not as a standalone business but as a branch of the Frankfurt homestead. In addition to running the traditional bill of exchange business, they issued government bonds for nearly all of Europe and a few Latin American countries. They also actively financed industrial enterprises and railroads and traded various commodities. While nominally independent, the houses co-ordinated many transactions, helped each other with temporary liquidity problems, and, most importantly, shared political and economic intelligence practically daily through extremely regular correspondence. They relied on a relatively extensive network of agents alongside five independent banks. The representative network was not developed according to a master plan but was formed according to the Rothschilds' changing business interests, opportunities, and market conditions. It was a dynamic phenomenon. Therefore, it should be noted that the Rothschild family initially formed an international network of so-called independent bank houses, and their intermediary networks developed together.

6.4.1 *Frankfurt House*

When Mayer Amschel died in 1812, his eldest son, Amschel Mayer (1773–1855), took over managing the Frankfurt house in the Rothschild Banking business. His brothers Salomon (1774–1855) and Carl (1788–1855) wandered from court to court, and from congress to congress; while negotiating connections and agreements, Amschel took the lead from Frankfurt in the government (sovereign) bond business. After the Napoleonic wars, Prussia had a 32 million pound debt and had severe financial difficulty. The Five Rothschild Brothers Maintained an Extensive Correspondence. In 1818, they sold a very successful bond for Prussia. The bond issuance in March 1818 was a great success, and indeed, this process is significantly included in the book of credit subscribers stored in the Rothschild archive. The first tranche of the loan was sold to 70% of the nominal value and soon began to bank much above this price. This financing strengthened their situation in Prussia. In 1822, Nathan won another credit agreement for Prussia for £ 3,500,000. The interest rate was also set at 5%, but this time, the issue price was sold on the international market for 84% of the face value of the Prussian loan. It was a more successful operation than expected (Subscription ledger for the Prussian Government loan, 1818, n.d.).

The Rothschild Brothers maintained consolidated financial accounts in Frankfurt, and each had a stake in the capital of each branch. According to a Document from 1828, The Five brothers together controlled assets totaling about 119 million francs. The resources of the Bank of France then amounted to about 60 million francs at that time (Gille, 1965).

Amschel received several orders and served as Royal Prussian Privy Councillor, Privy Councillor to the Electorate of Hesse, Royal Bavarian Consul, and Prussian Consul General. He died in Frankfurt in 1855 and had no child. The house passed to Carl von Rothschild (1820–1866) and Wilhelm Carl von Rothschild (1828–1901) as Joint Partners. By 1901, with the death of Wilhelm Carl, the Frankfurt bank's last remaining partner, Frankfurt was no longer a significant financial center. No family members in London, Paris, or Vienna wished to move to the Prussian city, and the decision was taken to close the Frankfurt house. The remaining business was transferred to the Disconto Gesellschaft of Berlin.

6.4.2 *London House*

Rothschild initially entered the London market as a Hesse-Kassel agency. This market was very competitive and prejudiced against the Jews. The most important feature of the period was the growing British economy and the Industrial Revolution in Europe.

After England's Great Revolution of 1688, democracy was well-developed, and the state was paying its debts seriously. The British had been trying to solve the public finance problem for a long time with the debt papers they issued, namely treasury bonds. This environment was an excellent chance for banks that gave loans to the state, such as the Rothschilds. In 1809, Nathan Rothschild began to deal with gold bullion, which he developed as a cornerstone of his business. The booming London market allowed Nathan to run very profitable operations. As a result of their intelligent banking operations, the brothers' business had grown exponentially since 1812 and gradually reached a global dimension. Nathan had left the traditional ways and created a new business. His wealth and resources had grown so much that conventional banking operations no longer interested him. During the Napoleonic wars, in 1811–1816, he cooperated with General J. C. Herries, the Commissary in Chief, and meeting the logistics requirements of the British army raised their reputation and enabled Britain's gates to be fully opened. As mentioned already, they organized transfer money to pay Wellington's troops on a campaign in Portugal and Spain against Napoleon, and later, they made subsidy payments to British allies when they arranged new troops after Napoleon's catastrophic Russian campaign. Their operations were enormous, and the success had increased in parallel. Nathan's leadership was successful because of the extraordinary financial operations that affected many European States then. He gave loans to various countries, especially the British Government, and entered into profitable and successful businesses such as managing state funds. In this way, between 1812 and 1830, the Rothschilds had power and wealth that no bank had before (Chapman, 1982).

Nathan Mayer Rothschild developed a robust and tight relationship with the Bank of England. He was a buyer and borrower of gold and silver from the Bank. In 1825, the Rothschilds prevented a financial crisis by providing a large volume of gold to the Bank of England when the Bank ran desperately out of coined gold. The Rothschilds reached the top of their power and international reputation in England in 1825 by solving the liquidity crisis. Another notable event was their move to support Britain during the Suez Crisis in 1875. These issues will be explained in detail in the next section.

After the Napoleonic wars, Britain had a severe financial deficit. Fixed interest paid by the government for bonds was reducing their risks. In addition, everyone could buy any amount of government bonds they wanted and freely sell them in the market. The bond market was growing. Companies' stocks could be traded in all major European markets. Unsurprisingly, the demand for these stocks increased steadily, and the bond markets became the most important in a few years. Nathan had taken full advantage of the opportunities provided by these markets, especially by investing in the bond markets.

Following the abolition of slavery in 1837, they also provided the money needed by the British Government for the payment of the Slave compensation. Rothschild and his business partner Moses Montefiore lent £ 15 million to the British Government. This money was used to compensate the slave owners in the British Empire (including himself) after the trade was abolished. The last part of the loan was paid back only in 2015 (Nathan Mayer Rothschild, n.d.)

While the Rothschilds carried out essential banking activities in leading European countries, the Rothschild Bank emphasized gold, diamonds, mines, and infrastructure projects. In the second half of the nineteenth century, the bank made an effort to develop the British South Africa Company. It became its largest shareholder, funding the De Beers diamond mines in South Africa.

The London banking house continued under the management of Lionel Nathan de Rothschild (1882–1942) and his brother Anthony Gustav de Rothschild (1887–1961) and then to Sir Evelyn de Rothschild (b. 1931). In 2003, following Sir Evelyn's retirement as head of N M Rothschild & Sons of London, the UK and French financial firms merged under the leadership of David René de Rothschild (Fig. 6.4).

Nathan Rothschild was a hard worker, even a workaholic. According to Nathan's great-great-grandson, the 4th Lord Rothschild, he (Nathan) was short, fat, obsessive, highly intelligent, and business-oriented. He was not a charming person to associate with. His cousin Evelyn had a similar view, "*I think he was very ambitious and determined, but I don't think he underestimates idiots.*" In a letter to his brothers, Nathan wrote (Parikh, 2008):

> I'm writing my opinion as writing to you is my damn duty. I read your letters not once but maybe hundreds of times. You can imagine this yourself. I usually have nothing to do after dinner. I don't read books, I don't play cards, I don't go to the theatre, my only pleasure is my job, and so I read the letters of Amschel, Salomon, James, and Carl... As for Carl's letter about buying a bigger house in Frankfurt, all this is ridiculous because as long as we have good jobs and are rich, everyone will praise us and envy all of us who are not interested in generating income through us.

Someone from that era described Nathan this way: "*The eyes are often called the windows of the soul, but when you see Rothschild, you feel that the windows are fake or no soul is looking out the window. Not a single glow from inside. All this makes you think of an empty body, and you wonder why it's standing upright with nothing in it*" (Morton, 1962).

6.4.3 Paris House

James de Rothschild (1792–1868) arrived in Paris in 1812, the last years of Napoleon's first reign, and for more than half a century maintained close ties to power and governments of all kinds. With the purchase of a hôtel in 1818 in the old rue d'Artois, now rue Laffitte, the richest, most animated, and modern part of Paris, James' lifestyle began to reflect the high social position he had attained as founder of the French Rothschild bank. In 1815, James Rothschild's Paris branch controlled just one-sixth of all Rothschild capital (approximately £36 million). By 1820, he was the richest merchant banker in Paris, and by 1821, his financial branch in Paris had become the most powerful within Rothschild's expanding financial empire.

The most profitable business after the Napoleonic wars was financing the indemnity that England and its allies demanded from the new French administration. They organized this syndicated loan together with Barings bank. In addition, by meeting the war pledge of the new king of France, their reputation in France increased considerably. They were the most respected bankers in France until the monarchy ended in 1848. In gratitude for his services to the French nation, King Louis Philippe (1830–848) elevated him to the dignity of Grand Officer of the Legion of Honour. James wrote in one of his letters (Chapman, 1982): "*We could obtain the title of "the King's Banker" if we wanted to, but it is better to do the King's business without the title. He promised that whatever he received he would place with us.*"

The family's most important activities outside of London were operated through the Rothschild Bank of Paris. The Rothschilds credited the state and were involved in various banking activities, including trading government bonds and bullion. They were also involved in financing Napoleon Bonaparte's army (Spagnol, 2019). They provided loans for the trade of various agricultural products. French Rothschilds also had the right to import the copper of the Russian Demidoff family. In the 1840s, they became increasingly interested in metals, and the Rothschilds were the only mercury mines in Europe (Kernan, 2009).

As James Rothschild's operations expanded with the restoration of Europe due to his network of financial relations, an antisemitic movement started in France in 1840. In addition, the death of 14 people due to an accident on the trains operated by the Rothschilds in 1846 increased the anger toward the family and the Jewish community. This anti-Semitic movement had turned into a European-wide campaign that blamed all Jews, including Rothschilds, who became very rich with alleged manipulation during the Waterloo war, where thousands of French soldiers were killed, with the claims of writers like Dairnvaell (Cathcart, 2015). Indeed, the anti-Rothschild emotion in France was also inspired by the dominance of James Rothschild in French finance and the scale of the Rothschild operations. Between 1823 and 1847, James had almost monopolized the French Government's finances by giving seven credits with a nominal value of 1.5 billion francs (£ 60 million) (Ferguson, 1999).

James had engaged in significant projects in France linked to his banking interests, such as the Compagnie des chemins de fer du Nord ("Northern Railway Company"), investing in coal mining, and various commercial activities in conjunction with his brothers. Additionally, the Rothschilds in France had become leaders in the viticulture industry (Ferguson, 1999).

Under Emperor Napoleon III's reign, Rothschild lost part of his political influence; France had become more nationalistic, and antisemitism was rising. The nationalists after the 1890s called them the demons of capitalism and transnationalism (Kernan, 2009). Despite difficulties, the family business survived and developed its activities under the new regime. In 1852, Rothschilds started the competition with the bank Crédit Mobilier. Nonetheless, Rothschild maintained the leading position in the finance sector (Muhlstein, 1983). Toward the end of the nineteenth century, with the increasing importance of oil, they were heavily involved in oil exploration in today's Baku region of Azerbaijan through the Caspian and Black Sea Oil Industry and Trade Association. Still, in 1911, the Royal Dutch Shell company was going to buy the Azerbaijan oil fields from the Rothschild family (Ferguson, 1999).

The Paris business suffered heavily in 1981 when the Socialist government of François Mitterrand nationalized the bank and renamed it Compagnie Européenne de

Banque. In 1987, a successor company called Rothschild & Cie Banque was created by David René de Rothschild, Edouard de Rothschild, and Eric de Rothschild. They built their small investment bank into a major financial institution in Europe. In 2003, the English and French firms merged into the Group Rothschild under the leadership of David René de Rothschild. In 2006, the French banking division extended into Brussels.

6.4.4 Vienna House

The House of Rothschild first dealt with Austrian finances during and immediately after the Napoleonic wars. In 1820, Austrian Foreign Minister Prince Metternich entered negotiations with the Rothschild Assembly for a large loan in the form of a lottery. He demanded the presence of a Rothschild in Vienna so that arrangements could be made for this enormous loan. So Salomon Mayer (1774–1855), who took over the Rothschild business with Austria, moved to the city and established a banking and investment establishment. He played an integral role in the development of the Austrian economy.

The Rothschild Bank facilitated lending to Austria as they gathered information about Austria's possibilities and willingness to meet its loan obligations in the early nineteenth century. No relationship has been as developed and essential as the Rothschilds' relationship with Austrian foreign minister Metternich. He was called "uncle" as an expression of affection and a code name in correspondence (Cowles, 1973). Internationally, the credit allowed Austria to pursue a foreign policy beyond its means. It also ensured the isolation of anti-war politicians. Metternich also benefited from the two-way exchange of information, taking advantage of the Rothschilds' impressive communication network (Shea, 2020).

The Austrian Emperor was very impressed by the commercial operations of the Rothschilds during the Napoleonic wars. He gave them great importance in providing financing and facilitating relations with England. Indeed, in 1822, the five Rothschild brothers, who headed the family banks in various parts of Europe, were given the hereditary title of Freiherr (Baron) in the Austrian nobility by the Emperor Francis of Austria. Nathan became the British honorary consul. This position would eventually pass to other family members, until 1914.

Austria's solvency became dependent on Rothschild's loans. High financial and economic instability, combined with the empire's continued currency depreciation and foreign policies, increased uncertainty about repayment (Mitchell, 1975). Austria also lacked democratic institutions and a properly functioning central bank to increase its credibility in the market (Schultz and Weingast, 2003). The Rothschild Bank could easily bankrupt Austria if it did not lend. The Rothschild Bank had the power to influence the state's warfare and diplomacy. Indeed, in the 1860s, the bank refused to give credit to Austria during the Prussian War, forcing it to accept Prussian demands (Steefel, 1936). The family's activities in Vienna would continue until the Nazis arrived in 1938.

6.4.5 Naples House

The forces that had defeated Napoleon at the Congress of Vienna in 1815 had decided that the Bourbons kingdom should be re-established in Naples. Ferdinand I thus ascended the throne of the new Kingdom of the Two Sicilies. However, the country had to pay Austria 10 million ducats for war reparations and maintenance of the Austrian army. Faced with a heavy debt burden, the government needed substantial loans. To support Ferdinand, the Austrian army entered the Kingdom of Sicily and occupied Naples. This event opened the door to Rothschild's interests. Carl von Rothschild was sent to Naples, where he founded CM de Rothschild & Figli as a satellite office to Germany's Rothschild banking family headquarters in Frankfurt am Main (Barbagallo, 2000).

The Bourbon's first 16 million ducats loan agreement was signed in May 1821. This deal was a syndicated loan with other Neapolitan commercial bankers, Appelts, Forquets, Falconnets and Meuricotrres, and Paris house Hagermann. The Rothschilds negotiated an additional loan of 16.8 million ducats with the Bourbon Government in December 1821. A third loan was applied for in August 1822, and the corresponding agreement of £2.5 million, equivalent to 15 million ducats, was signed in London in February 1824. Naples was now the fifth European capital, where a permanent branch of the Rothschild banking house acted as its sole lender and financial intermediary (Barbagallo, 2000).

The Bank financed the financial needs of the Treasury of the Kingdom of the Two Sicilies. It made the payments in the European financial markets, especially Vienna, the final destination of most resources. Local bankers were now buying and selling public bonds of the kingdom of Naples, which the Rothschilds had quoted on the London Stock Exchange at the request of the Minister of Finance, Luigi de Medici. As a result, the interests of the Bourbon Government, the Rothschilds, and the Neapolitan bankers were united to maximize the kingdom's revenues. In Naples, the Rothschilds were effectively integrated into the economic and cultural life of the Bourbon capital. Yet, like many foreign entrepreneurs who settled in southern Italy in the early nineteenth century, they lived in isolation; they were not inclined to mingle with the local bourgeoisie (Barbagallo, 2000).

1855 was wretched for the Rothschild banking dynasty: three of the Rothschild brothers died—Amschel, Karl, and Solomon; Nathan had already died in 1936. When the importance of the kingdom of Naples was lost, the Rothschild branch in Naples was transferred to Turin and Rome in 1863.

6.5 Other Notable Events in the Rothschild History

6.5.1 The Crisis of 1825 and the Bank of England

1825, the Rothschilds gained an international reputation due to their actions to save the Bank of England during the Panic of 1825. The background of the event was very complicated. At the end of the eighteenth century in England, more and more people were exchanging their banknotes for gold. Due to the overprinting of banknotes, the Bank of England lost its gold supply, and the value of each banknote decreased due to the gold standard. As banks in many cities were under attack of depositors, these banks began to demand monetary support from the Bank of England. Meanwhile, on February 22–24, 1797, French forces invaded England's land at Fishguard. When news of this event reached London, it was feared that there would be an even more remarkable run on the Bank of England, as many holders of bank notes tried to convert them into gold. It could reduce the bullion reserves of the Bank of England. Parliament decided to suspend these speculative payments immediately; this suspension was renewed every year until 1821. By 1821, however, radical economic policies initiated by Sir Robert Peel (the future prime minister who served as Chairman of the Bullion Committee) reversed the situation, and the British Government reintroduced "convertibility" on May 1, 1821. Interestingly, following the passage of the law, British right-wing politician Richard Brinsley Sheridan mocked the Bank of England for coming under the influence of William Pitt, describing the institution as "an old lady of the city, of great reputation and long-standing, but unfortunately in bad company." This led to the famous cartoon Political Ravishment; or the Old Lady of Threadneedle Street in Danger by James Gillray, well-known for his political cartoons, in which Pitt seduces the Bank of England for his fortune, depicted as an old woman dressed in £1 and £2 notes. The cartoon led to the Bank's nickname, "The Old Lady of Threadneedle Street," which is still used today (Bank Restriction Act, n.d.).

With the introduction of convertibility, the British economy entered a period of rapid expansion characterized by both an export and investment boom. In 1824, a temporary influx of gold created a massive expansion in banknote issuance. After that, they switched to a much more relaxed policy, which led to monetary ease. In between, the government was inflationary, refinancing its debt, leading to extra liquidity in the economy (Neal, 1998). The country banks added to this liquidity by issuing bank notes. This fueled the speculation that was already going on with the crisis. During this period, the country's economy grew rapidly, investments increased, and exports exploded. As the gaslighting of the cities and new railway projects were developed, there were mining projects in South America, some European and South American governments developed financial markets, and the stock market revived. Exports were mainly aimed at newly established South American countries. Meanwhile, the bonds of an imaginary South American country were also on the market. No one was searching if this was real; people were constantly investing to make money, creating a bubble in the securities market. The name of this imaginary country was

Poyais. The Scottish adventurer MacGregor, who fought for Venezuela in the war of independence against Spain, had created an entirely fictional state and convinced investors that the Central American Principality of Poyais had enormous resources. MacGregor was so persuasive that he could make a significant bond issue on the London Stock Exchange in 1822. He had successfully used the lack of information and the greed of investors during the market bubble (Morgan and Narron, 2015). Thus, like the French and English bubbles of the 1720s discussed in Chaps. 4 and 5, the market was poisoned by greed, and the banking system was flooded with risky loans (Bordo, 1998).

The Bank of England's gold reserves grew before 1825, so it issued more paper money on the market. It lowered interest rates, considerably increasing the amount of money in the market. The Bank of England was not yet the central bank it is today. It was not the only bank with this privilege; local banks in various parts of the country could also freely issue money and speculate in the stock market. There were also significant investment opportunities in England for those who did not want to be involved in South American investments. One was the Alliance Fire and Insurance Company, which the Rothschilds founded in March 1824. Nathan created this company when he could not agree with Lloyds Insurance, which discriminated against Jews and charged high insurance fees for shipping gold. Many investors who wanted to chase the success of Alliance Fire and Insurance tried to establish companies by developing various projects. At that time, permission to establish companies was given by the British Parliament. The number of applicants to set up new companies rose from 30 in March to 250 in April. However, some of the projects were entirely fictitious. However, a sharp contraction in banknote issuance followed in 1825. The reason for the contraction was that in 1825, the Bank of England realized that there was too much liquidity in the economy and tried to limit it. Meanwhile, the outflow of gold also contributed to the contraction. The government immediately curtailed spending but was forced to borrow both short and long terms. As Nathan predicted, this policy also led to a trade deficit. This outflow of gold was behind the sharp monetary contraction of 1825. Under these conditions, the high prices on the London Stock Exchange during the bubble of 1822–24 could not be sustained. In April 1825, the market began to fall. The sharpest falls were in British industrial bonds and Latin American bonds. But the bonds of the former Spanish republics performed even worse. Mexican, Colombian, and Peruvian bonds all fell below 20%. Even the best paper, the British 3% consolidated bonds, was affected. It was inevitable that such a severe asset devaluation would lead to a banking crisis (Ferguson, 1999).

Finally, a significant financial crisis had begun; the markets were upside down, and investors were selling their stocks. Concerned about the amount of money private banks gave, the Bank of England had taken control by reducing lending in August 1825. The Bank raised the discount rate from 4 to 5% on 14 December 1825 at the height of the crisis to increase its bullion reserves, which were too low. The Bank of England also began to issue one-pound notes for a short period as an emergency measure during the crisis. All small notes had been withdrawn from circulation in 1821. Parliament set up special committees to make advances to provincial towns in economic distress. In 1826, Parliament lifted the ban on joint-stock banking outside

London, which had been in force since 1708. These large banks gradually took over the provincial banks or caused them to cease operations. At the same time, the Bank of England tried to extend its reach beyond London by opening branches in seven major English cities. Since small notes were blamed for the crisis, in March 1826, Parliament declared that all private banknotes under five pounds should be withdrawn by 1829 (Black, 1995). Gold reserves had fallen to only 20% of the value of banknotes in circulation. At the beginning of 1825, when the markets were still alive and gold prices in London were low, the Rothschilds had taken a large loan from the Bank of England and sold gold to France. The Rothschilds had made a considerable profit by taking advantage of the bubble created by the excessive rise in the prices of securities in the markets. In London alone, six banks failed as one after another stopped payments. The bank's president had threateningly informed the government that suspending cash payments might be the only way to prevent a general financial collapse since Treasury bills would not be able to meet the demand for gold when they matured. Meanwhile, the bank's reserves of gold coins that could be used immediately were rapidly depleting. The British banker Henry Thornton had already realized that Rothschild had a stockpile of gold and demanded it with some persuasion and some threats. Nathan agreed, first by demanding a 2% commission, then by saying he was doing it for the public good (Ferguson, 1999).

When the crisis hit in the middle of the year, and the Bank of England found itself in a liquidity crunch, the Rothschilds kept their promise and played the savior bank role in rescuing the market within a few months. Nathan did two things: first, he advised the government to intervene in the money market by buying treasury bills to inject liquidity into the market; second, and more importantly, he started with £300,000 in gold and continued with more considerable sums over the following weeks until confidence was restored. Nathan would not have made such immense deliveries of gold without asking for a generous commission in return. This operation should be seen as part of a campaign to establish Rothschild as the dominant force in the London bullion market. The bank's rescue raised the international reputation of the Rothschilds (Ferguson, 1999).

After this operation, the Rothschilds became the official gold broker of the British state. One of the five members of the London Gold Exchange, the essential market pricing gold today, is selected from the Rothschild Company (Bank of England, n.d.). The Bank of England, which learned lessons from the crisis, started to give loans to banks in trouble, acting as a central bank to save the system (Winton, 2018). Meanwhile, as the Rothschilds' reputation rose, their position in the British State reached the highest level. Nathan's grandson, Alfred Charles Freiherr Rothschild, was appointed as one of the directors of the Bank of England in 1868 at the age of 26, and he held this position for 20 years until 1889. He became the first Jew appointed. After he left this position, no other Jew was in the directorate for more than fifty years. He left the Bank of England in 1889 because he was accused of investigating the private account of an art dealer whom Alfred suspected was asking him a disproportionate price. However, the matter was settled in 1894 when both sides exchanged apologies (The Rothschild Family, n.d.).

James (2012) characterizes the Bank of England's response to panics from 1790 to 1825 as "limited, episodic and inconsistent" but notes that the Bank played a more active role in managing the 1825 crisis through interest rate policy. This crisis made the country's economy more flexible and robust to external shocks by enabling Britain to make financial and political reforms. It ensured Britain's dominance over international finance until the First World War. In July 1826, the British tax system was overhauled, and bankruptcy laws were more modernized. Local banks could open branches nationwide, freeing them from being at the mercy of correspondent banks in other cities. Most importantly, the Bank of England became the first bank of the banks, learning how to behave when lending to the banking system. This reform reduced England's national debt and the cost of its debts, allowing the state to mobilize resources more effectively and wage wars cheaply throughout the nineteenth century (Winton, 2018). The Bank of England also officially received the privilege of issuing gold notes on behalf of the British State in 1844. The authorization of other banks with this privilege to print money expired in 1930. Today, this right continues in Scotland and Northern Ireland though. Thus, the Bank of England gradually became a modern central bank.

6.5.2 The Suez Canal Incident

Another event where the Rothschilds demonstrated their power was the Suez Canal crisis. In this incident, another Rothschild, Nathan's son Lionel (1808–1879), was the story's leading player (Fig. 6.5). Lionel had learned about the family business by graduating from the University of Göttingen and apprenticing in various banks in different countries. Meanwhile, like his father and uncles, he was also given the title of Baron by the Austro-Hungarian Emperor. Unlike his father, he always used this title. A crisis was created when Lionel, first elected as a Jew to the British House of Commons from the City of London constituency in 1847, refused to take the Christian oath to become a member of Parliament. Prime Minister Lord John Russell had legislated a Jewish Disability Act to solve the vow problem; however, although the Parliament approved the Act of Commons in 1848, it was twice rejected by the House of Lords. Finally, under the 1858 Jewish Relief Act, after the House of Lords passed a proposal that allowed each religion to take its oath, in 1858, Rothschild took the Jewish oath instead of the Christian oath, becoming the first Jewish member of Parliament (Roth, 1962). Baron Rothschild had raised considerable funds for the government and provided aid to the Irish famine victims, especially in the Crimean War. His most famous initiative was to lend the government £ 4 million to buy Suez Canal shares from Egypt (Fig. 6.5).

Egypt became a province of the Ottoman Empire after it was conquered in 1516 during the reign of Yavuz Sultan Selim. The powerful Egyptian governor of the Ottomans, Kavalalı Mehmet Ali Pasha, revolted in 1831 because he could not get the lands promised to him in return for suppressing the first Greek Revolt in 1821. As we will explain in Chap. 8 of our book, he made a series of wars with the

Fig. 6.5 Baron Lionel Rothschild (1808–1879). https://commons.wikimedia.org/wiki/File:Baron_Lionel_Nathan_von_Rothschild_1847_Allanson.png

Ottoman state and turned Egypt into an autonomous province in 1840, with the London Agreement. However, Egypt was still seen as a part of the Ottoman Empire on formal documents, and the governors of Egypt were called Khedives. Said Pasha, the fourth son of Mehmet Ali Pasha, was educated in Paris and made various reforms when he became the Khedive of Egypt. In 1856, French diplomat Ferdinand de Lesseps set up a project and received a concession from the Egyptian Khedive Said Pasha to establish a company that would build a canal open to ships of all nations. The Ottomans and the British were against this Project. Nevertheless, the watercourse was completed after 11 years of construction. The Ottomans thought that as a result of this project, Egypt would break away from them.

On the other hand, the British felt the Canal was an important trade route but perceived it as a French project and a threat to their geopolitical and financial interests. Initially, international circles approached the event with much skepticism, and there was not enough demand for the issued stocks to finance it. İsmail Pasha, who became Khedive after Said Pasha, faced heavy debts and offered his country's shares for sale. This time, quite unexpectedly, however, in 1875, the Rothschild Bank personally paid £4 million to Prime Minister Benjamin Disraeli to purchase Suez Canal shares without any collateral or documents (Fig. 6.6). Disraeli was a close personal friend of Lionel Rothschild and also a Jew. From the prime minister's point of view, "*it gave Britain a stake in a vital artery of imperial trade and security and symbolized her determination to assert her interests in regions of the world where they were under threat*" (Hicks, 2012).

Although the British Government repaid the debt within five months, Disraeli's purchase of the shares by borrowing from the Rothschilds was heavily criticized by

Fig. 6.6 British Prime Minister Benjamin Disraeli (1804–1881). https://commons.wikimedia.org/wiki/File:Benjamin_disraeli.png

his opponents. The prime minister was accused of undermining Britain's constitutional system with a loan not authorized by Parliament (Lionel de Rothschild and the Suez Canal, n.d.). Disraeli, one of the most distinguished Victorian politicians, told the Queen, "*We've got the canal done, now you own it, ma'am!*" he said. This event confirmed England's might on the sea routes. Sir Ian Malcolm, politician and author, called the Suez Canal stake "*the greatest love of Mr. Disraeli's romantic career*" (Baer, 1956). In the following years, the security of the Suez Canal, as the route to India, would become an essential part of British foreign policy. In 1882, Britain occupied the canal and took control of Egypt. In 1909, British Foreign Secretary Lord Curzon described the canal as "*the determinant of every significant movement of British power from the east to the south of the Mediterranean*" (Aldous, 2007).

6.5.3 The Rothschilds and the US Market

The weakest part of the Rothschild family structure was that their entrepreneurial spirit and ambition decreased as the new generations came to power. After the third generation of the Rothschilds, their operations began to weaken. This was especially evident in the indifference toward the newly developing continent of America. This period promised new opportunities for the Rothschilds. Another power emerged in the New World: the United States of America. Perhaps the Rothschilds had not sufficiently evaluated the economic potential of this country. Maybe there was no ambition and desire to acquire the same position here as in most European countries.

When the family did not choose to be a part of the booming economy of the USA, they lost some of their power and might as they entered the twentieth century. The Rothschilds expected the establishment of a central bank similar to the Bank of England in the USA. Had this been the case, they could have become part of the US system within their experience in England. However, unexpectedly, there was no demand for forming a central bank in the USA for a long time. The first two attempts for this purpose were unsuccessful. The First Bank of the United States was established in 1791 as a kind of central bank. President George Washington and Alexander Hamilton, the United States' founding fathers, mainly supported it. However, the states did not want a strong federal structure and asked for the states to have a more independent administration. Presidents such as Thomas Jefferson and James Madison did not like the bank for fear that a central bank would increase the federal government's power and weaken the state governments. In addition, the possibility that a significant part of the bank's shareholders to be established would be foreign was one of the most criticized issues. The first attempt failed, and the "First Bank of the United States" was closed in 1811.

In July 1832, President Andrew Jackson's veto of a bill establishing the United States "Second Bank of the United States" precluded the possibility of establishing a central bank in the United States. It would only be possible for the USA to have a central bank by 1913 (Federal Reserve Education, 2019). It was the consequence of the crisis of 1907 when the bank of J. P. Morgan saved the US financial system. Of course, the Rothschilds were also active in the US, with London as their base, especially in issuing government bonds. Occasionally, they collaborated and competed with J. P. Morgan. However, from 1879 on, Morgan preferred to remain independent from the Rothschilds in such issuing matters. London and Rothschilds were succeeded by the US and Morgan (Strouse, 2014). A significant hurdle for the family to become active in the US was that no family member wanted to go there to set up a bank. Since they were a family bank, a family member had to go and run the business.

6.6 The Banking Secrets of the Rothschilds

The Rothschilds are one of the most remarkable families in finance history. While many inevitably seek a mystery in their success, their success has depended mainly on their family members' solidarity, communication skills, and the global power and prestige they have earned.

6.6.1 Being Untouchable

In the nineteenth century, they said there were seven great European powers: Austria, England, France, Prussia, Russia, Rothschild, and Baring. Europe's proud representatives call for debt, hat in hand, negotiating with them as with any other power, and must be prepared to defend themselves against reprisals when negotiations fail (Steefel, 1936). Rothschild Bank was the largest bank of the nineteenth century; it was ten times the size of Barings, the second largest after it (The Rothschild Archive review, n.d.). Times had changed, and the bankers who depended on the kings were replaced by kings who depended on the Rothschilds. No bank established until that time had reached this capacity, and banks to be found in the future would not have such a chance. During this period, the Rothschilds were so powerful that they could influence the Bank of England's policies on the one hand, control the gold trade, and have a powerful bank in the world. They organize the French Government's borrowings. Austria's financial situation became utterly dependent on Rothschild's loans. The most significant source of this power was that besides being a multinational corporation, it was not easy for any king or ruler to influence or manage their wealth since they carried it in securities or movable commodities such as gold. They were so rich and powerful that no one dared to trip them anymore; everyone tried to win their friendship.

6.6.2 Being a Family Business

On the emblem of the Rothschilds, five arrows symbolize five brothers (Rothschild name and crest, n.d.). During the first three generations, the five branches carefully assisted each other. The partners' stakes were intertwined, and the operations in each center were cooperative. For example, Nathan and James collaborated to help the Bank of England out of the March 1825 crisis. "*I emptied my coffers for your gold*," James wrote to Nathan, having secured £10 million in gold from 1826 until September. The Rothschilds "bought gold from Russia, Turkey, Austria, and almost every part of the world" (Ferguson, 1999). Although this close cooperation began to deteriorate from the third generation, around 1860, when the partnership was in its golden age, the feelings and thoughts of the partners were inextricably linked, and various methods were developed to ensure the continuation of this cooperation and to maintain family solidarity to increase mutual trust. The brothers regularly visited each other and had regular meetings and holidays jointly. While Gutle, the widow of Mayer Amschel, was still alive, regular visits were made to Frankfurt for the new generation to get used to family affairs (Ferguson, 1998).

One of the issues that they paid the most attention to was marriage within the family. It did not matter what the lovers felt or thought. Thus, four of Mayer's grandchildren married other grandchildren, one to his uncle. In fact, between 1824 and 1877, 30 of the 36 Rothschild descendants married their cousins (Husband,

2015). Apart from these, they preferred to be related to the European royal families and married Danish, English, Greek, and Russian nobles. From the second half of the nineteenth century, more and more Rothschild women and married members of other religions disregarded this family order. Modern life has largely relaxed the Rothschild tradition.

The Rothschild House was a genuinely multinational bank with religious ties and strong family ties to the business, being far more homogeneous than most multinational banks today. It seemed sure that one Rothschild bank would support the other in a crisis, even if severe disagreements and arguments arose between them occasionally. They strictly followed their father's advice and maintained a high awareness of family and religion. Because the Rothschilds were a family business, they could quickly seize opportunities and take advantage of projects without conflict, unlike multi-partnership companies. They did not need short-term successes to satisfy shareholders like corporations or listed banks. There were no depositors in urgent need of money.

6.6.3 International Multicenter Structure

The Rothschilds established five centers in different countries and cities, such as London, Paris, Frankfurt, Vienna, and Naples. Only a dedicated family that trusted and cooperated could manage this complex structure, their most outstanding achievement. This unique multinational bank organization provided the Rothschilds with numerous opportunities, including intercountry arbitrage. More importantly, this international structure extended the bank's life by providing a kind of shield against crises and excellent investment diversity. Also, if there was a threat to the existence of one of the centers, they could help each other if they could not overcome it alone. In the nineteenth century, Europe's political and social environment was very active, monarchies gradually weakened, and there was always a crisis. Multinational organizations could only handle large-scale operations during the Spanish wars, such as sending gold from Europe to Spain. When England had a financial crisis in 1825, James and Nathan got together and survived this crisis, raising the Rothschilds' reputation to the highest point. Nathan had saved his brother James in Paris from France's financial collapse during the years of liberal democracy when King Charles X of France was deposed in 1830. In 1848, while revolutionary demonstrations took place across Europe, The family was better off as England was left out of this movement. Nathan came to help his other four brothers in Frankfurt, Paris, Vienna, and Naples. Neither the Vienna nor the Paris Centers could have survived 1848 without family support.

The Rothschilds had a privilege that the Medici or other ex-bankers did not have. Because they were well-equipped to issue bonds and organize government debt, they did not have to lend money to rulers and governments. Now, the monetary needs of the governments have increased so much that no bank can afford it. Instead, they either invested in government-issued bonds or their bonds were sold to investors as intermediaries. The risks were shared by selling the bonds in hand to various investors through stock markets. The Rothschilds had an excellent bond investment network through the stock exchanges in these five centers. When one of the countries failed, they could protect themselves because they never put all their eggs in one basket. In addition, since they had the opportunity to sell these bonds on the stock exchanges before maturity, they could always stay liquid. Most importantly, when the prices of these bonds differed between countries, they could earn from the price difference and benefit from arbitrage opportunities between countries.

Because the Rothschild Bank was so large, governments had to apply to them when issuing bonds. They knew that issuing bonds would not be successful without them; the absence of Rothschild support made it impossible for a country to raise funds. This situation sometimes reached the point that if the Rothschilds refused to support the bond issuance, the states would not have sufficient resources and would not go to war. It is known that the Rothschilds sometimes refused to participate in the allocation of war bonds, thinking that the possibility of the governments repaying the debt they took would decrease due to the economic problems that the war would bring. In 1838, when James Rothschild made a loan agreement with Belgium, he set the following condition: "If war were to break out or if any disputes were to arise, then we would be at liberty to annul our contract." The bank refused loans to Austria during the Prussian War (1860) and forced him to accept Prussia's demands (Ferguson, 1999). In 1861, in protest at the suppression of the Polish uprisings, Lionel Rothschild initially refused to contract a loan to Russia (Kutolowski, 1984).

6.6.4 Connection with Very Important People

Business success largely depends on whom you know in the business environment. Meeting people in strategic positions can open up new possibilities for business people. As explained in Chap. 5 of our book, John Law's most prominent supporter on his way to the French Ministry of Finance was Philippe, Duke of Orleans. Mayer Rothschild also became a respected banker through his relationship with a monarch, Prince William of Hesse-Kassel. However, the Rothschilds would take their business much further by reaching out to new and more powerful people. In many different countries, members of this family always did business with the highest officials, kings, and prime ministers. Thanks to the relations they established, they were given the title of Baron by the Austro-Hungarian Emperor, and Queen Victoria approved this title for England. This was also the case with the Medici Family and some important London Goldsmiths. However, none of them had previously had these relations in Europe, or even in the world geography. They were identified with their interests. The international character of the Rothschilds has made this more complicated and requires high standards of behavior. The Rothschilds held business meetings with influential people in the highest positions. Alfred Charles Freiherr Rothschild was the head of the Bank of England; Lionel Rothschild was a parliamentarian. This indicates that the family was identified with the British Empire.

The Rothschilds never had a problem contacting the people most important to them. Undoubtedly, it is very likely that such relationships have provided them with significant gains behind closed doors. One of the most common issues today is the relationship between politicians, bureaucrats, and people in business. While this relationship may benefit all directly involved parties, society and taxpayers may suffer. Due to their relationships, politicians provide tenders and similar privileges to the businessman while receiving clandestine commissions. The only way to prevent such corruption is to increase transparency in the economy and government. However, it is very likely that in nineteenth-century Europe, where these concepts were not sufficiently developed, the Rothschilds took advantage of the weaknesses of politicians and bureaucrats with the relations they established.

6.6.5 *Communication Skills*

About 120 years after Paul Reuters came to London from Berlin in 1851 and started giving financial news, the Reuters Company would go down in history as the first company to provide stock market news with a computer (Read, 1999). From this date on, financial news communication would develop so much that investors would have the opportunity to instantly turn the information in the market into money with high-frequency trading methods, which use even minutes, seconds, and still shorter intervals.

In the 1840s, perhaps sometime earlier, brothers began using pigeons to carry short and vital messages between them. Nathan Rothschild had a farm in Kent where he raised homing pigeons. An example of one or two letters held by pigeons is in the Rothschild Archive. These letters measure approximately 8 cm by 5 cm and were placed in a small pouch attached to the pigeon's leg. This communication method was one of Rothschild's in 1820–1850. A letter written by Nathan's son, Nathaniel Rothschild, from Paris in August 1846 contained the following statements: "*I hope our feathered ambassadors will bring you our fair prices on time. If the pigeon's message says A.D., buy stocks, it means the news is good; If it writes C.D., it means selling shares, the information is terrible*"(Rothschilds and pigeon post, n.d.).

Since the brothers lived away from each other, they needed to get the most out of the news. The Rothschilds habitually wrote detailed letters to keep others informed, closely examining what was happening in their area, investment opportunities, and prices in towns they visited. These letters need to be delivered quickly and safely. The Rothschilds relied on a reliable courier network in an age when the postal system was at varying speeds across Europe and was developing. The Rothschilds had the best horses from the start. They had invested heavily in building an infrastructure to keep the news confidential and the transportation fast and reliable. Reaching the news before others was more important than speeding up the information; it gave them a competitive advantage.

The Rothschilds had a network of trusted agents in Europe and America. The family placed great emphasis on trust when hiring agents. There were two main ways to gain confidence before becoming an agent: being a family relative or having worked in one of the households for a considerable time. Also, while many of Rothschild's trade agents were Jewish, many were not. The fraction of Jews working in banking was not high (Liedtke, 1998).

From the 1830s to the 1850s, the size of the network did not grow much, but its character changed in line with changing business needs. Some agents, such as Weisweiller in Madrid, Bleichroder in Berlin, or Morpurgo & Parente in Trieste, were more critical information hubs in the network. The news now contained far more political intelligence than at the beginning of the century. The development and spread of the electric telegraph and news agencies, especially from the 1840s, devalued pure business information. Strategic advice about the possible course of political events was now the kind of high-value information Rothschild banks expected from their representatives (Liedtke, 1998). Undoubtedly, as the communication network expanded, the Rothschilds were able to take more significant advantage of business opportunities and avoid risks.

By combining their communication infrastructure with their ability to make friends in the highest positions, the Rothschilds had taken their communication level one step further. In Paris, James could meet King Philippe and convey his views to his brother Salomon, who met in Vienna with Prince Metternich, the famous diplomat. After evaluating the news, Salomon could have shared his knowledge in a letter to Nathan in London. The family had reached a higher level where they could assess both the market news and the opinions of the influential people on the market. This communication superiority of the Rothschilds was much more advanced than the secret intelligence organizations of the states of that time (Ferguson, 1998).

6.6.6 Developing the International Bond Market

One of today's most important financial markets is the European bond market, the Eurobond market. While this market has developed since the 1960s and meets the long-term financing needs of both countries and leading companies, it has become much more critical in the second globalization period that started after the 1980s. The first establishment of this market dates back to the period of 1818–1822. In the first half of the nineteenth century, the European financial market began to develop rapidly, and the integration between the country's markets began. At the end of the eighteenth century, there were critical financial problems in the leading nations of Europe. After the 1789 French Revolution, the difficulties encountered in paying the debts of the Kings of France confused the markets. During this period, the Netherlands was exhausted after long wars and faced a financial crisis, while the Russian monarchy narrowly escaped bankruptcy through two foreign debt negotiations in 1797 and 1815. However, the Battle of Waterloo in 1815 boosted the popularity of the government bond market in England. While the development in England positively impacted other countries, the Rothschilds stood out as the most essential player in this market. They gained a great fortune from the growing market conditions.

On the other hand, technology was developing, and the telegraph was starting to be used in communication. The easy access of financial news to the markets, primarily via telegraph, made investment more secure (Standage, 1998). After the worldwide adoption of the gold standard in currency issuance during the second half of the nineteenth century, the countries allowed unrestricted capital flows, reducing currency risk across the continents (Obstfeld & Taylor, 2003). This period is known as the first globalization period in history. The second period of globalization would begin in the late 1980s when the Soviet Union collapsed, and the United States remained the only powerful state in the world. The Rothschilds were the most important players after 1810, with their international network and significant contributions to the development of the bond market (Swords, 2017).

The Rothschild Bank brokered the issuance of Prussian bonds in London in 1818 through an internationally integrated bank network. The bonds were issued in the pound sterling currency. The same practice applied to the Russian state in 1822. Although designed to yield as much dividends as the infinitive coupon payment, Russia's promise to pay the bondholder would cease with the 1917 revolution, as the Bolshevik Government rejected all foreign debt after the revolution. The novel interest payment practice was the most significant difference in Russian bonds. Interests could be paid in Paris, Vienna, London, and St. Petersburg in Pounds or Russian Rubles. Perhaps more importantly, dividends could be claimed in any of the above cities, effectively protecting the bondholder from the effects of a continental war. This means that currency risk was significantly reduced. Prussia and Russia also agreed to follow the Rothschild practice. They set up a sinking fund to amortize the loan, with regular remittances to London from the government to repay the capital. With a sinking fund to repay the principal, the schedule for eventual repayment was made explicit to the investor. These repayments were affected by the purchase of the bonds in circulation; if the bonds were being traded "above par"—that is, if their actual value were higher than their nominal value—then lots would be drawn to determine which bonds would be compulsorily redeemed at face value only. These bonds were innovative and unique, as no bonds with these characteristics had been issued. This would be a more significant pattern for future bond issues. The first tranche of the Prussian loan was sold at 70% of its nominal value and was soon trading well above that price. The interest rate, price of the issue, and the subsequent market price of a bond have often been seen as "opinion polls" of perceptions of a borrowing nation's creditworthiness, reflecting past performance in servicing loans, and contemporary views of a country's political and financial stability. Understanding this sensitive relationship was essential for success in this market. The Prussian and Russian bonds, issued in foreign currency on the international market, were unique and are described by Nial Ferguson as the first "Euro Bond" (Ferguson, 1998).

Government bonds provided a critical link between the financial markets in the US and the UK. After 1836, US bonds were traded on the London market, where the Eurobond market was born. Movements in bond prices initiated the link between the British and American financial markets. These bonds were the initial instruments of the London Bond Market and significantly contributed to the Eurobond market's development. Being an essential financial innovation, these bonds would set a new example for cross-border capital flows and herald a new era in global financial markets. Sylla et al. (2006) draw attention to the price balance between three types of financial assets traded in the London and New York stock exchanges: the bonds issued for establishing the First and Second (Central) Bank of the United States and the US quarterly government bonds. They were subject to arbitrage if there was a price difference between them. This movement of prices was the most important test of the international market equilibrium. The most important player in this market was the Rothschilds, and without their global relations and centers in different countries, the bond market could not have developed so much in this period.

6.7 Conclusion

The Rothschilds had the largest bank of the nineteenth century. Their influence on the world was greater than that of the Medici, JPMorgan, Citibank, or even the Industrial and Commercial Bank of China Ltd (IDCBY), the largest bank in the 2020s. In this success, Father Mayer Rothschild and his son Nathan Rothschild, who carried out banking activities in England, had an outstanding share of their extraordinary skills. Behind their success were the opportunities created by the turbulent business environment with the war and economic crises of that period. The Rothschild family had established a banking empire by wisely taking advantage of the chaotic environment created by the Napoleonic wars. While the Rothschilds attracted attention with daring speculative investments, they turned to risky areas that other bankers preferred to avoid.

The Rothschild family's most crucial banking secret is their ability to be untouchable. By reaching such a level, they have gained the appreciation of even their competitors and easily overcome the obstacles in business life. Banking relations based on strong family ties, a multi-center banking structure, the ability to reach influential people, and strong communication networks played an essential role in this success. While the Rothschild family was managing a vast organization with a highly disciplined family structure based on religious values, for a very long time, they showed the ability to manage this relationship without creating strife and jealousy among family members. By blending their communication skills with their fellowship, which is the highest strata of society, they had the power to direct the market entirely. They could carry out global banking operations that no commercial organization could handle. They also played a vital role in establishing the overseas bond market, which we know as Eurobonds today.

As observed in other important family-based companies, the Rothschild family and business disciplines decreased as they became wealthier. Instead of pursuing big projects, family members naturally turned to personal hobbies and less risky investments. The founders' superior banking skills, desire, and ambition did not pass on to their grandchildren, and new generations began to enjoy their wealth. Studies of family businesses partly explain how the Rothschilds lost their power. According to these studies, family businesses cannot be successful for more than three generations due to many reasons, such as positioning incompetent relatives, moving away from professionalism, inadequate education of family members, and inability to keep up with changes (Davis et al., 1997). The power of the family was weakened by the sharing of the Rothschild legacy among the heirs over time. Crucially, they missed a great opportunity by not entering the US market, which started to be the most important economy in the world since the beginning of the twentieth century. They quickly lost their status as the world's largest bank. While the role of the Rothschilds was decreasing, a new banking giant was emerging in the USA. This bank was made significant by John Pierpont Morgan, as to be discussed in Chap. 7, and is still known as JPMorgan Chase.

Today, although the Rothschilds are far from their glory days, there are still widespread conspiracy theories that they are behind many of the events taking place around the world. Undoubtedly, one reason for this is anti-semitism. But behind these family rumors is also the secluded appearance of the Rothschilds and the shadow of their past. While the new generations of the Rothschilds commemorate the glorious days of the past, perhaps from time to time, the lyrics of Waterloo, the song of the famous Swedish band ABBA that won the Eurovision Song Contest in 1974, rings in their ears: "At Waterloo, Napoleon did surrender, Oh yeah, and I have met my destiny in quite a similar way…".

References

Abraham Oppenheim. (n.d.). Abraham Oppenheim. *Wikipedia*. Retrieved April 7, 2023, from https://en.wikipedia.org/wiki/Abraham_Oppenheim

Aldous, R. (2007). *The lion and the unicorn: Gladstone vs Disraeli*. W.W. Norton and Co.

Arthur Wellesley, 1st Duke of Wellington. (n.d.). Arthur Wellesley, 1st Duke of Wellington. *Wikipedia*. Retrieved February 22, 2024, from https://en.wikipedia.org/wiki/Arthur_Wellesley,_1st_Duke_of_Wellington

Baer, W. (1956). The promoting and the financing of the Suez Canal. *Business History Review, 30*(4), 361–381. https://doi.org/10.2307/3111714

Bank Restriction Act. (n.d.). Bank Restriction Act. *Wikipedia*. Retrieved January 10, 2024, from https://en.wikipedia.org/wiki/Bank_Restriction_Act_1797

Bank of England. (n.d.). Bank of England. *The london gold market*. [online] bankofengland.co.uk. https://www.bankofengland.co.uk/-/media/boe/files/quarterly-bulletin/1964/the-london-gold-market.pdf

Barbagallo, F. (2000). The rothschilds in Naples. *Journal of Modern Italian Studies, 5*(3), 294–309.

Barbero, A. (2005). *The battle: A new history of Waterloo*. Atlantic.

Black, I. S. (1995). Money, information and space: Banking inearly-nineteenth-century England and Wales. *Journal of Historical Geography, 21*(4).

Bordo, M. D. (1998). Commentary on 'The Financial Crisis of 1825 and the Restructuring of the British Financial System'. *Review, 80*(3). https://doi.org/10.20955/r.80.77-82

Cathcart, B. (2015). *The news from Waterloo*. Faber & Faber.

Chapman, S. D. (1982). The establishment of the Rothschilds as bankers. *Jewish Historical Studies, 29*, 177–193.

Coleman, J. (2006). *The Rothschild Dynasty*. World Intelligence.

Coleman, D. (n.d.). *The battlefield of Waterloo—Waterloo*, Belgium. [online] Have Camera Will Travel. Retrieved April 4, 2021, from https://havecamerawilltravel.com/places/battlefield-waterloo-belgium/
Consol (Bond). (n.d.). Consol (Bond). *Wikipedia*. Retrieved April 8, 2021, from https://en.wikipedia.org/wiki/Consol_(bond)
Cowles, V. (1973). The Rothschilds: A family of fortune. Knopf, distributed by Random House.
Dairnvaell, G. (Satan). (1846). Histoire *édifiante et curieuse de Rothschild Ier, Roi des Juifs* (p. 4). Chez l'Editeur, Rue Colbert-Vivienne.
Davis, J. A., McCollom Hampton, M., & Gersick, K. E. (1997). *Generation to generation: Life cycles of the family business*. Harvard Business School Press.
Federal Reserve Education. (2019). *History of the federal reserve*. [online] Federalreserveeducation.org. Retrieved April 6, 2021, from https://www.federalreserveeducation.org/about-the-fed/history
Ferguson, N. (1998). *The world's banker: The history of the house of Rothschild*. Weidenfeld & Nicolson.
Ferguson, N. (1999). *The house of Rothschild: The world's banker, 1849–1999*. Viking.
Ferguson, N. (2008). *The ascent of money: A financial history of the world*. Penguin.
Gille, B. (1965). *Histoire de la maison Rothschild* (Vol. 1). Librairie Droz.
Gillerman, S. (2005). More than skin deep: Histories of the modern Jewish body. *Jewish Quarterly Review, 95*(3), 470–478. https://doi.org/10.1353/jqr.2005.0055
Hicks, G. (2012). Disraeli, Derby and the Suez Canal, 1875: Some myths reassessed. *History, 97*(326), 182–203. https://doi.org/10.1111/j.1468-229x.2012.00548.x
Husband, S. (2015). *Pedigree Chums: A history of aristocratic incest*. [online] The Rake. Retrieved April 6, 2021, from https://therake.com/stories/code/pedigree-chums-a-history-of-aristocratic-incest/
James, J. A. (2012). Panics, payments disruptions and the Bank of England before 1826. *Financial History Review, 19*(3).
Kernan, B. (2009). If I were a rich man: The Rothschilds and anti-semitism in 19th century France. *Historical Perspectives: Santa Clara University Undergraduate Journal of History, Series II, 14*(1), 8.
Kirby, T.T. (2011). *The Duke of Wellington and the supply system during the Peninsular War* [Master thesis, U.S. Army Command and General Staff College].
Kutolowski, J. F. (1984). British economic interests and the polish uprising, 1861—1864. *The Polish Review*, 3–25.
Liedtke, R. (1998). *Jewish Welfare in Hamburg and Manchester, c. 1850–1914*. Oxford University Press.
Lionel de Rothschild and the Suez Canal. (n.d.). Rothschild Archive. Retrieved January 25, 2024, from https://www.rothschildarchive.org/business/n_m_rothschild_and_sons_london/lionel_de_rothschild_and_the_suez_canal
Marengo (Horse). (n.d.). Marengo (Horse). *Wikipedia*. Retrieved April 6, 2021, from https://en.wikipedia.org/wiki/Marengo_(horse)
Mitchell, B. R. (1975). *European historical statistics 1750–1970*. Columbia University Press.
Morgan, D. P., & Narron, J. (2015). *Crisis Chronicles: The panic of 1825 and the most fantastic financial swindle of all time—Liberty street economics*. Liberty Street Economics New York Fed. Retrieved April 8, 2021, from https://libertystreeteconomics.newyorkfed.org/2015/04/crisis-chronicles-the-panic-of-1825-and-the-most-fantastic-financial-swindle-of-all-time-.html
Morton, F. (1962). *The Rothschilds: A family portrait*. Secker & Warburg.
Muhlstein, A. (1983). *Baron James: The rise of the French Rothschilds*. Vendome Press.
Nathan Mayer Rothschild. (n.d.). Nathan Mayer Rothschild. *Wikipedia*. Retrieved February 22, 2024, from https://en.wikipedia.org/wiki/Nathan_Mayer_Rothschild
Neal, L. (1998). The financial crisis of 1825 and the restructuring of the British financial system. *Review, 80*(3). https://doi.org/10.20955/r.80.53-76

Obstfeld, M., & Taylor, A. M. (2003). *Globalization and capital markets* (pp. 121–188). University Chicago Press.

Oman, C. W. C. (2015, reprinted from 1913). *Wellington's army 1809–1814*. Pickle Partners Publishing.

Parikh, C. (2008). *The Bonaparte of finance—Capital ideas online*. Capital Ideas Online. Retrieved April 5, 2021, from https://www.capitalideasonline.com/wordpress/the-bonaparte-of-finance/

Parys, W. (2024). Ricardo's finances and Waterloo: Legends by Samuelson and others lack historical evidence. *Cambridge Journal of Economics*, bead055.

Read, D. (1999). *The power of news: The history of Reuters*. Oxford University Press.

Reeves, J. (1887). *The Rothschilds. The financial rulers of nations*. Sampson Low, Marston, Searle, and Rivington.

Reeves, J. (2012). *The Rothschild: The financial rulers of nations*. CreateSpace Independent Publishing Platform.

Roth, C. (1962). *Essays and portraits in Anglo-Jewish history*. Jewish Publication Society Of America.

Rothschild Name and Crest. (n.d.). Rothschild Archive. Retrieved April 2, 2021, from https://www.rothschildarchive.org/family/the_rothschild_name_and_arms/

Rothschilds and Pigeon Post. (n.d.). Rothschild Archive. Retrieved July 25, 2021, from https://www.rothschildarchive.org/collections/rothschild_faqs/rothschilds_and_pigeon_post

Schultz, K. A., & Weingast, B. (2003). The democratic advantage: Institutional foundations of financial power in international competition. *International Organization, 57*(4), 3–42.

Shea, P. E. (2020). Money talks: Finance, war, and great power politics in the nineteenth century. *Social Science History, 44*(2), 223–249.

Spagnol, G. (2019). *Banksters and warmongers*. Institut Européen des Relations Internationales. Retrieved April 7, 2021, from http://www.ieri.be/en/publications/wp/2019/juillet/banksters-and-warmongers

Standage, T. (1998). *The Victorian internet*. Weidenfeld & Nicholson.

Steefel, L. D. (1936). The Rothschilds and the Austrian loan of 1865. *The Journal of Modern History, 8*(1), 27–39.

Strouse, J. (2014). *Morgan: American financier*. Random House Trade Paperbacks.

Subscription Ledger for the Prussian Government Loan, 1818. (n.d.). Rothschild Archive. Retrieved March 10, 2024, from https://www.rothschildarchive.org/collections/archivists_choice/march_2018_subscription_ledger_for_the_prussian_government_loan_1818

Swords, C. (2017). *Sovereign debt markets and political stability—Evidence from 19th century Europ. Economic History*. Retrieved April 5, 2021, from https://www.tcd.ie/Economics/assets/pdf/SER/2017/1sovereigndebt.pdf

Sylla, R., Wilson, J. W., & Wright, R. E. (2006). Integration of trans-Atlantic capital markets, 1790–1845. *Review of Finance, 10*(4), 613–644. https://doi.org/10.1007/s10679-006-9007-6

The Rothschild Archive Review of the Year April 2006 to March 2007. (n.d.). Rothschild Archive. Retrieved March 25, 2024, from https://www.rothschildarchive.org/materials/ar2007.pdf

The Rothschild Family. (n.d.). Rothschild Archive. Retrieved January 25, 2024, from https://family.rothschildarchive.org/people/62-alfred-charles-de-rothschild-1842-1918

Winton. (2018). *The panic of 1825: In quest of Aztec Gold*. Retrieved April 7, 2021, from https://www.winton.com/longer-view/the-panic-of-1825

Chapter 7
J.P. Morgan: The Banker Who Saved America (Nineteenth and Twentieth Centuries)

7.1 Introduction

On Saturday, November 2, 1907, like every weekend, Central Park was flooded with visitors. Although it was mid-autumn, the weather was fine. The vegetation covering the park fully reflected the season and offered New Yorkers a feast of colors with its golden, brown, and red tones. The pond, located in the southern part of the park, was an attraction for families with the famous Gapstow Bridge and the surrounding cherry, oak, and birch trees. Although the air had cooled, the sun's warmth was still felt. By contrast, the weather on Wall Street, the financial hub of the city's south end, had been frigid since September. Even though it was the weekend, bankers, investors, business people, and government officials roamed the streets with the utmost restlessness. They were all curious about the outcome of the ongoing meeting at John Pierpont (J.P.). Morgan's magnificent library with impressive architecture was built a few years ago on Madison Avenue. Leading Wall Street bankers attended and were discussing how to find money to save a brokerage firm, Moore & Schley. At that time, since there was no central bank in the USA and the Treasury did not have enough money, the critical players of the market had to find a solution.

The stockbroker Moore & Schley had borrowed heavily, using shares of the Tennessee Coal, Iron, and Railroad Company (TC&I) as collateral. Presumably, creditor banks would put up TC&I stocks on Monday to cash in on their collateral. This situation would cause the company's value to fall; furthermore, the brokerage house would not fulfill its obligations in the market, and this would trigger more panic. Many companies, including the American and Lincoln Trust, would inevitably go bankrupt, spreading the crisis throughout the country. The financial situation of TC&I had to be strengthened somehow; otherwise, the American economy would get into big trouble.

Commercial bankers had gathered in the east hall of the library. In the room, a carpet decorated with zodiac signs depicting the seven deadly sins could be viewed (Fig. 7.1). In the western hall, the heads of the trust companies had gathered. They

M. B. Karan et al., *A History of Banks*, Contributions to Economics,
https://doi.org/10.1007/978-3-031-62297-7_7

slumped into the classic red armchairs, lighting their cigars and discussing the markets fiercely. With a description of one of Morgan's colleagues, "*A more incongruous meeting place for anxious bankers could hardly be imagined. In one room were lofty, magnificent tapestries hanging on the walls, rare Bibles and illuminated manuscripts of the Middle Ages filling the cases; in another, that collection of the Early Renaissance masters—Castagno, Ghirlandaio, Perugino, to mention only a few—the huge open fire, the door just ajar to the holy of holies where the original manuscripts were guarded*" (Lamont, 2012). The famous banker of America, J.P. Morgan, was sitting in the library director's room between these two halls, watching his surroundings like an eagle and playing solitaire with cards, as he often did when he felt anxious.

A few days ago, TC&I's attorney, Lewis Cass Ledyard, offered to sell TC&I to Pierpont to strengthen Moore & Schley's collateral and prevent panic. That was precisely the proposal Pierpont had come up with to discuss. Since he did not have the cash to make this purchase, Pierpont had to provide the financial support of other banks and trusts. The loan he needed was approximately 25 million dollars, and everyone had to put their hands in their pockets to collect this amount. At 3 p.m., about 120 bank and trust company officials were listening to a report on the condition

Fig. 7.1 The Morgan Library & Museum, New York. https://commons.wikimedia.org/wiki/File:Morgan_Library_%26_Museum,_New_York_2017_25.jpg creativecommons.org-Creative Commons Attribution-Share Alike 4.0 International

of the trust companies, which were still in bad shape, and there was still disagreement over what to do. As the discussion dragged on, some bankers saw Pierpont locking them in the library and felt they could not leave the meeting even if they wanted to. Pierpont's tactic was to fasten the door of the meeting room; it was called Corsair. Corsair was the name of J.P. Morgan's yacht, and he would gather his competitors on his yacht for such negotiations and would not disembark anyone without reaching an agreement. In this critical meeting, he started to force them to find a solution by locking the door.

Participants were still reluctant to act, but Morgan insisted on telling them that the current situation would lead to a complete collapse of the banking system. Finally, at around 4:45 p.m., the Trust presidents were persuaded to sign the agreement. The bankers would follow them, and the American economy could breathe a sigh of relief. However, it was not over because J.P. Morgan would break US. Antitrust laws with this takeover operation. The deal would form a massive monopoly controlling 60% of the steel market. It would not be easy for US President Theodore Roosevelt to accept this offer. Since the beginning, Roosevelt waged war against companies that monopolized the market. He had been uncompromisingly enforcing antitrust laws. On Sunday, Pierpont and his delegation would travel to Washington by evening train, pulled by a private locomotive, to persuade the president. The president had to be convinced by sunrise; otherwise, it would have been a complete disaster when the markets opened on Monday. They organized a meeting with the president a few hours before the markets opened. The president refused this proposal at first. However, he began to soften next and then explained his confirmation as follows: "*I had to make a decision just before the stock market opened because the situation in New York was so tense that with each passing hour, investors were getting more and more depressed. It was not easy to object to*" (Bruner & Carr, 2007). When the news reached New York, there was a sudden relief in the markets, and the American economy was saved.

Although (John) Pierpont Morgan (Fig. 7.2), better known as J.P. Morgan, is known as the man who saved the USA with the above-described action, his move was better planned than it seemed; in fact, it was an extraordinarily clever one. In this way, he not only became the savior of the country but also bought the TC&I company, which he could not normally buy due to antitrust laws, thanks to the credit given by his competitors.

It was not the first time that J.P. Morgan & Co., which had a powerful influence on banking, business, and even government in America, saved the US economy. When the USA could not pay its debts during the 1893 economic panic, and the country's Treasury was about to go bankrupt in 1895, Pierpont gave some of his gold reserves to the Treasury and bought a considerable amount of treasury bonds. It was admirable that he became a savior by putting his hand under the stone when no one moved. However, each of his actions had made him big money. Therefore, a new system had to be developed to save the country from the saviors. At this stage, it was clear what to do: establishing a Central Bank.

J.P. Morgan (1837–1913) would become an important figure in banking history in the twentieth century. He may not have been America's most important citizen of all time, but he was one of its most outstanding business stars. While J.P. Morgan,

Fig. 7.2 John Pierpont Morgan (1837–1913). https://commons.wikimedia.org/wiki/File:John_Pierpont_J._P._Morgan.jpeg

respected by all who loved and disliked him, entered the history stage, the Rothschilds and also Barings, who had shaped European banking history in the nineteenth century, were slowly moving away from the scene. As we explained in the previous chapter, the new generations of Rothschilds were not interested in the US market. Baring Bank, the second largest bank, also slowed its activities, as it caused the biggest global crisis of the nineteenth century in the Argentine market, which it entered by taking an extreme risk in 1890 (Mitchener & Weidenmier, 2008). Pierpont's life is at the heart of the history of United States banking, not only about the past but also beyond it well into today.

7.2 Banking in the United States

While John Law was issuing paper money in France, paper money use had started at the local level in banks in the American colonies. The Bank of North America was the first bank to issue paper money at the national level in 1781. The United States Mint was founded after the Coinage Act of 1792 was passed by Congress after US independence in 1776. Its task was producing and distributing coins. The first Mint was in Philadelphia. Until 1873, it was part of the Department of the Treasury. It had the authority to refine any precious metal and convert it into a standard coin for anyone's account, with no seigniorage fees outside of transaction costs. There were no licensed American banks until 1781. The first was the Bank of North America, located in Philadelphia. Three years later, Boston merchants founded Massachusetts Bank. Then, the Bank of New York was founded. When George Washington became the first president in 1789, these were the only three licensed banks in the United States, with the fourth one being established in Baltimore in 1790 (Sylla, n.d.). They were all local institutions, but many different currencies were circulating.

Discussions on the establishment of a state bank that would print federal money had begun. State governments were concerned that if the federal government did have a central bank, it might become too powerful. Supporters of the bank were arguing that the nation needed a standardized coin, and only a national central bank could achieve it. In contrast, opponents of the central bank claimed that government monopolization of money was a corrupt practice that would impoverish the people.

In 1791, Congress granted a franchise to The First Bank of the United States as the first central bank of the United States. This bank was established by a partnership between the federal government and private shareholders. It was designed as a standard commercial bank to compete with the state banks while serving the federal government. In this form, similar to the Bank of England structure at the beginning of the eighteenth century, the bank's primary function was to provide loans to the government and private entrepreneurs for internal improvements and economic development. However, this project did not last long as it faced opposition from more than 100 state banks established in the last two decades. The New England region, which included Maine, New Hampshire, Vermont, Massachusetts, Connecticut, and Rhode Island, had become the principal place for banks (De Santis, 1973); see also Fig. 7.3. When the First Bank of the United States applied for renewal of its charter in 1811, it would therefore not be ratified (Bowden, 1989).

Fig. 7.3 New England region of the USA

The Second Bank of the United States was founded in January 1816. It aimed to prevent the economic turmoil and disorganization between currencies due to the Napoleonic wars of 1812. The charter of the Second Bank of the United States was established with a 20-year term. It should be renewed in 1836. Its role as the custodian of the federal government's revenues had become a political target of various state banks. Although the poor management of the bank in its early years played a role in this situation, especially President Andrew Jackson was strongly opposed to the renewal of the charter, considering it a mistake to give power and responsibility to a single bank. There was a widespread belief that real money was minted in gold or silver, and there was widespread opposition to central banking. The Second Bank would suffer the same fate as the First Bank (Dangerfield, 1965).

After 1837, a free banking era began in the USA. In this period, which would last until 1864, any bank would issue banknotes, and there would be no need for a central bank in the system. Previously, banks could obtain the privilege of issuing banknotes through a specific law; with the Michigan Act of 1837 no longer requiring special approval by state legislatures, banks could print notes directly without a concession. The Free Banking Act that was passed in New York the following year would contain similar provisions and was followed by other states. These banks would be able to issue banknotes in exchange for coins. The required reserves, loan and deposit interest rates, and required capital ratios of these banks would be regulated on a state basis (Rockoff, 1974). This system became widespread throughout the country for a while. However, with the laxity and abuse of laws in some states, banking had become an act of savagery with an extreme wave of credit spread, as banknotes were issued with little or no reserve. As a result, this system created a wave of financial crises and bankruptcies, and in particular, the diversity of state banknotes caused a great uproar (Rockoff, 1991).

***The huge US Civil War (1861–1865) costs made it urgent to revise the system. The National Banking Acts of 1863 and 1864 spurred the development of a national currency backed by the US Treasury and the banking system. Accordingly, the Department of the Treasury was empowered to review and regulate chartered banks on a national basis. It also encouraged many state banks to become national banks. The issuing of notes by state banks was discouraged by taxing these. The state bank notes disappeared eventually. National banks were allowed to issue bank notes backed by Treasury bonds, with a maximum of $500,000. Next to that, there were the Greenbacks, notes issued directly by the Treasury that were not convertible to gold but suitable for paying taxes and buying bonds. As a result of these developments, a dual banking system would emerge (Grossman, n.d.). Both national and state banks could be established in the US, and existing banks could choose either state or federal regimes. Nevertheless, all were subject to the laws of the State and governed in their daily course of business far more by the laws of the State than those of the Nation (Redford, 1966). An important difference between the two regimes was the minimum reserve requirements, the minimum ratio of reserves versus deposits. For the state banks, these minimum levels varied but were anyway below the 10%. For the national banks, it depends on the city where the bank is located. Banks located in central reserve cities, initially just New York City but later also Chicago and St.

Louis, were required to hold gold in their vaults equal to at least 25% of their note and deposit liabilities. Banks in other reserve cities were allowed to hold a portion of this required amount as deposits with central reserve city national banks. Finally, all other national banks, known as country banks, had a 15% reserve requirement of which a portion could be held as deposits with national banks in reserve cities or central reserve cities (Dunn & Wheelock, 2022). The reserves consisted of gold and silver coins, gold and silver certificates issued by the treasury, backed by gold and silver, and a fixed quantity of the greenbacks mentioned above. Since 1873, the US were on a gold standard, with silver only being secondary and strongly restricted (Elwell, 2011).

Within this federally regulated system functioned the private clearing houses. At the time, the use of checks against bank deposits grew rapidly (Gorton, 1984). Business people did not like to walk around with the money. First, banks settled the checks with each other with the aid of porters, running up and down with checks and gold. With the increasing number of banks, it got rather chaotic. In 1853, the New York banks established a clearing house. Other business centers followed in a couple of years. Instead of settling the checks with each other, they could now all settle the checks with the clearing house. The next step was to replace the gold with specie certificates. The certificates partly replaced the gold. The certificates were only for exchange between banks. They were fully backed by gold, and gold remained also in use for settling.

In the course of time, the clearing houses also started to play a role in dealing with banking panics. In case of a run on the banks, the banks were tempted to use certificates to settle the checks and keep the gold for anxious depositors. They started to issue temporary loan certificates that could be backed by different kinds of collateral. The loan certificates were used in the settling, just as the gold and the certificates. A bank generally paid 6% interest for its use. The final step was obviously to issue clearing house money to the public, backed by the loan certificates. This role of the clearing houses necessitated regulating, monitoring, and auditing the clearing house member banks. Together, the clearing houses were the forerunners of the Federal Reserve System.

7.3 The Banking Empire of John Pierpont Morgan

7.3.1 J.P. Morgan's Youth and Early Years

John Pierpont Morgan was a member of a distinguished family from Connecticut. He was born on April 17, 1837, in New England. Both of the parents' families had lived in this region for five generations. His mother, Juliet Pierpont, was the daughter of the famous minister and poet John Pierpont, and one of his grandparents was the founder of Yale University. His father's name was Junius Spencer Morgan (1813–1890). He was a reasonably wealthy businessman.

Pierpont had three sisters. His only brother died at the age of 12. Father Junius was born in West Springfield in 1813. He was the son of a wealthy businessman. He was a quiet, determined person, bright and smiling. He had a disciplined life that emphasized business ethics, as Chernow (2001) noted in his classic text published in 1990. Morgan's business career turned positive when he met the American George Peabody on a trip to Europe in 1853. Morgan moved to London in 1854 and became a junior partner in a British-owned merchant banking firm. This bank was aimed to facilitate the flow of British capital to America. Peabody retired 10 years later, and Morgan became a director of the firm, which was renamed J. S. Morgan and Company. He had transferred his business to England and moved his entire family to London. After that, while one foot of the family was in America, the other was in England. Junius Morgan became the most influential American banker in that part of the world. He later met Andrew Carnegie, who assisted him in business dealings. He also increased his reputation and wealth by chairing a syndicate that lent money to France after the Franco-Prussian War in 1870. J.P. Morgan suffered from a mysterious illness and spent most of his childhood at home. Initially an intelligent but apathetic student, Pierpont's grades began to soar when he attended English High School in Boston. Pierpont had just graduated from high school when the family moved to England. His father sent Pierpont to different countries to prepare him for an international banking career. After studying in Switzerland, Pierpont would complete his education at the University of Göttingen in Germany. Later, he lived for some time in the Azores Islands in the North Atlantic Ocean, which was good for his health. When Pierpont began working as a junior banker with the Duncan Sherman Company in New York at 20 in 1857, he was fluent in three languages. He was more familiar with the country's culture than most Americans of his time (Bruner & Carr, 2007).

J.P. Morgan, who had a natural leadership trait, founded his own company in 1860. In this period, when trade between England and America was booming, he wanted to make money by taking advantage of his relations in both countries. He met Amelia Sturges in 1858 while his commercial affairs were going well. Their 3-year friendship ended in marriage in 1861. Pierpont had fallen head over heels in love with Amelia. Unfortunately, she was a severe tuberculosis patient and had trouble walking when they got married. Although they went to Nice, France, where he hoped the weather would be good, he would lose his wife after 3 months (Bruner & Carr, 2007).

When the American Civil War (1861–1865) broke out, J.P. Morgan did not join the fight and paid someone else to go instead of him, as was customary at that time. However, he did not sit idle during the war and made a very profitable trade. He sold the rifles he bought cheaply from the government to the Northern army with a very high profit by renewing the barrels. In this transaction, John Pierpont Morgan bought more than 5,000 rifles at $3.50 each and sold them back to the government for $22. He never felt remorse for the incident, for which he was accused by some as a war profiteer (Wasson, 1941). During this period, Morgan was devoted entirely to his work and increased his wealth as quickly as possible. At the age of 27, he had become a well-known businessman in his region. A deeply religious and charitable person, Pierpont founded the Young Men's Christian Association (YMCA), an organization dedicated to improving the lives of young men. He regularly went to church. Meanwhile, he met Frances Tracy, a church member, and got married within a few months.

Now that Pierpont had almost completely recovered from his youth sickness, he was beginning to impress his surroundings with his strong shoulders, tall stature, piercing eyes, and leadership qualities. His biggest problem was "Acne Rosacea," known as Rose Disease, which settled on his nose. Because of this annoying disease, his big nose always looked red and spotty, and it always bothered him. At times, he would ask photographers to retouch them to show his nose better, and sometimes, he would pay them to destroy the negatives (Brands, 2010). He had four children, three girls, from his marriage. John Pierpont Morgan Jr., known as Jack Morgan, would later become head of his company.

Meanwhile, Pierpont sometimes went beyond the business world's ethical rules to turn every opportunity he had into a profit. In 1863, he started to speculate in gold together with his friend, Edward Ketchum. They bought gold for about $2 million, borrowing against the same gold to pay for it. Then, they exported the main part of the gold to London, contributing to a temporary perceived scarcity and a substantial price increase. In total, they had a profit of about $130,000. Although Wall Street bankers admired the plan, his father, Junius, was furious (Berfield, 2020). He accused Pierpont of being reckless and greedy. Junius first threatened to sever professional ties with his son and then decided to try to arrange for a senior partner in New York to guide him. In 1864, Pierpoint's own company was dissolved, and a partnership with the more experienced Charles Dabney was established: Dabney, Morgan & Co. Junius also participated. Pierpoint and Junius contributed most of the capital, Dabney his name, and a minor capital contribution. However, Pierpoint kept doing business with Edward Ketchum until Edward got arrested for stealing from his father's bank and forging gold certificates. It led to a loss of about $50,000 for Dabney, Morgan & Co. They kept it as secret as possible. Edward Ketchum went to the Sing Sing (Strouse, 2014). In 1871, Dabney announced his retirement. The trouble with his job and an excessive work tempo had pushed Pierpont into a psychological depression, and he started to think about also retiring from all his positions. However, his father saw other possibilities. He had contacts already with Tony Drexel, who, together with his brothers, was active in New York and Paris. They decided to combine the houses of Morgan and Drexel and saw a position for Pierpoint as senior partner in the New York-based Drexel & Morgan Company they were going to establish (Berfield, 2020). Pierpoint accepted but had one condition: he would go to Europe for an extended vacation of 15 months. After this date, Pierpont had gained the habit of going on vacation frequently and staying away from the stresses of business life. The partnership would last until 1893 when Tony Drexel died.

This period was called the Gilded Age (1860–1894). The term was inspired by the book "The Gilded Age: A Tale of Today," published in 1873 by Mark Twain and Charles Dudley Warner (Twain & Warner, 1873). As it is known, the word gilding means that some valueless materials are covered with glossy papers or gilded paints and shown as valuable things. In the book, the authors make fun of the vulgar rich people by drawing attention to their flashy activities, rude attitudes, corruption, and low morality. It was a period of turbulent industrial growth: railways all over the US, steel production developed and monopolized by Andrew Carnegie, oil production by John D. Rockefeller, development of electric light, mechanization in food processing, etc. Industry barons and bankers ruled the country. The US population doubled between 1870 and 1910, while the estimates of national wealth increased fourfold (Strouse, 2014). So, the average wealth increased, but that was only the average. It was combined with a long price decline, hurting especially the farmers, and partly corresponding with the Long depression (starting with the crisis of 1873). One of the causes was the lack of money. In 1873, the US switched from a bimetallic system with silver and gold to only gold, thus reducing the available liquidity and the growing costs of debts. It led to fierce political debates and conflicts about the role of silver. The most famous "Silverite" was William Jennings Bryan, also called "the great commoner," who was three times the Democratic nominee for the Presidency. In his speeches, he put the corporate interests, the moneyed interests, opposite the interests of the common people (William Jennings Bryan, n.d.). Most bankers, like Morgan, were in favor of only gold. They did not need silver for their dealings, and internationally, it worked better, creating more trust.

By 1900, Pierpoint Morgan specialized in restructuring and mergers and had one of the most influential banking organizations in the country. Apart from banking, J.P. Morgan would enter the railroad and steel industry. Maybe the railway industry was the most characteristic of the Gilded Age.

7.3.2 The Railways Investments

Railroads played an essential role in the development of the United States. At first, railroad investments had turned into a frenzy, attracting ambitious and adventurous businessmen. It all started with the construction of a long railroad stretching to the west in 1827, and fierce competition emerged in which more and more companies participated. For nearly 45 years, investors relentlessly built new lines until the Long Depression that hit the markets in 1873 bankrupted many companies and temporarily halted growth. In this period, investments in railways were in complete turmoil. The lack of government control left the market to dishonest players, and the railways became the plaything of uninformed investors and unscrupulous traders. They sold high-priced stocks and bonds, bribed politicians, and bought journalists to build railroad lines unlikely to be commercially successful. Meanwhile, they broke into the Indian regions, brutally killing the indigenous people and deporting them to other areas. Security measures were particularly lax, with tens of thousands of railroad workers dying each year, which was considered to be very natural (Berfield, 2020).

Large companies had become more assertive in the American economy, and monopolies were established in many sectors. At the end of the nineteenth century, it was considered normal for large firms to dominate various sectors. For example, Andrew Carnegie monopolized the iron and steel industry, while John Rockefeller owned 90% of the US oil industry. On the other hand, there was no strong firm in the railway sector, and intense competition prevailed. J.P. Morgan entered the industry in 1869 because he saw this as an opportunity. Being a brilliant businessman, Pierpont felt that he could make this business successful not only as an investor but also by taking an active role in the management of the company. Since the laws allowed it at that time, he started to place himself or a middleman in the director seat of the companies he financed. In this way, he could direct the company's management and access all the information about the company, increasing his power in the sector. Later, this practice became known as "Morganization" and became widespread in all his investments (Temin, 1991). Pierpont had developed and financed a railroad empire of more than 20 companies through restructurings and mergers throughout the United States and raised significant funds to attract European investors. Rather than just participating in projects as a financier, he helped reorganize the railroads and achieve greater efficiency, fighting speculators who were only interested in profit and forging a vision of an interconnected transportation system (Hayes, 2020).

The company of J.P. Morgan was operating the New York Central-Buffalo Railroad line in 1885. He reorganized the Philadelphia Reading in 1886 and the Chesapeake & Ohio Lines in 1888. In addition, he engaged in civil society activities in the railway sector. He showed that he was an indispensable player in the business world by organizing conferences that brought together the railway heads to enact new laws and monitor current practices. Being the first of their kind, these conferences increased interaction between rival railroads. They paved the way for significant mergers of the early twentieth century, making the initiator known throughout the country as the merge master. In addition, J.P. Morgan's banks financed many railroads between 1869 and 1899, especially street railroads in New York (Carosso & Carosso, 1987).

As Morgan became increasingly specialized in this business in the 1880s, he began to pursue aggressive methods of competition to attract European investors. In particular, he decided to restructure some loss-making lines in the industry. One was the West Shore Company, which operated the line between New York City and Buffalo. Pennsylvania Railroad was behind the West Shore. This company competed with Morgan's New York Central Company. In 1885, a fierce price war between West Shore and New York Central drove down both companies' stock and bond prices. In the spring of 1885, the West Shore went into receivership while the struggling New York Central postponed critical maintenance. JP Morgan knew these companies needed regular revenues to cover the fixed interest costs of bonds marketed in New York and London. By the mid-1880s, freight rates were plummeting under the pressure of savage price-fixing. Pierpont decided that "the main thing was to bring about a harmony between Pennsylvania and New York Central." On July 20, 1885, after picking up Chauncey Depew, president of the New York Central, he proceeded to a pier in New Jersey. He took George H. Roberts, president of the Pennsylvania Railroad, and Frank Thomson, vice-president, aboard. Pierpont has always denied that his yacht (Corsair) was chosen for secrecy. As the Corsair sailed up and down the Hudson, he sat under the rear awning, surrounded by railroad chiefs and smoking a nightmarishly huge black cigar. As he always practiced, the Corsair did not dock until the deal was done. He created a general "no exit" situation and added the threat that his rivals faced a deadline. He also underlined his position as an honest mediator by speaking little, allowing his adversaries to vent their anger. When the railroad presidents were released to their respective shores at seven o'clock that evening, they had agreed to buy each other's lines and give up their mutually destructive war (Chernow, 2001).

However, the war for railroads would heat up even more after 1895. There were two powerful rivals in the background of the story. James J. Hill, a railroad investor, was a businessman who, with the backing of J.P. Morgan, had turned a regional railroad in Minnesota into a successful transcontinental line connecting the upper Midwest to Seattle and Puget Sound. With Morgan's help, he merged the Great Northern and Northern Pacific. Hill had ambitions to integrate these railroads with the steamship lines that carried freight across the Great Lakes and the Pacific Ocean. He needed better rail connections to Chicago and other Midwestern points to accomplish these goals. The best solution was to buy the Burlington Railroad, a profitable line connecting Chicago to the Twin Cities (Minnesota) and the Midwest to the Northern Pacific in Billings, Montana. As a result, agreements could be made for tolls on both eastbound and westbound traffic. In contrast, another businessman, E.H. Harriman, had taken control of the bankrupt Union Pacific Railroad in 1897 and was pursuing his goals of rebuilding the original transcontinental railroad and improving its connections to Pacific ports. He was backed by Jacob Schiff, perhaps second only to Morgan in the American financial world. Harriman did not want Hill to buy Burlington. Offers to become partners were rejected. In 1901, Harriman and Schiff began quietly accumulating Northern Pacific stock to wrest control from Hill and Morgan and leave Burlington in the arms of Union Pacific (Haeg, 2013).

The Northern Pacific would run west from Wisconsin through North Dakota and Montana and terminate in Seattle, Washington. It was an extraordinarily bold plan because the House of Morgan had a significant stake in the Northern Pacific and could not tolerate such an attack. The raiders sneaked into the market and bought $78 million worth of Northern Pacific shares. It was one of the largest market operations at that time. Northern Pacific shares rose sharply in May. Sensing the danger, Morgan and their partners began frantic trading in the Northern Pacific. The jumps in the stock were phenomenal. Speculators were also involved, and it spread across the stock market. The stock market was in turmoil. In May 1901, after a few hectic trading days, shares of the recently bankrupt Northern Pacific reached $1,000 (Haeg, 2013).

Harriman lost the battle for control but still held a large block of shares in Northern Pacific. In the wake of this chaos, JP Morgan created a holding company, the Northern Securities Company, to hold shares in Great Northern and Northern Pacific (and Burlington along with them). However, Theodore Roosevelt soon became president. Roosevelt believed that large corporations and trusts created a monopolistic power and distorted business competitiveness. And the Justice Department challenged the legality of Northern Securities under the Sherman Anti-Trust Act of 1890. The Supreme Court narrowly declared the holding company illegal in 1903. The company was soon dissolved, but the Hill-Morgan railroads still had overlapping boards of directors and operated profitably as a "community of interest." (Berfield, 2020). While Morgan did not lose money on the project, his solid political reputation would suffer (Carosso & Carosso, 1987).

7.3.3 The 1895 Crisis and J.P. Morgan's Gold

The Panic of 1893 was one of the harshest financial crises in the history of the United States. The crisis started at interior banks. The problem was sourced from two reasons. Falling gold reserves because of European investors demanding payment in gold in a period of volatile global asset prices increased worries at home and abroad that the United States might have to stop the convertibility of notes, which might provoke depositors to withdraw notes and convert their funds into gold. Panic slowed down for a while when gold inflows from Europe lowered interest rates. Banks tried to get back to normal. Yet, in January 1895, US gold reserves were starting to run out; the Treasury was going into a troubled process. The second source of this inconstancy was the pre-panic deceleration in economic activity. The recession increased loan default rates. Draining bank raids swept through midwestern and western cities. More than a hundred banks paused their operations. In the summer of 1895, the panic was boosted, and 340 banks discontinued their operations. When these banks came under stress, they withdrew deposits from banks in New York City. To meet demands, banks began selling securities. Asset prices fell during the panic sale, jeopardizing the solvency of the whole banking system. The result was the incapacity of local banks to fulfill the demand for foreign currency in the country, and many of them went bankrupt. Worrying for the safety of their deposits, men and women began withdrawing money from banks. Fear spread, and withdrawals accelerated, resulting in widespread bank attacks.

Feeling the economy heading for the abyss, in mid February 1895, J.P. Morgan decided to go to Washington. He would present his thoughts to the president, explaining how the country's economy could be saved. When he heard that J.P. Morgan was coming, Grover Cleveland did not want to see him. He was timid about collaborating with big companies to avoid criticism from his Democratic party's left wing (Bard, 1985). A meeting would put him in a complicated political position. However, Pierpont insisted, and the president accepted it. Pierpont immediately got to the point at the meeting and explained that the country was in a stalemate. His sources had told him that Treasury reserves had dropped to $9 million. He also mentioned that an investor might have a $10 million gold bond and would soon apply to the Treasury for gold; maybe he was bluffing. Morgan said, "If this $10 million bond is presented, you cannot afford it; it will all be over before three o'clock." When President Cleveland said that this problem could be solved by issuing bonds and borrowing from the public, Pierpont explained that this process would take years and that a private bond sale in which he would be involved was necessary. According to this plan, Morgan would buy long-term government bonds and organize a group of banks (syndicate) to provide the Treasury with the gold it needed to survive. The amount of gold to be paid was $60 million. Then the president asked the critical question; "*Mr. Morgan, if we adopt this plan, what guarantee will you give that gold will not continue to be sent abroad and that while we receive it, gold will not leave the country and, above all, that we will achieve our goal?*" Morgan replied without hesitation, "*Yes, sir, I will guarantee this for the life of the syndication until this contract is completed and the goal is met.*" Cleveland knew that J.P. Morgan's word was as solid as gold. When this news was transmitted to New York and London by telegraph lines, the gold that Morgan promised to deliver was almost no longer needed, and the market relaxed (Brands 2011).

However, President Cleveland's problems were beginning. He would get into trouble with the left wing of his party, with his opponents accusing him of giving control of the state treasury to a bank boss, a symbol of capitalist power. Morgan would never reveal his profits from this operation to ease the pressure on President Cleveland. In an investigation that opened after this incident, Morgan told members of Congress, "*I refuse to answer. I am fully prepared to report every detail of the negotiations to the committee until the bonds are paid for and become my property. However, I do not wish to make a statement regarding my property after the purchase*" (Brands, 2011). The public thought that J.P. Morgan had earned significantly from this operation and that Cleveland and his party would pay the bill. The Democrats would not come to power again until 1910, after their defeat in 1896.

7.3.4 The Iron and Steel Investment

During the Gilded Age, the economy developed rapidly, and the commercial banking sector was also on the rise. While industrialists designed new projects and built factories with the loans they received from banks, many banks were established at the end of the nineteenth century, with capital flowing in from England. In America, there was jealousy between bankers and industrialists. Despite working together, their relationship was always distant. To industrialists, bankers were parasitic beings, and they viewed Wall Street bankers as arrogant, overbearing businessmen. They were people who exploited the labor of working people and were far from the realities of the USA. Therefore, Pierpont was formal and distant in his dealings with Andrew Carnegie and John Rockefeller. However, J.P. Morgan had taken his activities beyond trust and banking activities.

Morgan was now the most significant player in railways and train transport. He had begun to turn from the financial field to the industrial sector. He aimed to make a considerable investment in the iron and steel industry. Disliking competition, he wanted to be the strongest in this industry. While he was in contact with English and Scottish companies regarding this issue, he preferred to start with an American company. Two companies were on target; the first was Carnegie Steel, which controlled the US steel market, being the first corporation in the world with a market capitalization of over $1 billion. The other was Rockefeller's Minnesota mining company for iron ore.

On December 12, 1900, Pierpont attended an important dinner for Charles M. Schwab, a loyal employee of Andrew Carnegie, at the University Club in Manhattan. An eloquent orator and self-dramatizer, Schwab evoked for Morgan and 80 other financiers his vision of a steel trust that would handle all phases of the business, from mining ore to marketing steel products. After dinner, Morgan met for half an hour with Schwab, who was intrigued. It was clear that Morgan saw a light in him. Over the next 3 weeks, Morgan, his partners, and Schwab worked on a proposal at Morgan's library. It was never clear whether it was at Carnegie's behest or Pierpont's plan. The proposed trust would control more than half of the steel business. After a round of golf at the Saint Andrews Golf Club in Westchester, Schwab broached the subject with Carnegie. After some thought, Carnegie wrote down the sale price of $480 million on a piece of paper. He wanted the payment in bonds. When Schwab handed it to Morgan, Morgan looked at it and immediately said, "I accept this price." In his haste, Pierpont did not formalize the deal with a signature, and weeks later, he had to send a lawyer out of town for a contract. Carnegie's share of this amounted to $225.64 million, paid to Carnegie with a 5% interest, 50-year gold bonds.

In another story version, Carnegie's wife Louise wanted Carnegie to retire. In his book Brands (2011) describes what happened: "Louise Carnegie conspired with Schwab against her husband. Shortly after Schwab informed her of the merger plan, she telephoned to say that Carnegie would play golf the next morning at St. Andrew's Club in Westchester. He knew that he was always more cooperative after winning at golf. Schwab took the hint and deliberately lost the game. He then broached the subject of the sale. Carnegie didn't reject the plan outright, and Schwab took it as a good sign."

When Pierpont invited him to Wall Street, Carnegie insisted that Morgan come to his Fifty-first Street office instead. After a quiet 15-min conversation, Morgan said as he left: "Mr. Carnegie, I want to congratulate you on becoming the richest man in the world." Carnegie was delighted with the deal. The merger in 1901 included not just Andrew Carnegie's Carnegie Steel Company but also several other companies (Krass, 2011). Schwab subsequently became president of the company it created, US Steel. Later on, when he met Andrew Carnegie on the cruise, Morgan confessed that he was negotiating to buy a Scottish Steel company at the time and that the Scottish company wanted $100 million more than Carnegie for their business (Chernow, 1998b).

Pierpont then decided to buy iron ore mines and shipping ships from Rockefeller. Morgan could not afford to exclude such rich sources of raw materials from his investment. Although he did not like Rockefeller very much, he had visited him politely and, after some conversation, asked to reveal the price. Rockefeller had set a reasonable price without further ado, asking $88.5 million for ore and steamships. This amount was $5 million more than Pierpont had initially planned, but it was at a level that he could accept (Chernow, 1998a). The plans of J.P. Morgan, who had managed to become the most significant player in the steel market by now, were not finished yet. His target was the Tennessee Coal, Iron, and Railroad Company (TC&I), one of the largest companies in the industry. However, a merger of this magnitude might be prevented with antitrust laws strictly enforced by President

Theodore Roosevelt. He would have to wait a little longer for this but would have a great opportunity in the coming years.

7.3.5 The 1907 Crisis

The financial crisis of 1907 was the last crisis of the national banking era. It led directly to the establishment of the Federal Reserve in 1913. The trade-in agricultural products was an important factor in the crisis. The USA was a huge exporter of agricultural products. Most of it was exported through New York. The average balance of trade over the years 1900–1913 was (about) equal to 520 million dollars. More than half of it was realized in the last 4 months, the period of the harvest (Goodhart, 1969). During the harvest, the country banks needed a lot of cash to settle the transactions. Reserves they had in the form of deposits at national banks in (central) reserve cities were called back. It affected the cash reserves of the New York banks severely and made the fall always a season with more volatility in the money market.

The international trade was financed mainly with bills of exchange, generally in sterling. Import was paid for by bills drawn on correspondent banks in London. Exports could lead to a direct increase in US banks' balances with correspondent banks in London or the issue of bills of exchange by foreign banks. So, although most countries used the gold standard, international trade was financed without massive gold transmittances (Goodhart, 1969). This gold market was disturbed, however, in 1906, the year of the San Francisco earthquake. Insurance payments led to a gold drain to California (Tallman, 2012). The Secretary of the Treasury, Shaw, contributed to the disturbance by importing $50 million in gold from London to support the money market in New York in facilitating the issue of bonds to finance the Panama Canal works. London market makers reacted by making payments with bills of exchange less attractive, stimulating gold payments in this way.

So, while there was much instability in the fall, the trigger of the Panic of 1907 was F. Augustus Heinze. Heinze was a businessman who made a small fortune in the copper industry in those years but whose moral values were weak. He was planning considerable earnings with a market hit. Heinze had targeted the United Copper Company and arranged a manipulative transaction that would corner the company. It was not the first time he had done this. Years ago, he had formed a close relationship with Wall Street's notorious businessman Charles W. Morse. Together, they had made big bucks by successfully cornering the New York ice market. This manipulation was aided by Charles T. Barney, Chairman of the Knickerbocker Trust Company, New York's third-largest trust. With the help of his brother Otto, Augustus now wanted to corner investors who were short-selling on United Copper stocks. The Heinze family believed that it controlled most of the company's common stocks. Let us clarify the concept of short selling for our readers by taking a break here.

In short-selling operations, the speculator involved in this business immediately sells the stocks of the targeted company by borrowing them from the market. They expect that their prices will fall. When prices fall below a certain level in a few days or weeks, speculators will buy the company's stocks at a low price from the market and return the stocks they borrowed earlier. In short, they aim to make money from this transaction by selling at a high price and buying back at a low price. However, since the operation is based on borrowed stock for a few weeks, they will lose if prices do not fall or even rise in this short time; it is hazardous speculation. It is seen from time to time that some malicious players are trying to make money by artificially lowering prices. In January 2021, there was a similar transaction. In this case, Melvin Capital Management entered a short position with the expectation that the share prices of GameStop, which produces a video game company, would decrease. Melvin Capital even made an effort to reduce the company's stock prices. However, reportedly, for the first time in the capital market history, small investors had increased the value of GameStop with their organized purchases. Melvin Capital needed to buy the stocks it borrowed, so it had to repurchase them from the market at a very high price. Thus, small investors defended Gamespot and prevented Melvin Capital from having easy money (Financial Times, 2021).

In this case, Augustus and his brother Otto were acting on the assumption that speculators directed a significant portion of United Copper's shares to short-sell in anticipation of a decrease in prices. Just as the small investors in 2021 pressed on Melvin Capital, they thought that if they raised United Copper's share price, the speculators who had to close their positions would have to buy those shares no matter what the value was, so they could easily make money. According to their plan, the two brothers would aggressively buy stocks to raise prices for a while, waiting for the short-sellers to call in on them. They had asked for money from Barney, the Chairman of the Knickerbocker Trust, with whom they had previously collaborated, to obtain funding, but they could not get it. Confident in their plans, the brothers began collecting stocks on Monday, October 14. In one day, United Copper's stock price rose from $39 to $52. On Tuesday, October 15, the share price rose to $60, but no one would buy stock from them despite calls to short-sellers to return the borrowed common stocks. Speculators were able to find plenty of United Copper shares from sources other than the Heinze brothers. The brothers had misread the market, and after they could not find anyone to sell the stocks they bought on credit, the shares they bought for $39 would drop to $10 in a few days (Bruner & Carr, 2007).

The plan's failure left the two brothers helpless and led to the bankruptcy of the brokerage firm Gross & Kleeberg. On Thursday, October 17, the New York Stock Exchange suspended Otto Heinze's trading concessions. United Copper collapsed, and also the Montana State Savings Bank, owned by F. Augustus Heinze, declared bankruptcy. This affected, in the first place, the banks associated with Heize and Morse. The most important of these banks were clearing house members and could be provided with loans on the condition that Heinze and Morse resigned from their banking interests. The crisis would become widespread, however, because of the rumored association of Morse with Barney, the chairman of the Knickerbocker Trust Company.

In the early 1900s, trust companies had overgrown the banks, with their assets increasing 244% over the past decade. In contrast, national bank assets could only increase by 97%, and state bank assets in New York grew by 82% during the same period (Tallman & Moen, 1990). Trust companies of this type should not be confused with Industrial Trusts, like in steel or in railways. Industrial trust is a large grouping of business interests with significant market power, which may be embodied as a corporation or as a group of corporations that cooperate with one another in various ways. Trust companies were in the finance sector and comparable to banks but were more directed to investment than to facilitating trade. Their deposits were used as surplus funds for individuals and corporations and were not widely used as checking accounts. Trust companies were state-chartered institutions and were regulated much less stringently than national or state banks. While trust companies could compete with national banks in most banking activities, they also had investment opportunities that were prohibited to national banks. Restrictions regarding minimum reserves against deposits were much looser than for banks. Trusts gave a higher interest on the deposits but accepted a higher risk. In New York, the trust companies did not participate in the clearing house. They had to work with a correspondent bank to realize a broader access to the payment infrastructure.

The Knickerbocker Trust Company was the third-largest trust company in New York (Goodhart, 1969). It had the National Bank of Commerce as its principal correspondent bank, with J.P. Morgan as vice-president. Due to his past relationships with Morse and Heinze, on Monday, October 21, the Knickerbocker board requested Barney's resignation. The National Bank of Commerce requested a loan from the New York Clearing House on behalf of Knickerbocker. The request was denied, and then the National Bank of Commerce announced that it would not provide any further services to Knickerbocker. On October 22, Knickerbocker was forced to suspend banking activity when faced with a sudden demand for money from depositors who had lost confidence. Panic quickly spread to two other significant Trusts, the America Trust Company, and the Lincoln Trust Company. By Thursday, October 24, more than 10 trusts had stopped their activity (Bruner & Carr, 2007). A few weeks later, Charles T. Barney shot himself, and a wave of suicides among the bank's depositors followed. Soon, interest rates on loans would rise to 70%, and stock prices would fall to a low not seen since December 1900.

Between October 22 and October 24, the Treasury sent another 35 million dollars to the New York banks (Goodhart, 1969). Being all the Treasury could do, it was insufficient to dampen the crisis. During these hot days of the financial crisis, US President Theodore Roosevelt was out to join a bear hunt. Meanwhile, J.P. Morgan watched events closely, despite attending a church meeting in Virginia. Pierpont was not only the wealthiest and best-connected banker in the city, but everyone knew he had experience dealing with similar financial crises. J.P. Morgan was the leading character of every critical economic negotiation and the banker who solved the situation in 1895. When news of the problem came to light, he would return to New York as a responsible banker to make waves.

Pierpont and his experts set to work with a damage assessment as soon as they arrived. Financial reports showed that the Knickerbocker Trust had gone bankrupt. There was nothing they could do about it. The important thing was to stop the bank running and save healthy banks and trusts. He spent October 22 with meetings with the Ministry of the Treasury officials. The US Treasury had pinned almost all its hopes on Pierpont. The absence of a central bank to intervene in the market tied its hands. That evening, Morgan said: "*This crisis must be stopped at this point*" (Bruner & Carr, 2007). Otherwise, it would get out of control. He was trying to find money from the Treasury, big trusts, and banks, investing all the money he could see into the system to save the banks. The wealthiest man in the United States, John D. Rockefeller, had invested another $10 million in Stillman's National City Bank, now Citibank. He called the Associated Press news agency to instill public confidence and said he could pledge half of his fortune as collateral to protect the United States' reputation (Chernow, 1998b).

Despite the available cash flow, New York banks were reluctant to give short-term loans, which they usually provide to facilitate daily stock trading. Share prices were constantly falling. On Thursday, October 24, J.P. Morgan said that an early closure would be disastrous in response to Ransom Thomas, Chairman of the New York Stock Exchange. However, on Friday, there would be more panic in the stock market; everything was getting worse (Bruner & Carr, 2007). The essential players of Wall Street also joined hands. Wealthy businessmen such as John D. Rockefeller, George B. Cortelyou, Lord Rothschild, and James Stillman tried to restore economic confidence. Even the US Treasury was short on funds. The public trust had to be repaired. Two committees were formed to persuade the clergy to calm their congregations and to explain various aspects of the financial rescue package to the press. New York City needed at least $20 million by November 1. Otherwise, bankruptcies were inevitable. Meanwhile, the Mayor of New York, who stepped in, softened the problem a little by issuing bonds.

Although the market calmed down on Saturday, November 2, another crisis had emerged in New York. Moore & Schley, one of the stock market's largest brokerage houses, was heavily indebted and in danger of going bankrupt. The firm had borrowed a significant amount by collateralizing the Tennessee Coal, Iron, and Railroad Company (TC&I). If TC&I's position were not strengthened by Monday, the crisis would spread exponentially, and many trusts and banks would fail. To this end, as we pointed out in the introduction, Pierpont invited over a hundred financial institutions to a meeting at the Morgan Library. Participants were to discuss the problem of TC&I. It would solve the crisis if Morgan bought this company and strengthened his financial situation. However, other financial institutions were required to provide a loan of $25 million. The initial suggestion was made that the US Steel Corporation, the company of Morgan, would acquire TC&I. The management of US Steel analyzed the circumstances and offered either to lend Moore & Schley $5 million or buy TC&I for $90 a share. By 7 p.m., a consensus had not been reached, and the meeting was suspended. Finally, U. S. Steel Corporation acceded to a new plan to acquire TC&I. As suggested earlier, US Steel would purchase most of the company, but not by paying cash. US Steel would instead exchange its bonds for shares of TC&I stock at par. Precisely, US Steel would swap each of its 60-year, 5% sinking fund gold bonds, which had a par value of $11,904.76, for 100 shares of TC&I stock, which had a par value of $10,000. Still, the company asked for three essential conditions to be met. First, the Roosevelt administration must interpose no objections to the acquisition; second, this arrangement must "unquestionably save Moore & Schley" from collapse; and third, formal arrangements must be completed to track the city's working trust companies (Bruner & Carr, 2007).

Working at the library on Sunday, the parties had completed the purchase of TC&I by Morgan's company, US Steel. They traveled to Washington in the evening by a special train comprised merely of a locomotive and a Pullman sleeper car to request approval from President Theodore Roosevelt. At that time, private wagons could be pulled by a private locomotive, providing privacy to their passengers. Wealthy people used them for travel and entertainment, especially in the United States. If this agreement were not approved immediately, antitrust laws would void it. Grover Cleveland, who agreed with J.P. Morgan in the crisis of 1895, had lost the election. This incident is still fresh in my memory. Although the President's Secretary refused to meet with them, with the intervention of the Secretary of the Interior, they would meet with President Roosevelt and succeed (Chernow, 1998b). When the news reached New York, confidence in the market had increased. At the same time that newspaper headlines heralded that the crisis was over, the public was already starting to talk about Pierpont making the most profit. J.P. Morgan owned 60% of the steel industry by twisting the arm of his competitors and that of the president; he had been given the key to this industry.

Concerns about the concentration of financial power in the US had already been voiced. The crisis of 1907 showed this situation even more. In particular, a group of businessmen had amassed enormous wealth and power by building dominant roles in the banking, railroad, oil, and other industries that were the engines of the country's economy. The US Congress handled this situation through the Pujo Committee, called after its original chairman, Arsène Paulin Pujo. In 1913, it published an influential report concluding that a small group of plutocrats based in New York City had achieved de facto monopoly control over the American financial system. According to the Pujo Committee's report, financial leaders abused public confidence by consolidating control over many of its critical industries and, ultimately, the banking system, rapidly consolidating the operations of the nation's largest industrial and railroad companies in the hands of a few New York tycoons. They also concluded that the enormous combined wealth of their companies allowed them to exercise control over the country's leading banks and other financial institutions. In particular, the report revealed that some big banks like J.P. Morgan were able to advance their business and increase their profits through a network of "interlocking directorates" whose members serve as directors on the boards of companies that receive loans to protect their interests. The report pointed out that the J.P. Morgan Banking group had reached gigantic proportions, being represented on the boards of 112 institutions and client (lending) companies, including their own companies (Bruner & Carr, 2007). The Pujo Committee's findings impacted the passage of significant legislation during the administration of President Woodrow Wilson, including the Federal Reserve Act of 1913, which designated a decentralized national banking system, the Federal Trade Commission Act of 1914, which created a federal agency authorized to examine antitrust violations and the Clayton Antitrust Act of 1914, which handled interlocking directorates (Carosso, 1973).

In the Panic of 1907, industrial production fell more than during any other crisis, resulting in the second-highest wave of bankruptcies in US history. While production fell 11% and imports 26%, unemployment rose from 3 to 8%. Immigration to the country had dropped from 1.2 million 2 years ago to 750,000 in 1909 (Bruner & Carr, 2007). Now, the USA was on the verge of a new decision. It wished not to be helpless in the face of frequent crises and wait for wealthy cartels or trusts to save the country. Those who rescued the country were suspected of profiting from the chaos. A central bank had to be established. In May 1908, Congress began searching for a solution by passing a law establishing the National Monetary Commission to investigate panic and to regulate banking (Miron, 1986).

7.4 Establishment of the Federal Reserve Bank (Fed)

At the beginning of the twentieth century, the United States did not have a central bank, although almost every free country had one. In the crises of 1893 and 1907, this need was evident. The European states could maintain a balance in the economy by increasing the money supply when necessary. However, the absence of a central bank in the United States made its economy fragile. It was a politically sensitive topic, creating distrust of the big banks, tension between the responsibilities of the States and those of the Federation, and differences between Democrats and Republicans. To prepare for the transition, the Congress established the bipartisan National Monetary Commission, chaired by Senator Aldrich of Rhode Island. Given the sensitivity of the problem, he then organized a secret conference with the nation's leading financiers at the Jekyll Island Club on the coast of Georgia in November 1910 to develop a proposal. Most likely, J.P. Morgan had arranged for the Club's facilities to be used (Richardson & Romero, 2015).

The developed plan called for a National Reserve Association with 15 quasi-independent branches whose policies would be coordinated through a central national committee (Prins, 2014). Aldrich delivered the plan to the Congress in January 1911. President Taft promoted the plan, stressing that it would be an association. However, the Democrats had won control of the House in 1910 and blocked the proposal. They saw too much Manhattan influence. When Woodrow Wilson, a Democrat, was elected president in 1912, he had asked already Carter Glass, the representative of Virginia, and H. Parker Willis, an economist of the House Banking Committee, to make a new draft. Wilson insisted on one crucial change: having a Federal Reserve Board in Washington appointed by the president to control and coordinate the districts (Greider, 1987). It led to a fierce debate. The bankers would be represented heavily in the regional Federal Reserve Boards. They would be running these local boards in fact, but they also wanted to be represented in the Federal Reserve Board in Washington, the Board of Governors. The compromise was the introduction of the Federal Advisory Council, which advised on money issues.

Federal Reserve notes, issued by the Reserve banks, were going to replace the National Bank notes. They could be issued against gold reserves and certain types of commercial paper, eligible for rediscount at the Federal Reserve Banks. The Act reduced the reserve requirements for the member banks but determined that reserves had to be held in the Federal Reserve Banks. This made it possible to replace the private clearing houses. The Reserve Banks had the authority to engage in open market operations in gold, foreign exchange and a variety of domestic credit products. Coordination of these operations by the Board of Governors was essential.

In April 1914, the Reserve Bank Organization Committee announced that 12 Reserve Banks would be established. The New York Reserve Bank was the most important one, being located in the city of most central banks in the US and given the nearness of Wall Street. At first, it was formally not different from the other reserve banks. This changed over the course of time, though. It houses the open market desk for the whole Fed, it is the agent for the US Department of the Treasury, and it is the custodian of the world's most extensive storage of gold reserves.

The original Federal Reserve System was the product of a uniquely American political process of overcoming systemic problems with the US's money, existing banking, and payment deals. The main feature of the regulation was consensus enactment, which was in harmony with the US state and federal structure system. The highly structured system left space for limited private-sector participation in fulfilling a necessary public function. While establishing this system, considering the sensitivity of the US states to the central government, the term "central bank" was avoided (Parthemos, 1988).

Interestingly, although the Fed's roles and capabilities are concentrated in the new system, these powers are spread across the System's units. The system was uniquely different from any other central bank. The founders recognized that the dynamics of the US economy would require adjustments over time, given the US economy's future shape. The trials that the system faced in 1929–33 also revealed that this system was not able to solve all monetary problems. Therefore, in the mid-1930s, significant reforms led to the emergence of a system that was drastically different from the first system, both in structure and in approaches to money and credit control. Ten years after the Great Depression, the system became increasingly centralized, undeniably quite like other central bank systems. However, the System maintains its decentralized features and differentiates itself from other central banks. Its role in monetary policymaking today differs significantly from that envisioned in the original law, restructured to align more closely with radically revised views on money and credit control techniques. Central Bank directorates continue to take the initiative in determining the interest rate. More importantly, the executive chairpersons of the Reserve Banks are now formalized as chairmen rather than governors, serving actively on the Federal Open Market Committee, the System's main policymaking body (Parthemos, 1988).

7.5 The Death of J.P. Morgan and the Future of His Bank

J.P. Morgan died in his sleep on March 31, 1913, at 76, at the Grand Hotel Plaza in Rome, Italy, during a trip abroad. When his body was brought to New York by ship, the flags on Wall Street were at half-mast, and the New York Stock Exchange was closed for 2 h, as heads of state used to be honored. His son, John Pierpont "Jack" Morgan Jr, inherited the banking business while donating his painting and book collections to the Morgan Library in New York, which has been turned into a museum since. His fortune was worth $68.3 million that day's money, and he was one of the country's most prominent wealthy people when he passed away.

After his death, many positive and negative opinions about John Pierpont Morgan arose. Some described him as the man who saved the US economy, while others said he was a greedy, ruthless money baron, the true representative of the Baronial Age in which industry and finance had merged (Chernow, 2001). Indeed, he was the undisputed natural leader of Wall Street. He did not hesitate to take action in many cases where everyone panicked and did not take responsibility.

In the First World War, which started right after Pierpont's death, J.P. Morgan & Company supported the Allied armies by issuing war bonds for France and England. It survived the 1929 crisis without significant damage. The company had come to a crossroads in 1933 under the provisions of the Glass-Steagall Act, which was enacted to reduce market dominance by breaking up trusts and large companies. The law forced J.P. Morgan & Company to separate its investment banking from its commercial banking activities, and the family chose to operate as a commercial bank. In 1935, two J.P. Morgan partners established Morgan Stanley, one of the world's largest investment companies, together with Harold Stanley. By the 1950s, J.P. Morgan had lost its former power; it was only a medium-sized bank then. In 1959, J.P. Morgan merged with the New York Guaranty Trust to strengthen its position, forming the Morgan Guarantee Trust. Guaranty Trust provided substantial capital to this new venture, while the reputable name of J.P. Morgan attracted high-quality clients and bankers. In the 1980s, J.P. Morgan & Co., along with other commercial banks, moved toward investment banking, starting with issuing commercial papers. At the same time, in 1989, the Federal Reserve would allow J.P. Morgan & Co. to become the first commercial bank to operate in corporate public offerings. It would eventually merge with Chase Bank and be named JPMorgan Chase. This bank has become one of the largest banks in investment banking, commercial banking, retail banking, wealth management, private banking, and private equity operations in the US and globally.

7.6 J.P. Morgan's Banking Secrets

While J.P. Morgan earned an excellent reputation for his strong leadership capacity, he moreover used social networks wisely. While solving the crises he faced, he always managed to win and establish the most extensive banking and industrial empire in US history. When he died, he was a highly respected businessman at home and internationally.

7.6.1 Using Social Networks

Although studies on J.P. Morgan use various positive or negative adjectives about him, they agree that he was a respected businessman who kept his promises. In addition to him being the most influential timely person in the American financial market, it would not have been possible to judge otherwise. His response to prosecutor Samuel Untermyer's question at the Pujo Committee, a sub-committee of the House Committee on Banking and Currency, established in 1912, reflects his commitment to dignity and promise (Chernow, 2001).

"*Attorney Untermyer: Isn't your business credit primarily based on money or property?*

J.P. Morgan: Morgan: No sir; The first thing is character.

Prosecutor Untermyer: Before money or property?

J.P. Morgan: Before money or anything else. Money can't buy it."

Pierpont knew very well that dignity is hard-earned and easily lost. Undoubtedly, he sometimes bent the rules throughout his business life, and at one time, he even started to fall out with his father. However, within the framework of the nineteenth-century economic philosophy of "laissez-faire," he always tried to comply with the values of his business environment, even if he sometimes pushed the limits. The entire banking community thought that reputation was universally at the foundation of banking. In January 1925, Pierpont's son, Jack Morgan, wrote to his partner that the firm's reputation was his most excellent satisfaction. He stated: "*What is more important than the payment of the loans we give is the ever-increasing prestige and position in all the cities where our bank is located.*" One of the famous bankers of the time, Jacob H. Schiff, wrote to his partner: "*If our reputation is gone, we are done; only a show remains*" (Pak, 2013). Indeed, there are significant relationships between the reputations of investment banks and company performances (McLaughlin et al., 2000).

On the other hand, numerous studies suggest that J.P. Morgan was a ruthless and opportunistic businessman. However, it is necessary to understand that time's business ethics and values. In the USA, where J.P. Morgan lived, slavery was still not resolved, and the rights of Afro-Americans were not fully settled in all layers of society despite the Civil War. Workers' rights were inadequate, and large enterprises were exploiting workers' rights. It was considered normal for thousands of workers to die each year during the construction of railways. The business world believed in private enterprise, and it was thought that competition would solve all problems. The values of the elite that ruled the society were very different from those today. It would take another hundred years for business ethics and corporate governance principles to develop in the USA, namely after the financial scandals of companies such as Enron, Tyco, and WorldCom that emerged in 2001. Especially during the Gilded Age, the work ethic had collapsed entirely. The market was in the hands of robber businessmen. During this period, businessmen like Vanderbilt, Rockefeller, and J.P. Morgan were using their power without limit; the government was no match for them. Historian Howard Zinn writes that the US Government behaved as Karl Marx described capitalist states: "*It pretends to be neutral to maintain order, but only serves the interests of the rich*" (Zinn, 2005). Another historian, Historian Mark Wahlgren Summers, called this period "*the best period of theft*" (Summers, 1993).

In the early twentieth century, two factors were more important than the others in gaining prestige in US society. The first was to be religious and a distinguished member of the Church, and the second was to be accepted into businessmen's clubs and associations. Spiritual values in society were beyond moral values. Pierpont was a regular churchgoer and had strong support in religious circles as the founder of the Young Men's Christian Association. Being religious not only increased his reputation but also strengthened his social connections. During this period, social club membership and the principles of these social groups were different. Business people expanded their circles through the clubs. They were gaining a significant advantage in competition by cooperating in developing business contacts, making business deals, and ensuring the growth of their companies. Through the concept of social capital they created, gentlemen's clubs developed a system in which financial and social success depended on "*who you know, not what you know*" (Yee, 2015). They occupied the upper echelons of American society, representing the essence of high class, wealth, and privilege that others could not enjoy. Being a member of such clubs was a sign of exclusivity and prestige. J.P. Morgan was also one of the essential members of these clubs. The relations among the club members, almost all religious, were utterly different. In these relations, success in business life, power, and keeping promises made to each other was significant. Pierpont was socially trusted as a consistent and trustworthy person alongside unreliable businessmen who did a lot of dirty work. Even though Pierpont, who also had strong references in the Church, occasionally clashed with the Nation's rulers, everyone knew he kept his word.

To protect their prestige, bankers tried to maintain their eliteness by following each other and being aware of each other through social networks. They could showcase their distinguished lives and increase their prestige through magazines such as The World, the New York Herald Tribune, the New York Times, and Bankers Magazine. The Commercial & Financial Chronicle, one of the oldest newspapers in America, wrote that the reputation of bankers is a concept that is strengthened by their relationships with each other, based on many documents and information about the Morgans and other essential bankers. At the beginning of the twentieth century, bankers and elite business people were mainly university graduates who had social connections to universities (Yee, 2015). The business world in New York was utterly embedded in these social networks.

These complex social networks watched markets closely, strengthened cooperation, and filled in the gaps in economic relations by monitoring, deterring, and rewarding talented bankers from their perspective. When accurate financial information was difficult to access, naturally, personal relationships became more important. Therefore, social networks play an important role in maintaining and developing a bank's reputation. Being a member of these clubs was readily honored as they were dignified gentlemen who kept their promises. Bankers who came together in social environments were giving information to each other and forming a kind of communication network. Even though the members sometimes clashed, they could take up their relationship to a certain level. J.P. Morgan was born into a wealthy family. His father had strong connections. As a talented, hardworking, religious, and reliable person, he used his leadership qualities and gained a well-deserved reputation in business life. When he died in 1913, President Theodore Roosevelt, with whom he had conflicts occasionally, said that he had always been an honest banker.

During this period, the banking profession formed a private elite club owned by men, and members struggled to maintain this privilege. When Pierpont's son and heir, Jack Morgan, died, his obituary listed many memberships, such as Harvard University, a yacht club, and a tennis club, indicating the importance of such social groups. Although Knickerbocker's Chairman, Charles T. Barney, did not provide funding for the short-selling business to Augustus and Otto Heinze, the Knickerbocker Company had requested the resignation of Charles T. Barney, as it was known that they had a relationship in the past. This behavior showed how much importance the companies attached to reputation at that time.

Although social networks have changed over the past hundred years, some aspects of relationship banking have remained. Especially in the last 50 years, social relations established by university graduates have gained importance in bankers' careers. In the USA, employment opportunities are opened more quickly in the banking sector for those who have graduated from a top university, such as Harvard, MIT, Stanford, or Chicago. Almost all US Treasury Secretary or Central Bank Governors have graduated from the best schools in the country. Those with a Morgan, Chase, or Citibank background move up the career ladder more easily with established relationships. Henry Paulson, the US Secretary of the Treasury during the 2008 crisis, was a former Goldman Sachs employee. The legendary Chairman of the Fed, Alan Greenspan, was a former J.P. Morgan manager.

In Pierpont's time, these relationships were much more challenging, and there was an elitist approach. He managed social networks and relationships with his talents. During his visits to foreign countries, he was treated like a king. His statements to the Pujo Committee reflected the banking principles and understanding of the Gilded Age. Although he acquired a great fortune by exploiting the country's economy with other large companies, the strong image he reflected the society with the ties he established among themselves made him a respected person. Morgan's perceived power was far greater than the actual wealth he controlled. Morgan lived in an age where reputation was more important than the value of company stock. Therefore, society further cemented his reputation by identifying Morgan with Wall Street (Beattie, 2022).

7.6.2 Crisis Management

Pierpont had a worldwide network on which he could rely. He had overcome difficulties every time. Morgan had earned his first big profitable job in the filthy environment of the American Civil War. Undoubtedly, he was an ambitious young man with a temperament that was not afraid to take risks. His sale to the army by refurbishing used weapons was an example of opportunism. The point of contention was whether Pierpont was part of a conspiracy to defraud the Union. Historian Gordon R. Wasson published a lengthy study in 1943 arguing that there was no evidence that Morgan was committing fraud. Some historians have also suggested that Wasson's analysis is dubious, pointing out that Wasson became the vice-president of public affairs at J.P. Morgan & Co. after the exculpation of Morgan (Josephson, 1962).

J.P. Morgan transitioned from banking to the industry, and next to the steel sector, a preferred sector was the railroads. The main reason for investing in this area was the absence of a large company controlling the railway market and the chaotic structure in the railway sector. Too many companies were operating in this field because besides malicious business people, many journalists and self-interested politicians were involved in the dirty work related to the railways. Security measures were lax. As tens of thousands of railroad workers died each year, one railroad commissioner wrote in a report, "*Of course, workers will have to be maimed or killed in accidents for trains to work.*" The average life expectancy of workers on the railways was short (Berfield, 2020). Taking advantage of the crisis environment in the sector, Pierpont entered it step by step and indirectly solved the crisis and made a lot of money from this turmoil. Adapting to change became Morgan's calling card. He often rescued failing businesses as a powerful financier by facilitating their reorganization and restructuring. While J.P. Morgan saved the country in the crises of 1893 and 1907, he made a fortune, as detailed above. In 1895, he gave his gold reserves to the Treasury in exchange for long-term US Treasury bonds. Although Pierpont never disclosed how much he earned from this business, it was estimated that he made a pretty good profit and took over 60% of the iron and steel industry (Bruner & Carr, 2007).

Not all of Morgan's efforts were successful. His investments to consolidate the railroad companies failed due to political discontent. There was opposition in Parliament as he aimed to compete on London's underground railway. Also, a few large projects, such as those involving a Trans-Atlantic communications network, resulted in failures. However, in any case, Morgan displayed decisiveness while respecting opportunities for improvement. This dynamism was another courageous leadership trait he displayed throughout his life.

After J.P. Morgan's death, his son Jack Morgan made high returns by investing in the chaotic environment created by the First World War. At the beginning of the war, he organized the first loan of $12,000,000 to Russia, and by 1915, he lent

$500,000,000 to France and Britain. The British and French governments also gave Morgan a 1% commission on all his financial support, which would be $3 billion today (Horn, 2000).

7.6.3 Morganization

When J.P. Morgan started investing in railways, there were too many companies in the industry, price competition was very high, and many unrealistic projects were ongoing. It would be necessary to reduce the number of companies in this sector or to gather rival companies under one company through mergers to control the industry. Morgan had a large amount of capital to do this and planned to attract British investors to this sector. He would achieve his goal by combining his business circle and personal relationships. However, the method he used in this process was remarkable: putting himself or a middleman in the director seat of the company he financed. Later, "Morganization" became the name for the monopolization techniques used (Hayes, 2020). Using his reputation, Pierpont stabilized the sector by making his firm almost a monopoly after taking over the railway sector with the help of European financiers. Thus, he turned the railway sector into a profitable investment area that attracted more foreign investors. He would then apply this method to the iron, steel, electricity, and banking sectors. Morgan's tactics challenged the antitrust laws that the US administration tried to enact in the early twentieth century to break up many monopolies. As a method, Morganization first started with buying underfunded small companies. Later, J.P. Morgan, as a dominant partner or financier, was joining forces by controlling the companies with the members he placed on the boards of these small companies. In the last stage, small companies were reorganizing and increasing their efficiency. By acquiring small companies, Morgan lowered rail freight and ticket prices, causing competitors to face financial difficulties and go bankrupt. Chinese, Irish, Scottish, and Greek immigrants worked on the railways at that time. He had weakened their competitors' labor recruitments by offering these poor workers better prices.

The most remarkable example of Morganization is the monopolization of the iron and steel industry in 1907, becoming led by US Steel. At the end of the nineteenth century, the iron and steel industry would accelerate tremendously, leaving the railways industry behind. Steel was the primary raw material for developing the rapidly growing construction industry in the twentieth century. J.P. Morgan had established vertical integration in this industry. All stages of steelmaking were under his control, from ore to coal mines, blast furnaces, steel mills, finishing mills, and barges to railroad tracks. The last move was made during the 1907 crisis with the reluctant approval of President Roosevelt. After all, US Steel became the largest producer of the steel industry; it reduced its production costs by controlling the entire process (Berfield, 2020).

One of the most criticized practices of Morganization was the board network he established. Pierpont required that every company he financed, whether he was a partner or not, had one of his men on the board of directors. Thus, he had decisive power on the boards of directors of many companies and could learn their most confidential information, the company secrets. His board members gave him a tremendous competitive edge. Morgan used this power successfully in acquisitions and mergers. The 1912/13 Pujo Committee determined that J.P. Morgan had placed one or more of his men on the boards of 112 companies. By 1920, the Morgan Group had 167 representatives in various companies. It had established a network of 2,450 interconnected boards of directors, controlling 25% of all the companies in the United States. Even the Clayton Act of 1914 would not have prevented this. It was forbidden for a person to work in two companies competing, but this was possible in different sectors. However, it was not just the Morgans that had this practice; other bank leaders were doing it too.

7.6.4 Corsair Negotiation Method

In 1978, US President Jimmy Carter brought together Egyptian President Anwar Sadat and Israeli Prime Minister Menachem Begin at Camp David, a Maryland resort reserved for presidents. He was trying to create a peace process in this region by convincing the leaders of these countries to fight for 40 years. A successful peace agreement emerged during the 12-day meeting held in isolation from the world. The method applied here was similar to J.P. Morgan's Corsair management. When the two leaders met secretly, it was possible to put psychological pressure on the parties, as Morgan did. In particular, the influence of third parties who might have been involved in the discussion could be eliminated in interviews held in such isolated places (Parker, 1989). Applying the same method in 2000, President Bill Clinton brought together Israeli Prime Minister Ehud Barak and Palestinian National Authority President Yasser Arafat at Camp David, but the president was unsuccessful this time.

Pierpont was a very experienced businessman. In a bargaining process, he could sense all parties' strengths and weaknesses and knew how the groups could pressure each other. In particular, Pierpont considered the influence of third parties who would lose their interests due to the agreement. If the parties came together in isolation, the effect of the third party would be reduced, and he could more easily influence his opponents on his boat. Pierpont made them feel his power by hosting his opponents like kings on his yacht. He sensed that the party going to the opponent's home or office would always be weaker, especially in this negotiation process. Experts offer similar advice to Pierpont's method for successful bargaining. According to them, while approaching the problem harshly, being soft toward the person contributes to the solution. Also, while focusing on needs rather than positions, it is always beneficial to be creative about win–win options and negotiate well-defined deals (Fisher & Ury, 1981).

J.P. Morgan had also helped resolve a coal strike that had begun when Theodore Roosevelt was the new president and had earned the president's respect. In what became known as the 1902 coal strike, miners struck for higher wages, shorter working days, and union recognition. In this first labor dispute, the US federal government and President Theodore Roosevelt intervened as an impartial arbiter, again its dominant figure being J.P. Morgan. Pierpont had a vested interest in this business, and the Reading Railways he owned was on strike. He had persuaded War Minister Elihu Root to present a plan to the striking workers, and he was able to devise a reconciliation plan. Later, the president would thank him privately (Rhodes, 1923). Finally, while resolving the 1907 crisis, he first waited for the Bankers and Trust companies to reconcile separately, locked them all in a room, and endeavored to end the reconciliation as soon as possible.

7.7 Conclusion

John Pierpont Morgan was the most famous banker in the United States during the transition from the Gilded Age to the modern era. He made his mark in that period as a highly respected and renowned businessman. Many questions about him have remained unanswered to this day. Was he a banker who loved his country and saved it over and over? Or was he a ruthless businessman who took full advantage of his opportunities and did not hesitate to take risks? Choosing replies to any one of these questions is not easy at all. He was an intelligent businessman who took advantage of the opportunities in the unregulated competitive market of his age. He established good relations with the US administration and earned a high reputation with his skill and leadership as a businessman on Wall Street. Thanks to the relationships he found and his social environment, J.P. Morgan had the power to solve many problems he was involved in and established a strong immunity armor with business barons such as Rockefeller, Carnegie, and Vanderbilt, the creators of this system. The scandals that have emerged in recent years indicate that the armor of immunity continues to some extent today, and large companies can often stretch their activities beyond legal grounds by bending the rules, thanks to the relationships they have. The designers, who are the major players in the system, create a world where anything is possible while establishing a structure where their mistakes will be paid for by others, even if their greed endangers the economic order. They often use the excuse of being too big to fail and make taxpayers pay for their losses.

Despite the free-market tales told to emerging markets, as Nobel laureate Joseph Stiglitz (2002) claims, the market does not work the same in every country, and large companies can easily control the market. While large corporations may appear pro-competitive, as in the case of J. P. Morgan, they often dislike competition. They rarely hesitated to dominate the market when they got an opportunity, using their dominant power to the fullest. While Morgan and his likes could create a monopoly with the Morganization method, they could achieve their goals with the Corsair-type negotiation method they developed. The dynamics of modern times have transformed banking from a system where kings confiscated the money they borrowed 500 years ago to a system in which heads of state bow respectfully to bankers. Morgan's story has important lessons for everyone. While the USA and some European countries, who grasped this lesson well, achieved to become business partners of big financial giants with the system they established, developing countries could not readily learn the game. In today's globalized economy, developing countries, excited by the music of the free market, remain dependent on cash inflows like an alcoholic. When the music stops, namely when cash inflows pause, they find themselves either in the hands of the International Monetary Fund or on the deck of Corsair, bargaining desperately with a banker like J.P. Morgan.

References

Bard, M. (1985). Ideology and depression politics I: Grover Cleveland (1893–1897). *Presidential Studies Quarterly, 15*(1), 77–88.
Beattie, A. (2022). *The Kingpin of Wall Street: J.P. Morgan*. Investopedia. https://www.investopedia.com/articles/economics/08/jp-morgan-kingpin-wall-street.asp
Berfield, S. (2020). *The hour of fate: Theodore Roosevelt, J.P. Morgan, and the battle to transform American capitalism*. Bloomsbury Publishing.
Bowden, E. V. (1989). *Money, banking, and the financial system*. West Pub. Co.
Brands, H. W. (2010). *Upside-down bailout*. HistoryNet. https://www.historynet.com/upside-down-bailout.htm
Brands, H. W. (2011). *American Colossus: The triumph of capitalism, 1865–1900*. Anchor Books.
Bruner, R. F., & Carr, S. D. (2007). *The panic of 1907: Lessons learned from the market's perfect storm*. John Wiley & Sons.
Carosso, V. P. (1973). The wall street money trust from Pujo through Medina. *Business History Review, 47*(4), 421–437. https://doi.org/10.2307/3113365
Carosso, V. P., & Carosso, R. C. (1987). *The Morgans: Private international bankers, 1854–1913*. Harvard University Press.
Chernow, R. (1998a). *The deal of the century*. American Heritage. https://www.americanheritage.com/deal-century#1
Chernow, R. (1998b). *Titan: The life of John D. Rockefeller Sr.* Random House.
Chernow, R. (2001). *The house of Morgan: An American banking dynasty and the rise of modern finance*. Grove Press.
Dangerfield, G. (1965). *The awakening of American nationalism: 1815–1828*. Harper & Row.
De Santis, V. P. (1973). *The gilded age, 1877–1896*. Ahm Publishing Corporation.
Dunn, J., & Wheelock, D. C. (2022). *National banking acts of 1863 and 1864*. Federal Reserve History. https://www.federalreservehistory.org/essays/national-banking-acts
Elwell, C. K. (2011). *Brief history of the gold standard in the United States*. CRS Report for Congress. Congressional Research Service.
Financial Times. (2021). *Melvin capital, gamestop, and the road to disaster*. FT.com. https://www.ft.com/content/3f6b47f9-70c7-4839-8bb4-6a62f1bd39e0
Fisher, R., & Ury, W. (1981). *Getting to yes: Negotiating an agreement without giving in*. Reprint in 1991. Penguin Books.
Goodhart, C. A. E. (1969). *The New York money market and the finance of trade, 1900–1913*. Harvard University Press.
Gordon Wasson, R. (1941). *The hall Carbine affair: A study in contemporary Folklore*. Pandick Press Inc.
Gorton, G. (1984). *Private clearing houses and the origins of central banking*. NBER, Federal Reserve Bank of Philadelphia.

Greider, W. (1987). *Secrets of the temple; how the federal reserve runs the country*. Simon and Schuster.
Grossman, R. S. (n.d.). *US banking history, civil war to world war II*. Economic History. Retrieved March 20, 2024, from https://eh.net/encyclopedia/us-banking-history-civil-war-to-world-war-ii/
Haeg, L. (2013). *Harriman vs. wall street's great railroad war*. University of Minnesota Press.
Hayes, A. (2020). *Morganization definition*. Investopedia. https://www.investopedia.com/terms/m/morganization.asp#:~:text=Morganization%20refers%20to%20the%20strategy
Horn, M. (2000). A private bank at War: J.P. Morgan & Co. and France, 1914–1918. *Business History Review*, *74*(1), 85–112. https://doi.org/10.2307/3116353
Josephson, M. (1962). *The Robber Barons*. Harcourt Brace & Co.
Krass, P. (2011). *Carnegie*. John Wiley & Sons.
Lamont, T. W. (2012). *Across world frontiers*. Literary Licensing.
McLaughlin, R., Safieddine, A., & Vasudevan, G. K. (2000). Investment banker reputation and the performance of seasoned equity issuers. *Financial Management, 29*(1), 96–110. https://doi.org/10.2307/3666364
Miron, J. A. (1986). Financial Panics. The seasonality of the nominal interest rate. And the founding of the fed. *The American Economic Review*, *76*(1), 125–140.
Mitchener, K. J., & Weidenmier, M. D. (2008). The baring crisis and the great Latin American meltdown of the 1890s. *The Journal of Economic History*, *68*(2), 462–500.
Pak, S. J. (2013). Reputation and social ties: JP Morgan & Co. and private investment banking. *The Business History Review*, *87*(4), 703–728. https://doi.org/10.1017/S0007680513001104
Parker, T. (1989). *The road to camp David: U.S. negotiating strategy towards the Arab-Israeli conflict*. Peter Lang Publishing.
Parthemos, J. (1988). The federal reserve act of 1913 in the stream of US monetary history. *FRB Richmond Economic Review*, *74*(4), 1928.
Prins, N. (2014). *All the presidents' bankers: The hidden alliances that drive American power*. Hachette.
Redford, E. S. (1966). Dual banking: A case study in federalism. *Law and Contemporary Problems*, *31*(4), 749–773. https://doi.org/10.2307/1190836
Rhodes, J. F. (1923). *The McKinley and Roosevelt administrations 1897–1909*. Macmillan.
Richardson, G., & Romero, J. (2015). *The meeting at Jekyll Island*. Federal Reserve History. https://www.federalreservehistory.org/essays/jekyll-island-conference
Rockoff, H. (1974). The free banking era: A reexamination. *Journal of Money, Credit and Banking*, *6*(2), 141–167.
Rockoff, H. (1991). *Unregulated banking: Chaos of order?* Macmillan.
Stiglitz, J. E. (2002). *Globalization and its discontents*. Penguin Books.
Strouse, J. (2014). *Morgan, American financier*. Random House.
Summers, M. W. (1993). *The era of good stealings*. Oxford University Press.
Sylla, R. (n.d.). *The U.S. banking system: Origin, development, and regulation*. The Gilder Lehrman Institute of American History, AP US History Study Guide. Retrieved January 20, 2023, from https://ap.gilderlehrman.org/history-by-era/economics/essays/us-banking-system-origin-development-and-regulation
Tallman, E. W. (2012). The Panic of 1907. *The Federal Reserve Bank of Cleveland*, Working Paper 12–28. https://doi.org/10.26509/frbc-wp-201228
Tallman, E. W., & Moen, J. R. (1990). Lessons from the panic of 1907. *Economic Review*, May/June, 2–12.
Temin, P. (1991). *Inside the business enterprise: historical perspectives on the use of information*. NBER Books.
Twain, M., & Warner, C. D. (1873). *The gilded age: A tale of today*. American Publishing Company.
William Jenning Bryan. (n.d.). William Jenning Bryan. *Wikipedia*. Retrieved March 24, 2024, from https://en.wikipedia.org/wiki/William_Jennings_Bryan

Yee, R. (2015). Corporate governance and the rise of big business: Gentlemen's clubs among the social elite, 1899–1914. *An Undergraduate Journal of History*, 18–34.
Zinn, H. (2005). *A people's History of the United States: 1942—Present*. Harper Perennial Modern Classics.

Chapter 8
The Ottoman Bank: State Bank of the Empire (Nineteenth and Twentieth Centuries)

8.1 Introduction

In the first week of March 1853, Istanbul's Grande Rue de Péra was quite crowded despite the cool weather and a bit of rain. Many people filled this street and were talking loudly among themselves. The road had become Istanbul's most popular shopping center, with buildings made of stone, brick, or stone on the lower floors and wooden tops. As can be understood from their behavior and clothing, most were Orthodox Greek, Armenian, and Bulgarian Ottoman citizens living in the city. It was not unusual in recent years that non-Muslims, who also filled coffee shops and luxury restaurants, were crowding this region. Due to the privileges given to Western merchants by the Balta Port Agreement signed with England in 1838, foreign trade grew to unprecedented dimensions, transportation facilities improved, and the Grande Rue de Péra gradually became an international trade center (Pamuk, 2014). The Tanzimat Edict declared in 1839, transformed the economic and social environment into a more modern one, initiated the Westernization movement in the Ottoman Empire, and provided the citizens with the freedom to acquire property and the right to a fair trial. Taking advantage of these opportunities, many wealthy Christians, Jewish merchants, and businessmen flocked to this region to work with their European partners. However, more people than usual had gathered across the Russian Embassy in the middle of the Grande Rue de Perla today. This beautiful building, used as the Russian Consulate currently, was built just a few years ago on the old building site previously burned in the great Beyoğlu fire (Turanakinci.com, n.d.). The Embassy residence was created by the Architect Fossatti Brothers, using Renaissance architecture. It aroused interest among the Ottoman dignitaries, the representatives of foreign states in Istanbul, and the Levantines, and even caused rumors among the people that the Tsar was building a royal palace in Istanbul for himself (Skylife.com, n.d).

Suddenly, there was a scream; a woman shouted, "*He's here, he's here.*" The crowd swayed. A Russian officer dressed in a highly decorated uniform appeared in

M. B. Karan et al., *A History of Banks*, Contributions to Economics,
https://doi.org/10.1007/978-3-031-62297-7_8

the garden of his embassy. As the officer waved to the group, hundreds of people shouted, hooray, hurrah, and freedom to the Orthodox (Slade, 1943). This man was Prince Alexander Sergeyevich Menshikov, the ambassador of the Russian Empire, who had arrived in Istanbul a few days ago. Coming from a noble family, General Menshikov was one of the crucial statesmen of Russia, and he had a soldier and diplomat identity (Fig. 8.1). He had come to Istanbul as the special representative of the Tsar. The Tsar had been practicing a policy of weakening the state's authority by intervening with the minorities living in the Ottoman state, claiming to be the protector of the Orthodox. Menshikov's task was to convey the Russian demands regarding the holy places in the Ottoman Empire to the Sultan. They wanted to break up the Empire by imposing conditions unacceptable to the Ottomans, whom they considered a weak morsel. Among his wishes was the resignation of the pro-French Foreign Minister Keçecizade Fuat Pasha and granting concessions to the Orthodox in Jerusalem and its environs. The other demand was the official recognition that Russia was the patron of Orthodox Christians in Ottoman lands. In return, he had said that if Sultan Abdülmecid retracted his concessions to the French, a secret defense treaty could be signed that would protect the Ottoman Empire and the Sultan's throne (Palmer, 2002).

In recent years, the French, who got closer to the Ottomans and supported the Catholics in the settlement of the holy places, had not agreed with the Russians. Ottoman Foreign Minister Keçecizade Fuat Pasha, an experienced statesman, had sensed the intention of the Russians and got closer to France. Since he said that the key to the great door of the Bethlehem Church in Jerusalem would be given to Catholics, he was declared persona non grata in Russia. Before meeting with Sultan Abdulaziz, when Menshikov did not visit Fuad Pasha, the Minister of Foreign

Fig. 8.1 Alexander Sergeyevich Menshikov (1787–1869). https://tr.wikipedia.org/wiki/Aleksandr_Men%C5%9Fikov#/media/File:Aleksandr_Sergeevich_Menshikov_2.jpg

Affairs, contrary to diplomatic traditions, Fuat Pasha resigned to relieve the Sultan's politics (Köprülü, 1996). The famous Ottoman poet Ayaşlı Hayri Efendi poetically expressed Fuat Pasha's resignation in his work Hyderabad (Andic & Andic, 2002).

Menshikov came immediately after the incident
This was the reason for the confusion
He had come to Istanbul to create horror,
By entering into Bab-ı Âli recklessly
He never obeyed the rules

He never obeyed the rules of foreign affairs,
As he was pretending to support the state
Dear Fuat, the overseer of the century,
He gave importance to protecting his reputation,
He resigned immediately

This event ushered in a new era for the Ottomans. Throughout the nineteenth century, foreign ambassadors frequently interacted with the internal affairs of the Ottoman state (Bardakci, 2002). Ambassador Menshikov met with the Sultan on March 8, giving an ultimatum in diplomatic language. Continuing to pressure the Ottoman Government, which was trying to follow a restrained policy, Menshikov stayed in Istanbul until May. However, the Ottomans, who had the underhanded support of France and England, disagreed with the Russians despite the country's military and economic problems. With the expression of Grand Vizier Mehmet Ali Pasha, any concessions to the Russians would break the independence and dignity of the Empire (Andic & Andic, 2002). The Russians escalated the tension by invading Buğdan, the northern region of present-day Romania, on July 2, 1853. However, in the middle of June, British and French ships entered the straits, showing that they were on the side of the Ottoman Empire. Later, the Crimean War, in which the Ottoman Empire fought together with the French and the British, began, and the Russian army commanded by Menshikov was defeated.

This was the last war the Ottomans won against the Russians in the nineteenth century. Although it gave the country a sigh of relief militarily for at least 20 years, it opened the door to a financial disaster. The Ottomans had to borrow from abroad for the first time in their history in 1854. This initial borrowing of £5 million in return for the tax of the Egyptian province led to new borrowings. After that, the process of paying for debt with debt began, and the Ottoman State declared bankruptcy in 1876 by announcing that it could not pay its foreign obligations. Now, the Ottoman Empire was coming to the end of the road.

During this century, new financial institutions were established for the first time in the Ottoman Empire. The most important of these was the Ottoman Bank. Founded in 1856, this bank was to become the state bank of the Ottoman Empire, with an unexpected success despite the financial and political turmoil the country was experiencing. After the collapse of the Ottoman Empire in 1918, it served the young Turkish Republic as a central bank until 1930. Undoubtedly, the Ottoman Bank would play a significant role in the transition from an empire to a national state by substantially contributing to the development of banking in Turkish lands. The English and French capitals established the bank and recruited mainly non-muslims. The Ottoman Bank project, which started as the dream of two British entrepreneurs named Stephen Sleigh and Peter Pasquali in 1855, would be realized without them with the proclamation of Queen Victoria a year later. In 1863, the bank was renamed Bank-ı Osmanî-i Şahane. It served as the official bank and treasurer of the Ottoman Empire for many years and also served the Republic of Turkey for a while.

8.2 Politics and Economics in the Ottoman Empire

8.2.1 The Political Situation

The nineteenth century was, in the words of Prof. Ilber Ortaylı (2012), the Empire's Longest Century. In this century, as the Empire was gradually shrinking, the intellectual foundations of the modern Turkish Republic were being discussed. Events unfolded so rapidly that the country, which entered the century with a medieval economy, had to face the financial and political realities of the modern world by the end. As Table 8.1 shows, the Ottoman Empire faced significant external and internal developments throughout the nineteenth and early twentieth centuries. External influences were particularly decisive in the weakening of the Empire. Western Europe made a breakthrough in the political sphere and gained a significant economic and military advantage with the Industrial Revolution. Napoleon's invasion of Egypt in 1798 revealed the Ottoman Empire's military inadequacy, while Russia had become a powerful country due to Peter the Great's reforms. It had also started to put pressure on the Ottoman Empire from the north since 1760. The Ottoman Empire had to share the Black Sea with the Russians with the Kucuk Kaynarca Treaty signed with Russia in 1774. From this date onward, Russia began to destabilize the country by assuming the role of the protector of the Orthodox living in the Ottoman lands.

In the second half of the sixteenth century, socio-economic conditions in the Ottoman Empire deteriorated. From the seventeenth century onward, state authority in the center and provinces began to weaken, and political, military, economic, and demographic changes gradually disrupted the classical Ottoman order. A new social class emerged in this period: "Ayans (Notables)." This new class comprised soldiers, former rulers, wealthy merchants, and well-established families. In time, the Ayans became a power recognized by the state, and their powers and duties were defined. Ayans were tasked with preventing banditry and suppressing militia forces rebelling in the provinces. Ayans had become a kind of regional ruler. As of the early seventeenth century, the Ottoman central administration started to collect tax revenues mostly in cash and through Ayans, thus liquidating the traditional system with collecting taxes through "iltizam." It was a method of collecting a portion of the state revenues by transferring them to individuals by the state in return for certain upfront payments and installments. Iltizamwas similar to the tax farm system in France in the seventeenth century. Over time, the Ayans became a kind of state partner, were officially recognized, and were given political and military appointments. In short, they became representatives of the state and proxies of the provinces (Özdemir, 2018).

Table 8.1 Important political events of the nineteenth and early twentieth centuries

History	Events
1808	The Charter of Alliance
1826	Abolishing the Janissary Corps
1831–1833	First Ottoman Egyptian War
1832	Greek Independence
1833	Hünkar Pier Agreement
1838	The Treaty of Balta Liman
1839	Tanzimat Edict
1839–1841	Second Ottoman Egyptian War
1853–1856	Crimean War
1856	Edict of Reform
1876	1st Constitutional Monarchy
1877–1878	Ottoman-Russian War (93 War)
1878	Occupation of Cyprus by the British
1878	Closing the Assembly
1882	Occupation of Egypt by British
1908	Second Constitutional Era
1911	Tripoli War
1912–1913	Balkan War
1914–1918	World War I
1918	Armistice of Mudros
1920	Treaty of Sevres
1919–1922	Turkish Independence War
1923	Treaty of Lausanne

On the one hand, the Ayans contributed to the solution of the state's problems in the provinces; on the other hand, they weakened the central authority of the state.

During this period, the janissaries, known as the elite soldiers of the Ottoman army, became increasingly corrupt. They frequently revolted and could dethrone sultans who attempted to reform the state administration. The Janissary Corps had been established 400 years earlier as the first modern standing army in Europe. For centuries, they served as the Ottoman Empire's powerful infantry units. But now, they had become a force opposed to reform. In 1808, during an internal rebellion of the Janissaries, some Ayans, such as Alemdar Mustafa Pasha, suppressed the uprising and contributed significantly to the accession of Sultan Mahmut II (reign period 1808–1839) to the throne. Under Alemdar's influence, the Sultan invited all Ayans to Istanbul to resolve the "Ayans" issue, and an agreement was signed between the Ayans and the central government on September 29, 1808. With this agreement, the provincial administrations were given some broad powers. According to this agreement, the sovereignty of the Sultan would be accepted by the Ayans. Ayans would be the regional governor of their province. The two parties would trust each other. In addition, the Ayans would be responsible for ensuring the security of the people in their territories and making sure that the taxes collected from the people were not excessive. This agreement was called the Charter of Alliance. Some historians liken this agreement to the Magna Carta (1215) (Akşin, 1992). This event disturbed the sultan's close circle as it caused the central authority to be seen as helpless against the Ayans. When Alemdar Mustafa Pasha was killed a few months later in another revolt of the Janissary Corps, this agreement was canceled. Thus, the Ottomans missed a historic opportunity to transform the Empire into a more democratic structure (Shaw & Shaw, 2006). Finally, on June 16, 1826, Sultan Mahmut II destroyed the Janissary Corps with cannon fire and executed the survivors. Mahmut later established a new army, the Asakir-i Mansure-i Muhammediye. However, these events disrupted the Ottomans' relations with their provinces and weakened the army (Pamuk, 2014). Sultan Mahmud was a reformist sultan. The westernization of the Ottomans had started with him. These reforms immediately affected social and legal aspects of life in the Empire, such as European-style dress, architecture, legislation, institutional organization, modern schools, and land reform. Another significant development of the nineteenth century was the independence movement against the Ottomans led by Kavalalı Mehmet Ali Pasha, who took over the governorship and Ayan of Egypt after Napoleon's Egyptian campaign. Mehmet Ali Pasha was one of the most important commanders of the Ottoman Empire. At the end of 1827, Mehmed Ali Pasha demanded that Mahmud II grant him Syria in return for suppressing the Peloponnesian Revolt. He successfully suppressed the rebellion in the first phase. However, when Britain, which had contributed to the Greek independence movement with loans, and France and Russia, which had acted together, destroyed the Ottoman-Egyptian navy at the Battle of Navarin in October 1827, the balance tipped in favor of the Greek rebels. With the arms support provided to the Greek forces, the rebellion began to spread to northern Greece. The Treaty of Edirne, signed in September 1829 under pressure from Russia, which declared war on the Ottoman Empire, led to the independence of Greece in 1931.

In the meantime, M. Ali Pasha, who had successfully suppressed the rebellion in the first stage, did not receive Syria. In 1831, he started a war of independence against the Ottomans. The war in Egypt plunged the Ottoman Empire into a military and financial deadlock. With their newly formed army, the Ottomans could not stop the Egyptian forces from coming to Kütahya (mid-western Anatolia). While the French supported M. Ali Pasha and the British initially remained neutral, Mahmud II sought help from his old enemy, Russia. After the military success, with the contribution of the soldiers sent by the Tsar, the problem was partially solved by granting autonomy to Egypt. As a result of these events, he signed a non-aggression treaty with the Russian Empire in 1833 in the Hünkar İskelesi district of Istanbul.

Initially, indifferent to this event, Britain considered the Ottoman rapprochement with Russia an important threat to its interests. The Ottomans sought help from the British to stabilize their foreign relations. In return for this help, Britain demanded a trade agreement granting great commercial privileges. In the following years, the British supported Ottoman politics in Egypt and signed the Treaty of Balta Liman in

1838. Thus, for nearly 50 years from this date onward, protecting the Ottoman Empire became Britain's state policy. However, with this agreement, British merchants would pay lower taxes than local merchants in the Ottoman Empire. The Ottoman economy was weakened in the face of powerful European capital. Nevertheless, the Tanzimat Edict was considered a turning point in the foundation of modern Turkey. The Tanzimat Edict was a solid document of Ottoman intentions for Westernization and consisted of three rules. The first one was to guarantee the security of life of every subject. Secondly, it proposed an orderly system for assessing and collecting taxes and the length of service of soldiers. Finally, the third chapter deals with reforms in human rights and the justice system. In Prof. Dr. Halil İnalcık's (2017) words, "Tanzimat, together with the Westernization movement, continued as a life move in the Turkish nation….. In this respect, Tanzimat is a happy event in our history." The most important event after the Tanzimat was the Second Egyptian War with Kavalalı Mehmet Ali Pasha in Southeastern Anatolia and Palestine. The Treaty of London (1840), mediated by the great powers, ended the war, and Egypt remained an Ottoman province with special privileges. Mahmut died in 1839 and was replaced by Abdülmecid (reign period 1839–1861).

As mentioned in the introduction, the Crimean War was one of the most important events of the nineteenth century. From 1853 onward, Russia abandoned its policy of establishing a sphere of influence over a weak Ottoman Empire, which it had pursued during the Egypt crisis. Russia used the issue of holy places to weaken the Ottoman Empire. As a result of escalating events, the Crimean War broke out. Although the Ottoman Empire was among the countries that emerged victorious from this war, the country's finances deteriorated due to the decreasing state revenues from the loss of Egypt and the expenditures made during the wars. From this war onward, it was understood by the Western states that the preservation of the Ottoman Empire was essential for their own political and commercial interests. Otherwise, this region would fall under Russian domination, and its interests would suffer. Then, under the pressure of European states, the establishment of national assemblies in which non-Muslim communities would also be represented was demanded. With these assemblies, the people could discuss their affairs and make decisions (İnalcık, 2016). Despite the proclamation of the Edict of Reform in 1856, which granted new rights to non-Muslims, minority rebellions continued to increase. A new constitution prevented the great powers from exploiting the events. In 1861, Abdülmecid died, and his brother Abdülaziz (reign period 1861–1876) ascended the throne. The financial situation of the country was deteriorating, and minority revolts increased. The intellectuals' demands for constitutionalism were growing. Abdulaziz was widely criticized for allowing Egypt to borrow independently of the Ottoman Empire and extending Egypt's rights of autonomy despite the objections of Grand Vizier (Prime Minister) Mithat Pasha. Grand Viziers were responsible for the administration of the state when the Sultan was on campaign. The Grand Vizier, who chaired the cabinet meetings, presented his views on issues such as the economy, war, and religion to the sultan. From the nineteenth century onward, their role became stronger as the state weakened. As we will explain in Sect. 8.6.1, this borrowing of Egypt led ultimately to the definitive loss of the province along with Sudan in 1882. With a palace coup, reformists, including Mithat Pasha, dethroned Abdulaziz (1876). Later, it was announced that the sultan had committed suicide. When it was understood that the mental health of the new Sultan (Murat V) was not sufficient, Abdulhamid II, who promised to proclaim a constitutional monarchy, sat on the throne. Sultan Abdulhamid II (reign period 1876–1908) declared a Constitutional Monarchy by accepting the Legal Principle. However, the 1877 war with Russia that started damaged the state financially and politically. One of the reasons for this war was that the Ottoman Empire increased taxes on the Balkan peoples to pay its debts. This tax policy created a wave of discontent in the region and increased sympathy for Russia. The problem was not limited to this. Muslim groups such as Circassians and Abaza, who were placed to balance the Balkans population, caused conflicts in places and increased confusion in the region (Finkel, 2005). The rebellions that started in the area eventually grew and started a war (1877–1878) that caused the most significant defeat in Ottoman history. The Russian-Turkish War, which was called the 93 War because it was in 1293 in the Hijri calendar, would financially collapse the Ottoman Empire, which had already signed 16 debt agreements until that date (Yildiz, 2011). Using this defeat as an excuse, the Sultan ended the Constitutional Monarchy in 1878, establishing a 30-year autocratic regime. One of his actions was to exile and execute Mithat Pasha on the grounds that he had murdered Sultan Abdülaziz.

Britain's termination of its policy of protecting the Ottoman Empire after 1875 and its occupation of Cyprus (1878) also played an essential role in the end of the Constitutional Monarchy. After the invasion of Egypt (1882), the negative impact of capitalism on the Ottoman domestic market began to cause anti-Western sentiment within the country (İnalcık, 2016).

As the Ottoman Empire entered the twentieth century tired and weak, the Young Turk movement, supported by young officers and students who wanted to solve the country's problems, had begun. In the first months of 1908, internal turmoil in the Ottoman Empire increased considerably, and unrest broke out in Macedonia, the Ottoman homeland, due to ethnic problems. It was also claimed that the British and Russian rulers, who met in the Baltic city of Revan, now known as Tallinn, on June 9–10, began to discuss how to break up the Ottoman Empire. Rumors spread that Istanbul would be given to the Russians. The country was fog-covered; people were worried (Lewis, 2008). The revolution, which started first in Macedonia, began on July 3, 1908. The events resulted in the establishment of the 2nd Constitutional Monarchy and then the dethronement of Sultan Abdülhamid. After a brief period of fraternization between different ethnic groups, the Ottoman-Italian war began in 1911 with the Italian invasion of Tripolitania. While this war continued, the Balkan War broke out in 1913, and the Ottoman Empire lost most of its territories in the Balkans. Meanwhile, in Europe, the rivalry between Germany and other great powers was dragging the continent into a new war. The Ottomans, who could not receive sufficient interest from England and France, improved their relations with Germany. In 1908, after the declaration of the Second Constitutional Monarchy, the Unionist Progressive (İttihat Terakki) Party, the dominant power in the country, entered into a very close relationship with the Germans.

Finally, the First World War, which started in 1914, led to the collapse of the Ottoman Empire, which had aligned itself with Germany. The Turks were left with some territory in the middle of Anatolia with the Armistice of Mudros (1918) and the Treaty of Sevres (1920). The Greeks, who occupied Izmir with the support of the British, had advanced to Central Anatolia. However, under the leadership of Mustafa Kemal Atatürk, the Turks defeated the Greeks and won the war of liberation (1922). Turkey's independence was achieved with the Treaty of Lausanne (1923). Then, Atatürk established a secular and modern state with his revolutions.

8.2.2 *The Economic Situation*

The nineteenth century was a troublesome period for the Ottoman Empire in terms of the economy due to its wars, the compensations it paid, the loss of territory, and the internal and external rebellions. The most striking feature of this period is the interregional development disparity. Although some regions such as Istanbul, Izmir, Thessaloniki, and Beirut were developed due to trade, rural areas in Anatolia and Arabia were still living in the Middle Ages. Trade between the regions was minor, and international commerce was mainly conducted with neighboring countries. At the end of the century, exports were only around 2% of GNP. The population of the Ottoman Empire consisted of about 30 million people and only 20% of them lived in cities. There was even economic turmoil in the country; the loans received were spent on investments that did not yield any return, such as the Dolmabahçe Palace, the Beykoz Pavilion, and the Mecidiye Mosque. Perhaps the most critical assets of the Ottomans were the railways. These railways, shaped by external pressures and extending from the ports to the inner regions, served more the European traders than the country's interests. One of the essential methods used by the Ottomans in railway financing was granting railway construction as a privilege. In this practice, the companies' profits were guaranteed by the Ottoman Empire with a mileage guarantee system. The state covered the difference if the railway companies made a profit below the guaranteed profit. Agriculture was at a primitive level, and because transportation was not developed, it was difficult for agricultural production to reach cities and ports. The peasants were squeezed among the tax collectors, landlords, and usurers. The country had almost completely closed its doors to the industrial revolution. There were only a few industrial plants. Foreign trade was based on agriculture, and 60% of business was with England, France, Germany, and Austria (Tokgöz, 2000).

The society was divided into various layers; while the military layer constituted the governing group, the people were called the ruled (reaya). The military could generate income from fief holders, treasury, or foundations, and they were in the upper part of society. Reaya includes all the people outside the ruling class. The reaya, which consisted of guild members (tradesmen, merchants and jewelers) and peasants and nomads had to pay taxes. Most of the guild members were Greek, Jewish, and Armenian origin minorities. The Ottoman State did not allow the guilds to become overpowered. The guilds had close relations with the Janissaries, and the closure of the Janissary Corps was a significant blow to them. Initially, soldiers sold the spoils of war to guild member merchants. In time, numerous members of the Janissary Corps became their partners and became corrupt. However, trade liberalization with the Treaty of Balta Liman of 1838 significantly affected the guilds. It was difficult for the Ottomans to avoid the globalization and free trade practices initiated by European countries because of their financial weakness and need for Western currencies. The Ottoman rulers were in a deadlock. The European financial empire was pressuring them for free trade. The traditional economy was closed to international competition, and industry was weak and primitive. While free trade led to the closure of small businesses, accelerated financial collapse, plunged the country into a debt pit, and increased unemployment, there was no way the economy could develop with the old methods. But despite the war conditions, all the pressures, and the Western powers' economic superiority, governments tried to protect their economies. At the same time, free trade was influential after the Tanzimat Edict; after the financial deadlock of the Ottoman Empire in the last period of the nineteenth century (1878), in the first decades of the twentieth century, the supporters of the national economy (Young Turks and Union and Progress Party) prevailed over the supporters of free trade (Quataert, 2004).

Especially since the 1860s, due to the increasing relations with the European finance suppliers and the increase in the borrowing dependence of the Ottoman Empire, elites and the upper class of the society turned to consumption, interest income and games of chance, and imported goods such as hair dye and medical drugs (Kazgan, 2005b). At the same time, the excessive interest in European goods and customs among the Istanbul elite was criticized in Turkish literature. Ziya Pasha wrote in his poems, "*It is new to follow the ideas of Europeans by forgetting national unity and personality in everything we do.*" Even though conservation policies were followed at the end of the century, a significant change started in society, and the tendency to use foreign goods could not be controlled.

8.2.3 The Monetary Mechanism

The Ottoman monetary system, based on gold and silver coins, continued during the reign of Mahmud II. However, the country's revenues were insufficient, and the treasury financing problem deepened. The most used method in this period was to reduce the silver or gold content of the money. Monetary policy was based on debasement. In this period, the silver content of the Ottoman kurus, 5.9 g in 1808, decreased to 0.5 g by 1831. While the purchasing power of money was constantly falling, it was possible to make payments with this practice, but social stability deteriorated. The most interesting person of the period was the mint manager, Kazaz Artin Amira (Kazgan, 2005b).

The Ottoman trade with Europe and money management were carried out primarily by citizens of Jewish and Greek origin. While Muslims served as soldiers and administrators, commercial activities were left to minorities. Money traders and jewelers, who are called "Galata Bankers," gradually began to dominate the credit business after the Treaty of Balta Limanı, the finance and trade network of minority businessmen. They were a group of Greek and Jewish minorities based in the Galata district of Istanbul. Until 1855, they were exempted from military service by paying a tax. They were more successful in these fields by utilizing their ethnic advantages. The role of the Greek ethnic people decreased in the Ottoman administration after the separation of Greece in 1832. Armenian-origin Ottoman citizens replaced the Greeks in finance and trade issues. They became more involved in finance and foreign affairs. Kazaz Artin Amira (1771–1834) was the influential treasurer of the Ottoman Palace. Artin Amira became the personal advisor and close friend of Sultan Mahmud II. Thanks to his unique skills and relationships, he became the representative of the Armenian community in time. Kazaz Amira, who solved economic problems by finding efficient solutions, came to the fore when Russian ships blockaded the Bosphorus and created famine in the city during the Ottoman-Russian War in 1829. During the wheat and bread shortage that started in Istanbul, Kazaz proposed that the wheat trade should be released, and within a few days, the free-market dynamics solved the problem and prevented further wheat shortages. After this incident, Amira's reputation increased even more (Dadyan, 2012).

When money could not be found for war reparations to be given to the Russians in 1830, Kazaz Amira was summoned again. Kazaz, who told the Sultan he could solve this problem, collected the gold he could find from the wealthy Turks, Armenians, Greeks, and Jews residing in Istanbul and its environs in return for a loan bill stamped with the Sultan's seal. The gold was melted, copper was mixed into them, low-carat coins were minted, and the necessary compensation was provided (Atış, n.d.). In fact, this can be considered as the initial paper money used by the Ottomans. He would be more than rewarded for his success, as in the case of J.P. Morgan's story of saving the US treasury in 1895. These contributions of Kazaz Amira increased the Armenian community's prestige, and they were known as the "Loyal Community" for a while.

When Sultan Abdülmecid (1823–1861) throned in 1839, there was no gold left in the treasury, and the opportunity to produce new money was exhausted. To overcome the money bottleneck during his reign, "kaime" was created. The real name was "Kaime-ı Nakdiye-ı Mutebere." In fact, it was a borrowing instrument. This "banknote" was a money substitute, in a sense, a kind of debt note rather than money. It was a rather strange and complex instrument. Nevertheless, the government repeatedly declared that the kaime was issued to facilitate trade and would be accepted as legal tender just like gold and silver coins. It also announced that tax collectors would accept these notes in the provinces and the Treasury in Istanbul. Later, smaller denominations were also issued in order to increase their use in daily transactions. The first kaime was worth 500 kuruş, had an 8-year maturity, and gave 12,531 percent annual interest income. The interest was to be paid in two installments. A note of each payment was written on the back of the promissory note, by way of coupon payment. There were no specific reserves for the kaimes, but the Istanbul customs covered the interest to be paid. The total volume of the first and second rounds of notes in 1840 was equal to 40 million kurus (about £360,000). A high-interest rate was promised to incentivize its use. Circulation was initially restricted to Istanbul, hampered by the crude nature of the banknotes and the ease with which they could be counterfeited. The second printing was of better quality. Kaimas were now printed with the embossed seal of the sultan, and earlier issues were recalled and replaced with new banknotes. Initially, it was not enough for kaime holders to accept kaime as a mere savings instrument, and kaime only became more in demand when the interest payment approached. In the years between 1840 and 1844, the merchants of Istanbul gradually accepted these issues and the kaime entered circulation on an equal footing with the coins. In 1843, another issue of crimes was issued, with an interest rate reduced to 10% per annum in 1843 and 8% in 1844. Their denominations ranged from 50 kurus to 10,000 kurus. The government started to pay half of the salaries of civil servants in kaime. It also tried to encourage the use of the new banknotes by announcing that kaimes would be accepted in transactions like existing silver and gold coins and would be accepted by tax collectors. When the public became accustomed to them, the interest rate lowered, and then they were issued interest-free. Merchants mostly used the larger denominations.

By 1844, "Bimetallism," a system based on both gold and silver, was adopted by the Ottoman Empire and abandoned debasements. Bimetallism is a monetary standard or system traditionally based on using two metals, gold and silver. The typical nineteenth-century bimetallic system defined a nation's currency by law in terms of fixed amounts of gold and silver (thus automatically setting an exchange rate between the two metals). The system also provided an unrestricted market for both metals, imposed no restrictions on the use and coinage of either metal, and made all other money in circulation redeemable in gold or silver. The major problem with the international use of bimetallism was that, as each country independently determined its exchange rate between the two metals, the resulting rates often varied widely from country to country (bimetallism, n.d.). After this date, the Ottoman Lira, Mecidiye, and Kurus became the country's main currencies (Tekeli & Ilkin, 1997). Mecidiye is a silver coin minted in 1840 and was worth 20 kurus. The Mecidiye silver coin, minted by Abdülmecid I and named after him, consisted of 19.945 g pure silver and 4.110 g copper. Mecidiye, kurus and para were subunits. 1 lira = 5 mecidiye, 1 lira = 100 kurus, 1 lira = 4000 para. The gold lira weighed 7.216 g with a fineness of 22/24 or 91.67%, thus containing 6.6 g of gold (Pamuk, 2000).

The simultaneous circulation of a large number of different currencies in the Ottoman Empire led to the emergence of exchange rates that characterized the exchange transactions between them and indicated the exchange amounts. Coins, Kaime, and foreign currencies were in circulation at the same time, and exchange rates between them could change at any time. In addition to the exchange rates valid for the exchange of currencies of different denominations, there was a separate exchange rate used for foreign payments. It was very important to stabilize the value of the various currencies in the new system. That started with maintaining a more or less stable exchange of the Lira and the British pound sterling. This was rendered possible only by the creation of a stabilizing agency that would guarantee a constant supply of bills of exchange on London at the said rate (Eldem, 2006). The stability of the exchange rate was one of the most important elements of the monetary system.

A financial institution was needed to ensure this stability. Until 1845, there were no institutionalized banks; Galata bankers, lent money at interest, exchanged money, and acted as intermediaries for foreign bankers.

The first bank established in the Ottoman Empire was the Bank of Istanbul ('Banque de Constantinople'), founded in 1845 by two Galata bankers, Jacques Alléon and Manolaki Baltazzi, under government patronage. The bank aimed to stabilize the parity (Pamuk, 2000). For this, it would receive subsidies from the government. The bank's charter was terminated in 1847, and the bank was closed. Later, these two big Galata Bankers again agreed with the Ottoman Government, and the Dersaadet Bank was founded. The bank was undercapitalized but highly reputable. Its main function was to maintain the stability of the Ottoman Lira (One pound = 1.1 lira). In the period 1844–1914, this parity remained unchanged.

The bank accepted the bills of exchange in European countries. The Dersaadet Bank was responsible for keeping 1 pound sterling at a fixed value of 110 kurus in payments made abroad within the scope of foreign trade. In other words, it became a bank that would accept bills in London and Paris at this exchange rate, in order to avoid the appreciation of the pound sterling against the Lira. Appreciated sterling created a deficit in the balance of payments against the international trade of Ottomans. The state covered the resulting loss (Şenyurt, 2018). Since the state's balance of payments was always in deficit, the bank couldn't profit. However, even though the state covered the bank's losses, it could not pay its short-term debts and closed down in 1852. Although the Dersaadet Bank experiment partially succeeded in keeping exchange rates at the desired level, a high price was paid (Eldem, 2000).

A new phase in the history of the kaime began in 1852 when the first non-interest-bearing paper money entered circulation. 100,000 liras of interest-bearing kaime were withdrawn from the market and replaced by interest-free kaime of 20 kurus. These small denominations not only facilitated daily transactions but also helped the treasury to generate significant new revenues. While the interest-bearing banknotes made a premium in the hands of Galata bankers, which started to operate in Istanbul, the interest-free ones decreased to a quarter of their value. As the value of the kaimes decreased and imitations filled the market, some parts of the kaimes were burned in Beyazıt Square in 1852 following an intense collection campaign. This campaign was organized with donations from the public. In 1853, the volume of kaime in circulation had reached 175 million kurus, or about £1.6 million, which was still not a very large sum (Pamuk, 2000).

In 1854, new interest-free kaimes, called army kaime, were issued to finance the Crimean War. These kaimes were to be valid only in the provinces and regions where the war took place. This is paper money that does not rely on any reserve. The issuance of kaime was in large quantities, but the market price, expressed in one gold lira, fell to less than half of its nominal value. One gold lira began to be exchanged for 200 ± 220 kurus kaime. In 1861, 1,250 million kurus worth of kaime were issued, but their value continued to decline. In response to popular protests and general discontent, the government agreed to withdraw the kaimes from circulation in 1862 with the help of short-term loans from the Ottoman Imperial Bank (Pamuk, 2000).

With the Serbian uprising and the outbreak of the 93 War with Russia, the need to increase state revenues became even more urgent. Kaimes were issued in small and large denominations ranging from one kurus to 500 kurus and were declared legal tender throughout the Empire. In a very short time, their volume reached 16 million liras (£14.4 million). However, due to the large volume, the exchange rate of the kaime dropped to 450 kurus for the gold lira within two years. They remained in circulation for close to three years and were withdrawn from circulation at the end of the decade (Pamuk, 2000).

Financing the First World War. One of the important monetary developments during the war was the decision to reform the coinage. With a law of 1916, the government ended the circulation of all pre-1844 coins and adopted a standard where 100 silver kurus were equal to one gold lira. It also set a ceiling of 300 kuruş for all payments to the state in silver coins. It established gold as the sole standard for the Ottoman currency. The last kaime application took place during the First World War. The expansion of the paper money supply accelerated in the last two years of the war, making the kaime the main form of war financing in this final period. The volume of kaime reached 40 million liras at the beginning of 1917 and 100 million liras by the end of the same year. By the end of the war, the total amount of kaime reached 161 million, of which 158 million remained in circulation at the end of 1918. The Republic of Turkey allowed the circulation of kaimes until the wounds of the War of Independence were healed. As soon as these wounds were healed, it made attempts to print its own money, and on September 4, 1928, the Ottoman kaimes were abolished entirely (Akyıldız, 1996).

8.3 The Ottoman Bank

Two British people, Stephen Sleigh and Peter Pasquali, who knew the Egyptian and Ottoman markets very well, made a plan in 1855, thinking that Istanbul, which was developing rapidly, needed a bank. According to the project plan, a bank had to be established first. Then, this bank could become the state bank of the Ottoman Empire if they received the support of the Ottomans and England with an edict of the Sultan and a founding document of the Queen of England. Although the plan was initially well-received by both countries, after over a year of numerous meetings and difficulties, these two British entrepreneurs suddenly found themselves outside the bank's board of directors. Presumably, the British bureaucracy, sensing the opportunities this bank would bring, supported the idea while excluding the project owners. The bank's share capital was £500,000, consisting of 25,000 shares of £20 each. The bank's initial public offering was very successful, and although 25,000 shares were offered, demand exceeded 80,000. The first general manager of the bank was the British Charles Ede. Founded in 1856, the Ottoman Bank had no privileges but had solid capital with British and French support. However, it was still far from the expectations of the Ottoman Empire. Meanwhile, banks such as

Rothschild Bank approached the Ottoman Empire with different projects (Eldem, 2000).

The Ottoman Bank was initially established as a regular commercial bank. The bank was both lending and accepting deposits. Although the bank was profitable in its early years, its transaction volume was low. As the people in the country were not familiar with banking yet, note discounting and credit transaction services were not in demand due to financial insufficiency or religious reasons. The monetary instability in the country and the constant depreciation of the kaimes were also problems. Most of the bank's earnings were from government lending, so the bank had turned into a government-financing institution rather than a regular commercial bank (Eldem, 2000).

The Ottomans began to discuss their intention to establish a state bank from 1856 onward. They expected the new bank to find money from abroad for the Ottoman Empire with 5% interest. Although several financial groups, including the Ottoman Bank and the Rothschilds, made offers, none was sufficient. Initiatives such as for the Turkish National Bank and the Bank of Turkey could not be completed for various reasons. Despite everything, the Ottomans continued to borrow. In 1858, Istanbul customs revenues were used as collateral return for the principal and interests for borrowing approximately 5.5 million pounds. The borrowing agreement was signed with Dent, Palmer, and Partners, one of the prominent banking houses of London, and bonds were issued in the UK (Karabulut & Uğur, 2022). A significant portion of the money raised was spent on the withdrawal of the interest-bearing kaimes, whose market value had fallen by 30%. The remaining money was used to suppress the social turmoil in Lebanon and Montenegro (Kazgan, 2005b). The Ottoman Bank also played an essential role in realizing this borrowing. The European press ridiculed the increasing borrowings, and it was claimed that these funds were used for the personal expenditures of the sultans. In fact, according to historian Cevdet Pasha, who spoke of the extravagant abilities of the ladies of the palace, the newspapers were not so wrong (Eldem, 2000).

By 1861, the financial situation of the Ottoman Empire had become quite troubled, whereas domestic and foreign debts had accumulated. While 60% of the total debt was foreign, a significant portion of the domestic debt was borrowed from Galata bankers. The Ottomans declared that they would not pay their debts in full and Mires, who owned a newspaper in France and was a speculator banker, came to their rescue (Caty et al., 1999). The cost of the borrowing project prepared by Mires reached 13% with additional commissions. At a time when interest rates were 3–4% in Europe, this rate was excessive. This borrowing operation, which he claimed to be an April fool's joke in a British newspaper, became unsuccessful, and Mires was bankrupted and arrested at the end of this process. The impact of Mires' arrest on the Istanbul market was harrowing, and a series of bankruptcies occurred when the bills of exchanges drawn to the banks were not paid. This led the Ottomans to seek a new, urgent loan. The panic affected the entire city, including the bankers of Galata and even the Ottoman treasury. For this purpose, a borrowing agreement was signed with Deveaux and Partners in London in 1862. According to this agreement, the maturity value of the debt amount was 8,800,000 Ottoman liras, equivalent to 200 million francs. The interest rate was 6%, and the maturity was 23 years. As a result of this borrowing, the treasury received 5.984.000 Ottoman liras, and this money was used to remove most of the kaimes (including interest-bearing and non-interest-bearing) from the market. The kaimes were collected and burnt at the mint (Karabulut & Uğur, 2022).

However, this event began to shake the foundations of foreign investments in the Ottoman Empire. The Ottomans now had to find a reliable bank, which would become a state bank. When the Ottoman Bank, which also supported the previous borrowings of the state, made a successful loan of 8 million pounds with 6% interest in 1862, it had no rivals on the way to becoming a state bank. However, there was another problem: the Ottoman Bank was established with only British capital. Since the government wanted to balance the state's European policy, a French partner was searched for the bank. This partner was Credit Mobilier, led by the French Pereire Group.

8.4 The Bank-i Osman-i Sahane (The Imperial Ottoman Bank)

The name of the Ottoman Bank was changed to Bank-ı Osman-ı Şahane when it became a state bank. With the agreement signed on November 16, 1862, the bank's equity, divided into 135,000 shares, was determined as £2,7000,000. It was decided to give 80,000 of the bank's stocks to the British, 50,000 to the French, and 5,000 to the Ottomans. However, the inequality between these two foreign states would be resolved in a few years. Although the Ottomans initially wanted the bank's general manager to be an Ottoman citizen, they would fail. Whereas the primary control of the bank was in two committees in London and Paris, its headquarters was in Istanbul. The official establishment date of the bank was February 4, 1863. According to the agreement, the Ottoman Empire would no longer issue paper money, and the Ottoman Bank would be the only institution with paper money privileges.

As the Ottoman Bank became a state bank, it issued convertible banknotes. Thus, it was possible to liquidate the coins called'magsus' in the market from the country's coin stocks. The amount of precious metal in most of the magsus was manipulated. Even if low-denomination metal coins were withdrawn from the market, other metal coins were used. Coins were regulated after the gold-silver parity revolution. In any case, Ottoman Bank banknotes were larger than 200 kuruş and were not suitable for use in shopping. This amount was 25–30 times the daily wage of an unskilled laborer.

In the first years, the most critical problem was the reluctance of the people to use paper money due to the unpleasant experience of the previously issued kaimes. The Bank wanted to familiarize the population with banknotes by increasing the amount of money in circulation. By 1868, it had increased the amount of banknotes in circulation by 90%. In 1869, the emissions tripled compared to the previous year. After these promising developments, the markets were shaken by bad news. Because the French Emperor Napoleon III declared war on Prussia in 1870, this war caused panic in the Istanbul Stock Exchange (see below), and the government closed the stock market for a while. Panicked investors demanded gold from the Ottoman Bank in exchange for banknotes. This incident was the first crisis after the bank was established, and the problems were overcome, albeit with difficulty.

In 1850, gold discoveries in Australia and California significantly increased the global gold supply, and Germany had already adopted the gold standard. After the Franco-German War in 1870, there was a broad transition to the gold standard in the international markets under the influence of the victorious Germany. The gold standard replaced the bimetallism system. Following international developments, the monetary law of 1880 marked the official end of the bimetallic standard in the Ottoman Empire. According to the new regulation, as of March 1880, the monetary standard declared 100 kuruş equivalent to one gold lira, and free silver minting ceased. However, unlike the "full" gold standard, the new regulation allowed the Mint to accept unlimited quantities of silver at a discounted rate. The Ottoman Government moved toward a "limping standard," recognizing both gold and silver as legal tender but only allowing free coinage of gold. Ultimately, the Ottoman coinage system was dominated by several foreign and domestic standard and substandard silver coins (Tuncer, 2013).

An overexpansion in the economy, market manipulation, and the effect of the new gold standard collapsed the Wien Bourse on 9 May 1873. Viennese bank failures ensued, causing a contraction of the money available for business lending. Meanwhile, the Ottoman Bank succeeded in issuing bonds, providing new borrowing opportunities to the state, even though the war had overwhelmed the markets.

During the initial years of the bank, the Galata Stock Exchange was organized under Dersaadet Tahvilat Borsası in 1866, and the country had an official stock market from then onward. However, the newly developing Galata market was in turmoil. It was clear that there was a need for an institution to regulate the market. The stock market was highly speculative, and securities prices were volatile. It was a severe problem that the Dersaadet Bond Exchange was far from the European stock markets. In addition, many factors, due to the market's erratic nature, affected the value of the securities. Initially, while the Ottoman Bank, as a central bank, was expected to intervene in the monetary system, also in the functioning of the stock exchange, the state administrators prioritized eliminating the damage done by the crimes and preventing the issuance of unrequited paper money. The Stock Exchange became a market where bankruptcies and suicides became commonplace events in time.

The 93 War put the government in a difficult situation. Before the war, the Ottoman Empire could not pay its debts, and only half of the payments it had to make in 1875 could be made. In 1876, to cover the war expenses, the government wanted to set aside the money printing authorization given to the Ottoman Bank; however, since the contractors selling logistic materials demanded payment in gold or silver coins, the state had to buy gold and silver coins in exchange for kaime from the money changers in Istanbul (Pamuk, 1999). The Ottoman Bank initially opposed the Treasury's printing of banknotes due to the concession agreement. However, the bank had to accept the government's pressure on the condition that the banknotes would be under its control, would deal with the war's troubles during this period, and they would earn a good commission income. However, the cost of living caused by the increased emissions made the people miserable. A few years later, in 1878, the kaimes were collected again from the market and burned (Eldem, 2000). It led to a reduction in the state's reputation, but it increased the reputation of the Ottoman Bank. The bank would now play the role of a regulatory mechanism and become a significant player dominating the markets.

Until 1886, the Ottoman Empire would not be able to borrow again. The Ottomans tried to solve this crisis with the Galata Bankers. Galata Bankers were already creditors of the state for almost 9 million Lira. For this reason, various taxes, tobacco monopoly revenues, Istanbul, Bursa, Edirne, and Samsun silk cocoon revenues, Istanbul and its surroundings fishing tax, and salt monopoly revenues were left as collateral for this debt. The management concession of this business was given to a particular administration called "Rüsum-u Sitte İdaresi" (Six Tax Administrations) (1879–1880), which was established under the leadership of the Ottoman Bank. It was headed by Hamilton Long, a Frenchman who showed great success in Administration. Of the revenue to be collected by Rüsum-u Sitte, a quarterly portion of 275.000 liras was to be transferred to creditors and the remaining part to other debts of the State. It was established on 10 November 1879 and put into operation on 13 January 1880; this administration was to ensure the payment of debts to the Galata Bankers. So, The Rüsum-u Sitte Administration brought special privileges and solutions to the Galata Bankers and was objected therefore by the French and British governments and the bondholders. As a result of negotiations with a large group of creditors that started in 1880, the agreement known as the Muharrem Decree was signed on 28 Muharram 1299 (December 20, 1881), reducing the country's debt by half. In return, state revenues were transferred to the Public Debt Administration (Duyun-u Umumiye), and the debt payments were guaranteed. The Public Debt Administration became powerful, almost a state within the state (Kazgan, 2005a).

The Public Debt Administration, while stimulating the budget discipline of the Ottomans, reduced the borrowing as well as the cost of borrowing. While the state borrowed 245 million Ottoman Liras in the 1854–1874 period, 133 million Liras would be getting into debt in the 1886–1914 period. Before the Public Debt Administration, an average of 34% commission was paid for borrowing; this rate would decrease to 15% after 1886, and the average borrowing interest would drop from 5.67% to 4.24% (Öner, 2001). The Ottoman Bank and the Public Debt Administration's significant contribution ensured that borrowing operations were carried out more cost-effectively. They transformed the finance organization into a modern structure using the contemporary accounting system instead of traditional accounting.

The year 1895 was a pretty troublesome year for the bank. The reason for this was speculation by Sir Edgar Vincent, the Managing Director of the Ottoman Bank that an African company had found gold. Moreover, the bank exaggerated this news. There was intense demand for the company's stocks, and share prices had risen exaggeratedly quickly. The public raced to buy these shares, and the rising stock's value stirred the whole city. After a while, when the prices started to fall, the high demand gave way to panic, and the people rushed to the Ottoman Bank to sell the shares. The fact that the bank's general manager had an essential role in forming speculation put the bank in a challenging situation. Toward the end of the year, depositors began to form queues to withdraw their money from the bank. The bank's reserves were rapidly eroding. This time, the Ottoman Empire came to the aid of the bank. The bank's bankruptcy would have jeopardized not only the government's reputation but also its finances. With the government's support, the bank's payments were delayed, and the government stopped the payments until new gold reserves arrived from London.

Undoubtedly, this period of Abdulhamid II (1876–1908) was not going to be easy for the bank. The bank management had a somewhat negative view of the Abdulhamid II administration due to the poor management of its government spending and loan demands (Fig. 8.2). Although there was never a systematic incompatibility between the Ottoman Bank and the Abdulhamid regime, bank managers complained about the pragmatic behavior of the Sultan and the inadequacy of the government's fiscal practices. During this period, the state demanded endless short-term debt from the bank. Despite all the pressure on loan applications, the bank carefully negotiated the requests and did not accept the ineligible ones. While the bank frequently gave short-term advances to the government, it emphasized the guarantees and timely repayment of debts. However, it experienced difficulties from time to time due to the policy of "divide and rule" of Sultan Abdulhamid. Since the Ottomans received advances, it was not welcomed by the Ottoman bank that the Sultan entered into a financial relationship with the German Deutsche Bank. Payments due to the Ottoman Bank were spent while relying on revenues from the German bank (Eldem, 2000).

Sultan Abdulhamid was implementing a similar policy regarding the bankers of Galata. He was in close contact with them, obtaining loans and having his money managed by them. Interestingly, the bribes given by the pashas to rise to the upper echelons of the state were financed by the Galata Bankers (Meydan, 2017). Among these bankers, Yorgo Zarifi had a special relationship with Sultan Abdulhamid. According to the memoirs written by his grandson, who bears the same name as the banker himself, the Sultan had a large fortune, but the advisers mismanaged it, and this forced the Sultan into debt. Zarifi managed his wealth by paying off his debts and making significant money for the Sultan. He wrote, "Abdulhamid did not know how to express his gratitude and sympathy for my grandfather. My grandfather has turned into a hero in his eyes. With this enthusiasm, he calls him my father (Zarifi, 2002)." Tahsin Pasha, the Chief Clerk of Sultan Abdulhamid, said in his memoirs: "Monsieur Zarifi was crediting him in return to the salary of Sultan Abdülhamid Han as the banker of him. He did all his investment and charity work through Zarifi (Paşa, 2017)."

The most significant contribution of Banker Zarifi is that when the Russian army came to Yeşilköy in the 93 War in 1878 and was stopped by the intervention of the British, he became the banker who saved the country. He provided the war compensation that the Russians wanted. Zarifi, by paying the Russians for the gold he bought from Galata bankers, prevented the crisis, as did J.P. Morgan in the USA and banker Artin Kazaz years ago, and he earned a substantial fortune in return for

Fig. 8.2 Sultan Abdülhamid II (1842–1918). https://commons.wikimedia.org/wiki/File:Sultan_Abdulhamid.jpg

this skill. Historian Sinan Meydan wrote that Zarifi's relationship with the Sultan was based on mutual interests beyond true friendship (Kartopu, 2012).

8.5 The 1908 Revolution and Afterward

After the 1908 revolution, the administration was in the hands of the Union and Progress Party, and the finance minister was Cavid Bey. The Jewish-origin minister, who was to be executed due to his involvement in the assassination case against Mustafa Kemal Atatürk in 1926, was undoubtedly one of the most well-equipped statesmen in the field of money and finance of that period (Fig. 8.3). The new finance minister had very liberal opinions on economics, and believed that solid money was needed. While he advocated spreading paper money in rural areas, he thought circulation in the villages was more necessary than in the cities. For this reason, he began to press for the widespread use of Ottoman Bank banknotes in the country. Before entering the First World War, the government authorized the Ottoman Bank to issue one-Lira and half-Lira banknotes in August 1914. With this decision, the government authorized the issuance of small denomination banknotes, which had previously been excluded from the bank's privileges. Previously, gold and silver coins had been used in this area. It gradually began a transition to a financial system based on paper money. When the country entered the First World War, the bank eliminated the convertibility of banknotes to gold. The purpose of this decision was to avoid financial difficulties caused by the impending war (Eldem, 2000).

The money shortage that started with the Ottoman Empire's entry into the First World War began to cause a wedge between the Ottoman Bank and the government. There was a need for more loans and money printing, but the bank was very strict and did not show any flexibility. In addition, the central bank owners, the British and the French, were enemies in the war. The Ottoman administration asked the bank to issue 7 million Liras worth of banknotes, but the London and Paris committees of the bank did not accept this demand. The government started contacting German banks to finance the needs; 95 million marks were borrowed in 1914 and 80 million marks in 1915. Apart from this, the Ottoman Government had to issue banknotes by excluding the Ottoman Bank and presenting German treasury bills as collateral. However, the

Fig. 8.3 Minister of Finance Cavid Bey (1875–1926). https://en.wikipedia.org/wiki/Cavid_Bey#/media/File:Mehmed_Cavid_Bey.JPG

increasing budget deficit and the excessively printed new money created colossal inflation in the country, reaching 300% (Oktar & Varli, 2015).

Since the bank was Turkish by contract, at least three Turkish executives were appointed to head the bank. It was believed that it was now necessary to establish a national bank in the country, and initial steps would be taken in this regard. A delegation headed by Cavid Bey established the Ottoman İtibar-ı Milli Bankası in 1917. However, under war conditions, there was not enough interest in this bank's stocks, so German capital was required. The German equity would shadow the bank's reputation as a national bank. Despite all the good intentions and the legal and administrative support given to establishing the bank, this bank would not be successful.

After the Ottoman Empire lost the First World War and was occupied, the bank became a "stateless state bank" (Eldem, 2000). While the country was devastated, the British and French partners of the bank management were relieved. There was no longer a government to pressure them, but there was also no country where the bank could operate. The bank served the foreign soldiers who occupied Istanbul for a while. However, the fact that the bank had many branches in Anatolia enabled it to follow the events better. It drew its attention to the War of Independence started by Mustafa Kemal. The Ottoman Bank was one of the rare institutions that could see both sides of the line between the occupied territories of the period and the Anatolian resistance. Although the bank suffered some losses during the War of Independence, according to the reports from the general directorate, the total loss was less than expected. Interestingly, the fact that some accounts in the bank were under the name of Kemalist forces indicated that the bank observed the War of Independence thoughtfully. The bank operated without risking its future, serving the Istanbul and Ankara governments. Now, the bank was preparing for the new era (Eldem, 2000).

After the Turkish Republic was established, the most critical problem of the bank was whether it could continue its activities despite everything. The bank was a foreign bank, and the new state was not an Empire but a nation-state, and the hostility to Europe had increased. However, the bank's most significant advantage was the absence of any national institution to replace it. Since the new Republic needed foreign resources, their hopes were not lost. Another problem of the bank was the banknotes in circulation. In 1914, Cavid Bey prohibited the conversion of banknotes into gold due to war conditions. However, the war was over, and the bank could not immediately convert these coins into gold due to the increased printing of money during the Second World War. The bank had begun to reduce the banknotes it had issued in recent years unnoticeably, and as the new government would print its own money, this old money might become superfluous indeed. The excessive amount of banknotes on the market had to be discussed with the government. At the end of lengthy negotiations, the banknote problem was solved. The bank would no longer print money with a contract signed on March 10, 1924, after the War of Independence, and had to transfer this privilege to the Republic of Turkey. Plans to establish the Central Bank of the Republic of Turkey started in 1928. Dutch and Italian experts invited to Turkey stated that an independent and non-governmental central bank was necessary to ensure the stability of the Turkish currency. With the contributions of Prof. Leon Morf from Lausanne University, a draft law on the Central Bank was prepared. The Central Bank started its operations on 3 October 1931. As an indication of its wholly separate and independent status from other public institutions, the Ottoman Bank gained its legal existence as a joint stock company. However, until the Central Bank of the Republic of Turkey was established, it continued to carry out treasury operations and preserve its state bank character. In this period, it was named "Ottoman Bank" by the new political regime. The Ottoman Bank, structured as a private commercial bank with a contract signed in June 1933, became a national bank with another agreement signed in 1952 when it merged with Garanti Bank in 2001, ending its nearly 100 years of activity by then.

8.6 Imperialist Banking in the Nineteenth Century

Until the end of the eighteenth century, countries borrowed mostly for warfare. With the development of banking in the nineteenth century, this phenomenon began to change. While agriculture was losing importance, international trade and large international projects were much more critical for the banking system. Developed and underdeveloped countries started to seek finance (Ventura & Voth, 2015). The nineteenth century was unprecedented for underdeveloped countries regarding capital flow movements. As explained in this section, the Ottoman Empire followed this trend after the Crimean War and failed many times. In addition, Egypt and Greece, which had just gained their independence in the century, were also among the borrowing countries.

In 1820–1914, the London-based and Paris-based banks with significant capital accumulation were ready to make bold investment decisions in international markets. However, there was a problem; they had insufficient information about global markets, and there were no international banking regulations yet (Flandreau & Flores, 2009). The overseas loans were risky as the specific circumstances of countries such as the Ottoman Empire, Greece, or Egypt were unknown. In the initial step to reduce the anxiety of long-distance investing, banks began to seek information about foreign borrowers' trust and credit profiles by cooperating and relying on intermediaries and merchant banks. Apart from these mechanisms, they established organizations and shared information about the international markets. For example, the British Corporation of Foreign Bondholders (CFB) and similar committees became the critical forms of the London Financial Centre (Mauro & Yafeh, 2003). The Public Debt Organization was a system that allowed creditor banks to collect the debts of the Ottoman Empire in the nineteenth century when the IMF did not yet exist. Similar types of funds were established to manage the uncovered debts of Egypt (1876), Tunisia (1869), and Greece (1840, 1850, and 1898). They probably inspired the establishment of the IMF later.

However, the banks' mechanisms were not limited to these organizations. Undoubtedly, they also relied on the imperial power of their own country. For example, the British administration supported the overseas operations of its financial sector. British diplomats were frequently involved in finance committees. In addition, the British Government did not hesitate to protect the interests of British banks and investors using military force (Pénet & Zendejas, 2021). In the nineteenth century, big countries and banks worked together in what became known as financial imperialism (Laskaridis & Syrmaloglou, 2019).

Some scholars have used the term "informal empire" to refer to states colonizing countries by imposing financial conditions, without occupying any territory (Hopkins, 1994; Knight, 2008). If necessary, more punitive methods were also available, such as using the navy or threats to go further (Mitchener & Weidenmier, 2005). Colonial solutions to debt defaults led to new institutional relationships with creditors, with colonial powers offering explicit imperial guarantees against private investment losses. The process gradually turned into a debt trap and a method of exploitation by the great powers (Tuncer, 2015). However, colonial guarantees would start to show signs of weakening after the First World War (Pénet & Zendejas, 2021). After the Second World War, a more institutionalized international financing structure would be established. Today, financial imperialism still continues. As in the nineteenth century, it interferes with the political sovereignty of emerging countries by over-indebting them. The term debt trap was first coined in 2015 by the Indian researcher Brahma Chellaney, referring to China's predatory lending practices. The debt trap policy suffocates poor countries with unsustainable loans, forcing them to provide strategic leverage to China (Brautigam, 2020).

8.6.1 Egypt: A Country in a Debt Trap

Egypt was one of the most important and wealthy provinces of the Ottoman Empire since the sixteenth century. After a series of wars with the Ottoman Empire, Mehmet Ali Pasha made Egypt a privileged province due to the London Agreement of 1840. Now, the reign of Egypt and Sudan passed to the family of Mehmet Ali Pasha, and the country's presidents were called Khedive. As a successful state administrator, Pasha achieved his most significant success in Egypt by establishing state-run factories and thus laying the foundations of state capitalism reminiscent of Japan's Meiji period (Toussaint, 2016b). Moreover, under his leadership, Egypt attempted industrialization during the first half of the nineteenth century without resorting to external debt and by mobilizing internal resources.

By the 1860s, Egypt had a great opportunity because of the American Civil War. There was tremendous demand for cotton production areas to replace stalled production in America. The country had already embraced cotton as a valuable cash crop. Beyond Egypt's flax production, a significant income was opened up by producing high-quality cotton. Thus, Egypt doubled its cotton export revenue in 1863 (Earle, 1926). Although the increase in cotton income was a positive development, Egypt was now under the radar of European banks and merchants. Capitalists flooded the country quickly, and Mehmet Ali Pasha's successors implemented liberal policies, started free trade, and opened the country's resources to large projects based on foreigners and debt. Several European banks were established to regulate financial flows between Egyptian and European financial centers. London and French bankers specialized in long-term and short-term loans, respectively (Toussaint, 2016b).

The construction of the Suez Canal was significant for the country. Therefore, in 1860, the Khedive borrowed 28 million francs from a French bank from his account to fulfill his obligations to the Suez Canal. Later, in 1862, the Khedive applied for a state loan of £3.3 million with the permission of the Ottoman Sultan. This type of borrowing was the first time in Egyptian history. During 1862–67, the Egyptian Government was to borrow another £18 m in London and Paris with the support of several British and French banks, including Frühling & Goschen and the Anglo-Egyptian Bank. The revenues of the Delta, Dekahlieh, Charkieh, and Behera provinces of Egypt and the general revenues of the Egyptian state were given as collateral for these loans (Toussaint, 2016b). Also, some bonds, such as the 7% loan of 1866, were secured not on the state's revenues but on the large personal properties of the Egyptian Khedive and his family. In 1868, the Khedive succeeded in obtaining another £11.9 m loan at an effective interest rate of 8.86% through syndication of the Ottoman Bank, Société Générale, and Oppenheim. In 1872, the Egyptian Government was going to borrow again with the support of the Ottomans (Tuncer, 2015).

During the American Civil War, Egypt was making huge gains. When the war ended in 1865, the American market began to open up, and cotton prices began to fall. The decrease in export revenues caused Egypt to have difficulties in repayments. However, this did not prevent bankers, mainly the British, from giving long-term (20–30 years) loans to Egypt or French bankers from offering new, primarily short-term loans because the banks were charging high-interest rates. Finally, in 1873, the Egyptian Government obtained the largest foreign loan in its history, of £32 million, from the Ottoman Bank, Bischoffsheim, Société Générale, and other banking houses in Alexandria, Istanbul, and Amsterdam. This loan was secured by the revenues of the Lower Egyptian railways, the revenues of personal and indirect taxes, the salt tax, and various other taxes. In 1876, Egypt's debt was £68.5 million (vs. 3 million in 1863) and had reached unsustainable levels. In less than 15 years, foreign debts had increased 23 times, and revenues had increased only five times. The debt service absorbed two-thirds of the government and half of the export revenues (Toussaint, 2016b). Banks paid Egypt's debt with very high commissions. For example, the nominal value of the bonds issued in 1873 was £32 million, while the issuance price was 30% lower. As a result, less than £20 m fell into Egypt's treasury. With this borrowing with 11% coupon interest, the country would pay 77 million pounds in 30 years (Toussaint, 2016a).

Financial conditions imposed by the bankers made repayment unsustainable. Egypt had to borrow money to pay off its outstanding debt. In 1870, the bankers forced the Khedive Ismail Pasha of Egypt to sell infrastructure and make various concessions to obtain cash for debt repayment. He also had to raise taxes regularly. Egypt, which could not pay its debts, was giving up its sovereignty over the Suez Canal. The Khedive sold his shares in the Suez Canal Company, which was opened in

1869, to England in 1875. This sale was made on a loan from the Rothschilds to Prime Minister Benjamin Disraeli, as we remember from Chap. 6. With this sale, he could cover the large debt installments in December 1875 and January 1876 (Dawkins, 1901).

The Panic of 1873 was a financial crisis that triggered an economic depression in Europe and North America that lasted from 1873 to 1879 in France and Britain. This crisis also affected the debt-ridden Ottoman Empire, Greece, and Egypt. Egypt was finally forced to declare that it ceased paying its debts in 1876. Eventually, Egypt had to agree to create a Public Debt Fund ('Caisse de la Dette Publique') in agreement with the London bankers under the control of England and France (Dawkins, 1901). The Public Debt Fund had complete control over a range of government revenues. As soon as this fund was established, Egypt's debt was restructured. In this transaction, the bankers did not allow a part of the debt to be written off. The interest rate increased to about 7%, and repayments were planned for over 50 years. The political result of all these new arrangements was that the Khedive was now excluded from managing Egypt's finances, and the leading members of the Khedive administration now consisted of foreigners (Tuncer, 2015).

Although Egypt's financial problem was resolved, the international structure remained quite active. Britain, which bought the island of Cyprus from the Ottomans in return for the solution to the Egyptian issue, wanted to consolidate its control in the Eastern Mediterranean, which had increasing geopolitical importance. France's interest shifted to Tunisia during this period. However, not everything was perfect for the British in Egypt. The people of Egypt, complaining about the economic situation, started to be affected by the increasing nationalist movements. It led to the forming of the first nationalist groups under Ahmed Urabi in 1879. He became the war minister in the nationalist government headed by Mahmud Sami al-Barudi following a disagreement over the powers of the Egyptian Parliament regarding budget control. The slogan Egypt belongs to the Egyptians ('Misr li'l-Misriyin') made Arabi a national hero. Not only Khedive Tevfik Pasha but also England and France were worried about the increase in Arabi's prestige. Britain and France also sent a task force to Alexandria in 1882, using the rebellion as an excuse. In the end, England declared war on Egypt, organized a military occupation, and took the country under its protection. As a result, unconscious borrowings and mismanagement inevitably turned the country into a colony. Egypt joined the British Empire in 1882, not because of pressure from bankers and investors but because it was a critical location on the Indian road and threatened by anarchy within the country (Tuncer, 2015).

8.6.2 Greece: A Country Created by Debt

Another important region of the Ottoman Empire was the Peloponnese, for nearly 350 years. The Peninsula was simmering in the early nineteenth century. Then, the Greek uprising began in 1821. With the influence of intellectuals like Lord Byron, the people of England sympathized with the Greek war of freedom. But even though the bankers in London admired ancient Greece, that did not distract them from planning lucrative projects in the present Greece. A total of £2.8 million in loans was given to Greece in 1824 and 1825 to support the independence war. London bankers issued Greek Rebellion bonds and sold them on the London Stock Exchange. However, revolutionary Greece received only a portion of the Independence loans; the rest related to commissions, fees, and payments to brokers. Bonds were often sold for less than their par value. For example, in Greece's account, every £100 bond issued was sold for £60. The banks charged a high commission and paid Greece even much less than £60. Greece only had £1.57 m for a £2.8 m loan. On the other hand, 5% interest was to be paid on the nominal value, the interest rate of Greek bonds. Thus, the return of investors was over 8%. However, such a high rate was unsustainable (Laskaridis & Syrmaloglou, 2019). The reaction of the Turks to the uprising was very harsh. The Ottoman State brought an army under the command of İbrahim Pasha, son of the Egyptian governor Kavalalı Mehmet Ali Pasha, to the Peloponnese and suppressed the rebellion partly.

Nevertheless, the European financial support continued, but from 1826 onward, Greece began to disrupt payments. Also, in 1825, the first internally created crisis of international capitalism began (compare Chap. 6). This crisis caused a decline in economic activity, crashed many banks, and created risk aversion in financial markets. From December 1825, British bankers, then other European bankers, stopped lending, both externally and internally. Expecting to finance their debt payments by renewing bank loans, the Greeks could no longer find bankers to lend to them. The price of Greek Rebellion bonds fell very deeply, and the investors were at a loss. When the Great Powers (England, France, and Russia) took action on demand of the investors and destroyed the Ottoman-Egyptian navy in the Battle of Navarino in October 1827, the balance turned in favor of the Greek rebels (Harari, 2015).

However, Greece, exhausted by the war, could not pay its debts. Beginning in 1830, the three great powers of Europe formed the first Troika in modern world history and decided to establish a monarchy in Greece with a German prince at its head. The primary duty of Prince Otto, the new king of Greece, was to guarantee the debt payment. This was probably the first loan of this kind to be given an international guarantee. Under the agreement, all three parties had to agree unanimously on any request or action regarding Greece (Schönhärl, 2019). The Convention contained a right to "watch over" Greek public finances and provided for procedures such as diplomatic interventions in case the Greek state failed to fulfill its obligations to its debtors (Levandis, 1944).

Otto ruled Greece quite severely. He treated his people disrespectfully and did not comply with the Constitution. The country's income was insufficient, but Greece's debt payment conditions were quite harsh (Laskaridis & Syrmaloglou, 2019). Enraged by too much pressure on the people in September 1843, the Athenians rose against another tax increase. They wanted a more democratic government. The United Kingdom went so far as to threaten King Otto with military intervention if he did not raise taxes to meet his obligations to the Troika. The British and French navies occupied the port of Piraeus for two years, starting in May 1854, as a very effective way of efficiently handling the customs revenues received at the port. Otto was eventually overthrown and expelled by famous nationwide riots in 1862. After that, a new constitution was introduced in which royal powers were limited. The Troika agreed upon a Danish prince named Wilhelm as a new monarch. Since 1843, as promised to the banks, the Troika undertook the repayment of Greek debts when Greek revenues were insufficient to cover capital and/or interest payments. Troika repayments expired in 1871. In addition, 60 million French Franc credits were erased. However, Greece continued to allocate some of its revenues to debt repayment. France, Russia, and England demanded from Greece the sums they had paid to the bankers when Greece could not pay. These payments continued into the 1930s, but Russia received no further repayments after the 1917 revolution (Koliopoulos & Veremis, 2009).

These developments were only the beginning of the story. In 1897, a Turkish-Greek war broke out again. Although the war showed the superiority of the Ottomans, the intervening Troika finished the war. While each country gained almost nothing, they faced a heavy financial burden, and their debt to the banks increased. Greece has never been able to reduce its debts. While Greece, whose debts were more than twice its GNP after the 2008 crisis, jumped from one financial crisis to the next, with the wrong policies of populist politicians, Turkey, as the heir of the Ottomans, solved the debt problem with the 1923 Lausanne Agreement that ended the First World War of 1923 and paid the Ottoman debts off until 1954.

8.7 The Banking Secrets of the Ottoman Bank

By witnessing the last period of the Empire, the Ottoman Bank maintained its existence and prestige under challenging conditions. The bank owes its success to its management's ability to adapt to changing needs and maintain its independence.

8.7.1 Independence of Bank Management

Before the Great War, it was perceived as an unacceptable contradiction that a foreign bank managed by England and France was the bank of the Ottoman state. Toward the end of the year, when war became inevitable, the Ottoman Bank agreed to issue new banknotes printed first in Istanbul and then in London in a last-ditch effort to comply with the government's wishes. The already strained relations between the bank and the government had entered a breaking point with the Ottoman Empire's entry into the war on November 1, 1914. At that time, the appointment of Talaat Bey, the Minister of Internal Affairs and one of the regime's hardliners, as the acting Minister of Finance instead of Cavid Bey further increased the tension. When the government demanded an advance of 2,000,000 liras from the bank, ties were indeed severed. The general manager Nias and his deputy Steeg, who had conveyed the rejection of the Paris and London committees to Talaat Bey, received an ultimatum on December 31. They were asked to leave their posts because they were subjects of the enemy state. There was nothing to be done. The French and British managers withdrew, and the bank management was handed over to the Ottoman managers. Thanks to this concession to the government and Cavid Bey's continued support, the seizure of the Ottoman Bank by the government was prevented. Cavid remained an influential figure in the Empire's dealings with monetary issues. On the other hand, the British Government's decision restricted the bank's activities to 'friendly' countries. The Ottoman Bank, now divided in two and stripped of its power, had no choice but to wait for the end of the war. The Ottoman Government had entered the war in haste and was caught unprepared for the financial burden the war would bring. As it became clear that the Ottoman Bank could not—and did not want to—support the war, there seemed to be no choice but to print paper money once again to finance it. In 1876, the Ottoman Bank returned the privilege of issuing banknotes to the government, and in July 1915, the government issued the first series of paper money known as "evrak-ı nakdiye," a kind of kaimes. This series was cautiously issued with a gold guarantee. However, this caution was abandoned from the second series onward, and the issuance of nonrefundable paper money in increasing quantities and in different denominations began. These notes, which were printed in Germany of inferior quality, were easily counterfeited, and counterfeits were put on the market with the help of the chaos of the period (Osmanlı Bankası Muzesi, n.d.).

The pressure on the Ottoman Bank, considered to have failed to fulfill its duty as a state bank, was increasing. The insistence on the bank's participation in the 5% interest rate internal debt, issued by the government in May 1918, was a typical example. With the defeat of the Ottoman Empire and its occupation by the Allies in October–November 1918, life for the Ottoman Bank returned to some semblance of normalcy. The exiled managers returned and took back control of the bank. However, it was clear that the situation had not stabilized. Considering the possible success of the resistance movement that had begun in Anatolia, the bank's management started to provide advances to Mustafa Kemal's forces from the end of 1920. It tried to act as foresighted as possible regarding the country's uncertain future. By the end of the war, over 160,000,000 liras worth of paper currency had been issued, and the depreciation of this paper currency against gold had reached 80%. Adding to the currency's devaluation and the war's famine, the country's economy virtually collapsed, and prices increased more than 300% (Osmanlı Bankası Muzesi, n.d.)

Germany, the ally of the Ottoman Empire during the First World War, faced tremendous inflation between 1919 and 1923 after the war. Defeated, Germany had to pay the war reparations demanded by the Allied armies. The payments contributed to the inflation because they had to buy gold or other currency. In November 1923, inflation peaked; one dollar was worth 4,200 billion Deutsche Mark. In the end, the government in Germany had to put an end to inflation and began to curtail the money supply and stabilize the currency (Holtfrerich, 1986). After these horrors, the German Central Bank (Bundesbank) became the world's first independent central bank in 1951 (Uittenbogaard, 2015).

In the Ottoman Empire, the other defeated country of the war, inflation never exceeded 300%. However, the state issued German-made bonds and printed money outside the Ottoman Bank during the war. By current standards, the Ottoman Bank's banknotes, on the other hand, were much more valuable, although the bank did not fully function as a central bank. In the last quarter of the nineteenth century, when the 93 War took place, the Ottoman Empire issued kaimes under the partial control of the bank; this paper money was burned and taken out of circulation because it became worthless. These years were quite complex; there were constant rebellions and various wars. Despite this, the Ottoman Bank maintained the stability of its currency. From the perspective of the Ottoman Bank, the decisions made were broadly consistent. The Ottoman Bank did not print excessive money at the government's direction, as in post-war Germany. On the other hand, paper money issued by the Ottoman treasury, apart from the bank, was not managed well each time, and the value of the cash fell drastically. Clearly, the Ottoman Bank, as a private institution, would be in a difficult position if it printed excessive amounts of money and provided loans with insufficient collateral. Presumably, the bank resisted government pressure because of its reservations about this issue. Also, being a for-profit company with French and British capital and as an actual state bank and central bank, it did not stand behind the government in difficult times and was rather timid. As we explained before, during the world war, the Ottomans tried to establish a bank with national capital. Initially conceived as an alternative to the Ottoman Bank, the "Itibar-ı Milli Bank" managers continued to try to transform the Bank into a state bank in the last year of the war. However, the Bank, which faced significant difficulties during the armistice years and closed its balance sheets with successive losses, could not attain a structure that could fulfill the functions of the Ottoman Bank.

The Ottoman Bank was utterly foreign. As such, it was not eager to provide the Ottoman state with sufficiently cheap funds. However, being foreign was an advantage in a way, and the bank maintained its independence and stabilized the currency. Since the state's financial structure was fragile, the nationalization of the bank was out of the question. If a bank had been established with domestic capital during this turbulent period, it would not have withstood government pressure and would probably have failed. Central banks are critical institutions that back the states during troubling periods. They can provide low-cost financing to states in times of war. Countries with a central bank are pretty advantageous since they reduce countries' borrowing costs, especially in times of war (Poast, 2015). It is difficult to argue that the Ottoman Bank, under the control of hostile countries, helped the national interest as a national central bank. However, in this turbulent period, it was not easy for the Ottoman Bank to survive and maintain its stability under the influence of the government. In 1932, the Republic of Turkey established its national central bank. Under the fixed exchange rate regime implemented in this period, the authority to determine exchange rates belonged to the Government. The Central Bank's main policy instrument was the rediscount rates. In general, the 1930s were years when the independence of the Central Bank was at the forefront, and inflation remained at low levels. The 1940s, on the other hand, were the years when the adverse effects of the Second World War were felt, and Central Bank resources started to be used for public financing. Under the influence of this tendency, the Central Bank of Turkey was engaged in practices aimed at closing the financing gap of the public sector rather than conducting an independent monetary policy.

When we look at the performance of the Central Bank of the Republic of Turkey (CBRT) in the last 30 years, we see that, except for the 2001–2013 period, it could not maintain its independence as well as the Ottoman Bank. The CBRT could not stop the inflation, which rose to 70–80% in the 1990s, due to political pressures. Not only could it not reduce inflation, which reached two digits after 2015, but it also depleted the country's foreign exchange reserves by 2020 due to political pressures.

Today, a central bank's independence is evaluated in terms of four main elements: purpose, instrument, financial, and administrative autonomy. Within these factors, it is possible to say that the Ottoman Bank had financial and administrative autonomy. However, as a private company, the aim of the Ottoman Bank was naturally to make a profit, and from time to time, there was a conflict with the Ottoman Empire. At this point, it should be underlined that modern central banks do not aim to maximize their profit. In addition, under the conditions and understanding of that day, central banks did not have many tools, such as open market operations and interest setting. When we evaluate the Ottoman Bank within the scope of its purposes, it must be accepted that it was a success as an early-period central bank that preserved its independent structure in the Ottoman country under war conditions for nearly 50 years.

8.7.2 Adaptability and Flexibility

One of the most outstanding achievements of the Ottoman Bank was to ensure its continuity by adapting itself to changes in a turbulent period. The bank was established immediately after the Crimean War when the Ottoman Empire needed to attract foreign capital. By 1863, it had the privilege of being a state bank. Until it was accepted as a state bank, it competed on many projects with other banks, including the Rothschild Bank. It even had to compete with national bank projects such as the National Bank of Turkey and the Bank of Turkey. After becoming a state bank, it demonstrated its ability to survive with its strong capital structure. During the stock market crisis following the Franco-Prussian War of 1870 and the South African speculation of 1896 (the managing director of the Ottoman Bank, Sir Edgar Vincent, was involved), the bank met the demands of the public who twice rushed to the bank to convert their money into gold. Again, in 1895, the bank survived a raid by Armenian terrorists without much damage. It tried to work with the governments of the time within its principles and took a step back occasionally. However, the bank did not accept the unreasonable loans and advances requested during the reign of Sultan Abdulhamid; sometimes, however, convenience was provided to the state. When the Ottoman Empire wanted to issue kaime by the treasury for the second time, during the Russian War of 1987, the management of the Ottoman Bank followed a flexible policy, tolerating the issuance of extra paper money. The Bank agreed to issue the extra money on the condition that the banknotes would be under its control and that it would receive a commission of 1%.

After the 1908 Young Turk Revolution, the Ottoman Bank started working with the new government immediately. It tried to gain trust by informing the İttihat ve Terakki (Union and Progress) Government that it actively participated in projects. After working in harmony with the Union and Progress governments for a while, although resisting the government's increasing emissions demands during the First World War, it could not resist Ottoman demands for a Turkish manager to be appointed to the top level of the bank. At the end of the war, on the one hand, it got along well with the occupying forces; on the other hand, they entered into a money and deposit relationship with the Kemalist army. In this way, it could reach a position to cooperate with the young Republic of Turkey after the war. With the relations it established, it became the central bank of the Republic of Turkey until 1930, and it managed to survive until after the end of the twentieth century (Eldem, 2000). Undoubtedly, adapting to the time conditions with the policy they implemented was a significant success in such a difficult period.

8.8 Conclusion

On the night of February 6, 1923, those who entered the Lausanne Palace Hotel in Lausanne, Switzerland, saw that the hotel entrance was jam-packed with suitcases, bags, and boxes; the front of the hotel was full of taxis. Many Turkish journalists and diplomats walked around while the goods were loaded into the cars. The Turkish delegation was leaving Lausanne. When Ismet Pasha arrived at the hotel, journalists in the hall surrounded him. Someone asked, "What happened, Sir?" Ismet Pasha answered confidently, "What will happen... We did not accept being taken into captivity." The Lausanne conference, which started on November 11, 1922, was about to fall apart. Lord Curzon left Lausanne with the French representative, Monsieur Bompard, to pressure Ismet Pasha, the head of the Turkish delegation, who did not accept their offer. Earlier, when Lord Curzon said: "You reject everything. However, your country is in ruins. When you need money tomorrow, there is no country other than England where you can find money," the Turkish delegation was threatened. The purpose was clear: they wanted to put the Turks, who did not kneel on the battlefield, under economic pressure (Karacan, 2017). Mustafa Kemal and his friends, who founded the Turkish Republic, would never forget Lord Curzon's words and would carefully repay the money until the 1950s (Yavuz, 2009).

When Ismet Pasha's train arrived in Turkey at midnight on February 16, the Izmir Economic Congress continued. Mustafa Kemal wished to strengthen the independence he had gained through the war with a treaty. Meanwhile, he was starting a new struggle in the field of the economy before the guns of the independence war cooled down. In the economic congress that ended on March 4, 1923, it was again underlined that the capitulations were not accepted in any way. It was also decided that it was necessary to establish a national state bank that would provide loans to private enterprises. Ismet Pasha returned to Lausanne on April 23. When he completed his struggle there on July 24 and received the title deed to establish the Republic of Turkey, an economic war had just begun, and the way to go would be much longer.

M. Kemal Atatürk gave particular importance to the development of the economy. In 1924, the Turkish Government attempted to transform the Ottoman Bank into a state bank. Still, since the economic and financial conditions were not suitable for this, the banknote issuance privilege of the bank, which expired in 1925, was extended until 1935. Meanwhile, Atatürk commissioned a former banker, Celal Bayar, to establish a national bank for the Republic of Turkey. Bayar established Isbank, which would be the country's first local and national bank; its name was identified with the Republic. Lessons were learned from the experience of the Ottoman Bank, and it was understood that the State would not be politically independent without achieving economic independence.

Despite everything, the Ottoman Bank witnessed the last years of the Ottoman Empire from 1863 to 1918, served the state as an early period central bank, carried out the duties of a trade and investment bank, and endeavored to develop the insurance business in Turkey. While providing general service with its branches across the country, it enabled modern banking to be formed in the country. In a turbulent and challenging period, it adapted to the day's conditions and served as an independent institution without damaging its reputation. This process has taken many decisions that can be criticized, but it has had numerous benefits for the country. Today, if Turkish banking can compete with banks in Europe in terms of quality and size, and if Turkish banks can provide services to the farthest corners of the country, the success undoubtedly belongs to the Republic of Turkey. However, it should not be forgotten that the Ottoman Bank made a significant effort to introduce banking and modern Turkish banking with its widespread branch network at the end of the nineteenth century.

References

Akşin, S. (1992). Sened-i İttifak İle Manga Carta'nın Karşılaştırılması. *Tarih Araştırmaları Dergisi, 16*(27), 115–123.

Akyıldız, A. (1996). *Osmanlı Finans Sisteminde Dönüm Noktası Kağıt Para ve Sosyo-Ekonomik Etkileri* (A turning point in the Ottoman system. Paper money and its socio-economic effects). Eren.

Andic, F. M., & Andic, S. (2002). *Kırım Savaşı: Âli Paşa ve Paris Antlaşması* (Crimean war: Ali Pasha and the treaty of Paris). Eren.

Atış, B. (n.d.). *Kazaz Artin Amira*. Sufizmveinsan.com. http://sufizmveinsan.com/sohbet/kazazartinamira.html

Bardakci, M. (2002). *Dayılanan Elçiye Eskiden Temiz Bir Sopa çekerdik* (We used to draw a clean stick to the uncle who was unclean). Hurriyet.com.tr. https://www.hurriyet.com.tr/dayilanan-elciye-eskiden-temiz-bir-sopa-cekerdik-56166

Bimetalism. (n.d.). Britannica. Retrieved April 10, 2024, from https://www.britannica.com/money/bimetallism

Brautigam, D. (2020). A critical look at Chinese 'Debt-Trap Diplomacy': The rise of a meme. *Area Development and Policy, 5*(1), 1–14. https://doi.org/10.1080/23792949.2019.1689828

Caty, R., Richard, E., & Échinard, P. (1999). *Marseille - Les Patrons du Second Empire (Marseille—The patrons of the second empire)*. Picard.

Dadyan, S. (2012). Kazaz Artin Amira Bezciyan. www.academia.edu. https://www.academia.edu/8185584/Kazaz_Artin_Amira_Bezciyan

Dawkins, C. E. (1901). The Egyptian public debt. *The North American Review, 173*(539), 487–507.

Earle, E. M. (1926). Egyptian cotton and the American civil war. *Political Science Quarterly, 41*(4), 520–545. https://doi.org/10.2307/2142228

Eldem, E. (2000). *Osmanlı Bankası Tarihi* (Ottoman Bank History). Tarih Vakfi.

Eldem, E. (2006). Chaos and half measures: The Ottoman monetary 'system'of the nineteenth century. *The Economic Development of South-Eastern Europe, 1830–1914*, 251–305.

Finkel, C. (2005). *Osman's dream: The story of the Ottoman Empire 1300–1923*. Basic Books.

Flandreau, M., & Flores, J. H. (2009). Bonds and brands: Foundations of sovereign debt markets, 1820–1830. *The Journal of Economic History, 69*(3), 646–684. https://doi.org/10.1017/S0022050709001089

Harari, Y. N. (2015). *Sapiens: A brief history of humankind*. Vintage Books.

Holtfrerich, C. L. (1986). *The German inflation, 1914–1923: Causes and effects in international perspective*. De Gruyter.

Hopkins, A. (1994). Informal empire in Argentina: An alternative view. *Journal of Latin American Studies, 26*(2), 469–484. https://tr.wikipedia.org/wiki/Osmanl%C4%B1_Bankas%C4%B1_Bask%C4%B1n%C4%B1

İnalcık, H. (2016). *Devlet-i 'Aliyye: Osmanlı İmparatorluğu üzerine araştırmalar* (Studies on the Ottoman Empire) (Vol. 4). İşbank Publications.

İnalcık, H. (2017). *Tanzimat: Değişim Sürecinde Osmanlı Imparatorluğu* (Tanzimat: The Ottoman Empire in the process of change). Türkiye İş Bankası Kültür Yayınları.

Karabulut, R., & Uğur, A. (2022). OSMANLI DEVLETİNDE DIŞ BORÇLAR VE TASNİFİ. *Muhasebe ve Finans Tarihi Araştırmaları Dergisi*, (23), 17–36.

Karacan, A. N. (2017). *Lozan (Lausanne)*. İş Bankası Kültür Yayınları.

Kartopu, S. (2012). Duyun-U Umumiye İdaresi ve İdareyle İlgili Görüşler (Duyun-U public administration and opinions about the administration). *Global Journal of Economics and Business Studies, 1*(2), 32–40.

Kazgan, H. (2005a). *Galata Bankerleri I. Cilt* (Galata Bankers, Vol. 1). Orion Yayınevi.

Kazgan, H. (2005b). *Osmanlıda Avrupa Finans Kapitali* (European finance capital in the Ottoman Empire). Roma Yayınevi.

Knight, A. (2008). Rethinking british informal empire in Latin America (Especially Argentina). *Bulletin of Latin American Research, 27*(s1), 23–48. https://doi.org/10.1111/j.1470-9856.2007.00243.x

Koliopoulos, J. S., & Veremis, T. M. (2009). *Modern Greece: A history since 1821*. John Wiley & Sons.

Köprülü, O. F. (1996). FUAD PAŞA, Keçecizâde (Mehmed Fuad Pasha). In *TDV İslam Ansiklopedisi, 13. Cildinde* (TDV Encyclopedia of Islam, Vol. 13, pp. 202–205). Türkiye Diyanet Vakfı.

Laskaridis, C., & Syrmaloglou, A. (2019). Two sticks and one carrot: Public debt and the international financial commission in Greece 1854–1859. *Economia. History, Methodology, Philosophy, 9–4*, 797–829. https://doi.org/10.4000/oeconomia.7443

Levandis, J. A. (1944). *The Greek foreign debt and the great powers 1821–1898*. Columbia University Press.

Lewis, B. (2008). *Modern Türkiye'nin Doğuşu* (The emergence of modern Turkey). Turna, B. B. (Trans.). Arkadaş.

Mauro, P., & Yafeh, Y. (2003). *The corporation of foreign bondholders*. IMF Working Paper 03/107.

Meydan, S. (2017). *Zarifiden Zarrafa, Borç, Faiz, Borsa Batağında Osmanlı* (From Zarif to Zarrafa, debt, interest, ottoman in the swamp of the stock exchange). Sozcu. https://www.sozcu.com.tr/2017/yazarlar/sinan-meydan/zarifiden-zarraba-borc-faiz-borsa-bataginda-osmanli-2116491/

Mitchener, K. J., & Weidenmier, M. D. (2005). *Supersanctions and sovereign debt repayment.* NBER Working Paper 11472.

Oktar, S., & Varli, A. (2015). İttihat Ve Terakki Dönemi'nin Ulusal Bankası: Osmanlı İtibar-I Milli Bankası (National Bank of the union and progress period: Ottoman reputation). *Marmara Üniversitesi İktisadi Ve İdari Bilimler Dergisi (Marmara University Journal of Economics and Administrative Sciences), 27*(2), 1–20.

Ortaylı, I. (2012). *İmparatorluğun En Uzun Yüzyılı* (the longest century of the empire).

Osmanl Bankası Muzesi (n.d.). Salt. Retrieved May 10, 2024, from http://www.obmuze.com/#kronolojik

Osmanlı Bankası Baskını. (n.d.). Osmanlı Bankası Baskını. *Wikipedia.* Oxford: Oxford University Press. Retrieved April 08, 2024.

Öner, E. (2001). *Mali Olaylar ve Düzenlemeler Işığında Osmanlı İmparatorluğu ve Cumhuriyet Döneminde Mali Idare* (Fiscal administration in the Ottoman Empire and the Republican period in the light of financial events and regulations). T.C. Maliye Bakanlığı Araştırma, Planlama Ve Koordinasyon Kurulu Başkanlığı (Turkish Ministry of Finance Research, Planning and Coordination Board Presidency).

Özdemir, N. Ü. (2018). Ayanlık Kurumunun Gelişimi ve Anadolu ile Balkan Coğrafyasındaki farklılıkları üzerine bir değerlendirme. *Current Research in Social Sciences, 4*(1), 29–38.

Palmer, A. (2002). *Son Üç Yüz Yıl Osmanlı İmparatorluğu (Bir Çöküşün Tarihi)* (The decline and fall of the Roman Empire). Türkiye İş Bank Publications.

Pamuk, S. (1999). *Osmanlı-Türkiye İktisadi Tarihi 1500–1914* (Ottoman-Turkish economic history 1500–1914) (5th ed.). Gerçek Yayınevi.

Pamuk, S. (2000). *A monetary history of the Ottoman Empire.* Cambridge University Press.

Pamuk, S. (2014). *Türkiye'nin 200 yıllık İktisadi Tarihi* (200 years of economic history of Turkey). İş Bankası Kültür Yayınları (Bank Publications).

Paşa, T. (2017). *Abdülhamit: Yıldız Hatıraları* (Abdulhamid: Memories of stars). İmge Kitabevi.

Pénet, P., & Zendejas, J. F. (2021). *Rethinking sovereign debt from colonial empires to hegemony.*

Poast, P. (2015). Central banks at war. *International Organization, 69*(1), 63–95. https://doi.org/10.1017/s0020818314000265

Quataert, D. (2004). 19. Yüzyıla Genel Bakış: Islahatlar Devri—1812–1914 (Overview of the 19th century reforms period 1812–1914). In Andic, S. (Trans.) *Economic and social history of the Ottoman Empire* (pp. 885–1041). Eren Yayıncılık.

Schönhärl, K. (2019). Socially responsible investment in 19th century Greece. A case study of a Swiss Banker. *Vierteljahrschrift Für Sozial-Und Wirtschaftsgeschichte (Quarterly Journal of Social and Economic History), 106*(2), 167–190. https://doi.org/10.25162/vswg-2019-0007

Shaw, S. J., & Shaw, E. K. (2006). *Osmanlı İmparatorluğu ve modern Türkiye: Cilt 2* (The Ottoman Empire and modern Turkey: Vol. 2). Harmancı, M. (Trans.). E Yayınları.

Skylife.com. (n.d.). *Russian palace in Pera.* https://www.skylife.com/tr/1993-09/pera-da-rus-sarayi

Slade, A. (1943). *Türkiye ve Kırım Harbi* (Turkey and the crimean war: A narrative of historical events). Seyfi, A. R. (Trans.). Askeri Matbaa.

Şenyurt, A. (2018). Geç dönem Osmanlı maliyesinde poliçe kullanımı ve poliçeci esnafı. (No Title).

Tekeli, I., & Ilkin, S. (1997). *Para ve Kredi Sisteminin Oluşumunda Bir Aşama Türkiye Cumhuriyet Merkez Bankası (2.Edition)* (A stage in the formation of the money and credit system central bank of the Republic of Turkey, 2nd edn). Central Bank of the Republic of Turkey.

Tokgöz, E. (2000). 19. Yüzyılda Osmanlı Yüzyılda Ekonomisi (The Ottoman Empire in the 19th century). *Hacettepe Üniversitesi İktisadi ve İdari Bilimler Fakültesi Dergisi (Journal of Hacettepe University Faculty of Economics and Administrative Sciences), 19*(2), 365–376.

Toussaint, É. (2016a). Newly independent Greece had an odious debt round her neck. In *Greece and debt: Two centuries of interference from creditors.* Committee for the Abolition of Illegitimate Debt. www.cadtm.org/Newly-Independent-Greece-had-annh2-11

Toussaint, E. (2016b). *Debt as an instrument of the colonial conquest of Egypt*. Committee for the Abolition of Illegitimate Debt. https://www.cadtm.org/Debt-as-an-instrument-of-the

Tuncer, A. C. (2013). Black swan of the golden periphery: the Ottoman Empire during the classical gold standard era. London School of Economics CWPESH, (13).

Tuncer, A. C. (2015). *Sovereign debt and international financial control: The middle east and the Balkans, 1870–1914*. Palgrave Macmillan.

Turanakinci.com. (n.d.). *Beyoglu Rusya Sefareti (Russian Embassy in Beyoglu)*. https://www.turanakinci.com/portfolio-view/beyoglu-rusya-sefareti/

Uittenbogaard, R. (2015). *Evolution of central banking. De Nederlandsche Bank, 1814–1852*. https://doi.org/10.1007/978-3-319-10617-5

Ventura, J., & Voth, H. J. (2015). Debt into growth: How sovereign debt accelerated the first industrial revolution (No. w21280). National Bureau of Economic Research.

Yavuz, A. (2009). Başlangıcından Bugüne Türkiye'nin Borçlanma Serüveni: Durum ve Beklentiler (Turkey's borrowing adventure from the beginning to the present: Situation and expectations). *SDÜ Fen Edebiyat Fakültesi Sosyal Bilimler Dergisi (SDU Faculty of Arts and Sciences Journal of Social Sciences), 20*, 203–226.

Yildiz, A. (2011). Osmanlı Devletinin Borçlanmasında Osmanlı Bankasının Rolü ve Önemi (The role and importance of the Ottoman Bank in the borrowing of the Ottoman state). *Elektronic Sosyal Bilimler Dergisi, 10*(36), 318–330.

Zarifi, Y. L. (2002). *Hatiralarim: Kaybolan bir Dünya. Istanbul 1800–1920* (My memories: A disappearing world Istanbul 1800–1920). Literatür.

Chapter 9
The Rise (and Fall) of National Banking Champions (Nineteenth, Twentieth, and Early Twenty-First Centuries)

9.1 Introduction

When Harry Boessenkool re-entered the Netherlands in late 1961, aged 16 and 7 years after having left it for Canada with his family in 1954, he did speak Dutch but could barely write it. Nonetheless, he was hired by the Nederlandsche Handelsmaatschappij (NHM) to join the "Human Resources Department Foreign" on the third floor of the building at its headquarters at Vijzelstraat 32 (see Fig. 9.1). The impressive office was in the midst of the traditional Amsterdam banking area. Of course, the city had grown over the last three centuries, but its seventeenth century structure was still intact. Refer to Chap. 4 for more information on this or just take a stroll yourself through the still impressive neighborhood and be amazed by the Amsterdammers of the time of the height of the 1920s building.

Harry became involved with the affairs of the 41 foreign offices that the merchant bank maintained worldwide, being a Documentation Officer for incoming and outgoing mail. With his department being on the Executive floor, he did some interesting things that were extremely confidential. For four years, he was involved in doing the transfers of all annual "Tantièmes" (bonuses) to the Board of Directors of NHM and all the senior Managers overseas as well as the Executives of the Bank itself. He had memorized all the names of the expat officers, bank executives, and the names of the Board of Directors at that time. He still recognizes and smiles at the names when seeing them some 60 years later. Harry witnessed the 1964 merger with Twentsche Bank into the Algemene Bank Nederland. While enjoying working with economic and legal experts such as the future ABN AMRO chairman Jan Kalff whom we will meet later on, after 4 years, he decided that the still provincial atmosphere in crowdy Amsterdam did not suit him well. The bank gave him a nice letter of recommendation and so he left.

Harry returned to the openness of the Canadian cities and prairies, met his Canadian wife Joanne, and stayed in the "Land of Maple Leaf." He served the Bank of Montreal (BMO) in various provinces, including Alberta (various towns) in the West

M. B. Karan et al., *A History of Banks*, Contributions to Economics,
https://doi.org/10.1007/978-3-031-62297-7_9

Fig. 9.1 Meeting room in the former NHM head-office in the Vijzelstraat in Amsterdam, https://commons.wikimedia.org/wiki/File:Nhm2.jpg

and Ontario (Toronto) in the East, while ending up in the Far West (Vancouver) in British Columbia (B.C.). He worked in almost every area of the Bank in various branches and functions that included personnel, marketing, and treasury. Harry assisted to the provincial B.C. Strategy Vice President. He was General Manager in the Vancouver Downtown office and in the Main B.C. Office here. In this period, BMO did various large acquisitions, including in the nearby Chicago area in the USA, where it met ABN AMRO. Harry however maintains: "I am a conservative banker: when your grandma puts money in the bank, she wants to have it to be returned." Once, Harry came across a document on the US firm Enron, which little later caused *the* corporate accounting scam. "Already from page 1 onwards, I did not get what they were doing and decided to stay away from them," he says. Harry recalls his 70s and early 80s positions at BMO vividly.

- Training and Education Manager for the Alberta Division (124 branches and about 1500 staff) in Calgary (1973–76). "We found out quite quickly that MBAs were not the best hires. They wanted to be the boss before they wanted to file cheques. (When filing cheques in the first branch I worked at, I memorized all the data on them and soon found out who the best commercial customers were. The Manager was amazed that I could tell him which cheques to return for problem accounts.)"
- Administration Manager, Main Office Edmonton with a staff of 140 reporting, of whom some 135 were women. "I learned lot a about mining and oil and gas business. I cashed the biggest cheque of my career when we, on behalf of Ward Air had to send the gross lease for a BOEING 747 to Seattle for one hundred million dollars! I was there in the boom years with lots of problems with staffing.

Again, I made the habit of going through some one thousand cheques every day just to get a feel what was going on. I knew what I was looking for so could do it very quickly. The "girls" could not believe I was doing—they had never see anyone do it."

- Product Manager Sundry Services in Domestic Banking in Toronto for one year and two as Product Manager Guaranteed Investment Certificates also in Toronto but in the Treasury Division. "The main reason I got those jobs was that I knew how the branch systems worked. A lot of the H.O. guys and gals had never worked in branches. I learned from them, and they learned from me. The Asset & Liability Committee in H.O. was my most valuable experience. Matching Mortgage loans to GIC sales on a weekly basis was a high-stake business. With some 1,300 branches pumping out mortgage loans there was never a dull moment. Advertising our rates (and we did that in those years) was a real adventure with the Ad agencies I worked with."
- In 1981, Harry had an opportunity, kowing some senior staff by then, to return to Alberta. "The province was running a test phase on the roll out of ATM (Automated Teller Machines). The Division's Strategic Vice President (SVP) and Operations Manager had resigned, and the replacement SVP wanted me as his Administration Manager for the province. This was in the Bill Mulholland years, one of the Canadian banks first 'outside' CEOs. Because he liked the new SVP he was sending to Alberta, there was no objection for me to go there as well."

The American Mulholland made some major changes in the bank organization at the local level. During that time, Harry had two significant Area Manager jobs, one in Alberta (Lethbridge, covering Southern Alberta and Southeastern BC—some 600 km from Medicine Hat to Creston within 100 km (north) of the US border. Those two jobs led Harry to his final position at BMO. "In 1990, I became the Executive Assistant to the SVP of the British Columbia (BC) Division with 160 branches and some 2,000 employees. The BC Division was the most profitable Division in Domestic Banking in Canada. The job was also a grooming ground for Senior Executives. Matt Barrett went from that job to become the CEO of BMO in 1989 and from there, in 2004 to Barclays Bank in London where he retired in 2006."

Harry's new job was on protecting incumbent SVP from any major problems, except Credit and Loan problems. "Beside myself, the SVP had 6 Vice-Presidents covering the province. They were all men, except for the last two years, when we had female VP as well. Being a time of automation, the years from 1990 onwards involved a lot of changes, e.g., taking out Tellers and replacing them with Mutual Fund Salespeople or promoting them if they took the right courses. For 1996, the budgeting system (Income and Expense) for the Division required the elimination of positions that could not be achieved by normal retirements and turnover. This was the first time since the founding of BMO in 1817 that we would have to let people go and pay severances. This carried on in lessening degrees till I retired in 2002. The VPs oversaw selecting the people and I oversaw setting aside enough funds to meet the expenses challenges and divide them among the six districts we had in the province."

Harry concludes as follows. "One interesting project at that time was the selling of branches in rural B.C. to the local Credit Unions. Some bean counters in H.O. produced a list of twenty branches which we concurred and very secretly were passed on to the politicians (both Federal and Provincial) and to the BC Central Credit Union. They signed off on thirteen branches and they were sold. It saved a substantial number of severances and in general was well received in the communities, at least we did not close the branches like other banks had been doing." Indeed, many branches were closed nationwide, which helped to preserve interest margins (Calomiris & Haber, 2014). Moreover, Canadian banking became even more concentrated than before. It had already been differing from US banking in that banks branched out across provinces, whereas the US had a banking system with independent units.

Interestingly, Harry Boessenkool points at HSBC as a bank that is comparable to BMO. The Hong and Shjasnghai Banking Corporation that was found in 1865 (Roberts & Kynaston, 2015) at least resembles Canada's oldest incorporated bank in that they both have grown out of a British colonial base: BMO in North America and HSBC in East Asia. HSBC used its home base in 1842 and established British colony of Hong Kong to develop trade finance. The neighboring commercial center of Shanghai was vital, with other branches in China and beyond also being opened. The Bank was active in foreign trade finance, making currency operations also important. It operated via Chinese agents locally and did business with traditional Chinese banks, as well as with the Chinese government and beyond. King (1988) reports on railway investments and encounters with Deutsche Bank from Germany. Becoming active from Lombard Street in the London market on short-term loans and deposits, as well as long-term bonds, investment banking developed well. After World War I, the bank expanded by following its booming markets but also suffered with them in the Great Depression that followed. The Bank was a dominant factor in China, even assuming central bank functions and, e.g., topping the Dutch NHM in this respect.

Unlike BMO in the mostly de-colonized Canada, HSBC faced in 1941 a blow that heavily affected its position (Roberts & Kynaston, 2015). Although Japan had captured parts of eastern China earlier, business had been quite normal first. This changed when in the course of the Pearl Harbor incident not just the Shanghai International Settlement, but also Hong Kong and other parts of Eastern Asia were captured. When the Nationalists took over in China, affairs did not go well here. A new blow was the 1949 communist victory, leaving only the Shanghai branch open at a low scale. Hong Kong was still dependent upon Mainland China factories and other businesses (e.g., on foreign exchange) also continued. Although China's business picked up later, the now more rightfully called "Hongkong Bank" or "The Bank" felt urged to spread its wings. It did so by acquiring two British overseas banks and diversifying into small business finance, mortgage lending, and retail deposits. Important on the latter was a majority acquisition of the then-endangered Hang Seng Bank that later established the local stock exchange index. With the crown colony becoming a regional financial center, the bank was branching out way overseas. Strikingly, control was taken of Midland Bank in New York State (USA) in 1980 (King, 1991).

In the period just described, the Bank was thought to be as traditional, hierarchical, and introverted, but also as levering on self-reliance, flexibility, short communication lines, and clear desks (Roberts & Kynaston, 2015), making a comparison with Harry Boessenkool's BMO almost a trivial one. Also, the efficiency moves that followed suit in the 1990s may not surprise the reader. What makes the HSBC case differ, however, is the late ending of the British colonization in 1997, making Hong Kong's position in the region to give way to Shenzhen and Shanghai and even way beyond. The bank "took the plunge into South America" (Ibid, p. 214). Moreover, size ("being big") and shareholder orientation became an issue, with the US Citibank being an important competitor. Customer segmentation and flexible pricing were "in." With paternalism giving way, federalism was still around, and "collectivism" became a buzzword. The Asian financial crisis of 1998 was weathered and opportunities in the changing Europe were taken. Whereas business in China grew as well, Headquarters were moved to London, ending an era of some 150 years of banking growing out of imperialism. At the time, nearby "lions" were waking up.

Like Harry Boessenkool at the time, you may probably never have heard of the Industrial and Commercial Bank of China (ICBC). Nevertheless, its Shanghai Tower (2017) on a promenade ("Bund") that had hosted an iconic HSBC building, being taller than 100 m (see Fig. 9.2), may already give you a clue that ICBC is not exactly a tiny corporation. In fact, the mostly state-owned bank is the largest in the world if measured in terms of assets (S&P Global Market Intelligence, 2022) and it has already been like that for a decade. ICBC was not the only Chinese bank leading the "Top 5" list. The numbers 2, 3, and 4 were China Construction Bank (CCB), Agricultural Bank of China (ABC), and Bank of China (BoC), respectively, with JPMorgan Chase (USA) being the first Western bank at number 5. The US banks would have been ranked higher if they had reported under IFRS (international) reporting standards instead of under US GAAP rules. Moreover, according to ADV Ratings (2022), at around the same time, JPMorgan Chase was the largest bank in terms of stock market value (market capitalization), before respectively Bank of America (USA), ICBC (China), CCB (China), and Wells Fargo (USA).

The 2007 "Top 10" list looked very different from the more recent ones. Banks-Daily.com (2008) reported that the largest banking firm by assets was Royal Bank of Scotland (UK), closely followed by Deutsche Bank (Germany), BNP Paribas (France) and Barclays (UK), with Crédit Agricole (France), UBS (Switzerland), Société Générale (France), ABN AMRO (The Netherlands), ING Bank (The Netherlands) and the Bank of Tokyo-Mitsubishi UFJ (Japan) completing the list, in this order. In order of equity, Bank of America, Citigroup, JP Morgan Chase, and HSBC were the leaders, followed respectively by Mitsubishi UFJ Financial Group, Royal Bank of Scotland, ING Group, Crédit Agricole, Wachovia Corporation (USA, acquired by Wells Fargo in 2009) and BNP Paribas. Of course, the main difference is in the Chinese banks and this is often related to the growing size of their home economy and the more outward-bound approach of China in the later years. However, there was also something else that had happened in between the Global Financial Crisis and its aftermath.

The crisis appeared to affect many banks worldwide, even "too big to fail," so-called system banks. Harry Boessenkool's BMO had not been involved, but one of the examples included his root base that had become ABN AMRO, once the global

Fig. 9.2 ICBC building in Shanghai, by Peter K. Burian, https://commons.wikimedia.org/wiki/File:ICBC_building_on_the_Bund,_Shanghai.jpg

number 8 in terms of assets (BanksDaily.com, 2008). The bank underwent a complex bailout in 2008 and shriveled. Deutsche Bank, the world's number 2, German pride in terms of assets, barely survived, only to become the world's number 22 in terms of assets. The Swiss Credit Suisse was a leader in private banking until its collapse in 2023. On the other hand, the British HSBC navigated through the crisis quite well, being the world's number 8 bank at the time of writing. The four western banks just mentioned have much in common. They can show a long history and were co-leaders in their home countries. Although none of them was an outright market leader at home, one may rightfully label them as "National Champions". The issue is, however: how did they accomplish this? Moreover, what lessons can be learned from their experiences? Let us take a look and focus on the three who lost their games. We start with the one that has the longest history of all.

9.2 Dutch Banking and ABN AMRO

As shown in Chap. 4, despite losing its hegemony to other powers such as Great Britain, France, and the upcoming USA, the Netherlands was still the world's richest country by the end of the eighteenth century. However, the balance of power between the Stadtholders represented by the Orange family, the States General representing the provinces and the wealthy people in cities such as Amsterdam was falling apart, with Stadtholder Willem V being unable to manage the democratic uprising at the time. Although Prussia (the most powerful part of Germany) came to the rescue, he had to flee and the French captured the whole of the Netherlands by 1795. Interestingly, many reformations took place during the French occupation, e.g., a legal system that is basically still in use. The French were ultimately defeated in 1815 and this is how King William I, the son of Prince William V, came on the throne. In the course of a democratization movement, his son William II reigned in a less despotic way and the family's influence waned even more under William III. Although lagging behind economically, the Netherlands still had its most important colony: East India (now Indonesia).

ABN AMRO was and still is a large Dutch bank (ABN AMRO, 2022g). It is keen to find its traces back for over three centuries, with R. Mees en Zonen (founded in 1720) and Bank Hope & Co (founded in 1762) being among its ancestors (ABN AMRO, 2022e). These two banks capitalized on the good name of the Dutch financers in the eighteenth century and were, e.g., active in the slave trade, private loans, and government loans, financing the Russian Tsars and the French Emperor Napoleon Bonaparte. Their roles waned later on, but a series of mergers with especially the late nineteenth century founded investment bank Pierson, Heldring & Pierson, made MeesPierson become the specialized investment bank it was under the wings of ABN AMRO until 1997. Other banks merging into Mees Pierson include the Amsterdamsche Goederenbank ("Amsterdam Commodities Bank") and the Nederlandsche Bank voor Zuid-Afrika ("Netherlands Bank for South Africa"). The reader may recall from Chap. 4 that the Dutch had started a colony in South Africa and the latter bank was related to Dutch-origin settlers.

One of the more direct ancestors of ABN AMRO is the Nederlandsche Handelsmaatschappij ("Dutch Trade Company"). The NHM was founded in 1824 (ABN AMRO, 2022f), at the initiative of "King Merchant" William I, an indirect descendant of William of Orange, the one who launched the Dutch political and economic success story featured in Chap. 4. At first, the NHM was mostly active in the Dutch East Indies (especially on plantations) and other parts of East Asia, taking on much of the approach exemplified by the Dutch East India Company in the seventeenth and eighteenth centuries, but also acting as a banker of the Dutch State. The NHM was moreover involved with activities in the West Indies and the industrialization in its home country. After the renewed separation between The Netherlands and Belgium in the 1830s, and almost getting broke twice in its beginnings (Janssen, 2022), the NHM gradually became a merchant bank. It even took on central bank roles with the issue of banknotes in Eastern China ("Shanghai dollars") until 1946 and the former Dutch colony of Suriname until 1957. The Dutch branches were limited to one in Amsterdam and one in Rotterdam, but this changed much around the Second World War and the independence of Indonesia that followed suit.

The Twentsche Bank was founded in 1861 (ABN AMRO, 2022j). The bank financed the regional textile industry, while also being active in international trade, with bills of exchange, foreign exchange, and export financing in London and Amsterdam. Being the first Dutch bank with subsidiaries and branches, it did many greenfields and mergers in various Dutch regions and neighboring Germany. The bank introduced personal loans in 1958. It was keen to celebrate successes such as in a book issued at its centennial (De Twentsche Bank NV, 1961). The book breathes the atmosphere of a great past and a dooming electronic era, assessed with a mix of amazing, hesitation, happiness, mild irony, and norms setting. It is interesting to note that the bank aimed to behave as a man of standing in a fast-changing world. However, its merger with the NHM in 1964 rather marked the beginning of a new world. The Algemene Bank Nederland ("General Bank Netherlands," ABN Bank) as led by André Batenburg got far-reaching aspirations, especially after the merger with the Chicago-based LaSalle National Bank in 1979 (ABN AMRO, 2022b). LaSalle brought the bank a distinct position in the US Mid-West and a sound base for acquiring knowledge. The ABN Bank added many branches to its domestic presence. It also went into hire-purchase finance ("leasing").

Also in 1964, the Amsterdam(sche) Bank merged with the Rotterdam(sche) Bank to become the largest bank in the Netherlands. The Amsterdam Bank showed large ambitions right from the beginning in 1871, when it was founded as a Post Franco-Prussian War initiative by German banks serving a broad clientele consisting of, e.g., catholic and Jewish business owners, as well as investors in American railroad companies and planters in the Dutch East Indies (ABN AMRO, 2022d). In the early 1900s, the bank used the vehicle Amsterdamsch Wisselkantoor ("Amsterdam Exchange Office") for branching and it also acquired some smaller Dutch banks then. Losing much money in a German credit freeze and a large Dutch swindle in the 30s, it aimed to merge with its major competitor Rotterdamsche Bank in 1939, but turmoil on the global level made the plans to rest and after World War II had ended, the bank went on to consolidate local banks and expanding just in the nearby Belgium. It was also active in stocks and loans, as well as foreign exchange.

At its inception in 1863, The Rotterdam(sche) Bank was set up as a colonial bank, but quickly resumed its activities as a bank targeting just the Rotterdam trade and industry area (ABN AMRO, 2022h). With Willem Westerman ("William the Conqueror," indeed perhaps a distinct relative of one of the present authors) as a director, the bank took over some eighteenth-century old-style banks and numerous smaller banks, next to setting up various overseas branches. The latter had to be unwinded when the bank entered into a crisis. A new try was given after World War II, but repealed before the 1964 merger that created the AMRO Bank. The Amsterdam-Rotterdam Bank (ABN AMRO, 2022c), as led by Jan van den Brink, was keen on striking a balance between the two leading Dutch cities. After first trying to arrive at more international cooperation, the bank set up a foreign branch and representative offices network. The bank entered into factoring (making advance payments on selected company receivables) and bought an investment bank. A merger with the Belgian Generale Bank was strived for but appeared to be too complicated. Instead, a merger with the Dutch archrival ABN Bank was closed in 1991.

The motives for the ABN AMRO Bank merger were at least twofold (ABN AMRO, 2022c; Smit, 2008). Firstly, cost savings were assumed to occur, in the office network and beyond. Secondly, furthering international expansion was given priority. Despite differences between the gentleman-like decentralized ABN and the businessman-like centralized AMRO, with mergers, unwindings, and reorganizations being around all the time, whereas the efficiency ratio between the operating expenses and the gross margin went up steadily, especially the growth of the investment bank and the acquisitions in the USA and elsewhere made the bank grow toward a global Top 10 position anyway. In the consolidated Dutch banking landscape, with three banks largely dominating the market, an acquisition of the good-old Belgian Generale Bank (meanwhile with a Dutch presence) would be a logical step, but the Belgian/Dutch financial conglomerate Fortis Group was able to strike the deal in 1998. Anyhow, ABN AMRO opened a prestigious head office in the then newly created Amsterdam financial district ("Zuidas") in 1999.

In 2000, Jan Kalff retired as CEO of ABN AMRO after a long career that had started at the ABN predecessor NHM in 1964 (Wikipedia, 2022f). One year before, he had proudly presented a book on 175 years of ABN AMRO history to 108,000 staff members in 76 countries (De Vries et al., 1999). His successor was Rijkman Groenink (Wikipedia, 2022h), originally an AMRO Bank adept. Groenink inherited a bank that he had been co-shaping as director of the Dutch division, but that was not wholly in control, as signaled by its efficiency ratio. Issues included still uprising "tribe battles" between former ABN and AMRO staff and their heirs, an allegedly inert, over-staffed, and bureaucratic Dutch division, a generous promotion and bonus system at the investment bank, and the latter's distance from traditional operations. Groenink chose to focus on investment banking and wholesale above retail and private banking, a smaller role of country units and even contractions from various countries, less operational involvement of the Board of Directors, and above all, facing low share prices, creating shareholder value in terms of economic profit on all of the bank levels (Smit, 2008).

Value-based management is a concept that originates from the work of authors such as Rappaport (1986) and Stewart (1991). The idea is that a company should focus on its expected future cash flows and therefore not on its historical accounting profits, in relation to a true present economic cost of capital and not a hurdle rate drawn from internal or external benchmarks. The cost of capital is driven by the debt and equity investors, of whom the latter as residual claimants matter the most, with banks being price setters of debt anyway. Working on economic value is with banks by no means like a walk in the park and ABN AMRO was not alone in this respect. There are varying ways to calculate it, with the Economic Value Added (EVA) measure often prevailing. Forecasting EVA is difficult, compare it to calculating discounted cash flows with investment projects. However, also assessing the EVA in a past period is quite something, especially in a conglomerate type of company such as ABN AMRO at the time. The bank did the job with the help of no less than two consultancy firms and an investment bank (Smit, 2008). Despite an overall strive for accountability, it showed to be difficult to change the sales orientation that had characterized the bank for a long. After a few years, the focus on wholesale banking was given up, but also the Dutch division was reorganized.

Meanwhile, the price of ABN AMRO shares was lagging behind the aspirations of the bank (Smit, 2008). The low image in the stock market reflected various issues. Among others, the bank had been involved with various misjudges, including the scandalous initial public offering by the Dutch internet firm World Online, the acquisition and rapid sale of a Hungarian bank and a Dutch real estate development financing firm, a failed attempt to acquire the Generale Bank successor Fortis, compliance investigations opened by the Federal Reserve in the USA and more. At times, these were related to the not just to foreigners somewhat surpriseful personality of CEO Groenink and it was also a public secret that personal relationships in the top of the bank were sub-optimal to say the least, whereas the unrest that was characterizing the bank did also not help to boost internal feelings. Outsiders made jokes about the bank's slogan: Dè Bank ("*The* Bank") and criticized its strategic wobbling. Nevertheless, in the mid-2000s, the bank resetted its role in the industry landscape and went for a leading position in Europe.

In 2005, ABN AMRO entered into a proxy fight with a local bank, Fiorani, in order to buy Antonveneta, the number 8 bank in Italy (Smit, 2008). Despite of resistance by the Italian central bank and dubious tactics of Fiorani, ABN AMRO won the fight. However, it appeared to be a Pyrrhus victory, since its stock price soared and it readily became clear that Antonveneta would not swiftly contribute to the bank's profits. Nevertheless, the bank deliberated another takeover here, one in Brazil and even of the Lloyd TSB bank in the UK. Informal talks with the Dutch/Belgian ING on a merger of equals also became more concrete and there were even talks with the larger UK-based Barclays and Royal Bank of Scotland (RBS). Meanwhile, the bank had difficulties with the implementation of the complex matrix structure, as well as the realization of operational excellence and the ambition to be in the European Top 5 on shareholder value realization. By mid-2006, it became clear to Groenink that ABN AMRO would not be in the driver's seat anymore with the emerging bank consolidation race in Europe. Activist shareholders even indicate that a break-up of the bank, lacking synergies, would be welcome to them.

By the end of 2006, Michel Tilmant of ING entered into talks with his counterpart Rijkman Groenink of ABN AMRO on a merger of equals in which no merger premium would be paid (Smit, 2008). Nevertheless, ING would by far be the larger of the two equals in shareholder value terms. Meanwhile, the ABN AMRO share price went up on rumors and the activist shareholder TCI started to stir. ING felt that the bank had become too expensive and stopped the informal merger talks. Quickly, ABN AMRO reached a preliminary agreement with Barclays on a merger of equals, with Barclays acting as the bidder. RBS, Bank of Santander, and Fortis also formally showed interest on buying the bank jointly, but ABN AMRO was unpleased with this idea that effectively meant a break-up of the bank and even sold its US pearl LaSalle to Bank of America quasi overnight by way of a so-called poison pill. Nevertheless, the consortium came up with a bid that topped the one of Barclays, pending on LaSalle not being sold. Also, the shareholders showed in a meeting support for studying the consortium's bid.

The US investment bank Meryl Lynch had advised the consortium upon the $98.3 billion deal. RBS was at first largely interested in LaSalle and expected many synergies from this, but it could also settle with the investment banking division and the Asian network, whereas Fortis and Banco Santander went for the Dutch and Italian plus Brazilian operations respectively (Smit, 2008; Wikipedia, 2022a). Although Barclays arrived at an improved bid, its bid was still better in financial terms, and therefore ABN AMRO withdrew its support to the Barclays bid and took a neutral position from now onwards. The Dutch central bank, itself not leaning toward the consortium bid, took the 2007 summer to approve both bids. Barclays only received very limited support for its bid and therefore the consortium won. The ABN AMRO top managers cashed in on options and shares, as well as a leave bonus of in total of €1.4 billion. Groenink left the bank, after a career of 33 years. People seeing him later found him in a modest mood and with a sad feeling on the demise of *The* Bank. However, it appeared to be not really *The End*.

Soon after the completion of the deal, Banco Santander sold Antonveneta to an Italian bank. With also a credit crunch evolving, RBS had to make a rights issue, the largest one in British history by then, to increase its equity capital (Wikipedia, 2022a). Also, Fortis encountered into cash flow problems. CEO Jean Paul Vottron stepped down and a break-up became inevitable in October 2008, right after the Lehman Brothers collapse. The French bank Paribas, the Belgian State, and the Luxembourgian State stepped in. With ING readily refusing to take over Dutch parts, the Dutch State became the sole owner of the Dutch insurance branch, Fortis Bank Nederland, and ABN AMRO (The Netherlands). Observers felt that the joint value hereof would be 12 billion euros. By merging Fortis Bank Nederland and ABN AMRO, about 1 billion euros per year would be saved, representing 5 billion euros of total value. All in all, the assets could have been worth 17 billion euros. The price paid was about equal to 16.8 billion euros. Of this amount, 8.8. billion euros referred to ABN AMRO, at a loss for Fortis of roughly 15 billion euros (Michielsen & Sephiha, 2009). The often Belgian shareholders of Fortis lost a lot of money. By the end of June 2008, a Fortis share was still worth €15. Only half a year later, it was valued at about €1.

Initially, it was thought that the nationalization would be shortlived (Smit, 2008). The integration of the smaller Fortis and the larger ABN AMRO bank, less ABN AMRO commercial financing subsidiaries being sold to Deutsche Bank, had to go along with a 2.6 billion euro capital injection of the Dutch State and it took two years. As such, the restructuring did not affect major financial ratios (Bao, 2017). According to the company website, "The new ABN AMRO is focused on the retail market in the Netherlands and on private banking in the Netherlands and various countries in Europe and Asia, as well as on merchant and corporate banking in the Netherlands and abroad" (ABN AMRO, 2022a). The former Dutch Minister of Finance Gerrit Zalm led the reconstruction of the bank from 2009 to 2017. At the time of writing, ABN AMRO was partly privatized, but still majority owned by the Dutch State. Whereas the bank had abolished its defensive mechanism during the early-2000s move ahead, it was now owned for 50.1% by an administration office issuing certificates of shares to beneficiaries (ABN AMRO, 2022i). The much-reduced bank was as of 2022 planning to return largely to its pre-1999 head office.

At the time of writing, ABN AMRO was the third bank in the Netherlands in terms of asset size, with the first one being the already mentioned ING Group (Statista, 2022). When the Dutch financial landscape was consolidated around 1990, ING was created as a merger of a banking company and an insurance company (Wikipedia,

2022e). Rapidly, the bank part became known for its direct banking activities, absorption of the suddenly collapsed Barings (see Chap. 11), and takeovers in countries such as Belgium and Turkey. After a capital injection by the Dutch government during the financial crisis, the insurance part was unwound. The second Dutch bank in terms of asset size is Rabobank (Statista, 2022; Wikipedia, 2022g). It has a cooperative structure, with members instead of shareholders. Rabobank revoked its federative structure in 2006 but remained keen on local presence and local autonomy. Aiming to finance global agriculture, the overseas activities were stepped up from the 1980s onwards, but it is and cannot be a "Champions League" bank like ABN AMRO was.

9.3 German Banking and Deutsche Bank

Actually, up until around 1870, the German Confederation ("Deutsche Bund") was a hotchpotch of sovereign states and cities, even including a Dutch province (Limburg) and the Dutchy of Luxembourg. The leading state was Prussia, a Kingdom of its own, with large possessions outside of the Bund. It set up a so-called "Zollverein," which regulated cross-border taxes. Austria, although a part of the Bund, did not join it though. Despite of the Bund being weak, German trade and industry blossomed. Also, a liberalization movement started, leading to many democratic reforms, including the gradual introduction of a multi-party system. On top of this, German nationalism received an upheaval. During the victorious French/German War of 1870/71, the erection of the German Empire, under the strong leadership of Chancellor Otto von Bismarck, marked a new era. As a latecomer, rapidly, Germany captured various colonies and started to go for global hegemony (see Fig. 9.3).

In the nationalist climate of 1870, Deutsche Bank was founded by a group of Prussian bankers with various backgrounds (Gall, 1995). Interestingly, Ludwig

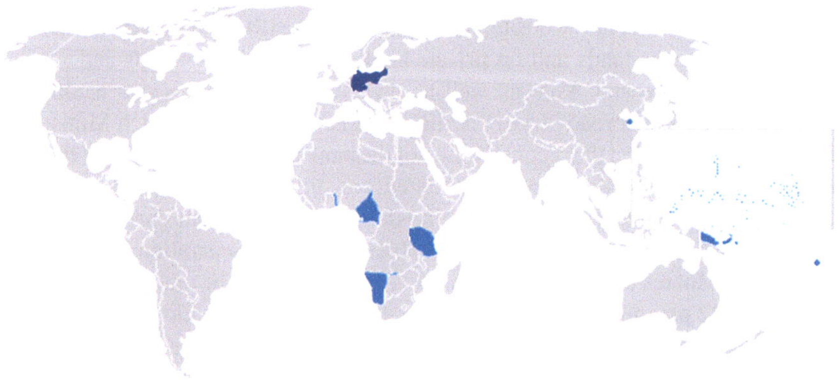

Fig. 9.3 Map of the German Empire—1914, https://commons.wikimedia.org/wiki/File:Map_of_the_German_Empire_-_1914.PNG

Bamberger, an economist, politician, and banker, who learned the banking job in London and participated in banks in Rotterdam and Paris, co-steered the unification of the German money system and its reform from a silver standard to a gold standard and the erection of the German central bank in 1876, was involved as a political advisor. The erection of Deutsche Bank was an initiative of Adelbert Delbrück, a Berlin-based banker and politician. Delbrück raised the capital to fund his idea from various domestic and foreign sources, but not from competing Hamburg and Munich houses though, whereas also the, e.g., Rothschilds (see Chap. 6) were not involved. Delbrück became the first Chairman of the Board, which was later split up into a Board of Commissioners ("Aufsichtsrat") and a Board of Directors ("Direktion"), thus creating the first genuine bank managers. The path setting directors were Georg Siemens and Hermann Wallich.

Whereas Siemens as a member of the well-known German industrial conglomerate family had experience with making business abroad, he was not raised as a banker but Wallach was (Gall, 1995). Siemens did have a nose for innovations though and he was a fast learner. Whereas the bank was meant to support German foreign affairs and to capture business from especially British banks, Siemens soon found out that it also needed to have a domestic base and so he attracted deposits from the public. The bank also went into industrial financing and supported bond and stock floatings. It became known for foreign projects including railways in the USA and the Ottoman Empire. Also, it opened branches in major German cities and abroad. The bank encountered bumpy roads on its way, including project losses and branch closures. Yet, its establishing of separate subsidiaries, notably the Deutsche Überseeische Bank ("German Overseas Bank") for South America and the Deutsch-Asiatische Bank ("German-Asian Bank") appeared to be useful. It was highly intertwined with German diplomacy, private companies, and military. It was dubbed to be the largest of the world, not in terms of assets or equity, but because of its diversity (Feldman, 1995).

Deutsche Bank lost some of its positions in the aftermath of the First World War, following the loss of German territory to especially Poland. The tremendous inflation of the early 1920s (see this chapter) forced an adjustment of its capital, but that was about it (Deutsche Bank, 2022; James, 1995). The Istanbul branch, closed in 1918, reopened in 1923. During the 1920s, the bank took over regional banks, strengthening its local presence. The bank was also involved with concentrations in the German industry, including the merger of the car manufacturers Daimler and Benz. Whereas a global economic crisis hit German banks massively in 1931, the Deutsche Bank did relatively well. However, it entered into a dark period in 1933, when three Jewish board members had to leave the bank, with the bank moreover taking part in the organization of Jewish-owned businesses and resuming the Bank Mendelssohn & Co., while also, e.g., even financing the building of the Auschwitz concentration camp (Wikipedia, 2022c). The bank resumed the management of banks in areas occupied by or allied with the Germans after the beginning of World War II in 1939. Moreover, branches were opened here (Deutsche Bank, 2022).

After the war, Deutsche Bank had to accept that almost all of its board members were suspended by the occupying powers (Deutsche Bank, 2022; Holtfrerich, 1995).

In the Western occupation zones, soon becoming the Bundesrepublik Deutschland (BRD, "Federal Republic of Germany"), a currency reform took place and the Deutschmark (DM) became the accepted currency. The bank had been broken up into 13 parts and in West Berlin it was not present at all. The situation was normalized after 1952, with mergers into three banks, for the north, south, and western areas. In 1957, they formally merged as Deutsche Bank, headquartered in Frankfurt. Whereas the DM had meanwhile become convertible, the bank was readily present abroad again, starting with a Deutsch-Asiatische Bank branch in Hong Kong in 1958. A Deutsche Überseeische Bank branch in the Argentine capital Buenos Aires followed suit.

With the examination of the need for establishments not being required anymore, the bank's inland network started to grow. The retail business started in 1959, with small personal loans to be repaid in installments in two years, soon followed by a medium-loan variant (Büschgen, 1995; Deutsche Bank, 2022). The bank did not just target the mass market and advertised actively on it, but it also supported the German "Wirtschaftswunder" (economic miracle) vividly. Moreover, it resumed its wholesale (large customer) banking and investment banking business, leading the privatization of the car manufacturer Volkswagen, most of the bond emissions by German firms in foreign markets, and a bond loan issued by the World Bank, as well as supporting domestic and foreign convertible bond and stock issues. Herman Josef Abs (1901–1994) was a key person in the transition period. He had joined the daily management already in 1937 (Wikipedia, 2022d). After advising the British occupiers and leading the Kreditanstalt für Wiederaufbau (KfW, "Reconstruction Credit Institute"), he led the bank's management board until 1967. Abs was fluent in several languages, assumed roles in up to 30 Boards of Commissioners, and played a semi-diplomat role for Western Germany, e.g., on the US Marshall Plan for post-war European recovery and the repayment of German foreign debts.

Büschgen (1995) describes the influence of electronic data processing improvements on the management accounting system. Much in line with other large banks globally, around 1970, the account calculation was broadened into revenue and cost oriented client calculation, whereas the corporate planning was enlarged from the short term to the long-term. Also, management changed from branch oriented to market oriented and from client oriented to target group oriented. The division between businesses became less emphasized. The cooperation between the main branches was increased, but the cooperation principle was maintained and the bank failed to align its organization structure across them. Management by objectives and management by delegation went along with management control. The dimensions "region" and "resort" were enlarged by "client group," thus adding a third area to the matrix structure. Holding staff was called for more mutual cooperation, newly appointed holding level directors took on operational issues and the management board focused more on strategic issues. Büschgen calls coordination the largest management task, given the continued enlargement of the activities. In the early 90s, a division structure was implemented.

The bank's equity-to-assets ratio varied around a minimal threshold of 5% in the post-war period, with periods of high growth showing sub-optimal levels (Büschgen,

1995). However, it should be noted that the bank had—common throughout banks all over the world—silent bulk reserves that were undisclosed. The ordinary shares were first traded at the "Deutsche Börse" in Germany, but also at 11 other exchanges worldwide later on, following the increased internationalization of the firm. Moreover, the trade in options and futures contracts started at the time. Whereas institutional investors became more important as shareholders from the mid-1980s onwards and firms also held a part of the shares, the general public gave way at the same time. With defensive mechanisms being common in Continental Europe at the time, it must be noted though that any investor votes were limited to 5% up until 1994. At that time, almost half of the shares could be considered to be possessed by foreigners. Relatively late according to Büschgen, an investor relations department was set up in 1988. Typical for not just the German banking landscape is that the bank itself also held positions in non-financial firms.

Typical for Deutsche Bank is that it started to contest the hegemony of the American banks on the foreign bond market and Eurodollar bond market at the time (Büschgen, 1995). Both of these markets had developed in the course of market inefficiencies and imperfections, by which issuers could arrive at volume advantages, cost advantages, and tax advantages, as well as to circumvent regulations at home or abroad. The difference between the two is that the Eurodollar market is about issuing dollar bonds not inside but outside of the USA jurisdictions, which made it especially attractive to Soviet bloc issuers. Often, Deutsche Bank operated as a leader of a consortium of international banks that supported the issue. However, Büschgen makes it clear that not every issue is successful. He also notes that these types of issues may go along with various financial derivatives constructions including so-called swaps. Whereas the stock market shows many peculiarities of its own, it is for the rest much alike the bond market and so it may not surprise the reader that Deutsche Bank also became much active here.

By the mid-1980s, Alfred Herrhausen had become "Vorstandssprecher": speaker or call it (co-) chairman of Deutsche Bank's management board. Indeed being a brilliant speaker and listener, he was often found in the media (Wikipedia, 2022b). He could be gruffly though, with Büschgen (1995) noting him replying in a shareholder meeting that silent reserves lose their character when one talks about them. He was considered to be a snob and encountered much resistance on his restructuring efforts throughout. He confirmed that Deutsche Bank had power, but that this should be used responsibly. Herrhausen was a visionary person, showing interest in international affairs and advising the West-German Chancellor Helmut Kohl, who worked on the German reunification. Herrhausen himself was able to announce the acquisition of the British investment bank Morgan Grenfell in late 1989. On 30 November 1989, three weeks after the fall of the Berlin Wall, Herrhausen's driver took him to his work. A bomb with a parked bicycle left the driver a little hurt, but Herrhausen himself was killed at 59 years. The assassination was claimed by the terrorist group Rote Armee Fraktion ("RAF"), which was shaking Germany at the time.

The above-mentioned acquisition of Morgan Grenfell, indeed a distinct heir of J.P. Morgan & Co (see the former chapter) was completed in 1990. It marked the start of a new era for Deutsche Bank, albeit that this initially did not show to be that fortunate

(Enrich, 2020). Deutsche Bank was a latecomer on the now sophisticated corporate finance market, despite of its experience in project financing, financial derivatives, as well as mergers and acquisitions. Thus, it was hoped that the acquisition would catapult the bank in the core of Wall Street, but this did not happen, yet. Senior Morgan Grenfell bankers left the bank for better opportunities than working with the "provincial" Germans. As it goes in (top) investment banking, a restless former Merrill Lynch banker, Edson Mitchell, created an exodus at this US investment bank. The "Wizard of Oz" started with around 2,500 of staff in 1995, but the meanwhile Deutsche Morgan Grenfell (DMG) named bank's headcount doubled within 1½ years. Among others, the opportunist Mitchell was also able to attract the competitive young derivatives trader Ashu Jain as well as his rather prudent Merill Lynch buddy Bill Broeksmit.

The business strategy at DMG was fairly simple (Enrich, 2020). Up so far, Deutsche Bank did have a position in lending money and supporting bond issues, but the customers went to competitors for hedging the associated risks and that should end. The derivatives team was led by Broeksmit. Mitchell secured the funding of DMG and resumed the lead over all of the Bank's investment banking. Mitchell also invested in building up a position in the American bond business, hiring staff originating from the US investment bank Goldman Sachs. Securitization of mortgages, the bundling of real estate loans into bonds packages and the subsequent trading of it, was an important business activity. One who made this business big was Boaz Weinstein, to finally make huge losses though. Overall, however, business went up too slowly to become a major player on Wall Street. Therefore, a new target was approached: Banker's Trust, a US investment bank, hit by the Asia Crisis of 1997 and thought to be a weak partner by people such as Jain anyway. Nevertheless, the buyout financing specialist was priced at a staggering amount of about 10 billion dollars in 1999. Interestingly, one of the new customers was the real estate tycoon and later US President Donald Trump, who was generally perceived to be a bad debtor.

Both the names of Morgan Grenfell and Bankers Trust disappeared. A planned merger of Deutsche Bank with its German competitor Dresdner Bank failed in 2000 (Enrich, 2020). Mitchell and his fellows had strongly opposed the deal. They even further extended their influence in the retail banking and private banking parts of the Bank and also acquired positions in the Vorstand. Whereas Broeksmit was retiring, Mitchell was in his top years now. He showed a nearly endless ambition, was an excellent recruiter and managed to steer staff to unintended highs. However, both his pilot and he himself were killed in a plane accident back home in the USA, right before Christmas 2000. The bank had now lost both a creationist and an integrator. The actual leader of the Bank, the Swiss citizen Josef Ackermann, promoted Anshu Jain to most of Mitchell's tasks. Of course, the 9/11 terrorist attacks in New York by Al Quaida had an impact, but less than a month later, on October 3, 2001, the Deutsche bank shares became listed on the New York Stock Exchange (NYSE). Under the ticker *DB* (at home in Germany in use as the abbreviation of the national railways company) it was up to make it in the USA.

Ackermann supported the idea that shareholders were the prime stakeholders of Deutsche Bank. In doing so, sufficing short-term (3-month) profit goals became leading throughout the Bank (Enrich, 2020). Bonusses became tied to accomplished profits, in an unlimited way. Risk management gave way to profit management. Relations with customers were supposed to make 25% and therefore customers had to be said farewell to. Calculations were however not aligned and therefore prices might differ throughout the Bank. The investment bank was thought to be *the* sell and trade profit maker, earning in a couple of hours the same amount of money as the global banking division. They did so in such a wild way that it might harm long-standing relationships. Deutsche Bank even became involved with the financing of bad regimes and terrorists. Moreover, the Bank saw opportunities in Rusland. Informal merger talks with first JPMorgan Chase and later Citibank failed, however. The latter would have brought together the then number 1 (Citibank) and number 2 (Deutsche Bank) in terms of assets.

Meanwhile, the collateralized debt obligation (CDO) market had rapidly developed. CDO's repackaged the underlying assets to make the debts easily tradeable and to mitigate risks. Deutsche Bank participated enthusiastically and successfully, by way of Weinstein's strategies and vehicles. A team led by Greg Lippmann was even betting against the market and made a fortune on it (Lewis, 2010). Recall that the bank had already been active in the securitization of loans. The resulting bond packages could be sliced again into more or less risky parts and exactly the latter was attractive. This kind of propriety trading of course did not go along with a free lunch, as we will see shortly. On top of this, the bank also did risky acquisitions and with one of them, MortgageIT, the bank also became specialized in so-called "Alt-A" (in between prime and subprime) US mortgages. This was in mid-2006, and in mid-2007 it became clear that a financial crisis was looming (Enrich, 2020). Bill Broeksmit was repealed from retirement and helped to stop the bleeding but it was inevitable that this could not be done all of a sudden, if only that the Bank had else to report losses, since the times of making use of silent reserves was over. However, in 2008 losses had to be reported anyway, albeit that they were dampened by profits made on crash bets, as well as insurance payments (Wikipedia, 2022c).

At the time, Josef Ackermann became the first real CEO at Deutsche Bank. He was happy to lead a bank that had been the global number 1 occasionally, almost topping the German economy as a whole. However, at a leverage ratio of 50 (assets) to 1 (equity) and with a derivatives portfolio that was making up almost half of these assets, it was probably not a good idea to buy the faltering Postbank in the German home market but Ackermann persevered on it anyway (Enrich, 2020). Meanwhile, he had become much intertwined with "Germany Inc." as a semi-statesman, alike his predecessors. However, the bank became more and more related to tricky affairs, including, e.g., the Greek debt crisis and the Libor scandal on interest rate fixing. Anyway, in 2012, Anshu Jain (representing the investment bank affairs) and Jürgen Fischen (representing the traditional German affairs) became co-CEO. Bill Broeksmit was refrained by the regulators of leading the risk management affairs and with accusations on malpractices rising, he committed suicide in 2014. The position of the CEOs also became soon untenable and after the British citizen John Croyon had first been co-CEO with Fischen and later sole CEO, Christian Sewing took the lead at the Bank in 2018 (Wikipedia, 2022c).

The German banking landscape differs from elsewhere in that Deutsche Bank was still by far the largest bank as of 2018, followed by the Commerzbank that had swallowed the Dresdner Bank in 2009, whereas also cooperative bank societies (e.g., DZ Bank), "Landesbanken" (state-owned district banks), regional banks and "Bausparkassen" (building societies) played an important role as well (TheBanks.eu, 2020). The German authorities, afraid of bailouts, probed a merger of the two largest German banks, but this initiative failed in 2019 (Enrich, 2020). Meanwhile, Deutsche Bank shares had lost 95% of their 2007 value. The Bank saw itself to be forced to do away with large parts of its derivatives and equity trading business. About 18,000 jobs were to be cut, leveling down the Bank's workforce by some 20%. Val Broeksmit, Bill Broeksmit's stepson who had used his father's files to act as a whistleblower on the Bank's affairs, died for undetermined reasons in 2022 (The New York Times, 2022). At that time, the bank's purpose was: "Deutsche Bank is here to enable economic growth and societal progress through its positive impact" (Deutsche Bank, 2022). Who would not want to cheer with us on this?

9.4 Swiss Banking and Credit Suisse

Switzerland is the 20th largest economy globally, with 8.6 million citizens in the middle of Europe and a per capita income of $76,026 as of 2021 (OECD, 2021). While staying out of the two world wars with its neutrality policy, it has remained economically strong. It has earned itself a well-deserved reputation at the international level with its high-technology products and quality services. Financial services and banking are among the most attractive economic activities of the country with the added value they create. Above all, Switzerland is a significant financial center in the middle of Europe. At first glance, it is surprising that a mountainous country that stood out with its livestock and agriculture in medieval times is such an important financial center today. Swiss banks have attracted many companies, investors, and illegal wealth holders with Private Banking: personalized and highly confidential financial services and products offered to their wealthy customers. Gaining so much trust is an unusual feature for a small country that has never been an imperialist power. Undoubtedly, it will be necessary to look for the backgrounds of this issue among the faded leaves of history.

In the twelfth century, Switzerland was a community of people living under the rule of the Roman and Habsburg empires and engaged in farming. With the opening of the Gotthard Pass that connects the country to Italy in the early 1200s, its strategic importance suddenly increased. Three Swiss cantons, Uri, Schwyz, and Unterwalden, lived autonomously under Habsburg rule. In 1291, cantonal representatives took the first steps in the independence movement. They signed a declaration against the Habsburg dynasty and committed to unification. The Swiss defeated a Habsburg army in the Battle of Morgarten on November 15, 1315 (Hanhart, 1847), securing the existence of the Swiss Confederation in the Holy Roman Empire this way. Little is known about the inner workings of the historic Swiss state. The country remains a great enigma. Although it has produced some of the strongest and most respected warriors for centuries, used as mercenaries, it has steadfastly maintained its neutrality over the centuries.

The first Swiss banks developed at a time when Italy became Europe's largest industrial and commercial power, at a time when Italian city-states gained dominance in trade and commerce and created a political and economic security environment for banks, enabling their growth and development in response to the needs of trade (De Roover, 1946). The Swiss were skillful businessmen and bankers after the disappearance of the Knights Templar, a European order of Christian warriors. Their engineering skills, being secretive and independent, and their religious tolerance could imply that they benefited from the Templar's historical heritage (Walker, 2017). Swiss Banking, applying universal banking practices, can offer all banking services at any authorized bank, with the exception of insurance, which requires a special license, and bank accounts have become attractive to depositors as they combine low levels of risk with very high levels of confidentiality, often referred to as the Swiss banking secrecy.

Bauer and Blackman (1998) hold that four historical events drive the origin of Swiss Banking:

1. Italian commercial banking practices introduced by the "Basel Council" (see Chap. 2).
2. The accumulation of capital due to the fighting skills of Swiss mercenaries.
3. The Protestant Reformation, differing from the Lutheran strand in Germany.
4. The banking philosophy of the nineteenth-century French bank Crédit Mobilier.

While merchant banking was developing in Italy, banking transactions in Switzerland started in Geneva with money-changing transactions. Its geographical position as an important center for medieval trade between southern and northern Europe was unique. It was both a warehouse and an important banking and exchange center. Some credit was provided to traders by goldsmiths. The Medici were represented in Geneva. Credit, primarily commercial, was organized on a "market to fair" basis, and interest was charged on loans, despite the Church's prohibition on usury. However, things changed when Louis XI passed decrees in 1465 that forbade the people of France from attending the fairs of Geneva and instead required them to use the newly created fairs in Lyon. The Reformation and the upheavals that followed caused Geneva to become a center of religious activity rather than a center of commerce.

With an influx of refugees from religious strife, another Swiss city, Basel, was starting to come to the fore, and as Geneva filled not only with Europe's best merchants but also with potential soldiers to serve as a means of defense (Bauer & Blackman, 1998). The Basel money trading system consisted of a relatively complex relationship between the mint managers, the mayor, and the money changers. While the mint director was under the direct control of the mayor, the money changers had a special relationship of trust with the coin lord (bishop). They had exclusive rights to exchange money and gold and made loans and advances to reputable businessmen. The economic development of Basel was due to it being a meeting place to resolve conflicts within Christianity. The Council of Basel (1431–1449) met in Basel to defend the faith and reform the Church. The prosperity was fuelled by the establishment of an imperial mint at Basel (Christianson, 2000).

The major Italian banks of the Medici, the Albertini, and the Gianfigliazzi were invited to the city of Basel to provide credit facilities. Thus, the money changers in Basel became acquainted with the techniques of Italian banking (Wills, 2015). The Italian bankers invited to the Assembly, especially the Medici, were not subject to the strict religious rules of the money changers and made substantial profits by lending to the clergy and the merchants. Undoubtedly, the free market economic environment prevailing in this region also facilitated their activities (Bauer et al., 1998). In 1504, the Basel city council took the first steps toward forming a modern bank in the form of a city exchange after establishing a city clearinghouse. The Bank of Basel was a city-owned commercial bank that handled the necessary banking business specific to the requirements of business activity. It accepted deposits and lent from these deposits mainly for trading purposes, offered interest on deposits, and received interest on loans. Undoubtedly, Basel owed its fame to the Italian bankers (Bauer & Blackman, 1998).

However, another factor in the origin of Swiss Banking, as important as the Italian bankers, was the Swiss mercenaries. There was also a kind of militia system in the cantons, in which the soldiers had to serve and were trained and equipped for it. More importantly, during the religious wars between Charles V (Spain) and Francis I (France), both sides eagerly sought out Swiss mercenaries (Rees, 1994). Switzerland was not a large country, but with the military system it developed, it not only protected its borders but also accumulated capital in the country. As a result, funds that could be invested began to accumulate, and Switzerland became a nation of relatively wealthy classes and abundant funds (Casparis, 1982). The Swiss learned to act as intermediaries to direct the available funds in the direction of needs and gave loans to Germany and many other countries and their enterprises, especially in France.

Moreover, an equally important factor was the Reformation period beginning in the early 1500s. It resulted in the creation of a branch of Christianity called Protestantism. In Switzerland, Calvinism was adopted as a specific strand. According to Bauer and Blackman (1998), first, by the breaking of the religious and social structure of the Roman Catholic dogma standing between man and God, it emerged that capitalism was not just a by-product but also a necessity for man's successful growth and development in his newfound freedom. Banks developed as partners or even equals of industrial enterprise and entrepreneurship, by transferring surplus funds against interest to enterprises with the permission of the new doctrine. Second was the sanctification of the work ethic. According to the new understanding, no institution like the Church should stand in the way of industry and wealth should be accepted. When lent at interest, albeit at only moderate levels, money will generate additional wealth.

One of the most famous philosophers of the eighteenth century was Henri de Saint-Simon. Saint Simon's ideas advocating that society should be organized according to the requirements of the industrial age and industry influenced the origins of Swiss Banking. Saint-Simonians focus is on the social aspect of banking, considering that the banking and monetary system is essential in establishing trust in society. The Saint-Simonians develop a particular argument for banking credit and money creation, arguing that banking credit alone has an instrumental position that not only increases wealth but also wealth formation. Emile and Isaac Pereire, creators of the French bank Crédit Mobilier in 1852, became prominent followers of these ideas (Eckalbar, 1979). The Crédit Mobilier practice would become a model to follow for Swiss bankers. The French writer and philosopher Voltaire praised the talent of the Swiss Bankers in 1794, saying, "if you see a Swiss banker jumping out of the window, do not hesitate to follow him, because there will certainly be a profit in it" (The Economist, 12 June 1997).

In 1713, the Geneva Grand Council passed a privacy law prohibiting banks from disclosing information to anyone other than the account holder or customer. Ultimately, since the end of the nineteenth century, the practice of secrecy became deeply rooted in Swiss banking. It was based on tradition rather than on specific laws. Banking secrecy was a matter of civil law, not criminal law. Its violation led to civil, not criminal, prosecution. Sanctions were only applied if a claim was made by the injured party and as compensation. The importance of banking secrecy began to increase when the wealthy were increasingly taxed. Swiss bankers could attract foreign capital to Switzerland this way. At the end of the First World War, they could withdraw the money of people fleeing financial crises. To hide cash by, but also used to withdraw cash from German Jews, Swiss banking secrecy was first enacted by the Banking Act of 1934. This criminal law act, combined with a stable Swiss frank and international neutrality, helped to attract deposits. In the 1940s, numbered bank accounts began to be used, creating an enduring principle of bank secrecy that is still recognized as a major aspect of private banking (Guex, 2000).

As of 2018, Swiss banks held 25% of all global cross-border assets, jointly holding US$6.5 trillion. The country ranked number two behind the United States and was on par with Singapore in the Financial Secrecy Index (2022). While the banking system keeps the money of people who want to hide their wealth, the biggest drawback of it is the threat that people with massive deposits suddenly withdraw their accounts due to distrust of the bank. Losing a few big depositors makes it then difficult for them to survive, unlike other commercial banks with thousands of depositors.

Although Swiss bankers know about the vulnerability of their reputation they built up over years, decades, and even centuries, a series of scandals have affected their credibility. The first major scandal broke out after the Second World War around Banque de Crédit International. The bank turned out to be serving Meyer Lansky, the accountant of the US mafia. In 1973, the American authorities started drafting an agreement with the Swiss government on mutual assistance in the fight against crime. The Luxembourgian Banque de Crédit et de Commerce International (BCCI) was suspected of laundering drug money and many bankers were arrested. During the investigation, police discovered that another Geneva-based bank—Banque de Commerce et de Places (BCP)—was also involved in criminal activities. In 1998, the biggest scandal in Swiss banking came to the fore. A Swiss commission estimated that the Swiss National Bank held $440 million ($8 billion in 2020 currency) Nazi gold. As money laundering scandals increased in Switzerland, the country's government began enacting laws to combat financial fraud. However, in 2009, another banking scandal erupted, still continuing presently. Bradley Charles Birkenfeld had put Switzerland's largest bank, UBS, in a difficult position by handing over information about more than 4,000 customers to US authorities (International Wealth, 2023).

Credit Suisse, the second biggest Swiss bank, was frequently involved in controversies and investigations. From a historical perspective, this is not much surprising. Whereas UBS was basically an amalgamation of various regional savings and commercial banks that were founded in the prosperous early 1860s (UBS, 2023), Credit Suisse was founded in Zurich by the business leader Alfred Escher as an investment bank, the Schweizerische Kreditanstalt (SKA) in 1856 (Credit Froelicher, 2023; Suisse, 2023). The bank has laid an emphasis on its entrepreneurial spirit since. Right from the start, it financed railroad constructions and other industrial ventures, fitting well with Escher's railroad interests. The bank loaded up much risk and had to reorganize often. Specific for Zurich was a liberal environment fuelling its rise as a financial center, much beyond which Escher played an important role in politics. Shifting from railroads to electricity supply, the SKA evolved into a reputed institute in a neutral, safe, and stable country, making domestic and foreign commercial loans to a growing network. It overcame the World Wars and captured a decent part of the Swiss capital inflow as a private banker. Under the leadership of Rainer Gut (1939), from the 70s onwards, the bank expanded, turning its eyes toward Wall Street and even taking a majority stake in the US investment bank First National Boston in 1990.

In 1977, the relationship of SKA executives with wealthy Italian tax evaders came to the fore. In 1995, Credit Suisse and some other Swiss banks were revealed to be keeping the money of the Philippine dictator Ferdinand Marcos. Now called Credit Suisse, the bank came across the dotcom crisis and the Global Financial Crisis of the 00s with relatively minor scratches. However, in 2009, Credit Suisse was fined for violating US sanctions against Iran and other countries. On May 19, 2014, Credit Suisse pleaded guilty to a conspiracy charge to assist US taxpayers in filing false income tax returns and other documents with the Internal Revenue Service (IRS). This resulted in the forfeiture of $2.6 billion in fines. Later, some dirty relations with the Republic of Mozambique were revealed, and the bank had to pay a fine of more than 300 million USD for these transactions in 2021 (Firstpost, 2023).

With the bankruptcy of Silicon Valley Bank and two small banks in the USA in March 2023, premiums to be paid by vulnerable banks increased in Europe, and the eyes were turned to Credit Suisse. On March 15, 2023, the share price dropped nearly 25 percent after Saudi National Bank, its largest investor, said it could not provide more financial assistance. The market price of the bank's unsecured bonds set for maturity in 2027 dropped to a low of 33 percent of their par value on that day, down from being valued at 90 percent shortly before. On March 19, 2023, fellow townsman UBS announced that it would acquire Credit Suisse for US$3.25 billion in an all-stock deal (Daga, 2023). The crisis was resolved now, but costly damage could hamper Switzerland's reputation as a safe investment destination.

9.5 Banking Secrets of the Champions

When looking at products and services that have been developed by the "National Champions" featuring above and their often at equal foot pioneering peers, it strikes that the list is quite long. First of all, there were the consumer credit products that added to the banking profile of investment banking and private banking a new consumer banking business. Selling to the people with mass communication techniques entered the scene and short-term consumer loans readily became long-term relationships. Of course, client payment systems provided a base, with bank accounts being a general product for almost all nowadays. With neighborhood ATM's replacing personal teller services in bank offices and paper cheques giving way to automated transfer systems, the banks were well able to control the costs of the high volume low margin business that had been added to their portfolio. Complex matrix structures were tried out and bank presidents became CEOs. Going for more business in terms of subprime mortgages did not show to be a viable way and made central banks nervous. The banks were well aware that becoming larger might not make them richer in terms of return on equity or rather shareholder return. In order to work on this ideal anyway, they pursued high margin business.

High margin business is either relatively risky or relatively scarce or even better both. Going for it provoked a drive with banks toward making a market in complicated financial products. All kinds of issues regarding seller and buyer gambling behavior, bank-client agency relationships, and bank control systems may go along with this. However, evermore stockpiling financial derivatives such as (mixes of) options, futures, and swaps, as well as complicated semi-insurance schemes with securitization packages, CDOs, CDSs, and way more, made it increasingly difficult for central banks to control the expanding monetary system as such properly. Moreover, falling leverage ratios enabled banks to expand their regular business and pursue corporate finance activities going far beyond traditional asset financing on well-established corporate financial ratio norms. Deutsche Bank was a relative latecomer, but a few well placed acquisitions and the combination of asset financing with derivatives trading made it soon a big player in a business where also minor players such as ABN AMRO tried their good luck. Obviously, this play did not just bring about winners and especially many small parties were forced to give way.

However, the losers did not give up that easily. One final way to become big was via takeovers. While not neglecting what happened during the expansionary post World War II period with foremost Citicorp's merger of equals with Traveler's Group, the then world's biggest merger ever, and less the various mergers that Deutsche Bank undertook in the same period, it is fair to say that the track record of ABN AMRO truly exemplifies the rise and fall of a "National Champion" with an ultimately failing aggressive acquisition policy. The background of the failure to use the hardly postcolonial NHM of Harry Boessenkool as the actual engine for international expansion can probably be traced back to a series of intra-Netherlands bank mergers in just a quarter of a century that led to strategy clashes, insufficient integration, and sticky cost levels. With share prices acting as ultimate judges in mergers and increasing shareholder activism, there was also not much for central banks to turn the tides.

When the bold merger wave in the banking sector gained global momentum, there was little left to make the Global Financial Crisis of 2008/09 to happen. Its aftershocks showed that it was no sinecure for central banks to retain control over the monetary system. At the time, it looks as if their "stress tests" and the like may indeed be of help, but do not cure the system as a whole. Not just giant general banks in developed countries have shown to be vulnerable to crises, but also the more specialized Swiss banks are, such as evidenced by the collapse of Credit Suisse in 2023. By way of tradition, these banks were highly trusted with private lending and investment, as underpinned by the Swiss banking secret. This also made Swiss banks a proper place to channel funds through. All of this has come at stake recently.

9.6 Conclusion

One can make a case that financial liberalization and deregulation have been the true engines of the rise (and fall) of the "National Champions". Liberalization refers to inter-country relaxation of rules and deregulation is its domestic counterpart, with especially liberalization provoking the growth of banks because of a cross-border scale effect. For example, as we will see in the next chapter, the ending of a century of (semi-) fixed exchange rates contributed to the growth of the global banking sector, given the extra demand for financial derivatives that it brought about from the '70s onwards. Also, the lowering and even abolishing of taxes on cross-country financial transactions, not just in Europe but also worldwide, encouraged the international trade of financial products and services. The growth dreams of many banks by way of establishing new branches or rather via making acquisitions, got new wings as cross-border growth became more feasible with the relaxation of regulation on, e.g., getting banking licenses.

Interestingly, there was quite a variety of strategies chosen by the "National Champions" whose faring we described in this chapter. Whereas the Canadian BMO and the Hong Kong/British HSBC took a modest approach by picking up major trends but leaving much risky business to others, ABN AMRO and Deutsche Bank were rather surfing on the waves of opportunities even trying to pick out the highest ones. ABN AMRO was likely the most vulnerable one of them, with a relatively shrinking home market along with a furthering decolonization and related decline of The Netherlands as a financial center. However, also Deutsche Bank, operating from a country that was re-emerging from a devastating war and a late reunification, was not in a good position to become a winner. Also, the unique Swiss banking model has lost momentum. Indeed, the US Citibank could have been the global winner, weathering a failed merger with Travellers Group, but it has to accept JPMorgan Chase as the largest US-based bank way ahead of it now. Its fascinating and unique story is told in the next chapter.

References

ABN AMRO. (2022a). *ABN AMRO, 1990–Present*. Historisch Archief (Historical Archive). https://assets.ctfassets.net/1u811bvgvthc/7GC2AGOzJYmenTcKNU86cr/e3c770aa1b5cafe994d6ceee9c5a5058/ABN_AMRO_geschiedenis_1990_present_UK.pdf

ABN AMRO. (2022b). *Algemene Bank Nederland, (ABN Bank) 1964–1991*. Historisch Archief (Historical Archive). https://assets.ctfassets.net/1u811bvgvthc/1hjvZaSt2uaMHzRm8snSip/db7f5179859927fe7a2461b49a83570b/ABN_AMRO_geschiedenis_ABN_UK__1_.pdf

ABN AMRO. (2022c). *Amsterdam-Rotterdam Bank (AMRO Bank*), 1964–1991. Historisch Archief (Historical Archive). https://assets.ctfassets.net/1u811bvgvthc/31yU6chjUm94qzQzdgteZA/6fae7a84d847627ea5cf8501775b6dad/ABN_AMRO_geschiedenis_AMRO_UK.pdf

ABN AMRO. (2022d). *Amsterdamsche Bank, 1871–1964*. Historisch Archief (Historical Archive). https://assets.ctfassets.net/1u811bvgvthc/5VrMu5q2bjpDZ7J4HrD7SQ/1c43ae28c962547570b00a6246b9c50a/Amsterdamse_bank_uk.pdf

ABN AMRO. (2022e). *Mees Pierson, 1720-Present*. Historisch Archief (Historical Archive). https://assets.ctfassets.net/1u811bvgvthc/5KmgqaFtv0IP5ulSrwV3Ob/747869e75e7d4f131862c2c0222c89c1/Mees_Pierson_history.pdf

ABN AMRO. (2022f). *Nederlandsche Handelmaatschappij 1824–1964 (Dutch Trade Company 1824–1964)*. Historisch Archief (Historical Archive). https://assets.ctfassets.net/1u811bvgvthc/4Q2bm2oxXNo3OcXeZr055o/a892b6def92a49cc3689d5f0162244ec/NHM__UK_.pdf

ABN AMRO. (2022g). *Our History*. https://www.abnamro.com/en/about-abn-amro/product/our-history

ABN AMRO. (2022h). *Rotterdamsche Bank, 1863–1964*. Historisch Archief (Historical Archive). https://assets.ctfassets.net/1u811bvgvthc/FtNRhVnYvvVW4LUmJRe2w/8bd90ca70b004245c5b47767c9d2dd0d/Rotterdamsche_bank__UK_.pdf

ABN AMRO. (2022i). *Shareholder Structure*. https://www.abnamro.com/en/about-abn-amro/product/shareholder-structure

ABN AMRO. (2022j). *Twentsche Bank, 1861–1964*. Historisch Archief (Historical Archive). https://assets.ctfassets.net/1u811bvgvthc/4qSUWB32uiOUVwLUN8HbeM/463288b4b407207ef46b60c98841ad69/Twentsche_bank_uk.pdf

ADV Ratings. (2022). *World's top banks by market capitalization*. https://www.advratings.com/banking/worlds-top-banks-by-market-cap

BanksDaily.com. (2008). *The world's 20 largest banks by total assets (2007) | The world's 20 largest banks by total eQquity (2007)*. https://banksdaily.com/topbanks/World/2007.html

Bao, H. (2017). Evaluation of pre and post demerger-merger performance: Using ABN AMRO bank as an example. *International Journal of Economics and Finance, 9*(2), 196–204. https://doi.org/10.5539/ijef.v9n2p196

Bauer, H., & Blackman, W. J. (1998). *Swiss banking: An analytical history*. Palgrave Macmillan.

Büschgen, H. E. (1995). Die Deutsche Bank von 1957 bis zur Gegenwart: Aufstieg zum Internationalen Finanzdienstleistungskonzern (Deutsche Bank from 1957 to the present: Ascent to become an international financial services group). In L. Gall, G. D. Feldman, H. James, C. L. Holtfrerich, & H. E. Büschgen (Eds.), *Die Deutsche Bank 1870–1995* (pp. 579–877). C.H. Beck.

Calomiris, C. W., & Haber, S. H. (2014). *Fragile by design: The political origins of banking crises and scarce credit*. Princeton University Press.

Casparis, J. (1982). The Swiss mercenary system: Labor emigration from the semi-periphery. *Review (Fernand Braudel Center), 5*(4), 593–642.

Christianson, G. (2000). Annates and reform at the council of basel. In T. M. Izbicki & C. M. Bellitto (Eds.), *Reform and renewal in the middle ages and the renaissance* (pp. 193–209). Brill Publishing.

Credit Suisse. (2023). *Who we are. Credit Suisse. Entrepreneurial from the start*. https://www.credit-suisse.com/about-us/en/our-company/who-we-are.html

Daga, A. (2023). *What happened at Credit Suisse and how did it reach crisis point?* Reuters, March 18. https://www.reuters.com/business/finance/credit-suisse-how-did-it-get-crisis-point-2023-03-16/

De Roover, R. (1946). The Medici bank financial and commercial operations. *The Journal of Economic History, 6*(2), 153–172.

Deutsche Bank. (n.d.). *Purpose.* https://www.db.com/who-we-are/

Deutsche Bank. (2022). *Deutsche Bank 1870–2020.* https://www.db.com/who-we-are/history/DB-CHRONIK-DEUTSCHE-BANK-1870-2020.pdf

Eckalbar, J. C. (1979). The Saint-Simonians in industry and economic development. *American Journal of Economics and Sociology, 38*(1), 83–96.

Enrich, D. (2020). *Dark towers: Deutsche Bank, Donald Trump, and an epic trail of destruction.* HarperCollins.

Feldman, L. (1995). Die Deutsche Bank vom Ersten Weltkrieg bis zur Weltwitschaftskrise 1914–1933 (Deutsche Bank from World War I to the great depression 1914–1933). In L. Gall, G. D. Feldman, H. James, G. E. Holtfrerich, & H. E. Büschgen (Eds.), *Die Deutsche Bank 1870–1995* (pp. 137–314). C.H. Beck.

Firstpost. (2023, March 17). *From Cocaine money laundering to fake names: The long list of scandals at Credit Suisse.* FP Explainers. https://www.firstpost.com/explainers/from-cocaine-money-laundering-to-fake-names-the-long-list-of-scandals-at-credit-suisse-12306982.html

Froelicher, L. (2023). *Credit Suisse began with a succesful bet, and ended with one that failed. The histtory of an extraordinary bnak in extraordinary times.* Neue Züricher Zeitung. https://www.nzz.ch/english/the-turbulent-history-of-credit-suisse ld.1732364

Gall, L. (1995). Die Deutsche Bank von ihrer Gründung bis zum Ersten Weltkrieg 1870–1914 (Deutsche Bank from its foundation to the First World War 1870–1914). In L. Gall, G. D. Feldman, H. James, C. L. Holtfrerich, & H. E. Büschgen (Eds.), *Die Deutsche Bank 1870–1995* (pp. 1–135). C.H. Beck.

Guex, S. (2000). The origins of the Swiss banking secrecy law and its repercussions for Swiss federal policy. *Business History Review, 74*(2), 237–266. https://doi.org/10.2307/3116693

Hanhart, R. (1847). *Erzählungen aus der Schweizer Geschichte: nach den Chroniken. 2* (Stories from Swiss History, after the Chronicles, Part 2). Schweighauser.

Holtfrerich, C. L. (1995). Die Deutsche Bank vom Zweiten Weltkrieg über die Besatzungsherrschaft zur Rekonstruktion 1945–1957 (Deutsche Bank from World War II to occupation to reconstruction 1945–1957). In L. Gall, G. D. Feldman, H. James, C. L. Holtfrerich, & H. E. Büschgen (Eds.), *Die Deutsche Bank 1870–1995* (pp. 409–578). C.H. Beck.

International Wealth. (2023, March 31). *Banking scandals in Switzerland: From past to present.* https://internationalwealth.info/en/offshore-banks-en/banking-scandals-in-switzerland-from-past-to-present/

James, H. (1995). Die Deutsche Bank und die Diktatur 1933–1945 (Deutsche Bank and the Dictatorship 1933–1945). In L. Gall, G. D. Feldman, H. James, C. L. Holtfrerich, & H. E. Büschgen (Eds.), *Die Deutsche Bank 1870–1995* (pp. 315–408). C.H. Beck.

Janssen, R. (2022). *Gokkers en Graaiders (Gamblers and Grabbers).* Follow the Money.

King, H. H. (1988). *The history of the Hongkong and Shanghai Banking Corporation, Volume II: The Hongkong Bank in the period of imperialism and war, 1895–1918.* Cambridge University Press.

King, H. H. (1991). *The history of the Hongkong and Shanghai Banking Corporation, Volume IV: The Hongkong Bank in the period of development and nationalism, 1941–1984.* Cambridge University Press.

Lewis, M. (2010). *The big short: Inside the Doomsday machine.* W.W. Norton & Company.

Michielsen, S., & Sephiha,M. (2009). *Bankroet: Hoe Fortis al zijn Krediet Verspeelde* (Bankruptcy: How Fortis Lost all its Credit). Lannoo.

OECD. (2021). *Switzerland—OECD Data.* data.oecd.org. https://data.oecd.org/switzerland.htm#profile-economy

Rappaport, A. (1986). *Creating shareholder value: The new standard for business performance*. Free Press.
Rees, V. (1994). Hungary's philosopher king Matthias Corvinus 1458–90. *History Today, 44*(3), 18–24.
Roberts, R., & Kynaston, D. (2015). *The Lion wakes: A modern history of HSBC*. Profile Books Ltd.
S&P Global Market Intelligence. (2022). *The world's largest banks*. https://www.spglobal.com/marketintelligence/en/news-insights/latest-news-headlines/the-world-s-100-largest-banks-2022-69651785
Smit, J. (2008). *De Prooi: Blinde Trots Breekt ABN AMRO (The Prey: Blind pride breaks ABN AMRO)*. Prometheus.
Statista. (2022). *The largest banks in the Netherlands in 2021, by total assets*. https://www.statista.com/statistics/762148/leading-banks-in-the-netherlands-by-total-assets/
Stewart, G. B. (1991). *The quest for value: The EVA management guide*. HarperBusiness.
The New York Times. (2022, May 15). *Val Broeksmit, 46, Who Blew the Whistle on Deutsche Bank, dies*. https://www.nytimes.com/2022/05/13/us/val-broeksmit-dead.html
TheBanks.eu. (2020). *List of top banks in 2018*. https://thebanks.eu/articles/top-100-banks-in-Germany-2018
The Economist. (1997, 12 June). *Fritz Leutwiler*. https://www.economist.com/obituary/1997/06/12/fritz-leutwiler
Twentsche Bank. (1961). *Bankspiegel 1861–1961*. De Twentsche Bank NV.
UBS. (2023). *Roots of UBS*. https://www.ubs.com/global/en/our-firm/our-history/roots-of-ubs.html
de Vries, J., Vroom, W., & de Graaf, T. (1999). *Wereldwijd Bankieren ABN AMRO 1824–1999 (Worldwide banking ABN AMRO 1822–1999)*. ABN AMRO Bank NV.
Walker, J. (2017). Sources for the Templar myth. In K. Borchardt, K. Döring, P. Josserand, & H. Nicholson (Eds.), *The templars and their sources* (pp. 360–371). Routledge.
Wikipedia Contributors. (2022a). *ABN AMRO*. Wikipedia. https://en.wikipedia.org/wiki/ABN_AMRO
Wikipedia Contributors. (2022b). *Alfred Herrhausen*. Wikipedia. https://de.wikipedia.org/wiki/Alfred_Herrhausen
Wikipedia Contributors. (2022c). *Deutsche Bank*. Wikipedia. https://en.wikipedia.org/wiki/Deutsche_Bank
Wikipedia Contributors. (2022d). *Herman Josef Abs*. Wikipedia. https://de.wikipedia.org/wiki/Hermann_Josef_Abs
Wikipedia Contributors (2022e). *ING Groep (ING Group)*. Wikipedia. https://nl.wikipedia.org/wiki/ING_Groep
Wikipedia Contributors. (2022f). *Peter Jan Kalff*. Wikipedia. https://nl.wikipedia.org/wiki/Peter_Jan_Kalff
Wikipedia Contributors. (2022g). *Rabobank*. Wikipedia. https://en.wikipedia.org/wiki/Rabobank
Wikipedia Contributors. (2022h). *Rijkman Groenink*. Wikipedia https://nl.wikipedia.org/wiki/Rijkman_Groenink
Wills, M. (2015). *The Origins of Secret Swiss Bank Accounts*. [online] JSTOR Daily. Available at: https://daily.jstor.org/origins-secret-swiss-bank-accounts/. [Accessed 8 Apr, 2021].

Chapter 10
Citibank: A National Champion Going Beyond Limits (Twentieth and Early Twenty-First Centuries)

10.1 Introduction

The seventies were a good period for the US and Citibank. Its leader, Walter Wriston, was at the top of his career. Of all the big bank leaders, he was the most articulate and a forerunner in the struggle against controls, especially government controls and Fed controls. The Bank was strong and Wriston was a giant, and he liked to show that. Limits and boundaries were there to fight. In 1973, he wrote the article "Freedom and Controls" (Wriston, 1973). It was triggered by a price and wage control introduced by President Nixon, but also inspired by the Credit Control Act of 1969.

Wriston writes: *There are those among us who wish to do away with the free enterprise system and force a new kind of society upon America. If this sounds extreme, perhaps we should speculate for a moment what kind of world we would have if the laws of the United States of America gave the President vast new power over the life of our credit and stock markets. Suppose the President, acting through some government agency, could require every borrower to obtain a license before he could have access to the market. Imagine that before any lender could lend, he must also get a license from an all-powerful federal agency. This power to license both borrowers and lenders would extend to the amounts involved, and, of course, would carry with it the authority absolutely to deny credit to brokers or bakers, to individuals or corporations. Imagine a law like this and then let yourself speculate upon the profound effect it would have on our marketplace and upon the entire fabric of our society. When you have thought about this for a moment, give it even more consideration, for such a law is now on the statute books of our country. It is called the Credit Control Act which was passed in 1969.*

Full implementation of this act, of course, would take us well down the road to economic serfdom. Fortunately, we currently have a President who believes in free enterprise and a market economy. The fact that our Congress passed such a monstrosity, however, should jolt us free of any day-dreams. What I find most appalling about this so-called Credit Control Act is that it was in fact a rider tacked

M. B. Karan et al., *A History of Banks*, Contributions to Economics,
https://doi.org/10.1007/978-3-031-62297-7_10

on to another more comprehensive bill that passed the Senate by a voice vote. No senator even stood up to have his name recorded on a basic reordering of American priorities. It is, in fact, ironic that credit market controls should even be considered seriously after the credit crunch of 1969 when interest rate ceilings not only hurt borrowers but produced pointless distortions in credit flows. If banks are discouraged from making loans, borrowers who are able will turn to the open market. Here the large, strong borrowers will fill their needs, but the small medium-sized companies are not likely to find the impersonal market as accommodating.

Wriston spent a good deal of his time as leader of Citibank in fighting the bank licensing and other such limits. He was looked upon and followed by his colleagues. In 2007, the then leader of Citibank, Charles Prince, had to explain why Citibank had continued to invest in leveraged buy-outs while there were plenty of warnings already of future crisis and he did not know better than saying: "As long as the music is playing, you've got to get up and dance" (New York Times, 2007). How is this possible? Maybe we can grasp it by reading the story of Citibank.

10.2 The First Century

Little known to many, the 1776-born United States of America (USA) already de facto had a central bank as of 1781 (see Chap. 7). Although operating nationwide, even its formal successor as of 1791, known as the First National Bank of the United States, merely served as a central bank in managing deposits and loans for the US Treasury and the public. It had its head office in Philadelphia, but also a branch in New York. When its charter was not renewed in 1811, next to already existing state banks, the City Bank of New York was erected in 1812. The publicly owned bank was involved with financing the US Treasury during the 1812 War with the British and served the cross-Atlantic merchant trade (Citigroup, 2012). It must be noted that New York was behind other US cities at the time and the operations were small. However, the client base readily became larger under the directorship of the business tycoon Moses Taylor. Also, a close alliance with America's first trust company, Farmer's Loan and Trust, was established. City Bank supported the Northerners in the American Civil War (1861–1865). In 1865, City Bank became a national bank and the name changed to National City Bank of New York (but we stick to Citibank here).

James Stilman became the Bank's director in 1891 (Citigroup, 2012; Huertas, 1985). He felt that successful banks had to go beyond receiving and loaning of money. Like his predecessors, he also had other activities, including managing an investment trust. With Citibank, he followed J.P. Morgan and other bankers who were developing stock and bond markets at the time. Citibank had a broad network of correspondence relationships, which helped when setting up a foreign exchange department, handling cash transfers, drafts (bills of exchange), and letters of credit. Stilman supported J.P. Morgan, one of Citibank's investors, in sustaining the Panic of 1907, a bank crisis described in Chap. 7. Citibank occupied a whole block on

Wall Street from late 1908 onwards. While remaining the Bank's largest shareholder, Stilman was succeeded by the self-made man Frank Vanderlip. He had been involved with financing the Spanish-American War of 1899, which led to the acquisition of i.a. the Philippines by the USA. With pressure from big clients such as Standard Oil, the Bank targeted South American markets with branches in countries such as Argentina, Brazil, and foremost nearby Cuba. Moreover, it acquired in 1918 the New York based International Banking Corporation (IBC), which had already been branching out of its state home base to, e.g., London.

The IBC was the first American bank with an Asian presence, namely in Shanghai (Citigroup, 2012). Actually, the US bank was a latecomer under the colonial banks that were already around here. Interestingly, two Deutsche Bank (see Chap. 9) trained IBC traders in New York were making much foreign exchange business, related to the complicated currency environment in China. The IBC rapidly developed branches in China and beyond. The collapse of the Chinese Empire in 1911 and the following unrest could be sustained. At home, Vanderlip supported the Federal Reserve System (Fed) starting in 1913 (see Chap. 7), which helped to stabilize US banking. A newly established investment bank affiliate brought World War I financing bonds to the masses and the Bank even had an advertising department as of 1919. In the same year, following severe losses in Russia, Vanderlip had to resign in favor of Stilman's son James, who in turn had to give up after facing the loss of about 80% of the Bank's capital in a Cuban sugar bubble crisis in 1920. The Bank set up a modest branch network in the war-inflicted Continental Europe. A drive into retail banking began after an acquisition and compound interest was paid to account holders. Most of the Far East Asian part of IBC was integrated in 1927. A panic in Japan was met with, but as President Charles Mitchell warned of in January 1929, a vast crisis was in the making at home.

10.3 Citibank and the Crisis of 1929

The Crisis of 1929 had a severe influence on the economy and banking in the US. One can really speak of "before" and "after." During this time, Charles Mitchell was first President and then Chairman of Citibank, and his career is closely connected with the crisis.

We follow Galbraith (1975) in a short sketch of the crisis. The twenties were a good time in the US. There was some extra wealth created because of war expenditures. Production and employment were high, wages were not going up much, and productivity increases were higher than wage increases. The income of the wealthy people was increasing. Wealthy and rich people saw opportunities to get richer by investing in securities. The prices of securities began to rise. The NYT average of the prices of the twenty-five most regular industrial stocks (the "Times Industrial") was equal to 106 by the end of May 1924. In December 1925, it was up to 181. People believed that this increase would last for some time and could not wait to participate. Moreover, companies started to use interest in securities to issue more than necessary in case of new activities, mergers, and centralization moves.

The most important vehicle to generate new securities was the investment trust. A trust company could diversify and reduce the risks for the participants and it brought the possibility to invest and participate in the boom to a broader public. The total assets of the trust companies in 1924 were estimated as less than $15 million (Committee on Banking and Currency, 1934), while it was more than $8 billion in the autumn of 1929. The way the funds of the trusts were invested was far from transparent. This was excused by referring to the sensitivity of the information, but it gave also much freedom. As long as the results were good, the participants tended to believe that the choices made by the management of the trusts were good. Nobody checked whether and how the funds available were invested. Diversification was not the main goal for the new trusts; it was rather a possibility to generate new ways to participate in the boom. It was quite possible that the volume of securities issued was much higher than the volume of the corporate assets. Part of the assets of trust A could be put in the common stock of trust B and part of the assets of trust B in the common stock of trust C, and so on, while the trusts involved could be managed by the same organization. Such a situation was created by Goldman Sachs, with the Goldman Sachs Trading Corporation, the Shenandoah Corporation, and the Blue Ridge Corporation. It created a lot of possibilities to manipulate. To realize more leverage for the common stock shares, it was attractive to issue also preferred stock and bonds. This extra leverage was attractive for people who believed in a continuing boom or just accepted the extra risk. The New York Stock Exchange facilitated the exchange of stock in trusts only from 1929 onwards and required a certain openness with respect to the securities held by the trusts, but there were other possibilities. A trust was generally established and managed by a bank or another already existing financial intermediary. That contributed to the confidence. Many of the sponsors were investment banking firms, making it easy to sell the securities to the trust and its participants.

In 1927 and 1928, the boom took speed. By the end of 1928, the Times Industrial stood at 331 and in January of 1929, there was another gain of 30 points. The Fed worried about the speculation and sent a warning to the banks to be careful with loans for speculation. The market started to get nervous and on March 25 and 26 the market crashed and the Times Industrial lost 25 points. Many of the brokers had sold "on margin" and needed more money. Mitchell was one of the directors of the New York Federal Reserve Bank but did not agree with the prudence of the Fed. He believed in the boom, expressed his confidence in the developments, and announced that Citibank was going to make $25 million extra available for the lack of margin resulting from the drop in value of the securities. His reputation as a successful investment banker and his position as chairman of Citibank made his move very reassuring and effective. The boom resumed. From May 31 until August 31, the Times Industrial rose from 339 to 449 points.

After the summer, the concerns about the boom increased. The volume of broker loans, to cover the margins, increased and increased, indicating the amount of speculation. In the first years of the twenties, it was less than $1.5 billion. In June 1928, it was $4 billion and in August 1929, it had increased to $7 billion. But most of the "experts" and, of course, the bankers remained positive. They found that too much attention was given to brokers' loans. But there were more signs. The real economy, as measured by the Federal Reserve Index of industrial production, was also shrinking a bit. In September the stock exchange was hesitating and fluctuating, but in the end of October the stock exchange really crashed. On November 13, the Times Industrial finally reached a provisional low of 224 points. Later, the decrease continued and the level was 58 on July 8, 1932.

The consequences were severe. Banks failed, people had severe financial problems and demand for luxurious goods fell. It contributed to the Depression of the thirties. Of course, it also had severe political repercussions. The Democrat Franklin Delano Roosevelt won the elections in 1932 and from 1933 on there was a Democratic majority in the Senate. The Senate Banking and Currency Committee hired Ferdinand Pecora to lead the investigations into the bankers' practices of the past years, the "Pecora Hearings" (Prins, 2014). The most important bankers then were Thomas Lamont of J.P. Morgan, Charles Mitchell of Citibank, and Albert Wiggin of Chase. Wiggin and Mitchell had to resign because of the investigations. Regarding Wiggin, the clearest case was that he appeared to have speculated in Chase stock. He short-sold shares in October of 29 and borrowed the money from Chase to buy shares in December. Mitchell had also traded in stock of his own bank, but his intentions were more constructive. In the fall of 1929, Mitchell had organized a merger with the Corn Exchange Bank. Corn Exchange stockholders would each get 4/5th of a share of Citibank or $360 in cash. At the moment of the deal, the Citibank stock stood at $500. So, it was to expect that none of the Corn Exchange shareholders would go for the cash. But then came the crash. The Citibank stock fell to around $425. Mitchell feared that all Corn Exchange shareholders would choose the cash now. Mitchell started to buy Citibank stock to support the price. To be able to buy more, he borrowed $12 million from J.P. Morgan. The support was insufficient. Then the Citibank management pushed the shareholders not to accept the deal. So far, it was more or less OK for Citibank, but Mitchell was left with a large debt to J.P. Morgan. Furthermore, his income over 1929 was high, much higher than 1 million, so he had to pay much tax. To circumvent this, he sold the stock to his wife: 18,300 shares for the then market price of $212 per share. A loss of more than $2 million removed the tax liability. Later he bought the shares back from his wife, again for $212 per share. Mitchell freely admitted to the Pecora Committee that he sold it to his wife for tax purposes. It was to explain his actions, but Mitchell was arrested because of it. Maybe President Roosevelt wanted also to show that he was able to bridle the bankers. Anyway, it resulted in the resign of Mitchell. In June, Michell was acquitted. Instead, the government entered a civil claim for the tax liability. Eventually Mitchell had to pay $1.1 million. The Senate committee revealed also a number of more structural malpractices: the use of preferred lists of how to distribute stock, depositors of a bank who were tempted to buy or keep stocks that were based on selective information about the stocks, and the misbehavior of the trust companies. It resulted in new legislation. Enter the Glass-Steagall Act.

10.4 The Glass-Steagall Act and Its Impact

The Glass-Steagall legislation was initiated by Carter Glass, former Secretary of the Treasury under Wilson and a Democratic member of the Senate for Virginia, and Henry Bascom Steagall, Democratic representative for Alabama and chairman of the Committee on Banking and Currency. The legislation changed the rules in the following way (Greider, 1987):

1. To protect depositors from bank failures, a deposit insurance was introduced, organized by the FDIC, the Federal Deposit Insurance Corporation. The banks contributed to the funds required to realize the guarantee. The limit of the guarantee was first $5000. Later it increased gradually to $100,000 in 1980. After the crisis of 2008, it was increased to $250,000. During the introduction of this insurance, there was already a fierce discussion on whether it would not lead to temptations for banks to take more risks. President Roosevelt was not in favor of it, but it was nevertheless decided by the Congress.
2. The separation of investment banking and commercial banking. Before 1929, the commercial banks with also an investment bank had the tendency to stimulate their depositors to buy stock that was difficult to sell otherwise. Chase and City Bank had already sold their investment bank before the act was signed. J.P. Morgan continued also as a commercial bank, while three of the partners established the investment bank Morgan Stanley.
3. Banks were prohibited to pay interest on checking accounts (part of Regulation Q). It was hoped that this subsidy by the depositors would lead to more relaxed practices with respect to loans: lower interest rates and more tolerance in case of payment problems. There were also limits on the interest that was allowed on savings deposits and time deposits (Beebe, 1981). It was to prevent competition in getting depositors, which could lead to instability of reserves.
4. To prevent too much speculation, the Fed was empowered to set limits on the collateral for credit in the stock market. One of the problems of the 1929 crash was the low margins that were practiced. The Fed could bridle that now. The margin limit was put on 50%. The tool (part of Regulation T) was applied until 1974, now and then. From 1974 onwards, the margin limit was fixed at 50% (Fortune, 2000).
5. The Fed was also reorganized. The Board of Governors ("Washington") was given authority over the Reserve Banks. Of course, with an exception for the New York Reserve Bank. Because of the proximity of Wall Street, this Reserve Bank has a special role in the execution of the open market operations of the Fed. The focus of the open market operations was on Treasury bonds.
6. To create more independence from politics, the Secretary of the Treasury and the Comptroller of the Currency were removed from the Board of Governors. And the control of the monetary policy was formalized in a new body, the Federal Open Market Committee, with an important representation of the Reserve Banks.

The banking system was already complex in 1863, viz. the dual banking system, with state-chartered banks and national banks and the rules varying over the states.

States could also issue rules regarding the national banks there, rules that could only partly be preempted by the Comptroller of the Currency. The establishment of the Fed led to more centralization and control, but it also added to the complexity. It was an extra regulating body, next to the Office of the Comptroller of the Currency (OCC). Complicating was also that part of the state-chartered banks became also member of the Fed. The new Glass-Steagall legislation made the system even more complex. All Fed members (national banks and Fed member state banks) were now also regulated by the Federal Deposit Insurance system with an own supervision body, the Federal Deposit Insurance Corporation (FDIC). The non-member state banks could also decide to participate in the Federal Deposit Insurance and were supervised then mainly by the FDIC. And then there were the savings & loans institutes, thrifts, state chartered and directed to the acceptance of savings and the provision of mortgages. They had an own regulating body (the Federal Home Loan Bank Board, FHLBB) and an own deposit insurance fund, organized by the Federal Savings and Loan Insurance Corporation (FSLIC).

Neither federally chartered banks nor state-chartered banks were allowed to branch over state borders. There could also be rules with respect to branching within the state. This made it difficult for big banks to acquire sufficient deposits that were needed as backings for loans. Banks tried to circumvent these rules by forming holding companies with banks (and also other types of firms) in different states. This made the regulations even more complex, with holding companies holding different types of banks. The Fed was losing control because of that and pressed for better legislation. Also, people in the country had the Depression in mind and feared that being too lax in this respect would lead to too much space and power for the big banks and threaten the development of small towns and communities (Mahon, 2013a). The variety in rules, the different regulating bodies, and the different political factions made American banking a landscape full of challenges and opportunities. Legislation was politically sensitive.

In 1956, after many years of Federal pressure and a long legislation process, the Bank Holding Company Act was signed into law. The law defined a bank holding company as any company that held a stake of 25% or more of the shares of two or more banks. A bank was defined as any institution that takes deposits and makes loans. Bank holding companies had to register with the Fed and to accept supervision. Planned expansions had to be requested at the Fed. The Fed gave special attention to interstate expansion. Practice was complicated however. The law did not prohibit expansion, but assumed that the Fed would judge whether the expansion was good for the community and for sound banking. The Fed was also required to ask the opinions of the Office of the Comptroller and of the respective state regulators. The definition of a bank holding company was also not very clear. What about a company with stakes in only one bank and in other companies? Another complication was that a bank was defined as an institute that took deposits and made loans, but what about an institute that only made loans, but not took deposits? That is why investment banks could easier engage in interstate branching than commercial banks. Finally, the law required all bank holding companies to divest themselves from ownership in any firms that were involved in non-bank activities but did not prescribe precise deadlines. So, the law resulted in much ambiguity and confusion and it certainly did not finish the tension between the banks, especially the big ones, the regulating bodies, and the political factions.

Citibank was a national bank in New York City and we sketch therefore the rules with respect to merging and branching in New York City and New York State. Only from 1898 on, branch banking was permitted in New York City. From 1919 onwards, it was also allowed in smaller cities. In 1934, New York State was partitioned in 9 banking districts (Federal Reserve Bank of New York, 1960). Branching within a district was allowed if the branch was not too close to the head office of another bank. The boundary of two of the banking districts ran through New York City. There it was allowed to branch over the district border. The extension of branching was also necessary because of the big holes in proper banking facilities resulting from the Great Depression.

The rule of 1934, with the 9 districts was also intended to restrict the growth of the big New York City (NYC) banks. It reflected the widely held fear that these banks would otherwise dominate the entire commercial banking system of New York State. Actually, the rule was indeed effective in that sense. The amount of deposits with the big NYC banks as a fraction of the total amount of deposits with all commercial banks was drastically declining, from 25.4% in 1941 to 13.9% in 1959. This led to more pressure on the NYC banks to open up the neighboring districts, especially Westchester and Nassau (Long Island), and, of course, more counter pressure of the local banks to keep the NYC "giants" out. In 1960, the state enacted the "Omnibus Banking Law" to settle this. It made it possible for NYC banks to open branches in Westchester and Nassau or merge with banks in these districts, and also the other way around. All such actions remained subject to approval by the State bank supervisory authorities. These authorities had to "prevent statewide control of a few giant institutions and foster a healthy and non-destructive competition among all types of banking organizations within natural economic and trade areas." The criteria were more or less comparable with those the Fed Board of Governors had to apply in judging a merger. They also had to look at the welfare of the communities involved and whether the bank holding company would not grow beyond limits consistent with "*adequate and sound banking, the public interest and the preservation of competition.*" Nice, but not easy to apply of course.

The development of bank holding companies and the Bank Holding Company Act was the most important domestic development between 1934 and 1960. For the rest, domestic banking was not very entrepreneurial by nature. Bankers operated according to the 3-6-3 rule: borrow at 3%, lend at 6%, and go to the golf course at 3 PM. Yet, this changed from the second half of the fifties onwards. Citibank was the forerunner in this respect. Walter Wriston, CEO of Citibank in 1967–1984, was very important for that development. It is the topic of the next section. We follow mainly the biography by Zweig (1995)

10.5 Wriston Wrestling with Regulations

Walter Wriston worked for Citibank from 1946 onwards, first in the auditing and credit department, but in 1950, he got actively involved in shipping finance and transportation finance in general. The Greek tycoon Aristotle Onassis was his first important client. Together with Onassis, he developed a loan with a charter as collateral instead of some physical property. In organizing such loans, Citibank worked together with a life insurance company, to have the longer-term liabilities taken care of by this company. Later, this type of loans was widely applied in transportation. In 1955, he joined the foreign division (see the next section) and he was appointed executive vice-president in 1960. In these first years of Wriston at Citibank, the chairman of the bank was James Stillman Rockefeller, a grandson of James Stillman. During the tenure of Rockefeller, the bank merged with First National Bank and was called thereafter First National City Bank of New York. This was shortened later to First National City Bank. For easiness, we keep talking about Citibank. When Stillman Rockefeller resigned in 1967, George Moore was appointed chairman and Wriston became President and CEO. When Moore left the company in 1970, Wriston became Chairman and CEO. Wriston's leadership was characterized by two features: in the first place the employment of high-quality personnel, with giving them sufficient freedom to operate and be entrepreneurial and in the second place the fight against government regulations in general and government interference with banking. The first characteristic resulted often in difficulties to control the company, the control got easily lagging behind business. Later, we come back to this point. Here, the topic is the fight against government interference.

Wriston was a convinced republican and liberal. Unsurprising to the reader of the opening vignette, he was very articulate in that. Being a son of Henry Wriston, an important Republican thinker (professor, dean, and later member of a think tank) with good contacts in Washington may have contributed to that. He was able to express himself clear and sharp and liked to use that to explore and stretch the freedom Citibank had.

10.5.1 The One-Bank-Holding Company Act and Amendments

An important goal was to extend geographically and to diversify. The former Comptroller of the Currency, James Saxon, was very much in favor of liberalization and had already arranged in 1963 that national banks were allowed to be active in leasing, data processing services, could operate travel agencies, act as agent in credit related insurance and provide tax preparation services. In 1966 though, under political pressure, the courts restricted these measures and Saxon had to step down. Now the banks had to fall back on the Bank Holding Company Act of 1956 and look sharper at the ambiguity and imprecision in this act to create more possibilities. The Congress was also aware of the shortcomings in the act and had already started discussions on how to amend it. Wright Patman was chairman of the House Committee on Banking and Currency and he was very alert on the power of big banks. In between, the big banks were forming so-called one-bank holding companies, to use the opening in the 1956 act (see above). Citibank formed such a holding company in 1968. Other banks followed suit. By the end of 1968, more than fifty banks had established bank holding companies. Some of them used the construction to include companies very far away of banking, e.g., TV broadcasting and furniture manufacturing. That was not the intention of Wriston. Citibank used the new structure right away to buy The Chubb Corporation, a major insurance company. In April 1969, the shareholders of both companies approved the merger. However, the antitrust department of the justice department blocked it and Wriston had to postpone this big step of including insurance.

In December 1970, the amendments were signed into law by President Nixon. The distinction between one-bank and more-bank holdings was removed and the 25% rule was replaced by a more precise description of "control." The amendments enabled the inclusion of certain non-banking companies that were closely related to banking. The Federal Board was important here. It had to judge whether its performance could reasonably be expected to produce "benefits to the public that outweigh possible adverse effects." The Board delineated a number of fields that could be seen as "closely related to banking." These included trust company activities, financial advice, leasing, data processing, and bookkeeping services, acting as underwriter of credit life insurance and credit accident and health insurance. Wriston decided that the right way to proceed was just to try. He ordered his people to buy all kinds of small "congenerics" (merchant banking, leasing, consumer finance, mortgage banking, ...) not too close to New York and not more than one in one area; the New York area was too sensitive for big banks. The message was: "Clerks follow the rules. You guys are hired to break the rules." As soon as the amendments were enacted, Citibank flooded the Fed with proposals for acquisitions (Zweig, 1995). By mid-1973, the Fed had settled on thirteen deals, ruled out seven and was still chewing over several others. The "guys" realized that the criteria were not easy to apply. In between, they had also bought a large consulting firm: Cresap, Mc Cormick & Paget. The Fed Chairman (Burns) was positive first, but the Fed Board did not accept. Citibank had to sell it within 10(!) years again. To be able to sell mortgages in a wider environment, it bought Advance Mortgage, in Detroit, in 1969. In 1973, the Fed rejected the acquisition but gave the opportunity to reapply. Citibank held on to it until 1979 and then there were other possibilities. Only with respect to expanding into insurance, the Fed was very prompt and strict.

Another step was to expand in New York State. Right after the enactment of the Omnibus Banking Bill of 1960, Citibank was active already in getting access to Nassau and Westchester. First it tried to acquire the National Bank of Westchester. This was denied by the Comptroller of the Currency, because it would change competition too drastically. Citibank did open various new branches in Nassau and Westchester though. Now, Wriston reconsidered the possibilities. The first move was to found the First National City Bank of Suffolk. In February of 1971, an application was sent to the Comptroller to charter the new bank. There was much opposition, of course, from within the Suffolk banking community. Yet, in June, Governor Nelson Rockefeller approved legislation permitting (all) New York banks to charter a new subsidiary in each of the nine banking districts, and allowing each subsidiary to open a limited number of branches. This legislation gave the existing banks the advantage to be able to acquire the best branches. By the end of 1971, Citibank was bidding aggressively for tiny banks in the outskirts of large upstate cities. The acquisitions were not very profitable, since competition was sabotaged by the local banks. In 1977, Citibank even considered the possibility to close some of the upstate branches again.

Wriston accepted the division between commercial banking and investment banking. However, when the securities industry started to lobby acts against bank underwriting of revenue bonds, he opposed and Citibank put merchant banking functions that were performed already (loan syndicating, private placements, risk management, foreign exchange trading, government bond underwriting, and advice with respect to corporate finance and mergers and acquisitions) together in a merchant group. However, he kept the group within the bank and did not let it grow into a standalone entity. Wriston was not interested in brokerage and underwriting of corporate securities.

10.5.2 Regulation Q and Reserve Requirements

The other field of rules that bothered Citibank was Regulation Q. Regulation Q placed limits on the interest banks could pay on deposits. In fact, it even prohibited completely the possibility to pay interest on demand deposits. The legal maximum interest rate on savings deposits was 5.25% and the maximum rate on time deposits was 5.75%–7.75%, depending on the maturity (Beebe, 1981). For thrifts, the limits were put 0.25% higher, to protect the flow of money into housing (Sherman, 2009). These limits were the legal maxima. The regulatory agencies were allowed and expected to impose lower levels (Ruebling, 1970). The Fed had to do that for the member banks. In 1933, it started to set the limits for all savings deposits and all tie deposits at 3%. Later, it distinguished between the various maturities of time deposits. The intention of the measure was to prevent runs for higher interest and create more stability in bank funding in that way.

Around 1960, the market interest started to grow above the Fed limits. Private depositors were not so sharp right away in looking for other possibilities to stall their superfluous liquidity; that was a major reason why Citibank liked to expand geographically and stay close to as many as possible private customers; the deposits were important for the funding of the bank. Corporations reacted sharper though, for instance by shifting their liquidity to short-term government obligations. So, there was always pressure from the big banks to increase the limits, but it was insufficient to keep the corporations. Then, Wriston and his colleague John Exter developed the

NCD, the Negotiable Certificate of Deposit, a large-denomination certificate (more than $100,000 generally) for corporations and foreign banks. To make the NCD's liquid, a secondary market for it was developed as well. The product grew fast. In 1967, the outstanding NCD's amounted already to $18.5 billion, a substantial part of the total amount of deposits at federal banks that was about $100 billion. The Fed put also limits on the interest on NCDs, depending on their maturity, but the most common maturity was rather long (3–6 months) and limits were rather high therefore (6% in 1968), while the liquidity of such NCDs, due to the secondary market, was comfortable. There were yet periods that the limits were lower than the market interest. During such periods the number of NCD deposits was sharply decreasing (Friedman, 1975); in 1969 about 50%.

In the course of the seventies, the market interest rates were further growing, also due to the increased inflation. Even the private depositor started to look for alternatives. The Savings and Loan banks tried to keep them by giving extra services, but that was not sufficient. So, they tried to work around the interest limits, especially the prohibition of interest on demand deposits. For instance, by guaranteeing, if necessary, an automatic transfer from a savings discount, it was possible to give better checking possibilities while keeping demand deposits low. Another possibility was to take, if necessary, a buffer period of some days before paying the check. This led to the so-called NOW (Negotiable Order of Withdrawal) account.

A new competitor in the acquisition of deposits was the Money Market Fund (MMF), developed in 1971/1972 by Bruce R. Bent and Henry B.R. Brown (coincidentally a former employee of Citibank). It is an investment in shares of a fund that invests in short-term securities, mainly government securities, commercial paper, and (ironically) NCDs. They were not at all subject to Regulation Q limits.

Deposits were important for funding the banks. Yet, the possibilities provided depended also on the Fed's reserve requirements. The more deposits and the lower the reserve requirements, the more freedom for the banks to provide loans. These requirements were to realize more security in bank lending and also to get more (monetary) control of the lending practices in general (Feynman, 1993). The reserve requirements varied also over time. In 1966, the reserve requirements for demand deposits were about 15% (for banks in reserve cities more, for country banks less), for time deposits about 5%.

Of course, the commercial banks were fighting these rules and they looked upon Wriston and Citibank for leadership. In Wriston's opinion, bank failures had nothing to do with reserve requirements and were rather a result of bad management. With respect to the monetary aspect of reserve requirements, he was convinced that high reserve requirements were not going to save any nation from inflation, "only a free market can equitably and efficiently allocate credit and capital" (Wriston, 1974). Smaller, state-chartered banks could decide to quit Fed membership and make use of easier state regulations. Indeed, this happened. Between 1959 and 1972, member bank transaction deposits as fraction of total transaction deposits decreased from 84 to 72%. The big banks, however, depended too much on the facilities of the Fed with respect to clearing and settlement. Their way to deal with restrictions was to find alternative ways of funding, and ways of borrowing that were not subject to reserve restrictions of the Fed.

An attractive instrument for Citibank seemed to be floating rate notes at variable interest tied to a benchmark rate. In 1974, it issued the first one, a $250 million offering of 15-year notes in $1000 units. To evade the Fed restrictions, it was issued by the Citicorp holding. The demand was overwhelming. Instead of $250 million, $650 million was issued. Yet, there was a lot of opposition, from the thrifts and from Congress. Also, the SEC (the Securities and Exchange Commission) had many critical questions. It was allowed after a lot of deliberations, but the interest rate had to stay within the Fed limits.

In the second half of the 70s, the market interest rose further, also due to the increasing inflation, and contributed to the pressure against Regulation Q. It finally led to the Depository Institutions Deregulation and Monetary Decontrol Act (DIDMCA), signed by President Carter in 1980. Regulation Q was going to be phased out in six years and the reserve requirements were lowered and simplified.

10.6 Intermezzo: Bretton Woods

The topic of the next section is the development of the LDC loans (Less Developed Countries). The international economic context was determined by, first, the introduction of the so-called Bretton Woods agreements and later the abolishment of these agreements. In July 1944, the bloodiest battles of the Second World War were taking place on the lands of France and Italy. It had been only a month since the Allied forces landed in Normandy, and the end of the war was almost a year away. Meanwhile, an exciting conference started in Bretton Woods, New Hampshire, USA. The meeting with 730 delegates from 44 countries was held in Mount Washington, the oldest and largest hotel in the region (Fig. 10.1). This hotel was known as a favorite retreat of poets and celebrities. Although it was the middle of the often-blustery summer, the weather was excellent, and the green hills of the White Mountain national forest from the hotel window exhibited an impressive view. The meeting was initially planned to be held in Washington DC. Yet, on request by the Soviet Union, the conference was taken here; the Russians wanted another place to limit the American influence. The participants were probably happy with this decision, as Washington DC's hot and humid weather would be difficult to endure during these months.

The conference's agenda was on what would be the world's monetary system after the Second World War. It was no longer possible to continue the gold system, that the country's banks issued money based on gold. The old system had not worked correctly, mainly because of the uncontrolled money supply caused by the wars and nationalism. There was significant inflation in the German economy after the First World War, and the US economy went into a great depression with the crisis of 1929. The death bells of the gold standard had begun to ring. When being in financial trouble, Britain started to abandon this system from 1931 onwards. While the USA left the gold system in 1933, most European countries would end it in 1936.

Fig. 10.1 Mount Washington Hotel, Bretton Woods. https://upload.wikimedia.org/wikipedia/commons/0/07/Mt._Washington_Hotel.jpg

In addition, after the war, all major countries except the USA were devastated and exhausted, and they had no gold reserves. A new world order had to be established.

The two most important participants were Harry Dexter White, the US delegate, Vice President of the Treasury, and John Maynard Keynes, who attended the meeting on behalf of England (Fig. 10.2). These two gentlemen would become the founding fathers of the new money order, the Bretton Woods system. Known for advocating interventionist monetary and fiscal policies in tackling recessions, Keynes had an excellent reputation as the twentieth century most influential economist. In response to the liberal economy's argument that the markets will stabilize in the long run he is known to have said, "in the long run, we will all be dead." White had supported the interventions of Roosevelt but had to represent now also the power of the US. All participants agreed that the international monetary system had to prevent competitive devaluations and ensure exchange rate stability, to promote international trade and economic growth (Kollen Ghizoni, 2013). Keynes and White agreed that this required the control of capital flows. Uncontrolled capital flows would disrupt normal international trade relations and become an independent and destructive force that could destabilize the market. Therefore, an international organization would be needed to meet the large or long-term capital outflow. Although White and Keynes agreed on creating a supranational institution such as the International Monetary Fund (IMF), they could not agree on its independence.

What the world needed, according to Keynes, was an independent institution that should counterbalance American economic power. Such an institution should have to be a kind of world central bank, capable of generating funds and regulating the flow of credit, using a new international currency, the *Bancor*. White disagreed; he asked the dollar to be the international reserve currency and suggested a gold-bound dollar system to run the world economy. Thus, the balanced growth of international trade could be promoted while maintaining the central role of the US dollar in global

Fig. 10.2 Harry Dexter White (left) and J.M. Keynes, Bretton Woods Meeting (1944). https://commons.wikimedia.org/wiki/File:WhiteandKeynes.jpg

finance. By the time the meeting was concluded at the end of the month, the power of the US had won and the proposal advocated by Harry Dexter White had been accepted. Accordingly, the US dollar would be tied to gold, and the currencies of all the countries would be linked to the dollar.

The IMF was established, not as a world central bank, but as an institution that promotes economic growth through international trade and financial stability. It was also decided at the conference to establish the World Bank. The bank's primary duty was to lend to the war devastated and exhausted countries. The Soviet Union, which attended the meeting, did not sign this agreement and did not join the IMF. Much later, it would join the IMF in 1992 as the Russian Federation, shortly after the Soviet Union collapsed (Mikesell, 1994). White regretted that and frequently stressed the importance of the participation of the Soviet Union.

When the IMF became operational in 1946, President Harry S. Truman appointed Harry Dexter White as the first US Executive Director. He was suspected then already by the FBI for having given people of the Soviet Union access to confidential information about the US. When this started to be investigated publicly in March 1947, he resigned. He has always denied the accusations and defended himself convincingly in August 1948, but died a couple of days later of heart failure.

The Bretton Woods system started a new era by creating a cooperative international exchange rate regime. Under the leadership of the USA, the world was shifting to a completely different order. While the dollar was getting its strength from the rapidly growing US economy, it made the world accept the US hegemony and its dollar as an international reserve. The USA would maintain this power uninterruptedly until the 1970s. Central banks and commercial banks, the playmakers of the traditional gold standard, now turned their eyes to the USA. Whereas it took up until 1958 to have the system, that priced gold at $35 per ounce and allowed currencies to fluctuate between −1% and +1% of their dollar parities, up and running, it would essentially be over in 1971, with a decision made by the then US President, Richard Nixon. He announced the ending of the dollar's convertibility into gold on Sunday, August 15. The US balance-of-payments deficits led to foreign held dollars exceeding the US gold stock, implying that the US could not fulfill its obligation to redeem the dollars for gold at the official price. The action of Nixon was very sudden and unilateral (the "Nixon shock," the IMF did not know it before and the other countries involved were "not amused"), but the decision itself was not unexpected and was widely discussed already (see also Chap. 11). Most bankers were in favor of keeping Bretton Woods. Walter Wriston was one of the few preferring a system with free exchange rates. Probably inspired by Milton Friedman, but maybe also because of the possibilities he saw for Citibank, with all her international subsidiaries, to become active in the foreign exchange market. One tried first to replace the system with a new one with pegged exchange rates and a somewhat higher price of gold for the dollar ($38 per ounce), the "Smithsonian agreement," but from 1973 onwards, all currencies were floating.

10.7 LDC Loans: Bankers as Warriors for America

Citibank was the most international of the big New York banks (see above). In 1930, it had 83 overseas offices and affiliates. That reduced till 63 in 1940 and 61 in 1955 (Zweig, 1995). During the Second World War the only branch that remained open in Europe was London. In the mid-1950s, there was also a branch in Paris. A large part of the business was to facilitate transfer payments for the Marshall plan. The activity in Asia was mainly concentrated in regions where the US was militarily present, Japan and the Philippines (Starr, 2002). There were also some branches in old English colonies, like Hong Kong and Singapore. The banking activities were restricted to foreign exchange and trade financing. They did not lend more than what was deposited locally. The Middle East market was just discovered as becoming important. In 1955, branches were opened in Egypt, Lebanon, and Saudi Arabia. Most of the Citibank activity was in Latin America. The lack of strong and dependable local banks made Citibank the best settled bank in Latin America. It had branches in all countries and most major cities. Cuba (11 branches) and Brazil (7 branches) were most important. Argentina had been important but was complicated now because of the socialistic Peron regime. In 1955, Wriston was appointed to the overseas activities of Citibank, first as head of the European division and from 1959 on, as head of the whole overseas division. It was time for a fast expansion in Europe, the Middle East, and Asia. The world economy was growing and the dollar was the stable, global currency. The banks served to grow the power of the US. The international activities of the big banks were aligned with the geo-political interests of the US. Many regimes in Latin America were instable and American economic activity and banks were important in consolidating the influence of the US. The fear of communism was well cultivated by Senator McCarthy. US oriented economic development was important to stop the influence of the Soviet Union in Europe, Asia, and Africa and the banks were important pivots here. And then there was the Middle East with its oil. American economic presence was required there as well. Politicians were aware of the importance of banks for developing geo-political ties. President Kennedy, e.g., initiated the Alliance for Progress, in 1961, to strengthen the ties between the US and Latin America and to prevent further communist influence. The 1959 revolution in nearby Cuba was threatening. The alliance was signed at an inter-American conference in Uruguay, August 1961. The big banks were asked to participate in the development of various economic activities. Wriston and his colleagues were not very positive about the initiative: it emphasized government-to-government grants and did little or nothing to create a free market environment. After the murder of Kennedy in November 1963, the initiative withered and it died after about 10 years. Yet, the principle that the cooperation of bankers is important to realize the geo-political goals was still alive afterward. There was a mutual interest. Also, Latin America was undoubtedly a region that had to be "Americanized."

Since Bretton Woods, it was clear that world trade was accounted for in dollars and soon it was also possible to deposit dollars abroad. Citibank was one of the first banks in London to give the possibility to deposit dollars. London was the first Eurodollar market. Later, Singapore and Hong Kong developed also such markets. A nice feature was that the Eurodollar markets were first largely free of American bank regulation. The Eurodollar market was the main facility to create big loans, generally syndicated. One of the first was for Shell Oil in 1960. Citibank put $100 million dollars together, with also contributions from two other American banks having a branch in London. London was the place to be for international finance, much to the chagrin of Wriston.

Governments of less developed countries (LDCs) and government related organizations were also interested in such loans. It was a time of economic growth and the LDCs wanted to participate. The bankers were however aware of the risks of sovereign loans (loans to governments and government backed organizations). Bunnell, Citibank's chief credit officer, retired in 1966 and warned at his farewell dinner against government loans. It was difficult to live to that principle. The opportunities were too attractive and the possibility to sell comparable loans in the US was diminishing, e.g., as big corporations issued their own commercial paper. In 1967, for instance, Citibank led a consortium of eleven American banks in providing a standby credit of $100 million dollar for Argentina.

The Eurodollar market got a boost with the first oil crisis, in 1973/74. The price of oil increased and the oil exporting countries were flooded with dollars. A major part of it was deposited at the foreign branches of the big American banks (Curry, 1997). The oil importing countries had to pay in dollars. They paid it from loans syndicated by the big American banks. It was called recycling of petrodollars. The Latin American debt increased between 1970 and 1978 from $29 billion to $159 billion. About 80% of it was sovereign debt. There were trials to organize this recycling more directly, by way of direct Arab investments in Brazil for instance, but that route did not work. It was much easier for the Arabs to use the American banks. Direct loans from Arab countries to LDC countries were also complicated because of Muslim rules prohibiting the payment of interest. The IMF and the World Bank tried to do something as well, but it all remained small. Wriston and his colleagues had anyway not much confidence in what the World Bank did: too socialistic and too bureaucratic. They accepted and even enjoyed that the recycling had to be done by the banks. The profits were secured against fluctuations of the market interest by coupling the interest to the LIBOR, a London-based variable interest rate floor. The routing chosen was stimulated by the government. Treasury Secretary Shultz for instance lifted the checks on foreign lending to facilitate the recycling. Burns, the then Fed Chairman expressed his worries and spoke about "bad loans" instead of about "recycling," but he was not taken very seriously.

To organize the "recycling" activities properly, Citibank established CIBL, Citicorp International Bank Limited. Wriston was hesitating here first. He accepted the Glass-Steagall separation of investment banking and commercial banking and saw the potential conflicts of interest. Citibank performed already a number of activities that fell loosely under investment banking, like government bond underwriting and advice with respect to mergers and acquisitions, but underwriting of corporate debt and equity was prohibited. By putting CIBL right under Citicorp and settling it in London, it was possible to cross this line. The CIBL bankers remained focused however on activities that were practiced already before, especially the organization of syndicated loans. In this, they were one of the market leaders. They organized the deals and then transferred parts of the loan to Citibank and the rest to other banks. There was generally more interest than could be awarded. Hundreds of banks were involved. For these banks, it was easy to participate and because the loans were organized by the big banks, participation looked risk-free. Most of the big syndications were for governments or for state-owned agencies. The principle was that the country officers, knowing the local situation, originated the loans and then CIBL was going to organize and sell them, but CIBL was already involved right from the start, and leading, with the support of the top of Citibank. In 1974, CIBL organized 40 deals, in total for $4.5 billion dollars, in 1975 this was 66 deals for more than $6.6 billion dollars.

In 1979, there was another oil crisis, due to the revolution in Iran and the diminished oil exports due to that. It led to new price increases. The Latin American countries kept heavily borrowing. Between 1979 and 1982, the Latin American debt increased from $159 billion to $327 billion. The debt to the eight biggest American money center banks increased from $36 billion to $55 billion. In addition to this, the value of the dollar compared to most other currencies increased by more than 10%. The LIBOR was extremely high these first years of the 1980s, more than 15%, partly due to the high-interest rates in the US. The debt-service ratios, the ratio of debt service payments and export earnings, of the Latin American countries increased. For Brazil, this ratio was even about 60%. Matters got worse because local money started to flow out of the LDCs. The political instability in these countries was also important of course: nationalization of banks in Mexico and the Falkland war in the case of Argentina. In August 1982, the Mexican finance minister indicated that his nation could no longer meet interest payments. By the end of 1982, 40 nations were in arrears with their interest payments and only a year later, 27 nations, including the four major Latin American countries, Mexico, Brazil, Venezuela, and Argentina were negotiating to restructure the existing loans. It was a rough year for international banking. Wriston tried to calm down the turmoil with an article in the New York Times (Wriston, 1982), stating that "countries don't go bankrupt." It is one of his most well-known statements, much criticized also and not very effective this time.

It would last more than a decade before the LDC countries and the banks involved reached stability again. Bank advisory committees were established to represent the banks in bilateral negotiations with individual debtor countries. These negotiations lasted until the end of the 1980s and were supported by creditor governments and international institutions (e.g., the IMF). The US banking officials did not immediately require the banks to set aside reserves on the loans involved. Such a policy was not feasible and might have caused panic since the LDC portfolio held by the money center banks was more than double their aggregate capital and reserves. According to Seidman, a former head of the FDIC, seven or eight of the ten largest US banks might have been deemed insolvent at the time, a finding that would have led to an economic and political crisis (Seidman, 1993). The big banks gradually built up their loan-loss reserves, but only from 1987 onwards, they explicitly recognized a loss. Citibank was the first, establishing loss provisions of $3.3 billion, more than 30% of its total LDC exposure. John Reed had succeeded Walter Wriston then already. The other banks followed suit. During the years 1987–1989, the money-center banks had in average negative returns. During the earlier years of the 1980s, the returns were already diminishing.

In 1989, Nicholas Brady, then-Treasury Secretary in the Bush administration, initiated a plan to settle the problems, recognizing that the debtor countries could not fully service their debts and seeking permanent reductions in the existing debt-servicing obligations. It shifted the focus of the negotiations between creditor banks and debtor nations from debt rescheduling to debt relief. As part of the process, substantial funds were raised from the IMF, the World Bank, and other sources to facilitate debt reduction. To qualify for such help, debtor countries had to agree to introduce economic reforms. It is estimated that under the Brady plan agreements, between 1984 and 1994, the banks contributed approximately $61 billion, 32% of the $191 billion dollars in outstanding loans, to the 18 countries that participated.

It was not that they were not informed. Al Constanzo, the head of the overseas division of Citibank, was a former top official of the IMF and to control the risks associated with LDC debts, Irving Friedman, also an ex-IMF official, was hired. It was however thought that the LDCs had to develop in this direction and that the banks were the most appropriate vehicle to facilitate it; the risks were accepted. Citibank was first among the banks in most of the LDCs, especially in Brazil. The earnings were plentiful there. In April 1978, Wriston mentioned to the shareholders that Brazil was the largest single source of earnings for Citibank, which was aiming at $1billion only from Brazil. This was interfering of course with the OCC rule that a national bank was not permitted to make loans to a single borrower in excess of the bank's capital. That is: if all loans to government or government related institutes of one country were aggregated to a "single borrower." There were more banks violating this rule. In January 1978, the OCC proposed to stress that this aggregation should be the norm. But in 1979, the final ruling was that it was up to the banks to judge whether the different agencies had to be aggregated in applying this rule. The OCC saw the problems coming and it was also clear from the deteriorating judgments of the rating agencies, but it did not like to interfere with the ongoing practice. There were concerns about the political aspect of such a decision and fears that it would lead to unattractive disturbances. It was preferred to let it go.

The LDC crisis was one of the important factors that weakened Citibank during the last years of the 1980s and the first years of the 1990s. Other factors were problems with corporate real estate and with leveraged buy-outs. It led to a severe crisis for Citibank in 1992. We come back to that.

10.8 John Reed and Consumer Banking

John Reed joined Citibank in 1965. He had an engineering education, with a master's degree in management from MIT. He fitted nicely in the recruitment policy of Wriston: hire high-performance recruits and then find them a good job. Reed started in the overseas planning department and was asked to redesign the accounting system and improve the operations. Citibank was lagging behind in automation and computerization. For bankers in the sixties, the computer was a mystery to stay far away from. Reed brought the innovations here—the first steps toward a Management Information System. That was urgently necessary with the shift to a matrix organization with country units meeting product lines. In 1968, Reed set up a subsidiary called Citibank Services, Inc. as his research and development arm. The ease with which he secured funding showed the confidence Wriston had in him. Citibank Services housed a mix of marketing, technology, and operations experts. In 1970, Reed was made senior vice president, the youngest vice president ever, and head of the operations division. With some early difficulties, he learned to find the right balance between new technology and insight and experience with the content. It was possible to limit the growth in back-office costs by improving the processes. The check processing was an important one for instance. Of course, there were now and then collisions with the more experienced banking-oriented people in the organization, but Wriston was always supporting Reed and his group. In 1971 the R&D activities of Scanlin Electronics were bought, combined with Citibank Services, and converted it to TTI (Transaction Technology, Inc.). An important activity was the development of well automated credit card processes.

The California-based Bank of America (BofA) was the first big bank being active in credit card development. There were already the entertainment and traveling oriented organizations Diners Club and American Express, but for banks it was all new. California was one of the most populous and wealthiest states and it allowed statewide branching. That made it most suitable for the development of a credit card system. It was also culturally predisposed to stay close to the people, not only to the bigger companies, being founded by Giannini, a son of an Italian immigrant who prided himself of serving "the little fellow" (Stearns, 2011). In 1958, they started to roll out their BankAmericard massively. They just sent millions of cards, unsolicited and unsecured. In the first years, this led to huge losses, the cards were just too easily issued, but from 1961 onwards, it became profitable. To extend it outside California, they created for other banks the possibility to license and established (1966) the BankAmericard Service Corporation (BASC) to organize this. Eventually this developed into VISA (1977). Other banks were less successful and joined their efforts in an initiative that led to the Master Charge card. Citibank tried first to develop its own card, the Everything card, but joined Master Charge, the later Mastercard alliance in 1968. As soon as dual membership was allowed, in 1977, Citibank joined VISA as well.

To be successful in the credit card business, secure and efficient transaction processing was absolutely necessary. So, it is understandable that Reed put so much focus on automation and computerization in this respect. Through TTI, Citibank played an important role in the further development of automated clearing, computer-aided design (CAD) technology, Automated Teller Machines (ATM) and image processing, with a strong tendency to stick to its own approach, sometimes in competition with the approaches of other important players. Occasionally, this went too extreme. Citibank wasted for instance $100 million on the development of a bank specific mainframe for online, real-time consumer banking. The support of Wriston was needed in such cases. Reed saw the current bank branches as completely out of date and envisaged a future with much more computerization, less dependence on human servers, more availability, and less waiting time. Together with Wriston, he rightfully foresaw that technological innovation would help Citibank to grow beyond its actual geographic boundaries. Citibank was present in upstate New York and, through the acquisition of Nationwide Financial, also in Florida, Georgia, and some western states, but this technological development would help to make Citibank a really national bank.

In 1974, Reed was given the responsibility for all of Citibank's domestic and worldwide consumer related businesses, the Consumer Service Group (CSG). With this jump from the back office to the front office, Reed got the opportunity to make his ideas come true. For Wriston and his peers, the consumer was mainly important because the consumer was also the depositor, a cheap source of reserves, but under the influence of Reed, this changed. Consumer banking, or broader: retail banking was going to be an important pillar under Citibank. Technology was important, but Reed stressed the necessity to develop a completely new business approach. In his well-known "Memo from the beach" (summer 1976), he writes: "*When I say that what we are building is new, I am not referring to these new technologies, nor to new delivery systems. Rather, I refer to a fundamentally new business, starting with a dedication to the consumer and to the proposition that we can offer a set of services, that will substantially satisfy a family's financial needs under terms and conditions that will earn the shareholders an adequate profit, while creating a healthy, positive and straightforward relationship with the customer.*" A dependable ATM was crucial in this new approach. The technology was not yet far enough to realize 100% availability and therefore, two ATMs were put in every New York branch. To extend the Citibank system and get it closer to the customer the Citibank Shopping network was established, consisting of more than three thousand locations with ATMs. Some of these were in fact in New Jersey and raised a discussion about the question of whether a free-standing ATM was a branch. In 1976 the Supreme Court determined that a free-standing ATM was indeed a branch, implying that the rules about branching had to be applied. Reed and Wriston realized that nationwide expansion could only be realized through agreements between states. There were more obstacles. The technology was mainly developed in house. Reed was not content with what was available on the market. Yet, it came at huge costs. The branch people had to get used to the new system, the new layout, with customers who were not any more connected to the branch but to Citibank. The float, the time between paying the merchant and subtracting the payment from the customer account, was reduced, leading to discontent with the customers. The credit card holders had to get used to paying a fee. Without a fee it was almost impossible to make the system profitable, but the fee was perceived as an unjust fine for the customers who paid in time. But they continued persistently. In 1977, Visa was joined and 20 million invitations were sent out to apply at Citibank for a Visa card. It led to 4 million acceptances. The business was growing fast, leading to many problems with respect to the customer service. It lasted long before profitability was realized. That was partly due to the huge investments, but also to huge credit losses. There were no dependable credit scorings yet, so, in trying to seduce millions of people to use a credit card, many were hit who just used it right away until its limit but who were never going to be able to pay. Reed knew and accepted that: "*We have red ink all over the place here, and we are going to lose some more money for a little while.*"

Most problems were growing pains, but there was also a more fundamental problem: the ceilings on the interest that could be applied on the credit balance of credit card accounts. There were state-dependent usury ceilings that also applied on the credit balance of credit card accounts. In 1980, a way was discovered to sneak around these ceilings. In some states these ceilings were relatively high and the Supreme Court decided in 1978, also in a credit card matter with the Marquette National Bank of Minneapolis, that the lending bank was allowed to apply the usury ceiling of the state where the lending bank was located. The Citibank people discovered that the ceiling was rather high in South Dakota, a state with only 700,000 residents then, and they explored the possibility to move the credit card subsidiary to Sioux Falls. The governor of South Dakota, William Janklow, appeared to be willing to increase the ceiling further and do whatever was necessary to make live for Citibank in South Dakota easy. So, in November of 1980, Citibank established a South Dakota chartered bank in Sioux Falls. It was approved by the Comptroller of the Currency and by the Fed, also because it fitted in the general deregulation trend. In the next years, more states were abolishing the usury ceilings and an intense competition was starting in the credit card business. Citibank was already far in front in between and to consolidate that, it bought Diners Club in 1981, a company with an established name but with relatively poorly organized back office and marketing processes.

10.9 The Prelude to the Financial Crisis

The LDC crisis had weakened Citibank already. Then the first years of the 1990s came with a recession, leading to severe problems in the commercial real estate market and Citibank was rather deeply involved. Wriston had always been hesitating with respect to getting involved in it, but the lack of other possibilities to increase the earnings had forced them to become active there, and after the change of leadership there was less control. Reed had not much experience with that aspect of banking and was also too busy with LDC loans. His style of leadership differed also very much from that of Wriston, more relying on management agreements and less keeping an eye on what was going on. The way Citibank was organized did not help either. The focus on hiring young and little experienced high-quality personnel, and incentives to become entrepreneurial, innovative, and independent, though highly profitable, could easily lead to a lack of prudence. The checks on the commercial real estate loans were insufficient. Rumors about a possible insolvency of Citibank were spread. The stock price plummeted and Citibank drew the attention of the regulators. It came under very close supervision from the end of 1990 until May 1993. The new rules of the Basle Accord with respect to capital ratios, approved by the Fed in 1988, were also important in stressing the norms. Reed was forced to reduce the dividend to zero, to cut expenses, to sell more stock, and to dispose of assets. This happened not fast enough at first, leading to a last warning, a Memorandum of Understanding (MOU) of the OCC in August 1992. Citibank sold more than $4 billion in new stock, partly to new investors, and partly to existing investors who were given the possibility to exchange preferred stock for common stock at a higher price. An important transaction was that with a Saudian Prince (Prince al-Waleed bin Talal), who bought for more than $500 million preferred stock with the right to convert it to common stock (eventually leading to a 4.9% stake in Citicorp). Yearly expenses on operations were cut with more than $1 billion, more than 11,000 employees lost their jobs, including an important part of the top management. And a number of subsidiaries were sold: some high-tech ventures, a student loan business and a couple of networking businesses. They also sold $1.5 billion of consumer receivables, packaged as securities, the largest of such transactions since the start of this type of securitization. In March 1993, Reed mentioned that Citibank would need until 1995 to recover completely. And it did, the 1995 profit appeared to be $3.5 billion, a record high. This was also partly due to the US support of Mexico during yet another Latin American debt crisis: the Peso crisis. But people involved were convinced that Citibank would never return to its past glory. Instability had slipped into the "institute" Citibank.

10.9.1 Further Deregulation

The banking environment was further deregulated during the 1990s (cf. Davison, 1997). An important first step was the DIDMCA of 1980, mentioned already above.

The DIDMCA established uniform reserve requirements for all depository institutions, to help the Fed to conduct monetary policy and to equalize the position of commercial banks and thrifts in this respect. All depository institutions now had access to the discount window of the Fed. The law provided also for the gradual removal of Regulation Q limits on the interest rates on deposit accounts, to help commercial banks and thrifts to compete with the money market funds run by the investment banks and to give small savers access to market interest rates. The phase out of Regulation Q limits had to be achieved by March 1986 and was to be overseen by the Depository Institutions Deregulation Committee (DIDC). To flatten the competitive environment further, all depository institutions, so including the thrifts, were allowed to provide checking account services. Thrifts were also granted the possibility to enter the consumer loan and credit card business. Another important point of the DIDMCA was the increase of the deposit insurance limit from $40,000 to $100,000.

The DIDMCA led to severe sourcing problems for the thrifts (Moysich, 1997). During the first three years of the 1980s, 118 S&Ls with $43 billion in assets failed. There were also about 750 mergers, many because of the same difficulty of getting or keeping sufficient payable deposits. To create the possibility to resolve this, a new law was adopted, the Garn-St. Germain Depository Institutions Act of 1982 (Garn-St. Germain). The act gave thrifts the possibility to invest in state and local government revenue bonds and to create money market deposits. They were also allowed to invest up to 5% of their assets in commercial loans. The DIDC was expedited to take care that differences in limits on deposit accounts between thrifts and commercial banks were removed by 1984. The law gave also more possibilities to the FDIC and the FSLIC to help troubled institutions: give loans, purchase assets, repurchase securities it had issued and assume liabilities. It gave all kinds of possibilities to FDIC and FSLIC to apply forbearance, to give the institutions time to return to sound conditions. An important measure in this respect was that, in case of troubles, interstate mergers were allowed. Everything was directed to a smooth continuation of the thrift business and an as small as possible use of FSLIC means. These means were anyway far from sufficient. That was also the main topic of the next law, the Competitive Equality and Banking Act (CEBA) of 1987. The FSLIC was recapitalized with $10 billion and the possibilities of interstate mergers and acquisitions were simplified and extended. Legislation directed to the problems of the thrifts was concluded with the Financial Institutions Reform, Recovery, and Enforcement Act of 1989 (FIRREA) and the Federal Deposit Insurance Corporation Act of 1991 (FDICA). In 1989, the FSLIC was replaced by the Savings Association Insurance Fund (SAIF), managed by the FDIC, next to the Bank Insurance Fund (BIF). The act imposed also stricter accounting standards and other standards for thrifts. It limited some of the activities of the thrifts and required that capital standards were at least as stringent as those for national banks. It gave the FDIC also more possibilities to intervene in the behavior of individual banks by terminating their deposit insurance coverage if there were reasons to doubt the liquidity or solvency. The act of 1991 further improved the authorities of the FDIC in monitoring and taking corrective action. The possibilities to borrow from the Treasury were also improved. Another important provision sought to limit the too-big-to-fail policy. The FDIC was now made to use the least-cost alternative in resolutions unless it was decided (with the agreement of the Secretary of the Treasury, in consultation with the President) that it constituted a systemic risk.

The act of 1991 was initiated by a proposal of the Bush administration to put forward a much broader plan that would not only reform the deposit insurance system and provide for increased supervision, but also to consolidate the regulatory structure, allow nationwide interstate banking, and allow commercial banks to perform investment bank services. The initiative was understandable; practice had grown into a very complex patchwork. Political controversies and differences in interests between the various agencies and banking groups led to the more restricted law, mainly focused on settling the Savings and Loan crisis. Other issues were still around. It would lead to three laws, the Riegle Community Development and Regulatory Improvement Act (1994), the Riegle-Neal Interstate Banking and Branching Efficiency Act (1994), and finally the Gramm-Leach-Bliley Act (1999). The first act was directed to simplifying the regulations. In 1978, Congress initiated the Federal Institutions Examination Council to coordinate and harmonize the activities of the various agencies, but the enduring Savings and Loan Crisis stressed that this was insufficient. The act resolved part of these problems. The second act facilitated interstate banking and the third act, finally, removed the barriers between commercial banking, investment banking, and insurance.

Practice was ahead of the law though, as well regarding interstate banking as regarding the permission to commercial banks to perform investment bank services. Interstate branching was not allowed until 1994, but acquiring a bank in another state was possible if and only if the state law authorized such out-of-state acquisitions. Maine was the first state who adopted such a law in 1975. By January 1986, 28 states had permitted some form of acquisition by an out-of-state bank holding company; 46 states did by May 1990 and when the Riegle-Neal act passed, only Hawaii did not have such a law. The practice of out-of-state acquisitions accelerated also with the Savings and Loan crisis. The legislation was basically making federal law consistent with reality. The law did establish limits on deposit concentration; the resultant bank holding company should not have more than 30% of the deposits in the home state of the bank to be acquired, but the host state could adapt this limit.

With respect to the permission to commercial banks of investment banking type of services, there was also a rather varied landscape. State-chartered non-member banks had always been exempted of Glass-Steagall and from the mid-1980s onwards, many states began allowing state-chartered banks to enter securities underwriting, real estate development, equity participation, insurance underwriting, and brokerage. Mostly just some combination of these was allowed. The FDIC had a say here, because it could refuse access to deposit insurance, but did in principle not object to the engagement of the banks in such activities. There were some worries, but because of differences in view between OCC, Fed, and FDIC that did not lead yet to regulations about this issue. The OCC was in such issues always the most liberal, mainly directed to realizing a fruitful competition between the commercial banks. In 1982, the Comptroller, C.T. Conover stated on the OCC position on bank applications for new activities: “Very simply, if a bank can make a strong case that a proposed activity is legal, our inclination is to approve it." During the early 1980s, for example, the OCC authorized national banks to offer brokerage and investment advisory services, to operate futures-commission merchant subsidiaries, and to underwrite credit life insurance. Legislation about this point came in 1999 with the Gramm-Leach-Bliley Act (Mahon, 2013b). The primary change in the law was the creation of a new kind of financial institution, the financial holding company (FHC). The FHC was an umbrella organization that could own subsidiaries in different financial activities. Security and insurance underwriting and sales by banks would still be restricted, but banks could be part of a large organization. The Fed was the supervising agent on the umbrella level. It had to rely primarily on the supervision of the appropriate state and federal organizations for the FHC subsidiaries. This could be the Securities and Exchange Commission for securities brokers and dealers and the state insurance commissioners for licensed insurance companies.

10.9.2 Sanford Weill, the Deal Maker

The 1980s and 1990s, with the deregulation regarding interstate banking and the growing possibilities of combining investment bank services with insurance and banking were a golden period for deal-making. The best deal maker of all was Sanford Weill ("Sanford I Weill"). Weill started as a runner for Bear Stearns and became a broker over there in 1956. Together with three others, he started a brokerage in 1960. He acted as chairman. Through numerous acquisitions, it led to the creation of Shearson Loeb Rhodes in 1979, the then second largest securities broker (after Merrill Lynch), with a capital of $250 million. Weill sold his firm in 1981 to American Express. Buying Shearson Loeb Rhodes was the latter's first step into the securities world. Weill began serving as president of the insurance subsidiary of American Express. Jamie Dimon, the later CEO of JPMorgan Chase, was his assistant here. In 1985, he resigned from American Express and Dimon followed him. In 1986, he bought Commercial Credit, a consumer finance company, a troubled subsidiary of Control Data Corporation, for $7 million. After layoffs and reorganization, the company was able to become profitable and could go public. During the next years, he acquired Gulf Insurance, Primerica, the parent company of Smith Barney, a retail broker, the A. L. Williams insurance company, the retail brokerage outlets of Drexel Burnham Lambert, and finally, in 1992 he paid $722 million to buy a 27% share of Travelers Insurance, which was possible because of the bad real estate investment portfolio of Travelers. The next year, he bought Shearson back from American Express and combined it with Smith Barney. By the end of that same year, he could take over Travelers completely, in a stock deal of $4 billion, and combine the whole conglomerate into Travelers Group. In 1996, he added to that the property and casualty insurance operations of Aetna, a $4 billion transaction, and in 1997, Salomon Inc. that held Salomon Brothers Inc., one of the main investment banks, was bought in a $9 billion transaction. All these acquisitions were organized by Well and Dimon jointly. Weill was the deal maker and Dimon was to align the companies and do the cost cutting (Barrett, 2009).

In 1998, Weill was 65 then, came the largest prey, Citibank. The merger was announced in April by Reed and Weill jointly, and completed in October. It led to a company, called Citigroup now, with almost $700 billion in assets. Reed and Weill were going to be co-chairmen and co-CEO. The merger was not yet legal then due to the leftovers of Glass-Steagall, but there was a two-to-five-year period allowed to act already as merged companies and they were confident that Congress would soon pass legislation removing the last thresholds. To help that process Gerald Ford, a past president, and Robert Rubin, the former Treasury Secretary, were invited in the board of Directors. The financial world was rather surprised by the merger and very sceptic about the idea of co-chairmen, given the huge differences in management styles. In an interview with Euromoney, a leading banking world periodical, Reed tells that he was well aware of these differences, but that he assumed then that it would be for a short period only (Lee, 2019). Maybe he had in mind that Weill would soon retire and that he would go on, together with Dimon (Lowenstein, 2000). Weill, the deal maker, had other plans though. Dimon was fired the next year and Reed was put on a side track and retired soon thereafter. Weill stayed as CEO until 2003 and as chairman until 2006. Rubin was added in between to the executive committee as advisor.

10.9.3 The Faring of Citigroup

Right after the merger, Citigroup operated in 52 countries, with 250,000 employees. The assortment of services varied over the countries. Citigroup provided, for instance, mortgages in Manhattan, loans in Malaysia, and credit cards in Bahrain (Rose & Sessia, 2011). Weill believed very much in the idea of a financial supermarket, with cross selling to exploit the synergy, already in his days with American Express. The first years were promising, Revenue and earnings were increasing, although more through new acquisitions than through cross selling. The market value increased from $155 billion in 1998 to $266 billion in 2001. In March 2002, the Travelers property and casualty division was spun off via an initial public offering, leading to new doubts with respect to the strategy. Cross selling of corporate products went well, but cross selling of the retail products was lagging behind. There were more problems around that time. Citigroup appeared to have been deeply involved with the Enron and WorldCom accounting scandals. It was accused of having given too positive information on Enron; they settled these claims for $2.7 billion later. With respect to WorldCom, the involvement was even deeper. Jack Grubman, the managing director of Salomon Smith Barney and its main telecom analyst appeared to have been too close with WorldCom and gave a too positive advice about investing in WorldCom. Grubman was fined by the SEC and banned for life from the financial industry. Citigroup was also charged. In 2004, it settled for $2.65 billion.

There arose some pressure on Well to organize his retirement and in 2003, Weill recommended the board to appoint Charles Prince as his successor. Prince was a lawyer by training and had worked for Weill since 1986. His main role was to execute mergers and acquisitions. To compensate his lack of banking experience, Robert Willumstad, head of the consumer bank as its chief operating officer, became in fact a kind of co-CEO. Weill stayed on as chairman. Some financial analysts suspected that Weill suggested a lawyer as successor to be better equipped to face all the lawsuits that were coming, and would be able as chairman to keep the reigns in between.

In 2003, Citigroup was active in about 100 countries and continued to focus on diversification, by product and by geographical region. According to the annual report of 2003, 20% of the revenues was due to cross selling. Nevertheless, the general perception within the company was that Citigroup was more a financial mall than a financial supermarket and Prince decided to put more focus on organic growth. That required product innovation and cost cutting. The 2004 earnings were a bit lower than those of 2003, mainly due to the settlements for Enron and WorldCom charges. But Citigroup was anyway underperforming compared to the other big banks and Prince started to accept a higher risk profile therefore. The mortgage-backed securities business was attractive then. So, a pool of mortgages was created and put in an SPV (Special Purpose Vehicle). The SPV could issue securities. The securities were combined in slices with increasing risk profiles. The mortgage-backed securities could be combined with securities backed by other income generating assets. One of the attractive points of an SPV was that it could legally be kept off the balance sheet of the bank. However, the reputation of the bank was at stake when an SPV got difficulties. That could enforce the bank to buy part of the riskier securities and/ or provide liquidity in another way. In case of serious problems, the best option could be to integrate the SPV in the bank balance sheet. It was a rather complex vehicle, requiring adequate risk control. A problem was that Citigroup was lacking such controls. That was also clear to the supervising agencies and in March 2005, the Fed prohibited Citigroup from making further acquisitions until improvement could be shown. Prince replaced some managers and took measures to improve ethics and control and the next year the ban was lifted again. Earnings over 2005 were more than 25% higher than the year before. But the expenses were still increasing and the market value did not reflect the earnings increase therefore. It became clear that the systems in use were outdated. Citigroup had overearned and underinvested. The systems were basically not integrated and the businesses did not communicate well. In 2007, Prince announced some concentration of activities and a 5% cut in the number of employees of 327,000 then.

10.9.4 The Start of the Crisis

His plans made sense, but Prince did not get the time to execute all these changes. During 2007, the poor quality of part of the mortgages became clear and had its effects, and Bear Stearns, the smallest of the five large US investment banks (Goldman Sachs, Merrill Lynch, Morgan Stanley, Lehmann, and Bear Stearns) got in trouble. Eventually it was bought by JP Morgan Chase. It fueled the start of the financial crisis of 2008/09. The trouble spread and in the fourth quarter Citigroup had to put part of her SPV's back on the balance sheet and announced a write off of $11 billion. Charles Prince resigned. Only a few days later, Weill asked Timothy Geithner whether he would be interested in succeeding Prince (Geithner, 2014). Geithner was then the chairman of the Federal Reserve Bank of New York, the supervising agent for Citigroup. It was a rather strange request, given the difficulties expected, but it was also showing how easy it was to switch from business to supervising agencies and the other way around. Geithner did not consider it very seriously. A year later, he would become Secretary of the Treasury, in the first period administration of Barak Obama. Vikram Pandit, a former Morgan Stanley executive was going to succeed Prince.

In Chap. 11, we give broad attention to the crisis. Here it suffices to tell that Citigroup came in severe problems. It had to be bailed out again and again. It would have been quite possible that Citigroup had gone under completely. All heads of the supervising agencies involved knew that Citigroup had underperformed and that its Chairman and CEO could be blamed here, but they differed very much in opinion about what to do. Most extreme were Geithner on one hand and Sheila Bair, the chair of the FDIC, on the other hand. Geithner stressed very much the importance of an as smooth as possible continuation of the current system, protecting especially the big banks as well as possible. Sheila Bair was in favor of a more drastic approach and proposed to call the problems by their names, organize haircuts, replace the management, split the healthy parts of the institute from the troubled parts, and protect the insured depositors (Bair, 2015). Others, like Larry Summers, then chairman of the National Economic Council (NEC), were in between. The approach of Geithner prevailed. That is how Citigroup survived the crisis: refreshed and shriveled, but still more or less the same. It was and is really too-big to-fail.

10.10 The Citibank Banking Secrets

Here we describe the most striking elements or aspects where Citibank was really ahead of the pack, its "banking secrets." We concentrate on the period from around 1960 onwards, where it started to deviate from other "National Champion" banks in the US and elsewhere. The first element is *international banking*. From around 1960 onwards, Citibank was fierce in having an affiliate in all countries with sufficient American influence. The Cuban revolution of 1959 was an unpleasant surprise. Wriston's focus on international banking was probably inspired by his early Citibank experiences with the finance of international transportation, starting with financing tankers for Onassis, growing out to all kinds of transportation: shipping, airlines, parcel service, trucking, car rentals, trains. Later, Citibank was also in front in organizing syndicated Eurodollar loans. And it was one of the important banks in

LDC loans. It also provided international transaction services and set up foreign subsidiaries.

Another feature where Citibank was a forerunner was *staff entrepreneurship*. When Walter Wriston started at Citibank, banking was a rather sleepy business. More than half of the assets were in US government obligations and only a quarter in loans. The growing economy forced all banks to become more entrepreneurial, but Wriston, together with his predecessor Moore translated it to the recruitment of high-level personnel. They wanted the best graduates of the nation's best colleges and business schools and gave them the freedom to innovate. One of these was John Reed. Reed who, supported by Wriston, built *consumer banking* within Citibank and showed the US and the world how that was going to be an important business, exploiting the new technological possibilities.

Finally, Citibank and Wriston were the main driving forces toward *deregulation*. There were many ambiguities, inconsistencies, dysfunctionalities, and anachronisms in the existing regulation. Nobody could show these so well as Wriston, and he loved to do that. No organization was so fierce in finding loopholes and workarounds as Citibank. Its officers did not ask, but just tried and awaited what happened. If the regulators forbade, it was always possible to go to court and fight it. If there was no success, it helped anyway to postpone the retreat and to find new opportunities.

10.11 Conclusion

This chapter covers important elements of the history of Citibank during the last hundred years. First a short overview of the first hundred years. We described how it was involved in the Great Depression. This crisis resulted in a whole bunch of new laws and regulations. Combined with the already existing ones the whole is a fragmented, complex, and inconsistent system, with loopholes of course. It is not strange that in the post-war period of growth, there was a broad movement from within the financial world to explore the loopholes and build pressure to change this. Wriston and Citibank were leading here. The international activities of Citibank were described and the dominant position of the dollar was important here. That is why we paid some attention to the Bretton Woods agreements. Irresistible temptations to lend also to LDC governments and government related organizations resulted in the LDC crisis of the 1980s. It contributed to the difficulties Citibank had in the 1990s. Problems with commercial real estate formed a major cause. Domestically, Citibank was a forerunner in the development of consumer banking, the use of credit cards, and the use of ATMs. A focus on the operations side of banking, the back office, an important contribution of John Reed, is essential here. We sketched how Citibank fared in the 1990s. Most important was the merger with Travelers, in 1998. That was the climax of a whole sequence of mergers and acquisitions by Sanford Weill. The deal-making abilities of Weill in combination with the accelerated deregulation of the 1980s and 1990s made it possible. It made Citibank, now Citigroup, a giant on clay feet. It survived the financial crisis of 2008, but only because it was too-big-to-fail.

The development of Citibank was on one hand the result of changes in political and economic circumstances, the economic growth of the post-war period, the dominant position of the dollar, the oil crises, the confusing regulating system, and the later deregulation move, also driven by technological developments. It shows also how three individuals, Wriston, Reed, and Weill had a lasting impact: Wriston as the articulate banker and inspiring leader, Reed as the passionate engineer with far-reaching ideas, and Weill as the deal maker with a sharp eye for weaknesses and other opportunities.

The Citibank example gives also an impression of American post-war banking, the role of the big US banks in international banking, the position of Savings and Loan institutions versus commercial banks, the role of state-chartered banks versus federally chartered banks, the rise of consumer banking and investment banking, the complicated regulation system, the influence of state politics and federal politics, as well as the steadiness with which bankers go to administration and to regulators and vice versa. The financial crisis of 2008 is more or less an apotheosis of all these developments. In Chap. 11, we pay attention to it.

References

Bair, S. (2015). *The bullies of wall street*. Simon and Schuster.

Barrett, P. M. (2009). *I, Banker*. A review of the book of Duff Mc Donald on Dimon: Last Man Standing. NY Times Book Review.

Beebe, J. (1981). "Deposit Deregulation" *Federal Reserve Bank of San Francisco*, April 10, 1981. http://www.frbsf.org/publications/economics/letter/1981/el81-15.pdf

Citigroup. (2012). *Celebrating the past*. Citigroup Inc.

Committee on Banking and Currency. (1934). *Stock exchange practices*. Senate Report 1455. June.

Curry, T. (1997). *The LDC debt crisis*. Chapter 5 of *An examination of the banking crisis of the 1980s and early 1990s*. Federal Deposit Insurance Corporation (FDIC). Washington DC. https://www.fdic.gov/resources/publications/history-eighties/volume-1/index.html

Davison, L. (1997). *Banking legislation and regulation*. Chapter 2 of *An examination of the banking crisis of the 1980s and Early 1990s*. Federal Deposit Insurance Corporation (FDIC). Washington DC. https://www.fdic.gov/resources/publications/history-eighties/volume-1/index.html

Federal Reserve Bank of New York. (1960). New York State's Omnibus Banking Law. *Monthly Review*, June, 94–107.

Feynman, J. N. (1993). *Reserve requirements: History, current practice, and potential reform*. Federal Reserve Bulletin, June.

Fortune, P. (2000). *Margin requirements, margin loans and margin rates*: Practices and principles. New England Economic Review. September/October 19–44.

Friedman, B. M. (1975, August). *Regulation Q and the commercial loan market in the 1960s*. *Journal of Money, Credit and Banking, 7*, 277–296.

Galbraith, J. K. (1975). *The great crash 1929*. Penguin Books.

Geithner, T. F. (2014). *Stress test: Reflections on financial crises*. Crown Publishers.

Greider, W. (1987). *Secrets of the temple: How the federal reserve runs the country*. Simon and Schuster.

Huertas, T. F. (1985). The rise of the modern business enterprise: The case of Citibank. *Business and Economic History, 14*, 144–157.

Kollen Ghizoni, S. (2013). *Creation of the Bretton woods system*. Federal Reserve Bank of Atlanta. https://www.federalreservehistory.org/essays/bretton-woods-created#maincontent

Lee, P. (2019). *The bankers that define decades: John Reed, Citibank*. Euromoney, June 18.

Lowenstein, R. (2000). *Alone at the top*. New York Times Magazine, August 27.

Mahon, J. (2013a). *Bank holding company act of 1956*. Federal Reserve History. https://www.federalreservehistory.org/essays/bank-holding-company-act-of-1956/

Mahon, J. (2013b). *Financial services modernization act of 1999, Commonly called Gramm-Leach-Bliley*. Federal Reserve Bank of Minneapolis. https://www.federalreservehistory.org/essays/gramm-leach-bliley-act

Mikesell, R. (1994). *The Bretton woods debates: A memoir*. Essays in International Finance 192. Princeton University.

Moysich, A. (1997). *The savings and loan crisis and its relationship to banking*. Chapter 4 of *An examination of the banking crisis of the 1980s and early 1990s*. Federal Deposit Insurance Corporation (FDIC). Washington DC. https://www.fdic.gov/resources/publications/history-eighties/volume-1/index.html

New York Times, The. (2007). Citi Chief on Buyouts: 'We're Still Dancing.', July 10. https://archive.nytimes.com/dealbook.nytimes.com/2007/07/10/citi-chief-on-buyout-loans-were-still-dancing/

Prins, N. (2014). *All the Presidents' bankers; the hidden alliances that drive American power*. Nation Books.

Rose, C., & Sessia, A. (2011). *What happened at citigroup?*, Harvard Business School.

Ruebling, C. E. (1970). *The Administration of Regulation Q*. Federal Reserve Bank of St Louis. https://files.stlouisfed.org/files/htdocs/publications/review/70/02/Administration_Feb1970.pdf

Sanford I. Weill (n.d.). Sanford I. Weill. *Wikipedia*. https://en.wikipedia.org/wiki/Sanford_I._Weill

Seidman, W. L. (1993). *Full faith and credit: The Great S&L debacle and other Washington Sagas*. Beard Books.

Sherman, M. (2009). *A short history of financial deregulation in the United States*. Center for Economic and Policy Research.

Starr, P. (2002). *Citibank: A century in Asia*. Citigroup.

Stearns, D. L. (2011). *Electronic value exchange*. Springer.

Wriston, W. B. (1973). *Freedom and controls*. New York State Bar Journal.

Wriston, W. B. (1974). *Capital formation-What is the question? Business Council* speech, October. https://exhibits.tufts.edu/spotlight/wriston-archives/feature/speeches

Wriston, W. B. (1982). "Banking Against Disaster." *The New York Times*, 14 September.

Zweig, P. (1995). *Walter Wriston*. Crown Publishers New York.

Chapter 11
Conclusion and General Discussion

11.1 Introduction

While Lehman Brothers Holdings Inc. was shaking, on Friday, September 12, 2008, Federal Reserve Bank of New York governor Timothy F. Geithner called the executives of major Wall Street firms to a meeting in Lower Manhattan (Geithner, 2014; Sorkin, 2009). Henry M. Paulson Jr., the US Secretary of the Treasury, requested the meeting. In were Christopher Cox, Chairman of the Securities and Exchange Commission, as well as leading Wall Street bankers: Lloyd Blankfein of the Goldman Sachs Group, James Dimon of JPMorgan Chase, John Mack of Morgan Stanley, Vikram Pandit of Citigroup, and John Thain of Merrill Lynch. Representatives from the Royal Bank of Scotland and Bank of New York Mellon also participated. The purpose of the meeting was to save Lehman Brothers, the fourth largest investment bank in the USA, and to stabilize the financial markets. Lehman was not invited to the meeting as the decision was related to it. The US economy was in trouble. Investment banks such as Lehman were investing in complex security schemes, assuming housing prices would increase continuously. However, they became worthless assets as homeowners were not paying a significant portion of their monthly mortgage payments for some time as housing prices were falling.

A decision had to be made before the markets opened on Monday. Paulson told his colleagues before that he would not let anyone leave until a decision had been made, just as J.P. Morgan had done when "saving the USA" 101 years ago. The room was tranquil, like before the storm. Unlike the Morgan library, decorated with classic office furniture, its walls' dark brown wood trim created a gloomy atmosphere in the dim light. The bank executives sat on one side of the big table, anxiously awaiting what Paulson would propose. In contrast, Paulson and other government representatives sat on the other side of the table. Interestingly, almost all the nervous bureaucrats were former Goldman Sachs or Morgan Stanley employees. For a long time, many of those in critical positions, such as the SEC or the Treasury Department, had previously worked at major investment banks and protected their interests. Now,

M. B. Karan et al., *A History of Banks*, Contributions to Economics,
https://doi.org/10.1007/978-3-031-62297-7_11

they had to serve the public interest. Coming from a similar culture, they could sense the dilemma of CEOs. One could feel the tension in the room. Occasionally, the eyes drifted to cell phones, and they nervously watched investment banks' constantly falling share prices. Bank executives only knew that if Lehman went bankrupt, the market would crash. Moreover, all of them had essential vulnerabilities. Merrill Lynch was in a fragile situation, and Goldman was also in financial difficulty. A few days ago, Paulson had called Warren Buffet, one of the most prominent players in the market, and asked him to support Lehman. Buffet turned down the offer, saying the investment banks were losing control as they were investing on their behalf. Koreans interested in the bank also retreated.

Henry M. Paulson began by indicating that Lehman could not meet its obligations by Monday and that none of the two potential buyers, Bank of America and Barclays Bank, wanted to buy it unless someone else would finance a part of the sale. The government would not be able to intervene in the market. He added: "If Lehman goes bankrupt, your situation will get worse." The meeting became tense; no one wanted to put their hands in their pockets. Paulson threatened them, saying, "We won't forget anyone to help." As the meeting continued the next day, it was clear that Bank of America preferred to save Merrill Lynch. Nobody wanted to mess up with Lehman, but the British Barclays had agreed to buy its good parts. The banks could not deny the plan and would take the risky parts. However, unexpectedly, Sir Callum McCarty, the head of the British banking regulator, did not approve the deal so this plan would not work either, making Lehman's bankruptcy inevitable.

Meanwhile, AIG, which insured mortgage securities against the risk of default, informed that it could not afford the $5 billion due on Wednesday. AIG had assumed the housing market would go up forever, but prices were now falling. A big crisis was coming up, and it would be impossible to resolve it without federal government support. Fed Chairman Ben Bernanke claimed that the entire financial system would collapse if measures were not taken. Before the press conference, Treasury Department spokesperson assistant secretary Michele Davis asked Paulson what to reply if someone asked her what the government was doing while all of this was happening. "Nobody wanted regulation; we were making a lot of money," Paulson said with a bitter smile, stating the truth. The apocalypse would break on Monday, and the most significant crisis after the 1929 one unfolded. As it ended and although the economy had collapsed, the CEOs of many firms directly involved in fanning the flames of the 2007/08 Global Financial Crisis received payouts and compensation handsomely. Later, despite protests such as those on Occupy Wall Street, the ongoing system continued with minor reforms and adjustments. Big banks were not easy to touch. The phrase "Too big to fail" was their perfect shield.

The events dramatized above are taken from the book of Sorkin (2009). As described in the book, Pandora's Box had opened, and banking had become the leading player in the 2008 crisis caused by an asset bubble. The road to the crisis began with an abundance of cash, which was channeled into the US housing market. In fact, the starting point of the story was the changing monetary system since 1944. Before the collapse of the Bretton Woods (1944) international monetary system in 1973, all money was backed by gold. In other words, paper money could be converted into gold—at least at the government level, even if the right of individuals to convert their paper money into gold was increasingly restricted as the twentieth century progressed. Gold has long been an internationally accepted store of value for many reasons, and governments cannot easily manipulate or devalue it. In contrast, throughout history, sovereign debt and paper money have often been worth far less than gold, sometimes even completely worthless. The collapse of Bretton Woods severed the last meaningful link between paper money and gold, and the US dollar quickly replaced gold as the world's reserve currency in which most international business transactions are conducted. However, since only gold (or currencies backed entirely by gold) was accepted as payment and the amount of gold was limited, the amount of money on the market was still limited. In 1971, everything would change. US President Richard Nixon's shock decision allowed governments to print paper money without limit. The influx of dollars would create asset bubbles, putting Lehman Brothers at risk, as in the story we told, and the entire world economy. Henceforth, the world would enter a different era in which asset price bubbles were more likely to lead to financial crises and public finances could not easily absorb the losses from banking (Duncan, 2011).

11.2 The Demise of the Gold Standard and the Failure of Lehman Brothers

The classical gold standard of the global monetary system was ended in 1944. The Bretton Woods system started a new era by creating a cooperative exchange rate regime. Under US leadership, the world was shifting to a completely different order. The asset of this order, as precious as gold, would henceforth be dollars. While the dollar was getting its strength from the rapidly growing US economy, it made the world accept the US hegemony and its dollar as an international reserve. The USA maintained this power uninterrupted until the 1970s. Central banks and commercial banks, the playmakers of the traditional gold standard, now turned their eyes to the USA. Whereas it took up until 1958 to have the system that priced gold at \$35 per ounce and allowed currencies to fluctuate between -1% and $+1\%$ of their dollar parities up and running, it would essentially be over in 1971, with a decision made by the US President, Richard Nixon. He announced the ending of the dollar's convertibility into gold on Sunday, August 15. This so-called "Nixon shock" was the inevitable result of a process characterized by an overly expansionary US economic policy and the leadership of a wild personality.

Richard Mulhouse Nixon (1913–1994) was born in a poor Californian Quaker family with strong Christian values (Richard Nixon, n.d.). At his high school, he won prizes for being a good debater. After receiving a bachelor's degree in history, he attended a prestigious law school, Duke, in North Carolina. After returning to California, he joined a law firm and married his wife Pat(ricia). To pursue better career opportunities and more excitement, he joined the US Navy in 1942, assuming logistics duties. Afterward, he returned to California and won a seat in Congress on behalf of the Republicans. He actively combatted communists and became a senator in 1950 after a campaign bringing him the nickname "Tricky Dick." Interestingly, while showing a liberal view on minorities and foreign aid, he, e.g., did not support price controls and other monetary restrictions. After a well-received speech on donations he had received from the largest-ever television audience, US Second World War hero General Dwight D. Eisenhower chose him as a running mate. They won the 1952 elections and were re-elected four years later. Eisenhower left much of the critical foreign and domestic affairs to Nixon. Looking pale in television debates against a fresh John F. Kennedy, he just lost the 1960 presidential elections. He returned to California, lost the run for the governorship in 1962, and went to New York to become a lawyer. Following a landslide Democrat victory in 1964, he ran for the presidency in 1968. He won upon vague peace promises during the devastating Vietnam War and appealed to socially conservative citizens. Indeed, Nixon, or maybe rather his Minister of Foreign Affairs Henry Kissinger, ended the Vietnam War in 1973 while supporting Israel against an Egyptian raid and following a "détente policy" throughout. He took on a modest racial integration and social policy. He won the "War in Space" that brought the first man on the Moon. His presidency ended unfavorably in 1974 after being accused of his re-election campaign supporting a burglary in the Democrat Party headquarters in 1972. After his resignation following the "Watergate Scandal," he took on the role of elder statesman and wrote no less than ten books.

An important economic policy event that Richard Nixon (see Fig. 11.1) will be remembered is the so-called "Nixon Shock" of 15 August 1971 (Nixon Shock, n.d.). Historians know much about it since Nixon had recently installed tape recording equipment in Washington D.C. office spaces, but unfortunately, not yet in the site 100 km away from the presidential retreat Camp David, where the decision was worked out by the presidential team. However, the television speech he made on the memorable day is well available at https://youtu.be/zD99SGj4IGM, the run-up is most fascinating, and there is much other descriptive material around, including an overview by Bordo (2020) and especially the article "Ending Bretton Woods: evidence from the Nixon tapes" by Butkiewicz and Ohlmacher (2021).

Nixon's shock on August 15, 1971, was one of the most critical events in the international monetary system. President Richard Nixon ended the history of gold convertibility that underpinned the Bretton Woods System and was the mainstay of the global monetary system for two centuries. The rest of the Bretton Woods System (adjustable peg) collapsed in March 1973 with the advent of generalized (managed) floating exchange rates. One of the driving motivations for President Nixon's actions was the perception that the growing imbalances between the United States, which was running exploding balance-of-payments deficits, and Germany and other Western European countries and Japan, which were running surpluses, were harming the competitive position of US manufacturing and the overall prosperity of the country (Bordo, 2020).

A case can be made that UK and especially US economic policies have already provoked the event from the early sixties onwards (Bordo, 2020; Butkiewicz &

Fig. 11.1 Richard Nixon in 1971. https://commons.wikimedia.org/wiki/File:Nixon_30-0316a.jpg

Ohlmacher, 2021). Upward pressure on the gold price was countered by establishing a Gold Pool maintained by eight countries in 1961. Also, the amount of gold in Fort Knox (USA) could not keep up with the demand for dollars due to the US balance of payment deficits and worldwide economic growth ("golden sixties"). Price stability was needed, but instead, inflation was soaring. A series of currency crises hit, e.g., the UK (1967), France (1969), Canada (1970), Austria and Switzerland (May 1971), Germany and the Netherlands (a day later), and again the UK (June 1971). Except for the UK pound and the French franc, national currencies bought more dollars. With US monetary controls already being established, wage and price controls seemed to be inevitable. Nixon, blaming his 1960 presidential election loss on rising unemployment levels, was in favor. He was even contemplating import controls, for that matter. However, there was an alternative.

According to the so-called "impossible trinity" or "trilemma," one cannot have it all together: no restrictions on capital flows, a fixed exchange rate, and domestic monetary autonomy (Bekaert & Mehl, 2019). If the US dollar were unpegged from gold prices and thus float, capital inflow and price controls could be given up, and interest rates would not have to rise. Nixon did not like soaring interest rates, being quoted from the "Nixon tapes" to have said "to hell with it" on the idea and added, "There is no dollar crisis." Yet, that was in May, and right afterward, a currency crisis broke out. Nixon would not grasp the interconnectedness of domestic and international policies (Butkiewicz & Ohlmacher, 2021), but he intended to show outstanding leadership in both. He was willing to combine the two in one policy. This led to the idea of a New Economic Program (NEP). Basically, it was about suspending the convertibility of dollars into gold or other reserve assets, floating the dollar, levying a surcharge on specific imports, temporary wage and price freezes, and various relatively small tax measures. The IMF was not informed upfront, and major countries were not amused, but domestically, and major countries were not amused, but domestically, the bold move was welcomed, and that was what it was about. The Camp David speech freed President Nixon from the difficulties posed by an inadequate gold supply. Gold would henceforth be an investment tool largely independent of the monetary system. Legal tender used after this date became Fiat Money and was valued according to a nation's financial power. Whereas the original US goal was to restore fixed exchange rates, with the so-called "Smithsonian Agreement" on it, being reached in December 1971, the idea was given up in March 1973 altogether, and all US capital controls were withdrawn in 1974.

The "Nixon shock" had major consequences on various levels. Politically, the US had cashed in its resentment against the outer developed world, with the President later being taped saying, "This country wants to kick foreigners the ass, correct?" (Butkiewicz & Ohlmacher, 2021). Economically, the high inflation in combination with economic stagnation ("stagflation") and the great uncertainty surrounding foreign exchange rates and interest levels of the '70s and early '80s can be related to the event. With the political and monetary decision-makers desperately trying to design a new sound and stable monetary system, the floor was opened to arbitrageurs, speculators, and passers-by to make money out of the increased financial market volatility. With a sound track record as traders on behalf of their customers and earning small fees, banks seemed well positioned to capture and control a large chunk of a virtually exploding market. Yet, where did they really fit for the deregulation that followed suit?

After the 1929 US stock market crash, the Glass-Steagall Act was passed in 1933. It made investment and commercial banking activities separate. The government eroded this law over time under the influence of lobbying bankers, as discussed in the chapter on Citibank (Chap. 10). The 1971 Nixon shock led to the sacrifice of the role of the US global currency system ruler to serve its own financial markets. Moreover, the growth of the Eurodollar market after 1973/74 increased the supply of dollars. This market was unregulated by the US. Undoubtedly, given the size of the Eurodollar market, over-leveraged Eurodollar lenders became a threat to global financial stability. Indeed, the 2008 crisis would be characterized by over-leveraged banks and a lack of liquidity (Fowler, 2021). In 1980, Regulation Q was phased out over six years, and reserve requirements were reduced and simplified. This regulation stated board-regulated institutions' minimum capital requirements and capital adequacy standards. In October 1982, President Ronald Reagan signed the Garn-St Germain Depository Institutions Act, which began the process of banking deregulation. The 1980s and 1990s saw continued deregulation of interstate banking and increased opportunities to combine investment bank services with insurance and banking. As late as 1997, Fed Chairman Alan Greenspan fought to keep the derivatives market unregulated. In November of 1999, President Bill Clinton signed into Law the Gramm-Leach-Bliley Act, which repealed part of the Glass-Steagall Act of 1933. This repeal made the already quite ineffective separation between commercial and investment banks break-up finally. In 2004, the Securities and Exchange Commission relaxed the net capital rule, which enabled investment banks to substantially increase the level of debt they were taking on, fueling the growth in mortgage-backed securities supporting subprime mortgages. Greedy bankers saw their opportunities. The lifting controls in financial markets deteriorated the old correlations between money and nominal income. In the aftermath of financial deregulation and innovation and the apparent breakdown of stable and predictable money demand relationships, there has been a move away from strict monetary targeting as the primary objective of monetary policy. However, the Lehman failure occurred after the initial collapses of Northern Rock (UK) and Bear Sterns (USA).

11.3 The Global Financial Crisis and Its Aftermath

Where were you on the day that Lehman Brothers (founded in 1852, see Fig. 11.2) went bankrupt: Monday 15 September 2008? Actually, the authors of this book barely remember it, if at all. Weirdly, many observers, of course, did witness a high street US investment bank (dubbed as the world's #1) going under and that financial markets did panic albeit in a concerting way, but they also often did not care too much about it, since the bank was not thought to be vital for keeping the US and global monetary system up. There was even some feeling of righteousness and gloating that after some bailouts, finally, a bank did fail. Banks had been making big money on deals in mergers and acquisitions, equities and bonds markets, and derivative markets, with their staff keeping a handsome amount of the fees themselves by way of base salaries, bonuses, and share plans. With deals that went evermore risky in a market facing a looming crisis, bankers had kept their business going up ever more and quoted Charles Prince of the US Citigroup stating, "As long as the music is playing, you've got to get up and dance" (New York Times, 2007). Much can be said about this infamous quote, but suffice it, for now, to note that many parties were able to dance on the Lehman Brothers' grave after the crisis and made buckets full of money on the failure.

Much evidence backs the idea that whereas the Lehman Brothers failure may have deepened the Global Financial Crisis, it was already underway at the time, and a correction was inevitable anyway. For quite some time already, banks have been securitizing mortgage loans, slicing them, and repackaging them for trading purposes to mitigate the risks involved (Patterson, 2010). Econometrical backing for the presumed low CDO risks came from the China-born financial engineer David X. Li. Unfortunately, he did not consider that CDOs could be used with subprime mortgages readily afterward (Patterson, 2010). Moreover, a JPMorgan team designed, tweaking prior modeling of pricing losses on loan portfolios (Islam, 2013), a product

Fig. 11.2 Headquarters of Lehman Brothers, one year before its collapse, https://commons.wikimedia.org/wiki/File:Lehman_Brothers_Times_Square_by_David_Shankbone.jpg

that did even better: the credit default swap (CDS). Other than a collateralized debt obligation (CDO), a CDS acts as an insurance product. In combination with spiking home prices, the rumbling volcano became higher and higher, with parties joining, such as the giants Citibank and Deutsche Bank, as well as the investment banks Goldman Sachs and Lehman Brothers. However, with the US housing market turning in late 2006, the CDO market also rapidly imploded. Infamous stories such as one on JPMorgan with so-called squared CDOs (CDOs on CDOs) even betting against its own customers show that winners and losers were difficult to point out from now on.

There was also something else. Regulators found it difficult to cope with the problems of the "shadow banks" that rapidly developed at the same time (Geithner, 2014). The term "shadow bank" was coined by economist Paul McCulley in a 2007 speech at the Kansas City Federal Reserve Bank's annual financial symposium in Jackson Hole, Wyoming (Taub, 2013). Commercial banks engage in maturity transformation when they use deposits that are normally short term to fund longer-term loans. Shadow banks do something similar. They raise short-term funds in the money markets (i.e., they mostly borrow) and use those funds to buy longer-term assets. But because they are not subject to traditional banking regulations, they cannot borrow from the Federal Reserve (the US central bank) in an emergency like banks can, and they do not have traditional depositors whose funds are backed by insurance; they remain "in the shadows." Banks typically have to operate under intense scrutiny from financial regulators in their home countries and around the world. Shadow banks, often referred to as non-bank financial companies (NBFCs), can typically operate with little to no regulatory oversight. Then President of the Federal Bank of New York Timothy F. Geithner refers in his famous book "Stress Test: Reflections on Financial Crises" to banks as depository-taking institutions. Investment banks and their slipstream entities, such as structured investment vehicles, private equity funds, money market funds, and hedge funds, but also insurance firms, clearance houses, exchanges, down-to-market brokers and dealers, and even individuals can perform bank-like functions but operate outside of the banking system. It takes too long to demarcate and describe the shadow banks exactly. Suffice it to say that during the peak years in the 2000s, their US GDP chunk topped one of the traditional banks, as it was also said to be when this book was written. An issue is that shadow banks are less regulated than traditional banks and may thus be able to charge lower costs and offer higher interest rates. Whereas traditional banks channel much of their affairs via shadow banks, the latter's growth does imply less grip on the monetary system.

Moreover, after the so-called internet bubble burst in 2000, hitting the US economy more than those of some of its competitors, interest rates were kept low (Davies & Green, 2010). This, however, meant that the banks had to lever up their assets to keep their returns steady. Later, the credit spreads (margins) were widening. Moreover, the fee business on non-core services ("structured finance") gained importance. Structured credit products had made the system riskier. It exposes an institution to other types of risk, such as market risk, liquidity risk, and operational risk. It was especially during the 2008 credit market turmoil that led to significant losses. All of this was also more or less true in the eurozone and several other parts of the world. As the US and other economies became more and more overheated, interest rates were raised, to only decrease effectively and rapidly when the Global Financial Crisis came in full swing after the Lehman Brothers debacle of September 15, 2008.

The crisis had started more than a year earlier, namely, in the summer of 2007. There were rumors that interbank markets would stop in mid-July. This occurred in the course of a subprime market implosion almost welcomed by central bankers because of the excess of "no-doc" loans (no proof of income loans), "liar loans" (loans on excessive expected incomes), and "NINJA" loans (to "No Income, No Job, No Assets" lenders) that had flooded the market (Geithner, 2014). Interestingly, a ninja was an "irregular" Japanese warrior in the feudal ages. Unfortunately, two hedge funds linked to the good-old American investment bank Bear Sterns collapsed, and the French bank BNP Paribas indicated that it could not price subprime securities anymore. Little later, the California-based mortgage lender Countrywide imploded, and Bank of America picked up its legacy. Citibank saw Charles Prince resign as its CEO for reporting losses. The next major victim was Bear Sterns, who had borrowed "too much and too short" (Geithner, 2014). Other than the non-Fed ruled Countrywide, it was much interwoven with the regular banks and, as Geithner puts it, "too interconnected" to fail. The New York Fed and JPMorgan Chase stepped on board, buying the shares at a scrap price. Also, the government-sponsored housing companies "Fannie Mae" and "Freddie Mac" were bailed out. The investment bank Merrill Lynch had made large write-offs, and it was sold to Bank of America on Sunday, September 14.

Lehmen's failure, which we told in a short story at the beginning of the episode, was the culmination of the crisis. Even more than a decade later, with lots of details having become known (Geithner, 2014; Patterson, 2010; Sorkin, 2009), it is still unclear to the public how it came about. By June 25, his team had shown Geithner that Lehman had borrowed too much, too short, and against too many illiquid assets. The Korea Development Bank and Bank of America failed to step in. The main players, some Lehman officials, New York Fed president Tim Geithner, and US Secretary of the Treasury Hank Paulson, gave it a final try on Saturday, September 13, only to find out the next day that the UK administration held back a probable deal with the British high street bank Barclays. Geithner (2014, p. 190) writes: "We had tried but failed to prevent a catastrophic default. That is still poorly understood." Hank Paulson and US Federal Reserve President Ben Bernanke did not want to admit failure since this might intensify the panic. Indeed, a panic there was. On September 15, US stocks fell by almost 5%, Citibank lost 15% of its value, the mortgage lender Washington Mutual lost 27% (it closed down in the same week), whereas the insurer AIG stocks were even down by 60%. The latter big fish was quickly bailed out by the Fed, albeit by way of a near-confiscation.

Measures to counter a crisis became implemented globally, albeit at often large delays, but things went on. As the money markets were essentially freezing, the Fed supported the liquidity with several facilities, of which many had already come in place before September 15. Short selling of many stocks, the timed disposal thereof with borrowed money, became forbidden. The deposit insurance limit for small savers went up. In the course of these events, a merger of two troubled banks, Wachovia (the global number 7 in terms of assets in 2007) and Citibank (the global number 2 in terms of assets in 2007), was agreed upon, but it was Wells Fargo (the global number 15 in terms of assets in 2007) that bought Wachovia in the end. A huge Troubled Asset Relief Program (TARP) facilitated the US Treasury to buy illiquid loans and shares of the banks involved. It helped to save the swiftly no longer partnership banks, Goldman Sachs and Morgan Stanley, with the latter also aided by a *typewritten* USD 9 billion check from the Bank of Tokyo-Mitsubshi UFJ, see Fig. 11.3 (Sorkin, 2009). It seemed as if control was lost. Paulson's cell phone rightfully became a museum object later. Being upset about the lack of command structure, Tim Geithner notes having used the term "banana republic" (Geithner, 2014). Even Citibank and Bank of America (the 2007 global number 1 in terms of assets) were to be bailed out via the TARP program for their mess of on-balance and off-balance mortgages and related derivatives, risky investment bank affiliates, and vulnerable funding bases. Of course, they had to reduce.

The reader may have arrived at the idea that the banking crisis was, in fact, a US phenomenon, although its key sequel—a steep economic crisis—might truly justify the label "Global Financial Crisis." Yet, this would be a misunderstanding. The then Bank of England (BoE) Governor Marvyn King (2016) recalls the misfit of Northern

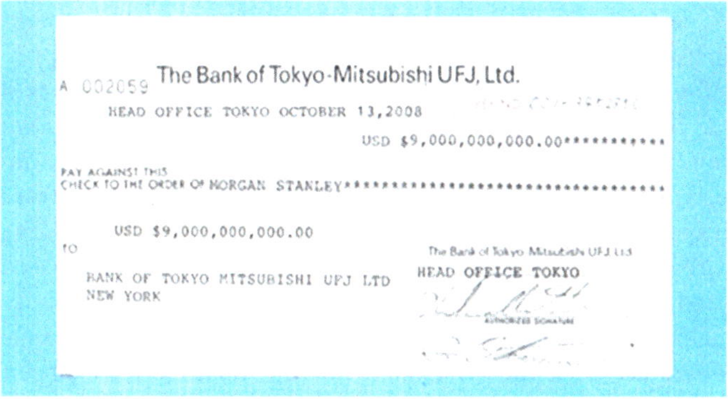

Fig. 11.3 The 9 billion dollar check that might have saved Morgan Stanley, https://twitter.com/morganstanley/status/1315673245291614208

Rock, a mutual building society that had converted into a stock-listed bank in the '90s. Actually, it was thought to be so shielded from the risk that it could return capital to its owners despite its leverage ratio being 60:1 or even lower. This became a problem when the mortgage markets closed, and following interim BoE loan support, the bank was nationalized. This occurred before the Lehman failure. Two days after it, Lloyds TSB agreed to step in HBOS, Britain's biggest home lender (2008 United Kingdom, n.d.). The mortgage lender Bradford & Bingley was nationalized. Her Majesty's Government also had to take stakes in the Royal Bank of Scotland, Lloyds TSB, and HBOS. In Germany, although the Dresdner Bank had to merge with the Commerzbank, government support to banks was limited to relatively small banks. The Netherlands, however, readily had to support the ING Group and nationalize ABN AMRO, with the small SNS REAAL also being nationalized ultimately.

In the countries mentioned above, the monetary system, jointly with the State to varying extents, was able to swallow the effects of the Global Financial Crisis (GFC) on its own. In other countries, it could not do so. Here, the GFC muddled along as a country debt crisis after 2009. Noteworthy European examples include Spain, Italy, Ireland, Cyprus, Greece and Iceland. Already in early 2008, or perhaps rather in 2001, Iceland took the lead ("2008–2011 Icelandic," n.d.; Islam, 2013). Just privatized Icelandic banks readily embarked from home. They especially targeted Great Britain and the Netherlands, offering high-interest rates to the flocking savers over there. Moreover, foreign capital was pouring into the country, making its GDP rise by more than 7% in 2004 and 2005. The Icelandic krona did relatively well initially but slipped away from early 2008 onwards, making the Icelandic foreign debt untenable. The Lehman Brothers failure in the USA was readily followed by the collapse of three major Icelandic banks: Glitnir, Kaupthing, and Landsbanki. The latter launched the label Icesave abroad by branching out. The so-called "Icesave dispute" on who had to compensate the small savers impacted Iceland's relationship with both the United Kingdom and the Netherlands for about a decade.

Greece is also a special case. Firstly, it was affected by the "credit crunch" appearing in its course elsewhere, with the Greek banking sector having been modest before and foreign bank funds being well around. Secondly, whereas the Greek economy had been doing very well over the last decades, the country was heavily indebted from its inception about 180 years earlier, as was indicated in Chap. 8. Thirdly, the expensive organization of the Olympic Games in 2004, other excessive government spending, and tax evasion exaggerated the government deficit. Fourthly, the actual Greek debt position was worse than shown, being partially covered by accounting and financing tricks. Fifthly, although Greece was hardly directly involved in the Global Financial Crisis, its consequences in terms of reduced economic growth did, of course, affect the country. With base interest rate levels having been high and only slowly reducing, the spread to be paid on top of it went up. One way or the other, as Islam (2013) writes, "By early 2012, Greece was not just officially in default—it was the world's biggest sovereign defaulter" (p. 18). However, the country was bailed out by the IMF, the Eurogroup, and private investors, albeit in a not that much-concerted way. Greece even stayed in the Eurozone.

What did change during and after the Global Financial Crisis? Firstly, although it is difficult to assess the numbers and with shadow banking still being all around, it is fair to assume that the banking sector declined in the course of higher reserve requirements, and at least the National Champions did so remarkably. Secondly, exciting and bold investment banking gave way to more traditional retail and private banking. It should be noted here that the role of "boutiques" (specialized houses) grew, and also new market niches were successfully explored. Thirdly, whereas shareholder value approaches gave way to broader stakeholder approaches and total compensation schemes became more modest throughout, they were unchanged in essence—many staff still go for bonuses and options on top of base salaries. Fourthly, staff was reduced, organizational structures were simplified, and small units were closed. Communication systems, IT systems, and control systems were scrutinized and improved, but it showed to be difficult to change cultures despite formal ethical reloadings. Lastly, formulas and algorithms were recorded, with, e.g., JP Morgan Chase later incorporating fat-tail distributions, calling them persistent outliers, in its own risk modeling. However, by definition, this does not include so-called "black swans" such as the Covid-19 crisis. It may also never preclude financial scandals provoked by slick traders, such as, e.g., JP Morgan Chase itself found out during one of the largest cases ever: the 2012 "London Whale" scandal.

11.4 The Secrets of the Banks: From the Knights Templar to the Present

The complete break of the monetary system's dependence on gold in the twentieth century, after Bretton Woods in 1944 and the Nixon Shock in 1971, not only created a glut of money in the world but also opened the door to a world in which we would become accustomed to living with crises. The banking system was now entering a different era. Before discussing the effects of this new era on banking, let us recall the thousand-year history of banking.

Notwithstanding earlier efforts, particularly by the Romans and the Arabs, the first corporate-like organization related to banking and finance emerged in the Crusades era. The Knights Templar was a primary supranational organization of medieval times. During the Crusades, the Templars earned rightful fame and established strong relations with popes, kings, and other segments of society. On the one hand, the order gained a solid reputation by having their trust; on the other hand, they provided them with various services. The Templars' ability to institutionalize their organization was the main driver of their success. Their vast organizations were based on collaboration and teamwork, though initially based on personal qualities and relationships. So they could maintain their power in Europe for 200 years. The Templars were honest and resourceful people; perhaps they would have survived for many more years if they had not suffered the wrath of the King of France. They developed many innovative practices, including money remittance systems, fund management methods, and cashier services no one had ever implemented. They had a solid religious reference, as they adhered to the solid Christian values of their time. This reference allowed them to be accepted by society as honest and good people. In addition, their founding purpose was to ensure that Christians could visit Jerusalem safely, which added a spiritual aspect to their mission. Although their religious side was strong, they had a secular understanding. They attached importance to the fact that their members were brought up with a secular sense and acted relatively independently of religious rules, like prudent merchants in the commercial field. Their global network enhanced their business skills. Maintaining a large number of branches was their strength. Not being a direct subject of any king made them accessible and independent. By influencing the Church, which had rigorous views on interest, and making it more flexible, they could run their banking business. Above all, they established a social balance between society and royalty by developing banking methods that prevented the despotic kings of the medieval age from greedily appropriating the property of the nobles. Their reputation in society was high. These features made them the essential bankers of the period and enabled their historical heritage to live forward with Swiss Banking until recent times.

Professor Galbraith (1990) said that banking belongs to the Italians if it is possible to look for ethnicity in business. Probably, Italian bankers benefited from the experiences of ancient Roman bankers and were impressed by the secular nature of the Templars, which softened the Church's view of the phenomenon of interest. In particular, the Medici family established good relations with the Church and wisely benefited from the economic conditions provided by the Renaissance. The Medici's dealings with Baldassare Cossa, the false Pope John, had earned them a fortune. They achieved extraordinary success and built the largest and most profitable bank in the world of that day, with its branches all over Europe. The Medici family was lucky because there was no authoritarian kingdom in Italy, and the assemblies were governed by republican city-states. Each Republic, and foremost Florence, practiced an elite form of male-dominated democracy. This moderate regime created a climate in which bankers could work more comfortably. There was no government to confiscate their money or threaten them. In addition, the leadership characteristics of the Medici family came to the fore. At the same time, they had the privilege of managing the funds of the popes with their charismatic abilities; they indirectly benefited from their power. Striving to keep a low profile, they could influence the administration of Florence. Undoubtedly, the most remarkable achievement of the Medici is the development and application of their organizational skills. Unlike the central administrations of other banks, they managed many of their subsidiaries with a holding-type organization model. In this model, although each company acted independently, it was also subordinate to the headquarters in Florence, and the managers could be paid according to their performance. This organizational model was quite progressive for its time and played a significant role in keeping the Medici Bank as an institutional structure for more than a hundred years. The Medici had felt the importance of public relations for centuries and established excellent relations with society; they strengthened their image by sponsoring art activities. The Medici had a robust communication network throughout Europe. With their ability to reach almost every region of Europe, they followed the exchange rates very well. Using these networks, they gained the opportunity to diversify their regional and product investments. They were one of the first banks to implement risk diversification in the modern sense. In addition, their increased capacity to monitor their customers by utilizing modern accounting practices has contributed to their prestige. As Western European countries strengthened economically with their colonization and global trading abilities, Italian banking lost its power and leadership in Europe.

During the late sixteenth century, the golden period of the Netherlands began, and the country became a financial center with the Amsterdam Stock Exchange, the East and West Indian Companies, and the Amsterdam Bank of Exchange. The Netherlands, which had undergone a tremendous evolution in banking and finance, was utterly different from its predecessors. Banking developed together with economic growth. The banking and financial sector grew even faster, as the Dutch had access to markets, not the least slave markets, and controlled them. Dutch investors' banking and financial skills improved as they invested in the country and abroad. Beyond a tolerant understanding of the economy, the Dutch had many city-like states, like the Medici's Italy, and lacked despotic rulers. The Dutch were not worried that their rulers might seize their money. Despite being at war, the moderate structure in northern Europe both attracted new investors and encouraged Dutch investors to invest without hesitation. By creating the bank money of the Amsterdam Bank of Exchange, they ensured financial stability and facilitated economic activity. For more than a hundred years since its establishment, the bank never deviated from its purpose and principles. The bank deposit was one hundred percent equivalent to precious metal, and the person who deposited gold in the bank could get it back whenever he wanted. In 1672, when the armies of Louis XIV approached Amsterdam, there was a great panic, and the depositors flocked to the bank, worried that their gold might have been spent. People would stop asking for their money when they saw that the bank was paying anyone who wanted it (Galbraith, 1990). In Dutch companies, institutionalization practices progressed one step further, and corporate governance principles were implemented. Both investors and company employees could claim corporate rights. Many countries in Europe admired the Bank and its institutions in the seventeenth century. The British carried out the Magnificent Revolution to establish a similar system in Britain, invited the Prince of Orange, William III, to their own country, and made him a king. Following this, England transitioned to a parliamentary democracy and became the most important country in Europe from the eighteenth century onwards, while Dutch banking began to lose its power.

The banking story in England started with the Goldsmiths at the end of the sixteenth century. They had begun to collect the money of wealthy people and traders as deposits. During the seventeenth century, the Goldsmiths learned that if they gained the public's trust, the people would not demand the gold they deposited in the bank but preferred to shop with the banknotes the bankers gave. Accordingly, the fractional reserve system started to emerge in England. The biggest threat to the bankers was the despotic kings who could confiscate their money. Instead of putting the funds entrusted to them in the safe, the Goldsmiths gave credit and distributed deposited cash to borrowers so the kings did not have any money they could confiscate. Kings could now face massive social opposition when they seized the people's money. The Goldsmith bankers did not hesitate to commit bribes when doing their job, though. Over time, they gradually institutionalized in the British Isles and became commercial banks. British society has broadly accepted this institutional structure and trusted the banks, and financial institutions such as Lloyds and Barclays have emerged among the Goldsmiths. The English Goldsmiths had drawn inspiration from the Dutch markets and further developed the methods of the early bankers. With the onset of Parliamentarism in England, banking evolved into a new stage. After the Glorious Revolution, the Bank of England was established, and the first model of modern central banking emerged with fractional banking in the driver's seat. As we have seen in previous cases, banking can especially develop in a moderate and liberal environment. As a result of the Glorious Revolution, the financial crises arising from England's monarchy system disappeared, the country's fragility decreased, and the role of the parliament in the economy increased. The predictability of government decisions grew as parliament unilaterally changed tax rates, increased spending, and prevented the king from arbitrarily seizing people's property. A factor behind the bankers' success was having a communication network to reach all European countries and cities. This network was critical for banks to provide loans and closely follow exchange rates. The British had established a highly developed communication system at the end of the seventeenth century, which, in time, went beyond the Dutch system, and even in the early years of the Bank of England, they could efficiently operate an international payment system. As the Bank of England became more robust, the British banking system's prestige increased and became a model for many states and neighboring countries.

John Law was the son of a Scottish Goldsmith who rose to the position of the Ministry of Finance in France, where he became an outlaw. He founded the Banque Générale, which would later become the Royal Bank of France, with authority given to it by the royal government. Observing the experiences of England and the Netherlands, the bank would issue banknotes in exchange for the gold being collected from the public. John Law was going to turn paper into money in one operation, to the envy of alchemists who could not turn matter into gold centuries ago in the laboratory. Backing the support of the regent Philippe, Law's plan was not limited to this; he also took the monopoly of collecting taxes while also undertaking investments to pay the state's debts. He opened the Mississippi Company, which owned the French colony of Louisiana in the United States, to the public. The bank investors initially earned considerable money from the bank, and after a while, the bank would disappear with a financial crisis. In 1720, when there was almost no gold reserve in the bank, the French Livre evolved into Fiat Money, which was not based on any valuable metal, as it is also common today. When his plan was unsuccessful, he was obliged to leave France with destroyed fortunes, falling prices, a stagnant business life, and endless doubt about the banks. After John Law, the reputation of banks was so degraded that for a long time, the French were suspicious of not only banks and paper money but also all money made of metal. Somewhat after these events, when the "assignats," which were the obligatory notes issued during the French Revolution and used as money, failed as well, the French would only use coins in transactions for a long time. Such events are quite instructive regarding what consequences a bank would feel when it lost its reputation. However, the John Law incident appeared as a highly negative model when general economic knowledge was minimal. Law's project was extremely radical and revolutionary. On the one hand, issuing paper money and investing in the Mississippi Company was a bold plan. Law also harmonized France's fiscal and monetary policies. Years later, Adam Smith, the founder of liberal economics, would write that he benefited from his experience. While John Law was already going very fast, the French, who did not show much prudence, caused the crisis to grow even more (Galbraith, 1990).

At the beginning of the eighteenth century, when the armies of Napoleon Bonaparte invaded Europe, the Rothschilds appeared on the stage of history. A Jewish banker, Mayer Rothschild, built a large banking empire by taking advantage of the post-Protestant Reformation in Germany. This Empire was based on the banking network of Mayer's five sons in major European capitals. The Rothschilds became the prime model of the influential Jewish bankers that would later emerge. Especially using the chaotic situation around the Battle of Waterloo, they increased their wealth and power as much as possible. The Rothschilds' greatest strength was that they were untouchable. Their capacity to circulate their money in different countries prevented any state from limiting their activities. Also, their strong family structure made them inaccessible. The loyalty of family members and the harmony between them was one of the strongest sides of the Rothschilds. The Rothschilds had established a strong communication network across Europe. This network was based on continent-wide relationships, skilled riders, and communication pigeons. They could wisely take advantage of investment opportunities using this network. Their Europe-wide network made it easier to organize money operations. They set up the European bond market and brought the financing of government projects to a more modern structure. The Rothschilds received the title of Baron and always had good relations with kings and prime ministers. Their relationships with the top-ranking people also made them more respectable. The Rothschilds were initially most successful in England, as Britain had more robust politics and market conditions than found elsewhere. Rescuing the Bank of England increased its reputation in England. After the French Revolution, they increased their presence in France by taking advantage of the moderate environment here. The Rothschilds had become so rich and powerful that they have been the subject of many conspiracy theories, and the rumors had also earned them global prestige. However, the Rothschilds would lose their importance in banking in the twentieth century, as the family could not adequately align with the tremendous economic development that began in the USA.

The most notable banker in America's Gilded Age was J.P. Morgan. Initially, he started his business life as a banker. According to a strong claim, he defrauded the State by trading weapons during the Civil War years and had success with the speculation in gold. Later, he was very successful also in the railways and steel industries and stood out as a businessman and a leader. When the USA did not yet have a central bank, he saved its economy from a crisis twice. J.P. Morgan had strong ties to British bankers and always believed that the dominant ideology of the USA should be based on free competition and democratic administration in the country. J.P. Morgan made his business life more respectable by wisely using social networks and also giving a lot of time and money to the support of art and culture in general. Being a good Christian, he was well-connected to the Church and became an essential member of social clubs and business associations. Although having occasional conflicts with government officials, he maintained his reputation as a committed and consistent businessman. J.P. Morgan even won the respect of Theodore Roosevelt, with whom he clashed at times. Morgan was handling crises very well. The railroad sector was in constant turmoil and was a good business target for him. J.P. Morgan took a strong position in the industry by solving its problems. With his leadership ability, he also played a profound role in the crises faced by the USA. He was a savior in the 1895 and 1907 crises; he also contributed to the resolution of the workers' strikes that put the economy in trouble. He cleverly used his breakthrough method of negotiation, which was called Corsair. J.P. Morgan's most outstanding business practice was "Morganization." In this way, he stabilized the markets by converting sectors to a monopoly and earning considerable money. He had an international reputation and was one of the most influential businessmen in the USA. Although the bank's power waned somewhat over time, its heirs maintained its reputation and influence and merged J.P. Morgan & Co. with Chase Manhattan in 2000.

Witnessing the last period of the Ottoman Empire, the Ottoman Bank was one of the oldest modern banks operating in a developing country. The bank was established with British and French capital and served as the central bank of the Turkish Republic after the Empire. It survived for nearly 150 years. Undoubtedly, the most outstanding achievement of the Ottoman Empire in the first 50 years, in the period of wars, revolutions, and rebellions, was to survive. The Tanzimat Edict and the relatively moderate state administration were essential to its success. The bank kept its power by maintaining its independence while wars had put great pressure on it. Inevitably, inflation had increased, and the country's financial situation deteriorated further. In this challenging situation, the Ottoman Empire tended to ask for the central bank's resources. Warfare was too expensive, and the debt credibility of the state decreased. Foreign ownership of the Ottoman Bank was a misfortune for the Ottomans because they could not sufficiently benefit from the bank's resources. However, from the bank's point of view, foreign ownership allowed it to maintain its independence, thus preventing its reputation from being tarnished. The value of the Kaimes issued by the State had decreased and failed. A success of the bank was its adaptation to the chaotic environment of the last period of the Ottoman Empire, even though its partners were foreigners. It survived despite changing administrations and various threats. Although the owners of the bank were enemies of the Ottomans during World War I, it could manage its relations. Interestingly, the Ottoman Bank had opened an account to M. Kemal's forces in the War of Independence. A flexible management approach allowed it to work with the newly established Republic of Turkey. The Ottoman Bank financed many essential projects, enabled commercial banking in Turkey, and became a bank model for Turkey; thus, it provided a strong reputation. However, its importance diminished over time, and the bank closed at the turn of the twentieth century.

The period of almost a century up until around 2010 can be thought to have been the era of the "National Champions," large banks that were (co-) dominating the banking business in their home country with also a (semi-) colonial heritage. Examples of these were the Bank of Montreal (BMO) in Canada and the Hong Kong and Shanghai Banking Corporation (HSBC) in China, banks that merged into ABN AMRO in the Netherlands, Deutsche Bank in Germany, and Credit Suisse in Switzerland. The National Champions developed consumer credit products and started selling them to the masses. The banks perfectioned client payment systems in terms of availability and automation. Going for more return went along with accepting more risk. The banks stockpiled financial derivatives, complicated semi-insurance schemes, and pursued corporate finance activities far beyond traditional asset and acquisition financing. Unscrupulous and even outright fraudulent activities by hungry traders made some of the banks shiver at times. By merging with other banks from far away, some national champions started striving for hegemony, such as ABN AMRO and Deutsche Bank. This way, their leaders, acting as genuine CEOs at the time, entered into a bold merger wave that ended in a bust by way of the Global Financial Crisis of the late 00s. The crisis had to be stopped by flabbergasted central bankers trying to regain control of an overexposed financial system that created many aftershocks. In tandem with some regional US banks, the secret-driven Swiss banking system encountered such a crisis in 2023, forcing UBS to swallow its townsman Credit Suisse. Like other National Champions, Credit Suisse had pushed for entrepreneurship too far, and the bank found itself involved in many investigations and scandals.

The leading banks in the USA are a special case of even expanding the boundaries of banking, and therefore, we treated Citibank as a typical example of a pathsetting National Champion separately. Citibank stood out in several respects during the period, especially in dealing with some 80 years after 1929. The bank was built on a strong international foothold in major European centers, such as China and Latin America. Later, Citibank served and benefited from the Americanization of the Free

World by its home country's government and leading companies. It performed large loans and arranged complex transactions. This was basically done by a young and brilliant staff, guided by strong leadership that stimulated entrepreneurial innovation but let discipline go. In this way, Citibank became, e.g., a global leader in transaction services. In particular, though, Citibank was found to push for the deregulation of financial markets that it aimed to service wherever possible. It sought loopholes and workarounds regarding, e.g., the in-principle strict rules in the USA on precluding interstate banking, the separation between commercial banking and investment banking, interest rates and reserve requirements, as well as mergers and acquisitions. The cross-sector merger with Traveller's Group, with a subsequent major spin-off and the use of complex financial vehicles that showed to be too risky, marked the end of a happy half-century. Citibank found itself to have overgrown and to have lost control over its activities, making it vulnerable during the Global Financial Crisis and in need of support from the US central bank system: the Fed. Like other National Champions, Citibank is fighting its way back to the top of the Western World.

11.5 Banking and Politics: About Countervailing Power

"The conflict between state and society, where elite institutions and leaders represent the state, creates a narrow corridor in which freedom flourishes," say Acemoglu and Robinson (2019), the world's best-known proponents of institutional economics. "This conflict must be balanced. Imbalance is detrimental to freedom," emphasizing the importance of preserving this narrow corridor for social and economic development. Staying within the narrow corridor is also important for the healthy development of banking. Therefore, it is useful to project the banking episodes we described regarding this concept of the narrow corridor.

An interesting example in this context is the role of the Knights Templar as a bank-like institution in opening a narrow corridor between the state and society in medieval society. The Templars dealt with two powers: the Popes and the Kings. As a sanctioned organization of Crusade warfare monks, the Templars cannot be related 1:1 to the Church. With their powerful institutional structure, they helped to develop a narrow corridor between the Kings, the Church, and the people (mostly nobles), creating the first bank-like institution in history. In fact, they stretched the Church's principles. As to the Kings, their relationship was friendly, at least in the beginning. The Templars provided loans to the Kings, and the Kings supported the Templars. Later on, the French King envied them, leading to a horrible raid. The Pope supported them halfheartedly, but he was too weak and too dependent on the French King. It finished the role of the Templars and the narrow corridor. Even before the Templars were wiped off the stage of history, there was vibrant commercial and financial activity in the city republics of Italy. Florence was special because of its elitist democracy, which was the right breeding ground for merchants and banking organizations. The commercial structure was quite liberal. The Bardi and

Peruzzi families had already traded wool with England in the 1290s. They made large loans to King Edward III. The king defaulted on his debts, and they went bankrupt. At that time, they couldn't stand against the Kings. The Medici, who rose after them, learned from previous experiences. While they controlled their business with a holding structure that gave their managers a share of the profits, they realized that they could not do banking unless they were politically powerful. They established a balanced relationship with both the city government and the church. They used the wealth generated by the bank to buy the support they needed to dominate the state's political life and keep the business conditions liberal (Goldthwaite, 1987). The Medici had a successful period with the creation of the narrow corridor. Their company and bank disappeared from the stage of history for external economic reasons, internal problems with management and control, and because they could not resist the temptation to lend to foreign "kings" and to interfere more and more in geo-political matters.

The next three episodes we considered were The Netherlands during the sixteenth and seventeenth centuries, England during the seventeenth century and the first half of the eighteenth century, and France during the first half of the eighteenth century. The stories are closely related, but the developments in these three countries were of a different nature. In the Netherlands, the merchants formed the government, especially the merchants from Amsterdam. The development of the stock exchange and the establishment of the Bank of Exchange were good for all merchants. It was infrastructure created by the government, taking into account the interests of all merchants. It was also the government that forced the merchants of the different provinces to work together in the VOC. That was not easy, but it was accepted, and most merchants participated. One could say that The Netherlands was in a narrow corridor then. Important was that there was no king. Now and then, there was a conflict between the Stadtholder, being pro-war, and the government with the merchants, being pro-trade, but in the end, the merchants determined the course. Maybe there was a lack of government control when the merchants became rentiers and started to invest in England and other countries, deteriorating the wealth of The Netherlands. In the case of England, there was a centuries-long struggle between Kings and Parliament over the lack of a proper tax system. The Parliament restricted the King's military activities and the King's means in general. The King reacted by seizing the mint, contributing to the distrust between King and the wealthy people. The civil war, the period of commonwealth without a king, the restoration thereafter, and finally, the Glorious Revolution with Prince William of Orange became King, together with his wife Mary, balanced the relationship between King and Parliament. From then on, they could work on the development of better possibilities for trade and manufacturing and better control of government finance. The Goldsmiths and the Bank of England were important beacons in this narrow corridor. The Glorious Revolution made the political system open and responsive to society's economic needs and aspirations. These inclusive economic institutions gave men of talent and vision the opportunity and incentive to develop their skills and ideas and to influence the system in ways that benefited them and the nation (Acemoğlu & Robinson, 2012). In France, on the other hand, the King had absolute power. Parliaments were only responsible for checking whether the laws were well implemented. An important quote of King Louis XIV is "L'Etat, c'est Moi," and the Regent for King Louis XV had 1715 almost the same absolute power. The bad monetary conditions and the terrible financial problems due to excessive military expenses and chaotic taxation forced him to give John Law the opportunity to introduce a completely new monetary system, money backed by equity, the shares of the Mississippi Company, and then converting the royal debt into this equity. It required huge changes that could only be implemented with the support of the absolute royal power. But, finally, that support crumbled due to the pressure from all segments of society, and the system failed, suddenly and completely.

With the Rothschilds, a new era in European banking had begun. Mayer Rothschild had reached a supranational position with his network spanning five countries and could operate powerfully with the relations he had established. Without the financing of the Rothschilds, even wars could not be fought. At the international level, there was no countervailing power yet. They could only flourish for so long by not abusing their power and by loyally fitting their national activities into the existing political system, not interfering with the possibly existing narrow corridor there. The best example of this is how Nathan Rothschild saved the Bank of England in 1825 and supported the development of English banking with the work of the Rothschilds in England. In the nineteenth century, when the Rothschilds were weakened by their failure to pay due attention to the economic potential of the rapidly developing USA, J. P. Morgan was one of the tycoons of the Gilded Age in the USA, the period of rapid growth that established America as the richest, most inventive and productive country on the planet. In the 1880s, there was extremely wild competition in the railway industry, comparable with the work of an unshackled Leviathan. Morgan saw and understood that and fought it by merging the companies and managing the resulting company or trust of companies. This was called Morganization. That led to new imbalances in the power distribution. The power of Wall Street began to grow as its leader. J.P. Morgan interpreted this role broadly and saved the economy twice, with the support of the President. However, after the crisis of 1907, business people and politicians realized that it was necessary to embed this power in society, and they created institutional structures such as the FED and the SEC, which were a step in the direction of a narrow corridor. But not in the narrow corridor yet; in the Citibank chapter, we describe how it resulted in the crisis of 1929. The regulations introduced thereafter made the imbalance switch to the other side: Too many and too complex regulations. Walter Wriston fought for sufficient freedom for his bank and for Wall Street in general. That took a long time, but with the push of the increased globalization, the Nixon shock, and the support of Reagan and later Clinton, Wall Street more than succeeded, leading to a situation with again too much freedom for financial intermediaries and eventually the crisis of 2008. Thereafter, the imbalance seems to have switched again to more power for the regulators.

Enforcing a balanced environment for the functioning of financial intermediaries is no longer a national problem. The proliferation of the financial crisis in 2008 was almost immediate. Much quicker than in 1929. In the chapter on the National Champions, we see that trust in the banks remained much longer there and that the reactions were very different from those in the US. Bretton Woods and the Nixon shock accelerated the globalization of finance. The International Monetary Fund and the Bank for International Settlements are the first steps to create balance in this system. But, it is far from sufficient yet. Especially the position of developing countries is poorly protected. In the episodes described, we find that back in the Ottoman Bank episode, the (semi-) colonial activities of the National Champions and the LDC loans of Citibank and other big Wall Street banks.

As we often emphasize in the book, the critical factor behind the success of banks is an environment of liberal democracy and economic freedom. Today, as Martin Wolf (2023) argues, this environment exists within democratic capitalism. When this environment did not yet exist, as described in this book, banks either benefited from moderate regimes and democratic values or were beyond the reach of rigid popes and greedy kings. While democratic standards have generally risen in recent centuries, the level of development has not always been the same in all countries. Although it is not easy for governments to confiscate people's savings directly in today's conditions, they can limit the working conditions of banks either by reducing the independence of central banks or by intervening in financial markets in various ways and on various grounds. Liberal democracy and economic freedom remain important for the sound development of banking.

Martin Wolf (2023) attributes the fragility of democratic capitalism to three factors. The first and most obvious is that democracy and a dynamic market economy depend on the existence of a chained Leviathan, i.e., a law-governed and effective state. In a structure where the law is not strong, fragility will emerge. Second, there will be no chained Leviathan without a balance between the political (democratic) and economic (market) aspects of civil society's relationship with the state. The third factor is that merely holding elections or liberalizing the economy is not enough to create and sustain the politics and economy of a chained Leviathan. This is why many attempts at democracy have failed. Last but not least, it is very easy to grow out of the narrow corridor, in both directions, by destabilizing the balance between the state, the people, and the economy. The walls that keep power and wealth separate can crumble, leading to plutocracy, demagoguery, or autocracy and thus to a departure from the narrow corridor. Accordingly, it is quite easy for these factors not to work sufficiently in a country. As the Turkish case shows, elected populist governments can easily turn into authoritarian regimes and close the narrow corridor.

Banking, with its wealth and relationships, has the capacity to destroy the narrow corridor. But we have to trust banks as an economic institution. For a system of democratic capitalism to work, politics is protected from the economy by norms, independent institutions, and laws regulating elections, civil participation, corruption prevention, and the role of the state in general, and the economy is protected from politics by norms, independent institutions and laws protecting property and transaction rights and regulating governance. This complex relationship between the market economy and democratic governance is, as we have seen, prone to failure. Economic institutions in a system of democratic capitalism are designed to allow free and safe transactions with foreigners anywhere in the world. In the modern economy, trust is built on reliable institutions like banks, including the rule of law.

And in modern politics, trustworthy institutions, including the rule of law, are the foundation of trust (Wolf, 2023).

For countries to remain within this corridor, reconciliation, and cooperation between the social, economic, and political actors of democratic capitalism must be achieved. Four aspects of this process of compromise and cooperation are particularly important. First, capitalist competition is not free for all. A free-for-all creates an environment in which bandits are powerful. However, the state must take the initiative to set the rules for a complex modern economy. But it, too, must not be captured by the most powerful actors in the economy. The possibility of regulatory capture of the financial sector, suggested by George Stigler (1971), is a problem in this regard. Banking should be prevented from becoming too powerful through lobbies. Second, the rules of the game are necessarily complex and changing. They include the rules that create and then govern the most important actors in the contemporary market economy—the corporations—as well as the rules that regulate the functioning of markets. As the economy has become more complex and interventionist and politics more democratic and demanding, these rules and regulations have inevitably and justifiably become more onerous and have created high costs. With its strong government relations, banking can use these issues as an excuse to remove regulations. Third, many of these rules have international implications. In today's global environment, the economic institutions of developed nations are designed to ensure that transactions can occur freely and safely, not just at home but worldwide. Making the whole system work is challenging and tricky. Finally, citizens have economic security and laws to protect them from exploitation. It is not easy to make all these things happen. All players need to make efforts to make the system work. In this context, in a modern economy, reliance on solid institutions, including the rule of law, is the foundation of trust and stability (Wolf, 2023).

11.6 The Power Game: Wall Street Versus Main Street

The Great Depression brought banking regulations back on the agenda. Regulation Q prohibited interest payment on demand deposits on August 29, 1933. It was also used to impose interest rate ceilings on various bank deposits, including savings and time deposits. Excessive bank competition for deposit funds was thought to encourage excessively speculative investment behavior by large banks. However, the cap on interest rates on savings deposits encouraged the emergence of alternative banks, including money market funds. An important possibility to avoid the regulations came from the eurodollar market.

After the Second World War, the amount of physical US dollar banknotes outside the United States increased dramatically, both due to dollar financing of the Marshall Plan and dollar revenues from European exports to the United States, which had become its largest consumer market. In 1956, during the Cold War, following the invasion of Hungary, the Soviet Union feared that its deposits in North American banks would be frozen as a sanction, so it sent them to UK banks. In 1957, in response to high inflation and the potential reduction in reserves caused by the Suez crisis, the British government imposed severe restrictions on sterling loans to non-residents, banned the use of sterling to finance third-party transactions, and began using dollar deposits as a means of credit for non-residents to circumvent the problem of exchange controls imposed by the UK. There were also lucrative investment opportunities in the UK, with the financial innovations that followed. With tight monetary policy in the US and the UK, relatively relaxed controls on the forward exchange market, and lucrative interest arbitrage opportunities, the eurodollar market began to expand rapidly. The Eurodollar market grew by over 252% from 1964 to 1969. As the US administration tried to control the outflow of dollars, multinational corporations, eager to use their surplus dollar balances profitably, and banks, equally keen to accommodate demand, found ways to circumvent the controls (Restrepo–Echavarría & Grittayaphong, 2022).

While expansionary fiscal and monetary policies had been in place since 1969, the crop failures of 1972 and 1973 and rising commodity prices, especially oil prices, which increased several times over, affected all countries. Above all, the public was convinced that inflation would never fall. This psychology made inflation even more resilient. Another issue was rising unemployment and the danger of stagflation. These factors in the 1970s and 1980s, notably the sharp rise in inflation and increased volatility in interest and exchange rates, put considerable pressure on banking institutions to develop new financial instruments. Banks also tried to get around the interest rate ban to increase their interest rates. NOW (Negotiable Order of Withdrawal) and Money Market Fund (MMF) were not subject to Regulation Q limits. Since the 1973 Nixon shock, the creation of banking money has also been growing uncontrollably. Reagan stabilized the economy after 1980 by implementing "Reaganomics." This policy involved economic deregulation and cuts in both taxes and government spending during a period of stagflation. He escalated an arms race and transitioned Cold War policy away from détente with the Soviet Union.. Over time, the Fed's commitment to low inflation gained credibility, unemployment fell, and the economy entered a sustained growth and stability. The Great Inflation was over.

However, the stabilized economy also reduced banks' profitability. Bankers argued that heavily regulated commercial banks were losing market share to less regulated and more innovative institutions. Moreover, US banks have started to lobby in the US political system and have begun to try to penetrate the views of legislators and regulators on significant issues, which is called regulator capture. This led to a wave of deregulation during the last two decades of the twentieth century. By 1999, banks could offer commercial banking, securities, and insurance services under one roof. Besides, the last two decades have seen fundamental changes in communications and computer technology that have irrevocably changed the way financial transactions are conducted worldwide. These innovations also meant increased risk for financial institutions. These innovations have encouraged or facilitated a high degree of leverage (borrowing) among very big institutions. It may cause more devastating spillovers in the event that a big bank or other highly leveraged firm fails. In the twentieth century, a narrow corridor had been established in the US and other developed countries, and an environment was created in which banking could flourish. However, developments during these last two decades showed that this time, the power struggle in the economy had taken a different turn. The financial lobby was now stronger and more demanding. Could this power lead it to go beyond its assigned role? Could it override the public interest? Was there a power struggle in this context? We simply call this the dance of Main Street and Wall Street. Main Street represents the public interest, and Wall Street is the greedy financial lobby.

To understand how this dance came about, we need to recall the original mandate of banks. The primary function of financial intermediaries, especially banks, is to overcome problems related to asymmetric information (Akerlof, 1970). According to traditional financial theory, market-created institutions such as banks allow the adverse effects of information asymmetries to be eliminated and balance the demands of savers and borrowers regarding maturity, amount, and risk. They also contribute to the monetary policies of governments by creating money and stabilizing liquidity by absorbing market shocks in the event of crises. Besides, financial innovations improve the banking system's ability to assess the quality of borrowers and investment projects to be financed. However, this 2008 financial crisis has led us to discuss whether banks fulfill their primary duty. Since the outbreak of the financial crisis in 2007–2008, there has been widespread public distrust of finance, banks, and bankers, and some questions were raised. Are banks playing their traditional role, or are they forcing markets to over-speculate, making extraordinary profits when things are going well and taking it out on the public when things go badly?

Schumpeter (1912), known for the theory of creative destruction, argues that finance is an essential element of the economic development process of a capitalist economy and that without a developed financial system, there can be no economic development. He argues that banks contribute by creating financial innovations. According to Schumpeter, there would be neither innovation nor economic development without bank money. His analysis of the role of bank money in the economic development process that characterizes capitalist economies used the concept of "good" finance as an example. More specifically, good finance is about entrepreneurship. Ventures with an appropriate level of risk will bring prosperity to society. In this context, the role of banking within the narrow corridor described by Acemoğlu and Robinson (2019) should correspond with the concept of good finance.

According to Minsky (1993), one of the leading representatives of the Post Keynesian School, the proliferation of "good" finance paves the way for the development of "bad" finance, i.e., excessive speculation and thus the outbreak of economic crises. Let us assume that banks fulfill their assigned economic roles within these limits. In this case, they would be fulfilling their responsibilities to Main Street (the real economy, ordinary people and small business owners, large national and international corporations, and in the US, the government, including the Fed and other regulatory bodies). In today's economic and monetary system, however, there is a real danger that Wall Street, which is all about banking and finance, will overstep these boundaries and turn to bad finance. In fact, as we will explain in a moment, bad finance is based on "money manager capitalism," which became widespread after a quarter of the twentieth century. The proliferation of a paradigm that neglected the distinction between good and bad finance provided a theoretical justification for the deregulation of financial markets and the liberalization of capital movements, which led professional intermediates, such as banks, to emphasize "speculation" over "enterprise" (Bertocco & KalaJzic, 2018).

Minsky (1989) distinguished between two forms of capitalism in the US economy during the period after the Second World War. He called the first form of capitalism, which characterized the period from the end of the war to the mid-1970s, "paternalistic, managerial, and welfare state capitalism." Paternalistic capitalism is based on the social regulation of aggregate demand since modern corporations cannot guarantee by their actions that the flow of aggregate demand will be sufficient to withdraw their planned production from the market at controlled prices. This burden falls on the State, which supports this through fiscal policy and monetary management. The second form of capitalism emerged after the mid-1970s, which he called "money manager capitalism." Minsky (1986) used this latter term to describe the characteristics of an economic system in which the financial system is dominated by agents whose ultimate goal is not to promote "entrepreneurship" but to maximize short-term profits through speculative trading activities. This paradigm eliminated the distinction between "enterprise" and "speculation," leading to the importance of "speculation" over "enterprise." It provided the theoretical justification for a political program based on the deregulation of markets (particularly, the deregulation of labor and financial markets) and the liberalization of the movement of goods and capital. This led to a clear break with the rules introduced after the Great Crash of 1929.

The theoretical justification for this program was simple: more deregulation meant more competition and more efficiency. The link between market liberalization, more competition, and a significant improvement in the functioning of market mechanisms may be valid in non-speculative markets. However, financial innovations can lead to instability and crises in a monetized economy. Keynes explained this: "Speculators may not harm bubbles on a steady stream of enterprise. However, the position is serious when enterprise becomes the bubble on a whirlpool of speculation. When the capital development of a country becomes a by-product of the activities of a casino, the job is likely to be ill-done." As Keynes pointed out, they can lead to the triumph of "speculation" over "enterprise." A clear sign of the increasing weight of speculation since the early 1980s comes from the misuse of securities.

According to Rajan (2006), the Chief Economist of the International Monetary Fund, two fundamental innovations have pushed the US banking system to create risk. The first is the standardization of financial instruments due to technology, information, and the computer revolution, which produced a higher availability of information that increased the liquidity of bank loans. Bank loans have thus become assets that can be sold in financial markets. The second innovation is the securitization process, which allows banks to sell some of their standardized assets in the market. This process fundamentally transformed the business model of banks and resulted in a shift from the traditional "originate-to-hold" model to a new "originate-to-distribute" model. While the securitization process has increased the efficiency of the financial system as the division of labor between banks and Special Purpose Vehicles (SPVs) has increased the diversification of financial assets, the ability of banks to transfer their loans and associated default risks through the securitization process has reduced the incentives for banks to assess the quality of loans rigorously. The liberalization of financial markets has encouraged distorted use of securitization techniques since the early 1980s. Second, the deregulation of the financial system has transformed the banking system into a homogeneous organism dominated by giant universal banks set up as joint stock companies that aim to maximize shareholder value through speculation. This paved the way for company managers to speculate to increase the value of the stock in the short term.

Rajan (2010) uses two concepts to explain the relationship between deregulation and speculation: tail risk and herd behavior. Tail risk describes decisions that generally offer very high returns while presenting a low risk of catastrophic loss. Rajan uses the concept of tail risk to explain the decision of bank managers to increase the supply of mortgages to low-income households. This decision stimulated housing demand and thus contributed to the development of a housing bubble. This was a speculative and risky policy. Its basic assumption was that house prices would rise continuously. Initially, however, this policy not only led to an increase in the price of stocks but also resulted in large bonuses for executives. But bankers took advantage of asymmetric information in the market to package high risk into high returns, easily disguised. It increased the risk of speculation, fraud, and systemic failure. Speculative behaviors have become widespread in a world where any kind of acknowledgment of debt or deed of ownership can be converted into a listed security and a world of unlimited creativity.

The second concept Rajan uses to explain the origins of the financial crisis is herd behavior. This concept explains banks' decision to hold many derivative asset-backed securities on their balance sheets. When the housing bubble finally burst, it became clear that banks were holding large amounts of asset-backed securities on their books. This surprised those who believed banks, which should have been aware of the poor quality of loans, avoided underwriting securitized mortgages. The bankers again took advantage of asymmetric information. Diamond and Rajan (2009) argue that bank managers, who were aware of professional speculators, continued to "follow the herd" by betting on the rise of house prices, even though they were already significantly overvalued. The concept of short-termism is widely used to illustrate the behavior of bank managers at the root of the contemporary crisis. It explains the iconic quote of Charles Prince: "As long as the music is playing, you have to get up and dance" (see the first section of this chapter and the previous chapter).

11.7 Central Bank Independence and Basel Accord

On the morning of March 20, 2021, even though it was a weekend, Turkish bank managers and international portfolio managers of Turkish funds in the London money market woke up early. They started an intense communication traffic between them. The news was very important. It turned out that the governor of the Central Bank of the Republic of Turkey (CBRT), appointed just four months ago, had been dismissed in the middle of the night and replaced by someone else. He was the fourth central bank governor to be dismissed in 20 months. He raised interest rates and stabilized the Turkish exchange rate during his tenure. But with this decision, the CBRT wholly lost its independence, and market players could not predict the bank's next steps. The markets started to react to the event on Monday. The Turkish Lira lost 10% of its value within a week, and foreign investors quickly sold their stocks, causing a sharp drop in market prices. The president argued that interest was forbidden by religion and demanded a radical cut in interest rates by the bank. In the following years, in an environment of high inflation, the deposits of low-interest depositors in banks were given to companies as loans at low-interest rates. Turkey experienced the most significant capital transfer in its history. Today, state administrators can no longer directly confiscate people's money; they can do so through different methods.

After this point, the narrow corridor in Turkey was out of sight, and a pessimistic atmosphere spread. As the question of whether foreign investors were leaving Turkey came to the fore, the economic policies of the 1980s–90s came to mind. Turkey, which has been transitioning to a liberal market economy since the 1980s, made similar mistakes in 1994 and 2001, and then mismanagement of the economy caused international capital to leave the country. During this period, the Turkish Lira depreciated sharply several times, and interest rates rose above 100%. However, thereafter, Turkey achieved a moderate economic environment for a decade.

The above story shows us how easily institutions like the central bank can lose their institutional power and independence and thus lose monetary stability. As Acemoglu and Robinson underline, it is not easy to maintain a constant balance between the state, the people, and the economy. The narrow corridor that had begun to form in the first decade of the twenty-first century had closed in Turkey. South American countries have repeatedly made the same mistakes over the last fifty years. South American banking has continuously drifted from one direction to another in the hands of populist and autocratic leaders (Ocampo, 2014).

Globalization, which accelerated with the collapse of the Soviet Union, has increased the interconnectedness of states and economies. It also raised the risk of contagion from speculation in financial markets, financial failures, and populist policies of governments. Therefore, national governments have started cooperating to promote stability and create a level playing field in international financial markets. Two significant trends have emerged in this context over the last 40 years. One is the need for central bank independence, and the other is the phenomenon of developing international banking standards. These approaches have increased the importance of international cooperation and fair rules worldwide. IMF encouragement and international agreements on regulatory and supervisory standards have tended to create a level playing field for global financial sector competition, preventing competition from unduly weakening the financial strength of institutions. Countries realized that financial crashes become more likely when they operate banking in excessively deregulated conditions. When they do occur, they are more severe and more likely to spread across borders. As we have explained in detail in this book, crises, and depressions in international banking and finance, have affected not only the country in question but also the countries with which it has economic relations. In the fourteenth century, when King Edward III of England defaulted on his debts, the Italian economy suffered, and the Mississippi and South Sea crises (Chaps. 4 and 5) affected many countries in Western Europe. Lehman's bankruptcy created a global crisis. World history is full of reckless behavior by the financial sector. Even if a bank or a country's Central Bank assesses their risk in a measured way, they may still not be prudent enough from society's point of view because some of the costs of failure fall on others, such as investors, shareholders and, in the case of a government bailout, taxpayers who ultimately have to pay. The emergence of this danger may even limit the flow of transnational capital to particular companies or countries, as we have seen in the case of Turkey.

The case for an independent central bank came to the fore due to four distinct and essentially simultaneous influences. First, the inflationary periods of the 1970s led to a great deal of dissatisfaction with central banks, which were blamed for allowing inflation to occur. Central bank organization, governance, and policymaking had to be rethought. Second, central banks were established or restructured in many countries—industrial countries, newly independent countries, and later transition countries that were transitioning from centrally planned economies to market-oriented economies (mostly Eastern European Countries). In each case, the role and place of the central bank within government structures had to be defined. Third, the rational expectations revolution in macroeconomics led to significant changes in thinking about the role of monetary policy. This hypothesis claims that people's expectations are the same as the estimation of the model being used to describe those people (Taylor, 2000). Particularly, the developments in macroeconomic modeling in the 1970s had important implications for understanding what a central bank could achieve. Accordingly, the advantages of delegating monetary policy to an independent body in a democratic society are strong enough. Finally, empirical research showed that countries with more independent central banks experienced lower inflation (Garriga & Rodriguez, 2020). By the 1990s, there was a consensus that central banks should be independent of political influence. However, just being independent is not sufficient; the modern central bank is a more complex institution with responsibilities that overlap with other government functions. Central bank efforts to prevent a systemic crisis may involve fiscal or spending decisions and have political and distributional consequences. Crisis intervention cannot be completely independent of political decisions. Central banks and governments have not fully worked out how to balance political responsibility and independence for central banks with a broad mandate. CBI is a more nuanced and complex concept than it seemed 30 years ago as the role of central banks has evolved (Wachtel & Blejer, 2020). On the other hand, in motivating countries to increase CBI, the IMF aims to insulate central banks from political interference and protect loan disbursements from government abuse. Moreover, some loan conditionality clauses give considerable power to independent monetary authorities in formulating economic policymaking. Such loans are usually conditional on the fulfillment of a condition aimed at helping the sovereign country to restructure or regain positive economic momentum. Thus, by pressuring the CBI, the IMF seeks to create a non-political player to support its economic policy reform agenda. This contributes to the Leviathan's chaining, as Acemoglu and Robinson suggested (Kern et al., 2019).

On the other hand, international finance today poses at least four significant challenges for national regulators and supervisors. First, it's not easy to assess the activities of financial institutions that extend beyond their home country. Second, financial firms may exploit regulatory differences across jurisdictions to locate their riskiest activities in less regulated areas. Third, complex institutions with activities across national jurisdictions are more challenging to resolve when they fail. Fourth, countries can actively compete for international financial business while supporting their domestic banks through lax regulatory standards. These factors undermine the global financial system's stability, especially as financial instruments and networks become more complex. To address these challenges, national supervisors began a consultation and coordination process in 1974 under the auspices of the Basel Committee on Banking Supervision. While the Basel Committee focuses on banking regulation with Basel I, II, and III accords, the Financial Stability Board, established by the G20 in the aftermath of the 2008 financial crisis, brings together national authorities, international financial institutions, and sectoral standard setters to coordinate the development of regulatory policy in the broader global financial markets. International financial cooperation remains essential for a strong and stable global economy (Adrian & Obstfeld, 2017).

11.8 The Future of Fractional Reserve Banking

As we stressed in Chap. 4, where we described the contribution of the Goldsmiths and the Bank of England to the financial revolution, the heart of the actual financial system is still formed by fractional reserve banking. It combines high flexibility with high vulnerability, which is characteristic and makes trust so important. Many technologically inspired developments are going on, and we will sketch whether and how these developments affect the functioning of fractional reserve banking. We pay attention to cryptography (combined with the increased importance of privacy protection), AI, open banking, e-money, cryptocurrencies, stablecoins, and CBDC (Central Bank Digital Currency). First again a simplified description of fractional reserve banking.

Payments are generally executed by using commercial bank money, i.e., demand deposits. If actor A pays an amount q to actor B and both have an account with some bank X, then X functions as a trusted third and subtracts, after some checks (authentication, authorization, anti-money laundering, and anti-terrorist financing), an amount q from the account balance of A and this to the account balance of B. If B has an account with another bank in the same country, bank Y, the country's CB, is also involved. Both banks have an account with the Central Bank (CB). The payment also necessitates a transfer from X's account to Y's. It reduces the reserves of X and increases the reserves of Y. In principle, it may lead to a shortage of reserves for X, but the total amount of reserves of all banks is not changing. So, the banks can resolve the problems mutually as long as they trust each other. If actor A prefers to pay B cash, he must first withdraw an amount q in cash. This reduces the reserves of bank X and all banks' reserves together. Actor A will only keep using his account if he trusts the bank sufficiently. This is the vulnerable kernel of the fractional reserve banking system. As long as the reserves are sufficient, a bank can issue new demand deposits by giving a loan without increasing the reserves. The CB tries to keep price development within limits by controlling the banks' access to the CB reserves.

The developments regarding *cryptography* have made it possible to improve the *privacy protection* of A and B so that it is not easily possible for the banks involved to monitor the information of A and B. It is even possible to make privacy protection absolute by using blockchain technology in combination with a distributed ledger. The checks and the transfer are performed by algorithms, so they are completely digital already. For the AML/ATF check, one can rely more and more on *AI*. *AI* is also useful in the risk assessment of new loans. The development of *open banking* is inspired by the principle that an actor who starts an account with a bank remains proprietor of his own information. This principle is the basis for PSD2, the payments directive of the EU, stating that an actor may give another party access to his account information. This makes it possible, e.g., to let this party initiate payments. This may help to realize a better integration of the payments with the actor's financial management. So far, the developments do not interfere with the fractional reserve banking principle. They lead to serious challenges for individual banks, but they fit well in the system.

This is already a bit more complicated for *e-money*. A financial service provider can create an e-money scheme by offering actors the possibility to convert their bank money or cash into some form of electronic money. They can pay other actors who also have an account in this e-money, with this e-money. If they like, they can withdraw their e-money again; ideally, e-money is full-reserve money. Many e-money providers work internationally. Then, the conversion is combined with a currency exchange. Examples of e-money are PayPal, Alipay (China), and the mobile phone money M Pesa in Kenya. A couple of years ago, Meta also had plans, the Libra, later renamed Diem. The Libra was said to be fully backed by a basket of currencies. US regulators blocked the introduction. There were fears that it would develop into a bank that, because of its really international character and its backing with a basket of currencies, did not quite fit in the financial system. The principle of full-reserve e-money fits in a financial system based on fractional reserve banking, but if free conversion is limited, it may lead to extra instability of the conversion flows that also impact the reserves of the commercial banks. And internationally working e-money schemes, like the Libra, do not easily fit into the regulatory structure.

New developments with respect to cryptography and a tendency toward libertarianism have also led to the development of cryptocurrency, with Bitcoin in the first place. For us, it is sufficient to know that a Bitcoin is a software-created entity that can be exchanged using DLT (Distributed Ledger Technology). It is something you may like to have, and it has a price therefore. All goods that people like to have and that can be exchanged, gold, silver, etc., can be used for payments. It misses, however, another property that is essential for money, already mentioned by Law (Chap. 5): stability of value. Therefore, pure cryptos are only suitable for speculation, not for payment. Their existence does not interfere with fractional reserve banking. The instability of cryptocurrencies has led to the development of *stablecoins*. A stablecoin is a crypto that is designed to remain stable relative to the dollar or euro. That is not easy. It is comparable to John Law's difficulties in stabilizing the Mississippi company's share price. Just as in the case of the Mississippi shares of Law, it is possible to manipulate the availability, but its effect on the price is not easy to predict. Guaranteeing a price may easily lead to bankruptcy. It would be interesting to make a more detailed comparison of the failure of the cryptocurrency exchange FTX (The Verge, 2022) and the bursting of the Mississippi bubble.

All these developments put pressure on the official financial world to come up with its own improvements. It was set against the almost failure of the financial system during the crisis of 2008 and led to the development of *Central Bank Digital Currency* (CBDC). CBDC is issued by the CB and is, in fact, just digital cash. If an actor wants to pay with CBDC, his account balance has to be reduced to the right quantity, and the payee's account balance has to be increased to that amount. The Federal Reserve has been thinking critically about whether there is a role for a potential US CBDC in the digital payments landscape of the future. It sets out four design principles that, according to analysis, would best serve the needs of the United States if a CBDC were created. These principles are that a potential CBDC should be privacy-protected so that consumer data and privacy are protected; financial intermediaries, rather than the Federal Reserve, should manage the CBDC accounts; it should be broadly transferable so that the payment system is not fragmented; and it should be authenticated so that law enforcement can continue to fight money laundering and terrorist financing ("Preparing for the Financial System of the Future," 2023). They add that to realize stability, it is necessary to limit the conversion of bank money to CBDC. Without such limits, a digital bank run could strike within seconds. Such a limit is also taken into account in possible pilot experiments that are going to be performed by the ECB (2023). Of all the developments mentioned, CBDC is the only one that seriously threatens the fractional reserve system. In between, the Positive Money movement is hoping for a complete switch to CBDC, paying only with CBDC instead of with commercial bank money (Huber, 2017; Jackson & Dyson, 2012). That would lead to a full-reserve system instead of a fractional reserve system, so a system with a less vulnerable heart than a fractional reserve banking system, but given what we have now, it is not very probable that such a switch will be realized soon.

11.9 Conclusion

The developments mentioned in the last section are not the only challenges for the banking sector. According to a report prepared by experts from the IMF, SAS, and the United Nations, five threats have emerged that will specifically affect the banking system by 2035. Accordingly, (1) the digital revolution is accelerating. Financial technology has evolved to a level where online banks and banking as a service are challenging incumbent banks and the nature of banking intermediation. While this threatens the actual banking model, it can create new markets and business opportunities. (2) Economic fragmentation is gaining momentum. Globalization, rising populism, nationalism, and protectionism are emerging. There is increasing uncertainty in global supply chains and international governance practices and agreements. (3) Common global challenges like climate change are multiplying and intensifying. (4) Ongoing economic and social inequalities and migration are significant challenges, and the deterioration of income distribution worldwide will affect business models. (5) Ethics is moving to the center of business practices. In the age of social media and activist investors, companies, including banks, must now be prepared to be accountable for their business's social and environmental impact (Banking in 2035, 2022).

This book is not the right place to try to develop possible scenarios to deal with all these challenges. But maybe it is good to refer to the introduction of bank money for international trade in Amsterdam. In the early seventeenth century, the Bank of Amsterdam issued bank money that was fundamentally no different from the digitized demand deposits of today's world. Since it is not easy to attribute great value to a piece of paper, it was natural that Amsterdam merchants were initially sceptical of money recorded in bank ledgers, much like the scepticism toward virtual currencies today. The Bank of Amsterdam quickly solved this problem with public confidence and became the first institution in history to issue dematerialized money. European merchants soon became accustomed to bank money and, within a hundred years, began to replace it with paper money. It can be said with certainty that the supremacy of paper money will not last for thousands of years like that of coins and will probably be replaced by digital money before the end of this century. In the fifteenth century, the Medici used Arabic characters to store their bank accounts in a libro segreto (secret book); in the twenty-first century, we are moving to an era where new digital accounts are stored in the clouds, and the development of distributed ledger technologies and cryptography is accelerating. This irresistible shift in technology is inevitably leading to branchless and unstaffed banks where decisions are made by artificial intelligence. Perhaps humanity's greatest strength is its instinct to adapt quickly to change.

Finally, in telling the banking history, we met colorful characters like the Medici, John Law, and J.P. Morgan, who took us from one country to another. We tried to understand their ambitions, passions, and mistakes. We left Goldsmiths' shops, came across a Citibank branch, almost only consisting of an ATM, and went to virtual branches. Instead of from the bank in town, we got a loan from the bank on our mobile phone. As we enter the second quarter of the twenty-first century, we will discuss technical issues like open banking, digital currencies, and artificial intelligence. In such a rapidly changing world, banks will face new problems. Perhaps the adventure of banking in the future will be even more fascinating than it was in the past. What do you think?

References

2008 United Kingdom bank rescue package. (n.d.). 2008 United Kingdom bank rescue package. *Wikipedia*. Retrieved August 5, 2019, July 7, 2023, from https://en.wikipedia.org/wiki/2008_United_Kingdom_bank_rescue_package

2008–2011 Icelandic financial crisis. (n.d.). 2008–2011 Icelandic financial crisis. *Wikipedia*. Retrieved August 5, 2019, July 7, 2023, from https://en.wikipedia.org/wiki/2008%E2%80%932011_Icelandic_financial_crisis

Acemoglu, D., & Robinson, J. A. (2012). *Why nations fail: The origins of power, prosperity, and poverty*. Crown Business.

Acemoglu, D., & Robinson, J. A. (2019). *The narrow corridor: How nations struggle for liberty*. Penguin UK.

Adrian, T., & Obstfeld, M. (2017). Why-international-financial-cooperation-remains-essential. https://www.imf.org/en/Blogs/Articles/2017/03/23/

Akerlof, G. (1970). The market for 'Lemons': Quality uncertainty and the market mechanism. *Quarterly Journal of Economics, 84*(3), 488–500.

Banking in 2035: three possible futures. (2022). Economic Impact. Retrieved April 05, 2024, from https://impact.economist.com/perspectives/sites/default/files/banking_in_2035_three_possible_futures_briefing_paper.pdf

Bekaert, G., & Mehl, A. (2019). On the global financial market integration, "swoosh" and the trilemma. *Journal of International Money and Finance, 94*, 227–245.

Bertocco, G., & KalaJzic, A. (2018). How much does finance benefit society? *PSL Quarterly Review, 71*(287), 419–437.

Bordo, M. D. (2020). The imbalances of the Bretton woods system 1965 to 1973: US inflation, the elephant in the room. *Open Economies Review [Online], 31*, 195–211. https://doi.org/10.1007/s11079-019-09574

Butkiewicz, J. L., & Ohlmacher, S. (2021). Ending Bretton Woods: Evidence from the Nixon tapes. *Economic History Review [Online], 74*(4), 922–945. https://doi.org/10.1111/ehr.13052

Davies, H., & Green, D. (2010). *Banking on the future: The fall and rise of central banking*. Princeton University Press.

Diamond, D., & Rajan, R. (2009). The credit crisis: Conjectures about causes and remedies. *NBER Working Paper*, no. 14739, February, Cambridge (MA): National Bureau of Economic Research.

Duncan, R. (2011). *The dollar crisis: Causes, consequences, cures*. John Wiley & Sons.

ECB. (2023). *A stocktake on the digital Euro*. ECB

Fowler, S. A. (2021). The monetary fifth column: The Eurodollar threat to financial stability and economic sovereignty, 47 Vanderbilt Law Review 825. https://scholarship.law.vanderbilt.edu/vjtl/vol47/iss3/5

Galbraith, J. K. (1990). *Money: Whence it came, where it went*. Golden Books.

Garriga, A. C., & Rodriguez, C. M. (2020). More effective than we thought: Central bank independence and inflation in developing countries. *Economic Modelling, 85*, 87–105.

Geithner, T. F. (2014). *Stress test: Reflections on financial crises*. Random House.

Goldthwaite, R. A. (1987). The Medici Bank and the world of Florentine capitalism. *Past & Present, 114*, 3–31.

Huber, J. (2017). *Sovereign money; beyond reserve banking*. Palgrave McMillan.

Islam, F. (2013). *The default line*. Head of Zeus Ltd.

Jackson, A., & Dyson, B. (2012). *Modernising money; why our monetary system is broken and how it can be fixed*. Positive Money.

Kern, A., Reinsberg, B., & Rau-Göhring, M. (2019). IMF conditionality and central bank independence. *European Journal of Political Economy, 59*, 212–229.

King, M. A. (2016). *The end of Alchemy: Money, banking, and the future of the global economy*. W.W. Norton & Company.

Minsky, H. (1986). Money and crisis in Schumpeter and Keynes. In H. J. Wagener, J. W. Drukker (Eds.), *The economic law of motion of modern society*: A Marx-Keynes-Schumpeter Centennial (pp. 112–122). Cambridge University Press.

Minsky, H. (1993). Schumpeter and finance. In S. Biasco, A. Roncaglia, & M. Salvati (Eds.), *Markets and institutions in economic development: Essays in honour of Paolo Sylos Labini* (pp. 103–115). Macmillan.

Minsky, H. P. (1989). Financial crises and the evolution of capitalism: The crash of '87—What does it mean? In M. Gottdiener & N. Komninos (Eds.), *Capitalist development and crisis theory: Accumulation, regulation, and spatial restructuring* (pp. 391–403). St. Martin's Press.

Nixon Shock. (n.d.). Nixon Shock. *Wikipedia.* Retrieved August 5, 2019, July 26, 2023. from https://en.wikipedia.org/wiki/Nixon_shock

Ocampo, J. A. (2014). The Latin American debt crisis in historical perspective. In *Life after debt. International economic association series.* London: Palgrave Macmillan.

Patterson, S. (2010). *The Quants: How a new breed of Math Whizzes conquered wall street and nearly destroyed it.* Crown Business.

Rajan, R. (2006). Has finance made the world Riskier? *European Financial Management, 12*(4), 499–533.

Rajan, R. (2010). *Fault lines: How hidden fractures still threaten the world economy.* Princeton University Press.

Restrepo-Echavarría, P., & Grittayaphong, P. (2022) Bretton-Woods and the growth of the Eurodollar market. Federal Reserve Bank of St. Louis. https://www.stlouisfed.org/on-the-economy/2022/january/bretton-woods-growth-eurodollar-market

Richard Nixon. (n.d.). Richard Nixon. *Wikipedia.* Retrieved August 5, 2019, July 26, 2023, from https://en.wikipedia.org/wiki/Richard_Nixon

Schumpeter, J. A. (1912). *Theorie der wirtschaftlichen Entwicklung, Duncker & Humblot, Berlin; English edition (1949).* Harvard University Press.

Sorkin, R. A. (2009). *Too big to fail: The inside story of how Wall Street and Washington fought to save the financial system—and themselves.* Penguin Books.

Stigler, G. J. (1971). The theory of economic regulation. *Bell Journal of Economics and Management Science, 2*, 3–21.

Taub, J. (2013). What we don't talk about when we talk about banking. In *The handbook of the political economy of financial crises* (pp. 447–466).

Taylor, J. (2000). How the rational expectations revolution has changed Macroeconomic Policy Research. *Stanford University.* https://web.stanford.edu/~johntayl/Papers/IEALecture.pdf

The New York Times. (2007). Citi Chief on Buyouts: 'We're Still Dancing', July 10. https://archive.nytimes.com/dealbook.nytimes.com/2007/07/10/citi-chief-on-buyout-loans-were-still-dancing/

The Verge. (2022). Here is everything that went wrong with FTX. https://www.theverge.com/2022/11/30/23484331/ftx-explained-cryptocurrency-sbf-sam-bankman-fried

Wachtel, P., & Blejer, M. I. (2020). A fresh look at central bank independence. *Cato Journal, 40*, 105.

Wolf, M. (2023). *The crisis of democratic capitalism.* Penguin.

The manufacturer's authorised [illegible] resentat[illegible] EU is Springer
Nature Customer S[illegible] GmbH, [illegible] latz 3, 69115 Heidelberg,
Germany. If you have any [illegible] ur products, please
contact ProductSafety@springernature.com

Printed and bound by CPI Group (UK) Ltd, Croydon, CR0 4YY
01/10/2026
02225852-0016